GW01250053

Guide to J2EE: Enterprise Java

Springer
London
Berlin
Heidelberg
New York
Hong Kong
Milan
Paris
Tokyo

John Hunt and Chris Loftus

Guide to J2EE: Enterprise Java

Springer

John Hunt
JayDee Technology Ltd, www.jaydeetechnology.co.uk

Chris Loftus
Department of Computer Science, University of Wales, Aberystwyth, UK
www.aber.ac.uk/compsci

British Library Cataloguing in Publication Data
Hunt, John
Guide to J2EE : enterprise Java
1.Java (Computer program language) 2.Application software - Development
I.Title II. Loftus, C. W.
005.7'1262

Library of Congress Cataloging-in-Publication Data
Hunt, John, 1964-
Guide to J2EE : enterprise Java / John Hunt and Chris Loftus.
p. cm.
ISBN 1-85233-704-4 (alk. paper)
1. Java (Computer program language) 2. Business--Data processing. I. Loftus, Chris, 1963- II. Title.

QA76.73.J38H855 2003
005.2'762--dc21 2003042427

ISBN 1-85233-704-4 Springer-Verlag London Berlin Heidelberg
A member of BertelsmannSpringer Science+Business Media GmbH
http://www.springer.co.uk

First published 2003

Typeset by Ian Kingston Editorial Services, Nottingham, UK
Printed and bound in the United States of America
34/3830-543210 Printed on acid-free paper SPIN 10895318

For my brother, Paul
JH

To Jonathan
CL

Preface

Why This Book?

This book aims to be a practical introduction to all you need to know to design, implement, deploy and run Java 2 Enterprise Edition (J2EE) technology applications. Such applications build on the technology provided in the Java 2 Standard Edition (J2SE) by exploiting Servlets, Java Server Pages (JSPs), Enterprise JavaBeans (EJBs) or some other server side technology (such as the Java Message Service).

A related question to "Why this book?" is "Why did we write this book?". The answer to this is that over the last three years we have trained a wide variety of developers in J2EE technologies. This has been both in industry and academia. We have also been involved in the design, implementation and deployment of several large J2EE technology applications. During this time we felt that there was no single book that presented the J2EE technologies as a whole in a coherent, cohesive and introductory form.

We did of course try to find appropriate books both to provide on our courses as well as to recommend. In general we found that the books available fell into one of two categories. They were either focused on one particular aspect of the J2EE (such as servlets/JSPs or EJBs) or they felt like reference material: to be dipped into as required, but not to be read cover to cover. This meant that if you wanted to learn a broad cross-section of J2EE technologies you had to take a course, buy multiple books or try to work through large reference style books with much information repeated in the standalone chapters.

This then is a book to read from cover to cover that will provide a detailed introduction to almost all aspects of the J2EE. Due to space restrictions it does not contain as much detail on EJBs as a dedicated EJB book; however, it does cover most of what you are going to need in the average project. The rest you can get from the EJB documentation provided with the J2EE or from tutorials on Sun's and others' Web sites (for example see `http://www.javaworld.com/` and `http://www.planetjava.co.uk/`). This is also true of servlets and JSPs.

Why Tomcat and JBoss?

A useful question to consider is why did we choose Tomcat and JBoss as the Web application and EJB application servers respectively? The answer to this is quite simple. We wanted to use freely available servers that could be accessed by readers of our book at little or no cost. However, we wanted these servers to be production quality servers that can and are used for real world systems. The obvious choices for these servers were therefore Tomcat (which is also Sun's reference implementation for a Web application server) and JBoss.

Tomcat

Tomcat is part of the Apache Jakarta project. The Jakarta Project creates and maintains open source solutions on the Java platform. Individual products are developed by and distributed through various sub-projects, of which Tomcat is one example. Each sub-project has its own team of developers and committees, and its own mailing lists and discussion groups.

Tomcat is developed in an open and participatory environment and released under the Apache Software License. It is one of the most widely used Java Web application servers around today. It is also used as the reference implementation by Sun for the Servlet and JSP specifications.

The version used for this book is Tomcat 4.0.3, which supports the Servlet 2.3 specification and the JSP 1.2 specification. Tomcat can be obtained from Apache using the following URL:

```
http://jakarta.apache.org/tomcat/index.html
```

Tomcat 5.0 will support version 1.4 of the J2EE SDK. However, at the time of writing this was currently in development and not yet available for general use. This version of Tomcat supports the Servlet 2.4 and the JSP 2.0 specifications.

JBoss

JBoss is an open source, standards-compliant, application server implemented in 100% pure Java and distributed for free. During 2002 there were over 150,000 downloads per month; JBoss is *the* most downloaded Web application server in the world based on the J2EE specification. In a poll carried out by TogetherSoft JBoss was the choice of 44% of respondents when asked which J2EE server they use for Enterprise Development, with closest competitor, BEA Weblogic, at only 23% (see `http://www.togethercommunity.com/index.jsp`). JBoss also won the *JavaWorld* Editor's Choice 2002 Award for Best Java Application Server. Therefore, although JBoss is open source it is the most used J2EE EJB application server currently available. Note that JBoss also provides implementations of the JNDI, Java Message Service, distributed transactions etc. It also includes a simple relational database known as Hypersonic.

When JBoss is combined with Tomcat it provides a complete J2EE stack – that is it offers support not only for the EJB server but also servlets and JSPs. Thus with JBoss and Tomcat you need nothing else. The version of JBoss used in this book is JBoss 3.0.0.

You can down load standalone JBoss (or JBoss with a built-in Tomcat) from:

```
http://www.jboss.org/
```

Versions of JBoss and Tomcat

As versions of both Tomcat and JBoss may have slightly different deployment requirements or changes in directory structures we have made the versions of both used in this book available on the Web site dedicated to this book.

Portability of Code

An import point to note is that J2EE-based applications should be cross-server. That is, if the developer follows the J2EE guidelines the source code should work whatever J2EE server it is deployed onto. This means that source code written to run on WebSpehere should run on JBoss/Tomcat or WebLogic. Therefore choosing the JBoss Tomcat stack combination for this book does *not* mean that you cannot use the material provided on other servers (although the way that the source is deployed may differ).

Guide to the J2EE Web Site

We have developed a Web site dedicated to this book and to the material in this book. The web site URL is:

```
http://www.guide-to-j2ee.net/
```

We both believe that software developers learn best by doing and by starting with some working code and experimenting. Therefore all the source code for the examples in this book is available on the Web site. Each chapter has its own directory within which the class files are listed individually. The source code has all been tested using the Java 2 Enterprise Edition (SDK 1.3.1) using Tomcat 4.0.3 and JBoss 3.0. As new versions of J2EE are released all examples will be tested against them using the relevant versions of Tomcat and JBoss. Any changes necessitated by a new release will be noted at the above Web site.

As mentioned earlier, we have also made available the versions of Tomcat and JBoss used with the examples in this book.

The Web site provides the following:

- The versions of JBoss and Tomcat used.
- All source code, XML files, JSPs and HTML files used in this book.
- Any updates necessitated by more recent releases of the Servlet/JSP or EJB specifications.

Structure of the Book

This book is divided into five parts.

Part 1: Background

This part presents the underlying J2EE or server-side technologies that EJBs, servlets, JSPs etc. rely on. This section therefore covers topics such as JDBC, RMI, JNDI and XML.

Part 2: Enterprise JavaBeans

In this part we present Enterprise JavaBeans (EJBs). EJBs are the J2EE technology used to represent application business logic, persistent data and, through message-driven beans, message-oriented logic.

Part 3: Servlets and JSPs

The presentation or Web tier of a J2EE application is made up of servlets and JSPs. This section therefore describes these technologies and associated issues such as securing Web applications.

Part 4: Additional technologies

We present a number of advanced J2EE technologies in this section, including J2EE transactions, EJB security, Web services and SVG (Scalable Vector Graphics, which is an XML technology).

Part 5: Design

This describes the design of J2EE applications and the use of the Design Patterns in Sun's J2EE Patterns Catalog.

Typographical Conventions

In this book, the standard typeface is Minion. However, source code is set in Letter Gothic (for example, `a = 2 + 3;`). A **bold** font indicates Java keywords, for example:

```
public class Address extends Object {. . .}
```

Trademarks

Java, Java 2 Standard Edition, Java 2 Enterprise Edition, Java Development Kit, Solaris, SPARC, SunOS and Sunsoft are trademarks of Sun Microsystems, Inc. MS-Windows and Windows 95, 98,

2000, NT and XP are registered trademarks of Microsoft Corporation. Unix is a registered trademark of AT&T. All other brand names are trademarks of their respective holders.

Acknowledgements

We have both benefited from discussions with colleagues both at work and within our social circles who have in their various ways contributed to this book. In addition all those students and course delegates that we have taught Java 2 Enterprise Edition technologies to have unknowingly helped to form the material in this book with their questions, comments and general feedback.

In particular we would like to thank Steve Mabbort, Ben Halton and Will Mepham of JayDee Technology Ltd, and Jon Adams, Denise Cooke and Alex McManus for proof reading various parts of this book. Thanks also to Steve Mabbort for technical input into the SVG and Web Services chapters.

John would also like to thank Jay Dee Technology Ltd (`http://www.jaydeetechnology.co.uk/`), and Chris would like to thank the Computer Science Department of the University of Wales, Aberystwyth (`http://www.aber.ac.uk/compsci/`), for their help and support. Both organizations allowed the authors time and materials to produce this book.

We have both been very lucky to have the help and support of both our partners – without whom neither of us would have got through this book.

John Hunt and Chris Loftus

Contents

Part 1 Background

Part 2 EJB Architecture

Part 3 Servlets and JSPs

Part 1

Background

Chapter 1

Why J2EE?

1.1 Introduction

In this introductory chapter our aim is to persuade you of the benefits of J2EE as a suitable technology to consider when building enterprise applications. This, you may think, has its risks, given that J2EE has only existed as a Java platform (as distinct from J2SE) since 1998, maturing sufficiently for many organizations only in the last two years. However, the latest release (1.4 (Proposed Final Draft) at the time of writing) includes many important new features essential for many enterprise applications, such as the automatic management of relationships between entity EJBs, support for EJBs that can handle asynchronous communication and Web Services.

Although concerns about the validity of J2EE technology in this context are understandable, other solutions have been far from ideal. In many cases you have been totally dependent on proprietary, non-standard solutions, making porting to other environments difficult and expensive. Also, solutions that are operating-system-specific are limiting given that some clients, over time, will want to change the operating systems they use. Moreover, proprietary solutions also tie you to a specific vendor, which introduces its own risks. Above all, the solutions provided are often incomplete, with significant effort needed to integrate the required solution parts obtained from different vendors. Also, as an enterprise application developer, you are forced to spend most of your effort solving distribution problems, such as database transactions, security, object to relational mappings, connecting Web components with business logic components, and so forth, rather than concentrating on writing business logic code.

We and many others believe that the comprehensiveness of J2EE will ensure that the majority of your requirements are addressed, including the user interface of your application (servlets and Java Server Pages), reusable business components (Enterprise JavaBeans), messaging (Java Messaging Service), distributed transactions, distributed security, and many others. Many have their own specification, but all sit under the J2EE specification umbrella, or are addressed across multiple specifications. This ensures that the technologies are coherent and well integrated. As we will see, J2EE also attempts to insulate developers from a multitude of application programming interfaces (APIs). We have yet to discover another set of technologies that do all of these things, not even .NET (Hunt, 2002)! Our confidence in J2EE is founded on experience gained developing enterprise solutions using it, believing J2EE to be by far the best set of technologies to use in this context. We are convinced that applications developed using the alternatives are more difficult to develop, maintain and port.

In the following sections we look at the IT challenges that face commercial organizations, and the requirements that such challenges place on the technologies they use. In the light of the other solutions available, we will make the case for Java and J2EE. However, a note of caution is needed because we realize that a knowledge of technologies is inadequate without the enterprise application developer being a skilled designer also. Such competence is founded on experience, but can be accelerated by the reuse of other developers' experience, encapsulated in published design patterns. Subsequently, the community has put together a set of server-side design patterns that should be invaluable to any enterprise application developer.

1.2 The Challenges Facing IT Organizations

A complex relationship exists between organizations (from hereon we use the term *businesses*) and information technologies. As technologies improve, businesses are presented with new or improved business opportunities. In turn, businesses push the technological envelope, demanding improved solutions to make customer to business and business to business interoperation easier and more efficient. Expectations, however, always outstrip the solutions available.

Increasingly, businesses wish to use IT to enable them link up electronically to other businesses and customers. An example is the automatic just-in-time ordering of parts from other companies as stock levels reach specified thresholds. Customers expect to be able to peruse online catalogues and order goods electronically, and then track the progress of their orders assuming secure and reliable access.

Enterprise systems within companies are also becoming more complex as business processes become more complex. Many companies have accounting systems that interwork with human resources and workflow management systems. The authors provided training courses and mentoring for a company developing an events tracking engine that would monitor assembly line operations, but that was also integrated with a workflow scheduling system; if the assembly line broke down the event would be reported to the workflow system that would call out the relevant engineer. To gain a competitive edge, many companies consider it essential to connect management information systems with other company systems.

In turn, these company systems are being opened up to network-based access to support:

- Customer to business access through the Web.
- Business to business access through the Internet or dedicated networks.

New technologies are being employed to make such access easier. For example, electronic data interchange (EDI) has up until now been supported by dedicated networks, and is mainly the domain of larger companies. The advent of Web services and efforts such as ebXML (Electronic Business using eXtensible Markup Language; `http://www.ebxml.org/`) should open up business to business interactions to SMEs. It is important though that new technologies adopted by companies are able to interoperate with existing legacy systems, such as large transaction processing systems or database management systems. Usually, companies cannot afford to replace such systems, but must leverage them when developing new enterprise applications.

In the commercial world businesses must make a financial case for the adoption of new technologies, and subsequently their inherent risks must be assessed. A major issue here is that of time to market. Technologies and software engineering processes used to develop enterprise applications must improve time to market. At the same time they must be open to change, with engineering practices that support such change.[1]

1.3 Requirements on Enterprise Application Development

Clearly, if applications are to come to market quickly, it is important that the technologies and processes used support their rapid development and deployment without compromising quality. A force that opposes this is the large number of APIs and technologies that must be learnt and used when developing distributed applications.

In enterprise applications, reliability and availability are qualities that must not be compromised. Reliability is concerned with application failure (mean time to failure) and availability is a combination of downtime caused by failure and disconnection for other reasons, such as maintenance. How often have you tried to access Web pages to be told that the page no longer exists, or is so slow that it is effectively unavailable? Perhaps the company's server has been disconnected due to network failure, overload or maintenance. Unreliable customer information may be another problem. Poor reliability and availability will lead to poor confidence in the Web site, and you may decide to delete it from your browser's bookmarks, which is clearly bad for business. The forces that militate against reliability and availability are:

- Using immature and therefore possibly unreliable technologies. Some of the first application servers that implemented J2EE had known problems. Most now have acceptable reliability.
- Poor understanding of new technologies. Before the dotcom collapse, there was a rush to train developers in the ways of J2EE. We know of cases where we taught core Java one week and J2EE the next and our client's developers were expected to implement complex applica-

1 The topic of software development processes used for developing enterprise applications is beyond the scope of this book. We advocate the reuse of design patterns, but do not discuss the kinds of development processes that might be applicable. The kind of process required will vary to some extent based on the kind of application or system being constructed and the nature of the project team. However, enterprise applications usually encapsulate business processes, which tend to be volatile, responding to changing client requirements or government regulations and laws. For these kinds of application, we think that agile processes should be used, such as eXtreme Programming (Auer and Miller, 2002), Feature-Driven Development (Palmer and Felsing, 2002), Agile Modeling (Ambler, 2002) or the lightweight application of the Unified Process (Hunt, 2000). These processes embrace change.

tions the week after that! Even with competent trainers and mentors it is unreasonable to expect developers to be fully conversant in core Java, let alone J2EE, within the space of three weeks. Such practices will lead to hacked solutions. As we will explain in this and the following chapter, J2EE is actually easier to learn than many of the alternatives, since it hides much of the distribution plumbing, lowering the learning curve, but not flattening it!

Security is another quality attribute that must be present in enterprise applications that manipulate customer information or could expose company-confidential information. In the e-commerce IT sector this is perhaps one of the most critical quality attributes. Breaches of security are newsworthy events and not only impact the Web site in question but also taint the whole sector. The accidental exposure of credit card information by one bank (and cases have been publicized) will dent confidence in online banking more generally. The forces that oppose good security are the use of public networks, complexity and unreliable technologies.

Some of those early dotcom companies were too successful for their own good, being swamped by large numbers of customers wishing to access their services. Consequently, the infrastructure in place could not cope with the increased level of demand because developers had lacked the foresight to use technologies that would scale up to meet it. The Internet exposes your online applications to a worldwide customer base and the demand might be unpredictably strong. Therefore, use technologies that will scale up to meet demand as it expands.

Often another requirement when developing enterprise applications is the need to integrate those applications with existing company information systems. Invariably, however, the existing investment base must be preserved. Integration is hampered by systems that are written in various languages, support varying API styles and which might not support operation within a distributed context. Therefore finding technologies that assist such integration is important.

As a developer of enterprise applications you may need to port them across multiple operating systems, a task that often consumes much effort. Similarly, significant effort may even be required when porting an application to the same operating system but at a different site. In both cases the database systems, security configuration and so on may be quite different at the two sites, often necessitating expensive changes to code to achieve such ports. Any technology that reduces the effort required to port applications will therefore be of great benefit.

1.4 Technological Choices

We need a set of technologies that helps us fulfil the requirements identified earlier but at the same time mitigates the forces that diminish quality. The choices available are threefold: .NET from Microsoft (Hunt, 2002), J2EE (specified by the Java Community under the stewardship of Sun Microsystems), proprietary solutions from specific companies (for example TopLink from WebGain: `http://www.webgain.com/`), and in-house solutions.

The two major technological solutions available commercially are .NET and J2EE. The former is quite recent and is focused on the Windows platform, although there are claims that the intermediate language (MIDL) used by .NET languages (such as C#) could be supported across multiple platforms. It is a good solution if Windows is the only platform used by your company and clients. The C# language sits on the shoulders of giants, such as Java, and adds useful features lacking in Java; syntactic support for performance optimization is an example. However, the platform requires integrated development environment support. In order to develop non-trivial applications it is essential to use a tool such as Visual .NET. Although .NET has a match for many of the distribution technologies defined within J2EE, it does not seem to have an equivalent to EJB. This is important for hiding distribution plumbing, which reduces the learning curve and improves portability.

The J2EE platform defines a programming model and an application infrastructure. The former consists of numerous APIs to distribution services. The latter provides a server-based framework of classes within which you plug your J2EE components. This framework supports the deployment and runtime operation of your components, performing many of the tasks you would otherwise have to code explicitly.

In addition to the above, there are some excellent proprietary integration solutions available, suitable for those who are happy to commit to a single vendor and a partial integration solution. Some of these vendors are now migrating their products to be J2EE-compliant, as is the case with TopLink, which among other services provides sophisticated object to relational mapping services.

Some larger companies, over several years, may have developed their own integration solutions. One advantage here is that the company has complete control over the solution implementation, thereby addressing the exact needs of the company. However, there are many problems with this approach. First, substantial effort is required to develop and then maintain the technology. Second, it is likely that many in-house solutions will be less robust and more poorly documented than commercial products. Third, the J2EE specification is managed by the Java Community Process, involving large numbers of experts drawn from many companies contributing their expertise across the many facets that make up J2EE. It is unlikely that in-house solutions can draw on such a large body of experts. Fourth, in-house solutions are likely to be targeted to specific platforms that may reduce porting possibilities. Finally, components developed for these integration platforms are specific to these platforms, again making it harder to export or import components to or from other integration technologies.

1.5 Why Choose Java and J2EE?

One of the main goals of Java is the provision of platform independence. Any computer with a Java virtual machine can run Java byte-code. Of course there can be small differences, particularly runtime behaviour associated with threads. However, this goal has been achieved and is one of Java's most endearing characteristics. For example, when developing applications for this book we were able to run them in the JBoss application server on both Solaris Unix and Windows 2000. No changes were required to either application code or even the configuration of the application server; it just ran. The same was true of the Tomcat Web server, also written in Java. Compare this to the C language, where the sizes of integer types are not specified. On one platform they might be 16 bit values, and on another 32 bit values. Your application might work on one platform but not another. Java's byte-code also gives us mobile code that can be squirted across a network and reconstituted as objects within a remote JVM, perhaps on a completely different operating system. Few languages support this.

When trying to integrate legacy systems, Java provides ideal platform-independent glue. Furthermore, Java provides APIs and implementations of CORBA, another standard integration middleware technology.

J2EE goes further by providing a sophisticated set of distribution APIs, with vendors and Open Source organizations providing implementations. These are necessary when developing enterprise applications, as discussed in Chapter 2. However, J2EE also defines an application server framework. This comprises two kinds of container, responsible for managing specific kinds of J2EE component. Web containers manage the life cycles of servlets and JSPs, EJB containers doing the same for EJBs. These containers perform much of the work that would normally have to be coded explicitly within your application, code that is often dependent on the environment your application operates within, or on volatile requirements, such as security and transaction needs. These are parts of your code that will need to be updated relatively often. Application servers enable us to generate such volatile code, with instructions as to what to generate being defined declaratively using XML. Changing the XML, especially if you have an appropriate XML editing tool, is much easier and less error-prone than tampering with application code, where you might accidentally alter business logic rather than change the distribution behaviour, as intended.

When using a J2EE application server you will develop application components that consist mainly of business logic code. The accompanying XML is used to configure these components for particular environments and distribution requirements. The value of these components is increased, since many will now form reusable business objects that can be configured for use in multiple applications. Examples include Account, Customer, Address and so on.

At a macro level, J2EE encourages a separation of concerns, with graphical user interface components supported within a Web tier (the Web containers) and the business logic supported within an EJB tier (EJB containers). Decoupling the user interface from the business logic and data is recognized widely as good practice, described by design patterns, such as Model–View–Controller and several J2EE design patterns (see Chapter 34). Other solutions might not encourage such a clear separation.

1.6 A Note of Caution

The J2EE specification provides not only for cross-hardware platform delivery, but also for cross-application server delivery. That is, if you program strictly to the J2EE specification then your code should run on the JBoss–Tomcat combination, on BEA's WebLogic, on IBM's Websphere etc. The benefit of this is that you are not tied to a single application server provider. If you are unhappy with the performance, reliability, cost or support from one server you should be able to move your code to another without the need for any redevelopment.

This ideal in reality is harder to achieve. There are three primary reasons for this:

1. In the above paragraph we have been careful to state that the "code" should be portable between servers. As you will see throughout this book, a J2EE application comprises more than

just Java code. At the very least, such an application also includes the XML files that define how the J2EE application should be deployed on your chosen application server. Although the J2EE specification does include a description of a set of XML files that are used for this purpose, in all cases there are additional deployment details that will determine whether server-specific XML files (such as the `jboss.xml` and `jboss-web.xml` files) or the equivalent specified through the application server's own user interface tools are required. This means that the information contained in these files will require porting from one application server to another. In many cases this is a trivial mapping; however, in some cases a whole new way of specification will need to be learned.

2. Many commercial application servers include proprietary extensions that can make some feature or other much easier to use, require less programming and be potentially more efficient. Often, unless developers or designers are particularly familiar with the J2EE specifications (which is no trivial feat), they may not realize they are using an application server-specific extension. As soon as this happens, the software is tied directly to that application server and the effort to port it to another server is that much greater. This is, of course, what the vendors want (they will dress it up as making things easier for the developer), as this means that the software developers are less likely to try to port the system to another application server. The JBoss–Tomcat combination has very few extensions.
3. Application servers are just software in their own right. In the case of the JBoss–Tomcat combination used in this book, the application server is just Java code that can be accessed from Apache's Web site. All software contains some bugs. You will encounter these as you develop your J2EE applications. The work-rounds that you will need to put in place to deal with the encountered "features" may make it harder to port your software from one application server to another.

You should not be put off by what has been said above; the fact that there is a J2EE standard that multiple application server vendors have implemented greatly increases your ability to move from one vendor's system to another. However, it should not be thought that this means that the software, XML files and database developed on one server will be portable to another without any changes at all. Equally, if you are doing such a port it should be considered as a "port" of the system rather than merely a test on another platform (which is closer to what is normally expected within the Java world).

1.7 Knowing the Technology Is not Enough

A common mistake made by many new developers is to think that after learning the J2EE APIs they are competent J2EE developers. In reality, complex APIs can give you lots of rope with which to hang yourself! Experience is needed to use these APIs efficiently and build well-designed applications. This can be learned by seeking design guidance from others with experience in this field, both generalists and those with more specific kills within the enterprise application development sector. Fortunately, our colleagues started to recognize this back in 1995 when Gamma, Helm, Johnson and Vlissades wrote the seminal book on software design patterns (Gamma *et al.*, 1995). Since then many others have encapsulated abstract design solutions as design patterns that can be used to help solve software problems that recur frequently. For J2EE, there is a J2EE

Patterns Catalog (Crupi *et al.*, 2001) that we overview in Chapter 34. Some of these patterns help us to build loosely coupled pluggable applications, whereas others aim to promote performance optimization. Others, furthermore, help with other design issues. We refer to design issues in various places within the book, with Chapter 35 presenting a complex example that employs a number of J2EE design patterns as a case study.

1.8 References

Ambler, S. W. (2002). *Agile Modeling*. Wiley, New York.

Auer, K. and Miller, R. (2002). *Extreme Programming Applied*. Addison-Wesley, Reading, MA.

Crupi, J., Alur, D. and Malks, D. (2001). *Core J2EE Patterns*. Prentice Hall, Upper Saddle River, NJ.

Gamma, E., Helm, R., Johnson, R. and Vlissides, J. (1995). *Design Patterns, Elements of Reusable Object-Oriented Software*. Addison-Wesley, Reading, MA.

Hunt, J. (2000). *The Unified Process for Practitioners*. Springer-Verlag, London.

Hunt, J. (2002). *Guide to C# and Object Orientation*. Springer-Verlag, London.

Palmer, S. and Felsing, M. (2002) *A Practical Guide to Feature-Driven Development*. Prentice Hall, Upper Saddle River, NJ.

Chapter 2

Introduction to Distributed Systems

2.1 What Is a Distributed Application or System?

In this book we define a distributed application or system[1] (we will use the more generic term *program* from here on) as one that comprises two or more components that at least occupy distinct address spaces. These components interact in a coherent manner in order to fulfil the task or tasks that the program implements. In contrast, a non-distributed program runs as a single operating system process that has its own memory address space, an example being an editor.

This simple definition means that a distributed program might run on both single or multiple processors, for example on a single laptop or a network. The distributed components may run sequentially or in parallel, with occasional synchronization. Indeed, depending on the way it is configured and deployed it may be possible for the distributed program to do all of these things. A platform that supports such flexibility would enhance business opportunities.

2.2 Why Build Distributed Programs?

Some of the benefits of or necessity for distribution are as follows.

The nature of your program might dictate the use of distribution. For example, a point of sale system will usually have a separate program running on each point of sale register that

1 The distinction between application and system is fuzzy and rather subjective. Enterprise applications are distributed, so the distinction cannot be on the grounds of distribution. We consider systems to be large, complex distributed programs that perform multiple tasks (e.g. a banking system). They may involve hardware as well as software. Applications can be non-distributed or distributed, but focus on supporting a specific task or business activity. Applications are comprised of software only.

requires access to a central server program that controls the tills as a group and provides common services, such as stock database access and management information services.

Speed optimization might be an issue. A program that consists of multiple distributed components that are able to execute in parallel on multiple processors should provide results more quickly than an alternative implementation that does not. However, we have to be careful and take into account the time needed for communication between these components. Sending data across a network is much slower than sending data across a computer's data bus. When evaluating the efficiency of a distributed as opposed to a non-distributed solution we need to analyse the degree of coupling required between components. If they are loosely coupled with just small amounts of communication, then a distributed system may be appropriate. We must also consider whether the program is inherently concurrent. If it is, then we know that distributed components can operate in parallel, and will not need to wait too long for data generated by other components. If the program is not naturally concurrent we might not gain an increase in speed.

There is another aspect of speed that may influence whether we choose to distribute. We might need to develop a program that requires extensive access to a company database system. Let us assume that the database is not distributed, being hosted on a particular server, and that our program needs to be accessed from user PCs. Also, let us assume that only one module within the program is tightly coupled with the database. If we develop a non-distributed program with a separate instance running on every user PC, then we know that there will be significant network traffic between user PCs and the database. However, if we split away the database-intensive module and locate it on the same host as the database, then we may find that the amount of network traffic generated by the program decreases. This, of course, requires that the main part of the program and its database-using component are themselves loosely coupled. So here, distribution gives us the opportunity to move tightly coupled components onto the same computer.

We may be forced to adopt distribution where our program needs to access an existing system. If we cannot co-locate our program with the system and the system does not support distributed access, then we will have to place a component on the same computer as the system. Additionally, we may find that the system presents an API (application programming interface) or framework architecture that is foreign to the language used for our program. If we are using Java, then the JNI (Java Native Interface) libraries might help bridge the gap. However, if JNI is not sufficient we might be forced to use a language-independent communication mechanism to allow our program to interoperate with the other system. We might also have to write some adapter code in the foreign language that supports the other end of the communication channel. Possible mechanisms include sockets or the Common Object Request Broker Architecture's (CORBA) Internet Inter-ORB Protocol (IIOP).

Using IIOP as our underlying transport protocol also gives us the flexibility to develop parts of our program in different languages. IIOP provides a standard language type mapping that enables data to be transferred between different type systems. We may find that the role of some components favours one language over another. For example, it might be more appropriate to use C or C++ than Java for a component that requires extensive access to Unix system calls. Furthermore, we might reuse existing components written in other languages that are difficult to integrate directly within the same address space as our main program. Again, IIOP may help in this situation.

Distribution also provides the possibility for runtime discovery of required services that are distributed. Web services (see Chapter 33) are an example. You can develop a program that interrogates a directory of published Web services for a service that the program requires. The Simple Object Access Protocol (SOAP) is then used to negotiate and allow communication between your program and the remote component (again see Chapter 33).

Another issue to consider is whether your program needs to be fault-tolerant. Are the reliability and availability requirements such that a failure of the program is unacceptable? If so, the critical components could be replicated across several computers, perhaps using a voting scheme to detect faults.[2]

There may be economic reasons for using distribution. Rather than reinventing service code within a monolithic program, a better solution might be to tap into an existing resource that is located elsewhere.

The above are just some of the reasons why distribution may be useful or necessary. There is another side to the coin, however, and we explore this next.

There are tradeoffs to consider when building distributed programs, including the following.

Network bandwidths in many western countries have improved in recent years. Even small towns may be connected to 100 Mbit/s links. For example, the University of Wales, Aberystwyth (where one of the authors works) is connected to the South Wales metropolitan area network by a 100 Mbit/s microwave link, and is due to be connected to a further high-bandwidth network later in 2002: the Wales Life-Long Learning network. Having said this, as capacity increases, it is well known that demand increases also. Even without competition for bandwidth, communication across large distances will be slower than data communication within the same computer. Typically, components that communicate via the Internet are likely to be loosely coupled,[3] requiring occasional data sharing. However, this might not be the case within company intranets. Developers of company-wide programs need to analyse carefully the levels of traffic expected between components, the bandwidth of the existing intranet and its current and projected usage statistics. Where distribution is optional, benefits must be weighed against communication costs. Where distribution is unavoidable, there may also be an unavoidable communication penalty, perhaps requiring improvements in the infrastructure.

One of the biggest problems associated with communication is security. The use of shared networks opens up the potential for malicious attack, snooping or accidental damage. There are several points of weakness. Connecting your program to the network presents a "door" into that program. Such an entry point would be harder or impossible to find for a non-distributed program. Such a publicly visible entry point requires authentication and authorization. You must devise a sufficiently robust authentication mechanism

---

2 To achieve this, an odd number of components are "asked" to compute some result concurrently. The result is returned to a voting component. The result that is the same from the majority of components is the result that is returned to the original caller. The duplicate components might be the same code or might be written using different designs and languages to guard against duplicated software faults.

3 There are plans afoot to develop an all-Wales bioinformatics supercomputer comprising clusters of computers talking to each other over a high-bandwidth network.

that cannot be subverted without substantial cost and effort.[4] Such a mechanism also requires appropriate procedures for its administration, such as changing passwords on a regular basis. Similarly, once access has been granted authorization checks need to be performed to limit access on a need-to-know basis. Even with such a mechanism, a malicious attack is possible. Denial of service attacks result from the site being bombarded with unwanted traffic, thereby denying access from legitimate users.

Another point of weakness occurs when data is transmitted between distributed components. Are we really transferring data to the correct component, or is there an impostor at the other end of the connection? Is the data commercially sensitive or personally confidential? If so, appropriate security mechanisms must be employed to prevent access or tampering and to validate the identity of both ends of the connection.

Exposing your enterprise programs to the public network makes the consequences of programming faults or maladministration of confidential information much more serious. An example was the unfortunate exposure of credit card account numbers by the UK Consumers' Association[5] (BBC News, 2001). 2700 customers who bought some online software from the Association's Web site discovered that their credit card details had been exposed accidentally. Ironically, this is an organization that campaigns for better Web security.

Dealing with security and optimizing the configuration and deployment of components to reduce network traffic are both complex issues and require complex analyses and solutions. Distribution introduces complexity not found with non-distributed programs. Debugging a distributed program is difficult. Partial failures can be difficult to detect and track. You have to rely on using complex communication protocols. You are more exposed to hardware failure, perhaps the failure of another organization's hardware. To enable flexible configurations you avoid hard-coding network addresses and use logical naming schemes instead. However, this adds further complexity as you need to devise a robust and accepted naming scheme that must be administered.

Clearly, building distributed programs is complex. There is a lot of distribution plumbing code that must be written that muddies the water and obscures the business logic code, making it difficult to maintain. Fortunately, some help is at hand, as we will see in the next few sections.

2.3 How Can Java Help With Distribution?

Fortunately, Java provides considerable support for building distributed programs. At the lowest level of abstraction Java provides an API to sockets and associated Internet protocols, TCP (Transmission Control Protocol) and UDP (User Datagram Protocol). The JDBC database connectivity API supports database drivers that can access remote database systems. Access to remote objects in a way that makes them appear local is provided by the Remote Method Invoca-

4 Unfortunately, even 128 bit encryption ciphers can be broken with enough brute force computing power.

5 The organization that produces the Which? magazines.

tion (RMI) API. There are APIs and implementations that grant you access to CORBA, and hence access to any CORBA compliant software, wherever it is located and whatever language it is written in. Asynchronous messages may be sent between components using the Java Messaging Service (JMS) API and associated messaging server. A more human-oriented version of this is provided by the JavaMail API and associated implementation servers. Remote objects can be discovered using the Java Naming and Directory Interface (JNDI) API and associated implementation servers. A security model is built into the core of Java so that you can define fine-grained authorization. An authentication and high-level authorization framework of classes and interfaces is provided by the Java Authentication and Authorization Service (JAAS). Hypertext Transfer Protocol (HTTP) is supported by the *java.net* package and servlet and Java Server Page (JSP) class libraries. Support is now provided for communication using XML, via Java's Web-service APIs. The distribution of mobile code is realized as applets and the Java WebStart mechanism.

The above is only a subset of Java distribution-related APIs, as the list is extensive. Of the above, CORBA and RMI can be termed distributed object systems. They are particularly interesting, since they aim to abstract away some of the complexities of distribution, hence making code development less difficult.

2.4 Distributed Object Systems

If you are familiar with Remote Procedure Calling (RPC), then you should grasp the ideas behind distributed object systems with ease. The key idea is that a client object views a distributed object as if it were co-located in the same JVM as the client. As far as the client object is concerned, method calls to the remote object appear to be local method calls (Figure 2.1).

In the case of CORBA and RMI this illusion is achieved by using proxy and skeleton objects. This is shown in Figure 2.2. The client obtains a local representative of the remote server object. This proxy object is of a class that has the same interface as the remote server class, allowing the client to treat it as if it were the remote server. In the case of RMI and

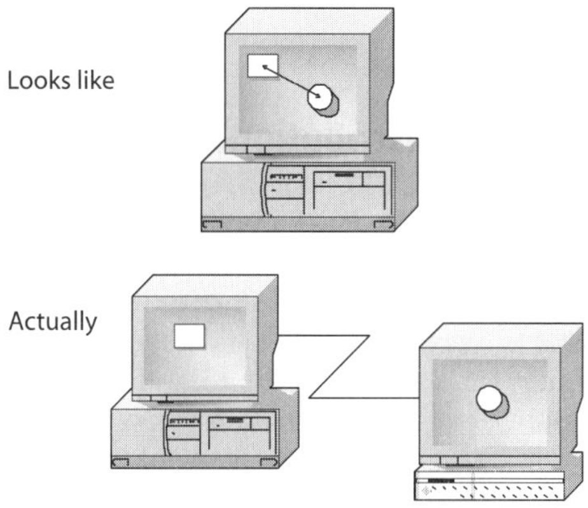

Figure 2.1 Appearances can be deceptive.

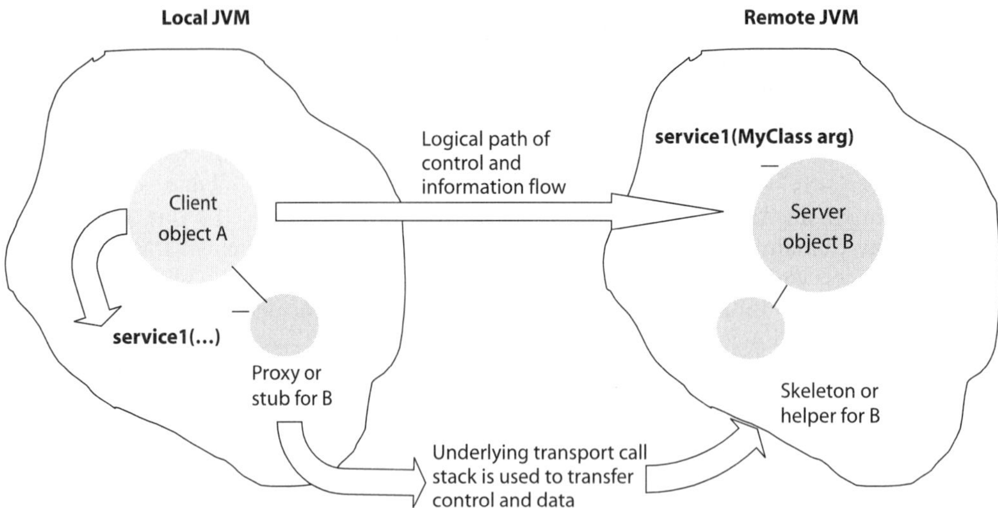

Figure 2.2 The use of proxy and skeleton objects achieve the illusion.

CORBA this proxy class is generated automatically by specialized tools. The proxy "knows" how to make a connection with the remote server object. This is achieved by using a lower-level communication protocol, such as TCP, UDP or IIOP. Clearly, the original method call and its data must be transmitted in the form required by the underlying transport mechanism (this is called marshalling). In some cases this is via a helper object, often called a skeleton; in other cases the interaction is directly to the server object. The helper is responsible for reformulating the original method call and making that call in the remote server's JVM. Results are returned in a similar fashion.

What are the benefits of distributed object systems? The main benefit is that you can design and write code that largely ignores the fact that distribution is taking place. You may need to write some bootstrapping code that obtains the proxy object, perhaps using JNDI to help you to find it. But once you have it you can treat it like any other local object, which is not surprising since it *is* a local object! However, all the work is, of course, delegated to the remote server object.

Consider one of the alternatives to using distributed object systems: that of writing socket code. In the example from Figure 2.2 you would be responsible for writing and maintaining the equivalent of the proxy and skeleton classes. This would require you to devise your own application-level protocol. Such a protocol would allow you to specify the method name and data corresponding to method parameters, as well as deal with return values. The helper class would probably contain a large `switch` statement or `if... else if` statements, where each case deals with a particular method. If you needed to publish a new method on class B, you would have to extend the protocol and include a new case in the `switch` statement. This would be time-consuming and error-prone. The use of code generation in object systems to achieve the same effect is much more efficient and will generate more robust code.

Object systems pose some problems. First, as a developer you may forget that there is a communication cost associated with using remote objects. Hiding the distribution plumbing may also help you to forget that the proxy will communicate over the network.

Second, on their own, object systems are not sufficient. As a developer you need access to many generic distribution services that support your distributed objects in various ways. One such service is a naming and directory service that allows you to find distributed objects prior to using them. Another is a security service that enforces authentication on first access to a security domain as well as providing authorization checks on client threads as they attempt to access your program's facilities. Likewise, we want distributed support for transactions to ensure that updates made to distributed data are performed in an atomic manner. Synchronous communication between objects through method calling is not the only form of communication. Asynchronous communication is often an important part of many applications, where it is not necessary for the message sender to wait for a response. Later in the book we provide an example of a Debug Monitor that is sent debug messages. The sender does not need to wait for the message to be processed; it just sends the debug message to a queue and then proceeds to its next task. Event notification is another service that may be required, where one part of the program registers its interest in the state of another part of the program. For example, you may have an assembly line monitoring and planning system. If part of the assembly line fails, it is important that interested parties are informed, perhaps to trigger a workflow scheduling system to call in the engineers.

Fortunately, Java provides APIs to most of these generic distribution services. Free implementations are provided for many. The CORBA naming service comes as part of the SDK. The SDKEE implementation of J2EE from Sun provides implementations, as does JBoss (the implementation used for examples in this book). CORBA also provides APIs for all of these services, and more.

However, although these services mean that you don't need to implement them yourself they pose problems of their own. Firstly, a process of intensive learning is necessary to become competent to know how to use these services. Worse still, in many cases there are multiple implementations and APIs for the same kind of service. For example, RMI comes with a naming service called the RMI registry. CORBA also has a specification for a naming service. Imagine a project where early on you use the RMI registry, but later you need to interoperate with another system that uses the CORBA Naming Service. You may end up having to maintain two naming services, each with its own API. Naming services also require you to define a naming scheme that your program components use when looking for components at runtime. Defining and maintaining this requires some effort and negotiation with other stakeholders. Also, although security and transaction services make the development of distributed programs possible, they are still complex to use. You are still required to write code that interacts explicitly with these services, obfuscating the business critical code, namely the code that implements business logic.

2.5 How Can J2EE Help?

The Java community recognized the complexities introduced by the burgeoning, albeit necessary, set of distribution services and APIs. In response, they decided to define a framework architecture called Enterprise JavaBeans (EJB) that would, by default, hide much of the "distribution plumbing". The idea was that you could develop a reusable business component where you chiefly write business logic code. In addition, you specify the public interface of this component, thereby defining the component's business methods available to other components and clients. You also write an XML deployment descriptor file that declaratively specifies the distribution properties of your component, such as the security authorization constraints to be placed on methods, where transactions should start and stop, whether the component should be synchronized with a database, and so on. You then deploy this component within an EJB server (which forms part of a J2EE application server). The deployment tools will read the XML and generate required distribution plumbing code on your behalf, no longer having to write or maintain this code yourself.

The outcome of this is that your components consist largely of business logic code. They are not tied down to a specific distribution configuration. Instead, by changing the XML deployment descriptors, these can be reused in multiple environments, even if the distribution requirements are quite different.

2.6 Online Reference

BBC News (2001). Red faces after credit card web blunder. 22 June 2001. `http://news.bbc.co.uk/1/hi/business/1401648.stm`.

Chapter 3

The J2EE Tour

3.1 Introduction

Two issues are explored in this chapter. Firstly, the relationship between the Java 2 Enterprise Edition (J2EE) and the Java 2 Standard Edition (J2SE) platforms is described. Secondly, we deconstruct the J2EE to take a tour of its constituent technologies. These technologies are revisited in depth in subsequent chapters, but here our aim is to give you an overview before plunging into detail later in the book.

3.2 The J2EE Platform

J2EE consists of a set of specifications (Shannon, 2001) and application programming interfaces (APIs) that build on top of the J2SE platform. J2SE provides APIs that are appropriate for the development of standalone applications, simple networked applications, or two-tier applications, for example client to database interaction. J2EE adds to the existing J2SE APIs by providing explicit support for developing server-side enterprise applications. These are applications that have the following characteristics:

- They are multi-tiered. Each tier has a particular responsibility, allowing both the separation of concerns and the physical separation of different aspects of the application. Physical separation provides for improved security, performance optimization and increased reliability.
- They are often accessed from clients via HTTP. This might support the customer-to-business model of interaction or indeed the business-to-business model of interaction, where HTTP or its secure form, HTTPS, is used as the transport protocol.
- They often have stringent security requirements. Enterprise applications act as a shop front to the outside world. Leaving the shop door unlocked at night or windows open will lead to unauthorized access or accidental exposure of confidential information. The consequences

of failing to take security seriously will be reported by the media, discrediting the industry, thereby reducing customer confidence. We have all read these press articles, such as the accidental exposure of customer credit card account numbers (BBC News, 2001). J2EE builds on the security model provided in J2SE, providing support for authentication (having, as it were, the right front door key), for authorization (having the right internal door keys and codes), and for encryption of data in transit.

- They must often integrate with existing legacy information systems. Many organization will want to *webify* existing internal applications. These will have their own information systems. It is essential therefore that J2EE provides mechanisms that enable a J2EE application to hook into these existing sources of business data.
- Many will require the use of both synchronous and asynchronous communication. Some client requests must be serviced immediately (synchronous handling of the request). Other requests might not demand an immediate response and can be queued for later processing (asynchronous handling of the request). J2EE supports both styles of communication.
- Many must be able to handle high volumes of incoming client requests. The J2EE specifications support concurrency and threading issues. However, it is the application server implementation of J2EE that will dictate the performance and reliability of your applications. You need to shop for J2EE application servers with care.
- They must support ACID (Atomicity, Consistency, Isolation, Durability) transaction principles, and within a distributed context. This is an important part of J2EE.

Projects developing server-side enterprise applications also have certain project requirements, in particular the requirement to get the product to market as soon as possible, without compromising the characteristics discussed above. Of course, this largely depends on the nature of the team and the development process followed. However, as mentioned in Chapter 2, J2EE provides a technological aid through its component technologies: EJBs and Web components. These technologies hide underlying APIs from the application's business logic code. The distribution properties of a component are specified externally of the component's code using XML. This also makes for rapid reconfiguration if the components need to be ported to other deployment environments.

Like J2SE, J2EE has a free Sun-provided implementation called the J2EE SDK (Software Development Kit).[1] This is a full J2EE application server. Lots of commercial implementations of J2EE exist[2] as well as open source implementations such as JBoss. Be careful not to confuse J2EE with its implementations. J2EE is comprised of a family of specification documents that can be downloaded from the Sun Web site. The API classes and documentation can also be downloaded from Sun. It is important to realize that these classes and interfaces are largely unimplemented. In fact, if you obtain any J2EE implementation it will come with these API classes and interfaces, but will, of course, also contain their full implementation. Although called a J2EE application server, in many cases the server consists of a federation of servers responsible for different aspects of J2EE; for example the EJB server, the HTTP server, the JNDI server and so on.

The J2EE specifications comprise:

---

1 http://java.sun.com/j2ee/

2 http://java.sun.com/j2ee/licensees.html

- A series of detailed J2EE technology-specific specifications, e.g. the EJB 2.1 specification and the JMS 1.1 specification.
- The J2EE 1.4 specification. This integrates the other specifications, dealing with issues that span the technologies, providing an overview of J2EE, and defining those J2EE features not dealt with elsewhere, such as the notion of the J2EE application (see Chapter 26).

Figure 3.1 provides an illustration of a generic, multi-tiered J2EE application where several clients interact with the application's Web and EJB components. The Web components interact with EJBs and also directly with databases in the Enterprise Information System (EIS) tier. Before dissecting this diagram further, it is important to realize that this diagram represents just one possible configuration of components and tiers. It is quite possible to have a J2EE application that leaves out one or more of the tiers, using a subset of the J2EE technologies. Also, for particularly complicated applications there might be any number of sub-tiers within one of the major tiers, perhaps dealing with separate subsystems.

Let us examine the diagram in more detail. There are four major logical tiers. The client tier contains the client components such as Web browsers, applets, Java applications, special J2EE clients, CORBA clients or other J2EE applications. Normally, they will be located on external machines. These clients communicate with the other tiers using a variety of mechanisms. HTTP and its secure encrypted form, HTTPS, will be used by Web browsers to send requests and receive responses. Other kinds of client may also use HTTP to communicate with the J2EE application server. A major advantage of HTTP is that firewalls allow communication on the default HTTP port, but for security reasons, prevent communication via other ports. The clients may also communicate with the other tiers using RMI, where the client makes a method call on a server object as if the server object was co-located with the client in the same JVM. This is particularly useful if the client is a Java application or applet. The disadvantage is that TCP/IP ports required by RMI may be barred by a firewall, although some servers (for example Weblogic) overcome this problem

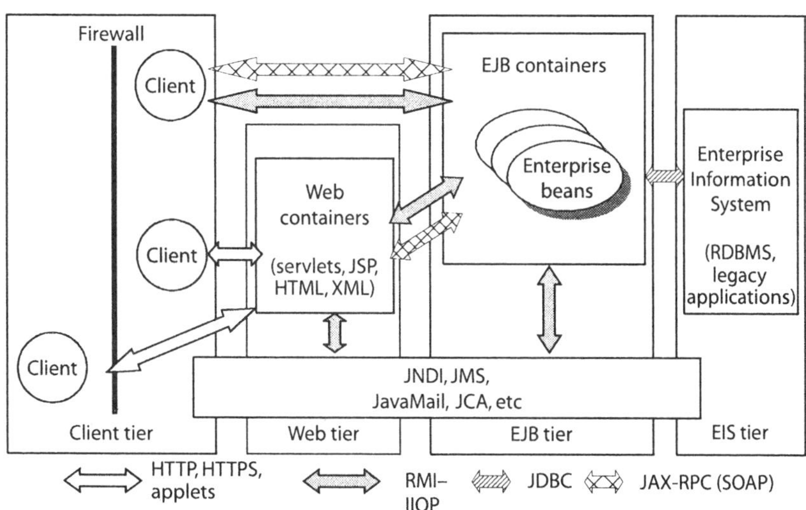

Figure 3.1 A multi-tier J2EE application.

by implementing RMI over HTTP. The clients could also use JMS to send messages asynchronously to the server-side application. Finally, and new to J2EE 1.4, clients may also communicate with certain kinds of EJB via the JAX-RPC API. This will send XML SOAP messages to the EJB. These messages ride on the back of HTTP(S) and so can bypass many firewall restrictions associated with other protocols.

The Web tier contains server-side components that are responsible for receiving, processing and responding to HTTP/S requests. Servlets and JSPs are the two J2EE technologies used in this tier. Servlets and JSPs may respond with HTML, XML, GIFs, applets etc. that are received by the original client. Normally, these Web components need to interact with business data, either directly from a database or via EJBs. Communication with EJBs is achieved using RMI, JMS or JAX-RPC. Communication with databases, and other external information systems, is achieved using JDBC or the Java Connector Architecture (JCA). JavaMail may also be used to communicate back with the client, e.g. to send purchase details to a customer.

The EJB tier contains server-side components that are responsible for encapsulating the application's business logic. For those familiar with the Model–View–Controller design pattern, the EJB tier implements the model, whereas the Web tier implements the view and controller. We will examine J2EE's version of MVC in Chapter 34. However, it is important that business logic remains separated from the code responsible for presenting the graphical user interface, thereby making it easier to change one without affecting the other, and to physically separate these subsystems for security reasons. For example, the Web tier may be exposed to the Internet; however, the EJB tier containing the business logic and associated data could be located on a separate machine that can only be accessed from within the organization's intranet. This is useful if you want to prevent direct access to the EJB tier from clients; that is, all client communication must be directed to the Web tier, enforcing a single point of entry.

The EJB business logic components may need to communicate with each other in the same J2EE server, but may also communicate with EJBs supported by other servers. Communication is achieved using RMI and JMS, although communication between EJBs in the same JVM can be achieved via simple method calls. EJBs are an in-memory representation of business data, some of which is persistent. An object to relational mapping between the EJBs and databases in the EIS tier is supported using JDBC and the JCA.

The Web and EJB components and special J2EE application clients are maintained in containers. Containers are responsible for maintaining the life cycle and operation of their components. In the case of Web and EJB components, they provide a buffer between the client and the component. Containers will also interact with various J2EE services on behalf of their components, for example, using the JAAS APIs to authenticate client requests before those requests are received by a specific component. Of course, components may also access these J2EE APIs directly themselves. We discuss the role of containers in more detail in Chapter 12.

3.3 J2EE Technology Tour

Contrived "hello world" examples are provided for some of the technologies to give you a flavour of the technology, without having to learn too much detail. A more realistic example will be developed during subsequent chapters.

The technologies have been divided into three groups:

- **Communication services.** These are the APIs and their implementations that enable either a component in one container to interact with a component in another, or even same, container, or to interact with components external to the J2EE platform, such as Web browsers and CORBA applications.
- **Horizontal services.** These are general services that may be required by several tiers in a multi-tier application. For example, authentication will be required on first access by a client to your enterprise application. This authentication could either be performed in the Web tier if access is required through a Web component, or performed in the EJB tier, if direct access is requested on an EJB component.
- **Component technologies.** As explained in Section 2.5, these are the "power tool" technologies that make developing enterprise applications more straightforward than they would be if you only had access to communication and horizontal services. For most J2EE applications these component technologies will insulate your business code from many of the underlying J2EE APIs.

However, be aware of the ambiguity of this grouping as, for example, JDBC (the database API) may fall under either horizontal services or communication services, since database interaction often occurs across a network, perhaps using RMI as the communication mechanism.

The full set of J2EE 1.4 APIs are as follows. The J2EE APIs that form part of the J2SE 1.4 platform are: Java IDL API, JDBC API (including its `javax.sql` extension), RMI-IIOP API, JNDI API, JAXP 1.1 API and JAAS API.

Those that are contained within Java Optional packages are: EJB 2.1, Servlet 2.4, JSP 2.0, JMS 1.1, JTA 1.0, JavaMail 1.3, JAF 1.0, JAXP 1.2, Connector 1.5, Web Services 1.1, JAX-RPC 1.0, SAAJ 1.1, JAXR 1.0, J2EE Management 1.0, JMX 1.2, J2EE Deployment 1.1 and JACC 1.0.

As you will notice, we focus on a core set of these APIs to keep the book to a manageable size.

3.3.1 Communication Services

Remote Method Invocation (RMI)

RMI enables communication between distributed objects. However, the programmer writes code at a level that largely ignores the presence of a network; for example, if object `A` needs to call a method on a remote object `B` then it simply makes the call `B.method(args)`. But how can `A` access `B` if it is remote? What actually happens is that the JVM containing `A` receives a local representative of remote `B`, often called a proxy or stub, which we now call `B'` to avoid confusion. The code for this is generated automatically and "knows" how to communicate using sockets with remote `B`. When `A` calls `B'.method(args)` the stub packages up the arguments and method name as a stream of bytes that are directed across a socket to remote `B`. Actually, there is some helper code at the remote end that reads from the socket, processes the bytes and makes the method call on `B` on behalf of `A`.

Why is RMI useful? It allows the programmer to concentrate on writing business logic rather than worrying about distribution details. In particular, the programmer does not need to maintain socket code in either the client or the server, since this code is generated automatically. Other reasons are discussed in Chapter 4.

Originally, RMI only permitted communication between Java objects. However, RMI now allows communication to objects written in other languages, which is achieved using RMI-IIOP (Internet Inter-ORB Protocol). IIOP is a CORBA (Common Object Request Broker Architecture) transport protocol that usually sits on top of TCP/IP. One of the key aspects of IIOP is that it provides a programming language-neutral way of transmitting data. Data in one programming language is mapped to its equivalent neutral form in IIOP that is then mapped to an equivalent programming language representation at the receiving end. These mappings are defined as part of the CORBA standard.

Listing 3.1 provides a simple example of the use of RMI. This implements a server object that publishes the `sayHello` method to the world. The code that registers the server has not been included, but could be placed either in `HelloServer` or in a separate class. More on this in Chapter 4.

Listing 3.1 A snippet of RMI code.

```
public interface HelloInterface extends java.rmi.Remote {
  public String sayHello() throws java.rmi.RemoteException;
}

public class HelloServer extends UnicastRemoteObject implements
    HelloInterface {
  public HelloServer() throws RemoteException {
  }
  public String sayHello() {
    return "Hello world" ;
  }
}
```

Java Messaging Service (JMS)

Figure 3.2 illustrates the main concepts behind JMS. Essentially, JMS supports asynchronous communication between producers and consumers. In other words, a producer sends a message to a queue or topic, but rather than waiting for a response it continues to undertake other tasks. When ready, consumers will consume messages from topics or queues.

There are two models of communication. The simplest involves the use of FIFO queues and normally supports one-to-one or many-to-one interactions between producers and consumers. Message objects are created by the producers and sent to a named queue. Consumers who wish to read messages from the head of that queue will need to obtain a reference to the queue and then can wait for messages to be placed on the queue. If a message is placed on the queue it will be read (and removed from the queue) by the listening consumer. The other model of communication is through the use of topics. Topics are analogous to newsgroups, since consumers, which we call subscribers, subscribe to one or more topics. Producers, which we now call publishers, publish messages to topics. A separate copy of a message is sent to each subscriber. Consequently, topics support many-to-many communication. We discuss JMS in some detail in Chapter 7 and its relationship to EJBs in Chapter 16.

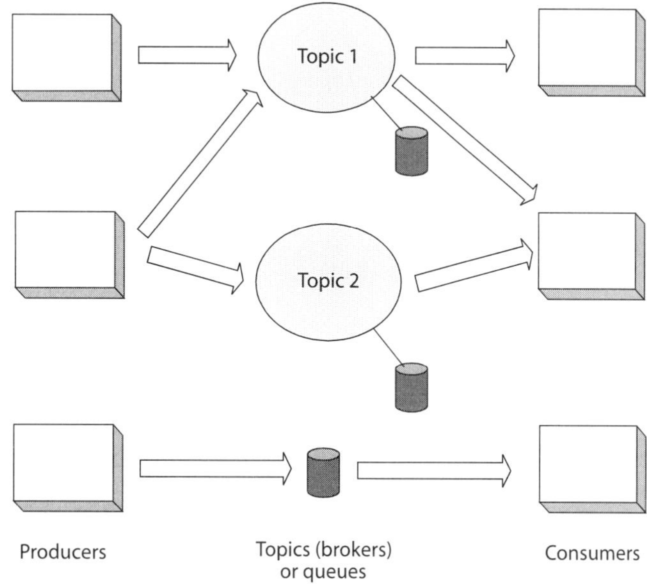

Figure 3.2 Overview of producers and consumers using JMS topics and queues.

JavaMail

JavaMail supports the sending and receiving of email from within a Java program. APIs are provided that allow you to construct MIME message objects, which are then sent and received via underlying mail protocols, such as SMTP, POP3 and IMAP4. Although a form of asynchronous communication, JavaMail is slower than JMS and should be used primarily where you need to interact with human users. We discuss JavaMail in Chapter 11.

HTTP/HTTPS

Hypertext Transfer Protocol is a text-based protocol used for communication across the Internet, and in particular, to support Web browser interaction with HTTP servers listening on server host machines. The protocol is stateless, in the sense that every request an HTTP client makes on the server will have to provide all the information needed to process that request; the server does not maintain any client state. Client requests are matched with server responses. Among other things, a client request identifies the resource target on the server (e.g. a particular HTML page or a servlet), the kind of request being made (HTTP supports several) and the nature of the client itself (such as the kind of browser, whether it can handle zipped data etc.), and any data to be sent to the server. Among other things, the server response will contain information about the status of the request (e.g. was the page found), the MIME type of the response data, and the response data.

HTTPS is the secure form of HTTP. It is where HTTP communication is transmitted over the Secure Socket Layer (SSL). SSL has its own handshake protocol that ensures that clients and servers can authenticate one another using verified digital certificates, and then transmit encrypted data.

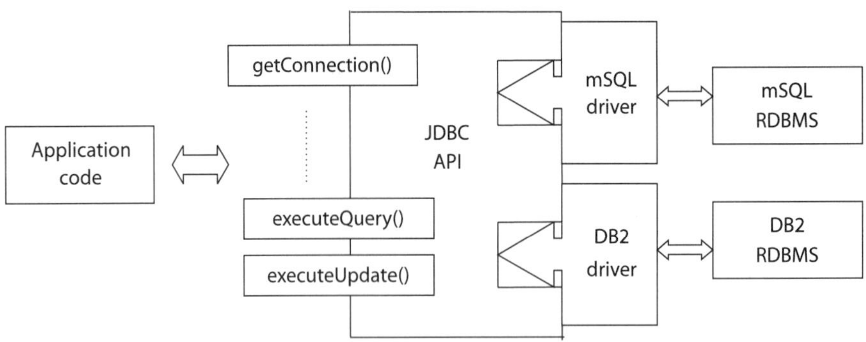

Figure 3.3 Conceptually how JDBC works.

3.3.2 Horizontal Services

JDBC

JDBC (unofficially, Java Database Connectivity) enables your programs to obtain database connections, execute SQL queries and updates via these connections, and process the results of such queries. The J2EE extensions to J2SE JDBC also provide support for connection pooling and distributed transactions. JDBC allows you to perform all these operations via database neutral APIs. Figure 3.3 illustrates this. The methods listed to the left of the diagram represent the neutral JDBC API, used to access any relational database system. The right-hand side of the diagram shows database driver modules (could be made up of several classes). There could be zero or many of these drivers plugged into JDBC. They have the responsibility of mapping a database neutral request onto the request expected by a real RDBMS. JDBC allows you to write much more portable code, since you pay less heed of the real database API, which can vary significantly.

Listing 3.2 is a very simple program that uses JDBC to query the `Messages` table for a row with the `id` column has the value 'world'.

Listing 3.2 A snippet of JDBC code.

```
try {
  Class.forName("sun.jdbc.odbc.JdbcOdbcDriver");
  String url = "jdbc:odbc:testDB";
  Connection con = DriverManager.getConnection(url);
  Statement st = con.createStatement();
  ResultSet rs = st.executeQuery("select message" +
    " from Messages where id = 'world'");
  if (rs.next())
    System.out.println(rs.getString("message"));
  rs.close();
  con.close();
} catch (Exception e) {}
```

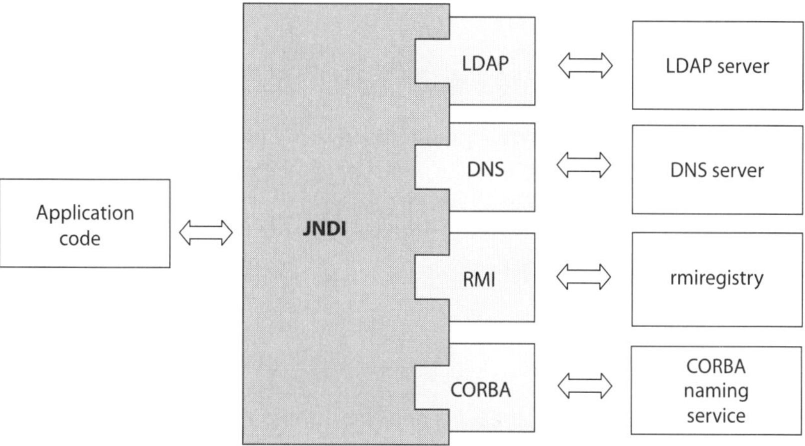

Figure 3.4 Overview of the JNDI architecture.

Java Naming and Directory Interface (JNDI)

Directory and naming services are common services across IT. They are used to map symbolic names or a set of search attribute values onto a resource. A file system is a naming service. A file resource is found by mapping a symbolic pathname onto a system file identifier (e.g. an inode in Unix). The Domain Name System maps symbolic host names onto their Internet addresses. Internally, J2EE application servers have a naming service implementation that is used by clients, Web components and EJBs to find J2EE resources using a symbolic naming scheme. All of these naming and directory services provide their own APIs and styles of interaction, and may be written in a variety of languages. JNDI provides a neutral API to these services, and in this respect is analogous to JDBC.

Figure 3.4 illustrates the main concepts. The API has methods such as `lookup`, `search`, `bind` and `rebind`. The application code uses `lookup` or `search` to locate some resource. However, before this can occur the application plugs in an appropriate mapping class, or classes (called the service provider). The application code will also need to tell the service provider where to look for the real server software. JNDI is discussed in more detail in Chapter 6 and subsequently in many other chapters, since it is the main mechanism for finding resources in J2EE.

Java Connector Architecture (JCA)

The JCA was new to J2EE 1.3. JCA provides mechanisms for integrating J2EE servers with heterogeneous Enterprise Information Systems (EIS) resources, such as Enterprise Resource Planning (ERP) applications, Customer Relationship Management (CRM) applications, RDBMSs etc. To comply with JCA, EIS vendors develop EIS specific resource adapters that are plugged into the JCA framework, which the J2EE server must support. Client applications access the EISs using the JCA's Common Client Interface API. This is analogous to using JDBC, except that this API does not focus on support for SQL. We discuss JCA in detail in Chapter 31.

Java Transaction API/Service (JTA/JTS)

JTS is a comprehensive transaction service that supports distributed transactions, and consequently two-phase commit protocol. For example, it supports a standard API that is called by a database's transaction manager when the database is ready to commit as part of a distributed transaction. JTA is a much simpler subset of JTS that is made available as a resource to J2EE applications. However, in most circumstances it is recommended that JTA is accessed by a container on behalf of its EJB components, rather than directly. We will discuss transactions in the context of EJBs in Chapter 27.

XML processing APIs

J2EE 1.4 includes the JAXP APIs. These APIs and their implementations support:

- Parsing of XML.
- Creation of in-memory representations of XML documents. This follows the Document Object Model defined by W3C (W3C, 2000).
- Parse-time triggering of callbacks. As the parser reaches a specific kind of tag or tag body, it can trigger the execution of a callback method that will take some application-specific action.
- Transformation of XML to some other representation, perhaps another XML document or an HTML document or even a PDF document. Transformation rules are encapsulated in an XSL file (W3C, 2002).

XML is becoming an important way of representing data in a standard format that can be validated against a Document Type Definition (DTD) or schema. This data can then be transmitted between various systems that convert the neutral format to system-specific formats, e.g. to a relational form. Just as Java provides code portability, XML provides data portability. XML is also used as the configuration language in J2EE. We provide a comprehensive overview of XML and related technologies in Chapter 10.

3.3.3 Component Technologies

Servlets

Servlets are server-side programs that execute in a servlet engine. This engine often forms part of an HTTP server, but may run standalone, being passed HTTP requests from a distinct HTTP server. A servlet is just a Java class that normally extends a `javax.servlet.http.HttpServlet` framework class. Servlet classes, JSPs and other resources can be packaged together as a Web component called a Web application. This is configured and then deployed within the J2EE server. Once deployed, an incoming client HTTP request to a servlet will cause an instance of the servlet to be created, unless one already exists. This then handles the request. Listing 3.3 provides an example of a simple servlet class. When a request is received, this servlet will send the "Hello World" HTML as part of an HTTP response back to the caller.

Listing 3.3 A snippet of servlet code.

```
public class Hello extends HttpServlet
{
  ...
  public void doPost(HttpServletRequest req, HttpServletResponse res)
  {
    res.setContentType("text/html");
    out = res.getWriter();
    out.println("<html><head><title>Hi world</title></head>");
    out.println("<body>Hello World!</body>");
    out.println("</html>");
  }
}
```

Java Server Pages (JSPs)

JSPs are servlets in disguise. As you can see from Listing 3.4, the format is HTML with additional JSP-specific tags. Although not shown here, Java code, called scriptlets, can be embedded in a JSP file. However, unlike HTML, the JSP source is translated automatically to servlet Java code prior to handling incoming HTTP requests. It is the generated servlet class, not the raw JSP, that handles the request.

Sun recommends the use of JSP where significant content is being developed. The aim should be to separate presentation and content from application logic, the JSP containing the presentation and content material. A JSP should be comprised largely of JSP and HTML tags, with little scriptlet code. Application-specific code can be encapsulated within developer-defined tags, JavaBeans or other Java classes called from the JSP. Avoid using servlets that contain large amounts of embedded HTML; use JSPs instead.

Listing 3.4 A snippet of JSP code.

```
<html>
<body>
<%@ page import="hello.BasicHello" %>
<jsp:useBean id="hello" scope="page" class="hello.BasicHello" />
<h1>Basic Hello World</h1>
This is a simple test
<p> <hr> <p>
Hello <jsp:getProperty name="hello" property="name"/>
<p> <hr>
</body></html>
```

Enterprise Java Beans (EJBs)

EJB components encapsulate business logic. Components have at least four parts:

- An implementation class that contains the business logic code.

- Two interfaces that advertise the EJB's methods to the outside world.
- A deployment descriptor: an XML file that is used to configure the EJB component before deployment within a J2EE server. For example, the security properties or transaction properties of EJB methods may be defined.

EJBs are container-managed components. That is, the container manages their life cycle and interacts with various J2EE services on behalf of the EJBs, based on configuration properties specified declaratively in their deployment descriptors. As mentioned in Chapter 2, the advantage of doing this is that 80% of the EJB code can be concerned with business logic and only 20% with issues of distribution. In non-EJB based applications this ratio may well be reversed, making maintenance and portability difficult.

3.4 References

Shannon, B. (2001). *Java 2 Platform Enterprise Edition Specification 1.3.* Sun Microsystems.

Shannon, B. (2002). *Java 2 Platform Enterprise Edition Specification 1.4.* Sun Microsystems, Proposed Final Draft.

BBC News (2001). Red faces after credit card web blunder, 22 June 2001. `http://news.bbc.co.uk/1/hi/business/1401648.stm`.

Java 2 Software Development Kit, Enterprise Edition. `http://java.sun.com/j2ee/`.

W3C (2000). *Document Object Model (DOM) Level 3 Core Specification, Version 1.0.* W3C Recommendation, November 2000, `http://www.w3.org/TR/DOM-Level-2-Core`.

W3C (2002). *XSL Transformations (XSLT) Version 2.* W3C Working Draft, August 2002, `http://www.w3.org/TR/xslt20`.

Chapter 4

Java and Remote Method Invocation

4.1 Introduction

In the last chapter we looked at some of the concepts underlying distributed applications – one of them being the ability to communicate between various parts of the distributed application. Java has a number of ways in which such communication can be achieved, including socket communication, CORBA-based communication and Remote Method Invocation (or RMI). Indeed, RMI is surprisingly simple to use and may well be preferable to sockets for Java to Java communication. This is because the resulting software is simpler and easier to maintain than using sockets. For example, a distributed software system resembles a software system executing within a single virtual machine except for the addition of one line to a client and two lines to a server!

4.2 Remote Method Invocation

RMI is similar in concept to Remote Procedure Calls (RPC) for procedural languages. Essentially, an object can invoke a method on another object in a separate process (potentially on a different machine).

RMI is surprisingly straightforward, merely requiring the developer to:

- Define a remote interface (which specifies what methods are available remotely).
- Subclass an appropriate RMI server class.
- Run the **rmic** compiler on the server class to generate the stub and skeleton files used with RMI.
- Rregister the remote object with the rmi registry.

The remote object is then available for use. In turn, the client need only obtain a reference to the remote object (via the registry) to be able to invoke remote methods on it. We will look at each of these steps in a little more detail.

Note that the registry is a central resource that records the names of remote objects and references to them. Using the registry clients can obtain a reference that allows them to communicate with the remote server.

4.2.1 The Remote Interface

A remote interface specifies the methods that will be available remotely from a RMI server object. All objects that are going to make themselves available remotely must implement a remote interface. To define a remote interface you must follow a number of steps:

- Define a new interface.
- Make this interface extend the interface `java.rmi.Remote`.
- Define any methods which are going to be available remotely (these methods must be public).
- Each method must declare that it throws the `java.rmi.RemoteException`.

As an example, consider the remote interface definition in Listing 4.1. This listing shows the `RMIInterface` interface to be used by the `RMIServer`.

Listing 4.1 The `RMIInterface` remote interface.

```
package myrmi;

/**
 * The remote interface used to indicate which
 * methods are remotely available.
 */
public interface RMIInterface extends java.rmi.Remote {
  public String query(String request) throws java.rmi.RemoteException;
}
```

4.2.2 Subclassing a Server Class

Once you have defined a remote interface, you can start to define the server class that implements this interface. To do this you need to:

- Specify the remote interface(s) being implemented by the server.
- Optionally subclass a remote server (e.g. `java.rmi.server.UnicastRemoteObject`). If you do not subclass a remote server you would need to write all the appropriate code that would otherwise be inherited.
- Provide implementations for the methods specified in the remote interface.
- Define a constructor for the server. This constructor must throw the `java.rmi.RemoteException`.
- Create and install the `java.rmi.RMISecurityManager`.

These steps sound complex, but are in reality straightforward. For example, Listing 4.2 illustrates the source code for the RMIServer remote object class. As you can see, it implements the RMIInterface interface and thus the query(String) method. It defines a null parameter constructor that throws the RemoteException exception (as indicated above). Within this constructor, it first calls super(). This invokes the null argument constructor[1] of the java.rmi.server.UnicastRemoteObject. By doing this, the remote object is 'exported' so that it can handle calls to the remote object on an anonymous port (actually 1099). Next the constructor calls the initialize() method. This method merely sets up a vector of vectors containing the test data. For a real system, this data might be extracted from other systems or a database. Once inside a try {} block, the constructor then uses the setSecurityManager() method of the System class to install a newly created instance of the RMISecurityManager. Note that we do not need to know much about this security manager to be able to use it. Also note that you can at this point get away without an RMISecurityManager if you ensure that the required classes are always on the classpath. However, later on we will need to be able to dynamically download appropriate classes to an RMI client, which can only be done when an RMISecurityManager is set, as this forces a security policy to be specified (see later).

Listing 4.2 The RMIServer class.

```
package myrmi;

import java.rmi.*;
import java.rmi.server.UnicastRemoteObject;
import java.util.Vector;

/**
 * An RMI server. This server records the partners of various people.
 * It will then return the name of a person's partner or the string
 * "Unknown".
 */
public class RMIServer extends UnicastRemoteObject implements RMIInterface {
  private Vector data = new Vector();

  /**
   * This constructor initializes the simple data structure holding the
   * information and registers this object with the rmiregistry.
   * @throws RemoteException
   */
  public RMIServer() throws RemoteException {
    super();
    initialize();
    try {
      System.setSecurityManager(new RMISecurityManager());
      System.out.println("Set security manager");
```

1 This would actually happen by default, but it is included here to indicate the operations occurring.

```
      Naming.rebind("//hal.dcs.aber.ac.uk/RMIServer", this);
      System.out.println("RMIServer bound in registry");
    } catch (Exception e) {
      System.out.println("RMIServer error " + e.getMessage());
      e.printStackTrace();
    }
  }

  /**
   * Initializes the internal data structure with sample data.
   * A better solution would be to hold this information in a
   * database, but for simplicity it is held internally.
   */
  public void initialize() {
    addRecord("John", "Denise");
    addRecord("Paul", "Fiona");
    addRecord("Peter", "Maureen");
    addRecord("Bernard", "Liz");
  }

  // Adds the information to the data structure. Note
  // the data is added twice so that if a name is found
  // the following name is always the persons partner (or null)
  private void addRecord(String s1, String s2) {
    Vector details = new Vector();
    details.addElement(s1); details.addElement(s2);
    data.addElement(details);
    details = new Vector();
    details.addElement(s2); details.addElement(s1);
    data.addElement(details);
  }

  /**
   * This method is the externally published method that may be called by
   * any remote object which has obtained a reference for the remote
   * object
   * @returns String
   * @throws java.rmi.RemoteException
   */
  public String query(String request) throws java.rmi.RemoteException {
    String result = "Unknown";
    for (int i=0; i < data.size(); i++) {
      Vector record = (Vector)data.elementAt(i);
      String person = (String)record.elementAt(0);
      if (person.equals(request))
        result = (String)record.elementAt(1);
```

```
      }
      return result;
    }

    /**
     * Test harness for RMIServer
     */
    public static void main(String args []) {
      try {
        new RMIServer();
      } catch (RemoteException e) {
        System.out.println("RMIServer error " + e.getMessage());
        e.printStackTrace();
      }
    }
  }
```

The other thing to note is the call to `rebind()` sent to the class `Naming`. This is actually the process used to register this object with the RMI registry. This allows another object in a different process to obtain a reference to this object. Essentially, the registry maintains a table of remote objects and how to reference them (i.e. the machine and port they are connected to). This process is illustrated in Figure 4.1.

If you do not want to use the default port, a different port can be specified when the object is registered with the registry. For example, `//hal.dcs.aber.ac.uk:1234/RMIServer` would connect the `RMIServer` to port 1234.

Note that the use of the class `Naming` only works when using RMI over the Java Remote Method Protocol (RMI-JRMP). If you are using RMI over IIOP (the Internet Inter-Orb Protocol) used by many (if not all) application servers then you will need to use the JNDI to access the naming service and then use the `PortableRemoteObject.narrow` method for

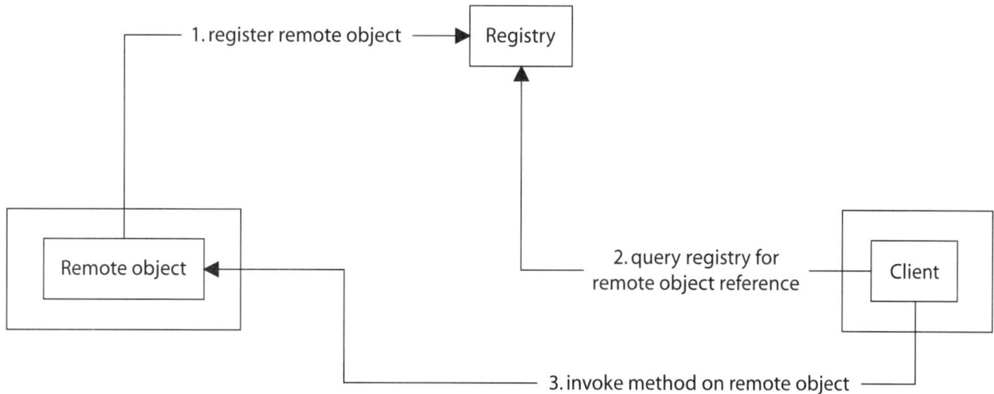

Figure 4.1 How the registry manages RMI references.

casting. Both of these topics will be covered later in this book and are only mentioned here for reference.

4.2.3 Running the rmic Compiler

Once you have defined the server class and successfully compiled it, you can then run the rmic compiler. This compiler is applied to the `.class` file rather than the `.java` file. For example, to execute the rmic compiler on the `RMIServer` class just created we would issue the following command at the command line:

```
rmic myrmi.RMIServer
```

Note that I have specified the package within which the `RMIServer` is implemented. This produces two additional `.class` files:

- `RMIServer_Skel.class`
- `RMIServer_Stub.class`

These files define the skeleton and stub files used to interface between the server and any clients. Essentially, the skeleton connects the server to the RMI framework while the stub acts as a proxy server in the client's environment. This is illustrated in Figure 4.2. Note that in Java 2 the skeleton is not required and can be omitted.

Figure 4.2 Using the skeleton and stub classes.

4.2.4 Starting the Registry

We are now nearly ready to deploy our RMI server object. However, we must first start the RMI registry so that it can record the location and name of the server object. This is done by executing the `rmiregistry` command. This command produces no output and is typically run in the background. For example, on Windows 95/NT you can issue the following command from the command line:

```
start rmiregistry
```

If `start` is not available, you can use `javaw`. In fact, on a Windows machine you can merely execute the `rmiregistry` within a DOS window and it will start to execute. However, if you terminate the window you will terminate the `rmiregistry` process (hence the use of `start` or `javaw`).

The registry runs on port 1099 by default. If you want to start the registry on a different port, specify the port number in the command. For example, to run the registry on port 1234 use:

```
start rmiregistry 1234
```

You can now start the server object. As the `RMIServer` class implements the `main` method, this remote object can be initiated in the normal manner:

```
java myrmi.RMIServer
```

4.3 The RMIClient

As we now have a server object that is running and has registered itself with the RMI registry, we can now create a client object. In our case we want to create a class which will obtain a string from the command line and print out the result returned from the `RMIServer` object. Listing 4.3 presents the `RMIClient` class definition.

Listing 4.3 The RMIClient class.

```
package myrmi;

import java.rmi.*;

/**
 * A simple client class used to connecct to the
 * RMIServer remote object and query it for the partner of
 * the specified person.
 */
public class RMIClient {
  private String question;
  public RMIClient(String string) {
    question = string;
    try {
      System.out.println("Attempting to gain reference to the remote
                          object");
      RMIInterface remoteObject =
            (RMIInterface)Naming.lookup("//hal.dcs.aber.ac.uk/RMIServer");
      System.out.println("Reference to remote object obtained");
      // Get string from remote object
      System.out.println("Issuing query to remote object");
      String reply = remoteObject.query(question);
      System.out.println(" \n" + question + "s partner is " + reply);
    } catch (Exception e) {
      System.out.println("RMIClient error " + e.getMessage());
```

```
        e.printStackTrace();
      }
    }

    /**
     * Test harness for RMIClientBean
     */
    public static void main(String args []) {
      if (args.length == 1)
        new RMIClient(args[0]);
      else
        System.out.println("Usage: java RMIClient <name>");
    }
  }
```

The `RMIClient` is an extremely simple class. It obtains the first command line parameter and uses that as the query to pass to the `RMIServer`. It obtains a reference to the `RMIServer` from the `rmiregistry` (the confusingly named class `Naming`). For example:

```
(RMIInterface)Naming.lookup("//hal.dcs.aber.ac.uk/RMIServer");
```

Note that it has to specify the machine on which the server is running as well as the name given to the server. Also, note that the object returned by the lookup method must be cast to the remote interface type (in this case `RMIInterface`). The resulting object can not be used in just the same way as a local object. In fact, it is a local object (the stub object). The calls are then passed onto the actual server object via the RMI framework.

The result of executing the `rmiregistry`, the `RMIServer` and the `RMIClient` are illustrated in the screen dump presented in Figure 4.3.

4.4 Performance

A concern that is often expressed with reference to RMI in Java is that there must be a performance penalty (compared to using plain sockets). As RMI is built on top of sockets, but provides additional support via the RMI registry for locating objects and providing skeletons and stubs as required, there must of course be some performance penalty. However, depending on how you use sockets in Java, the relative performance of RMI may be a surprise.

To illustrate this, Table 4.1 illustrates the performance of RMI versus two different implementations that make use of sockets. To keep the performance trials similar, all three applications passed one string from the client to the server and returned another string 100 times. Averages were calculated for the two-step send and retrieve process. One of the socket implementations uses the UTF read and write string methods. The other socket implementation uses serialization. In serialization, the object to be sent via the socket is "serialized" into a form that can be restored at the other end. At present, this approach can

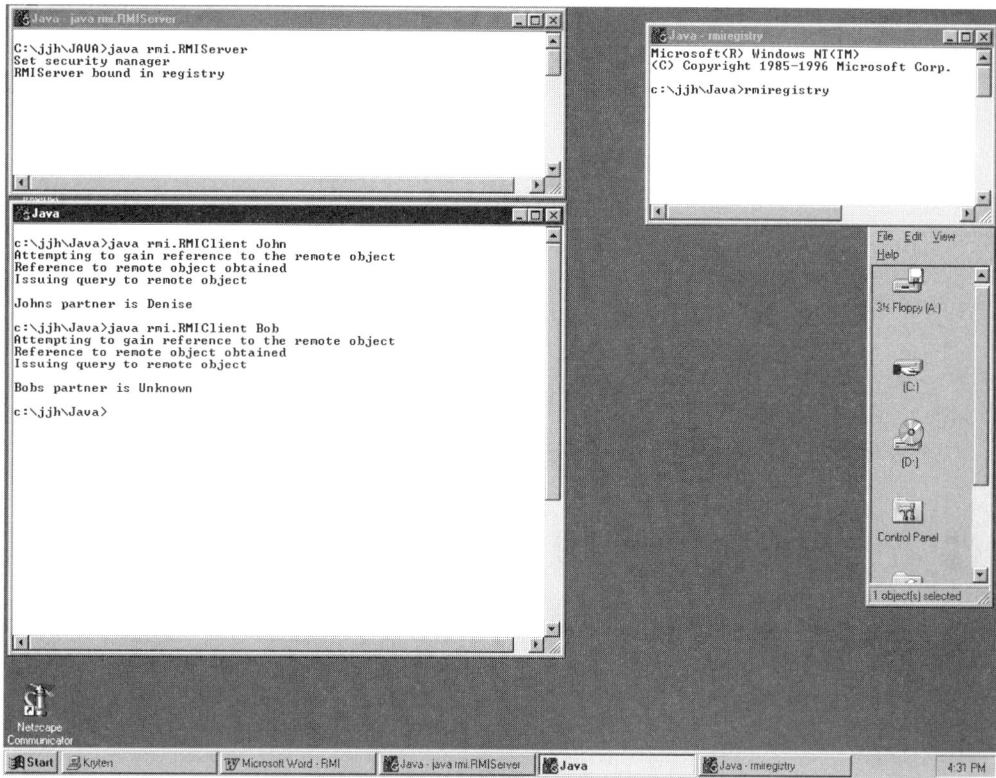

Figure 4.3 Running the RMI example.

Table 4.1 Comparative performance between RMI and sockets.

Test application	*Average of 100 exchanges (ms)*
RMI	39
Serialization and sockets	17
UTF conversion and sockets	4002

only work between Java programs (just as RMI-JRMP can only be used to connect different Java programs – note that RMI-IIOP is used between Java and other languages). In contrast, the UTF approach writes strings in a platform-independent manner that could be used between Java and any programming language.

All tests were carried out on a 133 MHz Pentium PC with 32 Mbyte of memory, using the standard JDK 1.1.5 virtual machine without optimization turned on (in the javac compiler).

As can be seen from Table 4.1, RMI is twice as slow as serialization and sockets; however, the conversion to UTF format strings is significantly slower (100 times slower!). This appears to be due to the `writeUTF()` and `readUTF()` methods. These methods are written in Java (as opposed to being part of the JVM, as is the case with serialization – which is also used by RMI) or implemented in native code. In addition, this Java does not look particularly optimal.

Thus the use of sockets in the blind belief that they will always be faster than RMI is not true. The performance penalty incurred by RMI (relative to serialization and sockets) does need to be considered; however, the resulting programs are far, far simpler. For comparison, the serialization test programs are presented in Listing 4.5. If you compare these with the RMI class presented earlier (upon which the test applications were based), you can see that it is quite a bit more complicated.

Listing 4.5 Serialization and sockets: server and client code.

```
import java.net.*;
import java.io.*;

/**
 * Simple server class which provides address for named people
 * using a simple protocol (e.g. name = 'John'). The socket to
 * socket communication facilities of Java are used to connect
 * a client to this server.
 */
public class SerializationServer {

  // Starts the server application
  public static void main (String args []) {
    SerializationServer s = new SerializationServer();
    s.start();
  }

  /**
    * Provides the main server loop:
    * 1. Wait for a connection
    * 2. Obtain a reuqest for an address
    * 3. Query the database
    * 4. Respond with a null string or the address
    */
  public void start() {
    // Set up the server socket
    ServerSocket serverSocket = null;
    Socket socket;
    InputStream socketIn;
    OutputStream socketOut;
    ObjectInputStream objectInputStream;
    ObjectOutputStream objectOutputStream;
    String queryString;
```

```
    // Register service on port 1234
    try {
      serverSocket = new ServerSocket(1234);
    } catch (IOException e) {System.out.println("Server socket
                            registration failed");}

    try {
      // Wait here and listen for a connection
      socket = serverSocket.accept();
      socketIn = socket.getInputStream();
      objectInputStream = new ObjectInputStream(socketIn);
      // Get a communications stream from the socket
      socketOut = socket.getOutputStream();
      objectOutputStream = new ObjectOutputStream(socketOut);

      queryString = (String)objectInputStream.readObject();
      // Wait for a data from a client
      while (!queryString.equals("end")) {
        // Return information to client
        objectOutputStream.writeObject("John");
        queryString = (String)objectInputStream.readObject();
      }

      // Now close the connections, but not the server socket
      objectInputStream.close();
      objectOutputStream.close();
      socketIn.close();
      socketOut.close();
      socket.close();
    } catch (Exception e) {
      System.out.println("Error during socket communications" +
          e.getMessage());
      e.printStackTrace();
    }
  }
}

import java.net.*;
import java.io.*;

/**
 * A simple client to test client/server via sockets
 */
public class SerializationClient {
  private String query = "name";
  private Socket socket;
```

```
private OutputStream outputStream;
private ObjectOutputStream objectOutputStream;
private InputStream inputStream;
private ObjectInputStream objectInputStream;

public static void main(String args []) {
  SerializationClient c;
  if (args.length == 0) {
    c = new SerializationClient();
  } else {
    c = new SerializationClient(args[0]);
  }
  c.test();
}

// Method used to initialize an applet.
// Sets up the applet panel.
public SerializationClient () {
  this("manuel.dcs.aber.ac.uk");
}

public SerializationClient(String s) {
  try {
    // First get a socket connection to the Server object
    socket = new Socket(s, 1234);
    outputStream = socket.getOutputStream();
    objectOutputStream = new ObjectOutputStream(outputStream);

    // Now get the input streams
      inputStream = socket.getInputStream();
      objectInputStream = new ObjectInputStream(inputStream);

    } catch (Exception e) {
      System.out.println("Error during socket communications");
      System.out.println(e.getMessage());
  }
}

public void test() {
  String result;

  long first = 0, second = 0, total = 0;

  try {
    for (int j = 0; j < 10; j++) {
      System.out.println("Round: " + j);
```

```
            first = System.currentTimeMillis();
            for (int i = 0; i < 10; i++) {
                // Now send a query to the server specifying the name to
                // search for
                objectOutputStream.writeObject("name");
                result = (String)objectInputStream.readObject();
            }
            second = System.currentTimeMillis();
            total = total + (second - first);
          }

          objectOutputStream.writeObject("end");

          System.out.println("total : " + total + " Average: " + (total / 10));

          // Close streams and socket
          objectOutputStream.close();
          objectInputStream.close();
          outputStream.close();
          inputStream.close();
          socket.close();

        } catch (Exception e) {
          System.out.println("Error during test method");
          System.out.println(e.getMessage());
        }
      }
    }
```

4.5 Passing Parameters

One issue that also needs to be discussed is that all parameters passed from an RMI client to an RMI server must either be serializable (i.e. they must implement either the `java.io.Serializable` or `java.io.Externalizable` interfaces) or they must be remote objects in their own right. If a parameter is serializable then its data is extracted from the local object and sent across the network to the remote server. The remote server then reconstructs the object with the data sent. This allows objects to appear to be created within one JVM and sent via RMI to another JVM. Remember though that a copy of the data is made and thus any changes made to the object in the RMIServer will not be reflected in the object held in the RMI client (and vice versa!). However, you should note that objects are not by default serializable (that is the class object does not implement the serializable interface). It is therefore necessary for any objects that need to be sent over RMI (and any objects they reference) to implement `java.io.Serializable`. As this interface does not specify any methods, this is straightforward.

The other option is to make an object remote in its own right. In such cases stub information is sent over RMI instead of a copy of the actual data. This allows a remote reference to be held to the parameter (that is the object does not "move" it remains on the JVM on which it was created). Any calls made to the parameter object actually become remote calls back to the actual object. This means changes made in one JVM are reflected in the original JVM.

A word of warning regarding treating remote objects as "local" objects. This has obvious performance implications relating to network latency, as each call goes across the network etc. In general it is better to group a set of smaller calls together into one call which will pull together all the information required.

4.6 Online References

The Java Remote Method Invocation (RMI) Home Page: `http://java.sun.com/j2se/1.4/docs/guide/rmi/`.

RMI Specification: `http://java.sun.com/j2se/1.4/docs/guide/rmi/spec/rmiTOC.html`.

Chapter 5

Activate Yourself!

5.1 Introduction

Remote Method Invocation (or RMI for short) was introduced in the last chapter. So why are we talking about it once again? Well the Java 2 Standard Edition (SDK 1.2) introduced a new and exciting feature to RMI – the ability to implement activatable servers! These are server programs that wake up and start to run when they are needed. This is in contrast to previous RMI servers (and indeed socket implementations of server programs), where the server program must be resident in memory all the time in case a client requests some information from it.

An activatable server is one that is executed only when the first request is made to it (it can optionally be turned of when it is not required). To do this, the RMI mechanism has been extended to include the ability to trigger a new Java Virtual Machine (JVM), instantiate a server program in this JVM and connect that program with the existing RMI mechanism. One of the really nice features of this extension is that no changes need to be made to any client of the server or to the interface specifying what methods the server makes available remotely – thus insulating the client side from the fact that the server is activatable or not.

In this chapter we will look at the use of activatable servers and present a simple activatable application based on that RMI application presented in the last chapter.

5.2 Extending RMI

Essentially RMI was extended so that everything that was true for the original version of RMI still holds. However, you can now make your servers activatable. Notice that in the previous section it was stated that the server was now loaded in memory and waiting for input all the time. However, let us say that we only want to actually use the server between 7.00 p.m. and 8.00 p.m. on a Sunday evening for some house keeping activities. In the previous section, either the server program was running the whole time with nothing to do except on a Sunday night, or some external entity needed to activate it when required. This latter approach is certainly possible, but requires more maintenance and administration.

With activation we can change all that so that the RMI framework instantiates the server program at 7:00 p.m. on Sunday when the first request is made of that server.

The way that this is handled is that a second program is now provided along with the `rmiregistry` naming service. This second program is called the rmid program. The rmid program (Java RMI Activation System Daemon) is a demon program that works with the `rmiregistry`. Essentially, the rmid program holds all the information necessary to start up a new JVM and load it with the server program. This means that the `rmid` program holds information about what the server is called, where to find the class files for the server, what initialization information to present to the server etc.

Now when a client requests a reference to the server from the `rmiregistry`, instead of holding a reference to the remote object the `rmiregistry` holds a reference to the rmid program and to the entry in the rmid program which holds the servers details. The rmid program is then requested to start up the server (which it does) and the resulting reference is returned to the client. The next time this (or any other client) requests a reference to this newly started server, the `rmiregistry` will be able to provide it directly. If for some reason the server is terminated (either programmatically or via external intervention), then any subsequent calls the server will cause the rmid program to start a new JVM.

5.3 Implementing an Activatable Server

To implement an activatable server you need to perform the following steps:

1. Subclass the `java.rmi.activation.Activatable` server class.
2. Implement a two-parameter constructor which takes an activation group id number and any initialization information (in the form of a `MarshalledObject`). For example:

```
public Server(ActivationID id, MarshalledObject data)
    throws RemoteException {
  super(id, 0);
}
```

3. Create an activation description that will allow the server to be instantiated by the rmid program.
4. Register the activation description with the rmid program and hold on to the reference returned.
5. Register the rmid reference with the `rmiregistry` program.
6. Then the activatable server must be compiled using javac and the rmic compiler as before.
7. The client should need no modification; nor should the remote interface.

Each of the steps will be considered below. For completeness we will also examine the remote interface and the client class.

5.3.1 Remote Interface

The following remote interface (which can be used with either the original form of RMI or the activatable form) states that a method `getMessage(String)` which takes a string and returns a string must be implemented by any class implementing the `HelloInterface` remote interface.

```
package remote;
public interface HelloInterface extends java.rmi.Remote {
  public String getMessage(String s) throws java.rmi.RemoteException;
}
```

5.3.2 The `Client` Class

The `Client` is an extremely simple class (see Figure 5.1). It obtains a reference to the `Server` from the `rmiregistry` (the confusingly named class `Naming`). For example:

```
(HelloInterface)Naming.lookup("rmi://hal.jdt.co.uk/Hello");
```

Having done this, it then calls the `getMessage()` method on the reference returned from the `rmiregistry`, passing in the string `"John"` as a parameter. Note that it has to specify the machine on which the server is running as well as the name given to the server. Also, note that the object returned by the lookup method must be cast to the remote interface type (in this case

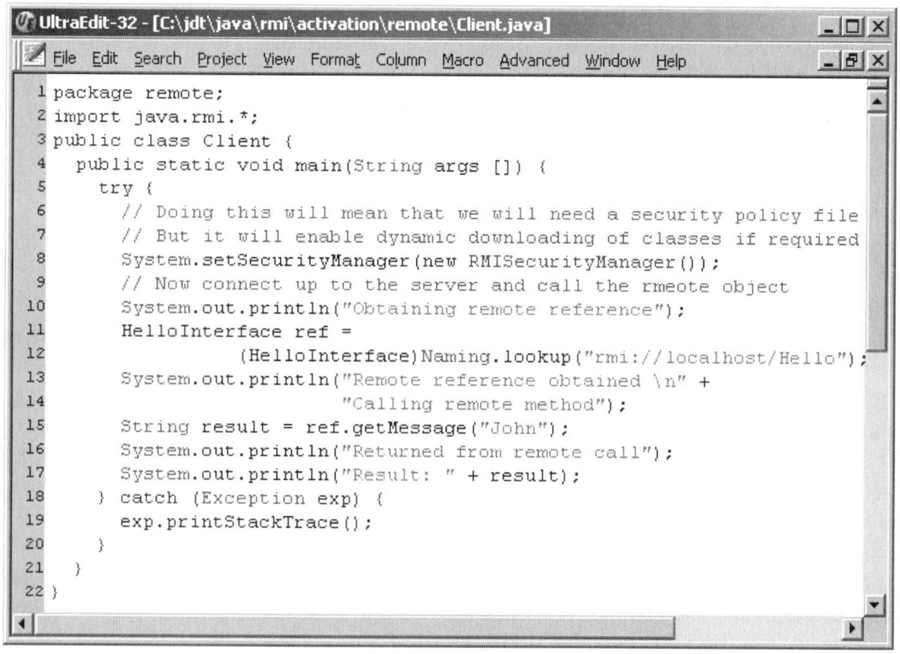

UltraEdit-32 - [C:\jdt\java\rmi\activation\remote\Client.java]

File Edit Search Project View Format Column Macro Advanced Window Help

```
package remote;
import java.rmi.*;
public class Client {
  public static void main(String args []) {
    try {
      // Doing this will mean that we will need a security policy file
      // But it will enable dynamic downloading of classes if required
      System.setSecurityManager(new RMISecurityManager());
      // Now connect up to the server and call the rmeote object
      System.out.println("Obtaining remote reference");
      HelloInterface ref =
                 (HelloInterface)Naming.lookup("rmi://localhost/Hello");
      System.out.println("Remote reference obtained \n" +
                         "Calling remote method");
      String result = ref.getMessage("John");
      System.out.println("Returned from remote call");
      System.out.println("Result: " + result);
    } catch (Exception exp) {
      exp.printStackTrace();
    }
  }
}
```

Figure 5.1 A simple RMI client.

HelloInterface). The resulting object can now be used in just the same way as a local object. In fact, it is a local object (the stub object). The calls are then passed on to the actual server object via the RMI framework. Finally notice that this code says nothing about the activation of the server obtained from the rmiregistry! Note that it installs a SecurityManager as the first operation it performs. This is so that it can have server classes delivered to it on demand.

5.3.3 The Activatable Server

As was stated earlier, to make a server activatable, it must extend the java.rmi.activation.Activatable class. The java.rmi.activation package is new in Java 2. It must also implement a two-parameter constructor, which throws the RemoteException. The activatable server for our example is presented in Figure 5.2.

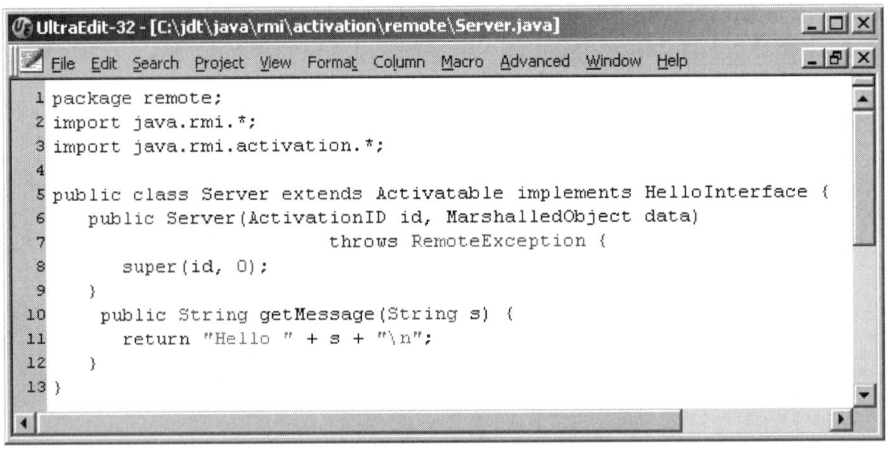

```
package remote;
import java.rmi.*;
import java.rmi.activation.*;

public class Server extends Activatable implements HelloInterface {
   public Server(ActivationID id, MarshalledObject data)
                        throws RemoteException {
      super(id, 0);
   }
    public String getMessage(String s) {
      return "Hello " + s + "\n";
   }
}
```

Figure 5.2 The Activatable server class.

There are a couple of things that you should notice about this class. Firstly, the method getMessage(String) does not throw the java.rmi.RemoteException. In contrast, the interface (HelloInterface) clearly specified that this method would throw the RemoteException (and indeed the client had to handle the possibility that the RemoteException may be thrown). So why doesn't the server say anything about the RemoteException? It is because it is not the server that will generate the RemoteException, but the RMI infrastructure. Thus it is the Stub class that would generate the RemoteException that the client must handle and not the server (for example, let us say we have lost the connection with the server because the server's machine has gone down – we still want to know about this and we will as the stub class will generate a RemoteException for us!).

The other thing to note about this class is that the ActivationId is passed straight on to the super class constructor. The activation id is used to obtain information about the JVM environment within which the server should be executing. Note that in this case we are not doing anything with the MarshalledObject; however, it is a bit like a vector and can hold (serializable) objects that we can extract in the server's constructor.

5.3.4 The Server Setup

We are going to use a separate program to set up the activatable server. We will do this to illustrate that the setup program has been terminated (by calling `System.exit(0)`), and thus the server program is initiated by the rmid program from scratch.

The setup program (presented in Figure 5.3) generates the activation description used by the rmid program to start up the server. It then registers this with the rmid program (via the class `Activatable` which via the register method acts as an interface to the rmid program). It completes its job by registering the reference returned by the rmid program with the `rmiregistry` naming service. It then terminates itself.

```
package remote;
import java.rmi.*;
import java.rmi.activation.*;
import java.util.Properties;

public class Setup {

  public static void main(String args[]) {
    try {
      // Doing this will mean that we will need a security policy file
      // But it will enable dynamic downloading of classes if required
      System.setSecurityManager(new RMISecurityManager());
      // Because of the 1.2 security model, a security policy should
      // be specified for the ActivationGroup VM. The first argument
      // to the Properties put method, inherited from Hashtable, is
      // the key and the second is the value
      Properties props = (Properties)System.getProperties().clone();
      props.put("java.security.policy",
                "/jdt/java/rmi/activation/remote/security.policy");
      ActivationGroupDesc agd = new ActivationGroupDesc(props, null);
      ActivationGroupID agi = ActivationGroup.getSystem().registerGroup(agd);

      String location = "file:/jdt/rmi/activation/remote/";
      ActivationDesc desc = new ActivationDesc(agi,
                                               "remote.Server",
                                               location,
                                               null);

      HelloInterface ref = (HelloInterface)Activatable.register(desc);
      Naming.rebind("Hello", ref);

      System.out.println("Activatable object registered " +
                         "and ready for activation");
      System.exit(0);

    } catch (Exception exp) {
      exp.printStackTrace();
    }
  }
}
```

Figure 5.3 The Setup program.

As this program is quite complicated we will now dissect it bit by bit. The first part we will look at is the use of the SecurityManager and the definition of the properties object. We will then look at the creation of the ActivationDesc object.

In this example we do set up a security manager. The use of the security manager requires a security policy file to be provided for use with the application (we will look at the file later). The reason we are using a security manager is that it allows the classes used by the server to be downloaded to a client program (if the classes are not found on the classpath when the rmiregistry starts up). This is useful if a server is made available over the Internet and the client needs to acquire the stubs dynamically.

Because the security manager requires a security property file the activatable server that this program is setting up needs to know which security property file to use. This is provided by the properties object used to represent the system properties. The property java.security.policy is used to specify the location of the security policy file (and its name). If you are trying to run this example you should change this property so that it points at the location of your own security property file. This file can be called anything, although by convention is has a .policy extension.

The creation of the ActivationDesc object is made up of three steps:

1. Create an activation group description. This is necessary even when there is only one server on its own (an activation group is a group of servers which will all be activated together when one of them is instantiated). It is necessary to create an activation group even if there is only one server, because it is the activation group that specifies the JVM environment (as described by the system properties).

```
Properties props = (Properties)System.getProperties().clone();
props.put("java.security.policy",
          "/jdt/java/rmi/activation/remote/security.policy");
ActivationGroupDesc agd = new ActivationGroupDesc(props, null);
```

2. Having created the activation group description we are now ready to create the activation group. There are a number of ways to do this, one of which is illustrated below:

```
ActivationGroupID agi = ActivationGroup.getSystem().registerGroup(agd);
```

This form uses the group description to create a new group and return a reference to that group (the ActivationGroupID).

3. We are now finally ready to create the actual activation description. To do this we need both the location of the class files for the server, the name of the server (in this case Server in the package remote), the activation group that this server is part of (held here by agi) and any initialization information (to be held in a marshalled object – in this case represented by null, as there is no information).

```
String location = "file:/jdt/java/rmi/activation/remote/";
ActivationDesc desc = new ActivationDesc(agi,
                                         "remote.Server",
                                         location,
                                         null);
```

We now have an activation description to register with the rmid program. This is done by calling register on the class `Activatable`. Note that the returned object must be cast to the interface:

```
HelloInterface ref = (HelloInterface)Activatable.register(desc);
```

This reference object can now be registered with the `rmiregistry` naming service:

```
Naming.rebind("Hello", ref);
```

We have now registered the server with both the rmid program and the `rmiregistry` (under the highly original name "Hello"). The set up program can now terminate! The final result is illustrated in Figure 5.4. Note that the server is in a dashed box because it does not yet exist!

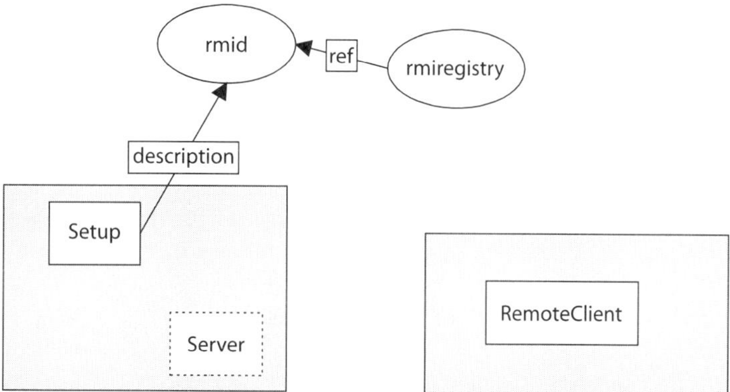

Figure 5.4 Installing an activatable server.

5.4 Running the Activatable Client–Server

Once you have compiled all the `.java` files and run the rmic compiler on the `Server` class file, you should then:

- Start the `rmiregistry`:
  `rmiregistry`
- Start the rmid program:
  `rmid -J-Djava.security.policy=rmid.policy`
- Start (and then terminate) the `Setup` program:
  `C:\jdt\java\rmi\activation>java -Djava.security.policy=/jdt/java/rmi/activation/remote/security.policy -Djava.rmi.server.codebase=file:///jdt/java/rmi/activation/remote remote.Setup`

- Start the `Client`:
  `java -Djava.security.policy=/jdt/java/rmi/activation/remote/security.policy remote.Client`
- Starting the `Client` program causes the `Server` to be initiated as well.

The result of doing this is illustrated in Figure 5.5.

There are a couple of things that need to be explained in more detail here. Firstly the rmid program: by default, rmid now requires a security policy file that is used to verify whether or not the information in each `ActivationGroupDescriptor` is allowed to be used to launch a JVM for an activation group. The `rmid.security` policy can contain `ExecPermissions` and `ExecOptionPermission`. The permission `com.sun.rmi.rmid.ExecPermission` is used to grant rmid permission to execute a command, specified in the group descriptor's `CommandEnvironment` to launch an activation group. The permission `com.sun.rmi.rmid.ExecOptionPermission` is used to allow rmid to use command line options, specified as properties overrides in the group descriptor or as options in the `CommandEnvironment`, when launching the activation group. For our example, the `rmid.policy` file is presented below:

```
grant {
permission com.sun.rmi.rmid.ExecOptionPermission
"-Djava.*";
permission com.sun.rmi.rmid.ExecOptionPermission
"-Dsun.*";
permission com.sun.rmi.rmid.ExecOptionPermission
"-Dfile.*";
  permission com.sun.rmi.rmid.ExecOptionPermission
  "-Dpath.separator=*";
  permission com.sun.rmi.rmid.ExecOptionPermission
  "-Duser.*";
  permission com.sun.rmi.rmid.ExecOptionPermission
  "-Dos.*";
  permission com.sun.rmi.rmid.ExecOptionPermission
  "-Dline.separator=*";
  permission com.sun.rmi.rmid.ExecOptionPermission
  "-Dawt.*";
};
```

The first two permissions granted allow rmid to execute commands that access any property information starting with `java` or `sun` (such as `java.vm`). The third allows information starting file (such as `file.separator`) to be used. The third allows any type of path separator to be used. The fourth allows user information to be used and the next allows the server to run on any type of operating system etc.

Note that if a second client were to request the services of this server it would already be resident in memory and would not require further activation by the rmid program (note if the server had printed any information to the standard output then that would have appeared in the same window as the rmid program was started in and not the window in which the set up program ran in – think about that one!).

The next aspect to look at is running the `Setup` program. As well as the `java` command and the fully qualified class name, we have also supplied two other items of information. These are:

1. A property `name` = `value` pair that specifies the location of the security policy file to be used to run the `Setup` program.
2. A property to specify where the stub code lives (no spaces from the "`-D`" all the way though the last "`/`"). These will be used to supply the classes on demand to clients. The options here are `file:` or `http`.

Finally, we start the client (Figure 5.5). This involves specifying the security policy file to use with the client (as it too uses a `SecurityManager`). This is the same security policy file as the server.

5.5 Summary

This chapter has described the new facility in Java 2 to implement activatable servers. Although at first sight the setup for the server may appear quite complex and unfathomable – it is actually quite straightforward (if long winded). It is likely that activation will be a very useful feature for very many developers.

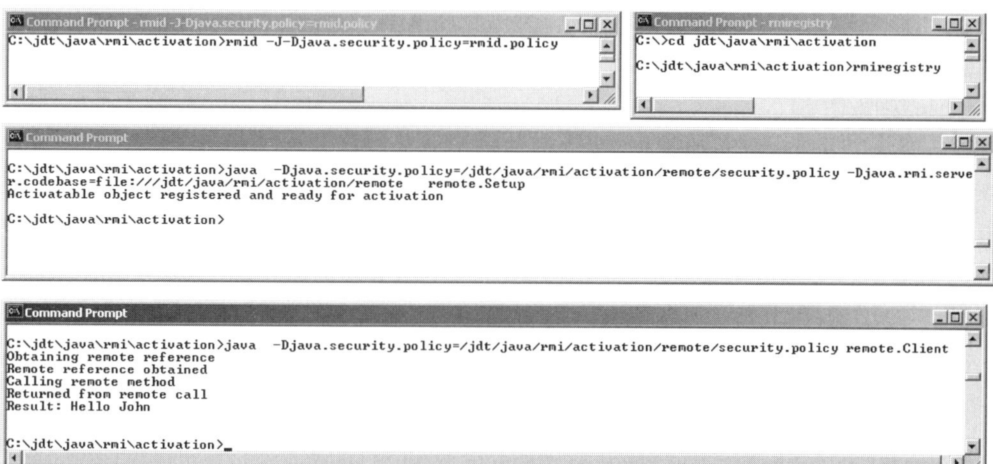

Figure 5.5 Running the activatable application.

5.6 Online Reference

Activation tutorial: `http://java.sun.com/j2se/1.4/docs/guide/rmi/activation.html`.

Chapter 6

JNDI

6.1 Introduction

The Java Naming and Directory Interface (JNDI) is designed to standardize access to directory and naming services such as NIS/NIS+ (Sun's Network Information Service) or LDAP (Lightweight Directory Access Protocol), or other naming services such as RMI's `rmiregistry` or a CORBA-compliant naming service.

A naming service is a bit like a dictionary (or a Java map) in that a key is mapped to a value. For example, DNS (the Domain Naming Service) is a naming service that provides mappings from domain names to IP addresses. For example:

```
www.jaydeetechnology.co.uk -> 123.145.169.29
```

DNS is essential to the operation of the internet. Humans are very good at remembering names such as `www.jaydeetechnology.co.uk`, but computers are very good at dealing with numbers, such as the actual IP address of the host machine. DNS provides the mapping between these two worlds.

Essentially all naming services provide this basic functionally. That is, they allow one system to register with the naming service providing a mapping from one value to another. They then allow another system to access that naming service to obtain the mapped information. Such interactions are essential for distributed enterprise-wide applications.

For example, within an enterprise there may be multiple software systems that wish to cooperate and communicate with each other. As a simple case, consider a payroll system that may wish to provide data to a pensions administration system (for calculating future pensions rights). In order for these two systems to communicate, the first thing they must know is where the other is. Each could be on a different server on a different part of the enterprise-wide network.

This information could be hard coded within the software. However, whenever a change was made to the location of the software the other system would need to be recompiled – this is less than ideal. Another approach in Java would be to encode the information within properties files. These are text files that can be loaded into the running system as a `Properties` object. The `Properties` object can then be queried at runtime for the actual values. This is certainly more flexible than hard coding the information. However, the issue of distributing updates to the properties file may now come into play. We would need to ensure that all software systems that need the updated properties file received it.

Neither of these approaches is ideal. Another approach is to have a third separate program that can be used to share information about the location of the software systems. This program is a naming service. Naming services are therefore very important within an enterprise.

Directory services take the naming service concept further by providing a hierarchical repository for enterprise-wide information. This is no longer a simple one to one mapping, but a hierarchy of information. In the case of directory services this hierarchy is usually optimized for search-style operations. It may also be distributed in nature or replicated across a network.

The sort of information a directory service can hold might include:

- user names and passwords
- user groups (for access control)
- computers (Ethernet and IP addresses)
- printers and their attributes (colour, A3, double-sided etc.)

The exact information and operations supported vary depending upon the directory service being used. Unfortunately, the protocols used to access different directory services also differ, necessitating the learning of multiple APIs.

This is where JNDI comes in. Just like JDBC, it acts as a common API or front end to various naming and directory services. Different back end adapters can then be used to connect to the actual service. This is illustrated in Figure 6.1.

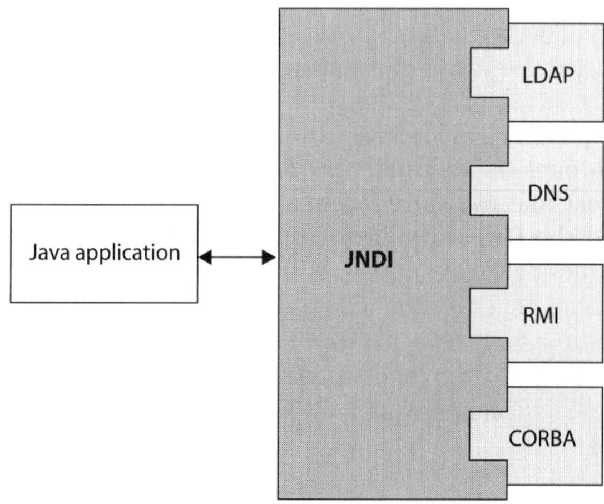

Figure 6.1 Using JNDI to interface to multiple naming and directory services.

As part of JNDI a standard interface has been specified that providers of a directory service can implement. This allows them to be plugged into the back JNDI. This interface is known as the Service Provider Interface (or SPI).

6.2 What You Need to Get Started

To use JNDI you will need at least version 1.3 of Java or any newer version, such as 1.4.1, as these versions include JNDI as standard. You will also need a directory service. In this chapter we will use LDAP as this is a widely available system. As we will be using LDAP as our naming and directory service we will look at LDAP next before returning to JNDI.

The Java 2 SDK, v1.3 includes three service providers for the following naming/directory services:

- Lightweight Directory Access Protocol (LDAP)
- Common Object Request Broker Architecture (CORBA) Common Object Services (COS) name service
- Java Remote Method Invocation (RMI) Registry

Other service providers can be downloaded from the JNDI Web site (`http://java.sun.com/products/jndi/serviceproviders.html`) or obtained from other vendors.

If you do not already have access to an LDAP server then you can obtain the OpenLDAP Software from `http://www.openldap.org/`, which is open source software.

6.3 LDAP

As we are going to be using LDAP we should say a little about it. LDAP stands for Lightweight Directory Access Protocol. It was originally developed in the early 1990s as a standard directory protocol. LDAP is an open standard maintained by the Internet Engineering Task Force (IETF), and is thus vendor- and platform-independent.

The LDAP v3 protocol is defined in RFC 2251 (`http://www.ietf.org/rfc/rfc2251.txt`) and is very mature. More recent additions to LDAP include the XML specification for LDAP, called the Directory Services Markup Language (DSML) (see `http://www.oasis-open.org/committees/dsml/`). This is intended to replace the more established LDAP Data Interchange Format (LDIF), which will be used in this chapter.

LDAP is now the most popular directory protocol in general use. It can be accessed by Java either directly using an LDAP API, such as the Netscape Directory SDK for Java (see `http://www.mozilla.org/directory/`) or via JNDI. A question you might ask at this point is why use the JNDI if there is a native LDAP API available? There are two answers to this:

1. JNDI is a standard API that is part of the J2SE.
2. JNDI is generic and thus you are not tied to LDAP.

One aspect of LDAP that is important to understand is that LDAP is a protocol that defines how client programs should access data on a server. It does not mandate how that data is stored. Therefore you can either obtain a directory service built specifically for LDAP (such as Sun's ONE Directory Server formerly known as iPlanet Directory Server) or get an LDAP front end to an existing directory service. However, in either case LDAP defines the interface and not the underlying data store.

6.3.1 LDAP Data

Within LDAP data is organized into a hierarchical tree. This tree is called a DIT, or Directory Information Tree. Each terminal node (or leaf) in the tree is called an entry. The first entry in the DIT is referred to as the root entry.

An entry is made up of a Distinguished Name (DN) and any number of key value pairs. The DN is the name of an entry and must be unique. The DN also shows how the entry fits into the hierarchical structure of the DIT. This is similar to the way in which the full path of a filename illustrates how the file fits into a hierarchical directory structure.

For example, the following DN (which is read right to left) defines a user `jjh`, within the group `employees`, within an organization `jaydeetechnology`.

```
uid=jjh, ou=employees, o=jaydeetechnology
```

Note that LDAP attributes often use shorthand forms (or mnemonics) as their names. In this case the following mnemonics have been used:

`o` = Organization
`ou` = Organizational unit
`uid` = userid

Other common mnemonics include:

`cn` Common name
`sn` Surname
`cn` Country
`mail` Email address

Note that attributes can have more than one value (for example, an employee may have more than one email address).

There is also a special attribute known as the `objectclass`. This attribute specifies what attributes are required and what attributes are allowed in a particular entry. The `objectclass` attribute is a little like a Java class, in that one `objectclass` can be extended to form a new `objectclass`. The new `objectclass` inherits all the parent's attributes and can add new attributes.

Attributes can also have rules applied to them that define how they should be matched when a client application searches LDAP. The possible matching rules are listed below.

DN	Attribute is in the form of a Distinguished Name
Case-Insensitive String (CIS)	Attribute is case-insensitive
Case-Sensitive String (CSS)	Attribute is case-sensitive and therefore can only be matched when the case is the same
Telephone	Same as CIS, but certain special characters are ignored (such as - and "(" or ")").
Integer	Attribute is treated as a number
Binary	Attribute is treated as a binary object and thus the two objects must be the same binary values (used with values such as photographs)

6.4 What LDAP Can Do

LDAP can be used for a variety of tasks, only some of which we have mentioned so far. These include registration of remote services, access control, yellow pages server and configuration data. Only the first of these has been discussed in previous chapters. Each of these uses will be outlined below so that you are aware of the roles LDAP can play.

Registration of Remote Servers

This is what we will be using LDAP for in this chapter and certainly what we have talked about so far. In this scenario, LDAP is used to allow remote servers to register their availability and then to allow clients to obtain that information and use the server. In some cases (for example RMI) this may mean storing serializable objects in LDAP and retrieving them at a later date (in a similar manner to the way in which the `rmiregistry` is used). One advantage that LDAP has over something like the `rmiregistry` is that LDAP can be searched, whereas the `rmiregistry` cannot.

Access Control

Many enterprise applications control who can access their services. This may be as simple as a login page to a Web application or as sophisticated as the use of digital signatures etc. Whatever approach is used, the information to be checked needs to be stored somewhere. One option of where to store the information is within LDAP. For example, we have already seen that we can store a user id within LDAP. It is merely a next step to store a password in LDAP. This password may be stored as a plain string or it may be encrypted (which is more normal). When information is sent to LDAP or retrieved from LDAP, technologies such as Secure Sockets Layer (SSL) may be used to ensure that the transmission of passwords is also encrypted. However, access control is not merely limited to logging into an application; it is also relevant for determining what operations within an application a particular user is allowed to perform. For example, a bank clerk may be allowed to read a customer's account details but not change them. In contrast, a bank manager may be allowed to read those details and also to modify them (for example, if an accounting error has been made).

White Pages Server

This use of LDAP (which acts a bit like a telephone directory – hence white pages) provides an information search facility. It is possible using LDAP to search for information based on attributes of an entry. For example, for user names, computers, printers etc. you could use LDAP to store information on all the employees in a company. You could then search on surname to find all the users with the surname "hunt" and retrieve their userids.

Configuration Data

LDAP can acts as a central resource of configuration information that is used by application at runtime. This is similar to using a properties file in a Java application, but rather than there being a properties file for each application, there is a single central repository which can be accessed and which must be maintained. For example, the name of a shared database that a particular set of application should use could be entered into LDAP. Thus if the database name changes there is only a single point that needs to be maintained for all the applications to move to the new database.

6.5 Using LDAP

There are four steps to perform in order to use LDAP. These steps are:

1. Connect to the LDAP server
2. Bind to the LDAP server
3. Perform any operations you require on the LDAP server
4. Disconnect from the LDAP server

We will examine each of these steps in a little more detail below.

Connecting

To use LDAP we must first obtain a connection to LDAP. To do this we need to know the host that LDAP is running on and the port to connect to. This is a bit like getting a phone line put into your house in order to be able to ring someone.

Binding

For LDAP there are usually at least two ways in which you can bind (login) to an LDAP server. That is, either anonymously or as a particular user. This is a bit like ringing a friend's number using the phone line put in by the phone company.

If you login anonymously then you will only have access to public data (which might include a list of employee email addresses etc.). If an application logs in as a specific user it will have access to all public data and whatever data that user is configured to access. This is determined by the Access Control Lists (ACLs) of the LDAP server. Essentially, an ACL specifies who can read, write or modify any data associated with the ACL. Within an entry different attributes may be associated with different ACLs. Thus different users may be able to see different items of data. In addition a particular attribute may be associated with more than one ACL, for example one ACL may provide read access to one group of users, but another ACL may allow write access for a different group of users.

Note that we are talking about LDAP v3 here. In LDAP v2 no anonymous binding was allowed.

Perform operations

It is possible to perform a range of operations on an LDAP server. These operations include:

Searching the server
Adding a new entry
Modifying an entry
Deleting an entry

Disconnecting from the LDAP server

Once an application has finished working with its connection to LDAP, the application should close the connection so that system resources are freed up.

6.6 Using JNDI

The JNDI is divided into five packages:

- `javax.naming` contains classes and interfaces for accessing naming services. In particular, it defines the `Context` interface and the `InitialContext` class.
- `javax.naming.directory` provides functionality for accessing directory services in addition to naming services. In particular, it defines the `DirContext` interface and the `InitialDirContext` class.
- `javax.naming.event` contains classes and interfaces for supporting event notification in naming and directory services.
- `javax.naming.ldap` contains classes and interfaces for using features that are specific to the LDAP v3 that are not already covered by the more generic `javax.naming.directory` package
- `javax.naming.spi` provides the means by which developers of different naming/directory service providers can develop and hook up their implementations so that the corresponding services are accessible from applications that use the JNDI.

To use JNDI to access a naming service or a directory service you need to follow these steps:

1. Set up a hashtable containing the properties that define the JNDI service you wish to use, the host you wish to connect to and the port that the LDAP server is working from.
2. Add any authentication or user login information to the hashtable.

3. Create an initial context object. If you are accessing a naming service you can use an `InitialContext` class. If you are accessing a directory service then you use an `InitialDirContext`.
4. Perform the required operation (for example adding a new entry or searching for that entry) using the context object obtained above.
5. Close the context object once you have finished with it.

We will look at these steps by examining the LDAPRead application presented in Figure 6.2.

We will work through the `LDAPRead` example, looking at each element of the program. In this program we first import the classes that we will be using. Note that the classes come from the core `javax.naming` package and the directory services extension

File Edit Search Project View Format Column Macro Advanced Window Help

```
import javax.naming.Context;
import javax.naming.directory.InitialDirContext;
import javax.naming.directory.DirContext;
import javax.naming.directory.Attributes;
import javax.naming.NamingException;
import java.util.Hashtable;

/**
 * Reads a simple attribute from LDAP
 */
class LDAPRead {
   public static void main(String[] args) {
      // Identify service provider to use
      Hashtable env = new Hashtable();

      // Specify the JNDI provider to use
      env.put(Context.INITIAL_CONTEXT_FACTORY,
            "com.sun.jndi.ldap.LdapCtxFactory");
      // Specify the the host and port to connect
      // to the LDAP server
      env.put(Context.PROVIDER_URL, "ldap://localhost:389/o=jaydeetechnology");
      try {
         // Now query LDAP for some data
         System.out.println("Create the initial directory context");
         DirContext ctx = new InitialDirContext(env);

         System.out.println("Search for John Hunt");
         Attributes attrs = ctx.getAttributes("cn=John Hunt, ou=JayDeeTechnology");

         System.out.println("Find the surname (\"sn\") and print it");
         System.out.println("sn: " + attrs.get("sn").get());

         // Close the context when we're done
         ctx.close();
      } catch (NamingException e) {
         e.printStackTrace();
      }
   }
}
```

Figure 6.2 The LDAPRead application.

javax.naming.directory. This is because LDAP is a directory service and we are exploiting those features in this example.

In this example we have define all the behaviour within the main method for simplicity. The first thing that the main method does is to set up the set of properties that will be used to create the initial context for the connection to the LDAP server. This first creates a Hashtable. It then provides the definition of the Initial Context Factory that will be used to generate an instance of a service provider (in this case the LDAP access service provider). The program next defines the context provider URL. In this case, as we are using an LDAP server, the protocol is "ldap". The LDAP server is running on the same machine as the Java program; therefore the host name is localhost and the port is 389, which is the default for this LDAP server. Should you be using an LDAP server on a different host then you would need to specify that host's name. Also, if a different port number is being used you would need to specify a different port. The final part of the URL is the LDAP namespace being used. In this case it is the namespace for jaydeetechnology (you may need to change this for your own environment). That is, the distinguished name (DN) o=jaydeetechnology is used for the root naming context.

```
Hashtable env = new Hashtable();
env.put(Context.INITIAL_CONTEXT_FACTORY, "com.sun.jndi.ldap.LdapCtxFactory");
env.put(Context.PROVIDER_URL, "ldap://localhost:389/o=jaydeetechnology");
```

Next, the main method enters a try...catch block. This is because connecting to the LDAP server or indeed querying the LDAP server may throw an exception. Therefore we handle the exception within the catch block. In this case we merely print the stack trace so that you can see what happens.

The program now takes the hashtable and uses it to configure the InitialDirContext used to connect to the LDAP server:

```
DirContext ctx = new InitialDirContext(env);
Attributes attrs = ctx.getAttributes("cn=John Hunt, ou=employees");
System.out.println("sn: " + attrs.get("sn").get());
```

Once a connection to the server has been established we can then perform a search on the LDAP server. In this case we are retrieving all the attributes associated with the object identified by the attributes "cn=John Hunt, ou=employees", essentially the attributes associated with the entry that has the common name "John Hunt" within the unit "employees". The retrieved Attributes object represents a collection of attributes retrieved. In this case we obtain from the Attributes object the attribute associated with the attribute id sn (or surname). We then use the get method on the returned attribute to obtain its value. If the attribute had more than one value then it would return the first.

When the LDAPReader class is compiled and run the result is that the value of the sn attribute is returned:

```
java LDAPReader
sn: Hunt
```

We have now accessed an LDAP server using JNDI from Java.

The `Context` interface defines a number of very useful methods which allow us to search, look up, list etc. information in a naming and directory service such as LDAP. Some of these are listed below:

- `list`: Enumerates the names bound in the named context, along with the class names of objects bound to them.
- `lookup`: Retrieves the named object.

The `DirContext` interface extends this with a further set of query facilities:

- `getAttributes`: Retrieves all of the attributes associated with a named object. See the class description regarding attribute models, attribute type names and operational attributes.
- `search`: Searches for objects that contain a specified set of attributes.

6.7 Placing Data Into LDAP

We have looked at reading data from LDAP first as it is the simpler example. In this section we will look at how we can add an entry to an LDAP server. Actually writing an object to an LDAP server is quite straightforward, as illustrated in Figure 6.3. However, there are a number of things you need to do to allow a Java object to be stored in LDAP. These are illustrated for a sample class employee, which illustrates the basic ideas. However, we will first focus on adding an entry to LDAP and then look at what we must do to the `Employee` class.

6.7.1 The `LDAPWrite` Application

The `LDAPWrite` application is presented in Figure 6.3. As can be seen from this figure, the way in which the application connects to LDAP is the same as was the case for reading an entry.

Once a connection has been established to LDAP we can then create an instance of the class `Employee` and bind it into LDAP. This is done by binding it to a Distinguished Name (DN). That is a unique name within the LDAP server. The context object has a method `bind` that takes two parameters. The first parameter is the Distinguished Name and the second is the object containing the information to add. We can then close the connection as we will have added the information to the LDAP server.

An interesting question at this point is why did we add an instance of the class `Employee` just to add the surname (`sn`) attribute for the John Hunt entry? In actual fact this is an area that is made more complicated through the use of JNDI (native LDAP APIs would be simpler). The problem is that JNDI is designed to read and write Java objects to and from naming and directory services. The result is that it is an instance of a Java class that must be added to an LDAP server even if that entry only holds a single string. You might at this point say that a string is a Java object. However a prerequisite of any object added via JNDI is that it must implement the `Referenceable` interface.

Classes that implement the `Referenceable` interface must implement a single method `getReference()`. This method returns a `Reference` object. A `Reference` object is an

UltraEdit-32 - [C:\jdt\java\jndi\LDAPWrite.java]

File Edit Search Project View Format Column Macro Advanced Window Help

```
import javax.naming.*;
import java.io.File;
import java.util.Hashtable;

class LDAPWrite {
    public static void main(String[] args) {
        // Set up the environment for creating the initial context
        Hashtable env = new Hashtable(11);
        // Specify the JNDI provider to use
       env.put(Context.INITIAL_CONTEXT_FACTORY,
               "com.sun.jndi.ldap.LdapCtxFactory");
       // Specify the the host and port to connect
       // to the LDAP server
       env.put(Context.PROVIDER_URL,
               "ldap://localhost:389/o=jaydeetechnology");
       try {
          // Now query LDAP for some data
          System.out.println("Create the initial directory context");
          DirContext ctx = new InitialDirContext(env);

            // Create the object to be bound
            Employee e = new Employee("Hunt");;

            // Perform the bind
          ctx.bind("cn=John Hunt", e);

            // Close the context when we're done
            ctx.close();
        } catch (NamingException e) {
            System.out.println("Operation failed: " + e);
        }
    }
}
```

Figure 6.3 The LDAPWrite application.

object that maintains a reference (pointer) to the original object. If that object is available in the current virtual machine then that original reference is used. If not, a factory class can be used to recreate the object with the data stored in the LDAP server. Thus as an object is not directly stored within LDAP a new instance of the class used to store the data can be created and populated with the original data. In our case the class `Employee` implements the `Referenceable` interface and the class `EmployeeFactory` can be used to recreate an instance of the employee class when needed.

The `Employee` class is presented in Figure 6.4. Note the `getReference` method, which creates an instance of the `Reference` class with the appropriate information required to rebuild the `Employee` class.

Note that the effect of storing the value of the instance variable surname into the new instance of the `StringRefAddr` class is that an attribute `sn` will be added to the DN entry "John Hunt" in the LDAP server.

```java
import javax.naming.*;

/**
  * This class is used by the Bind example.
  * It is a referenceable class that can be stored by service
  * providers like the LDAP and file system providers.
  */
public class Employee implements Referenceable {
    String surname;

    public Employee(String sn) {
        surname = sn;
    }

    public Reference getReference() throws NamingException {
       Reference ref =
           new Reference(Employee.class.getName(),
                         new StringRefAddr("sn", surname),
                         EmployeeFactory.class.getName(),
                         null);
        return ref;
    }

    public String toString() { return surname;  }
}
```

Figure 6.4 The referenceable Employee class.

The EmployeeFactory class is presented in Figure 6.5. It defines a single method getObjectInstance. This method takes a number of parameters. The parameter we are interested in here is the first parameter. This is the reference object. We can extract the information from the reference object that will allow us to rebuild the employee object. In this case it is the surname information for the object stored as an attribute sn in LDAP by the Employee class (via its getReference method).

If we ran the LDAPWrite program more than once we would generate the NameAlreadyBoundException. This is because the DN would already have a value bound for it. To allow for situations where we want to be able to bind to a DN more than once we should use the rebind method. The rebind() method is used to add or replace a binding. It accepts the same arguments as bind(), but the semantics are such that if the name is already bound, then it will be unbound and the newly given object will be bound. It is also possible to remove an entry from the LDAP server using the unbind method.

UltraEdit-32 - [C:\jdt\java\jndi\EmployeeFactory.java]

```
import javax.naming.*;
import javax.naming.spi.ObjectFactory;
import java.util.Hashtable;

public class EmployeeFactory implements ObjectFactory {
   public EmployeeFactory() {  }

   public Object getObjectInstance(Object obj,
                                   Name name,
                                   Context ctx,
                                   Hashtable env)
                                           throws Exception {
      if (obj instanceof Reference) {
         Reference ref = (Reference)obj;
         if (ref.getClassName().equals(Employee.class.getName())) {
            RefAddr addr = ref.get("sn");
            if (addr != null) {
               return new Employee((String)addr.getContent());
            }
         }
      }
      return null;
   }
}
```

Figure 6.5 The EmployeeFactory class.

6.8 JNDI, RMI and LDAP

One of the issues associated with using the rmiregistry with a production quality system is that Sun does not recommend that you do this. Firstly, rmiregistry is provided as an environment for testing RMI-based applications, and secondly it is not resilient to crashes. That is, if you have to stop and start the rmiregistry then you would need to re-register all of your objects with it.

One alternative option is to use JNDI and a different naming or directory service for your remote objects. For example, you could choose to use LDAP to store your remote objects.

To illustrate this idea we will present a very simple RMI application based on that presented earlier in this book. The remote interface is presented in Figure 6.6. This interface defines a single remote method query that takes a string and returns a new string.

The server class that implements this interface is presented in Figure 6.7. This server class is based on that presented in the RMI chapters earlier in this book. However, instead of using the rmiregistry and the Naming class it uses LDAP and the JNDI to connect to it. It does this in exactly the same way as presented earlier in this chapter. However, the object bound is the RMIServer remote object.

UltraEdit-32 - [C:\jdt\java\dist\jndi\RMIInterface.java]

File Edit Search Project View Format Column Macro Advanced Window Help

```
import java.rmi.*;

public interface RMIInterface extends java.rmi.Remote {
   public String query(String request)
                           throws java.rmi.RemoteException;
}
```

Figure 6.6 The RMIInterface.

UltraEdit-32 - [C:\jdt\java\dist\jndi\RMIServer.java]

File Edit Search Project View Format Column Macro Advanced Window Help

```
import java.rmi.*;
import javax.naming.*;
import javax.naming.directory.*;
import java.util.Hashtable;
import java.rmi.server.UnicastRemoteObject;

public class RMIServer extends UnicastRemoteObject
                          implements RMIInterface {
   public RMIServer() throws RemoteException {
      super();
      try {
        // Set up environment for context (need ldapbp.jar)
        Hashtable env = new Hashtable();
        env.put(Context.INITIAL_CONTEXT_FACTORY,
                "com.sun.jndi.ldap.LdapCtxFactory");
        env.put(Context.PROVIDER_URL,
                "ldap://localhost:389/o=JNDIExample");
        // Create the initial context
        DirContext ctx = new InitialDirContext(env);
        // Create RMI object and bind it
        RMIInterface rs = new RMIServer();
        ctx.bind("cn=RMIServer", rs);
     } catch (Exception exp) { exp.printStackTrace(); }
   }
   public String query(String s) {
        return s + " John";
    }
   public static void main(String [] args) throws RemoteException{
        new RMIServer();
   }
}
```

Figure 6.7 The RMIServer.

Note that we do not have to do any further work with our RMIServer (that is we do not need to implement the Referenceable interface). This work is done for us by the RMI framework.

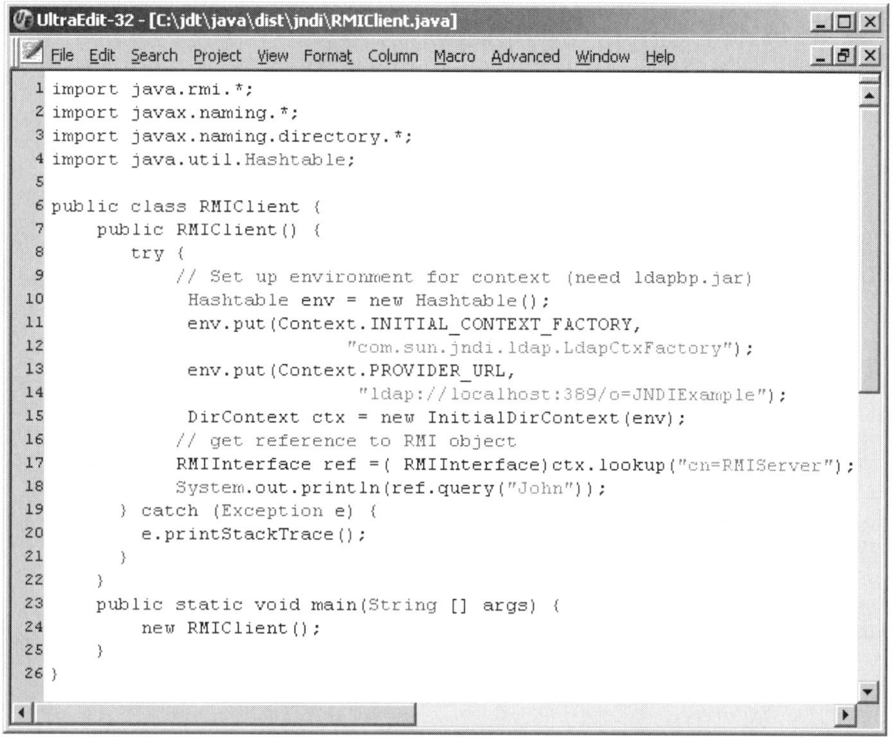

UltraEdit-32 - [C:\jdt\java\dist\jndi\RMIClient.java]

File Edit Search Project View Format Column Macro Advanced Window Help

```
import java.rmi.*;
import javax.naming.*;
import javax.naming.directory.*;
import java.util.Hashtable;

public class RMIClient {
    public RMIClient() {
       try {
           // Set up environment for context (need ldapbp.jar)
            Hashtable env = new Hashtable();
            env.put(Context.INITIAL_CONTEXT_FACTORY,
                          "com.sun.jndi.ldap.LdapCtxFactory");
            env.put(Context.PROVIDER_URL,
                           "ldap://localhost:389/o=JNDIExample");
            DirContext ctx = new InitialDirContext(env);
           // get reference to RMI object
           RMIInterface ref =( RMIInterface)ctx.lookup("cn=RMIServer");
           System.out.println(ref.query("John"));
        } catch (Exception e) {
          e.printStackTrace();
        }
    }
    public static void main(String [] args) {
        new RMIClient();
    }
}
```

Figure 6.8 The `RMIClient` using LDAP.

At this point we now have a remote object registered with the LDAP server that can be accessed by RMI clients. Such a client is presented in Figure 6.8. This client is just like the RMI client presented earlier in the book except that it now uses JNDI to access an LDAP server in order to obtain a reference to the remote object. This is done using the `lookup` method of the `initialDirContext` object. This returns something of type `Object` that must then be cast to the interface type in order that the remote method `query` can be called on it.

When this example is run the result is that the string "John John" is returned to the client from the server.

6.9 Summary

JNDI is a very important piece in the jigsaw of Java's enterprise facilities. It is used extensively with any CORBA application and with Enterprise JavaBeans. As you will see later on in this book, whenever you create a client for an Enterprise JavaBean you will use JNDI to obtain a reference to it.

Chapter 7

Java Message Service (JMS)

7.1 Introduction

In this chapter we will look at messaging services and the Java Message Service in particular. A message service is a peer to peer communications mechanism that allows for loosely coupled distributed communications. It is a very well established enterprise-oriented technology which is fundamental to many commercial applications.

7.2 Message Servers and JMS

7.2.1 What Is a Message Service?

A message service provides for distributed loosely coupled communication between software components or applications. That is, it allows an application running on one host using one particular technology to communicate with another application running on another host without the two clients needing to know anything directly about each other.

The basic concept in a message service is that two or more clients can communicate (in a peer to peer manner) by sending and receiving messages. A message is a "chunk" of data to be sent from one client to another via the message server. This data may be textual, it may be numeric or, in the case of a Java to Java application, it may include objects.

Typically a client that wishes to send a message does so to a "destination". In turn, the receiving client must access this destination to obtain the message sent. An important point here is that the clients do not need to be running at the same time. For example, the sending client may do so at one point in time. In turn, the receiving client may begin execution at a later point in time and receive that message.

7.2.2 Why Use a Message Service?

Why might such a service be useful in current, enterprise-oriented, environments? After all, we already have RMI, CORBA, TCP/IP sockets etc. There are a number of answers to this question, some of which were hinted at in the first paragraph of this section. The reasons include:

- **Loose coupling but high cohesion**. By loose coupling we mean that the clients involved in the messaging service do not need to implement a common interface, can be plugged together at runtime, can change over time and need to know every little about each other. However, it is a highly cohesive communication mechanism in that standard interfaces (at least with the JMS) have been provided that allow any client to work with a message service and to understand the steps involved and the information exchanged etc.
- **Avoids direct communication**. The clients involved in the communication never actual talk to each other directly. An intermediary, the message service, sits between the clients and thus acts as a buffer between the two applications. It can therefore provide additional security controls.
- **Guarantee of delivery**. A message service can be configured to ensure that a message is delivered. In the case of a JMS Provider the message can also be made durable. This means that if a client is not available when the message is sent, it can be held in the message server and delivered at a later date when the client becomes available again.
- **Asynchronous communications**. With RMI or socket-based communications, only synchronous communication is possible. That is, the sender of a message is blocked until the receiver replies. In some cases this is not what is required, and the sender wishes to send the message and carry on immediately. This is referred to as asynchronous communication. A message server typically supports both synchronous and asynchronous communication.
- **One to many, many to many and many to one communication**. A message service can be quite flexible on the numbers of clients involved in any particular communication. A typical queue-based application may involve one to one or many to one communication. A topic-based application may involve one to one, one to many, many to one or indeed many to many. It is thus a very flexible means of communicating between clients. Queues and topics will be discussed in more detail later in this chapter.

7.2.3 What Is JMS?

The JMS (or Java Message Service) is a standard API that can be used to access a variety of message servers. In this sense it is similar to the JDBC and JNDI in that it is trying to provide a standardized and unified interface to a variety of disparate vendor specific message servers. These servers often have their own native interface that can be used to access them directly. However, not only is the resultant code less portable, it also requires learning each new API whenever you wish to use a different message service. Using the JMS you can access IBM's MQSeries and the JBossMQ message server with the same API. This is of course the big benefit of the JMS, as it allows developers to avoid vendor-specific APIs.

Note that JMS is not a message service in its own right. It is still necessary to have a message server to connect to. In JMS terminology the underlying message server and the JMS interface to it are referred to as a JMS Provider.

7.2.4 JMS API Concepts

There are a number of core concepts within the JMS API that are mapped to the underlying message server. These are:

- **Administered objects.** These are objects created by an administrator for the use of the JMS clients. Examples of these are connection factories that are used to connect to the underlying message server and destinations (such as queues and topics). These are managed via JNDI and are accessed via a JNDI name. They are handled outside of a client application because they will differ greatly from one application to another. By requiring the message server provider to administer (handle) these objects JMS provides a buffer between the JMS clients and the actual JMS provider. As these applications are distributed JNDI provides an ideal way of accessing them. In the examples presented later in this chapter the administrator of these objects will be JBoss.
- **A JMS Provider.** This is the message server that implements the JMS interface and is referred to as a JMS Provider (examples include IBM's MQSeries and the JBossMQ message server).
- **JMS Clients.** These are producers and consumers of messages. As this is a peer to peer communications facility there is no concept of a client and a server. Also note that a JMS client can be both a creator of messages and a receiver of messages.
- **Messages.** These are the items of information sent between JMS clients.

Traditional message services have often supported one of two modes of communication, referred to as point to point or publish and subscribe. The JMS API defines support for both approaches. These two are described below.

7.3 Point to Point Communication

A point-to-point communication model is the simplest approach that can be used. In the point-to-point model a central queue acts as a published destination (administered object). One or more message producers can then send messages to the queue (note that messages are addressed to a specific queue). These messages are then picked up by a message consumer in the order they were sent. This is illustrated in Figure 7.1.

Typically the single message consumer can pick these messages up when it is activated, as the messages are held in the queue until they are consumed. The messages are sent by the producers asynchronously but can be received by the consumer either synchronously or asynchronously. That is, either the consumer can be waiting for the next message (i.e. it is blocked until a message is received) or it can be notified in a separate thread when a message arrives.

The messages in the queue may have an expiry time associated with them and may be stored either within the queue or in some external resource (such as a database) so that they can be recovered if the message service terminates for any reason. Note that in order for a message to be removed from the queue when it has been successfully consumed by the consumer, the consumer must acknowledge receiving the message.

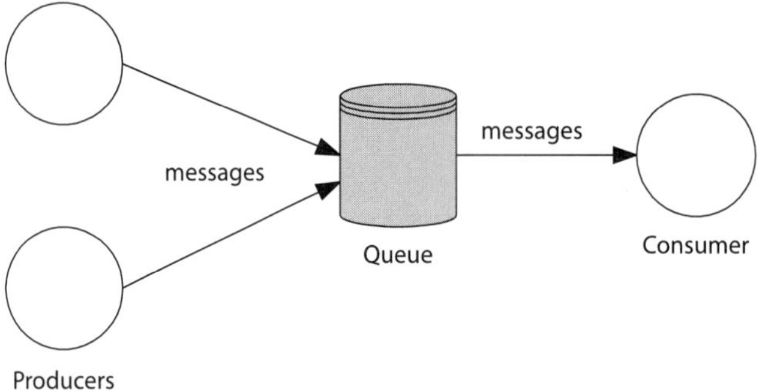

Figure 7.1 Point to point communication.

7.4 Publish and Subscribe Communication

The publish and subscribe communication model is based around the concept of a topic. A topic is a published destination (administered object) for messages. It differs from a queue in that it can have multiple clients for both message sending and message receiving. That is, each topic can have multiple subscribers (message producers) and multiple subscribers (message consumers). This is illustrated in Figure 7.2.

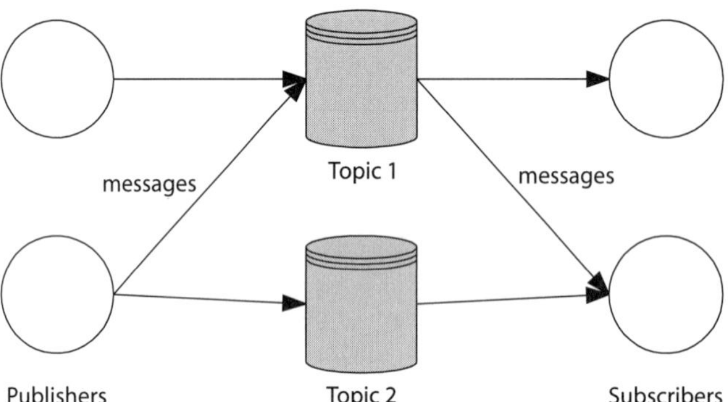

Figure 7.2 Publish and subscribe communication.

As with the point to point communications model, a JMS client can be both a publisher and a subscriber. However, clients only receive messages sent after they have subscribed to the topic. In some cases the topic can be durable. This means that if a client subscribes and then loses its connection to the topic, when it re-establishes that connection, it will receive all messages that it would have otherwise have missed.

Topics can also be ordered hierarchically. For example, a topic "holidays" may have a sub-topic "Menorca", which in turn may have a sub-topic "villas". However, what it means to subscribe to a topic with sub-topics depends on the message server. For example, subscribing to the "Menorca" topic may cause a subscriber to receive messages for the "villas" topic as well as the "Menorca" topic in some message servers.

7.5 The JMS API

The JMS API is defined within the `javax.jms` package. This package defines numerous interfaces, only two classes and a number of exceptions. It is interesting to note that almost all the elements in the JMS API are interfaces that must be implemented by a JMS Provider. This is a very similar picture to that for JDBC described in Chapter 9.

To use the JMS API involves creating a connection factory which provides a connection object. This connection object provides a connection to the message server. This is used to create a session that allows a message to be created. This message can then be sent via a message producer to a destination (a queue or topic). The message can then be delivered to a message consumer. This sequence of events is illustrated in Figure 7.3. We will look at the primary interfaces mentioned here in this section. The following sections will then look at applications that use point to point communication and publish and subscribe communications.

7.5.1 Connection Factories

A connection factory is an object that a client uses to create a connection with a JMS provider. It is an administered object and is therefore obtained via JNDI lookup. There are two types of connec-

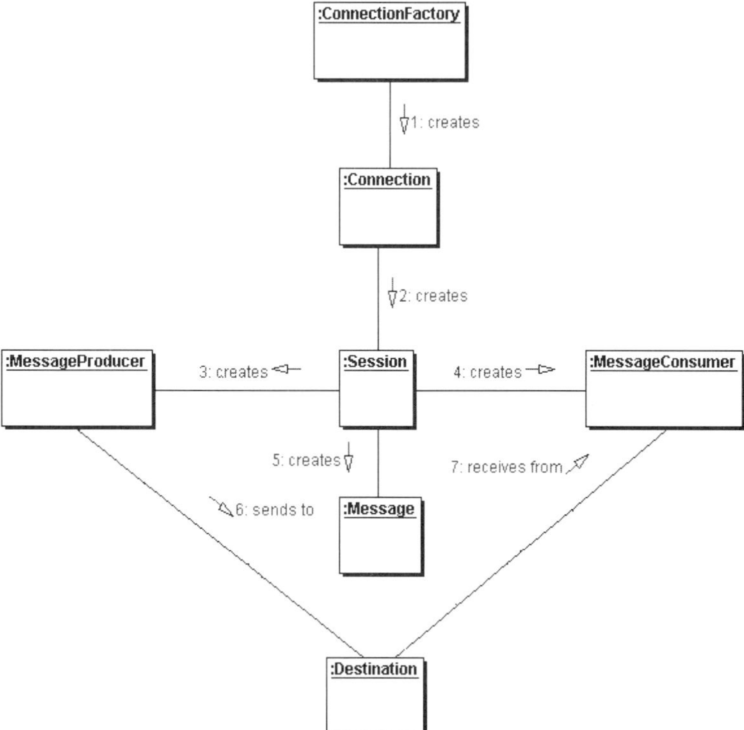

Figure 7.3 The basic structure of a JMS application.

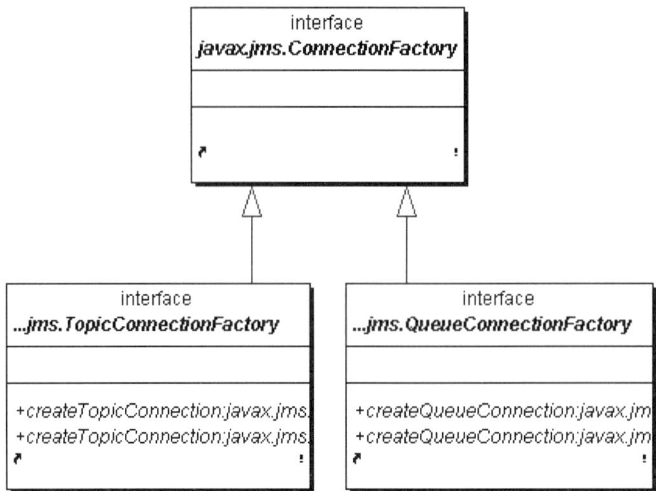

Figure 7.4 The `ConnectionFactory` interface and its sub-interfaces.

tion factory defined for the JMS API: the `QueueConnectionFactory` for point to point communications and the `TopicConnectionFactory` for publish and subscribe communications. These are illustrated in Figure 7.4.

7.5.2 Connections

A connection object is a communications medium to the JMS provider. The exact implementation of this communication will depend on the JMS provider (it could use TCP/IP sockets etc.). As well as the generic connection interface, there are also specific interfaces for queue-based and topic-based applications. These are presented in Figure 7.5.

7.5.3 Sessions

Sessions are used to create message producers, message consumers and messages. They are single threaded, so care should be taken in multi-threaded environments. They can also take part in transactions. That is, a session provides a transactional context with which to group a set of sends and receives into an atomic unit of work. Just as for connections there is a super interface for all sessions and two sub interfaces for queue- and topic-oriented applications (see Figure 7.6).

7.5.4 Messages

Messages are the items of information sent between clients via the message server. In JMS messages are quite straightforward objects to promote the cross-vendor nature of the JMS. As well as the root `Message` interface there are five other interfaces that define different types of message (such as `TextMessage`). These are presented in Table 7.1 and Figure 7.7.

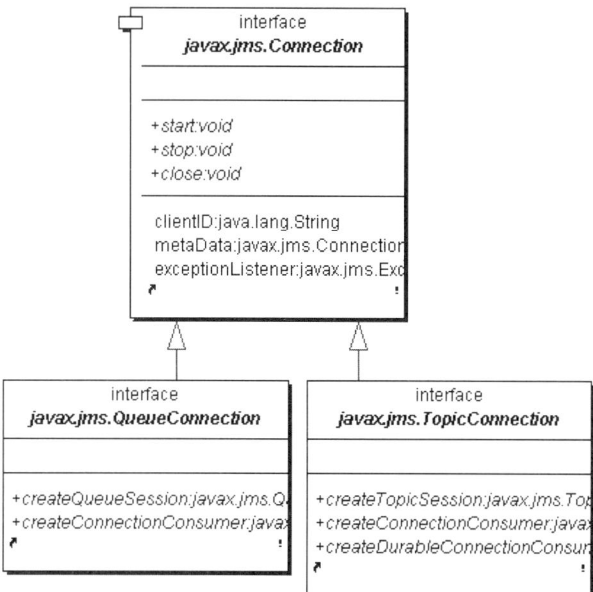

Figure 7.5 Connection interface hierarchy.

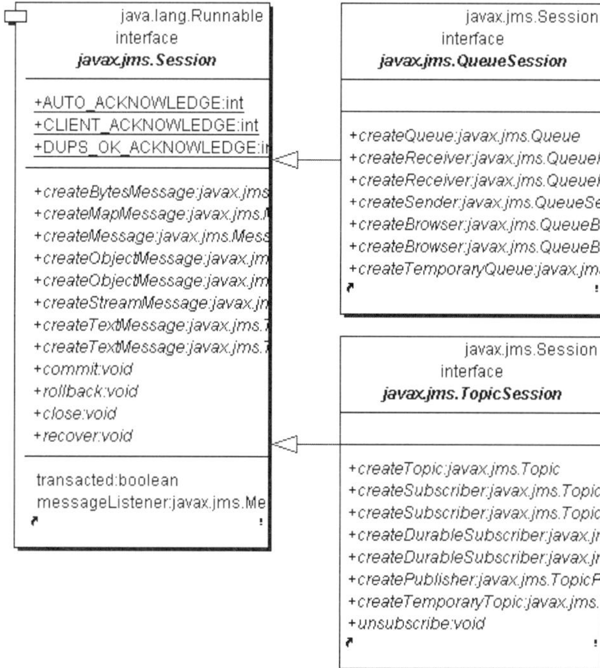

Figure 7.6 The `Session` interface hierarchy.

Table 7.1 Message types in JMS.

Message type	*Body contains*
`TextMessage`	A `java.lang.String` object (for example, an XML document). – `queueSession.createTextMessage()` – `tm.setText("")` – `tm.getText()`
`MapMessage`	A set of name/value pairs, with names as `String` objects and values as primitive types in the Java programming language. The entries can be accessed sequentially by enumerator or randomly by name. The order of the entries is undefined. – `queueSession.createMapMessage()` – `mm.setString(`*`name`*`, "")` – `mm.setInt(`*`name`*`, 5)` and other primitives – `mm.getInt(`*`name`*`)` and other primitives
`BytesMessage`	A stream of uninterpreted bytes. This message type is for literally encoding a body to match an existing message format. – `queueSession.createBytesMessage()` – `bm.writeBytes(`*`outByteArray`*`)` – `length = bm.readBytes(`*`inByteArray`*`)` – `bm.writeBoolean(`*`true/false`*`) etc.`
`StreamMessage`	A stream of primitive values in the Java programming language, filled and read sequentially. – `queueSession.createStreamMessage()` – `sm.writeString("")` – `sm.readDouble()` – `sm.reset() // take back to start of stream` – `sm.clearBody()`
`ObjectMessage`	A `Serializable` object in the Java programming language. – `queueSession.createObjectMessage()` – `om.setObject(`*`object`*`)` – `om.getObject()` – `object` must be serializable
`Message`	Root of interface hierarchy

Message Anatomy

A message is actually made up of a number of elements. These elements are the message headers, message properties and the actual message body (Figure 7.8). Each of these is briefly described below.

Message Header

The message headers are for standard, mandatory message information. For example, every message has a unique identifier (`JMSMessageID`); it also has a destination (`JMSDestination`), a priority (`JMSPriority`), a timestamp (`JMSTimeStamp`) etc. These are mostly set automatically by sending the message to the destination.

Headers can be accessed via get and set methods that have the form `set`*`JMSHeaderName`* or `get`*`JMHeaderName`* (for example `getJMSDestination()` and `setJMSDestination (Destination destination)`.

Message Properties

Message properties are for standard, vendor-specific or application-specific optional message information. Properties are often used to assist message filtering. For example, properties may include user id, debug class name etc. Properties are read-only in the receiving client and should

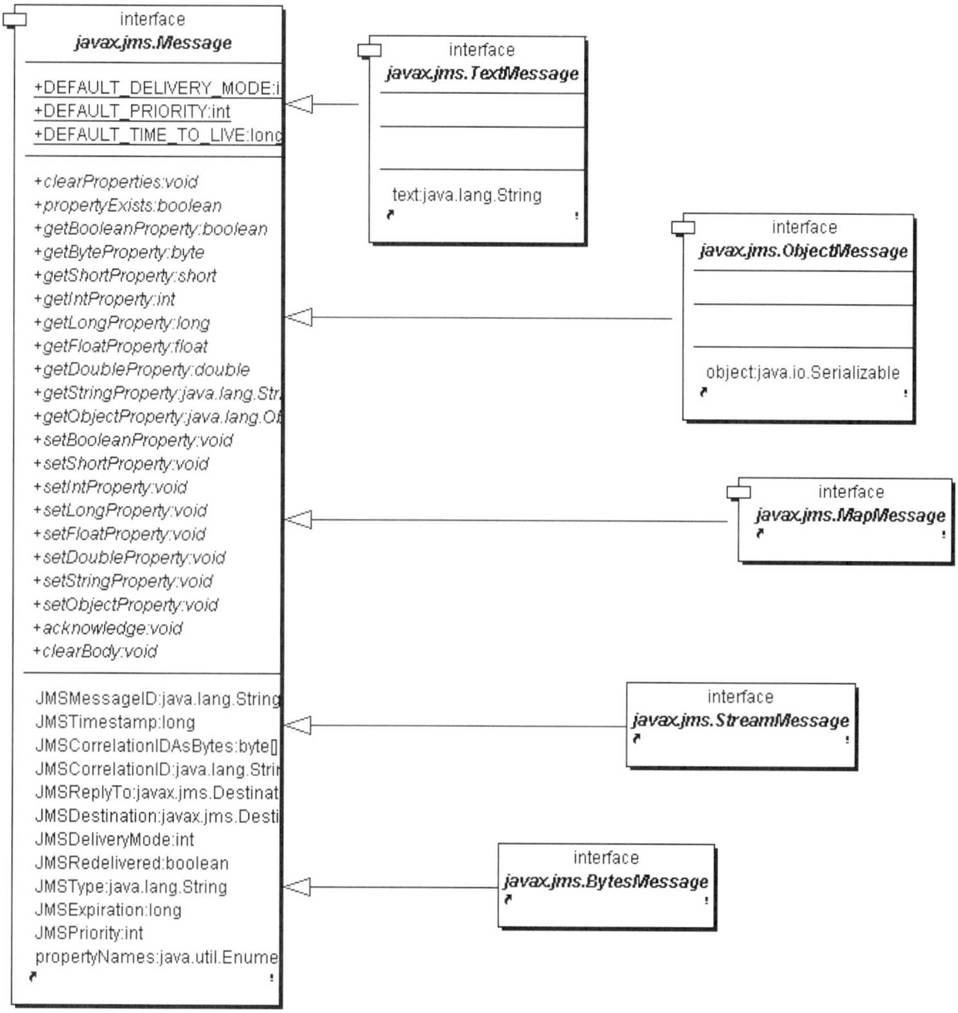

interface
javax.jms.Message
+DEFAULT_DELIVERY_MODE:i
+DEFAULT_PRIORITY:int
+DEFAULT_TIME_TO_LIVE:long
+clearProperties:void
+propertyExists:boolean
+getBooleanProperty:boolean
+getByteProperty:byte
+getShortProperty:short
+getIntProperty:int
+getLongProperty:long
+getFloatProperty:float
+getDoubleProperty:double
+getStringProperty:java.lang.Str
+getObjectProperty:java.lang.O
+setBooleanProperty:void
+setShortProperty:void
+setIntProperty:void
+setLongProperty:void
+setFloatProperty:void
+setDoubleProperty:void
+setStringProperty:void
+setObjectProperty:void
+acknowledge:void
+clearBody:void
JMSMessageID:java.lang.String
JMSTimestamp:long
JMSCorrelationIDAsBytes:byte[]
JMSCorrelationID:java.lang.Stri
JMSReplyTo:javax.jms.Destinat
JMSDestination:javax.jms.Desti
JMSDeliveryMode:int
JMSRedelivered:boolean
JMSType:java.lang.String
JMSExpiration:long
JMSPriority:int
propertyNames:java.util.Enume
interface
javax.jms.TextMessage
text:java.lang.String
interface
javax.jms.ObjectMessage
object:java.io.Serializable
interface
javax.jms.MapMessage
interface
javax.jms.StreamMessage
interface
javax.jms.BytesMessage

Figure 7.7 The `Message` interface hierarchy.

Message headers
Message properties
Message body

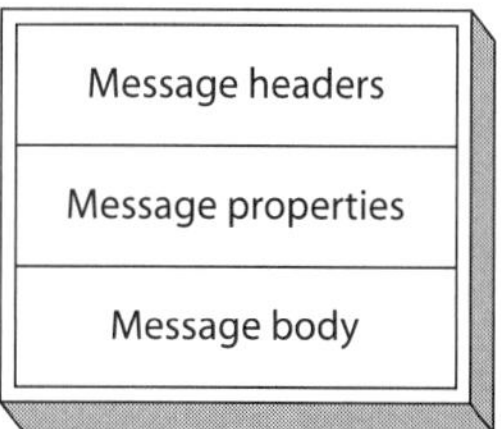

Figure 7.8 Structure of a message.

only be used for customizing headers or to aid in message selection, as they are less efficient than sending data in the message body.

Properties can be accessed via set and get methods, for example:

- `message.getTypeProperty(propertyName)`
- `message.setTypeProperty(propertyName, value)`

where `Type` is: `Boolean`, `Byte`, `Double`, `Float`, `Int`, `Long`, `Object` (primitive wrapper class objects only), `Short` and `String`.

The JMS API provides some predefined property names that a provider may support. All JMS-defined properties have a prefix of `JMSX`.

Message Body

The message body is the actual contents of the message. In JMS, various formats are supported.

7.5.5 Destinations

A destination is an administered object that represents either a queue or a topic within a JMS provider. That is, it is where messages are sent and where messages are read from. As an administered object they are obtained via a JNDI lookup. The `Destination` interface hierarchy is presented in Figure 7.9.

7.5.6 Message Producers

A message producer is an object that is used to send a message to a destination. It is created by the session object being used. There are two types of message producer. Which one should be used

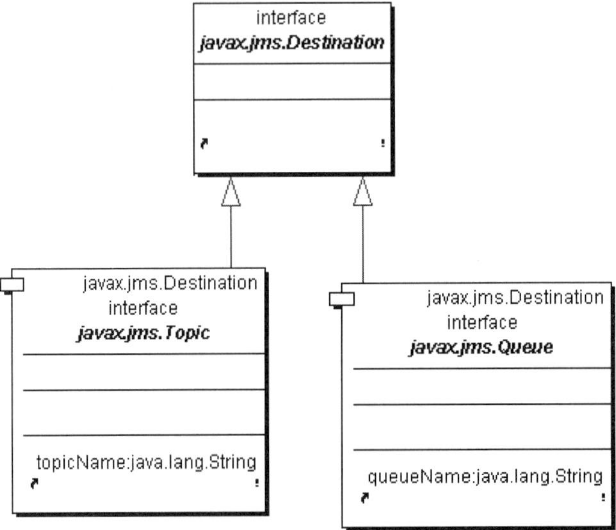

Figure 7.9 The `Destination` interface hierarchy.

depends upon wherther you are using point to point (queue-based) or publish and subscribe (topic-based) communication. The `QueueSender` is used with a queue and the `TopicSender` is used with a topic. The interfaces in the `MessageProducer` hierarchy are presented in Figure 7.10.

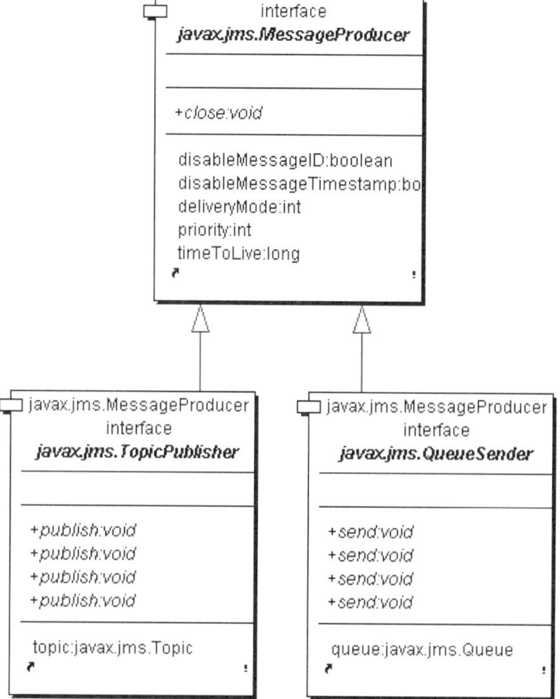

Figure 7.10 The `MessageProducer` interface hierarchy.

7.5.7 Message Consumers

Message consumers are generated by a session object and are used to obtain messages from a destination. If the destination is a queue then a `QueueReceiver` is used. If the destination is a topic then a `TopicSubscriber` is used. In either case, the consumer applications can either be synchronous (in which they call the receive method and wait for a response) or asynchronous in which case they register a message listener with message consumer object. The `MessageConsumer` hierarchy is shown in Figure 7.11.

7.6 Point to Point Application Development Steps

A prerequisite of any JMS application is that you need to have access to a messaging service in order to be able to send and receive messages. Examples of message services that you might look

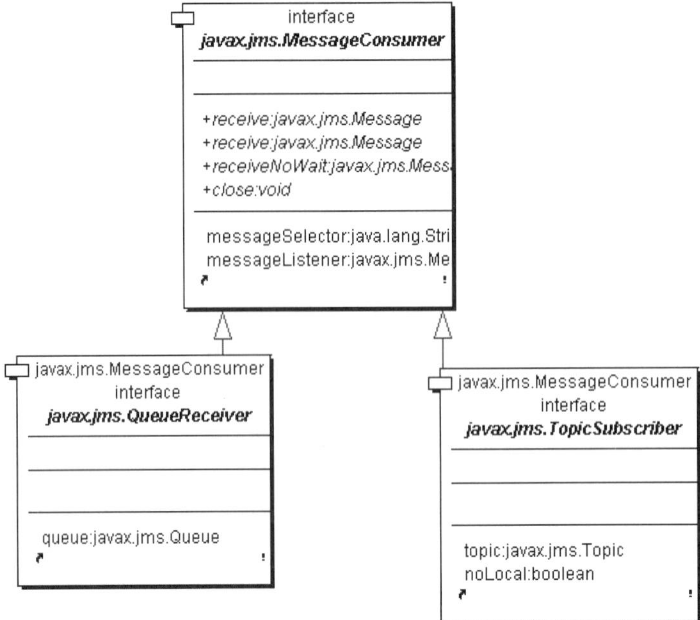

Figure 7.11 The `MessageConsumer` hierarchy.

at include IBM's MQSeries, the Sun ONE Message Queue (formerly iPlanet Message Queue for Java) and Microsoft Message Queuing (MSMQ). In this chapter we will actual use the message queue that is provided as part of the JBoss application server. This is because, first of all, it is free and secondly it is implemented in Java, and therefore whatever platform you are using these examples should work. See the preface of this book for information on how to obtain JBoss.

The Message queue provided with JBoss is the JBossMQ service. The JBossMQ is a JMS provider and is the part of JBoss that implements the JMS specification. To some extent using JBoss merely as a message service is something akin to hitting a pin with a sledge hammer. However, as we will be using JBoss later in this book for other features (including looking at Message-Driven Beans) it is a good starting point.

Once we have a message service available we can then start to develop a message-oriented application. To do this we must follow these steps:

1. Publish destinations (queues) using server-specified mechanism. This can be done in JBoss using the `jbossmq-destinations-service.xml` file. Essentially, a JNDI entry is registered for the destination.
2. Define clients that generate messages.
3. Define clients that receive messages (note that a client may be both a producer and a consumer).
4. Start the message server.
5. Compile and start the clients.

We shall follow each of these steps below for a simple queue based

7.6.1 Publish Destinations

How a destination is published is message service-dependent. In the case of the JBossMQ message server a destination can be published by providing an entry in the `jbossmq-destinations-service.xml` file. This file can be found in the `server\default\deploy` directory below your JBoss installation. This file defines the default Queues and Topics that JBossMQ ships with. It is possible to add other destinations to this file (which is what we will do below) or you can create other `*-service.xml` files to contain your application's destinations.

Figure 7.12 presents the `jboss-destinations-service.xml` file with some lines hidden. It shows the definition of a new queue: `jdt`. This will have a JNDI name of `queue/jdt`. As we have not defined any security information for this queue, all clients will be able to connect to this queue as a guest and will be able to write to the queue (produce messages) and read from the queue (consume messages).

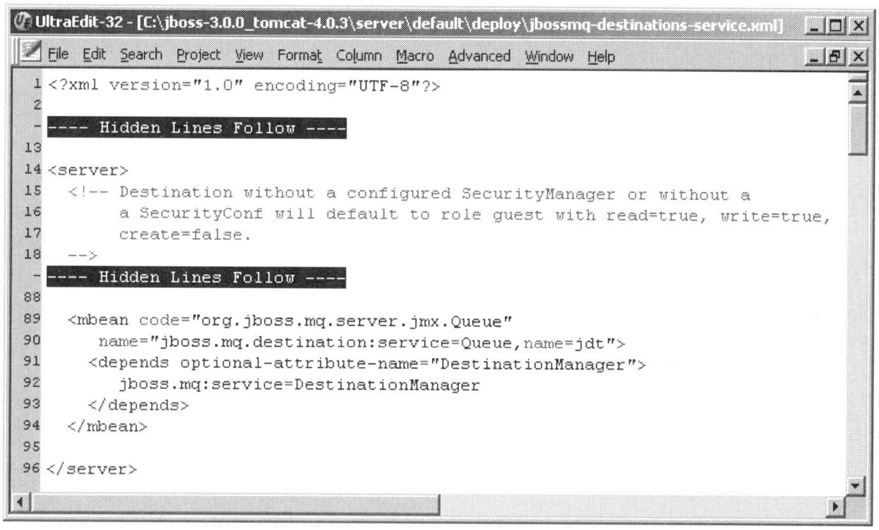

UltraEdit-32 - [C:\jboss-3.0.0_tomcat-4.0.3\server\default\deploy\jbossmq-destinations-service.xml]

File Edit Search Project View Format Column Macro Advanced Window Help

```
<?xml version="1.0" encoding="UTF-8"?>

---- Hidden Lines Follow ----

<server>
  <!-- Destination without a configured SecurityManager or without a
       a SecurityConf will default to role guest with read=true, write=true,
       create=false.
  -->
---- Hidden Lines Follow ----

  <mbean code="org.jboss.mq.server.jmx.Queue"
     name="jboss.mq.destination:service=Queue,name=jdt">
    <depends optional-attribute-name="DestinationManager">
       jboss.mq:service=DestinationManager
    </depends>
  </mbean>

</server>
```

Figure 7.12 Defining a new destination queue in JBoss.

Note that with JBoss, if you change this XML file, JBoss will notice the change and reload it. Thus the new queue should become immediately available.

7.6.2 Define a Client

To send a message to a JMS message server queue there are nine steps that must be performed. These steps are the same whether you wish to send the message from a standalone application, from a servlet or JSP or indeed from an Enterprise JavaBean. These steps, illustrated graphically in Figure 7.13, are described below.

Step 1: Obtain a queue connection factory. A queue connection factory is used to create the queue connection object used to handle the connection to the message servers queue. This factory class

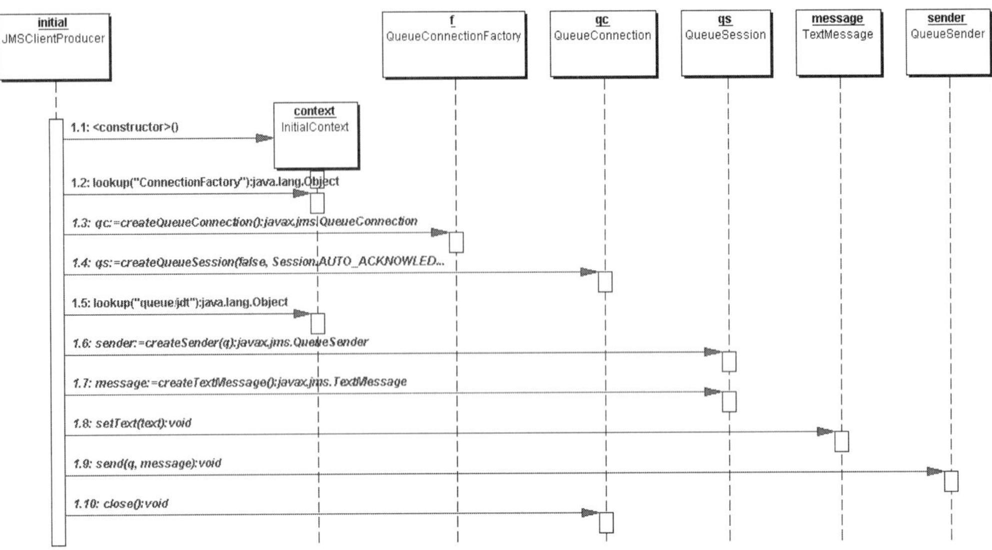

Figure 7.13 Steps taken by a message queue client.

follows the standard `Factory` pattern that is now widely used within Java and the J2EE. However in this case the `Factory` object is obtained from a naming service using the JNDI (described in the last chapter). This is illustrated below:

```
Properties evn = new Properties();
  env.put ("java.naming.factory.initial",
    "org.jnp.interfaces.NamingContextFactory");
  env.put("java.naming.provider.url",
    "jnp://localhost:1099");
  env.put("java.naming.factory.url.pkgs",
    "org.jboss.naming:org.jnp.interfaces");
  Context context = new InitialContext(env);
```

As we are only using a naming service here we use an `InitialContext` object (as opposed to the `InitialDirContext` object used in the LDAP example described previously). We are also using a `Properties` object. This is a direct subclass of the `Hashtable` class but only holds strings. As all our values are strings we have selected to use this. As with the examples in the last chapter we have provided the naming service factory class and the provider URL. In this case we are also providing some additional JBoss-specific information. This is the `java.naming.factory.url.pkgs` property. These properties together tell the initial context where to find the naming service and how to connect to it. They also tell the naming service provided with JBoss how we wish to communicate with it. Another option would have been to create a properties file called `jndi.properties` and instantiated the `InitialContext` using the default null parameter constructor. It would then have picked up the `jndi.properties` file from the classpath automatically.

To actually make the connect we instantiate the `InitialContext` using the property object we have created.

We are now in a position to obtain the actual connection factory using the context object obtained. This is done by using the lookup method on the context object. The connection factory is defined within JBoss using the JNDI name `ConnectionFactory`. The resulting object can then be cast to the `QueueConnectionFactory` class. For example:

```
QueueConnectionFactory f =
    (QueueConnectionFactory)context.lookup("ConnectionFactory");
```

Step 2: Create a queue connection. This is done by calling the `createQueueConnection` method on the factory object obtained, for example:

```
QueueConnection qc = f.createQueueConnection();
```

This returns a `QueueConnection` object. A queue connection is a connection to the JMS message server being used. There is usually one queue connection per client as it can be shared between all the queues you need to access. Its primary purpose is to allow the creation of queue sessions.

Step 3: Create a queue session. A queue session is obtained from the queue connection, as illustrated below:

```
QueueSession qs = qc.createQueueSession(false,
    Session.AUTO_ACKNOWLEDGE);
```

The first argument to the `createQueueSession` method above indicates that this is not part of a transaction. The second argument indicates that the queue session automatically acknowledges messages when they have been received successfully. Until a JMS message has been acknowledged, it is not considered to be successfully consumed. The successful consumption of a message normally takes place in three stages.

1. The client receives the message.
2. The client processes the message.
3. The message is acknowledged.

Acknowledgment of a message is initiated either by the JMS provider or by the client, depending on the session acknowledgment mode specified when the `createQueueSession` method was called.

The three possible argument values are:

- `Session.AUTO_ACKNOWLEDGE`. The session automatically acknowledges a client's receipt of a message either when the client has successfully returned from a call to receive or when the MessageListener it has called to process the message returns successfully.
- `Session.CLIENT_ACKNOWLEDGE`. A client acknowledges a message by calling the message's acknowledge method. In this mode, acknowledgment takes place on the session level: acknowledging a consumed message automatically acknowledges the receipt of all messages

that have been consumed by its session. For example, if a message consumer consumes ten messages and then acknowledges the fifth message delivered, all ten messages are acknowledged.

- `Session.DUPS_OK_ACKNOWLEDGE`. This option instructs the session to lazily acknowledge the delivery of messages. This is likely to result in the delivery of some duplicate messages if the JMS provider fails, so it should be used only by consumers that can tolerate duplicate messages. However, this option can reduce session overhead by minimizing the work the session does to prevent duplicates.

If messages have been received but not acknowledged when a `QueueSession` terminates, the JMS provider retains them and redelivers them when a consumer next accesses the queue.

Step 4: Look up the queue. We are now in a position to actually obtain a link to the queue that we wish to send messages to. This is done by using the initial context object we created earlier and looking up the queue using a JNDI name. In the case of JBoss all queues are prefixed with "`queue`"; thus the queue called `jdt` will have a JNDI name of `queue/jdt`. Therefore we can look up a queue in the following manner:

```
Queue q = (Queue)context.lookup("queue/jdt");
```

Step 5: Create a queue sender. A queue sender is a message producer that allows messages to be sent to the specified queue. A queue sender is created using the `createSender` method on the queue session:

```
QueueSender sender = qs.createSender(q);
```

The queue sender can be used to set the message priority, the delivery mode, the time to live for the message etc.

Steps 6 and 7: Create the message. The queue session also allows the message object to be created. In our example we are using a `TextMessage` and therefore the method called on the queue session is `createTextMessage`. Other types of messages were described in Section 7.5 and include `ObjectMessage`, `StreamMessage` and `MapMessage`. `QueueSession` provides appropriate create methods for each message type. As we are using a text message we must also provide the "text" to be sent. This is done using the `setText` method of the `TextMessage` class:

```
TextMessage message = qs.createTextMessage();
message.setText(text);
```

We now have a message object that can be sent.

Step 8: Send the message. Finally, we are in a position to send the message to the queue. This is done using the `QueueSender` object we created earlier. This object has a method `send` that takes two parameters, one for the queue to send the message to and the second for the message to send:

```
sender.send(q, message);
```

Step 9: Close the queue connection. We have now sent our message. If we have no further messages to send we can close the queue connection:

```
qc.close();
```

At this point we have successfully sent a message to the JMS message server available within the JBoss application server.

The complete program is presented in Figure 7.14. Note that the `main` method throws the `Exception` class. This is because various steps in the process of sending a message may

```
import java.util.Properties;
import javax.jms.*;
import javax.naming.*;

public class JMSClientProducer {

   public static void main(String [] args) throws Exception {
      if (args.length == 0) {
         printUsage();
      } else {
         String text = args[0];
         Properties env = new Properties();
         env.put ("java.naming.factory.initial",
                  "org.jnp.interfaces.NamingContextFactory");
         env.put("java.naming.provider.url",
                 "jnp://localhost:1099");
         env.put("java.naming.factory.url.pkgs",
                 "org.jboss.naming:org.jnp.interfaces");
         Context context = new InitialContext(env);
         // Get connection factory from naming service
         QueueConnectionFactory f =
                  (QueueConnectionFactory)context.lookup("ConnectionFactory");

         // Create the connection
         QueueConnection qc = f.createQueueConnection();

         // Create the session
         QueueSession qs = qc.createQueueSession(false,
                                                Session.AUTO_ACKNOWLEDGE);

         // Note queue must be placed before the queue name
         Queue q = (Queue)context.lookup("queue/jdt");

         QueueSender sender = qs.createSender(q);
         TextMessage message = qs.createTextMessage();
         message.setText(text);
         sender.send(q, message);

         // Must close the connection
         qc.close();
      }
   }
   public static void printUsage() {
      System.out.println("java JMSClientProducer <message>");
   }
}
```

Figure 7.14 A client that sends text messages to a queue.

throw an exception. In our case we are merely passing this exception up to the top level. However, in a real application we would want to catch the exception and present the user with some meaningful feedback.

7.6.3 Define Clients That Receive Messages

Next we will create a JMS client that will act as a consumer of messages. Just as with sending a message, there are a series of steps that must be performed. The first four of these are common to producing a message. However, we must then decide whether we are going to consume messages synchronously or asynchronous. In this example we will receive message synchronously. This means that we must create a queue receiver and then wait for messages to be received. Thus the steps to be followed for receiving a message are:

1. Obtain a queue connection factory
2. Create a queue connection
3. Create a queue session
4. Look up the queue
5. Obtain a queue receiver
6. Start the queue connection
7. Wait for a message to be received

As steps 1–4 are the same as before, we will jump straight to step 5: obtaining a queue receiver.

Step 5: Obtain a queue receiver. A queue receiver object is a message consumer. That is, it handles receiving messages from the message server. Once the connection is started it will handle receiving messages. You can stop the receipt of messages by calling the `close` method on the receiver. The receiver object is obtained from the queue session object, for example:

```
QueueReceiver rec = qs.createReceiver(q);
```

Step 6: Start the queue connection. Although creating a queue receiver gives you the facility to receive messages, you do not actually receive any messages until the start method has been called on the queue connection object associated with the queue session. The connection is started via the `start` method:

```
qc.start();
```

Step 7: Wait for a message to be received. As we are synchronously receiving messages we will call the `receive` method on the queue receiver once the queue connection has been started. By default this will cause us to wait until a message is received. The `receive` method can actually be used be used in several modes to perform a synchronous receive. If you specify no arguments or an argument of 0, the method blocks indefinitely until a message arrives:

```
Message m = queueReceiver.receive();
Message m = queueReceiver.receive(0);
```

For a simple client program, this may not matter. But if you do not want your program to consume system resources unnecessarily, use a timed synchronous receive. Do one of the following:

- Call the `receive` method with a timeout argument greater than 0:

```
Message m = queueReceiver.receive(1); // 1 millisecond
```

- Call the `receiveNoWait` method, which receives a message only if one is available:

```
Message m = queueReceiver.receiveNoWait();
```

In our case we are calling the `receive` method with a timeout of 1 millisecond and placing the call within a `while` loop that will monitor the queue receiver forever.

The `JMSClientConsumer` application is presented in Figure 7.15. At any time we could either temporarily stop the queue connection using the `stop` method or terminate it using the `close` method.

We could also have chosen to receive messages asynchronously using a message listener. A message listener is an object that implements the `MessageListener` interface and defines a method `onMessage`. The message listener object is registered with a `QueueReceiver` and will have its `onMessage` method called each time a message is received. The Message-Driven Enterprise JavaBean is a type of message listener.

7.6.4 Start Message Server

At this point we are now ready to start the JBoss application server, which will automatically start the JBossMQ message server. This is done by running the `run.bat` file (or `run.sh` if you are on Unix) in the `bin` directory of your JBoss installation. You will see very many messages being displayed – do not worry about this. What you should look for is a message similar to:

```
10:49:23,643 INFO [Server] JBoss (MX MicroKernel) [3.0.0
Date:200205311035] Started in 0m:27s:169ms
```

Obviously the time and date information is likely to be different, but the important point is that the JBoss server is Started.

7.6.5 Compile and Start the Clients

We are now ready to compile our clients. Both JMS clients need to have an appropriate J2EE jar available in order that the JMS classes and interfaces can be found. As we are using JBoss, we shall use the `jboss-j2ee.jar` file that contains the JBoss version of the J2EE jar (although we could have used the jar distributed with the J2EE from Sun). The `compile.bat` file used for compiling the JMS clients is presented in Figure 7.16. Note that the clients were compiled with version 3.0.0 of JBoss; if you have a different version then the classpath used for the JAR will be different.

Once the clients are compiled we can execute them. To do this we will need to setup another classpath. This is because when the clients connect to the naming service and to the message server they will need to access the classes used by JBoss. We will use two `.bat` files

```
public static void main(String [] args) throws Exception {
   if (args.length != 0) {
      printUsage();
   } else {

      Properties env = new Properties();
      env.put ("java.naming.factory.initial",
               "org.jnp.interfaces.NamingContextFactory");
      env.put("java.naming.provider.url",
              "jnp://localhost:1099");
      env.put("java.naming.factory.url.pkgs",
              "org.jboss.naming:org.jnp.interfaces");
      Context context = new InitialContext(env);
      // Get connection factory from naming service
      QueueConnectionFactory f =
               (QueueConnectionFactory)context.lookup("ConnectionFactory");

      // Create the connection
      QueueConnection qc = f.createQueueConnection();

      // Create the session
      QueueSession qs = qc.createQueueSession(false,
                                            Session.AUTO_ACKNOWLEDGE);

      // Note queue must be placed before the queue name
      Queue q = (Queue)context.lookup("queue/jdt");

      // Now wait to receive a message
      QueueReceiver rec = qs.createReceiver(q);
      qc.start();
      while (true) {
         Message m = rec.receive(1);
         if (m != null) {
            if (m instanceof TextMessage) {
               TextMessage message = (TextMessage) m;
               System.out.println("Message: " +
                                  message.getText());
            }
         }
      }
   }
}
public static void printUsage() {
   System.out.println("java JMSClientConsumer");
}
}
```

Figure 7.15 A JMS client used to receive messages.

to handle this: one for running the `JMSClientProducer` application and one for the `JMSClientConsumer` application. The two `.bat` files are presented in Figures 7.17 and 7.18.

The result of executing the `runProducer.bat` file is that the message is sent to the JBossMQ message server. For example:

```
runProducer "Hello JMS World"
```

The `.bat` file for running the consumer application is presented in Figure 7.18.

UltraEdit-32 - [C:\jdt\java\jms\bat\compile.bat]

```
echo on

set jbcp=C:\jboss-3.0.0_tomcat-4.0.3\client\jboss-j2ee.jar;..\classes

cd ..\source

javac -d ..\classes -classpath %jbcp% *.java

cd ..\bat
```

Figure 7.16 Compiling the JMS clients.

```
echo on

set jbdir=C:\jboss-3.0.0_tomcat-4.0.3\client

set jbcp=%jbdir%\jboss-client.jar;%jbdir%\jboss-j2ee.jar
set jbcp=%jbcp%;%jbdir%\jboss-common-client.jar;%jbdir%\concurrent.jar
set jbcp=%jbcp%;%jbdir%\jnp-client.jar;%jbdir%\jbossmq-client.jar
set jbcp=%jbcp%;%jbdir%\jboss-client.jar;%jbdir%\log4j.jar
set cp=%jbcp%;..\classes

java -classpath %cp% JMSClientProducer %1
```

Figure 7.17 Running the producer application.

```
echo on

set jbdir=C:\jboss-3.0.0_tomcat-4.0.3\client

set jbcp=%jbdir%\jboss-client.jar;%jbdir%\jboss-j2ee.jar
set jbcp=%jbcp%;%jbdir%\jboss-common-client.jar;%jbdir%\concurrent.jar
set jbcp=%jbcp%;%jbdir%\jnp-client.jar;%jbdir%\jbossmq-client.jar
set jbcp=%jbcp%;%jbdir%\jboss-client.jar;%jbdir%\log4j.jar
set cp=%jbcp%;..\classes

java -classpath %cp% JMSClientConsumer
```

Figure 7.18 Running the consumer application.

The effect of running this application is that it starts up and connects to the message server. When a message is received it prints that message out. It then waits for the next message. For example:

```
> runConsumer
> Message: Hello JMS World
--- waits for next message ---
```

7.7 Publish and Subscribe Application Development Steps

In this section we will explore the use of the publish and subscribe communications model also supported by the JMS API. We will follow a very similar set of steps to those described above in order to create a simple application that allows a client to publish messages to a topic and another client to subscribe to that topic. That is, we must follow these steps:

1. Publish destinations (topics) using server-specified mechanism.
2. Define clients that publish messages.
3. Define clients that subscribe to topics.
4. Start the message server.
5. Compile and start the clients.

As you can see, these are the same steps as those for creating a queue-based application. Below we highlight where the topic-based application differs from the queue-based application.

In essence, the changes are that we will use a topic wherever we previously used a queue. Thus the following changes will be made:

```
Queue class/interface Topic class/interface
QueueConnectionFactory  TopicConnectionFactory
QueueConnection TopicConnection
QueueSession  TopicSession
Queue Topic
QueueSender TopicPublisher
```

The only one of the above that does not follow the replacement of `Queue` with `Topic` is the `TopicPublisher`. However, even this is an obvious replacement. The other difference is that the JNDI name for the topic will be "`topic/<name of topic>`" rather than "`queue/<name of queue>`", for example "`topic/java`".

Below we will step through each stage of creating a topic-based application.

7.7.1 Publish the Topic

For JBoss this is done in a similar manner to publishing a queue. A new entry must be provided in XML in the `jbossmq-destinations-service.xml` file. The only difference is that the entry is for a topic. Again this can be done with a security manager in place or allow anonymous message sends. The specification of the topic for our application is presented in Figure 7.19.

7.7.2 Define the Publisher Client

To create a client that publishes messages to a topic we follow the same steps as those for creating a queue message producer (except using the `Topic` versions of the classes). Therefore we:

1. Obtain a topic connection factory
2. Create a topic connection

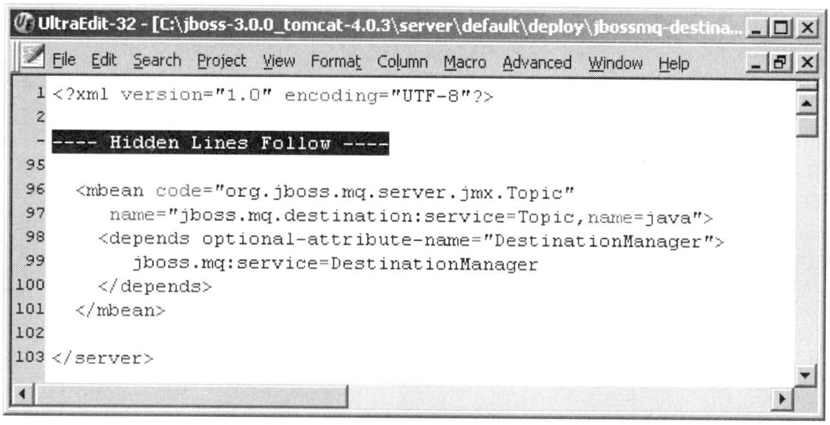

UltraEdit-32 - [C:\jboss-3.0.0_tomcat-4.0.3\server\default\deploy\jbossmq-destina...

File Edit Search Project View Format Column Macro Advanced Window Help

```
<?xml version="1.0" encoding="UTF-8"?>

---- Hidden Lines Follow ----

  <mbean code="org.jboss.mq.server.jmx.Topic"
     name="jboss.mq.destination:service=Topic,name=java">
    <depends optional-attribute-name="DestinationManager">
      jboss.mq:service=DestinationManager
    </depends>
  </mbean>

</server>
```

Figure 7.19 Defining a topic in JBoss.

3. Create a topic session
4. Look up the topic
5. Obtain a topic publisher
6. Create a text message
7. Publish it via the topic publisher
8. Close the topic connection

This is illustrated in Figure 7.20.

The main difference with topics is that we obtain a topic publisher. A topic publisher is a message producer, just like a `QueueSender`. It takes messages and publishers them to the topic its created for. This is done using the method `publish`, which takes a message as an argument.

7.7.3 Define the Subscriber Client

Creating a client to receive messages from a topic is essentially the same as defining a client to receive messages from a queue. Thus the steps are:

1. Obtain a topic connection factory
2. Create a topic connection
3. Create a topic session
4. Look up the topic
5. Obtain a topic subscriber
6. Start the topic connection
7. Wait for a message to be received

This is illustrated in Figure 7.21.

```
import java.util.Properties;
import javax.jms.*;
import javax.naming.*;

public class JMSClientPublisher {

   public static void main(String [] args) throws Exception {
      if (args.length == 0) {
         printUsage();
      } else {
         String text = args[0];
         Context context = new InitialContext();
         // Get connection factory from naming service
         TopicConnectionFactory f =
                  (TopicConnectionFactory)context.lookup("ConnectionFactory");

         // Create the connection
         TopicConnection tc = f.createTopicConnection();

         // Create the session
         TopicSession ts = tc.createTopicSession(false,
                                                Session.AUTO_ACKNOWLEDGE);

         // Note queue must be placed before the queue name
         Topic t = (Topic)context.lookup("topic/java");

         // Now handle publishing to topic
         TopicPublisher tp = ts.createPublisher(t);
         TextMessage message = ts.createTextMessage();
         message.setText(text);
         tp.publish(message);

         // Must close the connection
         tc.close();
      }
   }
   public static void printUsage() {
      System.out.println("java JMSClientPublisher <message>");
   }
}
```

Figure 7.20 The `JMSClientPublisher` application.

The main area of difference for a topic subscriber and a queue consumer is that a `TopicSubscriber` object is used. This is a message consumer (just like a `QueueReceiver`). Just as with the `QueueReceiver` it will only start to receive messages from the topic once the associated connection has been started (in this case a `TopicConnection` object).

It is possible to receive messages synchronously or asynchronously. In our case we have again chosen the asynchronous approach and therefore use the `receive` method with a timeout (as we did in the queue consumer example). Again we could have used a message listener and implemented an `onMessage` method.

7.7.4 Start Message Server

If you have not already done so, now is the time to start JBoss. If you already had JBoss running, you may note that it has picked up your changes to the XML configuration file and has registered your new topic.

```
import javax.jms.*;
import javax.naming.*;

public class JMSClientSubscriber {

   public static void main(String [] args) throws Exception {
      if (args.length != 0) {
         printUsage();
      } else {
         Context context = new InitialContext();
         // Get connection factory from naming service
         TopicConnectionFactory f =
                  (TopicConnectionFactory)context.lookup("ConnectionFactory");
         // Create the connection
         TopicConnection tc = f.createTopicConnection();
         // Create the session
         TopicSession ts = tc.createTopicSession(false,
                                                  Session.AUTO_ACKNOWLEDGE);
         // Note queue must be placed before the queue name
         Topic t = (Topic)context.lookup("topic/java");

         // Now handle subscribing to a topic
         TopicSubscriber sub =
                     ts.createSubscriber(t);
         tc.start();
         while (true) {
            Message m = sub.receive(100);
            if (m != null) {
               if (m instanceof TextMessage) {
                   TextMessage message = (TextMessage) m;
                   System.out.println("Subscriber Message: " +
                                        message.getText());
               }
            }
         }
      }
   }
   public static void printUsage() {
      System.out.println("java JMSClientSubscriber");
   }
}
```

Figure 7.21 The JMSClientSubscriber application.

7.7.5 Compile and Start the Clients

Now we can compile and run our clients. The clients are compiled in exactly the same way as before using the same compile.bat file (see Figure 7.16). The JMSClientSubscriber application can be run using the same classpath as the queue-based JMS clients. When it is run it will wait for messages to be sent to the topic. When they are it will pick up the message and print it out.

The JMSClientPublisher can also be run with the same classpath as the queue clients. It takes a string as an argument and sends it to the "java" topic. The result of doing this twice with the strings "help" and "Have a look at JMS" is that the subscriber applications receives two messages, as illustrated in Figure 7.22.

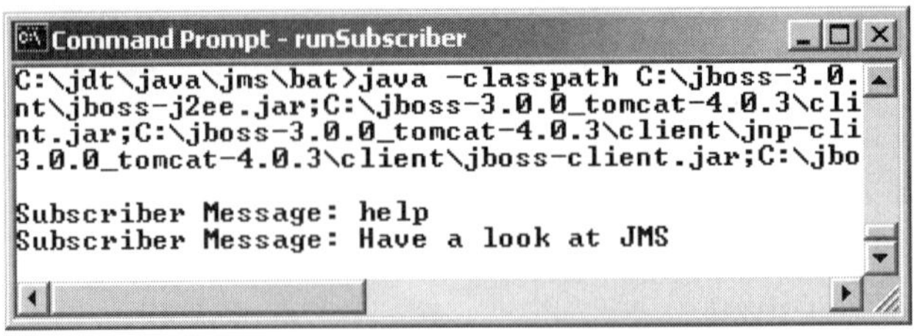

```
Command Prompt - runSubscriber
C:\jdt\java\jms\bat>java -classpath C:\jboss-3.0.
nt\jboss-j2ee.jar;C:\jboss-3.0.0_tomcat-4.0.3\cli
nt.jar;C:\jboss-3.0.0_tomcat-4.0.3\client\jnp-cli
3.0.0_tomcat-4.0.3\client\jboss-client.jar;C:\jbo

Subscriber Message: help
Subscriber Message: Have a look at JMS
```

Figure 7.22 Running the `JMSClientSubscriber` application.

7.8 Additional JMS Features

7.8.1 Specifying Message Persistence

Messages sent via the JMS can be persistent or non-persistent (the default is persistent). Persistent means that the message server should try to ensure that the message is not lost during transmission due to a failure of the JMS provider (message server). Non-persistent means that the JMS provider does not guarantee that messages will not be lost.

You can specify the delivery mode in either of two ways. You can use the `setDeliveryMode` method of the `MessageProducer` interface (the parent of the `QueueSender` and the `TopicPublisher` interfaces) to set the delivery mode for all messages sent by that producer. The other option is to use the long form of the `send` or `publish` methods to set the delivery mode for a specific message. The second argument sets the delivery mode.

7.8.2 Setting the Message Priority

It is possible to influence the order in which messages are delivered by a message server by altering the priority of a message. The priority of a message can be set by:

- You can use the `setPriority` method of the `MessageProducer` interface to set the priority level for all messages sent by that producer.
- You can use the long form of the `send` or `publish` methods to set the priority level for a specific message. The third argument sets the priority level.

There are currently 10 different priority levels ranging from 0 (the lowest) to 9 (the highest priority level). The default is 4.

7.8.3 Defining How Long a Message Lasts

By default, messages never expire. However, in some cases it may be necessary to say that if a message has not been consumed by a particular time it is no longer of interest. To support such situations it is possible to define a "sell by" date for a message, after which point the message is deleted. Setting the expiry date on a message can be done in one of two ways:

- You can use the `setTimeToLive` method of the `MessageProducer` interface to set a default expiration time for all messages sent by that producer.
- You can use the long form of the `send` or `publish` methods to set an expiration time for a specific message. The fourth argument sets the expiration time in milliseconds.

7.8.4 Durable Subscriptions

As mentioned earlier, a durable subscription is one that will maintain a list of messages that a client would miss while it was inactive. This of course has a higher overhead compared to non-durable subscriptions (the default), but may be desirable in some situations. To create a durable subscription the `createDurableSubscriber` method is used on a `TopicSession`. There may also be some configuration required by the message server to configure a topic for a durable subscription.

7.8.5 Topic Message Selectors

If you need to filter the messages you receive, then you can use the JMS API message selector. This is done by specifying to a session that you are interested in message filtering and providing an SQL-style query string. The query string is used by the JMS provider to filter the messages sent to a message consumer.

7.8.6 Client Authentication

In the examples presented in this chapter we have not worried about logging into a queue or topic. Instead we have relied on the use of the anonymous guest login. This has allowed us to send messages and receive messages. However, in enterprise-strength applications we may need to limit who can send messages to a queue or topic or who can read messages from a queue or topic. This can be done by requiring an application to authenticate itself with the JMS Provider (that is to log in to the JMS Provider). This is done by providing a userID and password when getting the initial connection to the JMS provider. The JMS provider must then be configured such that users can be associated with queue and topics etc. This is done in a vendor-specific manner.

7.8.7 Transactions

Message sends and receives can be grouped into a transaction. Just as with database transactions, this means that all messages are sent or (if one message send fails) no messages are sent. It also means that either all messages are received or no messages are received. To start a transaction you should use `true` as the first argument to the `createTopicSession` (or queue equivalent). The second argument is then ignored, so should be set to 0; for example:

```
ts = topicConnection.createTopicSession(true, 0);
```

The session can then be committed or rolled back as appropriate at a later date. For example:

```
ts.commit();
ts.rollback();
```

7.9 Summary

In this chapter we have explored the JMS API that is used for sending and receiving messages from a message service. We have explored both point to point and publish and subscribe communications models and have considered some of the more advanced features of the JMS API, such as message priorities and durable subscriptions. In Chapter 16, Message-Driven Beans, we will come back to the JMS and look at integrating an Enterprise JavaBean into this JMS model.

7.10 Online References

Archives of JMS Interest Group: http://archives.java.sun.com/archives/jms-interest.html
IBM's MQSeries: http://www-3.ibm.com/software/ts/mqseries/api/mqjava.html
OpenJMS Open Source JMS Provider: http://openjms.exolab.org/
SonicMQ: http://www.sonicsoftware.com/
Sun's JMS Tutorial: http://java.sun.com/products/jms/tutorial/index.html
Sun One Message Queue: http://wwws.sun.com/software/products/message_queue/home_message_queue.html

Chapter 8

Java, IDL and Object Request Brokers

8.1 Introduction

This chapter considers the new Java IDL facilities provided as part of JDK 1.2. To do this it is divided into two parts. The first part describes the CORBA standard for Object Request Brokers (ORBs). The second part then describes Java IDL and its interface to a CORBA-compliant ORB as well as the ORB provided as part of Java IDL.

8.2 CORBA

The Common Object Request Broker Architecture (CORBA) is a standard produced by the Object Management Group (OMG) in collaboration with many organizations (which are members of the OMG). The OMG adopts and publishes interfaces; it publishes "standards", but never gets involved in the creation, selling or re-selling of software. This is accomplished via a competitive selection process based on proposals generated outside the OMG. Interface documents published by the OMG give the standard interface; implementations of those specifications are available from other companies, such as Hewlett-Packard and Sun, which develop software systems that they can then sell as matching one of these specifications.

CORBA specifies the architecture of CORBA-compliant Object Request Brokers (ORBs). An ORB is a mechanism that allows objects to communicate between processes, processors, hardware, operating systems, etc. Calls in an ORB are treated as client–server calls. That is, the calling object is halted until a reply is received. The structure of a request from one object on one machine to another object on another machine is illustrated in Figure 8.1.

However, although the process is as illustrated in Figure 8.1, to the programmer, the call appears as illustrated in Figure 8.2. That is, it appears to the programmer that the server object is held locally and that the message is sent from the client to a local object. This greatly simplifies the programming task.

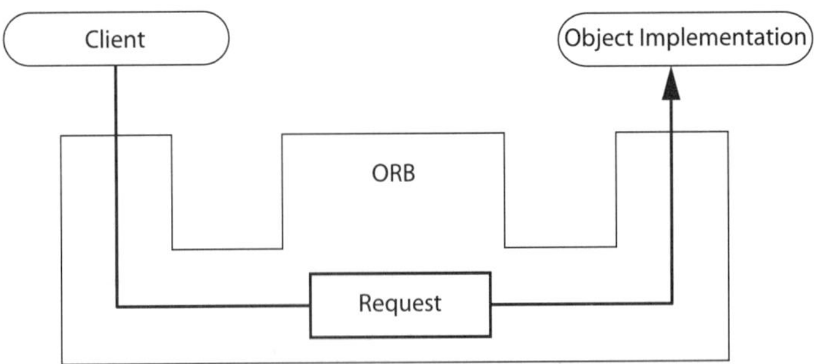

Figure 8.1 CORBA: what actually happens.

Figure 8.2 How the system appears to the programmer.

The way in which this process works is that, when a client requests information from, or a service provided by, a remote object, the client stub and the ORB cooperate to pass the request to the implementation skeleton. The skeleton then passes the request to the actual object. Once the object has processed the request (returning the required data etc.), the skeleton takes any results produced and uses the ORB to pass those results back to the client stub. The stub then passes the results to the client object.

In order to facilitate this process, the ORB needs to do a number of things. In particular, it needs to keep track of where the objects are and handle any conversions or translations required when crossing platform boundaries (both machine and operating system boundaries). It may also need to handle the creation and deletion of objects as well as activating objects before passing requests to them. In particular, it must handle object references persistently.

To facilitate the integration of different languages into the ORB framework, Interface Definition Languages (IDLs) are provided. A number of IDLs have now been provided for Java (for example, ORBIX provide a CORBA-compliant ORB and a Java IDL). An IDL defines the interfaces provided by an object. This information is used to produce client stubs and implementation skeletons (Figure 8.3).

8.3 Java IDL

In JDK 1.2 a new feature has been added called Java IDL. This allows an IDL specification to be compiled into Java interfaces so that Java programs can work with a CORBA-compliant ORB. This means that both Java applications and Java applets can now work seamlessly with any ORB and thus with any systems connected to that ORB (or via IIOP – Internet Inter-ORB Protocol – with other ORBs). Thus an applet can communicate with a legacy system via an ORB in a clean, implementation independent manner.

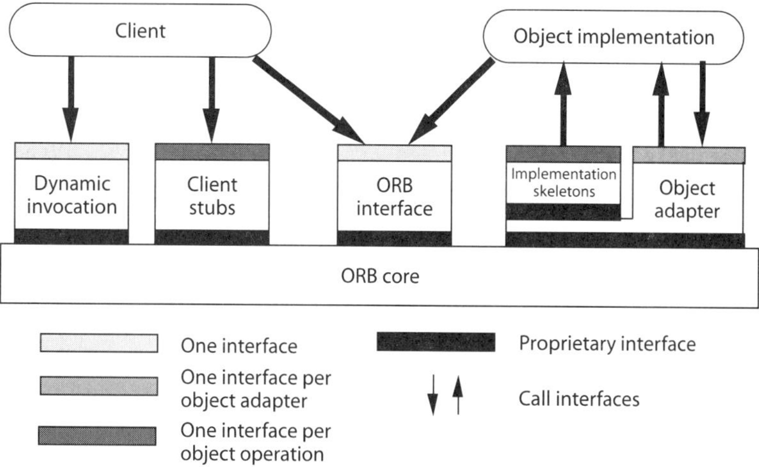

Figure 8.3 The components of CORBA.

To implement a distributed application which uses the Java IDL ORB you should use the following steps:

- Define an IDL interface.
- Use the idltojava compiler on the IDL specification to generate the appropriate Java interface and stub and skeleton files.
- Implement a `Server` class as a concrete implement of the appropriate Java interface.
- Implement a `Client` class as a concrete implementation of the appropriate interface.
- Compile all the Java code.
- Initiate the name server.
- Run the server and the client.

This section looks in more detail at Java IDL and works through a simple example client–server application.

8.3.1 Java ORB

Included in the Java IDL are a fully compliant Java ORB for distributed computing using IIOP communication and stub and server classes for linking Java objects to an ORB. The Java ORB is compliant with the CORBA/IIOP 2.0 Specification. The Java IDL ORB only supports transient CORBA objects. These are objects whose lifetimes are limited by their server process's lifetime. That is, once process is terminated the objects maintained by those processes are also terminated.

8.3.2 Java Name Server

Java IDL also provides a transient name server to organize objects into a tree directory structure. The name server is initiated by executing the tnameserv at the command line. For example:

```
tnameserv -ORBInitialPort 1234
```

The number following the -ORBInitialPort option indicates the port number to connect the name server to. In this case we have connected it to port number 1234. As described in Chapter 4, port numbers below 1024 are usually restricted for system services and so should not be used for the name server. The name server can be stopped by terminating the process running the name server.

The name server stores object references by name in a tree structure similar to a file directory. A client may look up or resolve object references by name. Because the name server is an ordinary Java IDL transient server, the entire directory structure of names is lost each time tnameserv stops running.

The name server is transient because when it is terminated all the references it maintains are lost. Thus they are not persistent between sessions of the name server. The name server is compliant with the Naming Service Specification described in CORBAservices: Common Object Services Specification.

8.3.3 Converting IDL to Java

To implement a object which will work with an ORB, it is necessary to map an IDL specification (the CORBA side of an object's interface) to the required implementation language – in this case Java. Note that in order to convert IDL specifications into Java specifications it is necessary to use the idltojava compiler. This tool must be downloaded separately from the JDK release (quite why this is so is unclear). The idltojava compiler can be downloaded from the following URL (note this URL takes you to the Java Developers Connection pages. To access these pages you must be a member of the JDC. Membership costs nothing and you can join at any time):

```
http://developer.java.sun.com/developer/earlyAccess/jdk12/idltojava.html
```

The result of downloading the idltojava compiler is a .exe file (if you are using Windows). This file will unbundle the idltojava compiler once run. You will then be ready to use the idltojava tool.

Using the idltoJava compiler you can now compile an IDL interface into a Java interface and the other .java files needed, including a client stub and a server skeleton.

For example, consider the following IDL specification for an interface called OrbHello which contains a single operation helloWorld:

```
module Hello {
  interface OrbHello {
    string helloWorld();
    };
};
```

Assuming that this IDL is defined in a file called OrbHello.idl, then using the idltojava compiler we would call the idltojava tool thus:

```
idltojava OrbHello.idl
```

Note that the idltojava compiler is currently hard coded to use the C++ preprocessor supplied with Microsoft Visual C++. To switch off the preprocessor use -fo-cpp as an option to the idltojava command, for example:

```
idltojava -fno-cpp OrbHello.idl
```

To change the pre-processor to be used set the two environment variables CPP and CPARGS. CPP should be set to the full pathname of the preprocessor to be used and set CPARGS to the complete list of arguments to be passed to the preprocessor.

The result of running the idltojava tool on the OrbHello.idl file is that five files are created in a subdirectory called Hello. These five files are:

- _OrbHelloImplBase.java This is an abstract class which will be used as the superclass of the server object once it is implemented. It provides the basic CORBA functionality for the server. It implements the OrbHello.java interface.
- _OrbHelloStub.java This is an abstract class which will be used as the superclass of any clients that wish to reference a server object. It provides the basic CORBA functionality for the client. It implements the OrbHello.java interface.
- OrbHello.java This is the Java interface version of the IDL interface presented above. It is presented below:

  ```
  package Hello;
  public interface OrbHello extends org.omg.CORBA.Object {
    String helloWorld();
  }
  ```

  As you can see from this, this is a normal Java interface version of the IDL interface. Note that it extends the org.omg.CORBA.Object, providing standard CORBA object functionality as well as specifying a single method helloWorld().
- OrbHelloHelper.java This is a final class that provides helper functions (including the narrow() method) required to cast CORBA object references to their Java types.
- OrbHelloHolder.java This is a final class that holds a public instance member of type OrbHello. It provides operations for out and inout arguments, which CORBA has but which do not map easily to Java's semantics.

You are now ready to implement the server and client classes. To do this you must provide concrete implementations for the _OrbHelloImplBase and _OrbHelloStub interfaces.

8.3.4 Implementing the Server

The server comprises two classes: the Servant class and the OrbServer class. The Servant class is a concrete subclass of the _OrbHelloImplBase abstract class. The Servant class implements the behaviour of all the operations and attributes of the interface it supports. In this case it only needs to implement the helloWorld() method. The OrbServer class initiates the application Servant. To do this it must first make a reference to an ORB instance so that it can make the Servant object available (register it with the ORB). To register the servant object, the OrbServer application must inform the name server of the Servant object and what it should be called by within the ORB.

Why is it necessary to have both Servant and Server classes? It is necessary because only servers can create new objects which can be registered with the ORB. Thus the OrbServer class is essentially a factory object which creates a new Servant object which is registered with the ORB.

The _OrbhelloImplBase class, which must be subclassed by Servant, is presented below:

```
package Hello;
public abstract class _OrbHelloImplBase extends
org.omg.CORBA.DynamicImplementation implements Hello.OrbHello {
  // Constructor
  public _OrbHelloImplBase() {
    super();
  }
  // Type strings for this class and its superclases
  private static final String _type_ids[] = {
      "IDL:Hello/OrbHello:1.0"
    };

  public String[] _ids() { return (String[]) _type_ids.clone(); }
  private static java.util.Dictionary _methods =
      new java.util.Hashtable();
  static {
    _methods.put("helloWorld", new java.lang.Integer(0));
  }
  // DSI Dispatch call
  public void invoke (org.omg.CORBA.ServerRequest r) {
    switch (((java.lang.Integer) _methods.get(r.op_name())).intValue()) {
      case 0: // Hello.OrbHello.helloWorld
        {
        org.omg.CORBA.NVList _list = _orb().create_list(0);
        r.params(_list);
        String ___result;
          ___result = this.helloWorld();
        org.omg.CORBA.Any __result = _orb().create_any();
        __result.insert_string(___result);
        r.result(__result);
        }
      break;
    default:
      throw new org.omg.CORBA.BAD_OPERATION(0,
          org.omg.CORBA.CompletionStatus.COMPLETED_MAYBE);
    }
  }
}
```

The Servant class is relatively straightforward. It merely implements the _OrbHelloImplBase interface, which in this case means that it implements a single method with the signature public String sayHello(). This method returns the string "Hello ORB of communications". Note that there are specific packages which need to be imported in order to implement the server, above and beyond the packages which are required for the actual Java application.

```
import Hello.*;  // The directory containing the stub files
import org.omg.CosNaming.*;
// Imports the naming service package
import org.omg.CosNaming.NamingContextPackage.*;
    // Specifies exceptions thrown by
    // the name service
import org.omg.CORBA.*;   // The main CORBA package
class Servant extends _OrbHelloImplBase {
  public String sayHello() {
    return "Hello ORB of communications.";
  }
}
```

The OrbServer class defines the public static void main method used to initiate the application. It performs the following steps:

- Obtains a reference to the ORB.
- Instantiates the servant class and registers it with the ORB.
- Obtains a reference to the name server, which is initially returned as a CORBA object and must be converted to the appropriate type.
- Binds the name to be used to identify the object within the ORB name server.
- Waits for a client to request a method on this object via the ORB.

The source code for the OrbServer class is presented below, it performs the above steps. Each step is commented in detail, and thus the source will be used as the main point of documentation. Note that a number of the ORB-related methods throw exceptions, and thus the whole method will be wrapped in a try...catch block.

```
public class OrbServer {

  public static void main(String args[]) {
    try {
      // Obtain a reference to the orb
      ORB orb = ORB.init(args, null);

      // Instantiate Servant and register it with orb
      Servant servant = new Servant();
      orb.connect(servant);

      // Next obtain a reference to the name server.
```

```
      org.omg.CORBA.Object nameServerObject =
        orb.resolve_initial_references("NameService");

      // Now need to perform the equivalent of casting
      // it to a name server as it is currently an
      // CORBA object this is done using the narrow
      // utility method.
      NamingContext nameServer =
          NamingContextHelper.narrow(nameServerObject);

      // Next bind the name to be used to identify the
      // object within the orb name server
      NameComponent name =
            new NameComponent("OrbHelloWorld", "");
      NameComponent path[] = {name};

      // Register the servant object with the given
      // name in the name server.
      // This means that a client can gain a reference
      // to servant by requesting "OrbHelloWorld"
      nameServer.rebind(path, servant);

      // Now wait for a client to request a method on
      // this object via the ORB. Note that we need to
      // specify which Object class we are referring to
      // as there is also a class called Object in the
      // CORBA package.
      java.lang.Object obj = new java.lang.Object();
      synchronized (obj) {
        sync.wait();
      }
    } catch (Exception e) {
      e.printStackTrace(System.out);}
  }
}
```

You are now ready to implement the client.

8.3.5 Implementing the Client

The `Client` class is a separate object which will communicate with the server via the ORB (in much the same way as the client example in Chapter 4). To do this the client must:

- Obtain a reference to the ORB.
- Using the ORB object, obtain a reference to the name server (once again converting it to the appropriate type).

- Next obtain a reference to the remote object. This is done by requesting that the name server "resolve" the reference for the remote object named OrbHelloWorld.
- Now call the appropriate method on the remote object.

The source code for the OrbClient class is presented below. Again note that the appropriate packages must be imported.

```
import Hello.*;
import org.omg.CosNaming.*;
import org.omg.CORBA.*;

public class OrbClient {
    public static void main(String args[]) {
      try {
        // create and initialize the ORB
        ORB orb = ORB.init(args, null);

        // Next obtain a reference to the name server.
        org.omg.CORBA.Object nameServerObject =
            orb.resolve_initial_references("NameService");
        // Now "cast" it to the name server class
        NamingContext nameServer =
            NamingContextHelper.narrow(nameServerObject);

        // Now obtain a reference to the remote object.
        NameComponent name = new NameComponent("OrbHelloWorld", "");
        NameComponent path[] = {name};
        Hello servant = HelloHelper.narrow(nameServer.resolve(path));

        // We can now call the remote method on the
        // remote object. Communication between this
        // object and the remote object are handled by the
        // ORB.
        String hello = servant.sayHello();
        System.out.println(hello);
    } catch (Exception e) {
        e.printStackTrace(System.out); }
  }
}
```

8.3.6 Compiling the Server and Client

You are now ready to compile your distributed application. This means that you must compile all the .java files that have been created by you and which have been generated automatically by the idltojava compiler. This should happen automatically for you when you run the javac compiler on the client and server classes.

8.3.7 Running the Application

You are now in a position to run your distributed application. To do this you should have already started the name server (we will assume it is running on port 1234). You can now initiate the `OrbServer` server application. This is done in the following manner:

```
java OrbServer -ORBInitialPort 1234
```

Note that a `-ORBInitialPort` command line option has been passed to the `OrbServer` application with the port number being used by the name server. This information is used by helper classes to connect to the name server.

The final part of this application is to run the client application. Once again you need to specify the port on which the name server is running. Thus the client is initiated in the following manner:

```
java OrbClient -ORBInitialPort 1234
```

8.3.8 Java IDL and RMI

As you can see from the description in this chapter, IDL and RMI are very similar in structure and concept. It is primarily the syntax used to initiate the operations and register the objects which differs, so why should you use one versus the other. Essentially it comes down to interoperability. RMI is a Java to Java mechanism, while Java IDL is a Java to ORB communications mechanism which allows it to communicate with a very wide range of languages (including C, C++, Cobol and Smalltalk). From a purely performance aspect, if you are performing Java to Java communications then RMI is a lot faster than an ORB (as it has less to do), whereas using Java IDL is more flexible. One interesting development is that work is currently being undertaken on an RMI to IDL interface which will allow MRI to communicate with ORBs as well as other Java applications – this will be extremely interesting!

8.4 Online References

CORBAservices: Common Object Services Specification: `http://www.omg.org/technology/documents/formal/corbaservices.htm`
Idltojava tool:
`http://developer.java.sun.com/developer/earlyAccess/jdk12/idltojava.html`
Object Management Group: `http://www.omg.org/`
OMG technical library: `http://www.omg.org/library/`

Chapter 9

Java Database Connectivity

9.1 Introduction

Officially, JDBC is not an acronym; however, to all intents and purposes it stands for Java DataBase Connectivity. This is the mechanism by which relational databases are access in Java. Java is an (almost) pure object-oriented language; however, although there are some object-oriented databases available, many database systems presently in commercial use are currently relational. It is therefore necessary for any object-oriented language which is to be used for commercial development to provide an interface to such databases. However, each database vendor provides its own proprietary (and different) API. In many cases they are little more than variations on a theme; however, they tend to be incompatible. This means that if you were to write a program that was designed to interface with one database system, it is unlikely that it would automatically work with another.

Of course, one of the philosophies of Java is "*write once, run anywhere*". This means we do not want to have to rewrite our Java code just because it is using a different database on different platforms (or even the same platform). JDBC is Sun's attempt to provide a vendor-independent interface to any relational database system. This is possible, as most vendors implement most (if not all) of the standard SQL, thus allowing a common denominator. SQL stands for Structured Query Language, which is used for obtaining information from relational databases. SQL is a large topic in its own right and is beyond the scope of this chapter. Reference is therefore made to appropriate books at the end of the article.

One potential problem with such an approach is that although the developers' interface is the same, different implementations of an application would be needed to link to different databases. In the JDBC this is overcome by providing different back-end drivers. Developers are now insulated from the details of the various relational database systems that they may be using and have a greater chance of producing portable code.

In the remainder of this chapter we consider JDBC and these database drivers in more detail. We then look at some examples of typical database operations and consider the implications for applets.

9.2 What Is JDBC?

The JDBC allows a Java developer to connect to a database, to interact with that database via SQL, and of course to use those results within a Java application or applet. The combination of Java and JDBC allows information held in databases to be easily and quickly published on the Web (via an applet). It also provides a bridge that supports the Open Database Connectivity (ODBC) standard. The first version of JDBC was released in the summer of 1996. The current release of JDBC in J2EE SDK 1.4 is JDBC 3.0. It is an important addition to Java's armoury, as the JDBC provides programmers with a language and environment that is platform- and database vendor-independent. This is (almost) unique. Most developers who use the ODBC C API are database vendor-independent, but find it non-trivial to port their C application to a different platform due to windowing differences, hardware-dependent language features etc.

ODBC is a database access standard developed by Microsoft. This standard has been widely adopted not only by the vendors of Windows-based databases but by others as well. For example, a number of databases more normally associated with Unix-based systems or IBM mainframes now offer an ODBC interface. Essentially, ODBC is a basic SQL interface to a database system that assumes only "standard" SQL features. Thus specialist facilities provided by different database vendors cannot be accessed. In many ways JDBC has similar aims to ODBC. However, one major different is that JDBC allows different database drivers (interfaces) to be used, one of which is the ODBC driver.

At present, the JDBC only allows connection to, and interaction with, a database via SQL. Features such as those found in tools like Delphi and Visual Basic are not available. For example, there are no database controls, form designers, query builders etc. Of course, it is likely that such tools will become available either from Sun or third-party vendors. This situation will change in the future as many JFC components (or Java Foundation Classes) are data-aware. The JFC provides an enhanced set of tools, including GUI components, in Sun's JDK 1.2.

The JDBC is able to connect to any database by using different (back-end) drivers. These act as the interfaces between the JDBC and databases such as Oracle, Sybase, Microsoft Access and shareware systems such as MiniSQL. The idea is that the front end presented to the developer is the same whatever the database system, while the appropriate back end is loaded as required. The JDBC then passes the programmer's SQL to the database via the back end. Java is not the first system to adopt this approach; however, a novel feature of the JDBC is that more than one driver can be loaded at a time. The system will then try each driver until one is found that is compatible with the database system being used. Thus multiple drivers can be provided, and at run time the appropriate one is identified and used. This is illustrated in Figure 9.1.

Figure 9.1 illustrates some of the most commonly used methods provided by the JDBC along with two database drivers (namely the Mini SQL driver – see Section 9.9 – and the ODBC driver; note that any number could have been provided). Such a setup would allow a Java program to connect to an mSQL database via the mSQL driver and to any database that supports the ODBC standard through the ODBC driver. The `getConnection()`, `executeQuery()` and `executeUpdate()` methods will be looked at in more detail later in this chapter.

There are an increasing number of database drivers becoming available for JDBC. At present databases such as Oracle, Sybase and Ingres all have their own drivers. This allows

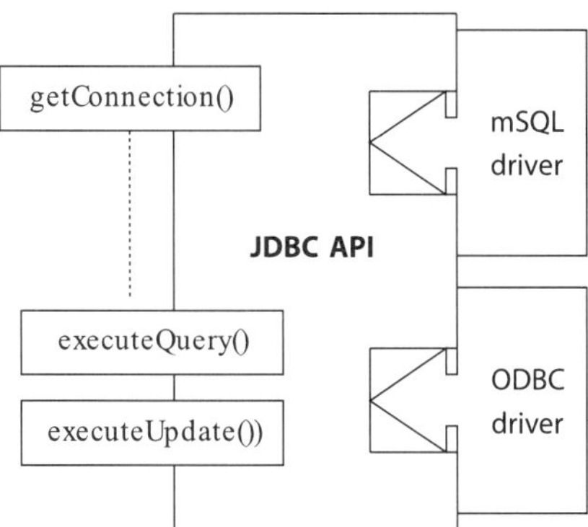

Figure 9.1 The structure of the JDBC.

features of those databases to be exploited. However, even databases that are not directly supported can be accessed via the ODBC driver, thus making a huge range of databases available to the Java developer.

There is a very definite series of steps that must be performed by any JDBC program. These involve loading an appropriate driver, connecting to a database, executing SQL statements and closing the connection made. These are discussed in more detail later in this article.

9.3 What the Driver Provides

What actually is a driver? In practice it provides the concrete implementation for a number of interfaces defined in the SQL package. In particular, it defines implementations for the interfaces and classes (such as `Driver`, `Connection`, `Statement` and `ResultSet`) which form a major part of the SQL API. Each of these will be considered in more detail later. However, essentially they comprise the way to connect to a database, to pass SQL statements to be executed to that database, and to examine the results returned. Note that, unlike some object-to-relational database interfaces, JDBC does not try to objectify the results of querying a relational database. Instead, the results are returned in a table-like format within a results set. It is then up to the developer to decide how to handle the information retrieved.

9.4 Registering Drivers

As part of the JDBC API a JDBC driver manager is provided. This is the part of the JDBC that handles the drivers currently available to a JDBC application. It is therefore necessary to "register" a driver with the driver manager. There are three ways of doing this:

1. Passing a command line option to a Java application using the `-Dproperty=value` parameter. For example:

   ```
   java -Djdbc.drivers=jdbc.odbc.JdbcOdbcDriver queryDB
   ```

2. For applets it is possible to set the `jdbc.drivers` system property. In HotJava this can be done in the properties file of the `.hotjava` directory. For example:

   ```
   jdbc.drivers=jdbc.odbc.JdbcOdbcDriver:imaginary.sql.iMsqlDriver
   ```

3. Programmatically by requesting the class of the driver to be loaded using the static method `forName()` in the class `Class`. For example:

   ```
   Class.forName("sun.jdbc.odbc.JdbcOdbcDriver");
   Class.forName("COM.imaginary.sql.msql.MsqlDriver");
   ```

   This will cause the associated class (in this case the driver) to be loaded into the running application.

As was mentioned earlier, you can install more than one driver in your JDBC program. When a request is made to make a connection to a database each one will be tried in turn until one accepts that request. However, using more than one driver will slow down both system start-up (as each must be loaded) as well as your run-time (as each may need to be tried in turn). For this reason, it may be best to select the most appropriate driver and stick with that one.

The JDBC ODBC driver is provided as part of Sun's JDK 1.1. However, other drivers can be obtained and used with the JDBC. For example, the mSQL driver mentioned above was downloaded from the Web and installed in an appropriate directory. In this way database vendors can supply their own proprietary database drivers, which developers can then utilize in their own applications.

9.5 Opening a Connection

Listing 9.1 presents a simple class that uses the ODBC driver to connect to a Microsoft Access database. We must first make the JDBC API available; this is done by importing the SQL package. Next the application loads the JDBC ODBC driver and then requests that the `DriverManager` makes a connection with the database `testDB`. Note that to make this connection a string (called `url`) is passed to the driver manager along with the user id and the password.

Listing 9.1 `TestConnect.java.`

```
import java.sql.*;
public class TestConnect {

  public static void main (String args []) {
```

```
    String url = "jdbc:odbc:testDB";

    if (args.length < 2) {
      System.out.println("Usage: java TestConnect userid password");
      System.exit(1);
    }

    String userid = args[0];
    String password = args[1];

    try {
      Class.forName("sun.jdbc.odbc.JdbcOdbcDriver");
      Connection con =DriverManager.getConnection(url, userid, password);
      con.close();
      System.out.println("All okay");
    } catch (Exception e) {
      System.out.println(e.getMessage());
      e.printStackTrace();
    }
  }
}
```

The string specifying the database to connect to is formed from a JDBC URL. This is a URL comprising three parts:

1. The JDBC protocol indicator (`jdbc:`)
2. The appropriate sub-protocol such as `odbc:`
3. The driver specific components (in this case `JdbcOdbcDriver`)

URLs are used as the Java program accessing the database may be running as a standalone application or may be an applet needing to connect to the database via the Web. Note that different database drivers will require different driver-specific components. In particular, the mSQL driver requires a URL of the following format:

```
jdbc:msql://hal.aber.ac.uk:1112/testDB
```

In this case it is necessary to provide the host name, the port on that host to connect to and the database to be used.

Once a connection has successfully been made to the database, the program then does nothing other than to close that connection. This is important, as some database drivers require the program to close the connection while others leave it as optional. If you are using multiple drivers it is best to close the connection.

Note that we placed the attempt to load the driver and make the connection within a `try {} catch {}` block. This is because both operations can raise exceptions and these must be caught and handled (as they are not run-time exceptions). The `forName()` method raises the ClassNotFoundException of it can't find the class which represents the specified driver. In turn, the getConnection() static method raises the SQLException if the specified database cannot be found.

The try {} catch {} block works by trapping any exceptions raised in the try part within the catch part (assuming that the exception raised is an instance of the specified class of exception or one of its subclasses).

An example of using this application is presented below:

```
java TestConnect jeh popeye
```

Here I am passing in the user id jeh and the password popeye.

9.6 Obtaining Data From a Database

Having made a connection with a database we are now in a position to obtain information from it. Listing 9.2 builds on the application in Listing 9.1 by querying the database for some information. This is done by obtaining a Statement object from the Connection object. SQL statements without parameters are normally executed using Statement objects. However, if the same SQL statement is executed many times, it is more efficient to use a PreparedStatement. In this example we will stick with the Statement object.

Listing 9.2 TestQuery.java.

```
import java.sql.*;
public class TestQuery {

  public static void main (String args []) {
    String url = "jdbc:odbc:testdb";

    if (args.length < 2) {
      System.out.println("Usage: java TestQuery userid password");
      System.exit(1);
    }

    String userid = args[0];
    String password = args[1];

    try {
      Class.forName("sun.jdbc.odbc.JdbcOdbcDriver");
      Connection con = DriverManager.getConnection(url, userid, password);
      Statement statement = con.createStatement();
      ResultSet results =
        statement.executeQuery("SELECT address FROM addresses
```

```
                                          WHERE name = 'John' ");
      System.out.println("Addresses for John:");
      while (results.next()) {
        System.out.println(results.getString("address"));
      }
      statement.close();

      con.close();
    } catch (Exception e) {
      System.out.println(e.getMessage());
      e.printStackTrace();
    }
  }
}
```

Having obtained the statement object we are now ready to pass it some SQL. This is done as a string within which the actual SQL statements are specified. In this case the SQL statement is:

```
SELECT address
FROM addresses
WHERE name = 'John'
```

This is pure SQL. The `SELECT` statement allows data to be obtained from the tables in the database. In this case the SQL states that the address field (column) of the table addresses should be retrieved where the name field of that row equals 'John'.

This string is passed to the `statement` object via the `executeQuery()` method. This method also generates an `SQLException` if a problem occurs. The method passes the SQL to the driver previously selected by the driver manager. The driver in turn passes the SQL on to the database system. The result is then returned to the driver, which in turn returns it to the user's program as an instance of `ResultsSet`. A results set is a table of data within which each row contains the data which matched the SQL statement. Within the row, the columns contain the fields specified by the SQL. A `ResultSet` maintains a cursor pointing to its current row of data. Initially the cursor is positioned before the first row. The `next()` method moves the cursor to the next row.

The `ResultsSet` class defines a variety of `get` methods for obtain information out of the `ResultsSet` table: for example, `getBoolean()`, `getByte()`, `getString()`, `getDate()` etc. These methods are provided by the JDBC driver and attempt to convert the underlying data to the specified Java type and return a suitable Java value. In Listing 9.2 we merely print out each address in turn using the `next()` method to move the table cursor on.

Finally, the `statement` and the `connection` are closed. In many cases it is desirable to immediately release a `statement`'s database and JDBC resources instead of waiting for this to happen when it is automatically closed; the `close` method provides this immediate release.

9.7 Creating a Table

So far we have examined how to connect to a database and how to query that database for information. However, we have not considered how that database is created. Obviously the database may not be created by a Java application; for example, it could be generated by a legacy system. However, in many situations it is necessary for the tables in the database to be updated (if not created) by a JDBC program. Listing 9.3 presents a modified version of Listing 9.2. This listing shows how a statement object can be used to create a table and how information can be inserted into that table. Again the strings passed to the statement are pure SQL; however, this time we have used the `executeUpdate()` method of the `Statement` class.

Listing 9.3 `TestCreate.java.`

```
import java.sql.*;
public class TestCreate {

  public static void main (String args []) {
    String url = "jdbc:odbc:testdb";

    if (args.length < 2) {
      System.out.println("Usage java TestCreate userid password");
      System.exit(1);
    }
    String userid = args[0];
    String password = args[1];

    try {
      Class.forName("sun.jdbc.odbc.JdbcOdbcDriver");
      Connection con = DriverManager.getConnection(url, userid, password);
      Statement statement = con.createStatement();

      statement.executeUpdate(
        "CREATE TABLE addresses (name char(15), address char(3))");
      statement.executeUpdate(
        "INSERT INTO addresses (name, address) VALUES('John', 'C46')");
      statement.executeUpdate(
        "INSERT INTO addresses (name, address) VALUES('Myra', 'C40')");

      statement.close();
      con.close();
    } catch (Exception e) {
      System.out.println(e.getMessage());
      e.printStackTrace();
    }
  }
}
```

The `executeUpdate()` is intended for SQL statements which will change the state of the database, such as `INSERT`, `DELETE` and `CREATE`. It does not return a result set; rather, it returns an integer indicating the row count of the executed SQL. You can either use this value or ignore it (as in Listing 9.3).

9.8 Applets and Databases

By default, applets are not allowed to load libraries or read and write files. In addition, applets are not allowed to open sockets to machines other than those they originated from. These restrictions cause a number of problems for those wishing to develop applets that work with databases. For example, many drivers rely on the ability to load native code libraries that actually generate the connection to the specified database. One way around these restrictions is to turn them off in the browser being used. This is acceptable for an intranet being used within a single organization; however, it is not acceptable as a general solution.

Another possibility is to use drivers that are 100% pure Java, such as the mSQL driver. However, even using an mSQL driver, the applet is still restricted to connecting to a database on the originating host. Thus the developers must ensure that the Web server that serves the applets is running on the same host as the mSQL daemon. This may or may not be a problem.

Another option is to use a separate database server application (note application and not applet) which runs on the same host as the Web server. Applets can then connect to the database server application requesting that it connect to databases, execute updates, perform queries etc. The database server application is then the program that connects to and interacts with the database. In such a setup the applet does not directly communicate with the database system and is thus not hindered by the restrictions imposed on applets. This is illustrated in Figure 9.2. In this figure a user's browser has connected to the Web server and downloaded the applet. The applet then connects to the database server application. The server application then connects to the database management system on another host.

With the advent of signed applets, some of the above problems go away; however, signed applets are far from universal. In addition, some organizations are still using browsers that do not support them.

9.9 Batch updates

In JDBC 2.0 the statement interface was enhanced to allow the batching of updates. This allows the submission of multiple update statements to the database in one go. These updates are then all performed together. This therefore reduces the communication overhead compared with multiple statements and can result in significant performance gains. For example:

```
con.setAutoCommit(false);
Statement st = con.createSTatement();
```

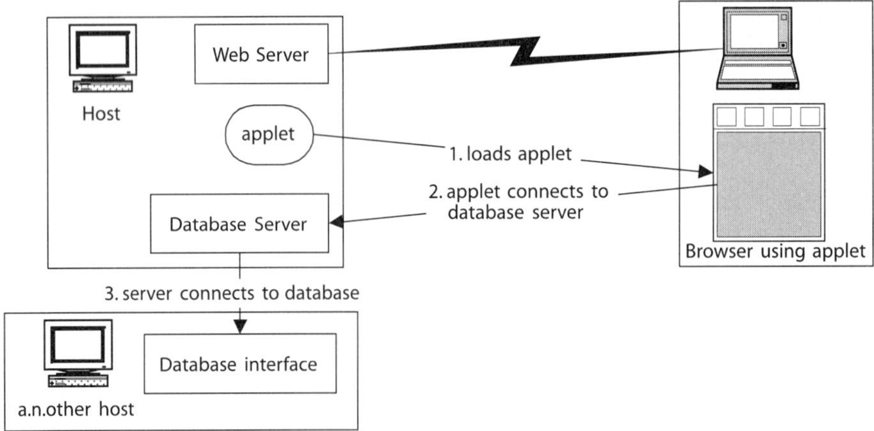

Figure 9.2 Using JDBC within an applet.

```
st.addBatch("INERT INTO ....");
st.addBatch("INERT INTO ....");
st.addBatch("INERT INTO ....");
int [] updates = st.executeBatch();
con.commit();
```

All statement types support the batching of updates. Note that by updates we are referring to inserts, deletions or updates.

9.10 Scrollable and Updateable ResultSets

In the description provided above the general assumption is that ResultSets are read only. That is, it is possible only to read data from the ResultSet (you cannot perform any form of update). In addition, the assumption has also been that it is only possible to move forward through a ResultSet. This was certainly true prior to JDBC 2.0, but in the 2.0 specification (which is part of the J2SE 1.2 and later) ResultSets where enhanced to provide:

- **Scrollability.** This means that it is possible to move both froward and backward through a ResultSet as well as to position the cursor at a particular row.
- **Scroll sensitivity.** This indicates whether the ResultSet always reflects the current state of the underlying database or whether it is a snapshot of that data taken when it is created. That is, a scroll-insensitive ResultSet will not attempt to update the data in the ResultSet as the cursor is moved back and forward. A scroll-sensitive ResultSet will update the data in each row. Note that scroll-sensitive ResultSets obviously incur a certain performance penalty, as they must constantly interact with the database to obtain any changes to the data they hold.

- **Updatability.** Updatable ResultSets allow the client program to modify the values held in the rows of the ResultSet. These updates can then be feedback to the underlying database.

These three features are supported by the `java.sql.ResultSet` interface.

9.10.1 Scrollable ResultSets

It is possible to determine whether the JDBC driver being used supports scrollable ResultSets from the `DatabaseMetaData` object. The `DatabaseMetaData` interface defines a method that allows the testing of the driver for the type of ResultSets supported. This method is listed below:

`boolean`	**`supportsResultSetType`**`(int type)` Does the database support the given result set type?

The types that can be specified are defined on the ResultSet interface and are:

`static int`	**`TYPE_FORWARD_ONLY`** The constant indicating the type for a `ResultSet` object whose cursor may move only forward
`static int`	**`TYPE_SCROLL_INSENSITIVE`** The constant indicating the type for a `ResultSet` object that is scrollable but generally not sensitive to changes made by others
`static int`	**`TYPE_SCROLL_SENSITIVE`** The constant indicating the type for a `ResultSet` object that is scrollable and generally sensitive to changes made by others

Thus we can write:

```
DatabaseMetaData md = connection.getMetaData();
Boolean okay = md.supportsResultSetType(ResultSet.TYPE_SCROLL_SENSITIVE);
if (okay) {
  ...
}
```

This is important, as not all JDBC drivers support scrollable ResultSets, and even if they do they might not support `SCROLL_SENSITIVE` ones. It is also worth noting that even some drivers that do support scrollability are worth monitoring, as some provide scrollability by loading the data from the underlying database into memory and then scrolling through this in-memory data structure. This can of course prove to be problematic, as a great deal more memory will be used by your Java application than might at first be expected (and in at least one application that the authors have been involved with caused a major problem!).

Having ascertained that what we are dealing with does support the appropriate type of ResultSet, we can indicate that this is the type of ResultSet to use when we execute a statement on the connection. For example:

```
Statement stmt = connection.createStatement(
  ResultSet.TYPE_SCROLL_SENSITIVE,
```

```
    ResultSet.CONCUR_UPDATABLE);
  ResultSet rs = stmt.executeQuery("SELECT a, b FROM TABLE2");
```

In the above code snippet we now have a variable `rs` that contains a scroll-sensitive ResultSet. Thus any changes in the underlying database will be reflected in the data held in the ResultSet as we move forward and backward through it. There are in fact three different aspects of sensitivity that can be monitored: updates, deletes and inserts. The `DatabaseMetaData` interface provides six methods that allow a client to determine what is and is not visible. These methods are:

`boolean`	**`othersDeletesAreVisible`**`(int type)` Indicates whether deletes made by others are visible
`boolean`	**`othersInsertsAreVisible`**`(int type)` Indicates whether inserts made by others are visible
`boolean`	**`othersUpdatesAreVisible`**`(int type)` Indicates whether updates made by others are visible
`boolean`	**`ownDeletesAreVisible`**`(int type)` Indicates whether a `ResultSet`'s own deletes are visible
`boolean`	**`ownInsertsAreVisible`**`(int type)` Indicates whether a `ResultSet`'s own inserts are visible
`boolean`	**`ownUpdatesAreVisible`**`(int type)` Indicates whether a `ResultSet`'s own updates are visible

The `ResultSet` interface defines several methods that allow for such navigation in addition to the `next()` method, including:

`boolean`	**`absolute`**`(int row)` Moves the cursor to the given row number in this `ResultSet` object
`void`	**`afterLast`**`()` Moves the cursor to the end of this `ResultSet` object, just after the last row
`void`	**`beforeFirst`**`()` Moves the cursor to the front of this `ResultSet` object, just before the first row
`boolean`	**`first`**`()` Moves the cursor to the first row in this `ResultSet` object
`boolean`	**`previous`**`()` Moves the cursor to the previous row in this `ResultSet` object
`boolean`	**`isAfterLast`**`()` Indicates whether the cursor is after the last row in this `ResultSet` object
`boolean`	**`isBeforeFirst`**`()` Indicates whether the cursor is before the first row in this `ResultSet` object
`boolean`	**`isFirst`**`()` Indicates whether the cursor is on the first row of this `ResultSet` object
`boolean`	**`isLast`**`()` Indicates whether the cursor is on the last row of this `ResultSet` object
`boolean`	**`last`**`()` Moves the cursor to the last row in this `ResultSet` object
`void`	**`moveToCurrentRow`**`()` Moves the cursor to the remembered cursor position, usually the current row
`boolean`	**`relative`**`(int rows)` Moves the cursor a relative number of rows, either positive or negative

We can now write code such as the following:

```
rs.absolute(2);
while (rs.previous) {
   ...
}
```

It is also possible to set the direction in which the scrollable ResultSet will normally move using the `setFetchDirection` method:

`void`	**`setFetchDirection`**`(int direction)` Gives a hint as to the direction in which the rows in this `ResultSet` object will be processed

The directions that are acceptable are defined on the `ResultSet` interface and are:

`static int`	**FETCH_FORWARD** The constant indicating that the rows in a result set will be processed in a forward direction; first-to-last
`static int`	**FETCH_REVERSE** The constant indicating that the rows in a result set will be processed in a reverse direction; last-to-first
`static int`	**FETCH_UNKNOWN** The constant indicating that the order in which rows in a result set will be processed is unknown

It is also possible to check the current fetch direction using the `getFetchDirection` method.

9.11 Updateable ResultSets

As mentioned earlier, prior to JDBC 2.0 ResultSets were read-only. That is, they reflected the data retrieved from the database in response to some query and that was all. However, in JDBC 2.0 changes were introduced that allowed a ResultSet to be updateable. Essentially this means that ResultSets become read–write and that when changes are made to the data held in a ResultSet those changes can be reflected in the underlying database.

Of course, once again it depends on the driver as to whether it supports updateable ResultSets or not. This can be determined using the `getConcurrency()` method on the ResultSet. This method will return a value indicating whether updates are allowed or not. This value is defined by two values on the `ResultSet` interface. These values are `CONCUR_READ_ONLY` and `CONCUR_UPDATABLE` and are described below:

`static int`	**CONCUR_READ_ONLY** The constant indicating the concurrency mode for a `ResultSet` object that may *not* be updated
`static int`	**CONCUR_UPDATABLE** The constant indicating the concurrency mode for a `ResultSet` object that may be updated

We can therefore write:

```
if (rs.getConcurrency(ResultSet.CONCUR_UPDATABLE)) {
  // perform some updates
}
```

The actual update methods in the ResultSet may be used in two ways:

- To update a column value in the current row. In a scrollable ResultSet object, the cursor can be moved backwards and forwards, to an absolute position, or to a position relative to the current row. The following code fragment updates the NAME column in the fifth row of the ResultSet object rs and then uses the method updateRow to update the data source table from which rs was derived.

```
rs.absolute(5); // moves the cursor to the fifth row of rs
rs.updateString("NAME", "AINSWORTH"); // updates the
  // NAME column of row 5 to be AINSWORTH
rs.updateRow(); // updates the row in the data source
```

- To insert column values into the insert row. An updateable ResultSet object has a special row associated with it that serves as a staging area for building a row to be inserted. The following code fragment moves the cursor to the insert row, builds a three-column row, and inserts it into rs and into the data source table using the method insertRow.

```
  rs.moveToInsertRow(); // moves cursor to the insert row
  rs.updateString(1, "AINSWORTH"); // updates the
    // first column of the insert row to be AINSWORTH
  rs.updateInt(2,35); // updates the second column to be 35
  rs.updateBoolean(3, true); // updates the third row to true
rs.insertRow();
  rs.moveToCurrentRow();
```

The updating methods on the ResultSet interface are:

void	**updateAsciiStream()** Updates the designated column with an ASCII stream value
void	**updateBigDecimal()** Updates the designated column with a java.math.BigDecimal value
void	**updateBinaryStream()** Updates the designated column with a binary stream value
void	**updateBoolean()** Updates the designated column with a boolean value
void	**updateByte()** Updates the designated column with a byte value
void	**updateBytes()** Updates the designated column with a byte array value

void	**updateCharacterStream()** Updates the designated column with a character stream value
void	**updateDate()** Updates the designated column with a `java.sql.Date` value
void	**updateDouble()** Updates the designated column with a `double` value
void	**updateFloat()** Updates the designated column with a `float` value
void	**updateInt()** Updates the designated column with an `int` value
void	**updateLong()** Updates the designated column with a `long` value
void	**updateNull()** Gives a nullable column a `null` value
void	**updateObject()** Updates the designated column with an `Object` value
void	**updateRow()** Updates the underlying database with the new contents of the current row of this `ResultSet` object
void	**updateShort()** Updates the designated column with a `short` value
void	**updateString()** Updates the designated column with a `String` value
void	**updateTime()** Updates the designated column with a `java.sql.Time` value
void	**updateTimestamp()** Updates the designated column with a `java.sql.Timestamp` value

The `deleteRow()` method can be used to delete a row.

9.12 JDBC Data Sources

Although all the examples so far in this chapter have used a DriverManager as the basis for obtaining a connection to a database, DriverManagers are not without their own limitations. For example, a DriverManager requires the Driver classes to be available on all JVMs in which the driver will be used. Thus it will need to be available to all clients of the database. Then to use the Driver with the DriverManager you must:

1. Load the Driver class.
2. Connect to the database using a URL-like string.

This URL might contain the driver protocol, machine name, port number and so on, all of which can easily become difficult to maintain even with the use of properties files etc.

However, with JDBC 2.0 DataSources were introduced. This allows JNDI to be used to map a *logical name* to the actual data source. Thus in the client (to the database) program the logical name can map to whatever data source is held in a naming service accessed via JNDI. This is easier to maintain, as the client program does not need to be changed if something changes in with the location or port used to access the database. Instead, a separate program that is used to configure the data source will need to be modified.

Thus the process of providing a connection between a database and the program accessing the database is broken down into the following steps:

1. Set up a data source with an appropriate driver and register with a naming service via JNDI.
2. In the client application program, access the data source from the naming service again via JNDI.
3. The client application program can then obtain a connection from the `DataSource` object.
4. The `DataSource` object in turn acts as a factory for connection objects.
5. The connection obtained from the data source is then used in exactly the same way as a connection obtained from a `DriverManager`.

The following code snippet illustrates this idea:

```
Context ctx = new InitialContext();
DataSource ds = (DataSource)ctx.lookup("jdbc/Personnel");
Connection con = ds.getConnection("jjh", "popeye");
```

This code snippet connects up to the current naming service (defined by the properties in a file called `jdbc.properties`). It will then look in this naming service for a DataSource object bound to the name `jdbc/Personnel`. For more information on JNDI see Chapter 6. These steps are illustrated graphically in Figure 9.3.

In many situations Step 1 will be performed by some form of application server such as an EJB server like JBoss. However, it is by no means the only way in which a DataSource could be registered with a naming service. For example, a separate setup program could be written to create a DataSource object and register it; for example:

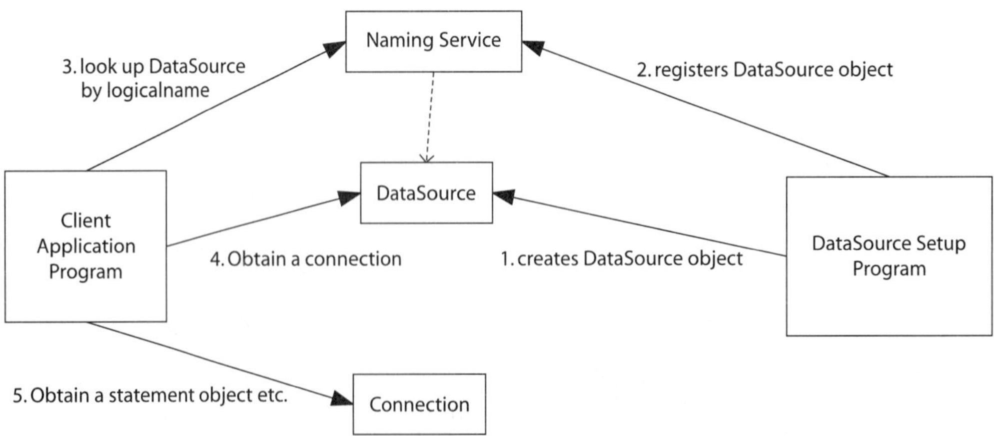

Figure 9.3 The steps taken to use a DataSource.

```
DataSource ds = new OracleDataSource();
ds.setServerName("thor");
ds.setDatabaseName("employees");
Contact ctx = new InitialContext();
ctx.bind("jdbc/Personnel", ds);
```

The above snippet creates an `OracleDataSource` object that will provide connections to a database called `employees`, running on the server thor. It can be accessed from the naming service being used via the name `jdbc/Personnel`.

It is interesting to note that originally it was expected that the use of DataSources would replace the sue of DriverManagers. However, what seems to have happened is that for simple single- or two-tier applications the DriverManager approach is still being used, but for EJB based applications the DataSource approach is used.

The methods defined by the `DataSource` interface are presented below:

`Connection`	**`getConnection`**`()` Attempt to establish a database connection
`Connection`	**`getConnection`**`(java.lang.String username, java.lang.String password)` Attempt to establish a database connection
`int`	**`getLoginTimeout`**`()` Gets the maximum time in seconds that this data source can wait while attempting to connect to a database
`PrintWriter`	**`getLogWriter`**`()` Get the log writer for this data source
`void`	**`setLoginTimeout`**`(int seconds)` Sets the maximum time in seconds that this data source will wait while attempting to connect to a database
`void`	**`setLogWriter`**`(java.io.PrintWriter out)` Set the log writer for this data source

9.13 Connection Pooling

The basic idea behind connection pooling is that a "pool" of connections is maintained and shared among several users. Why would this be a useful strategy? The answer is to do with both the overheads of creating a connection in the first place and the limit on the number of connections allowed by a database. We shall start with the first issue.

Although in many cases it may not be apparent, the creation of objects is both time-consuming and expensive in terms of memory, which may need to be later garbage collected. In the case of connections this is exacerbated by the need to make an external connection to the database, to authenticate users and verify their passwords etc., in addition to the allocation of memory by the JVM for the connection. It is not uncommon for this operation alone to take one, two or more seconds in heavily used applications. When we take into account that we are looking at server applications that service many clients (possibly thousands of clients), we can see that this overhead is very expensive for the system.

An additional concern is that it many cases there is some limit on the number of connections that are either allowed on a database system or that are in some way optimal. If we are considering a Web application being accessed worldwide we may be taking about thousands of concurrent users – few (if any) databases are able to deal with thousands of concurrent connections. However, in most cases most users are not using the connection all the time. Rather, they will perform some task and then need to read, consider and digest the information they receive. Thus one connection could be shared among several users, each getting a slice of the connection while the others are busy doing other things. In this way fewer connections can support a large number of concurrent users.

The two points discussed above are the basis for the need for connection pooling. In connection pooling a pool of connections is maintained. When a client needs to connect to the database it obtains a connection (temporarily) from the pool. It performs whatever operations it requires and then returns the connection back to the pool. When it needs to perform further database operations it will return to the connection pool and obtain another connection. If no connections are available (there is usually a limit on the number of connections held in the pool) the client is queued until such time as a connection is free.

There are some constraints on connection pooling. Firstly users who access the database must do so either through a single account or through a small set of common accounts. This is necessary as each connection is instantiated for a particular account. Thus it is not possible for each user to access the database with a separate account. If they do this, connection pooling is not appropriate. This is not as strict a restriction as it may seem. For example, Internet search engines do not require a user to log in; if they use a database a common account can be used to perform the search etc. Secondly, although users may log into an application via their own user id this does not mean that they have to access the database behind the application with that id. Rather, the application can perform some authentication operation and once logged in the users can be allocated an appropriate (but shared) database account etc.

The second constraint is that the application does not need to hold on to the connections for long periods of time. That is, the application can perform some operation and release the connection. if a permanent connection to the database is required connection pooling will not work. However, again the application can be designed around this. For example, in the next section two types of RowSet are described: a JDBCRowSet and a CachedRowSet. The JDBCRowSet requires a permanent connection to the database, whereas the CachedRowSet does not. Thus by choosing an appropriate RowSet we can work around the need for permanent database connections.

The `javax.sql` package provides for connection pooling in such a way as to hide the details of this from the application programmer. That is, the application server (such as JBoss) and the database driver (such as Cloudscape) handle the connection pooling behaviour internally. This, however, will only work if we use DataSource objects (and thus this is another compelling argument for using DataSources, particularly if you are using EJBs – see later in this book). In most cases it is necessary to configure the application server so that it will use connection pooling, but this is in general done externally to any Java program via what are called deployment descriptors (which are XML files used to configure the application server). This means that from the developers' point of view their programs do not need to change to use connection pooling and the hard work is done by the application server. This means that we can modify the diagram in Figure 9.3 to show the use of a connection pool. This modified diagram is illustrated in Figure 9.4. The changes from the earlier diagram are highlighted in bold.

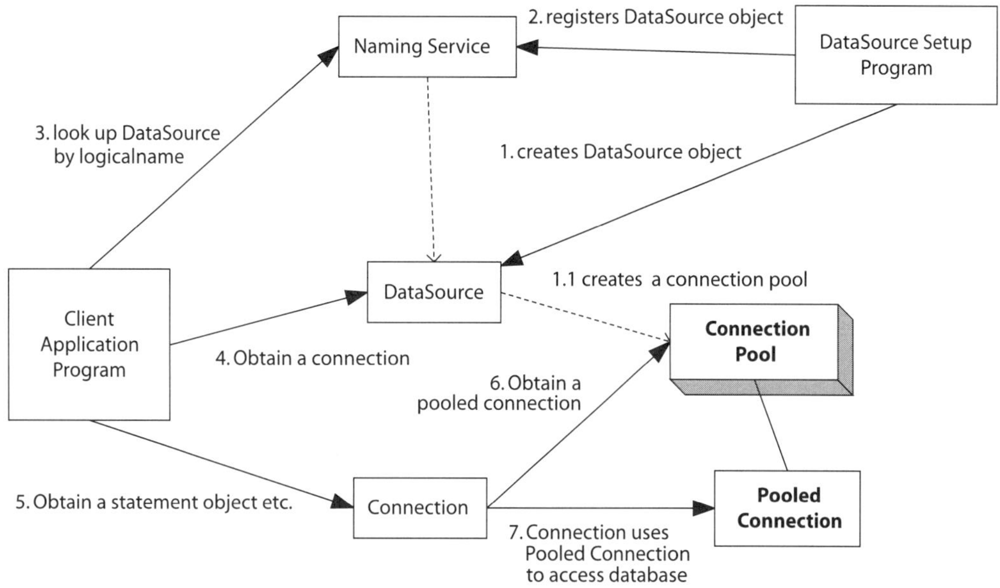

Figure 9.4 Using pooled connections with a DataSource.

Exactly how the application server is configured will differ from one server to another (e.g. from WebLogic to Websphere to JBoss). However, in general they will need to specify:

- The class implementing the `javax.sql.ConnectionPoolDataSource` interface
- The class implementing the `java.sql.Driver` interface
- The size of the connection pool (usually minimum and maximum size)
- The timeout period for a connection
- Authentication for the database

9.14 RowSet Objects

The `javax.sql` package defines an interface called `RowSet` which is a direct sub-interface of `ResultSet`. A RowSet is an object that encapsulates interaction with a database such as querying the database and accessing the results of a search. It is a JavaBean-compliant component and can therefore be used in a JavaBean development tool or as part of a JavaBean-based application.

Essentially the idea behind a RowSet is that this single object can be used to represent the connection to the database, a statement to execute and the ResultSet retrieved. Thus only one object is involved in the whole process with a simplified interface. For example, compare the two programs listed in Figure 9.5. the top program illustrates how we can use a connection, statement and separate ResultSet. In turn the bottom program presents the RowSet example. The two programs are exactly equivalent. the main difference is that

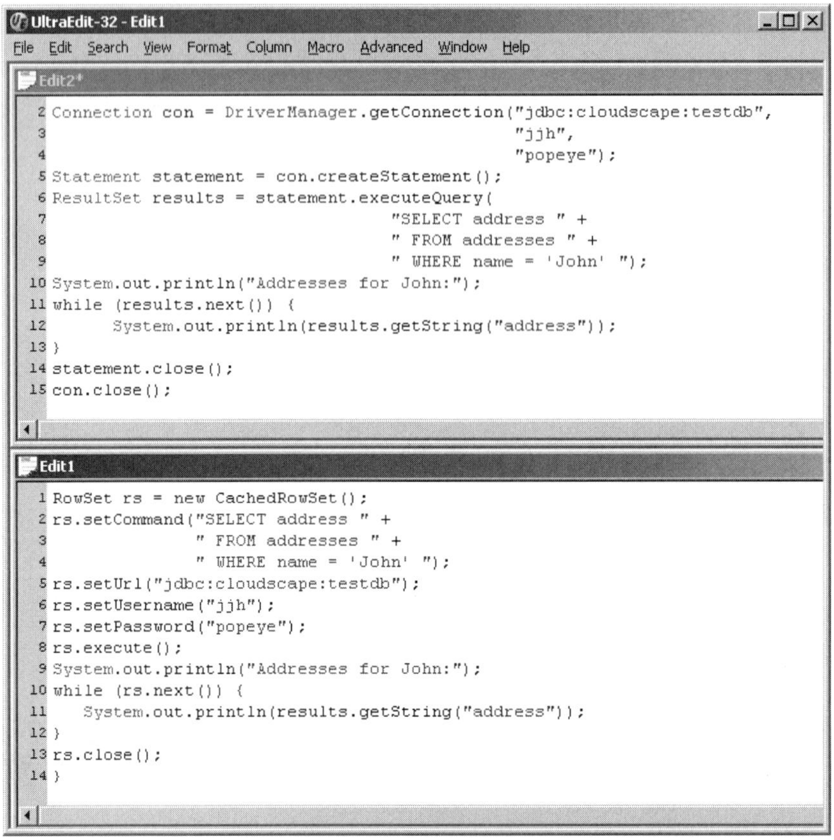

UltraEdit-32 - Edit1

File Edit Search View Format Column Macro Advanced Window Help

Edit2*

```
Connection con = DriverManager.getConnection("jdbc:cloudscape:testdb",
                                             "jjh",
                                             "popeye");
Statement statement = con.createStatement();
ResultSet results = statement.executeQuery(
                                   "SELECT address " +
                                   " FROM addresses " +
                                   " WHERE name = 'John' ");
System.out.println("Addresses for John:");
while (results.next()) {
      System.out.println(results.getString("address"));
}
statement.close();
con.close();
```

Edit1

```
RowSet rs = new CachedRowSet();
rs.setCommand("SELECT address " +
              " FROM addresses " +
              " WHERE name = 'John' ");
rs.setUrl("jdbc:cloudscape:testdb");
rs.setUsername("jjh");
rs.setPassword("popeye");
rs.execute();
System.out.println("Addresses for John:");
while (rs.next()) {
   System.out.println(results.getString("address"));
}
rs.close();
}
```

Figure 9.5 Using a RowSet.

rather than work with three different types of object that represent different aspects of the process of querying a database, in the RowSets example we only have to work with a single type of object. This can greatly simplify the process of accessing a database.

The advantage of a RowSet is that it can be used with other JavaBeans as it is itself a JavaBean. This not only includes the provision of accessor and setter methods, but also integration with the JavaBeans-style events. Thus other JavaBeans that are interested in the events being generated by the RowSet can register with the RowSet and be notified as and when they occur.

The `javax.sql.RowSet` interface (as mentioned above) builds on the `ResultSet` interface and thus provides all the methods in the `ResultSet` interface. In addition it also provides the methods listed below:

`void`	**`addRowSetListener`**`(RowSetListener listener)` RowSet listener registration
`void`	**`clearParameters`**`()` In general, parameter values remain in force for repeated use of a RowSet

void	**execute**() Fills the RowSet with data
java.lang.String	**getCommand**() Get the RowSet's command property
java.lang.String	**getDataSourceName**() The JNDI name that identifies a JDBC data source
int	**getMaxRows**() The maxRows limit is the maximum number of rows that a RowSet can contain
java.lang.String	**getPassword**() The password used to create a database connection
int	**getQueryTimeout**() The queryTimeout limit is the number of seconds the driver will wait for a statement to execute
int	**getTransactionIsolation**() The transaction isolation property contains the JDBC transaction isolation level used
java.lang.String	**getUrl**() Get the URL used to create a JDBC connection
java.lang.String	**getUsername**() The username used to create a database connection
boolean	**isReadOnly**() A RowSet may be read-only
void	**removeRowSetListener**(RowSetListener listener) RowSet listener deregistration
void	**setMaxFieldSize**(int max) The maxFieldSize limit (in bytes) is set to limit the size of data that can be returned for any column value; it only applies to BINARY, VARBINARY, LONGVARBINARY, CHAR, VARCHAR, and LONGVARCHAR fields
void	**setMaxRows**(int max) The maxRows limit is set to limit the number of rows that any RowSet can contain
void	**setUrl**(java.lang.String url) Set the URL used to create a connection
void	**setUsername**(java.lang.String name) Set the user name

In addition to the above methods there are also a set of setter methods for parameters, including setObject, setDate, setTime, setString etc.

The RowSetListener interface defines the methods that must be implemented by an object (or an adapter to an object) that wishes to be notified of events occurring in the RowSet. This interface has the following methods:

void	**cursorMoved**(RowSetEvent event) Called when a RowSet's cursor is moved
void	**rowChanged**(RowSetEvent event) Called when a row is inserted, updated, or deleted
void	**rowSetChanged**(RowSetEvent event) Called when the RowSet is changed

A RowSet event passed into these methods allows the original source of the event to be objected (i.e. the RowSet that originated the event).

It is also possible to obtain information about a RowSet from its metadata object. This is the `RowSetMetaData` object that is a sub-interface of `java.sql.ResultSetMetaData` interface. This can be obtained via the `getMetaData` method.

Sun provide some reference implementations of the RowSet interface that can be freely downloaded from Sun's Web site (see Section 8.16). These reference implementations are:

- A plain JDBC RowSet (`sun.jdbc.rowset.JdbcRowSet`). This is an implementation of the RowSet interface. It maintains a connection to the underlying database and uses this to retrieve data from. It is not serializable or cloneable and is dependent on the underlying ResultSet for features such as scrolling.
- A cached RowSet (`sun.jdbc.rowset.CachedRowSet`). This reads data into a local cache so that a permanent connection to the database is not required. It is also serializable (connections are not) and cloneable.
- A RowSet suitable for Web-based application (`sun.jdbc.rowset.WebRowSet`). The intention is that this RowSet can communicate with other component using XML over HTTP.

9.15 JDBC Metadata

Metadata is data about data. With respect to databases that means that it is data about the database or results obtained from the database: for example, the tables in a database, rows and columns in a table or the results set. This can be very useful information if you need additional flexibility in your application or if you need to adjust to the contents of a database or results set dynamically . For example, metadata can be used to create a database-aware JTable. Such a table could be given a database to connect to, login details and a select statement to be used to populate itself. It could then configure itself as appropriate, given the results obtained (for example the number of columns and their titles, the type of each column etc.). Note that it is up to the database driver to implement the metadata objects. However, not all drivers will provide all the information indicates via the various metadata interfaces.

9.15.1 DatabaseMetaData

The `DatabaseMetaData` object can provide information about the structure of a particular database. This metadata object is obtained from the connection to that database. For example:

```
con.getMetaData();
```

The `DatabaseMetaData` object is very comprehensive and provides over 130 methods. These are organized (loosely) into four categories:

- Methods that return a string
- Methods that return an int
- Methods that return a boolean
- Methods that return a ResultSet

String-returning methods provide information about the database, such as the user name, product name, version and driver name. They also provide information about database specifics such as:

- terms used for schema, procedure
- the actual database product name

The string-returning methods can also provide information on the SQL understood by the database and the escape character used etc.

The int-returning methods usually provide information on limits such as the maximum length allowed for a column name. They are generally of the form `getMaxXXX`; for example `getMaxColumnNameLength()` or `getMaxColumnsInTable()`.

The methods that return a boolean are the largest category (with well over 70 methods in all) and allow you to test for compliance with standards or for support for various features. They are ususally of the form `supportsXXX`, such as `supportsANSI92FullSQL`, `supportsFullOuterJoins()` and `supportsSelectForUpdate()`.

The final category are methods that themselves return a ResultSet. This is the most complex category of methods and needs careful examination of the methods to determine how to use them. For example, it is possible to obtain a description of the stored procedures in a database using the `getProcedures` method:

```
getProcedures(String catalog, String schemaPattern, String
procedureNamePattern)
```

However, the ResultSets retrieved by these methods may themselves be large and need analysis and processing in their own right.

9.15.2 ResultSetMetaData

It is possible to obtain a metadata object from a ResultSet (or RowSet). This is obtained from a ResultSet using the `getMetaData()` method. For example:

```
ResultSetMetaData md = resultsSet.getMetaData();
```

Thus the `ResultSetMetaData` object contains information about the ResultSet from which it was derived.

There are quite a lot of methods available on the `ResultSetMetaData` interface. The most commonly used are presented below:

`String`	**`getCatalogName`**`(int column)` Gets the designated column's table's catalog name
`String`	**`getColumnClassName`**`(int column)` Returns the fully qualified name of the Java class whose instances are manufactured if the method `ResultSet.getObject` is called to retrieve a value from the column
`int`	**`getColumnCount`**`()` Returns the number of columns in this `ResultSet` object

`int`	**`getColumnDisplaySize`**`(int column)` Indicates the designated column's normal maximum width in characters
`String`	**`getColumnLabel`**`(int column)` Gets the designated column's suggested title for use in printouts and displays
`String`	**`getColumnName`**`(int column)` Get the designated column's name
`int`	**`getColumnType`**`(int column)` Retrieves the designated column's SQL type
`String`	**`getColumnTypeName`**`(int column)` Retrieves the designated column's database-specific type name
`String`	**`getSchemaName`**`(int column)` Get the designated column's table's schema
`String`	**`getTableName`**`(int column)` Gets the designated column's table name
`boolean`	**`isCaseSensitive`**`(int column)` Indicates whether a column's case matters
`boolean`	**`isCurrency`**`(int column)` Indicates whether the designated column is a cash value
`int`	**`isNullable`**`(int column)` Indicates the nullability of values in the designated column
`boolean`	**`isSigned`**`(int column)` Indicates whether values in the designated column are signed numbers

As an example of using the metadata object look at the following code snippet:

```
ResultSetMetaData md = rs.getMetaData();
int cols = md.getColumnCount();
for (int i=1; i <= cols; i++)
    System.out.println(md.getColumnName(i));
// Note from 1 to cols, not 0 to cols-1
```

In this example we obtain the metadata for a ResultSet and then print out the name of each of the columns in that result set using the `getColumnCount()` method and the `getColumnName()` method. Note that the columns are numbered from 1 rather then 0.

9.16 Online References

Sun's JDBC home page can be found at `http://java.sun.com/products/jdbc`.

Information on available JDBC drivers can be obtained from `http://java.sun.com/products/jdbc/jdbc.drivers.html`.

mSQL is available by anonymous ftp from `ftp://bond.edu.au/pub/Minerva/msql`.

The mSQL JDBC driver is available from `http://www.imaginary.com/~borg/Java/java.html`.

9.17 References

Hamilton, G., Cattell, R. and Fisher, M. (1997). *JDBC Database Access With Java: A Tutorial and Annotated Reference*. Addison-Wesley, Reading, MA.

Jepson, B. (1997). *Java Database Programming*. John Wiley and Sons Inc., New York.

Microsoft (1997). *Microsoft ODBC 3.0 Software Development Kit and Programmer's Reference*. Microsoft Press, Redmond, WA.

Reese, G. (1997). *Database Programming with JDBC and Java*. O'Reilly, Sebastopol, CA.

Stephens, R. K. (1997). *Teach Yourself SQL in 21 Days*, 2nd edn. Sams, Indianapolis, IN.

Chapter 10

XML and Java

10.1 Introduction

By any standards XML is one of the hottest topics around at the moment. Almost everyone is talking about XML and the majority of modern programming languages now provide some way of accessing XML documents. Java is no exception, providing a number of ways of accessing the contents of an XML document. In this chapter we will look at the use of the DOM (Document Object Model) API defined by the World Wide Web Consortium (known as the W3C; see `http://www.w3c.org/`). This is a standard API that is specified in terms of interfaces that can be implemented in a particular language to provide a set of concrete classes for XML document creation, manipulation, searching and loading etc. This chapter begins with a brief overview of XML before covering Java's implementation of the SAX, DOM and Translation APIs.

10.2 XML Introduced

10.2.1 What is XML?

XML is a data markup language. That is, it is used to mark up or describe data elements. Markup languages are not new. They have been around for some time (and indeed are still often invented – any time you create a new syntax for describing data, say in a file, then you are marking up that data). Older markup languages include SGML (Standard Generalized Markup Language), LaTeX and nroff. The latter two languages are used for describing text for processing by a formatting program to create something that can be viewed or printed. Even HTML is actually a form of markup (indeed, it stands for HyperText Markup Language).

So if markup languages are nothing new, why have XML? Firstly HTML, LaTeX etc. are not extensible and are designed for a very specific purpose. For example, HTML is designed for describing the contents of a Web page for display within a Web browser. SGML, on the other hand, is extensible but very heavyweight, requiring extensive proprietary systems to manage and process it. XML is a compromise between the two. XML (which actually stands for eXtensible Markup Language) builds on the strengths of SGML, but does not try to provide the whole of the SGML model – only what is required most of the time. This follows the 80/20 rule: that is, 80% of the time only 20% of the functionality of, say, SGML is required.

As we have now seen, XML is designed for marking up data. However, XML itself is really very unsubstantial. It is necessary to define a vocabulary that creates the actual markup tags for the markup to have meaning. For example, we might create a definition for a set of tags to be used to "mark up" an invoice. The definition of the tags could be placed inside a DTD (a concept inherited from SGML) or the newer `XMLSchema`. In either case an XML file will be processed against the set of definitions to determine whether it is valid. That is, the XML file only contains tags defined in the definition and that the structure of the XML file matches that specified in the definition. One of XML's strong points is that it is possible to state that `tag1` must be placed inside `tag2` etc. In the case of `XMLSchemas` it is also possible to specify that a value must be a string, an integer, a positive value etc.

XML, however, is only about marking up data. It is not related to how that data is presented. This is in contrast, for example, to HTML. HTML is involved in both data markup and presentation. That is, HTML tells a browser how to present the data as well as the meaning of that data. In XML a separate file, for example an XSL file (XSL stands for XML Style Language) can be used to transform the XML into a presentation form. For example, it could convert an XML file into PDF format, Postscript format or indeed into HTML. This transformation aspect of XSL is referred to as XML Transformation or XSLT. An XSLT processor will apply an XSL specification to an XML document to convert the data in the XML file into the new format.

For any XML application we therefore need five things:

1. The definition of the XML tags to use
2. An XML document that marks up some data using the XML tags (for example in a file)
3. A parser that will compare the XML document with the definition
4. (Optionally) an XSL specification to describe how to translate an XML document into a viewable format
5. The application that will use the contents of the XML document

The above points are illustrated in Figure 10.1.

10.2.2 What Do XML Documents Look Like?

Figure 10.2 illustrates a very simple sample XML document that defines a set of contacts and their addresses. The first line of this document is a processing instruction that specifies the version of XML that this file corresponds to. Following this is the root element of the XML document: this is the `CONTACTS` element, which the remaining tags are defined within.

An important thing to remember about XML is that it is a hierarchical structure. This structure is illustrated in Figure 10.3. An XML document has a prolog that contains various information used by the XML processor (such as the version of XML being used) and a root element (that the rest of the XML document "hangs off"). The root element then holds the next level elements. In turn, these hold subsequent elements etc. (see also Figure 10.4).

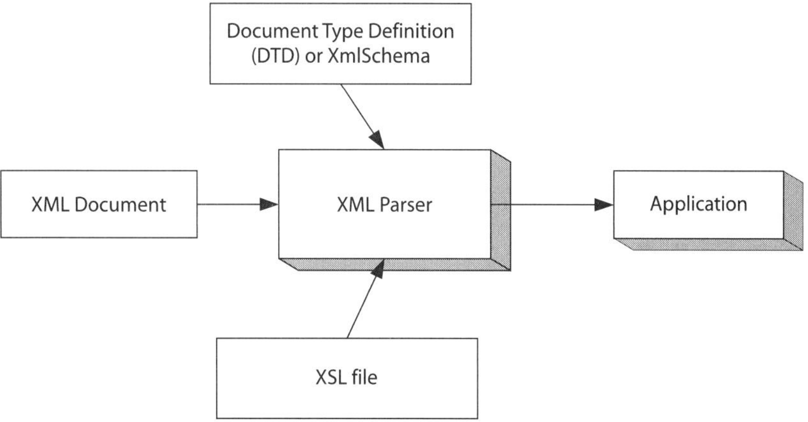

Figure 10.1 The components of an XML system.

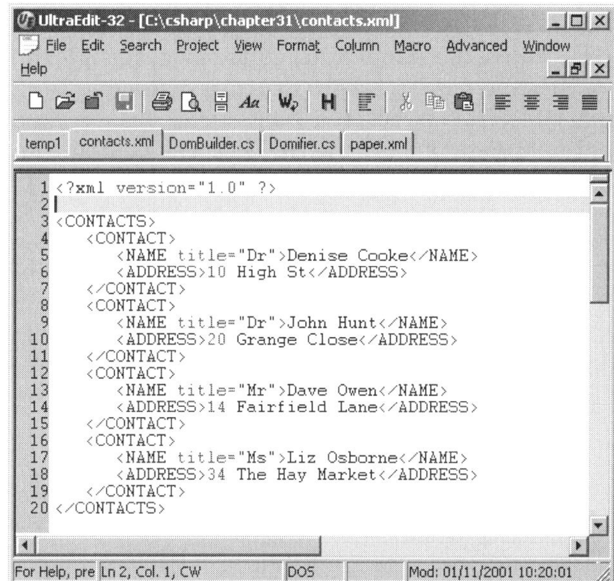

Figure 10.2 A simple XML document.

Within any element there can be a `CData` element (essentially data that should be left as is). An XML document can also have entity references. Entity references are a bit like shorthand for other things. They have the form &<name>; – for example & is the entity reference for an ampersand (&). We could, for example, create an entity reference for a company name. Thus each time we wanted to reference a company name we would use the entity reference that would be expanded to the full name when the XML document is processed.

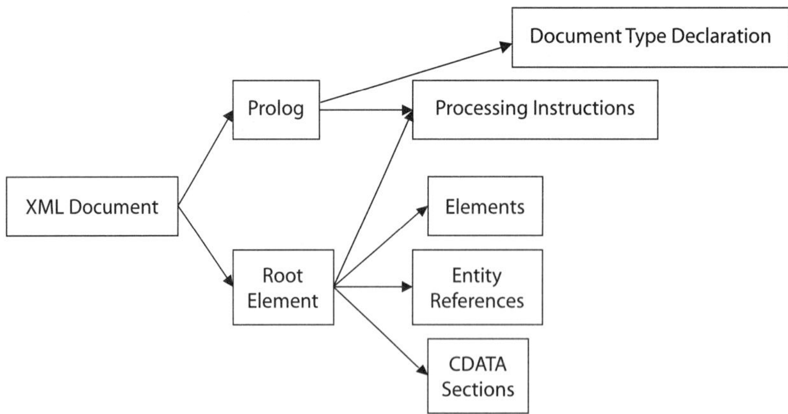

Figure 10.3 The hierarchical nature of XML.

We should also deal with some standard terminology at this point. Firstly, the phrase "XML Document" is used to refer to the XML structure defined by the XML markup. This could be coming from a file, from a socket or via C# remoting. Any text marked up by the document is referred to as Parseable Character Data. The concepts presented so far are illustrated in Figure 10.4.

Another point to note is that each of the tag pairs in the file (e.g. CONTACTS in Figure 10.2) is referred to as an element. Each element must be well formed. That is, each element must follow the rules of XML. There must be a starting tag and a corresponding closing tag (indicated by the start tag preceded by a forward slash); for example <CONTACTS>...</CONTACTS>. An element below the CONTACTS elements is referred to as a child element. For example, <CONTACT> is a child element of <CONTACTS>. In turn <CONTACT is a parent element for <NAME>.

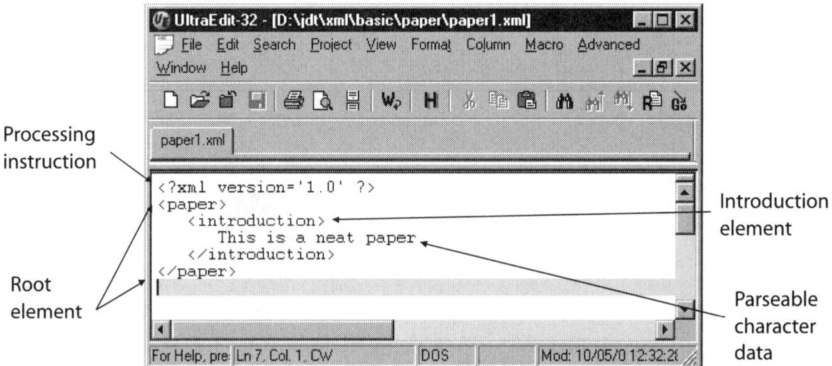

Figure 10.4 Parts of an XML document.

Elements can have attributes; for example, the `<Name>` tag in Figure 10.2 has an attribute title. This is a value (which must be in quotes – either double or single) that is linked directly with the element.

10.2.3 XML Vocabularies

XML vocabularies are XML specifications that define elements that can be shared among organizations. For example, the medical profession could create a vocabulary for describing diseases. This could then be used for passing information from doctors' surgeries to hospitals etc.

The actual set of vocabularies is growing all the time. Some of the early vocabularies (and thus the most developed) include:

- Mathematical Markup Language (MathML)
- Health Level 7
- Microsoft's BizTalk
- IBM's SpeechML
- Internet Open Trading Protocol (OTP)
- Open Financial Exchange Specification (OFE)
- Bioinformatic Sequence Markup Language (BSML)
- Development Markup Language (DML) for world development organizations – UNESCO

Some other vocabularies go beyond just the markup to include software systems that process those (see Figure 10.5). For example, Microsoft's Simple Object Access protocol (SOAP) is an XML vocabulary with extensive software support. Another example is SVG (Scalable Vector Graphics), which is an XML language for describing graphics that has a number of renderers available (the best being from Adobe).

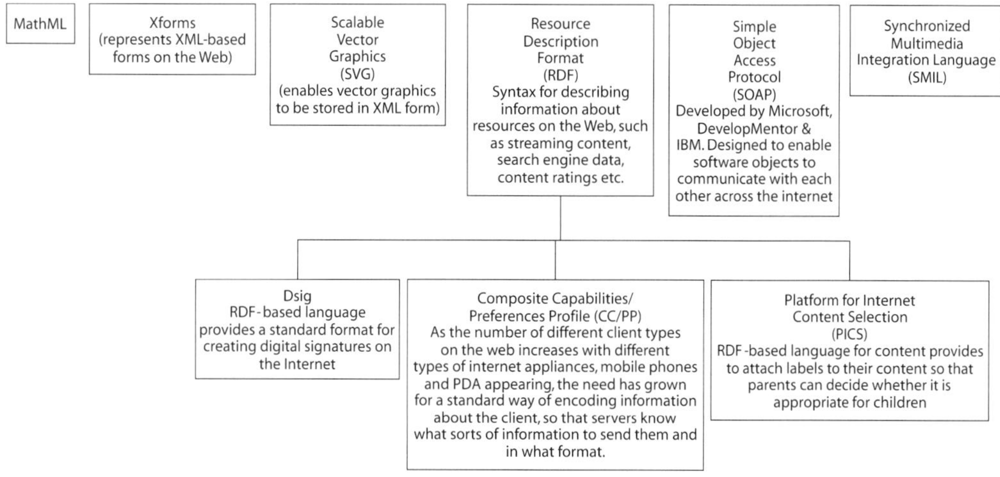
MathML
Xforms (represents XML-based forms on the Web)
Scalable Vector Graphics (SVG) (enables vector graphics to be stored in XML form)
Resource Description Format (RDF) Syntax for describing information about resources on the Web, such as streaming content, search engine data, content ratings etc.
Simple Object Access Protocol (SOAP) Developed by Microsoft, DevelopMentor & IBM. Designed to enable software objects to communicate with each other across the internet
Synchronized Multimedia Integration Language (SMIL)
Dsig RDF-based language provides a standard format for creating digital signatures on the Internet
Composite Capabilities/ Preferences Profile (CC/PP) As the number of different client types on the web increases with different types of internet appliances, mobile phones and PDA appearing, the need has grown for a standard way of encoding information about the client, so that servers know what sorts of information to send them and in what format.
Platform for Internet Content Selection (PICS) RDF-based language for content provides to attach labels to their content so that parents can decide whether it is appropriate for children

Figure 10.5 Established XML markup vocabularies.

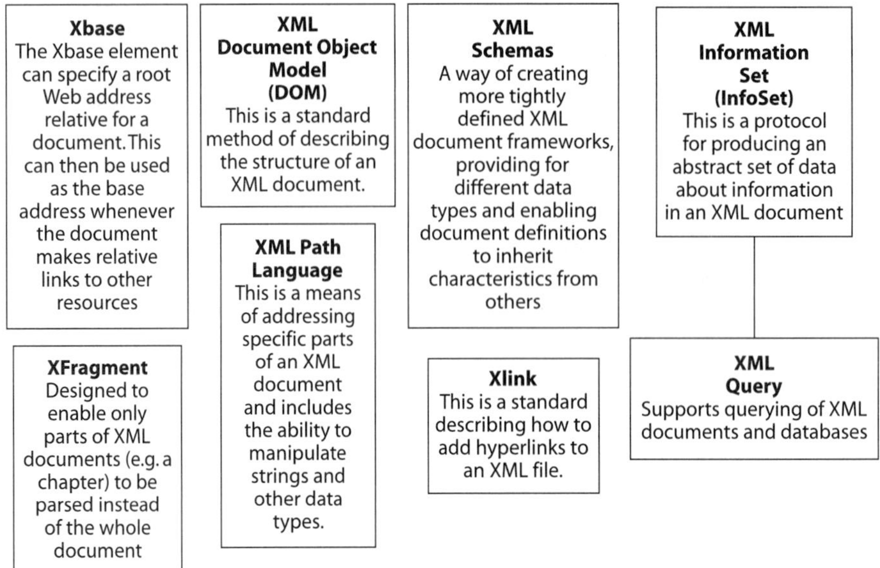

Xbase
The Xbase element can specify a root Web address relative for a document. This can then be used as the base address whenever the document makes relative links to other resources
XML Document Object Model (DOM)
This is a standard method of describing the structure of an XML document.
XML Schemas
A way of creating more tightly defined XML document frameworks, providing for different data types and enabling document definitions to inherit characteristics from others
XML Information Set (InfoSet)
This is a protocol for producing an abstract set of data about information in an XML document
XFragment
Designed to enable only parts of XML documents (e.g. a chapter) to be parsed instead of the whole document
XML Path Language
This is a means of addressing specific parts of an XML document and includes the ability to manipulate strings and other data types.
Xlink
This is a standard describing how to add hyperlinks to an XML file.
XML Query
Supports querying of XML documents and databases

Figure 10.6 Related XML technologies.

There are also a set of related technologies that are still growing to support the definition, analysis, manipulation and processing of XML files. These are summarized in Figure 10.6.

10.2.4 Working With a DTD

So far we have glossed over the issue of defining the elements to be used within an XML application. As mentioned earlier, this can be done via either an XML Schema or a DTD (Document Type Definition). In the case of a DTD this can be an internal DTD (contained within the XML document itself) or an external DTD (contained in a separate file). Figure 10.7 illustrates an XML file with an internal DTD. When an XML file is compared with its definition (e.g. a DTD) and is found to match the rules described in that definition, it is termed valid.

To link an external DTD to an XML file we could use a Document Type Declaration that contained a `SYSTEM` entry followed by the location of the DTD (Figure 10.8). For example:

```
<!DOCTYPE paper SYSTEM "paper.dtd">
```

There are four kinds of declarations in an XML DTD. These are:

- element declarations
- attribute list declarations
- entity declarations
- notation declarations

```
<?xml version="1.0" ?>

<!DOCTYPE paper [
   <!ELEMENT paper (introduction, section+)>
   <!ATTLIST paper
               title CDATA #REQUIRED
               author CDATA #REQUIRED>
   <!ELEMENT introduction (#PCDATA)>
   <!ATTLIST introduction
               heading CDATA #REQUIRED>
   <!ELEMENT section (heading, body)>
   <!ELEMENT heading (#PCDATA)>
   <!ELEMENT body (#PCDATA)>
]>

<!-- comment: XML document starts here -->

<paper title = "XML forever" author = "John Hunt">
   <introduction heading ="The history">
       The background to XML is interesting
   </introduction>
   <section>
       <heading>The main event</heading>
       <body>
           So what is XML all about
       </body>
   </section>
   <section>
       <heading>The Conclusion</heading>
       <body>
           Where is XML heading
       </body>
   </section>
</paper>
```

Figure 10.7 An XML document with an internal DTD.

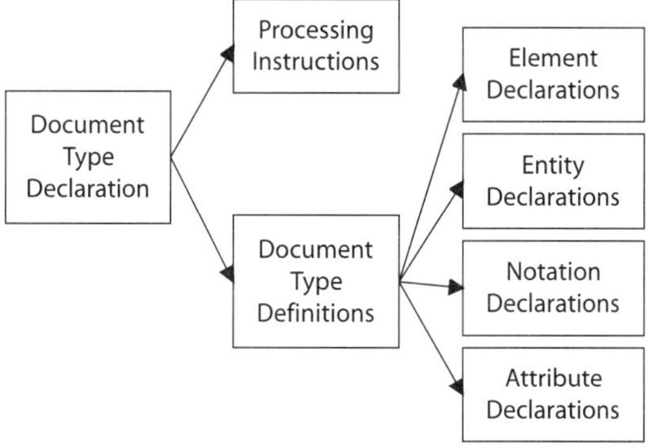

Figure 10.8 The structure of a DTD.

Element declarations define the names of elements and the nature of their content. For example:

```
<!ELEMENT paper (abstract, introduction, section+, conclusion,
bibliography?)>
```

This defines an element called `paper` and its "content model". The content model defines what an element may contain. In this case it contains an `abstract`, an `introduction`, one or more `sections`, a `conclusion` and (optionally) a `bibliography`. These elements in turn must be defined elsewhere in the DTD. Notice that `conclusion` was said to be optional and that there would be one or more `sections`. Where was this defined? It was indicated by the occurrence indicators following the relevant entities (the + and the ? above). The occurrence indicators that can be used in a DTD are:

- ?: zero or one occurrence
- *: zero or more occurrences
- +: one or more occurrence
- no symbol: one occurrence

At some point an element may wish to include some actual data (remember that XML is really about marking up data). Such data can be defined as parseable character data (indicated in a DTD by `#PCDATA`). For example:

```
<!ELEMENT author (#PCDATA | quote)*>
```

This states that author may contain 0 or more characters and a `quote` tag.

Finally, an element may also have attributes (as well as sub-elements or parseable characters). These attributes can be used to tell you more about the element. To define attributes for an element you need to identify:

- which elements may have attributes
- what attributes they may have
- what values the attributes may hold
- what default value each attribute has

An attribute in a declaration has three parts: a name, a type, and a default value. To define an attribute for an element an `ATTLIST` declaration is made. This contains all the attributes for that element, their type, whether they are required or not and any default values; for example:

```
<!ATTLIST paper
name  ID           #required
department CDATA   #implied
status ( accepted | submitted | inprogress ) 'inprogress'>
```

In the above example the paper element has three attributes. These are:

- name, which is an ID and is required
- department, which is a string (character data) and is not required
- status, which must be accepted, submitted or inprogress, and defaults to inprogress

10.3 XSL Transformations

To transform an XML document into, for example, an HTML document for presentation within a Web browser we can use an XSL file. This XSL file will contain a set of rules that define how the XML document should be transformed. That is, XSL is a transformation language, which in the case of XSLT is rule-based. This transformation could actually be into anything. For example, as well as HTML you might want to transform a document into another XML document, LaTeX, RTF or PDF etc.). To carry out this transformation you need the XML document, the XSL file and a Transformation Engine (the XSL Processor or transformer). Some applications come pre-built with such a processor. For example Internet Explorer 6 has an XSL processor built in so that XML can be presented as HTML via an XSL stylesheet.

XSL stylesheets are actually XML documents, so they must all start with:

```
<?xml version = "1.0" ?>
```

The XSL stylesheets contain the XSL declaration:

```
<xsl:stylesheet xmlns:xsl="http://www.w3.org/TR/WD-xsl">
```

This is actually a namespace that defines all the XSL elements. A namespace provides scoping to a set of elements so that there should be no ambiguity when a tag is referenced. In this it is a little like a Java package.

The XSL file must be closed by an xsl:stylesheet tag, for example:

```
</xsl:stylesheet>
```

The XSL stylesheet content itself is rule-driven. A pattern is looked for within the XML document. If it is found then the template that follows the pattern is applied. That is, if the pattern is found then whatever is provided as the template is generated in its place.

All XSL stylesheets start off by applying the stylesheet to the whole document. In the case of HTML output this allows the HTML header information to be output etc. This is done by telling the template to match the root of the XML document (the root is indicated by "/"), thus:

```
<xsl:template match="/">
```

Every stylesheet also has a match for the root element. For example, if we were writing a stylesheet for the XML file shown in Figure 10.9 (made up of a single contact entry) then we would write:

```
-<xsl:apply-templates select="CONTACT"/>
```

```
<?xml version = "1.0" ?>
<?xml-stylesheet type="text/xsl" href="simple-contact.xsl"?>

<CONTACT>
   <NAME>Denise Cooke</NAME>
   <ADDRESS>10 High St</ADDRESS>
   <EMAIL>denise.cooke@jaydeetechnology.co.uk</EMAIL>
</CONTACT>
```

Figure 10.9 A simple XML file for a contact.

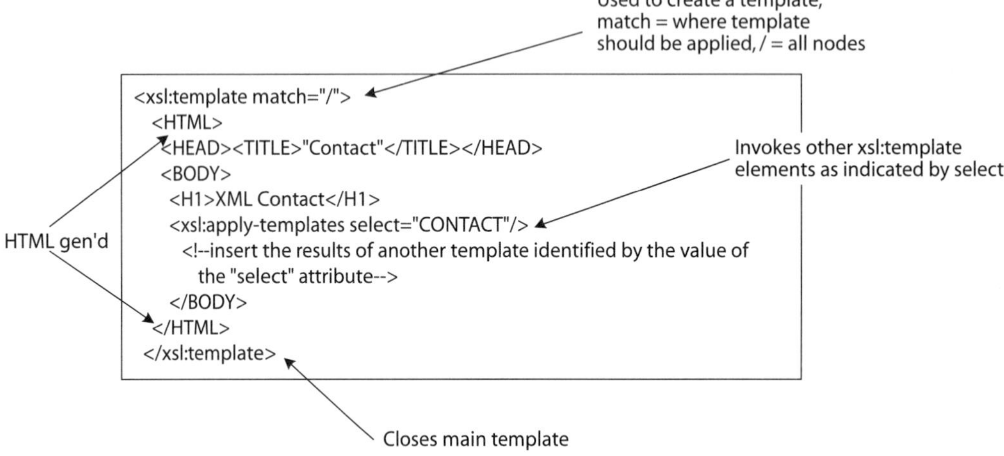

Used to create a template, match = where template should be applied, / = all nodes
<xsl:template match="/">
<HTML>
<HEAD><TITLE>"Contact"</TITLE></HEAD>
<BODY>
<H1>XML Contact</H1>
<xsl:apply-templates select="CONTACT"/>
<!--insert the results of another template identified by the value of the "select" attribute-->
</BODY>
</HTML>
</xsl:template>
Invokes other xsl:template elements as indicated by select
HTML gen'd
Closes main template

Figure 10.10 A sample XSL file.

Inside the template element, the result of the transformation is specified. This is illustrated in Figure 10.10.

The stylesheet in Figure 10.10 states that the whole stylesheet should be applied to the XML document. When this happens some HTML is output that defines an HTML header and a body. It then states that the contacts template should be applied. Once this is applied (and any output queued) the remaining HTML will be output. The `CONTACT` template is presented in Figure 10.11.

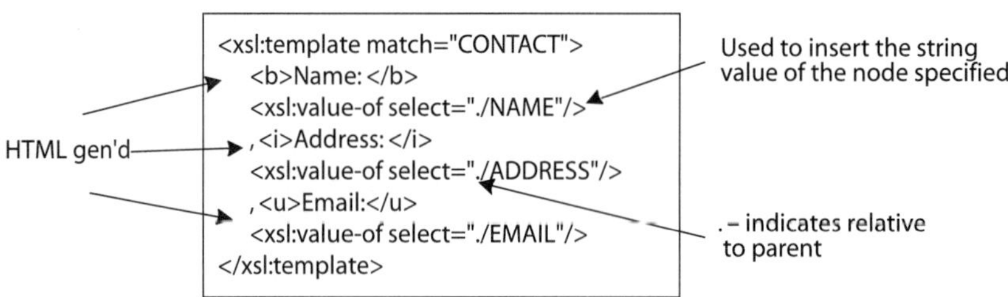

Figure 10.11 The `CONTACT` XSL template.

In Figure 10.11 the CONTACT template will be applied each time a Contact element is found in an XML document. When a Contact element is found, this template is applied and the specified HTML generated. In this case the HTML is supplemented with information extracted from the XML document. In this case it is the contents of the NAME, ADDRESS and EMAIL elements. This is done using the XSL element value-of.

The end result is that the XML file presented in Figure 10.9, when processed by the XSL presented above, generates the HTML illustrated in Figure 10.12.

Figure 10.12 The generated XSL HTML.

10.4 Processing XML

There are two standard APIs for processing XML documents. These are the SAX (Simple API for XML parsing) and the DOM (Document Object Model). The SAX provides access to the data in an XML document as it is read in. In contrast the DOM loads the whole XML document into memory in a hierarchical data structure (which is the document's object model). It is then possible to traverse the tree to access the information within it.

Why have two approaches? The SAX is excellent for situations where all you need to do is to access the data marked up by the XML document. However, if you need to manipulate that data, search it, restructure it or create new or modified XML documents, the DOM is much better.

10.5 The JAXP API

The JAXP API (Java API for XML Parsing) from sun (and bundled with Java 2 SDK 1.4) provides access not only to SAX and DOM parsers but also to XSL translators. These will be used in the filter classes to provide the XML to HTML translation.

One area of XML processing that can be confusing within the Java world is the relationship between the JAXP API and the actual SAX and DOM parsers and the translator. It might seem at first sight that having the JAXP API from Sun means that it is not necessary to have a separate SAX, DOM or XSLT parser. However, the JAXP API is really just a front end to such parsers and processors. It does provide a common front end to different parsers, but is not parser itself. This is very useful because the use of a SAX or DOM parser typically requires knowledge of the specific implementation of the parser.

The JAXP API is able to allow different parsers to be plugged in via a Pluggability layer. This Pluggability mechanism allows a compliant SAX or DOM parser to be "plugged in" with no visible affect on the JAXP interface.

This scenario is not unique within the Java world, as the JDBC (Java Database Connectivity) API provides a common front end to different database drivers but does not itself provide an actual connection to a database.

In our examples we have used the default distribution, which includes the Crimson SAX and DOM parsers. Crimson was derived from the Java Project X parser from Sun but is now available from Apache. The Xalan XSLT processor from Apache is also used. Note that the future plan is to move from Crimson to Xerces. These examples presented here should work with either parser plugged into JAXP 1.1.

The JAXP is made up of the classes in interfaces in the `javax.xml` package and sub-packages. There are four classes in the `javax.xml.parsers` package that are used enable an application to load XML documents. Two relate to the SAX API and two to the DOM API. These classes are:

DocumentBuilder	Defines the API to obtain DOM Document instances from an XML document
DocumentBuilderFactory	Defines a factory API that enables applications to obtain a parser that produces DOM object trees from XML documents
SAXParser	Defines the API that wraps an XMLReader implementation class
SAXParserFactory	Defines a factory API that enables applications to configure and obtain a SAX based parser to parse XML documents

We will use both pairs of classes in the following sections.

10.6 The SAX API

The SAX API has an interesting history. Originally it was a collaborative effort by members of the XML_Dev mailing list. This effort was coordinated and finalized by David Megginson, who is still considered the father of the SAX API.

The SAX API is the de facto standard for interfaces for event-based XML parsing. It is lightweight and fast with low memory overheads. This is because the SAX API merely informs the application using it of each element it has found in turn. It does not build up any in-memory structures, nor does it remember which elements it has already processed. It is up to whatever is using the SAX to do this. Interestingly, the SAX is often the basis of higher-level APIs such as DOM.

To develop a SAX-based application you need an XML parser that supports SAX, such as Apache's Xerces or Crimson, or as default implementations in the JAXP distribution. The SAX distribution is a collection of classes and interfaces that come with SAX-compliant parsers and as part of JAXP. In the case of Crimson, SAX can be found in the package

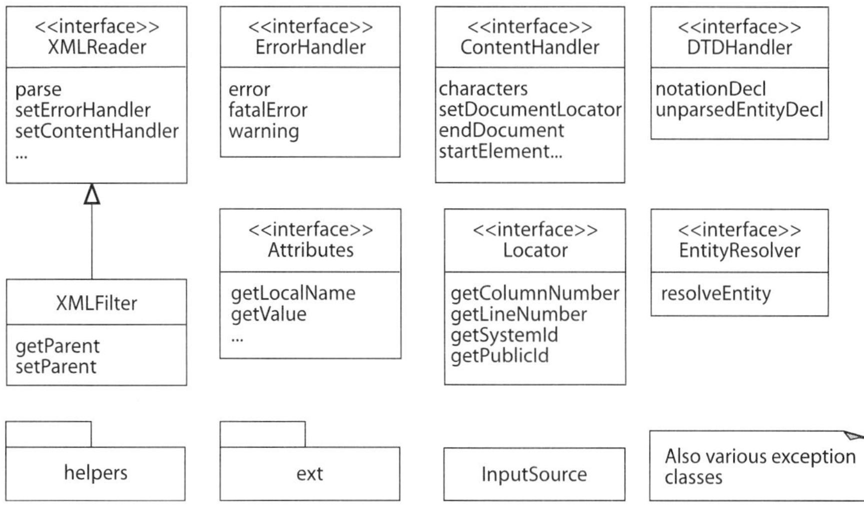

Figure 10.13 The SAX API interfaces.

`org.xml.sax` and its subpackages. From a Java point of view SAX essentially provides a set of event interfaces that must be implemented by one or more event handlers that will deal with document events such as "here is a new element".

The majority of the interfaces in the SAX API are used to represent the concepts that may be found in an XML document. These interfaces are then implemented as appropriate by different implementations of the SAX specification (such as Xerces and Crimson). The key interfaces are presented in Figure 10.13.

The key interfaces in the SAX API for processing an XML document are:

- `ContentHandler` This is the main interface that most SAX applications must implement whenever we want the application to be notified of the elements in the XML document. The application class must implement this interface and then call the `setContentHandler` method on the actual SAX parser used. The parser uses the instance to report basic document-related events like the start and end of elements and character data.
- `EntityResolver` If a SAX application needs to implement customized handling for external entities, it must implement this interface and register an instance with the SAX driver using the `setEntityResolver` method.
- `ErrorHandler` If a SAX application needs to implement customized error handling, it must implement this interface and then register an instance with the XML reader using the `setErrorHandler` method. The parser will then report all errors and warnings through this interface. Note that if no error handler is provided then no errors will be reported.
- `DTDHandler` If a SAX application needs information about notations and unparsed entities, then the application implements this interface and registers an instance with the SAX parser using the parser's `setDTDHandler` method. The parser uses the instance to report notation and unparsed entity declarations to the application. Note that this interface includes only those DTD events that the XML recommendation requires processors to report:

notation and unparsed entity declarations. This means that if what you want to do is to process the DTD used by an XML document then you need to look at the `DeclHandler` interface in the `org.xml.sax.ext` package.

SAX2 represents an extension of the original SAX specification and provides two interfaces in the `org.xml.sax.ext` package which can be very useful:

- `DeclHandler` This is an optional extension handler for SAX2 to provide information about DTD declarations in an XML document. XML readers are not required to support this handler, and this handler is not included in the core SAX2 distribution.
- `LexicalHandler` This is an optional extension handler for SAX2 to provide lexical information about an XML document, such as comments and CDATA section boundaries; XML readers are not required to support this handler, and it is not part of the core SAX2 distribution.

There are other interfaces, but the most important is the `org.xml.sax.XMLReader` interface. An `XmlReader` is an object that loads an XML document into memory. In essence the `SAXParser` class provided by the JAXP API wraps a class implementing the `XMLReader` interface inside it and uses that class to actually load the XML document.

When you are actually implementing a class or classes that will implement one or more of the interfaces in the SAX API for listening to events, it is common to start with the `DefaultHandler` class from the `org.xml.sax.helpers` package. `DefaultHandler` is a convenience base class for SAX2 applications: it provides default implementations for all of the callbacks in the four core SAX2 handler interfaces (that is, for `EntityResolver`, `DTDHandler`, `ContentHandler` and `ErrorHandler`). Developers can extend the `DefaultHandler` class when they need to implement only part of an interface.

To actually use the SAX to process the contents of an XML document you must therefore implement one or more interfaces (for example the `ContentHandler`), which can be done by extending the `DefaultHandler` convenience class. Create an instance of this class and register it with a `SAXParser` obtained from the `SAXParserFactory` provided as part of the JAXP API. Then when this `SAXParser` is used to load an XML document each element found will be reported to this instance.

The methods in the `ContentHandler` interface that can be implemented include:

- `startDocument()`: Notifies the beginning of a document
- `endDocument()`: Notifies the end of a document
- `startElement(String namespaceUri,`
`String localName,`
`String qName,`
`Attributes atts)`: Start of an element
- `endElement(...)`: Notifies end of element
- `characters(char ch[], int start, int length)`: Notifies character data

To illustrate the use of the SAX API we will look at a simple program that uses the SAX to verify whether an XML document in a file is both well formed and valid. This program is called `Verifier`. The `Verifier` class itself extends `DefaultHandler` and therefore implements the four core interfaces of the SAX API, including ContentHandler and ErrorHandler. We can therefore register the Verifier instance with the parser object we obtain from the SAXParser.

To obtain the SAXParser we first obtain a SAXParserFactory class using the newInstance() method and then configure the SAXParserFactory object we obtain. This configuration allows the SAXParserFactory to determine which SAXParser to provide. You can then either work with the SAXParser object obtained, or, as we do in the Verifier class, obtain the implementation of the XMLReader that it wraps. This allows us to work directly with the XMLReader instance and to request that the XML document is parsed by the XMLReader.

Once the application has set up the parser it then calls the parse method on the XMLReader within the Verifier.verify() method. This forces the XMLReader object to notify the Verifier class of any errors and XML elements. This is done by calling the startDocument, endDocument, startElement, endElement etc. methods in the order that matches the contents of the XML file.

The Verifier application is presented below:

```
package jdt;

import java.io.File;
import javax.xml.parsers.SAXParser;
import javax.xml.parsers.SAXParserFactory;
import org.xml.sax.Attributes;
import org.xml.sax.Locator;
import org.xml.sax.XMLReader;
import org.xml.sax.SAXException;
import org.xml.sax.SAXParseException;
import org.xml.sax.helpers.DefaultHandler;

public class Verifier extends DefaultHandler {
  private String uri;
  private XMLReader parser;
  /**
   * Runs the application
   **/
  public static void main(String args[]) {
      if (args.length != 1) {
        System.err.println(
                "Usage: java jdt.Verifier xml-file");
        System.exit(1);
      }
      Verifier v = new Verifier(args[0]);
      v.verify();
  }
  /**
   * Constructor for the class
   * @param file the name of the XML file to load
   **/
```

```
public Verifier(String file) {
    try {
      // Set the URI for the file to load
      uri = "file:" + (new File(file)).getAbsolutePath();
      // Obtain the parser provided by the SAXParser factory pattern
      SAXParserFactory spf = SAXParserFactory.newInstance();
      spf.setValidating(true);
      spf.setNamespaceAware(true);
      parser = spf.newSAXParser().getXMLReader();
      // Set this object to receive notification of both
      // XML elements and of any errors
      parser.setContentHandler(this);
      parser.setErrorHandler(this);
    } catch (Exception e) {e.printStackTrace();}
}
/**
 * Initiates the processing of the XML file
 **/
public void verify() {
    try {
      parser.parse(uri);
    } catch (Exception e) {e.printStackTrace();}
}

//*********************************************************
// DefaultHandler methods
//*********************************************************

public void setDocumentLocator(Locator l) {
  // Useful if need to resolve relative URIs
}
public void startDocument() throws SAXException {
  System.out.println("<?xml version='1.0'?>");
}
public void endDocument() throws SAXException {
  System.out.println(
             "XML verification of " + uri + " complete");
}
public void startElement(String namespaceUri,
                         String localName,
                         String qName, Attributes atts)
                             throws SAXException {
  System.out.print("<" + qName);
  for (int i=0; i < atts.getLength(); i++)
    System.out.print(" " + atts.getLocalName(i) + " = \"" +
                           atts.getValue(i) + "\"");
```

```
  System.out.println(">");
}
public void endElement(String namespaceUri,
                       String localName,
                       String qName) throws SAXException {
  System.out.println("</" + qName + ">");
}
public void characters(char buf[],
                       int start,
                       int length) throws SAXException {
  String output = new String(buf, start, length);
  if (output.length() != 0)
    System.out.print(output);
}
public void ignorableWhitespace(char buf[],
                                int start,
                                int length)
                                      throws SAXException {
// Ignorable - so we do
}
public void processingInstruction(String target, String data)
              throws SAXException {
  System.out.println("<?" + target + " " + data + "?>");
}
public void startPrefixMapping(String prefix, String uri)
              throws SAXException {
  // We ignore the prefix and uri as namespaceAware
  // property is true
}
public void endPrefixMapping(String prefix)
              throws SAXException {}
public void skippedEntity(String name) throws SAXException {
  // Most parsers will not skip entities so we can ignore
}

//*********************************************************
// Error handling methods
//*********************************************************

public void error(SAXParseException exp)
              throws SAXException {
  System.out.println("** Error" +
                     ". line " + exp.getLineNumber() +
                     ", uri " + exp.getSystemId());
  System.out.println(" " + exp.getMessage());
}
```

```
  public void fatalError(SAXParseException exp)
              throws SAXException {
    System.out.println("*** Fatal error" +
                       ". line " +
                       exp.getLineNumber() +
                       ", uri " + exp.getSystemId());
    System.out.println(" " + exp.getMessage());
    throw exp;
  }

  public void warning(SAXParseException exp)
              throws SAXException {
    System.out.println("* Warning" +
                       ". line " + exp.getLineNumber() +
                       ", uri " + exp.getSystemId());
    System.out.println(" " + exp.getMessage());
  }
}
```

The text XML file we will use is contacts.xml presented in Figure 10.14.

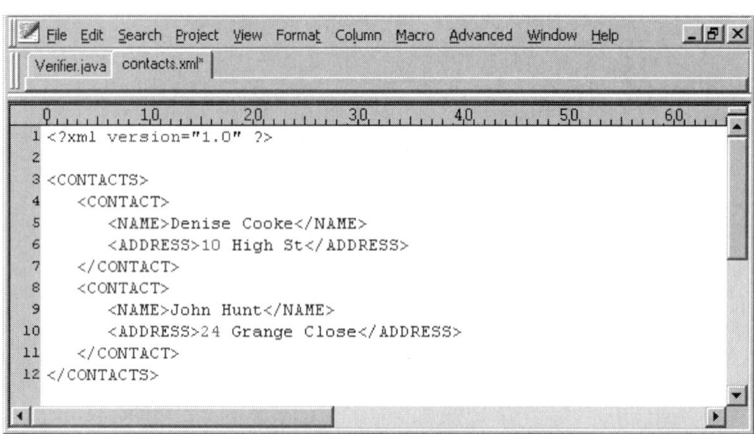

Figure 10.14 The contacts.xml file.

The result of running the Verifier application on the contacts.xml file is presented below:

```
C:\ >java jdt.Verifier contacts.xml
<?xml version='1.0'?>
* Warning. line 3, uri file:C:\contacts.xml
  Valid documents must have a <!DOCTYPE declaration.
** Error. line 3, uri file:C:\contacts.xml
  Element type "CONTACTS" is not declared.
```

```
<CONTACTS>
  ** Error. line 4, uri file:C:\contacts.xml
  Element type "CONTACT" is not declared.
<CONTACT>
  ** Error. line 5, uri file:C:\contacts.xml
  Element type "NAME" is not declared.
<NAME>
Denise Cooke</NAME>
  ** Error. line 6, uri file:C:\contacts.xml
  Element type "ADDRESS" is not declared.
<ADDRESS>
10 High St</ADDRESS>
  </CONTACT>
  <CONTACT>
      <NAME>
John Hunt</NAME>
      <ADDRESS>
24 Grange Close</ADDRESS>
  </CONTACT>
</CONTACTS>
XML verification of file:C:\contacts.xml complete
```

10.7 The DOM API

There are in fact two standards for DOM: DOM Level 1 and DOM Level 2 Core. Together these define interfaces with methods and properties used to manipulate XML (see `org.w3c.dom`).

In this section we will concentrate on the DOM. The DOM takes an XML document and builds a tree-like structure that represents that XML document (as illustrated in Figure 10.15). It is now possible to get hold of any element in the tree (which is represented by a node object) and ask that element for its attributes, its child nodes, its value etc. This is done by a standard set of specifications. That is, the W3C specification for the DOM is actually a set of interfaces specifying what the various elements of the DOM API should do. Then in a particular language (for example Java) the interfaces are implemented to create concrete implementations. This means that moving from one DOM implementation to another should be straightforward.

As may be expected, J2EE comes with an implementation of the W3C DOM API. These interfaces and classes can be found in the `org.w3c.dom` package.

The Java implementation of the DOM API supports all of DOM Level 1 and DOM Level 2 Core. One aspect of the DOM which is not specified is how an XML document should be loaded. This is again where the JAXP API comes in. The JAXP API provides the `javax.xml.parser` package with the `DocumentBuilderFactory` and `DocumentBuilder` classes. These classes together allow a parser-independent approach to loading an XML file and creating a DOM tree. The approach is similar to that used with the SAX API. First a `DocumentBuilderFactory` object is obtained using the `newInstance()` static method on the class. This factory object can

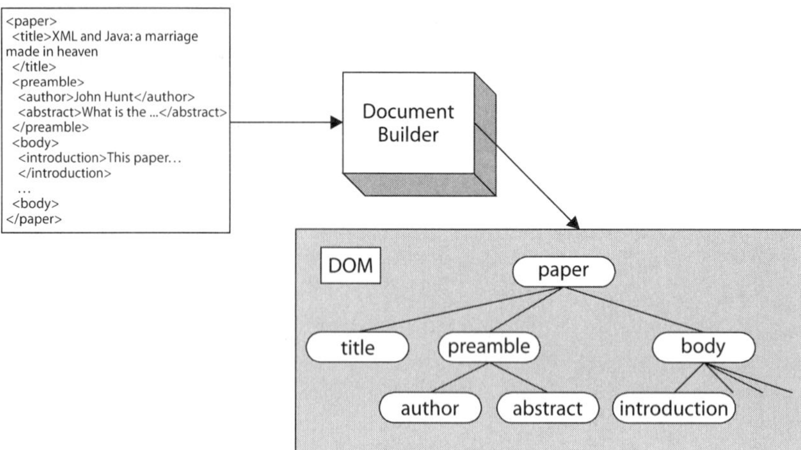

Figure 10.15 Creating a DOM from an XML document.

then be configured as required (here "factory object" indicates that the role of this object is to create other objects). It can then be used to create instances of the `DocumentBuilder` object. This is done using the `DocumentBuilderFactory newDocumentBuilder()` instance method.

Of course the JAXP API is merely a façade (or layer) on top of an actual DOM parser (such as Crimson or Xerces). In some cases these parsers provide additional (but non-standard) facilities for reading and writing XML documents.

The DOM API also does not say how an in-memory XML DOM tree should be written out to a file. In the case of Crimson an additional method, `write`, has been added to the root document node object that can be used to write the XML out to a file. This works but is not transferable between parsers. To overcome this a generic approach has been provided by the JAXP API which is a little more convoluted but is cross-parser-compliant. We shall look at this later.

There are a variety of node types in the DOM that represent different types of element within an XML document. The class hierarchy for these is presented in Figure 10.16 and the key nodes are described briefly below:

- `Node` – root of node type interface hierarchy
- `Document` – root of tree structure (one per XML document)
- `Element` – represents an XML element
- `Text` – represents text within an element
- `Attr` – Attribute of an element
- `CDATASection` – represents CDATA
- `NodeList` – collection of child nodes
- `ProcessingInstruction` – represents instructions, e.g. <?xml-stylesheet type="text/xml" href="prf.xsl"?>
- `Comment` – contains information from a comment

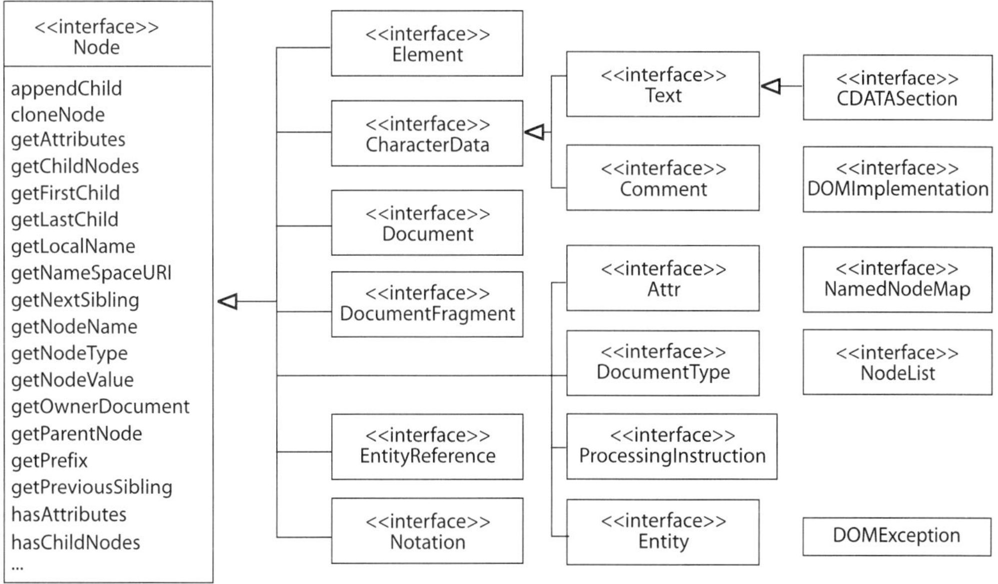

Figure 10.16 The node types in the DOM.

- `DocumentFragment` – cut-down version of a `Document` node - used for moving nodes around the tree
- `DocumentType` – represents a (subset of) document type definition. In DOM 2 DocumentType has list of entity nodes and little else (`getEntities()`,`getNotations()`) DOM 3 will probably cover other DTDs
- `Entity` – represents an entity tag in a DTD
- `EntityReference` – represents a reference to an entity in an XML document
- `Notation` – represents a notation tag in a DTD

The way in which the nodes in the DOM tree actually map onto an XML document is illustrated by example in Figure 10.17.

There are a couple of things to note about this tree. The first is that it is a little more complex than might at first be expected. For example, a node representing the element `<NAME>Denise Cooke</NAME>` actually contains a `NodeList` object which in turn contains a `Text` node that actually holds the text "Denise Cooke". This is because an element may have multiple sub-elements in general. All these sub-elements must be held in something. They are therefore held in a `NodeList`. A `NodeList` is therefore somewhat similar to an `ArrayList`. For example, if you wanted to represent a one to many relationship between a father and two children, you might use an `ArrayList` to hold the references to each of the children in a "children" instance variable in the father object. This is exactly what is happening within a DOM tree.

Secondly, note that the processing instruction `<?xml version="1.0"?>` does not get represented explicitly in the tree. This is because it is considered an instruction directed at the parser and not at the application that will use the XML!

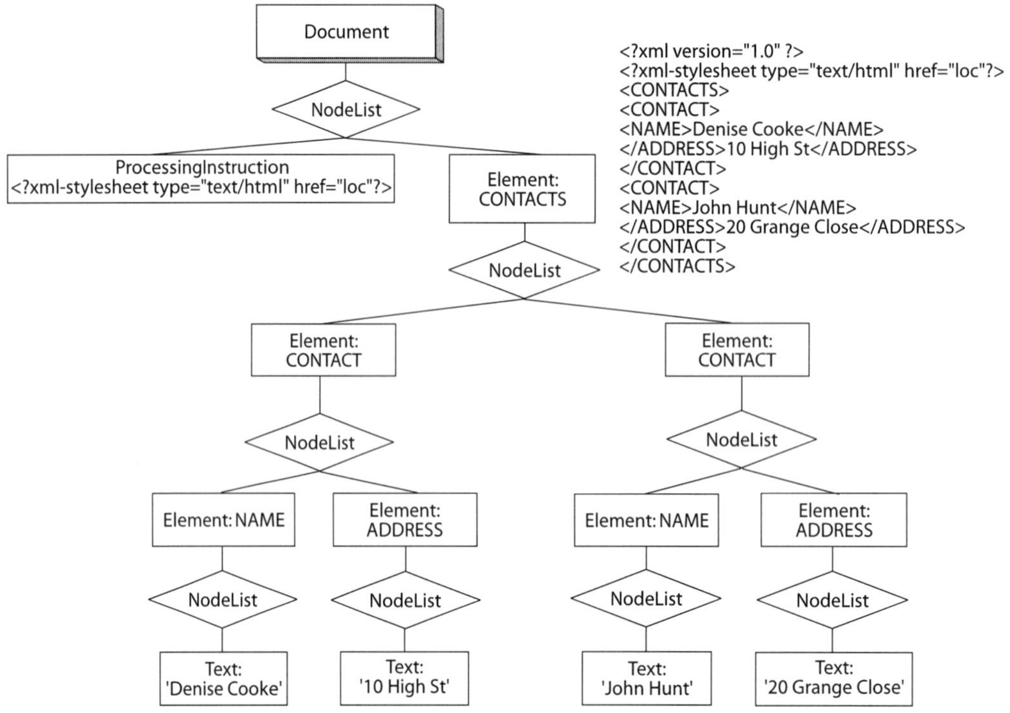

Figure 10.17 Mapping an XML document to a DOM tree.

This particular example does not contain any attributes; however, they are included in the DOM if present. Attributes are not distinct parts of the tree (that is, they are not separate nodes in the tree); rather, they are internal to elements. Each element contains a `NamedNodeMap` (probably a hash table) with `Attr` nodes. Each `Attr` node contains a value for the attribute.

10.8 Loading an XML Document

This section presents a Java program that loads an XML file into a DOM and then traverses the DOM tree printing out the elements, their values, their attributes etc. Note that this program can either perform validation or not. Remember that an XML file must be well-formed, but it is optional as to whether it is validated against a DTD. The `Domifier` program presented below can either be run in validating mode or in standard mode. If it is run in validating mode then it will check the XML file against the DTD. Figure 10.18 presents an XML file that contains an internal DTD (the `Domifier` program can work with external DTDs as well, but we are keeping things simple here). If the `Domifier` is run indicating that validation should be performed, then the internal DTD will be used to check the XML in the file.

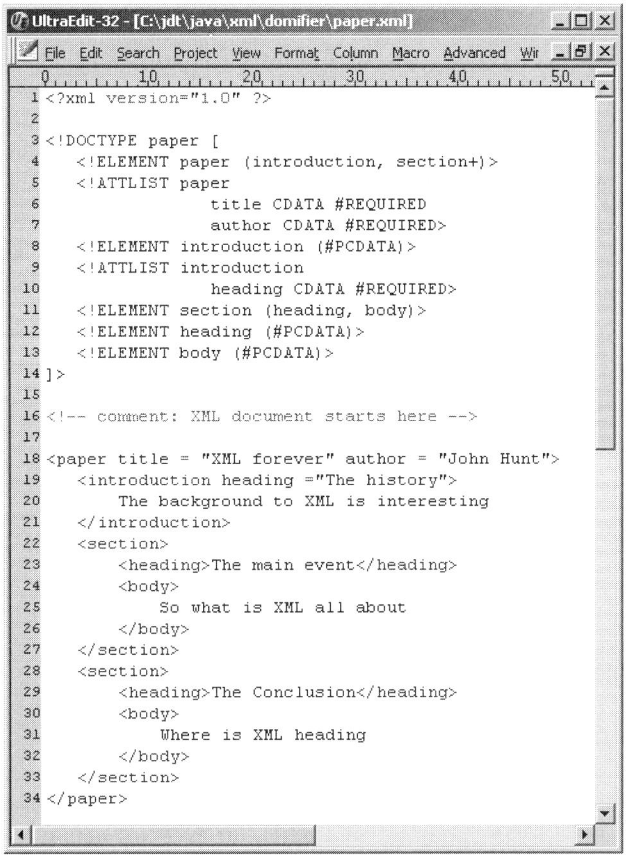
UltraEdit-32 - [C:\jdt\java\xml\domifier\paper.xml]
File Edit Search Project View Format Column Macro Advanced Wir
<?xml version="1.0" ?>
<!DOCTYPE paper [
<!ELEMENT paper (introduction, section+)>
<!ATTLIST paper
title CDATA #REQUIRED
author CDATA #REQUIRED>
<!ELEMENT introduction (#PCDATA)>
<!ATTLIST introduction
heading CDATA #REQUIRED>
<!ELEMENT section (heading, body)>
<!ELEMENT heading (#PCDATA)>
<!ELEMENT body (#PCDATA)>
]>
<!-- comment: XML document starts here -->
<paper title = "XML forever" author = "John Hunt">
<introduction heading ="The history">
The background to XML is interesting
</introduction>
<section>
<heading>The main event</heading>
<body>
So what is XML all about
</body>
</section>
<section>
<heading>The Conclusion</heading>
<body>
Where is XML heading
</body>
</section>
</paper>

Figure 10.18 An XML file containing an internal DTD.

The `Domifier` application first initializes the `uri` string as appropriate. The `uri` string is a string that represents a URI specification. In this case the protocol used is "`file:`" to indicate that we are accessing a local file. However, other protocols could be used (such as HTTP). We also set the validating flag as appropriate.

The `main` method (at the bottom of the listing) then calls the `load` method and the `displayDOM` method. The `load` method actually loads the document into memory. The `displayDOM` method merely traverses the DOM tree and prints out the results.

To load an XML file into the `Document` object the `Domifier` uses two clases from the JAXP API. These are the `DocumentBuilderFactory` and the `DocumentBuilder`. They work together in a two-step process to load a document.

A `DocumentBuilderFactory` is an object that can supply an appropriate `DocumentBuilder` on demand. An instance of the `DocumentBuilderFactory` is obtained using the `newInstance()` method. This new instance can then be configured to supply an appropriate `DocumentBuilder` (in this case we configure it to generate a validating document builder).

In turn, a DocumentBuilder is an object that can load an XML file and create an in-memory DOM structure. This object is obtained from the DocumentBuilderFactory instance using the newDocumentBuilder() method.

To actually load a document into memory we use the parse method on the DocumentBuilder. This overloaded method can take a number of different parameters, including a File object, an inputstream and, as in this case, a URI-like string.

```
package jdt;

import java.io.*;
import javax.xml.parsers.*;
import org.w3c.dom.*;

public class Domifier {
  private String uri;
  private Document doc;
  private boolean validating;

  public Domifier(String file) { this(file, false); }
  public Domifier(String file, boolean validating) {
    uri = "file:" + new File (file).getAbsolutePath();
    this.validating = validating;
  }
  public void load() {
    try {
      DocumentBuilderFactory dbf =
              DocumentBuilderFactory.newInstance();
      dbf.setValidating(validating);
      DocumentBuilder db = dbf.newDocumentBuilder();
      doc = db.parse(uri);
      doc.getDocumentElement().normalize();
    } catch (Exception exp) { exp.printStackTrace(); }
  }
  public void displayDOM() {
    println("Domifying " + uri);
    displayDOM(doc.getDocumentElement(), 0);
  }
  private void displayDOM(Node node, int level) {
    println(node.getNodeName());
    if (node.getNodeType() == Node.ELEMENT_NODE) {
      indent(level);
      println(node.getNodeName());
      NodeList children = node.getChildNodes();
      level++;
      for (int i=0; i<children.getLength(); i++)
        displayDOM(children.item(i), level);
```

```
    } else
      System.out.println(": " + node.getNodeValue() );
  }

  //============================================
  // Utility methods
  //============================================
  private void println (String s) {
    System.out.println(s);
  }

  public void print(String s) {
    System.out.print(s);
  }

  public void indent(int number) {
    StringBuffer sb = new StringBuffer(number);
    for (int i=0; i < number; i++) {
      sb.append(" ");
    }
    sb.append("+-");
    print(sb.toString());
  }

  //============================================
  // Main method
  //============================================
  public static void main(String [] args) {
    Domifier dom;
    if (args.length < 1) {
      System.err.println ("Usage: java Domifier xml-file <validating>");
      System.exit (1);
    }
    if (args.length == 1)
      dom = new Domifier(args[0]);
    else
      dom = new Domifier(args[0],
                (Boolean.valueOf(
                      args[1])).booleanValue());
    dom.load();
    dom.displayDOM();
  }
}
```

In the above listing the recursive `displayDOM` method actually does the work of traversing the DOM tree and displaying the results. It does this by checking to see the type of the node currently being visited. It then extracts either name and the value of the node, or if it is an element node (as opposed to a text node for example), then it checks to see if the element has any children. If so, it calls itself recursively on each of the children. Note that an XML element that contains some text, will be represented in the DOM as a node (of type element) with at least one child (of type text) that represents the text from the XML.

The effect of compiling and running this program is presented below:

```
C:\jdt\java\xml\domifier>javac -d . Domifier.java
C:\jdt\java\xml\domifier>java jdt.Domifier paper.xml true
Domifying file:C:\jdt\java\xml\domifier\paper.xml
paper
+-paper
#text
:
introduction
  +-introduction
#text
:
      The background to XML is interesting
#text
:
section
  +-section
#text
:
heading
    +-heading
#text
: The main event
#text
:
body
    +-body
#text
:
          So what is XML all about
#text
:
#text
:
section
  +-section
#text
:

heading
```

```
    +-heading
#text
: The Conclusion
#text
:
body
    +-body
#text
:
          Where is XML heading
#text
:
#text
:
```

10.9 Creating an XML Document in Java

The following Java program, called `DomBuilder`, using the DOM API to create a (very) simple XML document. This document is then saved to file. The XML file created is illustrated in Figure 10.19. Notice that the program takes the file name to save the XML to as a command line parameter. Also notice that the `Document` object (held in the `DomBuilder` instance variable) is used to create the elements contained within the XML document.

The use of the document object to create the nodes that can then be added to the DOM tree may at first seem confusing. However, the document object is playing the role of a factory object here. That is, it acts as a factory that produces DOM nodes that can be used to construct the DOM tree. To do this the document class provides a host of creation method that allow appropriate nodes to be created. For example:

- **`createAttribute`**`(String name)` Creates an `Attr` of the given name. Note that the `Attr` instance can then be set on an `Element` using the `setAttributeNode` method.
- **`createComment`**`(String data)` Creates a `Comment` node given the specified string.
- **`createElement`**`(String tagName)` Creates an element of the type specified. Note that the instance returned implements the `Element` interface, so attributes can be specified directly on the returned object. In addition, if there are known attributes with default values, `Attr` nodes representing them are automatically created and attached to the element.
- **`createTextNode`**`(String text)` Creates a `Text` node given the specified string.
- **`createCDATASection`**`(String text)` Creates a `CDATASection` node whose value is the specified string.

Once a node has been obtained it can then be added to the document object or any node below that using the `appendChild` method, defined in the `Node` class and inherited by every type of node.

- **`appendChild`**`(Node n)` Adds the node `newChild` to the end of the list of children of this node. If the `newChild` is already in the tree, it is first removed.

If you wish to work with namespaces (namespaces are a little bit like Java packages – they providing scoping of element definitions), there are versions of the create methods that take a namespace parameter. These methods all include `NS` for namespace in their name. For example:

- **`createElementNS`**`(String namespaceUri, String qualifiedName)` Creates an element of the given qualified name and namespace URI.

The following program illustrates how some of these methods are used to construct an in memory DOM tree.

```
package jdt;

import org.w3c.dom.*;
import javax.xml.parsers.*;
import javax.xml.transform.*;
import javax.xml.transform.dom.DOMSource;
import javax.xml.transform.stream.StreamResult;

import java.io.*;

public class DomBuilder {
  private Document document;
  private String filename;

  public static void main (String [] args) {
    try {
      DomBuilder db = new DomBuilder(args[0]);
      db.create();
      db.save();
    } catch (ParserConfigurationException exp) {
      exp.printStackTrace();
    }
  }

  public DomBuilder(String file) throws ParserConfigurationException {
    filename = file;
    DocumentBuilderFactory factory =
              DocumentBuilderFactory.newInstance();
    DocumentBuilder builder = factory.newDocumentBuilder();
    document = builder.newDocument(); // Create a new XML document
  }

  public void create() {
      Element root = document.createElement("employee");
    document.appendChild (root);
```

```
    Element name = document.createElement("name");
    name.appendChild(document.createTextNode("John"));
    root.appendChild(name);

    Element dept = (Element)document.createElement("dept");

    root.appendChild(dept);
    dept.appendChild(document.createTextNode("Support"));

    Element manager = (Element)document.createElement("manager");
    manager.appendChild(document.createTextNode("Andy"));
    dept.appendChild(manager);
  }

  public void save() {
    try {
      TransformerFactory tFactory = TransformerFactory.newInstance();
      Transformer transformer = tFactory.newTransformer();
      DOMSource source = new DOMSource(document);
      transformer.setOutputProperty(OutputKeys.INDENT,
                                    "yes");
      PrintWriter pw = new PrintWriter(new FileOutputStream (filename));
      StreamResult result = new StreamResult(pw);
      transformer.transform(source, result);
    } catch (TransformerException te) {
      te.printStackTrace();
    } catch (IOException exp) {
      exp.printStackTrace();
    }
  }
}
```

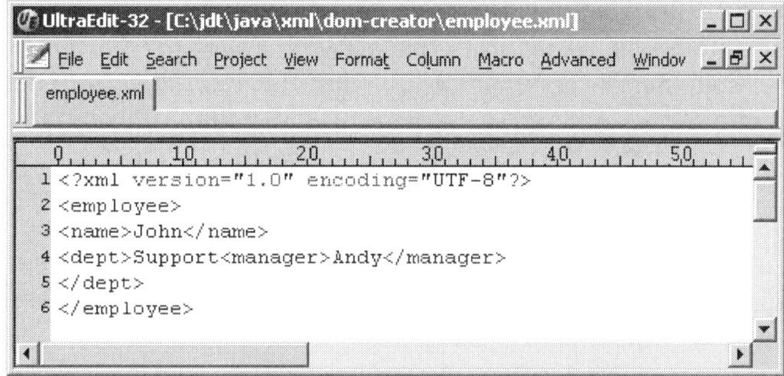

Figure 10.19 The XML file created by the DomBuilder.

For the moment we will skip over the `save` method other than to say that this writes the in-memory structure out to a file. We shall look at the use of Transformers more in the next section.

The result of compiling this program and running it with the following statements:

```
javac jdt/DomBuilder.java
java jdt.DomBuilder employee.xml
```

is the XML file displayed in Figure 10.19.

10.10 Performing XSLT in JAX

In this final section we will briefly examine the XSLT transformations supported by the `javax.xml.transform` package. JAXP 1.1 introduced a vendor-neutral XML document transformation API. This is very useful, as previously there was great variation in the APIs provided by XSLT processors. This also means that the JAXP 1.1 is more than a parser API.

The API for transformations in JAXP is modelled after the TrAX (Transformation API for XML) specification and may in time adopt the TrAX directly. As of JAXP 1.1, the XSL transformation support is provided by Apache's Xalan implementation for XSLT 1.0. The actual JAXP façade to this lower level implementation is provided by the classes and interfaces in the `javax.xml.transform` package and its sub-packages.

Performing XML transformations requires three basic steps:

1. Obtain a Transformer factory
2. Retrieve a Transformer
3. Perform operations (transformations) on an XML file in line with the rules in an XSL file.

The `TransformerFactory` in the `javax.xml.transform` package acts as a factory for Transformers (and operates in a similar manner to the SAX and DOM equivalents). Thus to obtain a new `TransformerFactory` you use the static method `newInstance()`. You can then configure the `TransformerFactory` object obtain with various attributes used to set up the XSL processor chosen (by default Xalan, but others could include SAXON, Oracle's XSL processor or any TrAX-compliant processor).

You can then use the `newTransformer()` instance method on the `TransformerFactory` to create a new instance of the `Transformer` class to perform the actual transformation. A difference here is that the `newTransformer()` method can take a `StreamSource` which allows it to obtain the contents of an XSL file that will provide the processing rules to use (if one is not provided, then the XML is passed without modification through the transformer).

A `StreamSource` is an object that can act as a holder for a transformation `Source` in the form of a stream of XML markup. It is a class defined in the `javax.xml.transform.stream` package. It provides constructors that can take a file name and a `File` object or an `InputStream` (and a `Reader` object).

There is a corresponding `StreamResult` class that can receive the results of the transformation. This class can then write the new XML to another DOM, to a file, to an output stream or to a writer object. It is this facility that was used in the save method in the last section to write the contents of a DOM tree out to a file (in this case no modification of the XML took place). Instead, an in-memory structure was "transformed" into a file.

However, the most common use of the Transform API in the JAXP is to apply some XSL transformation file to an XML document. In the Translator application presented in Figure 10.20 we do exactly this.

```
package jdt;

import java.io.*;
import org.w3c.dom.Document;
import javax.xml.transform.*;
import javax.xml.transform.stream.*;
import javax.xml.transform.dom.DOMSource;
import javax.xml.parsers.*;

public class Translator {
   private String xmlfile, xslfile, outputfile;
   public Translator(String xmlfile, String xslfile, String outputfile) {
      this.xmlfile = xmlfile;
      this.xslfile = xslfile;
      this.outputfile = outputfile;
   }
   public void translate() {
      try {
         // Load an XML file into a DOM tree
         DocumentBuilderFactory dbf = DocumentBuilderFactory.newInstance();
         DocumentBuilder db = dbf.newDocumentBuilder();
         Document doc = db.parse("file:" + xmlfile);
         // Set up the transformer
         TransformerFactory factory = TransformerFactory.newInstance();
         Transformer transformer =
                     factory.newTransformer(
                              new StreamSource(
                                "file:" + xslfile));
         // Define the output file for the StreamResult
         PrintWriter pw = new PrintWriter(new FileOutputStream (outputfile));
         StreamResult result = new StreamResult(pw);
          // Transform source xml to pathname destination file
         transformer.transform(new DOMSource(doc), new StreamResult(sr));

      } catch (Exception exp) {
         exp.printStackTrace();
      }
   }
   public static void main(String [] args) {
      if (args.length != 3) {
        System.out.println("Usage run <xmlfile> <xslfile> <destination>");
        System.exit(1);
      }
      Translator t = new Translator(args[0], args[1], args[2]);
      t.translate();
   }
}
```

Figure 10.20 The Transformer application.

The Transformer package has a main method that drives the application and a constructor that sets up the name of the XML file, the XSL file and the output file. The translate method is the method that does the work. This method first loads the specified XML document into memory (as described in the section relating to the DOM). It then creates a TransformerFactory object.

The TransformerFactory is then used to create a new Transformer object using the specified xslfile name.

A StreamResult object is then created that points to the outputfile via a PrintWriter wrapped around a FileOutputStream. The in-memory document is then transformed into the output file using the transform instance method of the Transformer class.

Note that the DOM tree was wrapped inside a DOMSource object. This is a class in the javax.xml.transform.dom package. This class acts as a wrapper around the DOM tree that allows it to be processed by the transformer. There is also a DOMResult class that allows the result of the transformation to be another in-memory DOM tree rather than an external file. There are also SAXSource and SAXResult classes if you wish to use the SAX API with the transformer class (see javax.xml.transform.sax).

To illustrate the result of this process we will apply the Transformer application to the XML file presented in Figure 10.21.

```
<?xml version = "1.0" ?>

<!-- comment: XML document starts here -->

<paper>
   <section>
     This is my paper, written in XML. This
     version is very basic but will illustrate
     the use of a very simple XSL deifnition.
   </section>
</paper>
```

Figure 10.21 The paper.xml XML file.

To do this we will of course need an XSL file. A sample XSL stylesheet is illustrated in Figure 10.22.

The paper.xsl stylesheet merely extracts the text held in the section of the paper and places horizontal lines around it.

The Transformer application can be applied to the paper.xml file using the paper.xsl stylesheet in the following manner:

```
java jdt.Transformer paper.xml paper.xsl paper.html
```

The end result of this is an HTML file, illustrated in Figure 10.23.

```
<?xml version='1.0'?>
<xsl:stylesheet version="1.0"
     xmlns:xsl="http://www.w3.org/1999/XSL/Transform">
  <xsl:template match="/">
<!--this template is applied to the root element-->
    <HTML>
      <HEAD><TITLE> "Paper" </TITLE></HEAD>
      <BODY>
        <xsl:apply-templates select="paper"/>
<!--insert the results of another template identified by
    the value of the "select" attribute-->
      </BODY>
    </HTML>
  </xsl:template>
<!--closes out main template-->

  <xsl:template match="paper">
<!--This template creates a table and begins populating it -->
     <HR/>
       <xsl:value-of select="section"/>
     <HR/>
  </xsl:template>
<!-- close the template that creates the table -->
</xsl:stylesheet>
```

Figure 10.22 The `paper.xsl` XSL stylesheet.

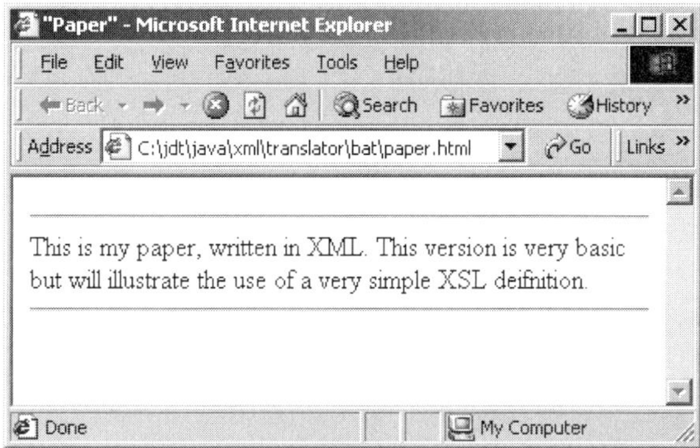

Figure 10.23 The `paper.html` file generated from the `paper.xml` file using the `paper.xsl` stylesheet.

Chapter 11

JavaMail API: the Mail Is in

11.1 Introduction

There are many situations in which an application may need to send an email: for example, when an error situation occurs, or when the next step in some workflow must be started, or in response to some event that has occurred. Java applications are no exception to this, and many Java standalone applications as well as two-, three- or *n*-tier applications may need to send email. In some cases these applications will also need to support the retrieval of email (although this is probably less common, as many users will read email with one of the leading solutions such as Eudora, Outlook or similar).

Java provides access to email systems through the JavaMail API. The JavaMail API has been developed over a number of years, and the current release version is version 1.3. It is possible to obtain the JavaMail API either as a separate downloadable jar from Sun's Web site or as part of the Java 2 Enterprise Edition (also known as J2EE). You need to be careful with the two approaches as the Enterprise Edition Release 1.3.1 currently contains version 1.2 of the JavaMail API, whereas from the Sun Web site it is possible to obtain both the 1.2 release and the current version of the 1.3 release. J2EE SDK 1.4 uses version 1.3, which is also used in this chapter.

In this chapter we will look at creating a basic email message, sending an email message with an attachment and receiving an email message. This will cause us to examine the core aspects of the JavaMail API and thus provide a sound basis for anyone wishing to get started with this very useful set of packages.

11.2 The JavaMail API

The version of the JavaMail API used in this chapter is based on the 1.3 release provided as part of the current J2EE release. The JavaMail API is made up of four packages. These are:

- `javax.mail` This package provides the core classes for generating, sending and reading email.
- `javax.mail.event` Event listeners and associated events for notifying application classes of mail-related activities.
- `javax.mail.internet` Classes specific to Internet mail systems, including MIME type emails.
- `javax.mail.search` Provides for searching through emails during the process of retrieving emails from a server-centric email system.

As you will see from the above list, all the packages start `javax`, and thus the JavaMail API is a standard language extension (and thus an optional package).

It is important to realize that the JavaMail API focuses on email user agent type programs such as Eudora, and not on implementing an email server. Thus the API provides for reading, constructing and sending electronic messages via a server that understands en email protocol such as SMTP or POP. SMTP stands for Simple Mail Transfer Protocol (SMTP) which is the protocol most often used to send email. POP stands for Post Office Protocol (currently in version 3 and often referred to as POP3), which is the protocol most often used to receive email.

Like a number of other APIs in Java (most notabley JDBC), JavaMail is not tied to one particular protocol or one particular type of email server. Instead, JavaMail relies on the appropriate protocol implementation, known as protocol-specific providers. Sun provides a set of protocol-specific providers with JavaMail. These include SMTP, POP and IMAP. If you have used older versions of the JavaMail API (for example 1.1.3) then you will probably be pleased to see that a POP provider is now supplied with JavaMail (previously it was necessary to download from Sun a separate jar that would add a POP provider to your JavaMail installation).

11.3 Setting up JavaMail

If you are going to use the JavaMail API directly from the J2EE 1.3.1 release then you do not need to do anything special to get things to work (other than making sure that the `j2ee.jar` file is on your classpath). If you intend to use the JavaMail API independently of the J2EE installation then you will need to follow the installation instructions provided with the version of the JavaMail API you obtain.

11.4 Sending Email

We will start off by sending a very simple email to a single user. The email will contain only text. This is the simplest example, but in many cases is also exactly what is required. For example, if a server application needs to send an email to a support engineer informing them of some problem, then it is likely that the email message will be textual and include the error message.

Thus although this is a simple example, it is both very useful and one on which we will build in the rest of the chapter.

We shall be using classes in the javax.mail package and in some cases the javax.mail.internet package.

The steps that we must follow to create an email and send it are:

1. Create and initialize a session object.
2. Create and put text into a message object.
3. Send the message using the static Transport.send() method.

The session object represents a basic email session. That is, it represents a single communication channel with an email server. It is through this session object that everything else operates.

The session object needs to know some details in order to connect to the appropriate mail server. This information is passed to the session object via a Properties object. A Properties object is part of the java.util package (and not part of the javax.mail package or sub-packages). It is used in many situations and provides dictionary-like lookup facilities. That is, given a key it will return a string value. Thus it is possible to place configuration information into a Properties object that can be picked up by the session object. One such example is the mail.smtp.host property. This can be defined within a Property object by defining mail.smtp.host as a key and setting the value to be "thor" if thor is the name of the SMTP host. Of course, you should replace "thor" with the name, usually a full URL, of your target email server.

Figure 11.1 presents a very simple email program (called JDMailer). This Java application takes three parameters: the email address of the recipient of the message, the subject heading of the email and a string for the contents of the email message.

Notice that the code imports the java.util.Properties class and two of the JavaMail packages, namely javax.mail.* and javax.mail.internet.*. We need to import these two packages, as the Session, Message, Address and Transport classes are defined in the javax.mail package. In turn, the MimeMessager and InternetAddress classes are defined in the javax.mail.internet package.

The first thing that the JDMailer class does is to create a Properties object and store the mail.smtp.host property in it. Note that you should replace this with the address of whatever mail server you are using.

Next we create an instance of the Session object. This can be done in a number of ways, but here we are creating the session object using the "factory" method getDefaultInstance. This method takes two parameters, the properties indicating which mail server to use and an authenticator object if one is being used. At the moment we are not using an authenticator, so we will pass in null here. Following this we set the session debug flag to be true so that some output will be generated by the JavaMail classes to indicate what is happening behind the scenes:

```
Session session = Session.getDefaultInstance(props, null);
session.setDebug(true);
```

Now we come to the first point where the program has been protocol specific. We need to create a message object suitable for the mail system in use. In this case it is a MimeMessage object:

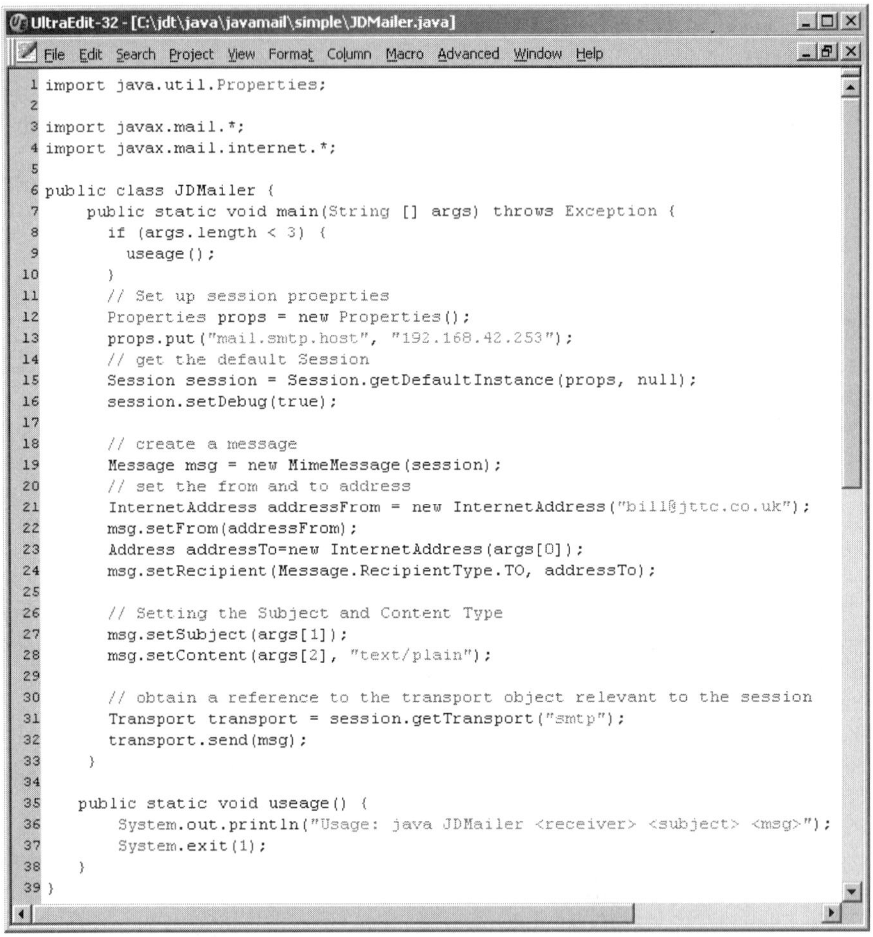

UltraEdit-32 - [C:\jdt\java\javamail\simple\JDMailer.java]

File Edit Search Project View Format Column Macro Advanced Window Help

```
import java.util.Properties;

import javax.mail.*;
import javax.mail.internet.*;

public class JDMailer {
    public static void main(String [] args) throws Exception {
      if (args.length < 3) {
        useage();
      }
      // Set up session proeprties
      Properties props = new Properties();
      props.put("mail.smtp.host", "192.168.42.253");
      // get the default Session
      Session session = Session.getDefaultInstance(props, null);
      session.setDebug(true);

      // create a message
      Message msg = new MimeMessage(session);
      // set the from and to address
      InternetAddress addressFrom = new InternetAddress("bill@jttc.co.uk");
      msg.setFrom(addressFrom);
      Address addressTo=new InternetAddress(args[0]);
      msg.setRecipient(Message.RecipientType.TO, addressTo);

      // Setting the Subject and Content Type
      msg.setSubject(args[1]);
      msg.setContent(args[2], "text/plain");

      // obtain a reference to the transport object relevant to the session
      Transport transport = session.getTransport("smtp");
      transport.send(msg);
    }

   public static void useage() {
       System.out.println("Usage: java JDMailer <receiver> <subject> <msg>");
       System.exit(1);
   }
}
```

Figure 11.1 The basics of sending email with JavaMail.

```
Message msg = new MimeMessage(session);
```

We now have a message object that will represent our email message. However, we need to set up a number of attributes for the message, such as who sent the message and where it should go. This is done by creating an instance of the `InternetAddress` class (from the `javax.mail.internet` package) and then using the constructed object as the parameter for either the `setFrom` or `setRecipient` methods. As well as the `set` versions of these methods there are also `add` versions.

Also note that the `setRecipient` method takes two parameters. The first parameter is the recipient type (such as `TO`, `CC` or `BCC`) and is defined by the `Message` inner class `Message.RecipientType`. The `JDMailer` example uses the `TO` type, but there are also `Message.RecipientType.CC` and `Message.RecipientType.BCC`. The snippet of code that illustrates this from the JDMailer example is presented below:

```
InternetAddress addressFrom = new InternetAddress("bill@jttc.co.uk");
msg.setFrom(addressFrom);
Address addressTo=new InternetAddress(args[0]);
msg.setRecipient(Message.RecipientType.TO, addressTo);
```

Note that as far as SMTP is concerned the "from" field is optional. We could have left this out and this example would still have worked. In fact, when we send an email in this way we can make up a "from" email address (such as "Bilbo.Baggins") and the email will still be sent! We can now set up the subject header for the message and the content of the email message. In our example we take them from the command line:

```
msg.setSubject(args[1]);
msg.setContent(args[2], "text/plain");
```

Note that for the content of the message it is necessary to set the content type. In this case we are using `"text/plain"` to indicate that the content type is plain text. We could have used the `setText` method on the message, which would have set the text and the content type in one step. This is fine if all you ever want to do is to send text. However, we could change the content type to be `"text/html"` if we wished to send HTML by email using `setContent`.

We now have an email message which is ready to be sent to the recipient. This is done using the `Transport` class. There are two ways in which we could use this class. For instance, we could use the static method `Transport.send()`. In our example we obtain the `Transport` object from the session and then use the instance method `send` on the `Transport` object obtained.

Finally, note that the whole `main` method throws an `Exception`. This is because numerous steps in the creation and sending of an email message may throw exceptions. To keep this example simple we are merely passing the exception out of the `main` method. In most cases you will need to handle the exceptions locally in a `try...catch` block.

Figure 11.2 illustrates a simple `compile.bat` file used to compile this code and Figure 11.3 shows a simple `run.bat` file that illustrates how the `JDMailer` is executed. Note that it is necessary to add the `j2ee.jar` to the classpath.

You should now be able to send an email message. The end result, as displayed in Eudora, is presented in Figure 11.4.

Now that you have looked at an example of a program that can send a message to a single email address it is straightforward to extend this principle to multiple email addresses (Figure 11.5). The `JDManyMailer` does just this. It takes a list of email addresses and sends a

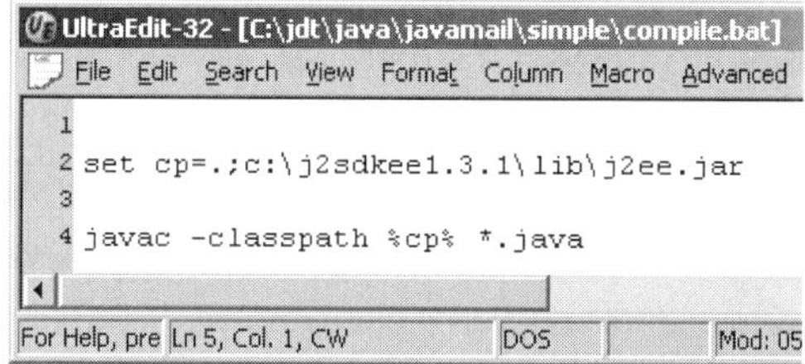

Figure 11.2 A `.bat` file set up to add the `j2ee.jar` to the classpath for compilation.

```
set cp=.;c:\j2sdkee1.3.1\lib\j2ee.jar

java -cp %cp% JDMailer jit@bizt.co.uk Hello "This is a short message
```

Figure 11.3 A .bat file for running the JDMailer example with appropriate parameters.

Figure 11.4 An email message sent by JDMailer and read by Eudora.

message with the provided subject and content to each. This is done by creating an array of InternetAddress objects and using the msg.setRecipients(Message.RecipientType.TO, addrs) method (note that extra "s"). Note that in the JDManyMailer example the recipients' addresses are provided at the end of the command line options.

11.5 Receiving Messages

So far in this column we have focused on sending emails. The other aspect of an email tool is receiving emails. We will now look at what support the JavaMail API provides for reading emails from an email server. As the most common way in which email is read is from a POP3 server, we will focus on this example. Figure 11.6 illustrates a simple program, called JDMailReader, that will read email from a POP3 server.

Just as with sending emails, the starting point is the Session object. However, note that this time we do not need to define any specific properties. Instead, our Properties object is left empty.

```
Properties props = new Properties();
Session session = Session.getDefaultInstance(props, null);
```

When reading email we have to get hold of a store object. The store object obtained must be appropriate for the specified protocol. For example, as we are using POP3 we must specify the

UltraEdit-32 - [C:\jdt\java\javamail\simple\JDManyMailer.java]

File Edit Search Project View Format Column Macro Advanced Window Help

```java
import java.util.Properties;

import javax.mail.*;
import javax.mail.internet.*;

public class JDManyMailer {
    public static void main(String [] args) throws Exception {
      if (args.length < 3) {
        useage();
      }
      String subject = args[0];
      String content = args[1];
      // Set up session proeprties
      Properties props = new Properties();
      props.put("mail.smtp.host", "thor");
      // get the default Session
      Session session = Session.getDefaultInstance(props, null);
      session.setDebug(true);

      // create a message
      Message msg = new MimeMessage(session);
      // set the from and to address
      InternetAddress addressFrom = new InternetAddress("bill@jttc.co.uk");
      // To send the message to many users - loop
      // creating an InternetAddress object for each
      msg.setFrom(addressFrom);
      Address [] addrs = new InternetAddress[args.length - 2];
      for (int i=2, j=0; i<args.length; i++, j++) {
         addrs[j] = new InternetAddress(args[i]);
      }
      msg.setRecipients(Message.RecipientType.TO, addrs);

      // Setting the Subject and Content Type
      msg.setSubject(subject);
      msg.setContent(content, "text/plain");

      // obtain a reference to the transport object relevant to the session
      Transport transport = session.getTransport("smtp");
      transport.send(msg);
    }

   public static void useage() {
       System.out.println("Usage: java JDManyMail <subject> <msg> " +
                          "<receiver1>..<receivern> ");
       System.exit(1);
   }
}
```

Figure 11.5 Modifying the `JDMailer` class to send an email message to multiple recipients.

"`pop3`" protocol. A `Store` is an object that models a message store and its access protocol for storing and retrieving messages. Once the `Store` object has been obtained it is necessary to connect the store to the email server that will supply the email messages. This is done using the `connect` method of the `Store` object. This comment takes the name of the server (e.g. thor), a user name and a user password. This is used to authenticate the user to the email server and identify the email messages for this user. An alternative to providing the user name and password directly is to use an `Authenticator` object. An `Authenticator` object is one which will supply

File Edit Search View Format Column Macro Advanced Window Help

```
import java.util.Properties;
import javax.mail.*;
import javax.mail.internet.*;

public class JDMailReader {
    public static void main(String [] args) throws Exception {
      if (args.length < 2) {
        useage();
      }
      // Set up session proeprties
      Properties props = new Properties();
      // get the default Session
      Session session = Session.getDefaultInstance(props, null);
      //session.setDebug(true);

      // Obtain the store object
      Store store = session.getStore("pop3");
      store.connect("thor", args[0], args[1]);
      //Get Folder
      Folder folder = store.getFolder("INBOX");
      folder.open(Folder.READ_ONLY);
      // get Directory
      Message messages[] = folder.getMessages();
      for (int i=0; i<messages.length; i++) {
         messages[i].writeTo(System.out);
         System.out.println("--------------------");
      }
      folder.close(false);
      store.close();
    }
   public static void useage() {
       System.out.println("Usage: java JDMailReader <username> <password>");
       System.exit(1);
   }
}
```

Figure 11.6 A Java application that reads email from a POP3 email server.

the username and password on demand (for example by promoting the user for these items of information). The two statements that obtain and connect the store are presented below:

```
Store store = session.getStore("pop3");
store.connect("thor", args[0], args[1]);
```

We are now in a position to be able to obtain a `Folder` object that will supply the actual email messages. A POP3 server has only one folder, the "INBOX" folder. This folder holds the emails held on the email server that have not yet been downloaded. Note that an IMAP server could have additional folders that can be managed and searched by the JavaMail API.

```
Folder folder = store.getFolder("INBOX");
```

At this point we have something that can be used to read the contents of the "INBOX", but which has yet to do so. To actually download the messages it is necessary to open the folder. This can be done in a number of ways. For example, it is possible to indicate that the folder should be opened in read-only mode so that messages are not actually removed from the server (useful for testing your applications). The class `Folder` defines several constants that allow you to control how the folder is opened, for example `Folder.READ_WRITE` and `Folder.READ_ONLY`. We will use the read-only option here:

```
folder.open(Folder.READ_ONLY);
```

Now we have the messages in the `folder` object we can start to make use of them. You can retrieve the messages using the method `getMessages()` on the `folder` object. This returns an array of `Message` objects that you can now loop through:

```
Message messages[] = folder.getMessages();
for (int i=0; i<messages.length; i++) {
  messages[i].writeTo(System.out);
  System.out.println("--------------------");
}
```

Note that the messages are actually only retrieved from the server when you access them. Thus if you only access the first message and exit the others will not be retrieved.

Finally you have to close the folder and store:

```
folder.close(false);
store.close();
```

Replying to a message is very straightforward. The `message` class contains a reply method that can be used to generate a reply message object. This message object can then be set up as appropriate, for example:

```
Message reply = message.reply(false0;
reply.setFrom(new InternetAddress("bill@jaydeetechnology.com");
reply.setText("Thanks");
Transport.send(reply);
```

The only question that really remains is how do you delete an email? The answer is that you must first open the folder in read–write mode:

```
folder.open(Folder.READ_WRITE);
```

After this you can set the flag for each email you retrieve to "deleted":

```
msg.setFlag(Flags.Flag.DELETED,true);
```

The email is not actually deleted until you close the folder with "`true`" as the parameter:

```
folder.close(true);
```

Notice that this is the only flag that the POP3 server takes any notice of.

11.6 Replying to Messages

Having read an email one of the most common things that you want to be able to do is to reply to that email. The JDMailer2 application does exactly that. It builds on the concepts presented in the JDMailReader program by making the class more object-oriented and by adding the ability to reply to received emails. This is done in the sendReply method. As this example is intended to be simple, an automatic reply is sent to each email received, notifying the sender that the receiver is on holiday. The source for the JDMailer2 program is presented below:

```
import java.util.Properties;
import javax.mail.*;
import javax.mail.internet.*;
import java.io.*;

public class JDMailer2 {

  private static final String EMAIL_SERVER_IP_ADDRESS = "192.168.42.253";

  private Session session;
  private String user;
  private String password;

  public static void main(String [] args) {
    if (args.length < 2) {
      System.out.println("Usage: java JDMailer2 <username> <password>");
      System.exit(1);
    }
    JDMailer2 jdm = new JDMailer2(args[0], args[1]);
    jdm.readMail();
  }

  public JDMailer2(String user, String password) {
    this.user = user;
    this.password = password;
    // Set up session
    Properties props = new Properties();
    props.put("mail.smtp.host", EMAIL_SERVER_IP_ADDRESS);
    session = Session.getDefaultInstance(props, null);
    session.setDebug(true);
  }
```

```
    private void readMail() {
      try {
        // Obtain the store object and in box
        Store store = session.getStore("pop3");
        store.connect(EMAIL_SERVER_IP_ADDRESS, user, password);
        Folder folder = store.getFolder("INBOX");
        folder.open(Folder.READ_ONLY); // As this is just for testing
        // Get Messages in In box
        Message messages[] = folder.getMessages();
        for (int i=0; i<messages.length; i++) {
          messages[i].writeTo(System.out);
          System.out.println("--------------------");
          // Now let's automate a reply
          sendReply(messages[i], user);
        }
        folder.close(false);
        store.close();
      } catch (Exception e) {
        e.printStackTrace();
      }
    }

    private void sendReply(Message message, String from) {
      try {
        // Obtain the reply message
        boolean replyToAll = false;
        MimeMessage reply = (MimeMessage)message.reply(replyToAll);
        // Set the from address
        InternetAddress addressFrom = new InternetAddress(from);
        reply.setFrom(addressFrom);
        // Set the reply text
        reply.setText("I am on holiday but will get back to you when I
                       return");
        // obtain a reference to the transport object relevant to the
        // session
        Transport transport = session.getTransport("smtp");
        transport.send(reply);

      } catch (Exception e) {
        e.printStackTrace();
      }
    }
  }
```

We will examine the sendReply method in detail, but first note that the session object used to read email and send email is the same instance. You need to be careful here. It is not necessary to provide any properties to obtain a session that will allow you to access a POP3 account (indeed the JDMailReader application did exactly that). However, as this becomes the "default" session instance, if we first read email from a POP3 account and later try to send email via an SMTP server, as we have done earlier, with the JDMailer program, we would have a problem. This is because the default session was configured first for the POP3 account, but is not shared by the SMTP session. This means that no SMTP server will have been configured, and it will default to localhost (even if we supply some properties specifying the SMTP to connect to).

There are two or three ways around this. One is to obtain a new instance of the session object when sending email via the SMTP server using the getInstance(Properties) static method on the Session class. However, you would then have two session objects around, which is inefficient. Another approach is to set up the SMTP properties when you first need to get a default session, even if at that point all you are trying to do is to access a POP3 server. This then means that the default session is configured for SMTP access as well as for POP3 access. However, this of course could be confusing to the reader.

In our case we initialize the session in the class constructor for use throughout the JDMailer2 class. Once this issue has been resolved we can read email messages from the POP3 server as before. We can then send replies to each of the messages received (by calling the sendReply method each time a message is received).

The sendReply method itself uses the reply(boolean) method on the message object to generate a message which is appropriately configured. That is, the new message will have its attributes and headers set up appropriately. For example, the subject will have a "Re:" added if one is not already present.

Note that the boolean parameter is used to indicate whether the reply message should be sent to all recipients of the original message or just the sender. If the value is true it is sent to all.

We can then treat the new reply message just like any other email message we wish to send. We can set the "From" address, indicate who should be CCed on the message etc. Note that the "From" address is not automatically filled in when the reply object is created – you must do this yourself.

We can then place some text in the message indicating that the receiver is on holiday and then send the message. The end result of such a message when received in a tool such as Eudora is presented in Figure 11.7.

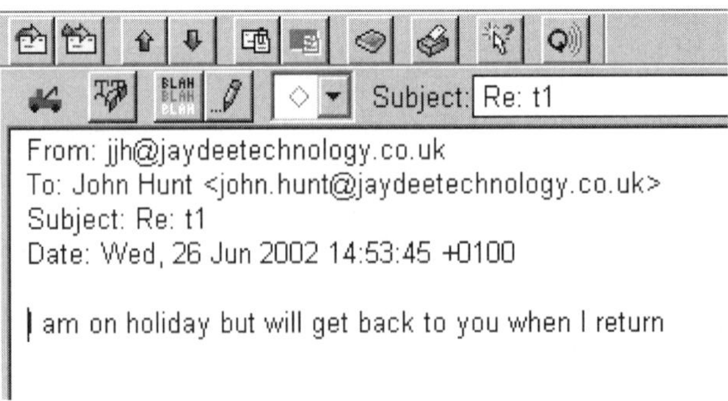

Figure 11.7 The reply in Eudora.

One thing you may note from the figure is that the reply does not contain the original text – only the text sent as a reply. This is because the reply does not automatically receive the original text. To add the text we need to look at multipart MIME messages.

11.7 Multipart MIME Messages

We now need to have a short aside to talk about multipart MIME messages. All email messages are made up of multiple "parts". All of these parts together comprise the multipart that is the email message, and each part is referred to as a body part. To work with MIME there are specific subclasses in the JavaMail API for `MimeBodyPart` and `MimeMultiPart`.

To work with multipart messages we must first create our own `MimeMultiPart` object and then create each of the `MimeBodyParts` that will be added to the `MimeMultiPart`. The `MultiPart` object is then added to the `Message` object using the `setContent` method.

11.8 Adding the Reply Text to a Reply

We can now look at how to include the original text in our reply example. The example is called `JDMailer3`. This version of the `JDMailer` application replies to the original sender, including their email in the message.

This is done by first creating a `MimeMultiPart` object. Next each of the individual body parts is created. Note that the message indicating that the receiver is only holiday is also a body part. Each body part is then added to the multipart. The multipart object is then added to the reply object. However, notice that to obtain the original message we had to go to the original message object and obtain a `DataHandler` object.

A `DataHandler` is actually a class from the `javax.activation` package, which is part of the JavaBeans Activation Framework (JAF). This is part of the infrastructure for JavaBeans and is not provided by default with the Standard Edition of the Java 2 SDK. However, it is provided as part of the Java 2 Enterprise Edition SDK.

The idea behind `DataHandlers` is that the `DataHandler` class provides a consistent interface to data available in many different sources and formats. It manages simple streams, string conversions and related operations using `DataContentHandlers`. For multipart messages this is a very useful feature. Each part of a message could be different type of data; for example, it could be text, attached images or word processor documents, or a spreadsheet or a Java class file etc. `DataHandlers` can provide access to such data and handle the management necessary for these different data types.

In terms of replying to an email we can effectively treat the `DataHandler` as providing a way to access the content of the original email message. The modified `sendReply` method is presented in Figure 11.8.

The result of including the original text in the reply is presented in Figure 11.9.

```
    private void sendReply(Message message, String from) {
        try {

            // Obtain the reply message
            boolean replyToAll = false;
            MimeMessage reply = (MimeMessage)message.reply(replyToAll);
            // Set the from address
            InternetAddress addressFrom = new InternetAddress(from);
            reply.setFrom(addressFrom);

            //------------- New in JDMailer3 ----------------------
            // Now get hold of the Multipart object
            Multipart multipart = new MimeMultipart();
            // Next create the body for the reply text
            BodyPart bodyPart = new MimeBodyPart();
            bodyPart.setText("I am on holiday but will get back to you when I return\n\n");
            multipart.addBodyPart(bodyPart);
            // Next retrieve the message text being replied to
            bodyPart = new MimeBodyPart();
            bodyPart.setDataHandler(message.getDataHandler());
            multipart.addBodyPart(bodyPart);
            // Now associate the multi part object with the reply
            reply.setContent(multipart);
            //------------- New in JDMailer3 ----------------------

            // obtain a reference to the transport object relevant to the session
            Transport transport = session.getTransport("smtp");
            transport.send(reply);

        } catch (Exception e) {
            e.printStackTrace();
        }
    }
}
```

Figure 11.8 The modified `sendReply` method.

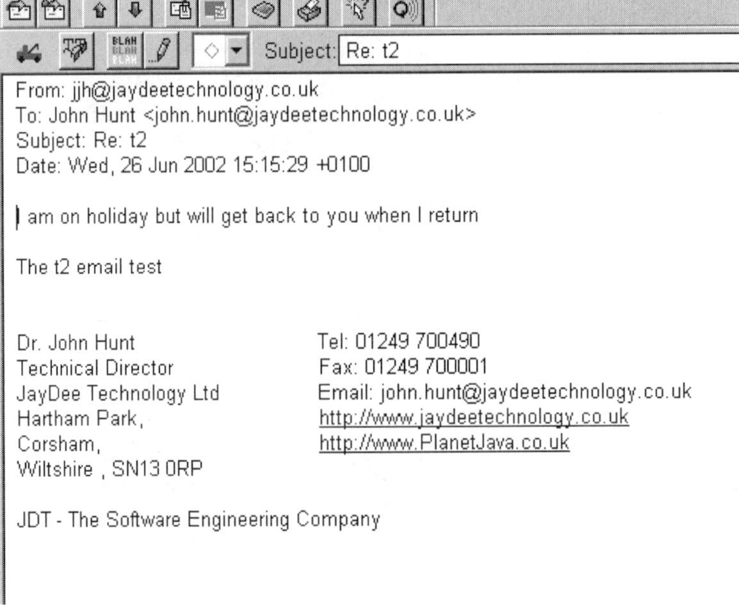

Figure 11.9 A reply message.

11.9 Message Forwarding

Message forwarding is similar to replying, if a little more work. There is nothing in the JavaMail API that directly supports forwarding. Instead, you have to do all the work from scratch yourself. This means that you have to create an empty message and fill it out with the appropriate subject, "From" address, "To" addresses and content.

To place the content of one message inside another message we follow the same steps as we followed when replying to a message. This is illustrated in the `forward` method in Figure 11.10.

File Edit Search Project View Format Column Macro Advanced Window Help

```
    private void forward(Message message, String from, String to) {
        try {

            // Obtain the reply message
            boolean replyToAll = false;
            MimeMessage fromMessage = new MimeMessage(session);
            // Set the from address
            InternetAddress addressFrom = new InternetAddress(from);
            fromMessage.setFrom(addressFrom);

            //-------------- New in JDMailer4 ----------------------
            fromMessage.setSubject("Fwd: " + message.getSubject());
            fromMessage.addRecipient(Message.RecipientType.TO,
                                     new InternetAddress(to));
            //-------------- New in JDMailer4 ----------------------

            // Now get hold of the Multipart object
            Multipart multipart = new MimeMultipart();
            // Next create the body for the reply text
            BodyPart bodyPart = new MimeBodyPart();
            bodyPart.setText("This could be of interest to you:\n\n");
            multipart.addBodyPart(bodyPart);
            // Next retrieve the message text being replied to
            bodyPart = new MimeBodyPart();
            bodyPart.setDataHandler(message.getDataHandler());
            multipart.addBodyPart(bodyPart);
            // Now associate the multi part object with the reply
            fromMessage.setContent(multipart);


            // obtain a reference to the transport object relevant to the session
            Transport transport = session.getTransport("smtp");
            transport.send(fromMessage);

        } catch (Exception e) {
            e.printStackTrace();
        }
    }
```

Figure 11.10 The `forward` method of JDMailer4.

11.10 Sending Attachments

One of the most common things people do with email today is to add an attachment. An attachment is an external resource such as a file that is added to the email message and sent along with, but external to, the main content of the email. When an email program receives the email message it typically indicates the attachment as an external entity to the email (accessed by a double click or by opening the attachment in some other way).

JavaMail is no exception to this, and it is possible to attach external resources to a mail message and send them. In turn it is then possible to obtain those attachments when the email is received using JavaMail. We will look at both scenarios below.

We will first consider sending an email with an attachment. This is not as straightforward as it possibly could be because of the use of the Java Activation Framework (JAF) and data handlers, but we will step through the process to make the procedure clear.

The first thing to do is to attach a resource is to create a new `MimeBodyPart`. Next we create a `DataSource` object. This is part of the JAF and thus is defined in the `javax.activation` package. A `DataSource` is a source of an arbitrary type of data that can be accessed via an input or output stream and can handle any encoding required. In our case we are attaching a file; therefore we create an instance of the `FileDataSource` object. This implements the `DataSource` interface. It can return its content type to indicate the type of data it holds.

Once we have obtained a `DataSource` object we must then wrap it inside a `DataHandler` object. This will allow us to pass the `DataHandler` to the body part object. Once we have done this the operation of linking the body part to the message is the same as for any other body part. We can then link the body part to the multipart object and add the multipart object to the message. The message can then be sent in the normal way.

This will work, but if you do this you will find that the filename of the attached object is a system-generated filename. To overcome this you must provide your own filename. This filename can be anything you like (it does not have to be the same as the name of the file the attachment was loaded from). It will, however be used as the name of the attachment file when the file is accessed by an email client such as Eudora.

The source code for this example is defined in the `JDMailer5` application and presented in Figure 11.11. The end result of sending this email is presented in Figure 11.12.

We have now successfully sent an email with an attachment. We can now look at receiving an email with an attachment. This is more complex than sending attachments, because MIME has no simple notation of what an attachment is.

To obtain an attachment you must first obtain the multipart object contained in the message. This is done from the message using the `getContent` method. This can then be cast to a multipart object. However, what you receive may not be a multipart object, so you therefore need to test to see what type of object you have actually received. In the example presented in `JDMailReader2` we ignore the mail message if it is not a multiple object. Once we have the multipart object we can then test it to see how many parts it has. Each of these parts can be retrieved using the `getBodyPart(int)` method. We can then find out if the part is an attachment by testing its "Disposition". The disposition describes how the part should be presented to the user.

Body parts with a disposition of either `Part.ATTACHMENT` or `Part.INLINE` indicate that the body part is an attachment. It is then possible to obtain the filename of the attachment and an input stream, from which it is possible to read the contents of the attachment. This can be used to write the contents of the attachment to a local file. This is exactly what has been done in the `saveAttachment` method of the `JDMailReader2` application. Note that we test to see whether a file with the same name as the attachment already exists. If it does we follow the standard convention of adding a number to the filename until the file does not exist.

```
File Edit Search Project View Format Column Macro Advanced Window Help
        Properties props = new Properties();
        props.put("mail.smtp.host", "192.168.42.253");
        // get the default Session
        Session session = Session.getDefaultInstance(props, null);
        session.setDebug(true);

        // create a message
        Message msg = new MimeMessage(session);
        // set the from and to address
        InternetAddress addressFrom = new InternetAddress("bill@jttc.co.uk");
        msg.setFrom(addressFrom);
        Address addressTo=new InternetAddress(args[0]);
        msg.setRecipient(Message.RecipientType.TO, addressTo);

        // Now get hold of the Multipart object
        Multipart multipart = new MimeMultipart();
        // Next create the body for the reply text
        BodyPart bodyPart = new MimeBodyPart();
        bodyPart.setText(args[2]);
        multipart.addBodyPart(bodyPart);

        // ------- New in JDMailer5 ----------------------
        // Next handle the attachment
        bodyPart = new MimeBodyPart();
        // Create a data source object
        DataSource source=new FileDataSource(args[3]);
        // Now link the body part to the attachment via the data handler
        bodyPart.setDataHandler(new DataHandler(source));
        // Givce it a meaningful file name
        bodyPart.setFileName(args[3]);
        // Add the attachment to the multipart object
        multipart.addBodyPart(bodyPart);
        // Link the multipart object to the message
        msg.setContent(multipart);
        // ------- New in JDMailer5 ----------------------

        // obtain a reference to the transport object relevant to the session
        Transport transport = session.getTransport("smtp");
        transport.send(msg);
```

Figure 11.11 JDMailer5 sending an attachment.

Figure 11.12 An attachment in an email sent by JavaMail.

The listing for JDMailReader2 is presented below:

```
import java.util.Properties;
import javax.mail.*;
import javax.mail.internet.*;
```

```
import java.io.*;

public class JDMailReader2 {
  public static void main(String [] args) throws Exception {
    if (args.length < 2) {
      useage();
    }
    // Set up session properties
    Properties props = new Properties();
    // Get the default Session
    Session session = Session.getDefaultInstance(props, null);
    //session.setDebug(true);

    // Obtain the store object
    Store store = session.getStore("pop3");
    store.connect("192.168.42.253", args[0], args[1]);
    // Get Folder
    Folder folder = store.getFolder("INBOX");
    folder.open(Folder.READ_ONLY);
    // Get Directory
    Message messages[] = folder.getMessages();
    for (int i=0; i<messages.length; i++) {
      Message msg = messages[i];
      Object obj = msg.getContent();
      if (obj instanceof Multipart) {
        Multipart multipart = (Multipart)obj;
        for (int j=0; j<multipart.getCount(); j++) {
          Part p = multipart.getBodyPart(j);
          String disposition = p.getDisposition();
          if (disposition != null) {
            if ((disposition.equals(Part.ATTACHMENT)) ||
              (disposition.equals(Part.INLINE))) {
                saveAttachment(p);
            }
          }
        }
      }

    System.out.println("--------------------");

  }
  folder.close(false);
  store.close();
}

private static void saveAttachment(Part part) {
```

```
    try {
      String filename = part.getFileName();
      File f = new File(filename);
      InputStream input = part.getInputStream();
      int count = 0;
      while (f.exists()) {
        count++;
        f = new File(filename + count);
      }
      FileOutputStream output = new FileOutputStream(f);
      byte[] bytearr = new byte[512];
      int len = 0;
      try {
        while ((len = input.read(bytearr)) != -1) {
          output.write(bytearr, 0, len);
        }
      } catch (IOException exp) {
        throw exp;
      } finally {
        input.close();
        output.close();
      }
    } catch (Exception exp) {
      exp.printStackTrace();
    }
  }

    public static void useage() {
      System.out.println("Usage: java JDMailReader2 <username> <password>");
      System.exit(1);
    }
  }
```

11.11 Sending HTML

The final JavaMail feature we will look at is sending HTML. If you are merely sending text marked up with HTML then all you need to do is set the content type of the email message to "text/html". However, you may wish to embed an image within your email message. this could be done using standard HTML and requiring the email client to access the image via the Internet. Another option is to embed the image within the email message itself as another body part. The HTML can then refer to this using a local reference name that is associated with the message body part via a header ("`Content-ID`"). This is illustrated in the `JDMailer6` application in Figure 11.13.

```java
        // Set up session properties
        Properties props = new Properties();
        props.put("mail.smtp.host", "192.168.42.253");
        // get the default Session
        Session session = Session.getDefaultInstance(props, null);
        session.setDebug(true);

        // create a message
        Message msg = new MimeMessage(session);
        // set the from and to address
        InternetAddress addressFrom = new InternetAddress("bill@jttc.co.uk");
        msg.setFrom(addressFrom);
        Address addressTo=new InternetAddress(args[0]);
        msg.setRecipient(Message.RecipientType.TO, addressTo);

        // Now get hold of the Multipart object
        Multipart multipart = new MimeMultipart();
        // Next create the body for the reply text
        BodyPart bodyPart = new MimeBodyPart();
        String text = "<h1>Message</h1><hr><img src='cid:logo'>";
        bodyPart.setContent(text, "text/html");
        multipart.addBodyPart(bodyPart);

        // Create image body part
        bodyPart = new MimeBodyPart();
        DataSource source=new FileDataSource("logo.jpg");
        bodyPart.setDataHandler(new DataHandler(source));
        bodyPart.setHeader("Content-ID", "logo");

        // Add the multipart object
        multipart.addBodyPart(bodyPart);
        // Link the multipart object to the message
        msg.setContent(multipart);

        // obtain a reference to the transport object relevant to the session
        Transport transport = session.getTransport("smtp");
        transport.send(msg);
```

Figure 11.13 Embedding an image in an email message for an HTML content type message.

11.12 Summary

In this chapter we have looked at the JavaMail API. This API allows a Java program to create and send emails, to read emails and to reply to them. In addition to what has been presented here it is also possible to send attachments and to deal with multipart MIME messages.

11.13 Online References

jGuru JavaMail FAQ page: `http://www.jguru.com/faq/JavaMail`
Sun's JavaMail home page: `http://java.sun.com/products/javamail/`
Sun's JavaMail Tutorial: `http://developer.java.sun.com/developer/onlineTraining/JavaMail/`

Part 2

EJB Architecture

Chapter 12

The EJB Architecture

12.1 Introduction

Enterprise JavaBeans are server-side components that take the struggle out of developing distributed enterprise applications. EJB components, by their very nature, are reusable, without requiring extensive forethought to achieve this. Normally, the effort required to achieve reuse militates against its implementation. Why is it easier with EJBs? The main reason is that EJBs are surrounded by a "womb" of software that does much of the work that would previously have been programmed explicitly within the application. This "womb" consists of the EJB server, static container code and container code that is generated automatically prior to EJB deployment within a container.

The EJB framework (container and server) allows you to focus on writing business logic code within your EJBs. Rather than 80% of the code being concerned with distribution plumbing code and only 20% with business logic, this distribution code is moved out into the framework, leaving 80% of the code devoted to business logic and only 20% to other issues. Much of this distribution plumbing code is generated automatically prior to deployment. This means that your EJBs are less complicated and easier to maintain, and are far more portable. Distribution code is notoriously non-portable. Although this sounds like magic, it is achieved in a straightforward way. EJB components are configured using XML deployment descriptors. XML files are written that describe the required distribution properties for EJBs. So rather than explicitly writing the distribution code within the EJBs, you declare them using XML tags. With an appropriate XML deployment descriptor editor, you are able to display and alter these deployment properties with ease.

So what kinds of properties are defined in this way? The main ones worth mentioning now are security, transaction scope, persistence requirements, composition, the type of EJB, and the name with which the EJB is to be published. We will examine these deployment descriptor files in some detail in subsequent chapters. The security properties allow us to say who is allowed to invoke which methods. Logical security role names are used. These are independent of any real security principal names in the deployment environment and must be mapped onto real environment security names during deployment. Transaction scope can also be declared. For example, you may wish to ensure that when a particular method is invoked a new transaction is started, and that any other methods called by the first method also run in the context of the transaction, and also that any external resources accessed by these methods are also included in the scope of the transaction. You will also wish to indicate to the container the kind of EJB you have developed and, if a persistent EJB, the parts of the EJB that should be synchronized with a table in an underlying RDBMS. If you wish to change any of these distribution properties it is a simple matter of editing the XML deployment descriptor files, using container tools to generate the distribution code and redeploying the EJBs and newly generated code. None of this requires direct changes to the EJB source code.

So EJBs are like JavaBeans in the sense that they are reusable, configurable components. But that is as far as the similarity goes. JavaBeans are simple classes that follow a particular coding style (have `setter` and `getter` methods). EJBs, however, are built to deal with the complexities of distribution, and must operate within the context of a container.

There are three kinds of EJB. Session EJBs are used to encapsulate business logic. Their data is not synchronized automatically with an underlying persistent store by the container. Two variants of session beans exist. Stateful session EJBs are able to store client-specific data across method invocations, whereas stateless session EJBs are unable to store client-specific data.

Entity EJBs also encapsulate business logic. Their data, however, is synchronized with an underlying persistent store. This synchronization can either be at the control of the container entirely, termed container-managed persistence, or can be partially the responsibility of the EJB code, termed bean-managed persistence. Where container-managed persistence is used, you do not have to use persistence APIs such as JDBC to write data to a database; this is done for you by the container.

The third kind of EJB is the message-driven EJB. This is new to EJB 2.0 and supports asynchronous communication. Session and entity EJBs support synchronous communication; that is, a client making a call on an EJB method must wait for the EJB to return a result, just like normal Java method calls. Message-driven EJBs, on the other hand, read message objects off an associated destination, called a queue or topic (both are essentially queue structures). Clients sending messages to the destination do not wait for a response – they simply continue some other task. At some point, one of the message-driven beans attached to the destination reads a message from the head of the "queue".

The definitive definition of EJBs can be found in the EJB specification 2.1 (DeMichiel *et al.*), a comprehensive 640 page document providing very detailed explanations. In this book we do not attempt to provide the same level of detail, but rather to provide you with a good introduction to EJBs and how to use them in practice as part of multi-tier application development.

12.2 EJB Server Elements

Figure 12.1 shows just a small part of the overall J2EE application server, namely the EJB server and the naming service (JNDI server).

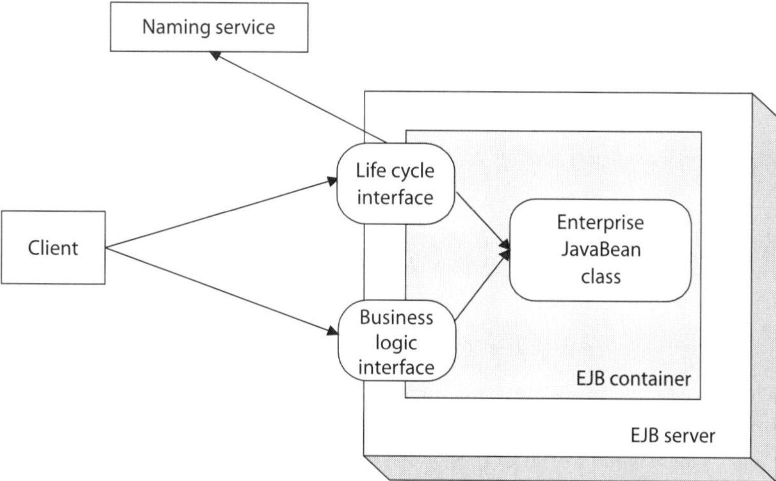

Figure 12.1 The EJB architecture.

The EJB server holds containers and provides generic EJB server services required by all containers, including transaction monitoring services, generic security services and administration service. The transaction monitoring service is responsible for maintaining information about transactions, their state, and the resources that are encompassed by transactions, so that if a transaction is committed or rolled back, the transaction monitor "knows" which resources it needs to synchronize as part of the commit or rollback.

The precise demarcation of responsibilities between the server and its containers is not defined by the EJB specification. Vendors are at liberty to decide whether services should be placed in the server or the containers. However, containers are responsible for managing the runtime behaviour of EJBs. An EJB will be deployed into a specific container, thereby creating instances of the EJB, removing instances of the EJB, passivating and then reactivating instances of the EJB and synchronizing entity EJB data with an underlying data store. The container is also responsible for registering session and entity beans at the point of deployment within the JNDI naming service, allowing clients to access deployed EJBs. The container will also need to maintain versions of EJBs with the same deployment name. For instance, a new version of an EJB may be deployed so that it can be used by new clients. However, an existing version of the EJB may still be in use by an existing client. The container therefore will have to make sure that the old EJB remains accessible until it is no longer being used.

A vendor is at liberty to create specialized containers, for example those that handle only entity EJBs or session EJBs. Although leaving the decision of what goes where to vendors gives them flexibility, for example, to optimize performance, it means that containers cannot be unplugged from one server product and plugged into another. The specification does not define the server-to-container API.

The container to EJB interface is part of the specification. For every EJB component you must implement certain methods. These are called callback or life cycle methods. The container will invoke these methods when certain life cycle events occur. For example, a method is called just after a component instance is created, or just before it is destroyed, or just prior to its passivation (i.e. a form of serialization) or reactivation. This gives you the opportunity to write code that can react to these events, for example to open or close a database connection. We will discuss this container to EJB interface in some detail when discussing types of EJBs in subsequent chapters.

Figure 12.1 shows three other elements within the EJB server. For the moment let us think of this diagram as a kind of class diagram rather than an object diagram. The three elements comprise a single EJB component. In a real server there would probably be many EJB components deployed; here, for simplicity, we show one only. The implementation class contains the business logic code. The two interfaces publish the services of the EJB to the outside world, in the same manner as RMI remote interfaces. The outside world could be external Java application clients, CORBA application clients, or other EJB components. The key point is that all interaction with a session or entity EJB component must be via one of these gateway interfaces, or rather the implementations of these interfaces. No client is allowed to execute methods on the component implementation class directly. This is extremely important, since this indirection allows the container to undertake certain distribution activities before passing on a client request to the implementation class. Although you are responsible for writing the life cycle and business logic interfaces, their implementation classes are generated automatically prior to deployment by container tools. These container tools read your XML deployment descriptor files and generate distribution code based on the XML declarations. This code may, for example, check the security principal of the calling client to see if the client is allowed to access a particular component class method, or it might start a transaction before the client request is forwarded to the component instance.

The next section explores these elements in more detail.

12.3 EJB Component Elements

There are four basic elements that make up an EJB component, namely the business logic interface (also known as the object interface), the life cycle interface (also known as the home interface), the EJB component class and the XML deployment descriptor. The component class is where you write the business logic code and implement certain life cycle callback methods. The life cycle interface is where you define methods concerned with creating new instances of EJBs and finding existing EJBs. The precise semantics of these methods depends on the kind of EJB you are dealing with. The business logic interface is where you define the business methods for the EJB, such as `addToCart` or `getItems`. The XML deployment descriptor file is where you declare the distribution properties of one or more EJB components. The file may be shared by several EJBs. Entity EJBs may also have a fifth element called a primary key class, a description of which will be given in Chapter 14.

Since EJB 2.0, two new kinds of interface have been introduced: the local life cycle interface and the local business logic interface. These are discussed next. Since EJB 2.1, a further client interface has been introduced, namely the Web service endpoint interface, allowing access to stateless session EJBs via JAX-RPC (Java's API to SOAP). We discuss this further in Chapter 33.

12.3.1 Local and Remote Interfaces

Until EJB 2.0 there was only one type of life cycle and business logic interface, namely the remote type. These interfaces are actually RMI remote interfaces, and hence support remote communication via the RMI distribution mechanism. Since EJB 2.0, a second type of life cycle and business logic interface is available, the local type. As these interfaces are not RMI interfaces, they only support communication within the same JVM.

In Section 12.3.2 we will examine the steps that must be followed to define a local or remote interface. What therefore are the characteristics of these two types of interface?

Remote clients are supported by remote interfaces:

- EJBs communicating with each other via remote interfaces are location-independent of one another. That is, the client bean could be located on a completely different EJB server to the one supporting the server EJB. This provides loose coupling between EJBs, giving you the flexibility to move server EJBs without affecting the clients, since RMI hides their true location. The client and server EJBs may even be collocated in the same JVM.
- RMI-IIOP (Internet Inter-ORB Protocol) must be supported as a possible communication protocol. This means that in addition to calls made from Java application clients and EJBs, calls to EJBs may also be made by CORBA clients, written perhaps in languages other than Java.
- Method parameters are passed by value. Primitive parameters (`int`s, `double`s etc) are copied across the network. Parameters of a type `rmi.Remote` are not copied. Instead, a new remote reference (object stub) is created within the server. Other kinds of object are copied, but only if they are of type `java.io.Serializable`. Actually, the specification states that the parameters must be CORBA-compliant.
- Communication using the RMI call stack is an expensive operation. Several levels of software must be passed through during the call, a stub object must be created, distributed garbage collection must be managed, and method parameter values must be marshalled into byte streams that are then unmarshalled in the server. It is therefore a good idea to design J2EE software that requires the minimum number of RMI calls to be made. This leads to coarse-grained EJBs, where the EJBs form the master components in a master-to-detail relationship between EJBs.
- Since communication occurs across the RMI-IIOP and TCP/IP transport stacks, communication failures may occur. This might be because the physical communication link goes down or the remote server becomes unavailable. Consequently, your code will need to be able to handle such communication failures.

Local clients are supported by local interfaces:

- A local interface may be accessed exclusively by local EJB clients. Both must be deployed in the same container.
- The RMI-IIOP call stack is not used during communication. Instead, normal Java method calling is used. However, it is important to realize that EJB client calls are made via local interface objects that delegate to the server EJB object. This gives these interface objects the opportunity, among other tasks, to validate the caller's security principal against allowed security roles for the target method, and to start or propagate a transaction.

- The use of normal method calling means that object parameters are passed by reference; that is, the target EJB receives an object reference rather than a copy of the object. Primitive values are copied in the normal Java way. Remote reference objects are passed like any other kind of object reference. For those reasons, this difference between remote and local interface parameter passing semantics must be taken into account when developing EJB components. First, it has an impact on communication performance. Local interfaces allow for a relatively low communication overhead, whereas remote interfaces lead to high communication overheads, resulting from the expense of marshalling and unmarshalling parameters and the copying of objects. Second, changes made to a non-primitive object parameter received by a target EJB through a local interface will affect the client's copy of the object, that is, normal Java semantics. However, changes made to an object parameter received by a target EJB through a remote interface will not affect the client's copy of the object. Third, since communication is local it is unnecessary to program for RMI `RemoteException` exceptions.
- The implications of local interfaces are that they are particularly appropriate in containers where EJBs are tightly coupled and where the use of remote interfaces would prove to be too slow and unnecessary. Local interfaces are therefore useful when supporting the master-to-detail relationship between entity EJBs, this relationship being maintained internally within the container.

An EJB component can have both remote and local interfaces. For instance, an entity EJB could expose infrequently called business logic interface methods that convey coarse-grained data through remote interfaces and expose frequently called business logic interface methods that convey fine-grained data through local interfaces.

12.3.2 The Process of Developing and Deploying EJB Components in a Nutshell

There are a number of steps you need to follow when developing an EJB component. Most are common to all EJBs. These generic steps are described below.

First, define the business scope of your EJB and represent its business interface as one or two business logic interfaces. You need to decide what the business methods are and whether they are to be published remotely or constrained to be accessed locally within the same container by other EJBs. Performance issues that must be considered when defining these methods and deciding whether they are local or remote. You should also apply the usual object-oriented design principles. Will the EJB have a high level of cohesion? That is, do the business methods belong to the EJB or should the EJB be split into two EJBs? Only logically related methods should be grouped. Also, try to reduce coupling between the EJBs, especially between remote EJBs. Where there is a high level of interaction between the two EJBs, this may indicate that the EJBs should be coalesced, or perhaps the methods redesigned to reduce the number of interactions required.

Next, define the life cycle interfaces for your EJB. Will you only, for instance, allow the EJB to be created, destroyed and found locally within a container, or will remote clients be granted access to this interface? The methods defined in the life cycle interface also vary depending on the kind of EJB you are defining.

Once you have defined the external interfaces of your EJB, you can define the substance of the EJB as the EJB component class. You will have to write the code for all the business methods defined in the business logic interface and you will also need to define some of the methods defined in the life cycle interface, depending on the kind of EJB you are developing. Moreover, you will also need to write certain container life cycle callback methods, discussed in later chapters.

The final major development task is to define the deployment descriptors for one or more EJBs. These are written in one or more XML files. One of these files will contain standard EJB descriptors, whereas other files will container EJB server-specific deployment information not defined in the EJB specification. Among other things the standard descriptors define:

- the elements of each EJB; for example, the fully qualified names of the local and remote interfaces and the component class
- the type of each EJB; for example, whether it is a session, entity or message-driven bean
- the transaction properties of each EJB business and life cycle method
- the security properties of each EJB business and life cycle method
- the external resources required by each EJB

We will look at these descriptors in some detail in each of the EJB chapters.

Finally, after compiling the Java class files, we combine them in a standard directory structure with the XML deployment descriptor files. Usually, this structure is packaged up into a jar file. The deployment process is server-specific. In JBoss the jar file, or directory structure, can simply be placed within a directory called `deploy` that forms part of the JBoss installation. JBoss will detect this and deploy the EJBs. Weblogic 6+ has a similar mechanism, but requires a pre-processing step that generates the code classes for the EJB local and remote interfaces. We discuss JBoss-specific deployment issues in subsequent chapters. We now examine the EJB elements in more detail.

12.3.3 The EJB Component Classes and Interfaces

The classes and interfaces that comprise an EJB component are shown in Figures 12.2 and 12.3. Figure 12.2 contains the classes and interfaces for a shopping cart EJB that has remote interfaces. Figure 12.3 is a version that has local interfaces.

In both figures the light grey boxes denote J2EE predefined framework interfaces. The full package names are given. The white boxes denote the interfaces and classes that you write, and the dark grey boxes denote classes that are generated automatically by container tools.

To define a remote EJB, you must write interfaces that extend the predefined `EJBHome` and `EJBObject` interfaces. These, in turn, extend the `java.rmi.Remote` interface discussed in Chapter 5. This shows the link with RMI, since RMI is used as the transport mechanism by J2EE servers to achieve remote communication. The methods defined in `EJBHome`, `EJBObject`, `EJBLocalHome` and `EJBLocalObject` are shown in Figures 12.4 and 12.5. We will discuss these methods in later chapters. After defining the interfaces you write the component class, in this case `ShoppingCartBean`. This must implement one of three interfaces: `SessionBean` (as in this case), `EntityBean` or `MessageDrivenBean`, depending on the kind of EJB you are developing. These interfaces are shown in Figure 12.4, and are

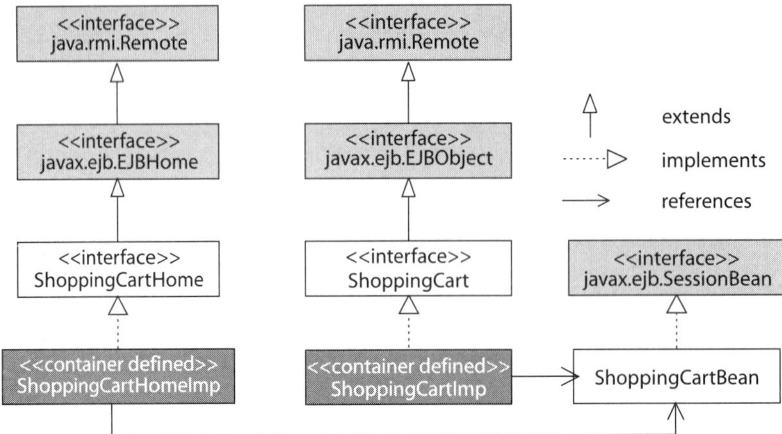

Figure 12.2 The elements that make up a remote EJB.

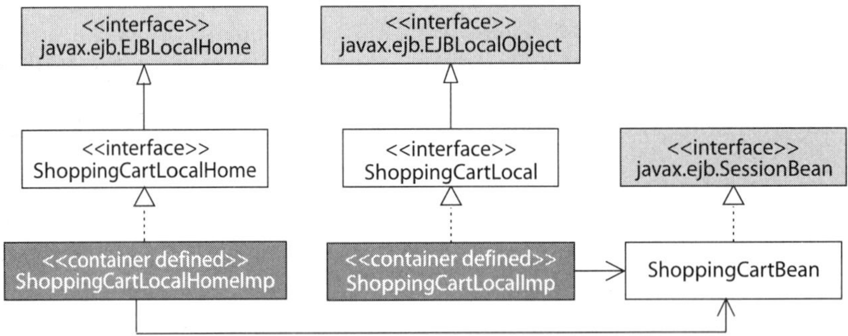

Figure 12.3 The elements that make up a local EJB.

discussed further in later chapters. The final pieces of the EJB are generated automatically by container tools; that is, `ShoppingCartHomeImp` and `ShoppingCartImp`. The actual names of these classes will vary between servers. Objects of these classes act as a gateway to your component class object; that is, all incoming client communication must go via one of these gateway objects. They check for security violations, start transactions and undertake other distribution plumbing tasks on behalf of your implementation class. Notice that they have references to your component class; that is, they will "know" how to forward client requests to relevant methods in your class. Precisely how this is done is server-dependent. It is also important to note that your component class does not directly implement these interfaces. We will discuss the reasons for this in Chapter 15.

Defining a local EJB is done in almost the same manner as defining a remote EJB. In this case the `ShoppingCartLocalHome` extends `EJBLocalHome` and `ShoppingCartLocal` extends `EJBLocalObject`. Of course, you could define a hybrid EJB with four interfaces, two being remote and two being local. Other combinations are also possible.

There are some common class and interface naming conventions that you may wish to follow. For remote EJBs, all life cycle (home) interfaces have the name of the EJB, in this case `ShoppingCart`, with the word `Home` appended. The business logic interface has the name of the EJB. Local interfaces also have the name `Local` inserted into the interface name. For both remote and local EJBs, the component class has the EJB name appended with the word `Bean`. Of course, you might decide to use a different naming convention, but make sure you are consistent in its use to avoid confusion.

The methods that you write in each of the interfaces and the class depend partly on the kind of EJB you are developing, and we will look at this in detail in later chapters. However, we can make a few general remarks here. First, all methods in the remote interfaces must declare that they throw either `java.rmi.RemoteException` or `java.lang.Exception`. This is because communication failures of various kinds may occur when clients interact with remote EJBs. Note that any corresponding methods in the component class do not necessarily have to declare that they also throw `RemoteException` or `Exception`. This makes sense, since the exception will normally be generated as a result of a communication failure somewhere between the component class and the client, and not by the EJB itself. Also, all remote interface object parameters must either be serializable or remote references.

Finally, the predefined interfaces and classes available to you are shown in Figures 12.4 and 12.5. Apart from `java.rmi.Remote` they all belong to the `javax.ejb` package. Notice the three types of EJB that are supported and that they are related through a common

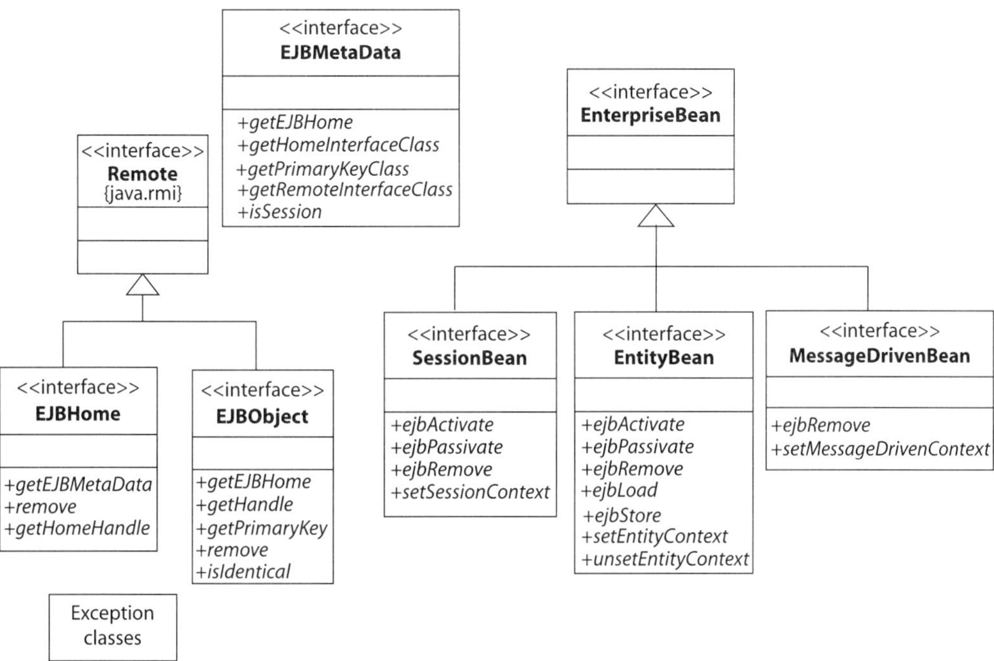

Figure 12.4 Interfaces of the `javax.ejb` package (1).

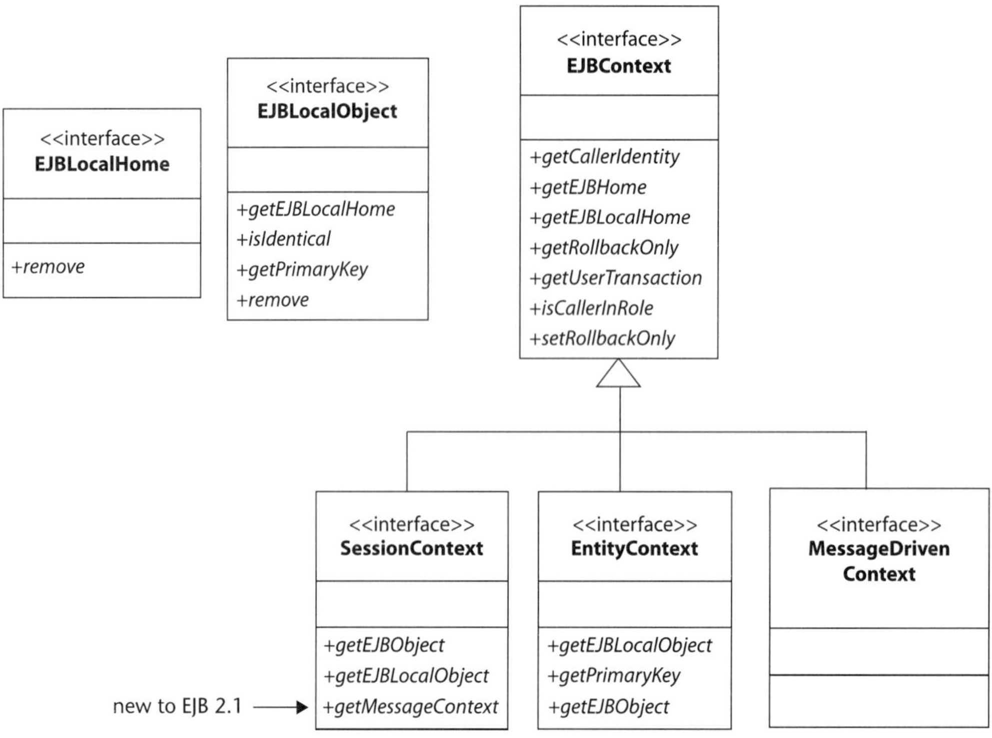

Figure 12.5 Interfaces of the `javax.ejb` package (2).

super-interface. Also notice the `EJBContext` interfaces. As we will see later, these allow your component class to obtain information about itself.

12.4 Accessing EJBs From a Java Application Client

Once we have defined and deployed an EJB, how do we access it from a client? A client could be a Java application, applet, servlet, JSP, another EJB or a CORBA client. Listing 12.1 contains a simple client application that uses JNDI (see Chapter 6) to obtain a remote reference to the `ShoppingCartHome` life cycle interface object. We assume in this application that the system properties contain appropriate values for, at least, `Context.INITIAL_CONTEXT_FACTORY` and `Context.PROVIDER_URL`. This could be done on the command line (as a `-D` option) or as a properties file placed on the classpath. Alternatvely, you can supply a `Properties` object with appropriate values as a parameter to the `InitialContext` constructor. For JBoss the values required are:

```
Context.INITIAL_CONTEXT_FACTORY:
  java.naming.factory.initial=org.jnp.interfaces.NamingContextFactory
```

```
Context.INITIAL_PROVIDER_URL:
  java.naming.provider.url=jnp://localhost:1099
Context.URL_PKG_PREFIXES:
  java.naming.factory.url.pkgs=org.jboss.naming:org.jnp.interfaces
```

The value for the provider URL will depend on where the JBoss server is running and the port number it is listening on.

In J2EE, there is a recommended naming convention for J2EE resource entries stored in the J2EE naming service. EJBs remote references are placed somewhere under the `ejb` context, data sources under the `jdbc` context, JMS resources under the `jms` context, and so on.

Listing 12.1 Java application access to an EJB using JNDI.

```
import store.*;
import javax.rmi.PortableRemoteObject;
import javax.naming.*;
public class Client {

  public static void main(String args[])throws Exception {
    // Obtain the default JNDI naming service initial context
    Context jndiCtx = new InitialContext();
    // Search for a particular EJB and narrow the type
    Object objRef = jndiCtx.lookup("ejb/cart");
    ShoppingCartHome shopH =
        (ShoppingCartHome)PortableRemoteObject.narrow(objRef,
                ShoppingCartHome.class);
    // We now create a new cart
    ShoppingCart cart = shopH.create("cwl");

    // Now exercise the business methods
    cart.add("Bread");
    // Etc...
  }
}
```

Examples discussed in Chapter 6 used a Java cast to narrow the type of the value returned by `lookup`. This cannot be done when accessing EJB resources from a J2EE naming service. Instead, a special `narrow` method must be used. The reason is that the naming service may contain references to CORBA server objects. CORBA allows you to develop server objects using a variety of languages. Many of these languages do not support a cast operator. Consequently, CORBA provides an alternative mechanism to achieve the same result. This is the `narrow` method. In Java, this can be found as a static method in the class `PortableRemoteObject`. This method is defined to take the object reference returned by `lookup` and the type of the object you wish to narrow to, in this case `ShoppingCartHome`.

The `class` attribute will generate a `Class` object that can then be used internally by `narrow` to create and return the remote reference.

Once a remote reference to the life cycle interface object has been obtained, the application uses it to create a new `ShoppingCart` business logic interface object on the server and to return a remote reference to this object to the client. This `create` method takes an initialization parameter, in this case a user identifier. We will look at `create` and other life cycle methods in more detail in later chapters. Finally, as shown in the listing, once we have a remote reference to the business logic interface object we can call its business methods, in this case `add`.

12.5 Reference

DeMichiel, L. G. *et al.* (2001). *Enterprise JavaBeans Specification Version 2.0.* Sun Microsystems.

DeMichiel, L. G. *et al.* (2002). *Enterprise JavaBeans Specification Version 2.1*, Sun Microsystems, Proposed Final Draft.

Chapter 13

Stateless Session EJBs

13.1 Introduction

The first kind of EJB we will look at is the session EJB, and in particular its lightweight incarnation, the stateless session EJB. We will look at its other form, the stateful session EJB, in Chapter 30.

What are the main characteristics of both kinds of session EJB? Unlike entity EJBs, session EJBs do not represent persistent data; that is, if they contain data the container will not automatically synchronize that data with an underlying data store. If you wish to make a session EJB's data persistent, then you must do it explicitly in your code using an appropriate API, such as JDBC. The main reason for using session EJBs is to encapsulate business logic, where each EJB contains a coherent set of business methods. Very often, they act as coordinators of other EJBs as part of a business control workflow, for example a funds transfer handler session EJB that will contain a `transfer` method that coordinates the transfer of funds between two account entity EJBs and records that transfer in a transaction audit entity EJB. They also often act as a façade between client code and other EJBs, in particular entity EJBs. Indeed, such façade session EJBs may represent a client login session of some kind, hence the name. We discuss these issues further in Chapter 15. Use session EJBs if you do not need to store persistent data, and/or where your EJBs need to coordinate other EJBs, and/or where you need to insulate a client from too much detail. There are other reasons why you might wish to use session EJBs over entity EJBs. We will discuss this further in Chapter 15.

What are the distinguishing characteristics of stateless session EJBs? Unlike stateful session EJBs, stateless session EJBs do not retain client-provided data between method invocations. If a client calls method `addBook` on a `cart` session EJB that happens to be declared as being stateless, then a call of `getBooks` on the same EJB will probably not return the book previously entered, even though the `cart` component class stores the books in an instance variable. At first sight this appears very strange, but the reasons will become apparent in the next section, where we also discuss the motivation for using stateless session EJBs.

Another distinguishing feature of stateless session EJBs is their ability to act as Web service end-points. No other kind of EJB can be used for this purpose. This feature is new to the EJB 2.1 specification. We discuss this further in Chapter 33.

13.2 Stateless Session EJB Life Cycle

Figure 13.1 is a state diagram that illustrates the states that a stateless session EJB instance can be in during its lifetime! This sounds like an oxymoron. However, there are two meanings attached to the word *state*. "Stateless" refers to that fact that these EJBs do not store client-specific state. The "state" in state diagram refers to life cycle states, of which there are two, *does not exist* and *ready pool*.

An EJB is in the *does not exist* state prior to its instance creation or just after it has been garbage collected. The EJB is in the *ready pool* state when an instance has been created from its component class. The container, and only the container, is responsible for moving stateless session EJBs between these two states. The transition to the *ready pool* state will occur for several reasons. Just after the EJB component has been deployed, the container reads the EJB's deployment descriptor and discovers that it is a stateless session EJB. For performance reasons, the container maintains a free pool of instances for a stateless session EJB. Consequently, at the point of deployment the container usually populates this pool with *N* instances if the EJB. Normally, the value of *N* is calculated from information provided in server-specific deployment descriptors and the current server resource usage statistics. The latter will also influence the transition to the *does not exist* state; that is, the container may decide to conserve and balance resources by removing some instances of the EJB from the free pool. Instances will also be removed at the point of server shutdown, EJB undeployment, or when an instance throws an unchecked exception or `RemoteException`.

There are two methods that get called by the container when the EJB transitions between the two states. These methods must be declared in your implementation class. They are life cycle callback methods invoked by the container to let your EJB "know" that it is moving between life cycle states. You may wish to write code in these methods to react to these events. Although typically empty, you may wish to open a handle on a resource (such as a database)

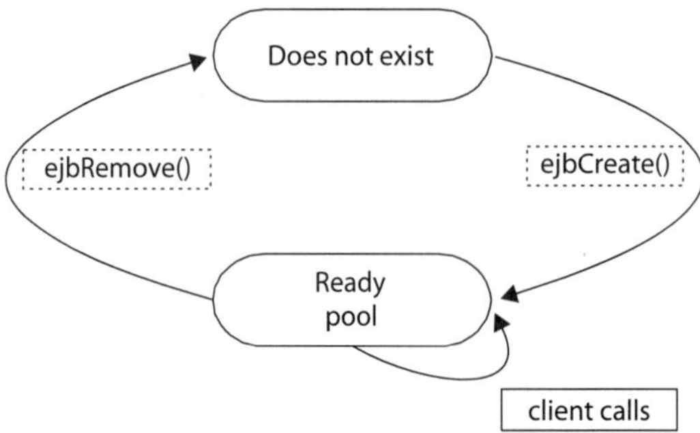

Figure 13.1 The life cycle of the stateless session EJB.

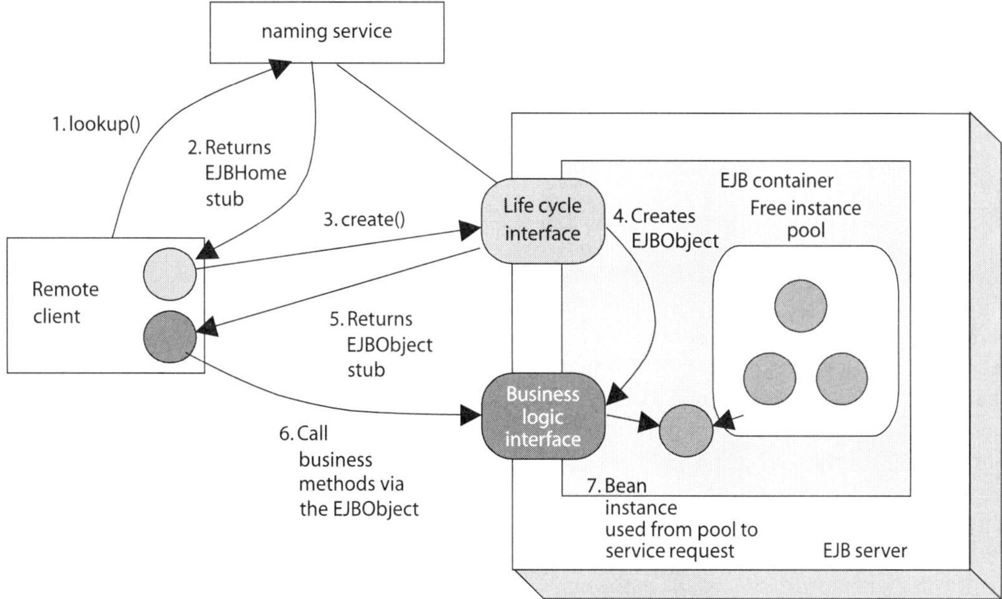

Figure 13.2 A scenario of interaction between a client and a stateless session EJB.

in `ejbCreate` and then close it in `ejbRemove`. When a stateless session EJB is in the *ready pool* state it can service incoming client requests. Let us examine this in more detail.

Figure 13.2 illustrates a sequence of interaction events between a client and a stateless session EJB. This scenario involves the client obtaining a stub (remote reference) to the EJB's life cycle interface, and then calling the `create` method on this stub, which returns a stub to the EJB's business logic interface. Once it has obtained this stub the client is able to invoke business methods on the EJB.

Before looking at the interactions in detail we need to go back one step to the deployment stage. At deployment, the container will do three main things. First, it will populate a free pool with EJB instances. Second, it will create an instance of the EJB's life cycle interface class. Depending on the server, it may need to generate the code for the interface's implementation class. JBoss is an example of this. Alternatively, the code may have been generated using some other server tool at an earlier stage (e.g. the `ejbc` command in Weblogic). Third, the container registers the life cycle interface object with the J2EE naming service. The name used to bind the object within the naming service name tree (such as `ejb/till`) is specified in the deployment descriptor files. Let us now examine the sequence of interactions in more detail:

Steps 1–2: The client does a JNDI lookup (using a lookup name such as `ejb/till`) to obtain the stub for the EJB.

Steps 3–4: The client calls the `create` method on the stub. The life cycle interface object will ensure that the client has sufficient security access rights to perform this operation. In stateless session EJBs the `create` method does not create an instance of the implementation class; rather, it creates an instance of the business logic interface class. Remember, it is only the container that initiates the creation of instances in the free pool.

Step 5: The stub for the business logic interface object is returned to the client as the return value of `create`.

Step 6: The client can now execute business methods by using the business logic interface stub.

Step 7: When the business logic interface object receives a client request, it will do several things. First, it will check that the client has sufficient security access right to invoke the method. Second, it may start a transaction (discussed in Chapter 27). Third, it invokes the real business method on an arbitrary but currently unused EJB instance in the free pool. As soon as the method returns control to the container, the EJB will be free to service another client request.

Step 7 is important, and distinguishes stateless session EJBs from their stateful cousins. An EJB instance is not permanently associated with the client's business logic interface object. Instead, a different instance is used to service each incoming request. The advantage of this is that a small number of instances can service a large number of client requests. If an instance was permanently associated with a specific client (as is the case with a stateful session EJB) then that instance would be free to service only that client's requests; more EJB instances would be required within the container. For this reason, stateless session EJBs are often referred to as lightweight session EJBs, whereas stateful session EJBs are considered heavyweight.

This sharing of instances among clients is also the reason they are termed stateless. Client-provided data passed into an instance (such as using the `cart.addBook` method referred to at the start of this chapter) will be stored in that instance of the EJB. However, when the client calls `cart.getItems` to retrieve the list of his or her books the call may be directed to a completely different instance, containing quite different data. Consequently, stateless session EJBs are not suitable for storing client specific data. Imagine using stateless session EJBs for storing account information! However, although they are termed stateless, there is nothing preventing you from storing shared, non-client data within stateless session EJBs. This could include shared database or JMS connections, perhaps to hook into read-only resources such as stock quote feeds.

From the above we can see that stateless session EJBs are useful, for performance reasons, if you want to encapsulate business workflow, and where you do not need to store client-specific data between client method calls on the EJB. Of course, this does not mean you should never pass client-specific data into a stateless session EJB. It is not a problem if this data is only used by the business logic for the duration of the call, or the EJB passes the data onto another kind of EJB that can store client-specific data.

Figure 13.2 shows only one scenario of interactions. Other scenarios are also possible. For example, the business logic interface inherits the `remove` method from `EJBObject`/`EJBLocalObject`. If the client calls this method then the business logic interface object is destroyed. Note that this does not cause an EJB instance to be removed from the free pool; only the container decides when that should happen. Another possibility is that the remote stub goes out of stack-scope within the client, leading to its garbage collection. As mentioned in Chapter 4, if a reference to a remote RMI server object is not used within a certain leasehold time period, the remote reference count for that object is decremented by one. It is eligible for garbage collection if this becomes zero and there are no local references to the object.

13.3 The Process of Developing a Stateless Session EJB

The process is almost identical to that described in Section 12.3.2. Let us summarize it again here:

- Write the local and remote business interfaces; what the EJB does.
- Write the local and remote life cycle interfaces; how to "create" a stateless session EJB.
- Write the implementation class; the implementation of the business logic.
- Write the deployment descriptors as part of one or more XML files.
- Deploy on the EJB server. The exact process depends on the server.

Each of these will be examined in the following sections, using the bookstore application to illustrate each step. Figure 13.3 shows the interfaces and component class for the `Till` stateless session EJB. This EJB forms a small part of the bookstore application, being responsible for calculating the price of the contents of a shopping cart. A stateless session EJB can be used for this task, since no client-specific state is stored in the `Till` EJB. Also, the `Till` encapsulates business logic that can be reused both at runtime by many clients and, because it is sufficiently generic, during project development in several different projects. An alternative approach could have been to create an ordinary `Till` class and used that internally by other EJBs. This would be fine if you knew that the `Till` did not require its own security and transaction properties, and was always collocated with those EJBs. Making the `Till` an EJB provides you with a greater degree of deployment flexibility. However, the trade-off is the performance overhead associated with the `TillHomeImp` and `TillImp` objects intercepting all client requests.

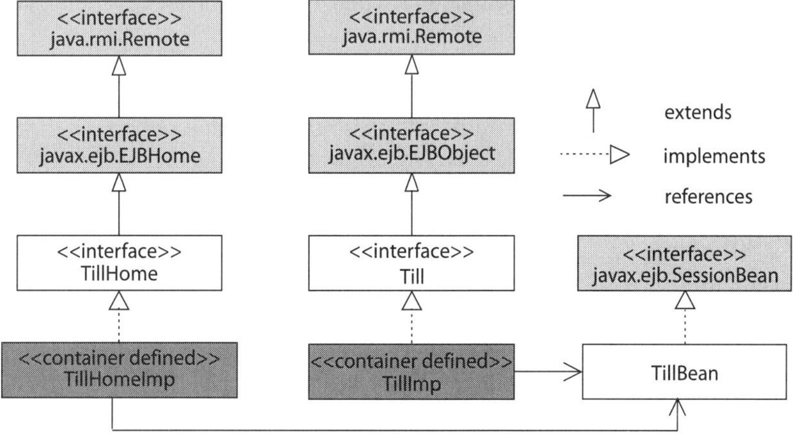

Figure 13.3 `Till` interfaces and implementation class.

13.4 The Business Logic Interface

Listing 13.1 is the code for the Till remote business logic interface. This is also often referred to as the remote EJBObject interface. The interface declares the business methods of the EJB. In this case there is a single method, getTotal that takes an array of Book objects and returns the total price of those books as a double. The parameters must either be primitive, serializable or remote references. More precisely they must conform to CORBA's Java parameter typing rules. Declaring Till to extend EJBObject means that the interface is remote. That is, distributed clients are able to access the Till EJB over an RMI protocol, either JRMP (Java Remote Method Protocol) or RMI-IIOP (Internet Inter-ORB Protocol). The latter must be supported by all J2EE 1.3, and above, compliant servers.

Listing 13.1 The Till remote business logic interface.

```
import javax.ejb.EJBObject;
import java.rmi.RemoteException;
public interface Till extends EJBObject {
  public double getTotal(Book[] items)
    throws RemoteException;
}
```

The super-interface, EJBObject, contains the methods:

```
public EJBHome getEJBHome() throws RemoteException;
public Handle getHandle() throws RemoteException;
public Object getPrimaryKey() throws RemoteException;
public void remove() throws RemoteException, RemoveException;
public boolean isIdentical(EJBObject other) throws RemoteException;
```

The getEJBHome method returns the life cycle interface stub for the EJB. For a stateless session EJB the remove method removes the container's business logic interface object. It does not remove an instance of the EJB. The RemoveException is thrown by the container if the operation is not permitted, perhaps for security reasons. This is more likely to be the case with other kinds of EJB. The getHandle method returns a handle object that can be safely serialized and then deserialized at a later date. The isIdentical method returns true if the two business logic interface objects are the same. The getPrimaryKey method is only applicable to entity EJBs. Calling it on another kind of EJB will result in RemoteException being thrown. This exception is also thrown for all the methods if there is a communication problem or the business logic interface object is unavailable for some reason; perhaps it has been garbage collected due to a connection leasehold timeout (see Chapter 4).

The local interface version of Till is shown in Listing 13.2.

Listing 13.2 The TillLocal business logic interface.

```
import javax.ejb.EJBLocalObject;
public interface TillLocal extends EJBLocalObject {
```

```
  public double getTotal(Book[] items);
}
```

Extending EJBLocalObject declares the interface to be local. Notice that getTotal does not throw RemoteException. The super-interface EJBLocalHome contains the same methods as EJBObject except that getEJBHome is replaced by getEJBLocalHome. Also, all the methods throw EJBException rather than RemoteException, the latter being inappropriate for local error reporting. EJBException is an unchecked exception used to wrap up other kinds of exception. Chapter 27 will discuss this exception further in the context of transactions. For stateless session EJBs it is unlikely that the container will have cause to throw this exception. This is not the case for other kinds of EJB, where EJB component class instance life cycles are more under the control of a client.

13.5 The Life Cycle Interface

Listing 13.3 is the code for the TillHome life cycle interface. For stateless session EJBs, the only method you can define in this interface is create. Also, this method must not take any parameters. This is because the create method is really just a request to the container to create a business logic interface object, not an component class instance. Consequently, the container does not delegate the create request to an instance. Also, for other kinds of EJB, create is used to pass in client-specific initialization data to a newly created EJB. Stateless session EJBs cannot support this kind of data, for reasons discussed earlier.

The create method must be declared to throw CreateException and RemoteException. CreateException can be thrown by the container if it fails to create the business logic interface object.

Listing 13.3 The TillHome life cycle interface.

```
import javax.ejb.EJBHome;
import java.rmi.RemoteException;
public interface TillHome extends EJBHome {
  public Till create()
          throws CreateException, RemoteException;
}
```

The super-interface, EJBHome contains the following methods:

```
public EJBMetaData getEJBMetaData() throws RemoteException;
public HomeHandle getHomeHandle() throws RemoteException;
public void remove(Handle handle)
       throws RemoteException, RemoveException;
public void remove(Object primaryKey)
       throws RemoteException, RemoveException;
```

The getEJBMetaData method returns an object that can be used to obtain further information on the EJB, such as the Class objects for the life cycle and business logic interfaces and for the implementation class. This is useful if you have a generic application that wishes to discover, through Java reflection, the interface methods of the EJB. The EJBMetaData class also has the methods isSession and isStatelessSession that allow a client to test what kind of EJB it is dealing with.

The getHomeHandle method returns a HomeHandle object that can be safely serialized and then deserialized at a later date. The remove method that takes a Handle will remove the business logic interface object identified by that handle. The other remove method is only applicable to entity EJBs.

Listing 13.4 is the code for TillLocalHome. It is identical to TillHome except that all references to RemoteException are removed, and we inherit from EJBLocalHome.

Listing 13.4 The TillLocalHome life cycle interface.

```
import javax.ejb.EJBLocalHome;
public interface TillLocalHome extends EJBLocalHome {
  public Till create()
    throws CreateException;
}
```

The super-interface, EJBLocalHome, contains just one method, remove, which takes a primary key. This is not used by stateless session EJBs.

13.6 The Component Class

The component class contains the actual business logic code. Listing 13.5 contains code for the TillBean implementation class.

Listing 13.5 The TillBean component class.

```
import javax.ejb.SessionBean;
import javax.ejb.SessionContext;
public class TillBean implements SessionBean {
  private SessionContext ctx;

  public void setSessionContext(SessionContext ctx) {
    this.ctx = ctx;
  }

  public void ejbActivate() {}
  public void ejbPassivate() {}

  public void ejbRemove() {
    // Close any resources prior to garbage collection
```

```
  }

  public void ejbCreate() {
    // Open any required resources when free pool populated
    // by the container
  }

  // Business logic methods
  public double getTotal(Book[] items) {
    double cost = 0.0;
    for (int i=0; i<items.length; i++) {
      cost += items[i].getPrice();
    }
    return cost;
  }
}
```

Since the Till is a session EJB we must implement the SessionBean interface. The other two interfaces are EntityBean and MessageDrivenBean. The SessionBean interface declares the methods:

```
public void setSessionContext(SessionContext ctx) throws EJBException;
public void ejbActivate() throws EJBException;
public void ejbPassivate() throws EJBException;
public void ejbRemove() throws EJBException;
```

These methods are called by the container when it wishes to "tell" your EJB that a certain life cycle event has occurred. The ejbRemove method is called by the container just prior to garbage collection of the EJB implementation object. This gives your EJB the opportunity to close any open resources, such as database or JMS connections. In our example, there were no resources to close.

The methods ejbActivate and ejbPassivate are not invoked on stateless session EJBs since they are specific to stateful session EJBs and will be discussed in Chapter 30. These methods will always be empty in stateless session EJBs.

The final life cycle method is setSessionContext. This is discussed below.

There is only one business method to implement, getTotal. This takes an array of books and calculates the overall cost of these books as a double. This is then returned to the caller.

13.6.1 The Session Context Object

The setSessionContext method is called by the container just after it has created the EJB object. It takes a SessionContext object that is maintained by the container. It is good practice to save this object reference in an instance variable, as the object provides life cycle context information about the EJB that may be required by the EJB's methods at a later stage. The SessionContext interface is declared as follows:

```
public interface SessionContext extends EJBContext {
  public EJBObject getEJBObject() throws java.lang.IllegalStateException;
  public EJBLocalObject getEJBLocalObject()
    throws java.lang.IllegalStateException;
}
```

The super-interface, EJBContext, is declared as:

```
public interface EJBContext {
  public java.security.Principal getCallerPrincipal();
  public EJBHome getEJBHome() throws java.lang.IllegalStateException;
  public EJBLocalHome getEJBLocalHome()
    throws java.lang.IllegalStateException;
  public boolean getRollbackOnly() throws java.lang.IllegalStateException;
  public javax.transaction.UserTransaction getUserTransaction()
  public Boolean isCallerInRole(String roleName);
  public void setRollbackOnly() throws java.lang.IllegalStateException;
}
```

The methods getEJBObject, getEJBLocalObject, getEJBHome and getEJBLocalHome all return a reference to the EJB's respective interface object. The exception IllegalStateException will be thrown if the implementation object is not associated with the relevant interface object. For example, when an EJB is deployed the container will create instances of the EJB component class, call their setSessionContext methods and then create instances of the life cycle interfaces. The exception will be thrown if the EJB calls getEJBHome or getEJBLocalHome before the life cycle interfaces (i.e. home interfaces) have been created. The exception will also be thrown if your EJB calls getEJBObject or getEJBLocalObject while waiting in the free pool to service client requests. Stateless session EJBs are only associated with business logic interface objects while servicing a client request. The exception will also be thrown if your EJB tries to obtain a reference to a local interface where you have only defined a remote interface, or vice versa.

Why would the EJB need access to its own interface objects? Sometimes it is useful for an EJB to pass a reference to itself to another EJB. For example, a stock portfolio EJB might want to register itself with a stock feed EJB, with the intention that the portfolio EJB is "told" of any changes to that stock. This is analogous to Swing, where listener objects are registered with Swing components, so that when a GUI event occurs the listeners are informed. Since all EJB communication is via reference objects, it is these reference objects (or stubs in the case of remote interfaces) that are passed as method parameter values. We cannot pass the reference "this" to another EJB.

The other EJBContext methods will be discussed in later chapters.

13.6.2 Why Doesn't the Component Class "Implement" the Business or Life Cycle Interfaces?

You might be surprised to see that TillBean does not directly implement the TillHome and Till interfaces. This is because these interfaces inherit system provided methods from EJBObject,

EJBHome and their local counterparts. Clearly, you should not have to implement these methods. Rather, these methods are implemented within classes automatically generated by the container tools prior to deployment.

The consequence of this is that the compiler will not check that TillBean implements all the business logic interface methods defined in Till, in this case just getTotal. Any inconsistencies will not be found until deployment, and deployment error messages are notoriously difficult to understand. However, there is a way of forcing compile-time checking. Listing 13.6 illustrates how to achieve this for the Till EJB. We have introduced another interface, TillMethods, that contains the business method declarations. We then implement this within TillBean using Java's implements clause. The compiler will now check that TillBean has implemented getTotal correctly. The Till interface will extend both EJBObject and TillMethods, and so will declare getTotal as being a client accessible business method.

Listing 13.6 Forcing compiler checking of business methods.

```
import java.rmi.RemoteException;
public interface TillMethods {
  public double getTotal(Book[] items) throws RemoteException;
}

import javax.ejb.EJBObject;
public interface Till extends EJBObject, TillMethods {
  // No business methods are defined here
}

import javax.ejb.SessionBean;
import javax.ejb.SessionContext;
public class TillBean implements SessionBean, TillMethods {
  // Code as before
}
```

13.7 The Deployment Descriptor Files

The final development step is to configure the deployment properties of the stateless session EJB. In EJB 1.1 and above standard deployment descriptor information is specified using XML and saved in a file called ejb-jar.xml. Container tools use this information when generating implementation code for the business logic and life cycle interfaces and for configuring the J2EE application server.

The standard deployment descriptors specify information such as:

- The elements that comprise an EJB component.
- Whether a session EJB is stateful or stateless.
- The transaction and security properties of the EJB.

Other server-specific deployment files allow you to define server-specific configuration information.

13.7.1 The ejb-jar.xml File

Listing 13.7 is a listing of the ejb-jar.xml file for the Till EJB. The first line declares the version of XML. This is followed by the document type declaration. This declares that the root tag is ejb-jar and gives the URL for the document type definition (DTD) file. The DTD is a Sun standard DTD for EJB 2.0. In XML, DTD files define the tags allowed in an XML document and their ordering and structure.

The remainder of the file defines the deployment properties of the Till EJB. Usually several EJBs are defined in the same descriptor file and then packaged and deployed together. We will see examples of this in later chapters.

After the <ejb-jar> root tag, there is a mandatory <enterprise-beans> tag. This will contain one or more EJB definitions, in this case just one. The optional <session> tag declares the properties of a session EJB. As with other types of EJB, this starts with the mandatory <ejb-name> tag. This declares a unique name for the EJB that can be referred to from other parts of the file and from server-specific deployment files. This is followed by between two and four tags that declare the business logic and life cycle interfaces for the EJB. In this example, there is a remote life cycle interface (the <home> tag) and a remote business logic interface (the <remote> tag). Other EJBs might also, or instead of, declare local interfaces with the tags <local-home> and <local>. The <ejb-class> tag identifies Till's implementation class. All these tags contain a fully qualified class name.

The mandatory <session-type> tag declares whether the session EJB is Stateful or Stateless. The mandatory <transaction-type> tag declares whether the Container manages transactions or the Bean explicitly manages transactions. We discuss this in Chapter 27.

Listing 13.7 The ejb-jar.xml file for the Till EJB.

```
<?xml version="1.0"?>
<!DOCTYPE ejb-jar
  PUBLIC '-//Sun Microsystems, Inc.//DTD Enterprise JavaBeans 2.0//EN'
        'http://java.sun.com/j2ee/dtds/ejb-jar_2_0.dtd'>
<ejb-jar>
  <enterprise-beans>
      <session>
        <ejb-name>Till</ejb-name>
        <home>store.TillHome</home>
        <remote>store.Till</remote>
        <ejb-class>store.TillBean</ejb-class>
        <session-type>Stateless</session-type>
        <transaction-type>Container</transaction-type>
      </session>
  </enterprise-beans>
  <assembly-descriptor>
    <container-transaction>
```

```
        <method>
        <ejb-name>Till</ejb-name>
              <method-name>*</method-name>
            </method>
        <trans-attribute>Required</trans-attribute>
      </container-transaction>
    </assembly-descriptor>
  </ejb-jar>
```

We discuss the role of the <assembly-descriptor> tag and substructure in later chapters. However, notice the reference to the Till identifier, thereby linking this bit of the file to the main definition of Till.

Listing 13.8 is the equivalent for J2EE 1.4. In this version an XML schema reference is used instead. For a discussion of the differences between DTDs and XML schemas see Section 25.11. Note that in this example it is only the schema or DTD references that are different. For both listings the remaining tags remain the same. However, note that J2EE 1.4 has introduced new tags, and many of these are highlighted in subsequent chapters.

Listing 13.8 The ejb-jar.xml file for the Till EJB.

```
<?xml version="1.0"?>
<ejb-jar version = "2.1"
  xmlns = "http://java.sun.com/xml/ns/j2ee"
  xmlns:xsi = "http://www.w3.org/2001/XMLSchema-instance"
  xsi:schemaLocation = "http://java.sun.com/xml/ns/j2ee
                        "http://java.sun.com/xml/ns/j2ee/ejb-jar_2_1.xsd">

<ejb-jar>
  <enterprise-beans>
    <session>
      <ejb-name>Till</ejb-name>
      <home>store.TillHome</home>
      <remote>store.Till</remote>
      <ejb-class>store.TillBean</ejb-class>

      <session-type>Stateless</session-type>
      <transaction-type>Container</transaction-type>
    </session>
  </enterprise-beans>

  <assembly-descriptor>
    <container-transaction>
      <method>
        <ejb-name>Till</ejb-name>
        <method-name>*</method-name>
      </method>
```

```
      <trans-attribute>Required</trans-attribute>
    </container-transaction>
  </assembly-descriptor>
</ejb-jar>
```

13.7.2 The JBoss jboss.xml File

Listing 13.9 is a listing of the jboss.xml file for the Till bean.

Listing 13.9 The jboss.xml deployment descriptor file.

```
<?xml version="1.0"?>
<jboss>
  <enterprise-beans>
    <session>
      <ejb-name>Till</ejb-name>
      <jndi-name>ejb/till</jndi-name>
    </session>
  </enterprise-beans>
</jboss>
```

This JBoss-specific file mirrors the ejb-jar.xml file quite closely. It contains an <enterprise-beans> tag that declares properties for one or more EJBs, in this case just the Till session EJB. Among other things, this file provides us with the opportunity to specify the JNDI name for the TillHome object. We will see later that the client will refer to this name when executing a jndiCtx.lookup method.

When using JBoss, the jboss.xml file is optional. If it is omitted then the server will provide default configuration property values for server-specific properties, such as the JNDI name. For the latter, the server will use the value of the <ejb-name> tag as the EJB's JNDI name.

13.8 Deploying the EJB Component

Deploying an EJB component will vary between J2EE application servers. However, deployment units must conform to a standard directory and file structure. Figure 13.4 illustrates the standard structure. The deployment unit is represented by a file system directory and its contents. In this example the directory must contain a sub-directory called META-INF. This is where deployment descriptor files are placed, in this case ejb-jar.xml and jboss.xml. The server-specific deployment files will vary between servers and types of EJB.

The deployment unit also needs to contain all the class files that comprise the EJB components, in this case just the classes for the Till EJB. The directory structure reflects the Java package structure used for Till; that is, all the Till classes belong to the store

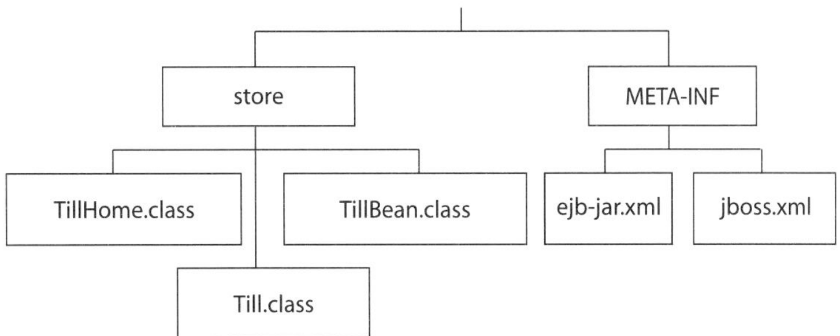

Figure 13.4 The deployment structure for the `Till` component.

package. Some servers will require you to generate and then include the implementation classes for your interfaces. This is true of Weblogic, but not of JBoss.

Most servers will allow you to deploy the directory structure in its uncompressed form. However, they all allow you to package up the deployment unit into a jar file:

```
jar -cf till.jar ./store ./META-INF
```

How you deploy this unit then depends on the server you use. On JBoss you simply copy the directory or jar file to the directory: `jboss-installation/.../deploy`. The JBoss server will detect the presence of the deployment unit, read the deployment descriptor files, generate and compile the implementation classes for the interfaces and then deploy your EJBs in appropriate containers. JBoss will also detect and deploy new versions of the same deployment unit.

13.9 Accessing the EJB From a Java Application Client

Listing 13.10 is a test Java application that exercises the `Till` EJB. The comments embedded in the code describe the algorithm.

Listing 13.10 A client application that uses the `Till` EJB.

```
package client;

import java.util.*;
import javax.naming.*;
import javax.rmi.*;

import store.TillHome;
import store.Till;
import store.Book;

/**
```

```
 * A simple client to test the Till EJB.
 * This simple client exercises the Till stateless EJB.
 * The client first creates an array of book items<br>
 * It then passes these books to the Till EJB requesting the total price<br>
 * It prints out the result returned by the (remote) EJB<p>
 */
public class Client {
  private TillHome home;

  public static void main(String [] args) {
    Client cl = new Client();
    cl.init();
    cl.pay();
  }

  /**
   * Initializes the JNDI initial context for the naming service lookup.
   * Obtains a reference to the TillHome object via the JNDI name "ejb/
   * till".
   */
  public void init() {
    try {
      InitialContext ctx = new InitialContext();
      Object obj = ctx.lookup("ejb/till");
      home = (TillHome)PortableRemoteObject.narrow(obj, TillHome.class);
    }
    catch (Exception exp) {
      exp.printStackTrace();
      System.exit(1);
    }
  }

  /**
   * Uses the home object obtained in init() to obtain a reference to the
   * Till session EJB. The session EJB then calculates price of the books.
   */
  public void pay() {
    Book[] books = {new Book("Java", "John Hunt", 29.50, "1111"),
                    new Book("XML", "Chris Loftus", 45.00, "1112"),
                    new Book("UML", "Denise Cooke",19.90, "1113") };
      try {
        System.out.println("You must pay:");
        Till till = home.create();
        System.out.println(till.getTotal(books));
      }
      catch (Exception exp) {
```

```
        exp.printStackTrace();
        System.exit(1);
      }
    }
  }
```

The Till EJB and the client both use a utility class called Book. This is shown in Listing 13.11.

Listing 13.11 The Book JavaBean class.

```
package shop;

public class Book implements java.io.Serializable {
  private String title;
  private String name;
  private double price;
  private String isbn;

  public Book(){}

  public Book(String title, String name, double price, String isbn) {
    this.title = title;
    this.name = name;
    this.price = price;
    this.isbn = isbn;
  }

  public void setTitle(String title) {
    this.title = title;
  }

  public void setName(String name) {
    this.name = name;
  }

  public void setPrice(double price) {
    this.price = price;
  }

  public String getTitle() {
    return this.title;
  }

  public String getName() {
    return this.name;
```

```
    }

    public double getPrice() {
      return this.price;
    }

    public String getIsbn() {
      return this.isbn;
    }

    public void setIsbn(String isbn) {
      this.isbn = isbn;
    }
    public String toString() {
      return this.title + ':' + this.name + ':' + this.price + ':' + this.isbn;
    }

    public boolean equals(Object other) {
      boolean result = false;
      if (other != null && other instanceof Book) {
        Book otherBook = (Book)other;
        result = otherBook.isbn.equals(this.isbn);
      }
      return result;
    }
  }
```

The client was executed using a `Till` EJB deployed on JBoss. The properties required by JNDI to hook into the JBoss naming service were defined in a Java properties file containing the lines:

```
java.naming.factory.initial=org.jnp.interfaces.NamingContextFactory
java.naming.provider.url=localhost:1099
java.naming.factory.url.pkgs=org.jboss.naming:org.jnp.interfaces
```

Finally, a Jakarta Ant (`http://jakarta.apache.org/ant/index.html`) build file was written and then executed to compile the source code, construct the deployment unit JAR file, and then deploy that file into JBoss's `deploy` directory.

Chapter 14

Entity EJBs: How to Implement a Container-Managed Entity EJB

14.1 Introduction

Entity EJBs are beans that represent persistent data. An entity EJB's data is an in-memory representation of data held in a persistent database, usually a relational database management system (RDBMS). When an entity EJB is created, its data will be inserted into the database, for example, as a row in a relational table. When, therefore, an entity EJB is removed, the corresponding data in the database will be removed. It is also possible to search for entity EJBs. If the data being searched for exists in the database, then one or more entity EJBs will be created in the container. Conceptually, as far as the client application is concerned, all the data is resident in memory. In reality, some is cached in memory, but the bulk will reside on disk. Another major characteristic is that all entity EJBs have a unique key, namely the primary key. Every entity EJB can be identified uniquely and searched for based on this key.

There are two kinds of entity EJB. The first, discussed in this chapter, has its data synchronized with the database automatically by the container. The EJB developer does not have to write the code that will read data from the EJB and write it to the database and *vice versa*. Instead, the container generates this code during deployment. This kind is called the container-managed persistence (CMP) entity EJB. The second kind, discussed in Chapter 29, requires the EJB developer to write the database access code and is called the bean-managed persistence (BMP) entity EJB.

Entity EJBs are used to represent business data such as accounts, customer records and orders – indeed any data that must last across client sessions. Otherwise, if your data only lasts as long as a client access session then use a session EJB. In true object-oriented fashion, entity EJBs should only encapsulate data concepts. For example, you would not have an entity that encapsulates customer details and their bank account. Also, the entity EJB's business logic should only be concerned with accessing and manipulating data within that EJB. It might, for example, check that an account balance update is within a certain threshold, or that only the bank manager is allowed to increase the balance above this threshold. Such logic should not be concerned with accessing other EJBs directly. There is an exception to this, however, that we will examine later. Instead, where several entity EJBs need to be accessed as part of a single business transaction, this should be undertaken from a session EJB.

Why use entity EJBs? One reason is that CMP entity EJBs insulate you from an important part of the distribution plumbing, that being access to one or more, possibly remote, databases. In CMP entity EJBs the code for persistence plumbing, usually code that uses the JDBC API, is generated automatically prior to deployment according to instructions within the deployment descriptor files. One benefit of this is that you avoid having to maintain this code. If you port your EJB to another application server that uses different database management systems, then, at most, you only need to update the relevant deployment descriptors and re-deploy the EJBs. This also makes it easy to switch between database systems over time within the same environment.

Another reason for using entity EJBs is that they provide an object-oriented view on your data; they abstract away from a specific persistence mechanism and represent business entities at the appropriate level. Other EJBs use your entity EJBs at a level of abstraction that is meaningful within the business workflow, such as a call to `updateBalance` on an `Account` EJB rather than calling a JDBC `executeUpdate` method. Of course, you could write your own data access object classes (see J2EE design patterns in Chapter 34) that encapsulate the database handling code. Although this would also provide a high level of abstraction, you have to make a conscious design decision to develop these classes, and they still require you to provide explicit operations to open and close their data sources, and to synchronize their state with the underlying database at the right time. They may also need to be maintained, and are likely to be more error-prone than container-generated code. Clearly, writing such data access object classes is better than sprinkling your EJBs with direct JDBC calls, but it still has its drawbacks.

A further reason for using entity EJBs is that the container "tells" them when it is appropriate to synchronize their state with the database; either to load data or store data. The timing of EJB to database synchronization depends on many factors, and these will be examined later. One major factor is transaction context. The container may instruct an EJB to load its state at the start of a transaction and to store its state when a transaction is committed.

However, there are some pitfalls to be aware of when using entity EJBs. The persistence code generated will tend to be JDBC code that uses standard, but basic, SQL statements. This least common denominator approach allows containers to work with many database systems, but removes some of the performance optimization possibilities open to the developer who programs to a specific system. Where this is an issue it may be better to use BMP entity EJBs. Additionally, there are other performance issues associated with entity EJBs that you need to be aware of when designing your application, and these will be examined in Chapter 15.

14.2 Entity EJB Life Cycle

Figure 14.1 illustrates the life cycle states of an entity EJB. An EJB is in the *does not exist* state prior to its instance creation or just after it has been garbage collected. The EJB is in the *pooled* state

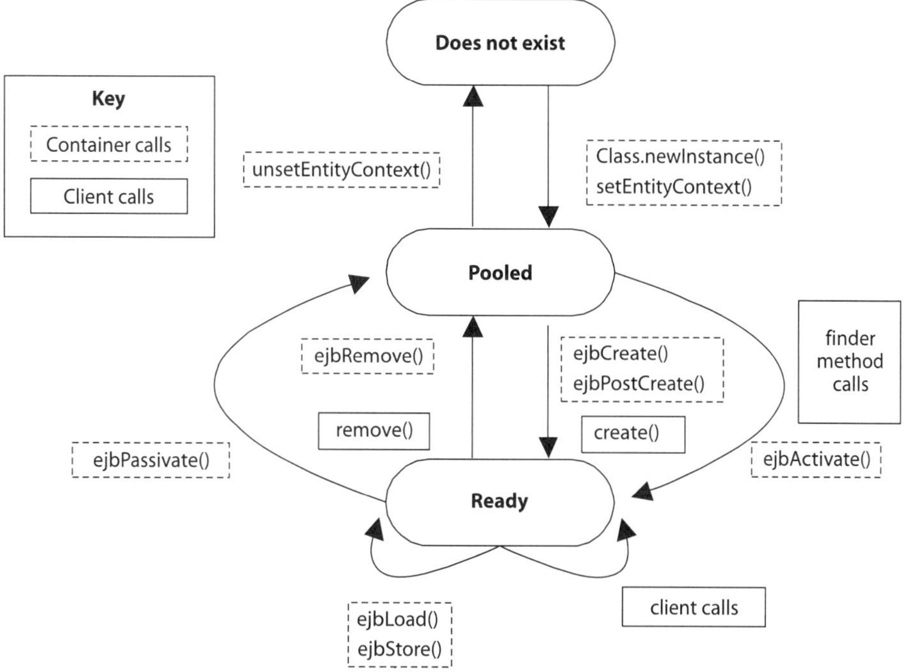

Figure 14.1 The entity EJB life cycle state diagram.

when an instance has been created from its implementation class. The container, and only the container, is responsible for moving entity EJBs between these two states.

The transition to the *pooled* state will occur for several reasons. Just after the EJB component has been deployed, the container reads the EJB's deployment descriptor and discovers that it is an entity EJB. For performance reasons, the container maintains a free pool of instances for an entity EJB. Consequently, at the point of deployment the container usually populates this pool with *N* instances of the EJB. As with stateless session EJBs, the value of *N* is calculated from information provided in server-specific deployment descriptors and the current server resource usage statistics. The latter will also influence the transition to the *does not exist* state; that is, the container may decide to conserve and balance resources by removing some instances of the EJB from the free pool. Instances will also be removed at the point of server shutdown, EJB undeployment, or when an instance throws an unchecked exception or `RemoteException`. During the transition to the pooled state, the container will call the `setEntityContext` method on your EJB. This passes in an `EntityContext` argument that provides the EJB with information about itself. We discuss this further in Section 14.7.1.

The transition from the *pooled* state to the *ready* state occurs under two circumstances, namely creation and reactivation. The first is triggered when a client invokes a `create` method on one of the EJB's life cycle interfaces, leading, additionally, to the creation of new data in the underlying database. The second is triggered when the container needs to obtain a pooled EJB to represent an existing database entry in memory.

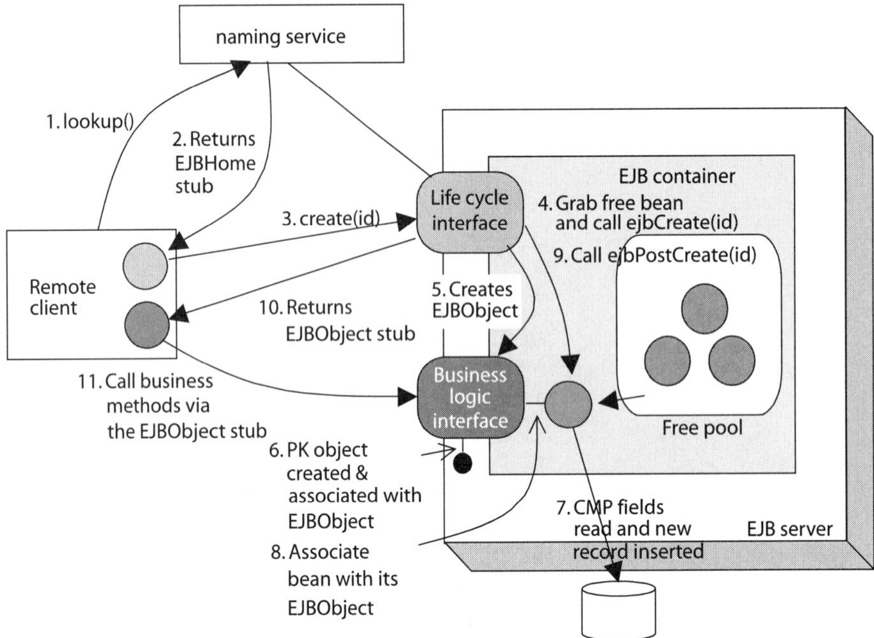

Figure 14.2 Scenario showing a client obtaining and using an `EJBObject` stub.

Figure 14.2 illustrates the former:

Steps 1–2: The client obtains a stub to the life cycle interface object by calling the JNDI `lookup` method.

Step 3: The client calls `create` on the stub. This particular `create` method takes a single parameter, `id`. In this case, it will be used to construct a primary key, but in other scenarios additional initialization parameters might have been provided.

Step 4: The container grabs an unused EJB instance from the free pool and calls `ejbCreate` on that EJB passing in the `id` parameter. You are responsible for writing the implementation of `ejbCreate` in your component class. One of the tasks this method must perform is to store the initialization data in container-managed fields within the EJB. We will see how this is done in Section 14.7.

Step 5: The container creates a business logic interface object.

Step 6: The container obtains the primary key data from the EJB (in this case `id`) and associates it with the business logic interface object. In some circumstances this will result in the creation of a primary key wrapper class. We will look at this in Section 14.6.

Step 7: The container will read the container-managed field data from the EJB and insert it as a new database entry; usually a new row in an RDBMS table.

Step 8: The EJB instance is associated with its corresponding business logic interface object.

Step 9: The container calls `ejbPostCreate`. This method is used to undertake any final initialization before the EJB is made accessible to the client. This includes initialization that could not be performed in `ejbCreate`, such as the creation of container-managed relationships between EJBs. We will examine CMRs in Section 14.11.

Step 10: The EJB moves to the *ready* state when `create` returns the stub to the EJB's business logic interface object. It is now ready to receive client business method requests.

Passivation and reactivation are two events initiated by the container when it wishes to manage resources. Passivation results in an EJB instance being disassociated from its business logic interface object and sent back to the free pool; it can then be reused by some other client. This happens because the container has to manage limited resources, such as memory or the number of instances permitted in the free pool and it must share these resources between competing clients. Part of this sharing involves returning infrequently used "ready" EJBs back to the pool. This may happen even if these EJBs are part of a transaction (Chapter 27).

When the container passivates an EJB:

Step 1: The container calls the `ejbStore` method on your implementation object. This method has a greater significance in BMP entity EJBs and is usually empty in CMP entity EJBs. However, if you need to change the representation of your EJB's data before it is stored in the underlying database then `ejbStore` is where you write this conversion code. For example, you might be using a database that cannot store objects (e.g. `ArrayList` objects), but your EJB contains such objects as its data. In this case you would use `ejbStore` to convert such object to a string form, and rely on the container to store these strings in the database rather than the objects.

Step 2: The container reads the EJB's CMP fields and uses the primary key field value to find the corresponding database record. This record is then updated with the field values.

Step 3: The container calls the `ejbPassivate` method on your implementation object. This gives you the opportunity to close external resources (e.g. a JMS connection) before the EJB is placed back in the free pool for general use. There might also be non-CMP, client-specific data stored in instance variables that you wish to clear.

Step 4: The EJB instance is disassociated from its business logic interface object and placed back in the free pool ready for reuse.

If the client then calls a business method on the EJB's stub, the container will have to reassociate an EJB instance with the business logic interface object. This is called activation:

Step 1: The container grabs an instance from the free pool and associates it with the business logic interface object.

Step 2: The container calls the `ejbActivate` method on your EJB. This gives you the opportunity to re-establish connections to external resources (e.g. a JMS or JavaMail connection) and to reinitialize non-CMP client-specific data.

Step 3: The container uses the primary key value stored with the business logic interface object (see Figure 14.2) to search the database for the relevant record. If found the data is read from the database and written to the EJB's CMP fields.

Step 4: The container calls the `ejbLoad` method on your EJB. This is normally empty for CMP EJBs, but, as with passivation it can be used to change the representation of EJB data. For example, you might wish to change CMP-string data to its object representation.

The `ejbStore` and `ejbLoad` methods are called at other times, not just during passivation and activation. The container will synchronize an EJB's CMP fields with the underlying database at various times in order to keep them consistent. Just before it stores CMP data the container will call `ejbStore`, and just after it has read CMP data the container calls `ejbLoad`. This gives you the opportunity to change data representations, as discussed above.

When does the container decide to store or load CMP field data? This depends on a variety of factors such as the transactional state of the EJB, and various configuration properties set in server-specific deployment descriptor files. The worse case scenario leading to poor performance is as follows:

Step 1: The client makes a method call on an EJB business logic interface object.

Step 2: Before the call is forwarded to the EJB instance, the container loads the EJB's data from the database.

Step 3: The business method call is now performed on the EJB instance.

Step 4: The EJB instance method returns. However, just before control is returned to the client, the container stores the EJB's CMP data back in the database.

This is clearly very inefficient and in most cases unnecessary. Normally, it is only necessary to load data into an EJB at the start of a transaction; that is, when the EJB is accessed for the first time as part of a transaction. Also, it is normally only necessary to store data when the transaction commits. There may be many method calls on the EJB between these two events. If the database is not being shared by non-EJB applications then the degree of container-to-database interaction may be reduced still further. Some application servers also allow an entity EJB to be defined as being read-only. In this case `ejbStore` will never be called.

Figure 14.1 shows that an EJB also moves from the *ready* state to the *pooled* state when the client invokes the `remove` method on the EJB. This leads to the following:

Step 1: The container calls `ejbRemove` on your EJB. This gives you the opportunity to free up resources before the EJB is placed back in the free pool.

Step 2: The container removes the EJB's corresponding database entry, and disassociates the EJB from the business logic interface object. The EJB instance is placed back into the free pool.

Step 3: The business logic interface object is marked for garbage collection.

The final transition in Figure 14.1 is the transition from the *pooled* state to the *does not exist* state. This will either occur when the container wishes to free up resources by reducing the pool size, or when an EJB instance throws an unchecked exception or `RemoteException`. In these situations the instances will be marked for garbage collection. Just before this is done the container calls `unsetEntityContext` method on your EJB. This gives you a last chance to free up any resources.

14.3 The Process of Developing an Entity EJB

The process is similar to that described in Chapter 13. Let us summarize it again here:

- Write the local and remote business interfaces; what the EJB does.
- Write the local and remote life cycle interfaces; how to create and find entity EJBs.
- Write the component class; the implementation of the business logic.
- If compound primary keys are needed, create a primary key class.
- Write the deployment descriptors as part of one or more XML files.
- Deploy on the EJB server. The exact process depends on the server.

Each of these will be examined in the following sections, using the bookstore application to illustrate each step. Figure 14.3 shows the interfaces and implementation class for the `BookItem` entity EJB. This EJB represents a book reference within the online bookstore. We have decided to represent book items as entity EJBs since they must be persistent. However, due to performance

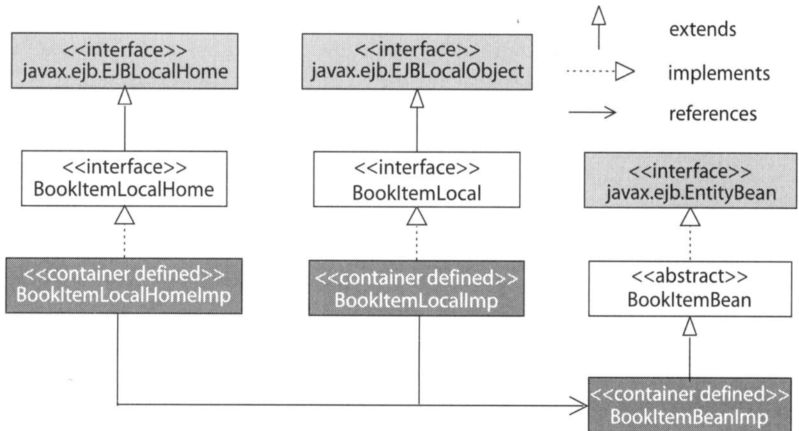

Figure 14.3 The `BookItem` entity EJB.

reasons, using an entity EJB for such a fine-grained data item might not always be appropriate. We discuss this further in Chapter 15.

For the BookItem entity EJB we decided to provide both local and remote interfaces. The local interfaces prevent direct access to the book items by Web applications. The remote interface (not shown here, see Chapter 15) provides bulk accessor methods allowing limited access to the EJB by remote clients. The remote interface will be discussed further in Chapter 15. As we will see in Chapter 15, most access to the BookItem EJBs is achieved via a local Cart entity EJB. Notice also that, unlike session EJBs, in EJB 2.0 entity EJB implementation classes must be declared as abstract. The container tools will generate a concrete implementation class during deployment.

14.4 The Business Logic Interface

Listing 14.1 is the code for the BookItemLocal interface. The JavaDoc comments describe each method. The only set method provided is setPrice, since all the other details are fixed at the point of creation. The price, however, may change over time. The BookItem EJB is used by the Cart entity EJB. We explore this relationship in Chapter 15. The use of bulk data accessor and updator methods such as getData will be explored in Chapter 15.

In addition to the methods declared in the interface, several predefined methods are inherited from the super-interface. For the EJBObject interface these are:

```
public interface EJBObject extends java.rmi.Remote{
  public EJBHome getEJBHome() throws RemoteException;
  public Handle getHandle() throws RemoteException;
  public Object getPrimaryKey() throws RemoteException;
  public void remove() throws RemoteException, RemoveException;
  public boolean isIdentical(EJBObject other) throws RemoteException;
}
```

The methods getEJBHome and getHandle were discussed in Chapter 13. The getPrimaryKey method returns the primary key object for the entity EJB. The remove method will destroy the EJB and its corresponding database entry. The isIdentical method will only return true if the two EBJs have the same primary key value. The EJBLocalObject interface defines the getPrimaryKey, remove and isIdentical methods, all with the same semantics as their remote counterparts.

Listing 14.1 The BookItemLocal interface.

```
package store;

import javax.ejb.EJBLocalObject;
public interface BookItemLocal extends EJBLocalObject {

  /**
```

```
     * Gets the price of the book.
     * @return The price of the book.
     */
    public double getPrice();

    /**
     * Resets the price of the book.
     * @param The new price of the book.
     */
    public void setPrice(double price);

    /**
     * Gets the ISBN of the book.
     * @return The ISBN of the book.
     */
    public String getIsbn();

    /**
     * Gets the author of the book.
     * @return The author of the book.
     */
     public String getAuthor();

    /**
     * Gets the title of the book.
     * @return The title of the book.
     */
     public String getTitle();

    /**
     * Gets the complete book data.
     * @return The book data as a Book object.
     */
    public Book getData();
}
```

14.5 The Life Cycle Interface

Listing 14.2 is the code for the BookItem life cycle interface. You can define three kinds of method in an entity EJB's life cycle interface. Finder methods allow clients to find existing entities based on some lookup data. Creator methods enable clients to create new entity EJBs, thereby creating a corresponding entry in an underlying database. Finally, any other method whose identifier does not start with create or find is known as a home method. The life cycle interface will also inherit a remove method. This method takes a single argument: the primary key of an entity EJB that the client wishes to remove.

In addition to the methods declared in the interface, several predefined methods are inherited from the super-interface. For the EJBHome interface these are:

```
public interface EJBHome {
  public EJBMetaData getEJBMetaData() throws RemoteException;
  public HomeHandle getHomeHandle() throws RemoteException;
  public void remove(Handle handle)
         throws RemoteException, RemoveException;
  public void remove(Object primaryKey)
         throws RemoteException, RemoveException;
}
```

The getEJBMetaData and getHomeHandle methods were discussed in Chapter 13. The two remove methods allow a client to destroy an entity EJB, using either a handle object as the reference or a primary key object.

Listing 14.2 The BookItemLocal interface.

```
package store;

import javax.ejb.EJBLocalHome;
import javax.ejb.CreateException;
import javax.ejb.FinderException;

public interface BookItemLocalHome extends EJBLocalHome {

  /**
   * Finds a BookItemLocal based on the books ISBN.
   * @param isbn The unique ISBN lookup key.
   * @return a reference to the BookItemLocal business logic
   * interface.
   * @exception FinderException is thrown if the book item
   * is not available from the bookstore.
   */
  public BookItemLocal findByPrimaryKey(String isbn)
    throws FinderException;

  /**
   * Finds all the book items written by a given author.
   * @param author The author's name. An attempt will be made
   * at a crude match with author details stored in the
   * bookstore. Recommend that only the surname is provided.
   * @return a Collection of BookItemLocal objects, one for each
   * book item authored (or co-authored) by the author. If no
```

```
     * entries are found an empty Collection is returned.
     * @exception FinderException is thrown if a database error occurs.
     */
    public Collection findByAuthor(String author)
      throws FinderException;

    /**
     * Creates a new book item reference for the online bookstore.
     * @param newBook A new book that must at least contain a valid ISBN.
     * @return a BookItemLocal object.
     * @exception CreateException is thrown if either an entry for
     * the ISBN already exists or the ISBN is null or empty or
     * a general database error occurs.
     */
    public BookItemLocal create(Book newBook)
      throws CreateException;
  }
```

14.5.1 Creator Methods

Creator method identifiers must start with the word `create` but, optionally they can be followed by further characters. Also, creator methods with the same identifier can be overloaded in the normal Java way. All creator methods will result in an entity EJB being created with the corresponding entry being created in the underlying database. Usually, at least one of a creator method's parameters must correspond to the entity's unique key, although it is possible for the component class object to generate a unique key using some other mechanism. All creator methods must return an object of the corresponding business logic interface. Local creator methods will return local business logic interface objects and remote creator methods will return remote business logic interface objects.

Creator methods are optional. If you want to define a read-only entity then leave out the creator methods. You may wish to do this where you are providing access to legacy data, or where you have a local interface that allows local client EJBs to create instances, but a corresponding remote interface that does not, or vice versa.

All creator methods must declare that they throw `CreateException`. This can be thrown by the container if it cannot create the entity, for example if an entity with the same primary key already exists or the database update fails for some other reason. Your EJB component class can also throw this exception. Remote life cycle interface creator methods must also declare that they throw `RemoteException`. Application-specific exceptions may also be declared.

Listing 14.2 has a single creator method that takes all the information needed to construct a new `BookItem` entry. The `isbn` value will be used as the primary key. We will see how this is specified later.

14.5.2 `find` Methods

`find` method identifiers must start with the word `find`, which can optionally be followed by further characters. There must be one method called `findByPrimaryKey` that takes a single primary key argument, compound primary key values being wrapped up in a user-defined primary key class. All `find` methods must declare that they throw `FinderException`. For the `findByPrimaryKey` method, the container will throw this exception if it is unable to find the database entry. For all `find` methods this exception may also be thrown if the database selection fails for some other reason. The `findByPrimaryKey` method must return a business logic interface reference, a local one if the `find` is local and a remote one if the `find` is remote.

Other `find` methods are optional and are application-specific. In Listing 2 the *findByAuthor* method enables clients to obtain references to all the book items authored (or co-authored) by a given author. All application-specific `find` methods will declare that they return a `java.util.Collection`, a `java.util.Set` or a local or remote business logic interface. This collection will either be empty, where no database entries matched the search parameters, or will contain a business logic interface reference for each match found. These references will be either local or remote, depending on whether the life cycle interface is local or remote.

The container will generate code for `find` methods at the point of deployment. For application-specific `find` methods you need to specify their semantics in some standard way. In EJB 2.0 this is achieved using a declarative query language called EJB-QL. We look at this in Section 14.9.

14.5.3 Home Methods

Any method that does not start with `create` or `find` is, by default a home method. Home methods are akin to stateless session EJB methods; that is, the container will execute them on an EJB instance in the free pool. The container does not need to associate an entity EJB instance with a business logic interface object in order to execute one of these methods. Home methods are appropriate if the method code does not need to access the EJB's CMP state. For example, an `Employee` entity EJB might have a home method:

```
public double calculatePay(double basicPay, double bonus)
```

that returns the actual pay after applying a formula that uses both the basic pay and the bonus. If this method does not need data from the EJB's database entry then it should be declared as a home method rather than a business logic interface method. Home methods execute much more efficiently than business logic interface methods, since they avoid any database access, and can be executed without the need to create a business logic interface object, and avoid having to associate an EJB instance with that object.

14.5.4 Select Methods

Select methods were introduced in EJB 2.0. They are similar to `find` methods since their implementations are generated by container tools during deployment, based on EJB QL query statements. This allows you to define their implementations at deploy-time using an SQL-like query language. However, unlike `find` methods, they are not declared in life cycle or business logic interfaces, and consequently are not exposed to client applications or EJBs. Instead, they are used internally by an entity EJB instance, and are therefore akin to private utility methods on that instance. They allow the EJB component object to query the database about itself, or, via CMR fields, related entity EJBs.

How do we define a select method? Let's say we wished to define the select method `selectBooksBetweenPrices(double p1, double p2)` that would query the database to return all `BookItem` references that cost between `p1` and `p2`. You would declare this as an abstract method within the implementation class:

```
abstract java.util.Collection
  ejbSelectBooksBetweenPrices(double p1, double p2)
  throws FinderException;
```

Note the mandatory use of the `ejbSelect` prefix. The behaviour of the query would then be defined in the `ejb-jar` deployment descriptors for the entity EJB using EJB QL (see Section 14.9).

The return type can be a `Collection` or `Set`, a local business logic interface, a remote business logic interface or a type that is also used for a CMP field. `select` methods, unlike `find` methods, may return CMP values (or collections) as well as business logic interface objects. The container will throw a `FinderException` if the EJB QL statement fails; for example, if the `select` method declares that it returns a single value, but the query maps onto multiple values.

14.6 Primary Keys and the Primary Key Class

Every entity EJB has a unique key that differentiates it from other entity EJBs of the same type within the same EJB container. Usually, server-specific deployment descriptors are used to define the mapping of this key onto one or more primary key columns in a database table. The key enables:

- the container to uniquely select and update the database entry that corresponds to the EJB
- client code to compare two entity EJBs to see if they are identical
- client code to find an entity EJB by providing a primary key value as an actual parameter to the `findByPrimaryKey` method

In CMP a primary key object is created by a container when an entity's `ejbCreate` method returns (see Figure 14.2). At the point of creation, the container will read CMP fields that represent primary key values from the entity EJB and insert these values into identically named fields in the primary key object. The standard deployment descriptors define which of the EJB's CMP fields represent primary keys. The newly created object is then associated with the new business logic interface object for the lifetime of that BLI object.

The primary key is defined by a primary key class. This must be a legal RMI-IIOP type, which effectively means that it must be serializable or a remote reference. This is because keys may be marshalled and transmitted across the network. Where a single-valued key is sufficient, a predefined Java class is usually selected as the primary key class, typically `java.lang.String`. Where a compound key is required or the key is a primitive type, an application-specific key class must be defined. In both cases the class must provide both a `hashCode` and an `equals` method. Why are both required? It is likely that the container will use a hashtable to store entity business logic interface objects. Their associated primary key objects will be used as the lookup keys for such a table. The hashCode method will return a hash value that identifies a location within the table. In the majority of cases (where a good hash function is used) each primary key will map to a unique location in the table. However, this is not guaranteed, and it is possible for two different keys to return identical hash code values, and hence map to the same hashtable location. When this occurs the container may chain the collisions as a list. When a lookup on the hashtable is performed and a chain is found, the equals method could be used to find the correct entry from the chain.

The BookItem entity EJB has a single primary key, namely the ISBN. Consequently, we don't need to define our own key class and instead use java.lang.String. However, our online code does define a user-defined primary key class for the Cart EJB, called CartPK. Although contrived, this is included to illustrate how such a class could be defined. To illustrate an example where two primary keys are required we refer to the Fault Tracker application, described in Chapter 35. Listing 14.3 shows the CRFPrimaryKey class. In the application, a requirements change report form (CRF) is represented as an entity EJB. Each CRF is identified by a project name and a project-unique CRF "number" (actually it may take many forms, not just numbers).

The key values must be represented by public instance variables. The names must be the same as the CMP field names used in the component class. There must be a no-argument constructor. This is used by the container when it creates the primary key object. We have also provided a convenience constructor to assist client code developers. The equals and hashCode methods have been implemented. They rely heavily on the equivalent methods in the String class. We have also included getter convenience methods and a toString method, again to assist the client code developer.

Although we discuss the deployment descriptors in detail later, to complete this example we show in Listing 14.4 a snippet of the ejb-jar.xml deployment file for the Fault Tracker. You might want to refer to Section 14.8.1 before studying this example. However, the <prim-key-class> tag specifies the name of the class being used as the primary key.

Listing 14.3 The CRFPrimaryKey class.

```
package com.jaydeetee.ft.model.crf;

import java.io.Serializable;

public class CRFPrimaryKey implements Serializable {
  public String crfNumber;
  public String project;

  public CRFPrimaryKey() {
  }

  public CRFPrimaryKey(String project, String crfNumber) {
    this.crfNumber = crfNumber;
    this.project = project;
  }
```

```
  public String getCrfNumber() {
    return this.crfNumber;
  }

  public String getProject() {
    return this.project;
  }

  public int hashCode() {
    // Assumes key cannot be null
    return (project + crfNumber).hashCode();
  }

  public boolean equals(Object other) {
    if ((other==null) || !(other instanceof CRFPrimaryKey)) {
      return false;
    }
    CRFPrimaryKey otherPK = (CRFPrimaryKey)other;
    return crfNumber.equals(otherPK.crfNumber) &&
           project.equals(otherPK.project);
  }

  public String toString() {
    return project + ":" + crfNumber;
  }
}
```

Listing 14.4 A snippet of the ejb-jar.xml file for the Fault Tracker application.

```
<ejb-jar>
  <enterprise-beans>
    <entity>
      <ejb-name>crfBean</ejb-name>
        <home>com.jaydeetee.ft.model.crf.CRFHome</home>
        <remote>com.jaydeetee.ft.model.crf.CRF</remote>
        <ejb-class>com.jaydeetee.ft.model.crf.CRFBean</ejb-class>
        <persistence-type>Container</persistence-type>
        <prim-key-class>
          com.jaydeetee.ft.model.crf.CRFPrimaryKey
        </prim-key-class>
        <reentrant>False</reentrant>
        <cmp-version>2.x</cmp-version>
        <abstract-schema-name>crfbeanschema</abstract-schema-name>
        <!-- Other descriptors omitted -->
      </entity>
      <!-- Other descriptors omitted -->
```

```
    </enterprise-beans>
    <!-- Other descriptors omitted -->
</ejb-jar>
```

A key object should remain immutable; that is, once it has been assigned key values those values should not be changed. It is possible that a client EJB will share a primary key object with the container. If the client EJB changed the value of the key object this might cause erroneous behaviour in the container.

In some applications you will not know what type of key to use; perhaps the type can only be ascertained at the point of application assembly. In this situation you can declare the type to be `java.lang.Object` and an appropriate mapping to the actual type defined in the deployment descriptors.

Finally, in some applications you will not know the value to use for a primary key when creating an entity EJB. Remember that typically one or more of the actual parameters in the entity EJB's `create` method contain primary key values. However, you may want these values to be generated automatically. This could be achieved by having a stateful session EJB that generates and manages a set of key values that it provides to entity EJBs. This might require the session EJB to query the database using a database vendor-specific mechanism to obtain this set of values.

14.7 The Component Class

For entity EJBs the component class must implement the `javax.ejb.EntityBean` interface. This interface defines life cycle callback methods that are called by the container when the entity enters various life cycle states. The interface defines the following methods:

```
public interface EntityBean{
  ejbActivate()
    throws EJBException, java.rmi.RemoteException;
  ejbPassivate()
    throws EJBException, java.rmi.RemoteException;
  ejbLoad()
    throws EJBException, java.rmi.RemoteException;
  ejbStore()
    throws EJBException, java.rmi.RemoteException;
  ejbRemove()
    throws RemoveException, EJBException, java.rmi.RemoteException;
  setEntityContext(EntityContext ctx)
    throws EJBException, java.rmi.RemoteException;
  unsetEntityContext()
    throws EJBException, java.rmi.RemoteException;
}
```

The purposes of these methods, apart from the context methods, were discussed in Section 14.2. The setEntityContext method is passed an EntityContext object by the container. Normally, you should store this in a private instance variable within the component class, for later interrogation. We discuss the purpose of this object in Section 14.7.1. The EJBException is thrown by your code if you want to indicate that a system-level exception has occurred; for example, if a database exception is reported (SQLException) you can wrap this exception in EJBException and throw it up into the container. This impacts transactions and will be discussed in Chapter 27. The RemoteException is defined for backward compatibility with EJB 1.0. You should not use it, but rather use EJBException instead. In CMP entity EJBs the ejbRemove method is generated by container deployment tools. The code generated will attempt to remove an entry from an appropriate database table. If it is unable to do this, the code will throw the RemoveException back to the client (EJBHome, EJBObject and their local equivalents all define a remove method that throws a RemoveException).

Listing 14.5 contains code for the BookItemBean implementation class.

Listing 14.5 Code for the BookItemBean class.

```
package store;

import javax.ejb.EntityBean;
import javax.ejb.EntityContext;
import javax.ejb.CreateException;

/**
 * The bookItem entity bean represents a book item entity. This is quite a
 * fine-grained bean and should, for performance reasons, only
 * be accessed via local interfaces
 * @author Chris Loftus
 * @version 1.1
 */
abstract public class BookItemBean implements EntityBean {

  private EntityContext ctx;
  // Container managed fields follow (defined in ejb-jar.xml)
  /**
   * Gets the ISBN primary key value
   * @return The primary key for the book
   */
  abstract public String getIsbn();
  /**
   * Sets the ISBN CMP field
   * @param isbn should be a non-null valid ISBN
   */
  abstract public void setIsbn(String isbn);
  /**
```

```
 * Gets the book's title
 * @return The title of the book
 */
abstract public String getTitle();
/**
 * Sets the title of the book
 * @param title is the new title for the book
 */
abstract public void setTitle(String title);
/**
 * Gets the author of the book
 * @return The author of the book
 */
abstract public String getAuthor();
/**
 * Sets the author's name for the book
 * @param author is the new author name for the book
 */
abstract public void setAuthor(String author);
/**
 * Gets the price of the book
 * @return The price as a double
 */
abstract public double getPrice();
/**
 * Sets the price for the book
 * @param price is the new price for the book
 */
abstract public void setPrice(double price);

// Life cycle callback methods

public void setEntityContext(EntityContext context){
  ctx = context;
}

public void unsetEntityContext(){
  ctx = null;
}

public void ejbActivate(){
}

public void ejbPassivate(){
}
```

```
public void ejbRemove(){
}

public void ejbStore(){
}

public void ejbLoad(){
}

/**
 * Checks that a valid book has been provided and if so
 * stores the book's details as CMP values
 * @param newBook The new book to add as a BookItem
 * @return A primary key value. Since a CMP EJB, returns null.
 * @exception CreateException is thrown if newBook is null or
 * the book's ISBN is null or of length 0
 */
public String ejbCreate(Book newBook)
  throws CreateException{

  if (newBook == null || newBook.getIsbn() == null ||
    newBook.getIsbn().length() == 0)
    throw new CreateException("Null or empty ISBN key provided");

  this.setIsbn(newBook.getIsbn());
  this.setTitle(newBook.getTitle());
  this.setAuthor(newBook.getAuthor());
  this.setPrice(newBook.getPrice());

  return null;
}

public void ejbPostCreate(Book newBook)
  throws CreateException {
}

// Business methods
// Methods to set and get the data in one method call to
// improve performance when this is required. Based on the
// Value Object J2EE pattern

/**
 * Resets the book item's CMP fields with data provided
 * in bookData. The ISBN field will be ignored.
 * @param bookData Contains the data that will be assigned
 * to CMP fields, including null values
```

```
    */
    public void setData(Book bookData) {
      //this.setIsbn(bookData.getIsbn());
      this.setTitle(bookData.getTitle());
      this.setAuthor(bookData.getAuthor());
      this.setPrice(bookData.getPrice());
    }

    /**
     * Gets the book item's data as a Book object
     * @return A Book object populated with data from the CMP fields
     */

    public Book getData() {
      return new Book(this.getTitle(),
                      this.getAuthor(),
                      this.getPrice(),
                      this.getIsbn());
    }
  }
```

The JavaDoc comments describe the application-specific methods that comprise this class. However, there are some general comments that apply to all EJB 2.0 entity beans. First, the class must be declared to be abstract. Container deployment tools will generate a concrete subclass of this class. In particular, the generated subclass will contain code for each of the abstract methods. These methods correspond to the CMP fields defined in the `ejb-jar.xml` deployment descriptor file (described in Section 14.8). From the setter and getter methods it can be seen that the entity EJB is also a JavaBean, with properties that correspond to the CMP fields. Container-Managed Relationships (CMRs) are declared similarly, and will be discussed later.

An `ejbCreate` method should check whether the formal parameter values are valid. If not, the method should normally throw a `CreateException`. In CMP entity EJBs, this method must return null. The container will create the primary key value. As we will see later, this is not the case with BMP entity EJBs. There may be many `ejbCreate` methods, each corresponding to a `create` method defined in the remote or local home interfaces. Each should have the same name as the corresponding interface method name, except for the "`ejb`" prefix.

Each home interface `create` method also has a corresponding `ejbPostCreate`. Again the name should be identical to that used in the interface except for the prefix "`ejbPost`". Why have a post create method? In many cases this method will not be required and will remain empty. However, there are occasions when certain initialization cannot be undertaken until a valid business logic interface object has been created, along with its primary key object and associated with the component object. Since the container creates the primary key object after the `ejbCreate` method returns, it is impossible for `ejbCreate` to undertake any initialization task that requires this object. In this situation `ejbPostCreate` should be used since it is executed after the primary key has been created. Also, there are cases where the EJB needs to obtain a reference to its own business logic interface object. Again this cannot be done in `ejbCreate`, but can be done in `ejbPostCreate`. Another reason for using `ejbPostCreate` is to establish CMRs.

14.7.1 The `EntityContext` Object

What role does the `EntityContext` object play? It provides the EJB with a way of obtaining information about itself. The interface contains the following methods:

```
public interface EntityContext extends EJBContext {
  public EJBLocalObject getEJBLocalObject()
    throws java.lang.IllegalStateException;
  public EJBObject getEJBObject()
    throws java.lang.IllegalStateException;
  public java.lang.Object getPrimaryKey()
    throws java.lang.IllegalStateException;
}
```

The `EJBContext` super-interface was described in Chapter 13. The `getPrimaryKey` method enables your EJB class to obtain its own primary key object. It may wish to do this when calling a method on another EJB, thereby passing its identity to the other EJB. The other way of passing the EJB's identity to another EJB is to obtain a reference to its `EJBLocalObject` or `EJBObject`. This is the mechanism to use if you wish to provide a callback reference to another EJB; you are not allowed to pass the EJB's `this` reference to another EJB. The `IllegalStateException` will be thrown if the required business logic interface object or primary key object has not been created by the container. For example, the exception will be thrown if your code attempts to call any of these methods within `ejbCreate` methods. However, all three can be called from `ejbPostCreate` methods.

14.8 The Deployment Descriptor Files

There is much persistence-related information that must be defined in the XML deployment descriptor files. In the standard `ejb-jar.xml` file this information includes:

- CMP fields and their types
- the name of the primary key class
- identification of the CMP field that acts as a primary key
- whether the EJB is container-managed or bean-managed
- the definition of CMRs
- the definition of finder and select methods using the EJB Query Language

In JBoss there is an entity EJB-specific XML deployment file called `jbosscmp-jdbc.xml` that contains further persistence-related information, such as:

- the mapping of CMP fields to database columns
- the association of an EJB with a specific data source and table within that data source
- the mapping of CMP types to appropriate data source types
- the mapping of CMRs to foreign keys and tables within the data source

There is also the JBoss `jboss.xml` file. All three files assist the container's deployment tools when they generate the code for the concrete implementation class. The two JBoss deployment files are optional, and JBoss will attempt to generate appropriate default code if they are not provided. They are overviewed in later sections. We now examine the entity EJBs deployment descriptors in more detail.

14.8.1 The `ejb-jar.xml` File

Listing 14.6 contains the `ejb-jar.xml` descriptors for the `BookItem` EJB.

Listing 14.6 The `BookItem` EJB part of the `ejb-jar.xml` file.

```
<ejb-jar>
  <!-- Some descriptors omitted -->
    <entity>
      <ejb-name>BookItem</ejb-name>
      <home>store.BookItemHome</home>
      <remote>store.BookItem</remote>
      <local-home>store.BookItemLocalHome</local-home>
      <local>store.BookItemLocal</local>
      <ejb-class>store.BookItemBean</ejb-class>
      <persistence-type>Container</persistence-type>
      <prim-key-class>java.lang.String</prim-key-class>
      <reentrant>False</reentrant>
      <cmp-version>2.x</cmp-version>
      <abstract-schema-name>bookitemschema</abstract-schema-name>
      <cmp-field>
        <field-name>isbn</field-name>
      </cmp-field>
      <cmp-field>
        <field-name>title</field-name>
      </cmp-field>
      <cmp-field>
        <field-name>author</field-name>
      </cmp-field>
      <cmp-field>
        <field-name>price</field-name>
      </cmp-field>
```

```
      <primkey-field>isbn</primkey-field>
      <!--Any query tags can go here. To be described later. -->
    </entity>
    <!-- Further descriptors omitted -->
</ejb-jar>
```

As with other types of EJB the BookItem entity EJB has an EJB name, and at least one life cycle interface and business logic interface. In this case four interfaces are defined to allow both efficient access from other EJBs in the same container (the local interfaces) and remote access (the remote interfaces defined by the tags <home> and <remote>). The local interfaces are used for fine-grained data access (e.g. getting the value of an individual book item CMP value), whereas the remote interfaces only allow macro-operations to occur (e.g. getting all the book item details in a single getData operation).

The EJB component class is defined next. This is followed by the <persistence-type> tag. This should have the values Container for container-managed entity EJBs and Bean for bean-managed entity EJBs.

The <prim-key-class> tag defines the class to be used for the primary key. In this case we wish to use a predefined class (see Section Listing 14.4 for an example of a user-defined primary key class). Notice the use of the full package name. If we wish to defer the type of the primary key until deployment time we can specify a primary key class of type java.lang.Object, which would also be the type returned by ejbCreate and the type used by the getter and setter methods for the primary key's CMP field. When an entity is created the ejbCreate method will need to obtain appropriate key values from an external source, since the key type is not known during code development, and hence cannot be provided by client code.

The <reentrant> tag is specific to entity EJBs. This indicates whether direct loopbacks are allowed on your EJB. If set to True, BookItem would be allowed to call a method on another EJB, which could then call a method on BookItem. It also allows recursion within the EJB. This is discouraged by the EJB specification, since it also allows multithreaded access to the EJB from other sources that form part of the same transaction, not just from the callback. This can lead to potential corruption of data within the EJB. However, it is there if you really need to use it.

The <cmp-version> tag simply specifies the version of container-managed persistence that is required for the entity EJB. The values can be 1.x (for EJB 1.1 persistence mechanisms) or 2.x (for EJB 2 persistence mechanisms), the default being 2.x. If 2.x is specified then an abstract schema name must be defined. The <abstract-schema-name> tag is used to define this name. This name is referred to within EJB Query Language statements, thereby tying those statements to a particular EJB. We will look at this further in Section 14.9.

There is then a separate <cmp-field> tag for each container-managed field (including primary key fields). Each has a <field-name> tag that defines the name of the CMP field. Each of these CMP fields must have corresponding abstract setter and getter methods in the component class.

If a predefined class is used as the primary key, then you must specify, using the <primkey-field> tag, which of the CMP fields will be used to store the key value.

Tags required to specify the CMR properties of EJBs are discussed later.

14.8.2 The JBoss jboss.xml File

Listing 14.7 shows the deployment descriptors relevant to the BookItem and Cart entity EJBs.

Listing 14.7 The jboss.xml file.

```
<?xml version="1.0"?>
<jboss>
  <enterprise-beans>
    <entity>
      <ejb-name>Cart</ejb-name>
      <local-jndi-name>ejb/cart</local-jndi-name>
    </entity>
    <entity>
      <ejb-name>BookItem</ejb-name>
      <jndi-name>ejb/bookItemR</jndi-name>
      <local-jndi-name>ejb/bookItem</local-jndi-name>
    </entity>
    <session>
      <ejb-name>Till</ejb-name>
      <local-jndi-name>ejb/till</local-jndi-name>
    </session>
    <session>
      <ejb-name>Purchase</ejb-name>
      <jndi-name>ejb/purchase</jndi-name>
    </session>
  </enterprise-beans>
</jboss>
```

The <jndi-name> and <local-jndi-name> tags provide the JNDI names to be used when deploying the local and remote home objects in the server's JNDI naming service.

14.8.3 The JBoss jbosscmp-jdbc.xml File

Listing 14.8 shows the JBoss specific deployment descriptors that map logical persistence definitions onto environment-specific persistence definitions.

Listing 14.8 The JBoss jbosscmp-jdbc.xml file.

```
<?xml version="1.0"?>
<jbosscmp-jdbc>
  <defaults>
    <datasource>java:/DefaultDS</datasource>

    <type-mapping>Hypersonic SQL</type-mapping>
    <type-mappings/>
```

```
    <create-table>true</create-table>
    <remove-table>true</remove-table>
    <tuned-updates>true</tuned-updates>
    <read-only>false</read-only>
    <time-out>300</time-out>
  </defaults>

  <enterprise-beans>
    <entity>
      <ejb-name>Cart</ejb-name>
      <table-name>CARTTAB30</table-name>
      <remove-table>false</remove-table>
      <cmp-field>
        <field-name>id</field-name>
        <column-name>id</column-name>
      </cmp-field>
    </entity>
    <entity>
      <ejb-name>BookItem</ejb-name>
      <table-name>BOOKITEMTAB01</table-name>
      <remove-table>false</remove-table>
      <cmp-field>
        <field-name>isbn</field-name>
        <column-name>ISBN</column-name>
      </cmp-field>
      <cmp-field>
        <field-name>title</field-name>
        <column-name>TITLE</column-name>
      </cmp-field>
      <cmp-field>
        <field-name>author</field-name>
        <column-name>AUTHOR</column-name>
      </cmp-field>
      <cmp-field>
        <field-name>price</field-name>
        <column-name>PRICE</column-name>
      </cmp-field>
    </entity>
  </enterprise-beans>

  <!-- Relationship definitions go next and are described later -->
</jbosscmp-jdbc>
```

This example and the following description are not comprehensive, but rather give a flavour of what this JBoss-specific deployment descriptor file looks like. The JBoss documentation can be consulted for more details (Fleury *et al.*, 2002).

The descriptors start with an option `<defaults>` tag. This allows you to define default properties that will apply for each of the subsequent entity EJB definitions. These defaults can be overridden on an EJB by EJB basis if required. The child tag `<datasource>` is the mechanism used to identify the database to use. It is specified as a JNDI name, the mapping of this JNDI data-source name to a physical database being defined in a separate JBoss configuration file. The type mapping tags refer to a type mapping scheme defined in a separate JBoss configuration file. If necessary we can provide our own Java to database type mapping scheme; however, JBoss provides several default mappings, including those for DBMSs, such as Hypersonic, bundled with JBoss. The other child tags are concerned with automatic table creation, destruction and timeouts. Consult the JBoss documentation for more details.

Within the `<enterprise-beans>` section of the file, each entity EJB is defined within an `<entity>` tag, each having an `<ejb-name>` that corresponds to the name used in the `ejb-jar.xml` file. The `<table-name>` tag provides the mapping of the EJB to a specific database table. Notice how the `<remove-table>` tag overrides the default specified earlier in the file. Each CMP field is then mapped onto a column name using the `<cmp-field>` tag. Normally you only want to do specify this mapping if the table names and column names are different from the EJB name and CMP field names, since the latter are used as default names if an explicit mapping is not provided.

The mapping of CMR fields to foreign keys and tables is discussed in a later section.

14.9 The EJB Query Language

Since EJB 2.0 the EJB specification has been extended to define an SQL-like query language that may be embedded within the `ejb-jar` deployment descriptors. This language allows you to declaratively define the query behaviour of `find` (other than `findByPrimaryKey`) and select methods, which may involve traversing across relationships. EJB QL is useful for CMP entity EJBs where you rely on the container tools to generate code for find and select methods. Prior to EJB 2.0, vendors provided proprietary languages and mechanisms, thereby reducing portability of EJBs across application servers. Defining queries declaratively rather than hard-coding within BMP EJBs, provides potential efficiency gains, since the query language is compiled at deployment to a repository's native language and uses the repository's API in an optimal fashion. In this section we give a flavour of the language rather than a comprehensive survey.

14.9.1 Query Language Statements

The basic form of an EJB QL statement contains three clauses:

- A `SELECT` clause. This defines the type of objects or values to be selected.
- A `FROM` clause. This defines from where the objects or values will be obtained.
- An optional `WHERE` clause. This places constraints on what should be returned.

The following is an example of an EJB QL statement.

```
SELECT OBJECT(b) FROM bookitemschema AS b
                 WHERE b.author = ?1
```

This query will return a collection (or set) of bookitem local or remote business logic interface objects, but only those where the author CMP field has a given value. The "?1" will be substituted by the value of the first actual parameter of the associated find or select method. The variable b is known as an identifying variable. If the variable contains an EJB reference then the QL statement may refer to a CMP or CMR field supported by that EJB (defined as part of its schema in the ejb-jar file). These CMP and CMR fields must have getter methods.

The SELECT OBJECT(b) statement will return either a single object or a collection of objects, depending on the return type specified on the associated find or select method. For find methods, the type of object or objects returned will be either a remote business logic interface or a local business logic interface, depending on the return type specified on the associated find method.

For select methods, by default it is assumed that a local business logic interface object (or collection/set) will be returned. If remote interface objects are to be returned then this needs to be specified in the deployment descriptors.

If DISTINCT is inserted after SELECT, then any duplicates found by the query will be removed from the collection. If the associated find or select method returns a java.util.Set then DISTINCT is implied.

The SELECT statement can also have the form:

```
SELECT b.isbn FROM bookitemschema AS b
              WHERE b.author = ?1
```

Here we are referring to a CMP field defined as part of the bookitemschema. The intention is that the find or select method will return a collection or set of ISBN strings for a given author.

The FROM clause identifies a schema name. The schema name must be defined in the same ejb-jar file as the query, and effectively identifies an entity EJB. In the previous two examples the target of the query was the entity EJB. The clause can also range over a collection of relationships, as demonstrated by the following example:

```
SELECT Object(bi) FROM cartschema AS c, IN (c.cartItems) AS bi
```

Two identifying variables are used in this example: c, as in previous examples, and bi. The IN subclause allows the query to range over the cartItems CMR. This is a one-to-many relationship between Cart EJBs and the contents of the Cart, the BookItem EJBs. The bi variable provides access to members of the cartItems CMR collection. This query will return all the contents of the Cart.

Queries may contain the relational operators >, <, <>, =, >= and <= and logical operators AND, OR and NOT. An example is shown below:

```
SELECT Object(b) FROM bookitemschema AS b
                 WHERE b.price <= ?1 AND >= ?2
```

A more concise way of expressing the above would be:

```
SELECT Object(b) FROM bookitemschema AS b
                 WHERE b.price BETWEEN ?1 AND ?2
```

Comparisons between values can be achieved by declaring two identifying variables. The following will search for the most expensive book written by a particular author:

```
SELECT DISTINCT Object(ba) FROM bookitemschema AS ba, bookitemschema AS bp
                           WHERE ba.price > bp.price AND ba.author = ?1
```

There are many more features supported by EJB QL. Table 14.1 lists these features.

Table 14.1 Further EJB QL expressions.

LIKE	Checks for similar values, e.g. b.author LIKE '%Loftus'. The "%" maps to zero or more characters in b.author followed by "Loftus". An "_" maps to any character in the source string. The second operand must be a string literal
IS EMPTY or IS NOT EMPTY	Checks for an empty collection, e.g. WHERE bi IS NOT EMPTY
IS NULL or IS NOT NULL	Checks for a null valued CMP or CMR value. Used where single values are returned, rather than collections/sets
Functional expressions	String CONCAT(String, String), String SUBSTRING(String, start, length), int LENGTH(String), int LOCATE(String, String [, start]), ABS(number), SQRT(double)

14.9.2 The <query> Deployment Descriptor

How do we declare EJB QL queries in the ejb-jar.xml file? Listing 14.9 contains the XML query descriptor for the findByAuthor method.

Listing 14.9 Declaring an EJB QL query.

```
<ejb-jar>
  <!-- Some descriptors omitted -->
    <entity>
      <!-- Some descriptors shown earlier are omitted -->
      <abstract-schema-name>bookitemschema</abstract-schema-name>
      <!-- Some descriptors shown earlier are omitted -->
      <query>
        <query-method>
          <method-name>findByAuthor</method-name>
          <method-params>
            <method-param>java.lang.String</method-param>
          </method-params>
        </query-method>
        <ejb-ql>
          <![CDATA[SELECT OBJECT(o) FROM bookitemschema AS o
                   WHERE o.author = ?1]]>
```

```
        </ejb-ql>
      </query>
    </entity>
    <!-- Some descriptors omitted -->
</ejb-jar>
```

Each query on the given entity EJB starts with the <query> tag, embedded as a sub-tag of <entity>. The <query-method> tag identifies the name of the find or select method that the query statement will define. The <ejb-ql> tag's body contains the EJB QL statement. Since EJB QL is not well-formed XML, we are forced to embed the statement within a CDATA section; that is, instructing the XML parser to treat the statement as raw data, not XML. This is preferable to using XML entity references such as > instead of >.

A <result-type-mapping> tag may be inserted prior to the <query-method> tag. This can have the value Remote or Local and indicates to container code generation tools whether a select method must return remote business logic interface objects or local business logic interface objects. If the tag is omitted, the default is Local. This is not required for find methods, since the find methods are declared within local or remote life cycle interfaces; a local find method will return local objects, and a remote find will return remote objects.

14.10 Accessing the EJB From a Java Application Client

Listing 14.10 illustrates how a Java application client can access the remote life cycle and business logic interfaces of the BookItem entity EJB. For reasons explained in Chapters 13 and 15, direct access from application code to entity EJBs is not recommended; however, BookItemClient was used legitimately as a simple test harness. Remember that only remote interfaces can be accessed from non-EJB clients. If an EJB client were used then the local interfaces would also be available.

The class obtains a reference to the life cycle interface using a JNDI lookup. In queryByAuthor the findByAuthor find method is called. This returns a Collection of remote BookItem business logic interface objects. The findByPrimaryKey method is also called, to check that the ISBN key found the correct BookItem EJB. The isIdentical method can be used to determine whether two entity EJBs have the same primary key.

Furthermore, to ensure their correct operation, the class calls create and remove within the createNewEntry and removeEntry methods.

Listing 14.10 The BookItemClient application client.

```
/* Generated by Together */

package client;

import store.BookItemHome;
import store.BookItem;
```

```
import store.Book;
import java.util.Collection;
import java.util.Iterator;
import javax.naming.InitialContext;
import javax.rmi.PortableRemoteObject;

public class BookItemClient {

  private BookItemHome biHome;
  private static final String AUTHOR = "Chris Loftus";

  public static void main(String[] args){
    BookItemClient client = new BookItemClient();
    client.init();
    Book newBook = new Book("J2EE", "Chris Loftus",20.99, "1240");
    client.createNewEntry(newBook);
    client.queryByAuthor(AUTHOR);
    client.removeEntry(newBook);
    client.queryByAuthor(AUTHOR);
  }

  private void init(){
    try{
      InitialContext ctx = new InitialContext();
      Object objref = ctx.lookup("ejb/bookItemR");
      biHome = (BookItemHome)
        PortableRemoteObject.narrow(objref, BookItemHome.class);
      }
    catch(Exception e){
      e.printStackTrace();
    }
  }

  private void queryByAuthor(String author){
    try {
      BookItem bookItem = null;
      Book book = null;
      Collection books = biHome.findByAuthor(author);
      Iterator it = books.iterator();
      System.out.println("Books authored by: " + author);
      System.out.println();
      while (it.hasNext()){
        bookItem = (BookItem)it.next();
        book = bookItem.getData();
        System.out.println(book);
      }
```

```
      // Now find a specific book using an ISBN derived from
      // the last book found earlier. Compare the two book items
      // to make sure they are identical
      if (bookItem != null){
        String isbn = bookItem.getData().getIsbn();
        BookItem duplicateItem = biHome.findByPrimaryKey(isbn);
        if (bookItem.isIdentical(duplicateItem))
          System.out.println("findByPrimaryKey correctly found " +
                             "book " + isbn);
        else
          System.out.println("findByPrimaryKey did not find " +
                             " the same book as " + isbn);
        }
      }
    catch(Exception e){
      e.printStackTrace();
      System.exit(1);
    }
  }

  private void createNewEntry(Book bk){
    try{
      System.out.println("About to create book: " + bk);
      BookItem newItem = biHome.create(bk);
      System.out.println("New book entered");
    }
    catch(Exception e){
      e.printStackTrace();
    }
  }

  private void removeEntry(Book bk){
    try{
      System.out.println("About to remove book: " + bk);
      biHome.remove(bk.getIsbn());
      System.out.println("Remove the book");
    }
    catch(Exception e){
      e.printStackTrace();
    }
  }
}
```

14.11 Container-Managed Relationships

In this final section we overview EJB 2.0's support for container-managed relationships.

One of the limitations of pre-EJB 2.0 versions was the lack of automatic container support for the maintenance of relationships between entity EJBs. The programmer was obliged to maintain explicitly in code the referential integrity of inter-entity relationships. Typically, this took the form of private instance variables of the appropriate business logic interface type (or `Collection` of such objects), declared in the component classes. However, these would have to be set up and removed explicitly within your code, leading to complex code. For example, if the target of a "relationship" was removed, the source end of the relationship would either need to be "told" that the target was about to be removed, or else your code would have to cope with "dangling relationships"! Also, although (with difficulty) one-to-one and one-to-many relationships could be maintained in this way, many-to-many relationships would require you to create an intermediate entity EJB explicitly. All of this detracts from the business logic code of the EJB, which is unfortunate given that EJBs were developed to hide distribution plumbing and allow developers to focus on business logic. Also, the network of relationships was hard-coded within the entity component classes; the `ejb-jar` descriptors were not used to define these "relationships", which meant losing the flexibility of descriptor-driven, deployment-time code generation.

EJB 2.0 solves these problems by providing a descriptor-based mechanism for defining inter-entity EJB relationships: one-to-one, one-to-many, many-to-one and many-to-many. The descriptors also allow you to define unidirectional or bidirectional relationships, and whether or not to cascade a delete operation; that is, if entity A is removed, then remove any entity EJBs to which it has relationships. These descriptors are used by the container tools during deployment to generate code that will automatically maintain their referential integrity, and create extra database tables to support many-to-many relationships.

Within the `BookStore` application we define a CMR between the `Cart` entity EJB and the `BookItem` entity EJB, shown in Figure 14.4. It illustrates the many-to-many relationship required between shopping carts and their items. Each book item can be referenced in zero or more shopping carts, and each shopping cart can contain zero or more references to book items. The arrow at the target end of the `bookItems` association (the UML term for this kind of relationship) indicates that the relationship is unidirectional; that is, it can be navigated from `CartBean` to `BookItemLocal`, but not the other way. Note that navigation is only allowed to an entity EJB if it has a local business logic interface.

14.11.1 Declaring Container-Managed Relationships in a Component Class

Container-managed relationships (CMRs) are declared in the entity component class in a similar fashion to CMP fields. Listing 14.11 contains part of the code for the `CartBean` component class (see Listing 15.12, for the full listing), where the bold text highlights CMR-specific code.

The code contains a pair of abstract CMR getter and setter methods: `getCartItems` and `setCartItems`. These represent the CMR defined in the `ejb-jar.xml` file and their methods are implemented automatically by container deployment tools. For a one-to-many or many-to-many relationship, the return type must be either of type `java.util.Collection` or of type `java.util.Set`. For the one end of a relationship the method will return a

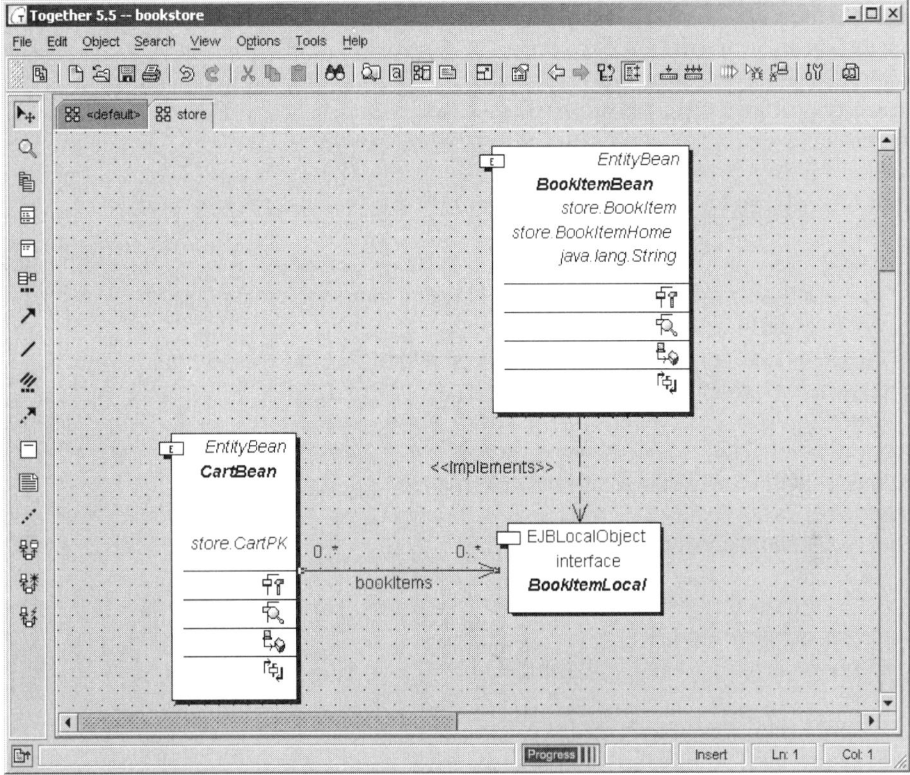

Figure 14.4 Part of the class diagram for the BookStore, showing the bookItems relationship.

single value, so the return type should be the local business logic interface of the target entity EJB.

Relationship links can be added or removed from cartItems using the setter and getter methods. For non-collection types this simply involves passing the business logic interface object as an actual parameter or receiving it as a return value. Collections can be treated in a special way. In Listing 14.11, the add method finds the relevant BookItem EJB, obtains the current collection of relationship links, and uses the Collection API to add the new bookItem link. It is not necessary to call setCartItems; rather, the Collection object is maintained by the container, which will detect the addition or removal of entries. If an attempt is made to add an object of the wrong type or a null then the container will throw an IllegalArgumentException.

Listing 14.11 Part of the CartBean implementation class.

```
package store;

import java.util.*;
```

```
import javax.ejb.EntityBean;
import javax.ejb.EntityContext;
import javax.ejb.EJBException;
import javax.ejb.CreateException;
import javax.ejb.FinderException;
import javax.naming.InitialContext;
import javax.rmi.PortableRemoteObject;

/**
 * The cart entity bean is a simplified shopping cart as used
 * by many online shops.
 * It is possible to add items to a shopping cart, remove them
 * determine how they cost, etc.
 * @author John Hunt & Chris Loftus
 */
abstract public class CartBean implements EntityBean{
  private EntityContext ctx;
  private BookItemLocalHome itemHome;

  // Environment naming context lookup names for the cart and till beans
  static private final String bookItem_ref =
    "java:comp/env/ejb/bookItemBean";

  // Container managed fields follow (defined in ejb-jar.xml)
  abstract public String getId(); // Key
  abstract public void setId(String id);

  // Container managed relationships (defined in ejb-jar.xml)
  abstract public Collection getCartItems();
  abstract public void setCartItems(Collection items);

  // Some of the code listing omitted here

  // Business methods

  /**
   * Adds a book to the shopping cart
   * This actually involves adding the book to the cartItems many-to-many
   * relationship. We need to find the item from the BookItem table first
   * and then add it to the cartItems Collection.
   * @param Item the item to add
   * @exception FinderException thrown if the book's ISBN is unknown
   */
  public void add(Book item) throws FinderException {
    BookItemLocal bookItem = itemHome.findByPrimaryKey(item.getIsbn());
    Collection items = this.getCartItems();
```

```
    items.add(bookItem);
  }

  /**
   * Removes a book from the shopping cart.
   * Need to remove the item from the cartItems relationship
   * @param Item the item to remove
   * @exception FinderException thrown if the book's ISBN is unknown
   */
  public void remove(Book item) throws FinderException {
    BookItemLocal bookItem = itemHome.findByPrimaryKey(item.getIsbn());
    Collection items = this.getCartItems();
    items.remove(bookItem);
  }

  // Other business methods etc. omitted here

}
```

Referential integrity will also be maintained. Figure 14.5 illustrates the effect of resetting the link for a one-to-one relationship. Assume that b1 has a cmr link to b2. In this case the relationship is between EJBs of the same type. If b1.setCmr(b3) is then called, the container will automatically remove the previous link between b1 and b2. Now, b2.getCmr() will return null, and b3.getCmr() will return a reference to b1.

As mentioned earlier, for one-to-many or many-to-many relationships, collection types are used for the "many" end. Figure 14.6 illustrates the use of the bookItems relationship. Here, a new BookItem is created and added to the bookItems Collection. This leads to the automatic addition of a link to the bookItems relationship. If the new book item EJB is removed, for example directly from the database, then the container will automatically remove its entry from the items Collection.

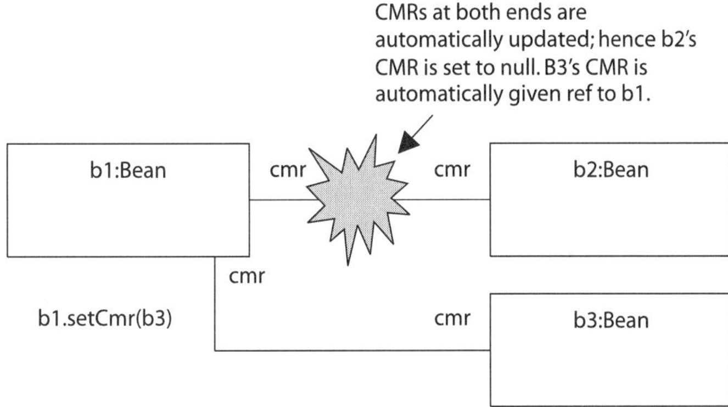

Figure 14.5 Effect of setting the link for a one-to-one relationship.

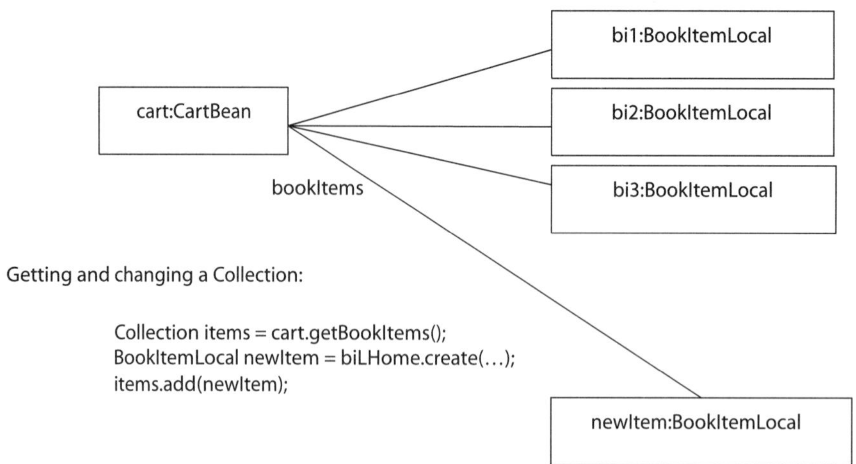

Figure 14.6 Getting and setting the `bookItems` relationship.

14.11.2 The Relationship Deployment Descriptors

The `ejb-jar.xml` file contains a `<relationships>` tag that may be inserted after the `<enterprise-beans>` tag. This is used to define relationships between entity EJBs defined within the same `ejb-jar` file. Listing 14.12 shows the `BookStore` `ejb-jar.xml` file again, this time with the `<relationships>` tag displayed.

The `<relationships>` tag may contain one or more `<ejb-relation>` tags; in this example just one is used. The `<ejb-relation>` tag and sub-tags define a container-managed relationship. The `<ejb-relation>` tag contains an optional `<description>` tag and an optional `<ejb-relation-name>` tag followed by two `<ejb-relationship-role>` tags. The relation name must be unique within the `ejb-jar` file and is often referred to in vendor-specific deployment descriptor files, as we will see later.

The two `<ejb-relationship-role>` tags define the two ends of the relationship. Each has an optional `<description>` tag, followed by an optional `<ejb-relationship-role-name>` tag, followed by a `<multiplicity>` tag, followed by an optional `<cascade-delete>` tag, followed by a `<relationship-role-source>` tag, followed by an optional `<cmr-field>` tag. The `<ejb-relationship-role-name>` tag must be unique within an `<ejb-relation>` and is often referenced by vendor-specific deployment descriptor files, as we will see later. The `<multiplicity>` tag can have the value `Many` or `One`. In the example, `Cart-Has-Books` has a `Many` value. This is because we want to define a many-to-many relationship. If we had wanted a one-to-many relationship, then this `<multiplicity>` tag would be given the value `Many` and the `<multiplicity>` tag in the `Book-Item-Used-In-Carts` would have the value `One`.

The `<relationship-role-source>` tag contains the `ejb-name` for the source entity EJB for the current role, in the case of `Cart-Has-Books` this is `Cart`. If navigation is allowed from the source entity EJB, then a `<cmr-field>` tag is included. This will map to a pair of getter and setter methods in the source entity component class. As we saw earlier, CartBean has abstract getter and setter methods that correspond to the <cmr-field-name> cartItems. If the multiplicity is Many, then we must specify the <cmr-field-type>, which can either be java.util.Collection, or java.util.Set. Otherwise it can be omitted.

Listing 14.12 ejb-jar.xml file highlighting the <relationships> tag.

```
<ejb-jar>
  <!-- Descriptors omitted -->
  <enterprise-beans>
    <!-- Descriptors omitted -->
  </enterprise-beans>
  <relationships>
    <ejb-relation>
      <ejb-relation-name>Book-Items-In-Cart</ejb-relation-name>
      <ejb-relationship-role>
          <ejb-relationship-role-name>
            Cart-Has-Books
          </ejb-relationship-role-name>
          <multiplicity>Many</multiplicity>
          <relationship-role-source>
            <ejb-name>Cart</ejb-name>
          </relationship-role-source>
          <cmr-field>
            <cmr-field-name>cartItems</cmr-field-name>
            <cmr-field-type>java.util.Collection</cmr-field-type>
          </cmr-field>
      </ejb-relationship-role>
      <ejb-relationship-role>
        <ejb-relationship-role-name>
          Book-Item-Used-In-Carts
        </ejb-relationship-role-name>
        <multiplicity>Many</multiplicity>
        <relationship-role-source>
          <ejb-name>BookItem</ejb-name>
        </relationship-role-source>
      </ejb-relationship-role>
    </ejb-relation>
  </relationships>
  <!-- Descriptors omitted -->
</ejb-jar>
```

Notice that in the Book-Item-Used-Carts role, we have omitted the <cmr-field> tag. This is because the relationship is unidirectional; we only want to allow navigation from the cart to its book items and not vice versa.

A `<cascade-delete>` tag was not required in this example. If included, then it indicates that the lifetime of one of more entity EJBs is dependent on the lifetime of another entity EJB. If the `cartItems` relationship had been one-to-many, then we could have included a `<cascade-delete>` tag to the `Cart-Has-Books` end of the relationship. If we then removed a `Cart` entity EJB, any `BookItem` entity EJBs linked to the `Cart` would also be removed. Note that this action is not transitive, so any entities related to the removed `BookItem` EJB would not also be removed, unless the `<cascade-delete>` tag had been specified for those relationships also. Automatic deletion made no sense in the `BookStore` application since the book items were meant to represent long-lived stock information referred to from multiple carts. Indeed, the EJB specification prohibits the use of `<cascade-delete>` if the other relationship role has the multiplicity value `Many`.

14.11.3 The JBoss `jbosscmp-jdbc.xml` File

This file enables you to map logical relationships onto RDBMS tables and foreign keys. Listing 14.13 shows the mapping for the `BookStore` `bookItems` relationship. This example and the following description are not comprehensive, but rather give a flavour of what this JBoss-specific deployment descriptor file looks like. Consult the JBoss documentation for the complete picture (Fleury *et al.*, 2002).

Listing 14.13 Using `jbosscmp-jdbc.xml` to map the logical `bookItems` relationship to a mapping table.

```
<jbosscmp-jdbc>
  <!-- Some descriptors are omitted -->
  <relationships>
    <ejb-relation>
      <ejb-relation-name>Book-Items-In-Cart</ejb-relation-name>
        <table-mapping>
          <table-name>
            CARTBOOKITEMTAB01
          </table-name>
          <create-table>true</create-table>
          <remove-table>false</remove-table>
          <ejb-relationship-role>
            <ejb-relationship-role-name>
              Cart-Has-Books
            </ejb-relationship-role-name>
              <table-key-fields>
                <table-key-field>
                  <field-name>id</field-name>
                  <column-name>CART_ID</column-name>
                </table-key-field>
              </table-key-fields>
          </ejb-relationship-role>
```

```
        <ejb-relationship-role>
          <ejb-relationship-role-name>
            Book-Item-Used-In-Carts
          </ejb-relationship-role-name>
            <table-key-fields>
              <table-key-field>
                <field-name>isbn</field-name>
                <column-name>ISBN</column-name>
              </table-key-field>
            </table-key-fields>
          </ejb-relationship-role>
      </table-mapping>
    </ejb-relation>
  </relationships>
</jbosscmp-jdbc>
```

Each relationship mapping is defined as using an `<ejb-relation>` tag within the `<relationships>` tag. The `<ejb-relation-name>` tag refers to the logical relationship defined in the `ejb-jar.xml` file. The `<table-mapping>` tag supports a relation table mapping that is mandatory for many-to-many relationships and may also be used for one-to-many and one-to-one relationships. The `<table-name>` tag names the table onto which the `Book-Items-In-Cart` relationship is to be mapped. In this case the table will be called `CARTBOOKITEMTAB01`. The `<create-table>` tag indicates that, on first use, the table should be created automatically. Setting `<remove-table>` to `false` ensures that the contents of the cart remain persistent.

In a similar fashion to the `ejb-jar` file, two `<ejb-relationship-role>` tags are defined, one for each end of the relationship. Each has a `<ejb-relationship-role-name>` that ties the role to the corresponding logical role in the `ejb-jar` file. Each role must have one or more `<table-key-field>` tags. Each has a `<field-name>` tag that identifies the logical primary key CMP field for the source entity of that role. The `<column-name>` tag defines the actual name to use for the mapping-table column.

Normally, an extra table is not required for one-to-one or one-to-many relationships. In this situation a `<foreign-key-mapping>` tag is used instead of the `<table-mapping>` tag. Listing 14.14 shows an alternative one-to-many version of Listing 14.13. For one-to-many relationships, only one role (the many end) has a non-empty `<foreign-key-fields>` tag (as in the example). Each `<field-name>` must use the same name as the logical primary key CMP field in the target entity EJB. The `<column-name>` tag identifies the name of the foreign key column in the source table. Notice that in this example the `Cart-Has-Books` role should not have a foreign key, hence the `<foreign-key-fields>` tag is empty. For one-to-one relationships either or both roles can have a non-empty `<foreign-key-fields>` tag. The placement of the non-empty `<foreign-key-fields>` tag does not affect the navigation directionality of the relationship. This is determined solely within the `ejb-jar` file.

Listing 14.14 Using `jbosscmp-jdbc.xml` to map the logical `bookItems` relationship to foreign keys.

```
<jbosscmp-jdbc>
  <!-- Some descriptors are omitted -->
  <relationships>
    <ejb-relation>
      <ejb-relation-name>Book-Items-In-Cart</ejb-relation-name>
      <foreign-key-mapping>
        <ejb-relationship-role>
            <ejb-relationship-role-name>
                Cart-Has-Books
            </ejb-relationship-role-name>
              <foreign-key-fields/>
          </ejb-relationship-role>
          <ejb-relationship-role>
            <ejb-relationship-role-name>
              Book-Item-Used-In-Carts
            </ejb-relationship-role-name>
              <foreign-key-fields>
                <foreign-key-field>
                  <field-name>isbn</field-name>
                  <column-name>ISBN</column-name>
                </foreign-key-field>
              </foreign-key-fields>
            </ejb-relationship-role>
        </foreign-key-mapping>
      </ejb-relation>
  </relationships>
</jbosscmp-jdbc>
```

14.12 Reference

Fleury, M. and JBoss Group (2002). *The Official JBoss Development and Administration Guide.* Sams.

Chapter 15

Gluing EJBs Together

15.1 Introduction

The EJBs we have been discussing so far have, in the main, been discussed in isolation of each other, and, apart from the Cart to BookItem relationship, we have not considered issues with tying them together. This chapter will revisit the Till, Cart and BookItem EJBs and will introduce the Purchase EJB that coordinates the Till and Cart.

Section 15.3 presents the Environment Naming Context, an important mechanism used when tying EJBs together and when connecting the Web tier with the business logic tier.

We then examine several design issues concerned with developing multi-tier applications. Section 15.4 discusses five such issues. Some of these issues will be revisited in a more formal manner in Chapter 34 when we consider J2EE design patterns.

Finally, and new to EJB 2.1, we present J2EE's Timer Service, where EJBs can be registered to receive temporal event notifications.

15.2 The BookStore EJB Interactions

The UML collaboration diagrams in Figures 15.1 to 15.3 illustrate the kinds of interactions supported by the BookStore application. Note that the boxes represent EJB components that consist of a life cycle interface object, a business object and an EJB component object, and for entity EJBs a primary key object.

Figure 15.1 represents the selection and addition of a book item to a shopping cart. The set of collaborations for this operation involve the Cart and BookItem EJBs. We have also defined a new EJB, the Purchase session EJB. Initially, this will be a stateless session EJB. In Chapter 30 we reimplement it as a stateful session EJB. The reasons for including this EJB are discussed in Section 15.4.1.

Following the numbered messages, we start with the client code creating a Purchase business logic interface object (message 1). The client then places a book into the shopping

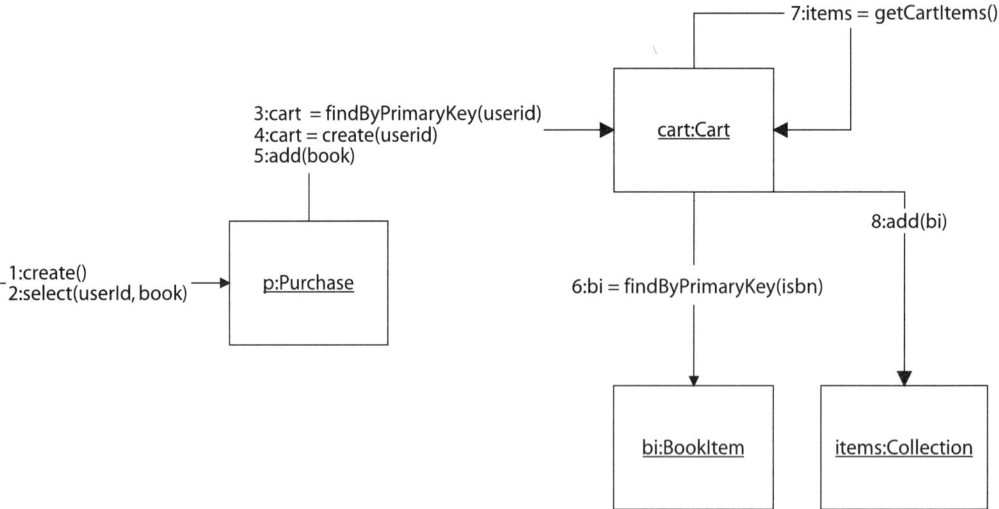

Figure 15.1 Interactions required when selecting a book.

cart using the select call (message 2). Notice that the client's user identifier is passed as a parameter, which is used to uniquely identify the shopping cart. An attempt is made to find an existing cart with the userid primary key (message 3). In this scenario, the cart does not exist, so a new one is created (message 4). The Purchase EJB will then call the add business method on the cart (message 5). In response, the Cart EJB needs to check that the bookstore stocks the book, achieved by calling findByPrimaryKey, using the book's ISBN value as the primary key (message 6). If the book is stocked, the Cart obtains a handle on its cartItems CMR (message 7) and adds the book as a new relationship link by adding it to the Collection (message 8).

Figure 15.2 illustrates the set of interactions required for the balance operation. This obtains the current value of the books held in the user's shopping cart. Notice that the balance method takes a userid value (message 1). This is because client-specific state cannot be stored in the Purchase EJB, since it is stateless. The Purchase EJB "creates" a Till business logic interface object (message 2). The user's cart is then obtained (message 11) and a copy of the current contents of the cart retrieved (message 12). The Cart EJB finds its contents by calling the CMR getter method getCartItems (message 13). Finally, the Purchase EJB calls total on the Till, passing in the list of books. An alternative approach would be to pass the Cart reference as a parameter to the total method. Where remote references are used, this would reduce the amount of serialization and copying of data across the network. However, in our implementation this would not improve performance, since we use local interfaces, removing the need for serialization and pass-by-copy semantics. Also, this alternative approach reduces the reusability of the Till EJB since it would always have to be used with the Cart EJB.

Figure 15.3 illustrates the find collaboration, this time to support the payment operation. In response to calling the pay business method (message 1), the Purchase EJB finds the appropriate cart (message 2), undertakes the payment transaction for the cart's

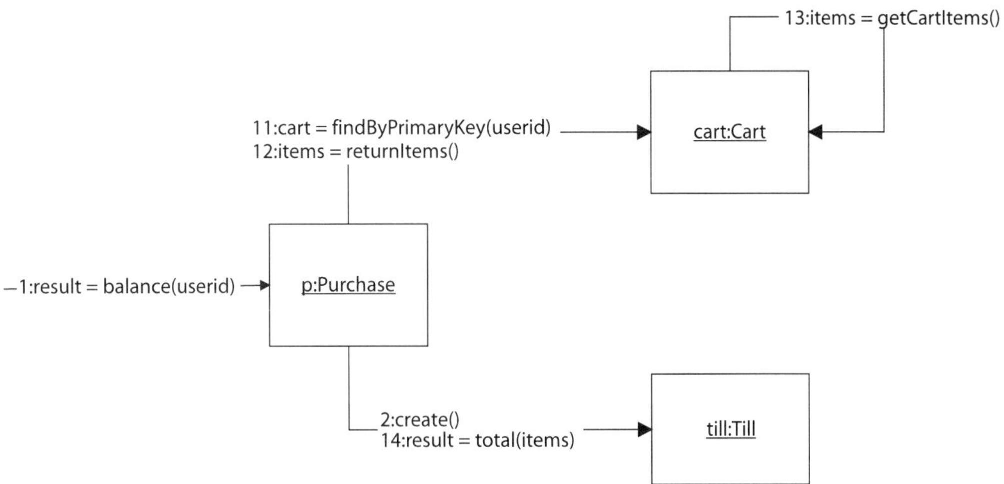

Figure 15.2 Interactions required when finding the cost of the books in the cart.

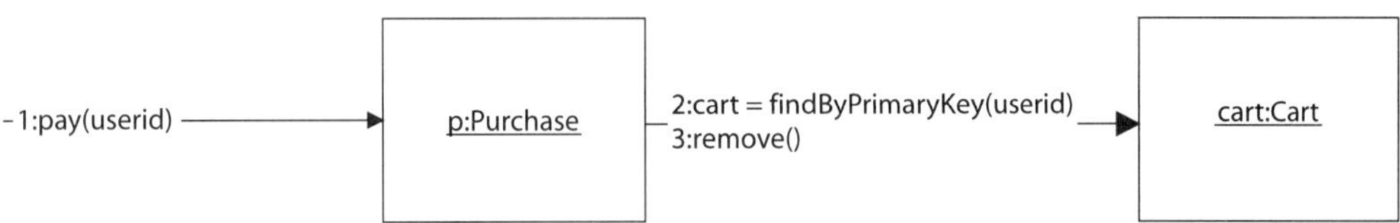

Figure 15.3 Interactions required when paying for the books in the cart.

contents (not implemented), and discards the cart (message 3). Calling `remove` will remove the database entry for the shopping cart.

These diagrams simplify the actual sequence of interactions. The collaboration diagram in Figure 15.4 provides a more detailed view of Figure 15.2's interactions. Message 1 is sent to the `Purchase` EJB's remote reference (stub). This request is forwarded via RMI/IIOP across the network to the `Purchase` EJB's business logic interface object (message 2). This, in turn, delegates the request to the component object (message 3). The `PurchaseBean` object uses the JNDI `InitialContext` to obtain the `TillLocalHome` life cycle interface object (message 4). This is used to "create" a `TillLocal` business logic interface object (message 5). The `PurchaseBean` object also uses the JNDI `InitialContext` to obtain the `CartLocalHome` life cycle interface object (message 6). This is used via its `findByPrimaryKey` method to obtain the relevant `CartLocal` business logic interface object (message 7), upon which `returnItems` is called (message 8). At this point, the container might refresh the cart's CMP fields with data from the database (message 9). The `returnItems` method is called on the `CartBean` object (message 10). At this point, the container might save the CMP fields back to the database[1] (message 11). Finally, the

1 Although you should write deployment descriptors that prevent this, since `returnItems` does not update the EJB's state.

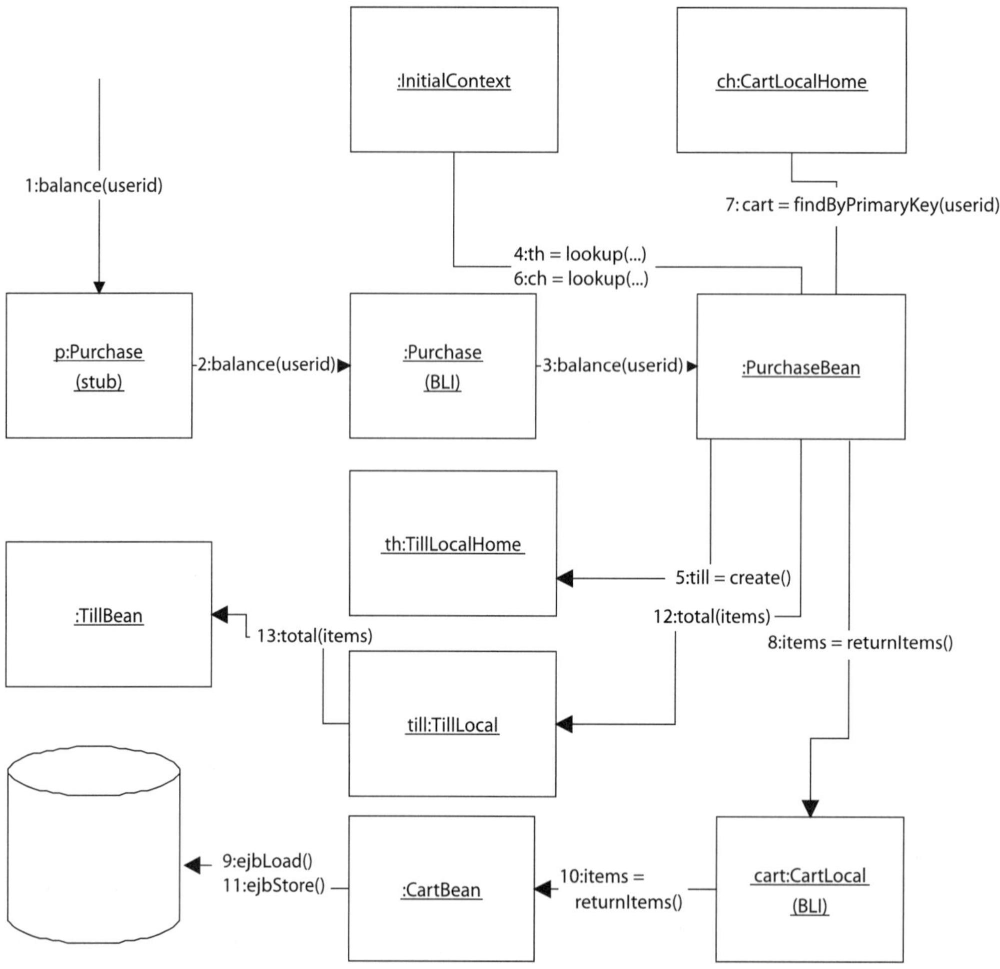

Figure 15.4 Collaborations at a more detailed level.

PurchaseBean object calls total on the TillLocal object (message 12), which in turn delegates this call to a free TillBean object (message 13).

Listing 15.1 shows the life cycle and business logic interfaces for the Purchase EJB. Listing 15.2 shows the component class. The comments in Listing 15.1 describe the functionality of the EJB. Let us consider the component class. The first point to mention is the declaration of the class variables cart_ref and till_ref. These lookup strings are a little different from those we have seen before. Part of each string references what is called the EJB's Environment Naming Context (ENC), which we will look at in Section 15.3. None of the life cycle callback methods are implemented, apart from setSessionContext, which simply saves the SessionContext reference in a private instance variable.

The business methods select, remove, pay and returnItems all start by obtaining a local reference to the Cart EJB. They do this by calling the utility method getCart. This uses the InitialContext to obtain the CartLocalHome interface object, which in turn is used to obtain the CartLocal business logic interface object. An attempt is made to find an existing cart with the given user identifier. If a FinderException is thrown, then a new shopping cart is created for the user.

The balance business method obtains both a local reference to the cart and the till, the latter being used to calculate the cost of the books, the former to obtain the current contents of the cart.

The code for the Cart EJB is shown in Listings 15.8–15.14 at the end of this chapter.

Listing 15.1 The Purchase EJB remote life cycle and business logic interfaces.

```
package store;

import javax.ejb.EJBHome;
import javax.ejb.CreateException;
import java.rmi.RemoteException;

public interface PurchaseHome extends EJBHome {
  /**
   * Creates a purchase Stateless session EJB
   * @exception CreateException thrown if the remote business logic
   * interface object cannot be created
   * @exception RemoteException thrown if there's a communication failure
   */
  public Purchase create() throws CreateException, RemoteException;
}

package store;

import javax.ejb.EJBObject;
import java.rmi.RemoteException;
/**
 * Remote business logic interface for the Purchase EJB.
 * @author Chris Loftus
 * @version 1.0
 */
public interface Purchase extends EJBObject {
  /**
   * Allows you to place a book in the shopping cart
   * @param userid the customer's id
   * @param item the item to place in the cart
   * @exception FinderException thrown if book ISBN not known
   * @exception RemoteException thrown if there's a communication error
   */
```

```
    public void select(String userid, Book item)
      throws FinderException, RemoteException;
    /**
     * Allows you to remove a book from the shopping cart
     * @param userid the customer's id
     * @param item the item to remove from the cart
     * @exception FinderException if the book ISBN is unknown
     * @exception RemoteException thrown if there's a communication error
     */
    public void remove(String userid, Book item)
      throws FinderException, RemoteException;
    /**
     * Allows you to buy the contents of the shopping cart.
     * This will also remove the Cart bean
     * as a side effect!
     * @param userid the customer's id
     * @param creditCardNumber a number of your choice
     * @return returns a transaction id
     * @exception RemoteException thrown if there's a communication error
     */
    public int pay(String userid, int creditCardNumber) throws
      RemoteException;
    /**
     * Allows you to get the balance of books in the shopping cart
     * @param userid the customer's id
     * @return the current value of the books in the shopping cart
     * @exception RemoteException thrown if there's a communication error
     */
    public double balance(String userid)throws RemoteException;
    /**
     * Allows you to get a list of the books in the shopping cart
     * @param userid the customer's id
     * @return returns an array of Book objects
     * @exception RemoteException thrown if there's a communication error
     */
    public Book[] returnItems(String userid) throws RemoteException;
  }
```

Listing 15.2 The Purchase EJB implementation class.

```
package store;

import java.util.*;
import javax.ejb.SessionBean;
import javax.ejb.SessionContext;
```

```
import java.rmi.RemoteException;
import javax.ejb.EJBException;
import javax.ejb.CreateException;
import javax.ejb.FinderException;
import javax.naming.InitialContext;
import javax.rmi.PortableRemoteObject;

/**
 * A stateless session bean for coordinating the purchase of items (books)
 * including obtaining current
 * balance of such items and initiating payment of thee items.
 * @author John Hunt and Chris Loftus
 * @version 2.0
 */
public class PurchaseBean implements SessionBean {
  private SessionContext ctx;

  // Environment naming context lookup names for the cart and till beans
  private static final String cart_ref = "java:comp/env/ejb/cartBean";
  private static final String till_ref = "java:comp/env/ejb/tillBean";
  public void setSessionContext(SessionContext context){
    ctx = context;
  }

  public void ejbActivate(){
  }

  public void ejbPassivate(){
  }

  public void ejbRemove(){
  }

  public void ejbCreate(){
  }
  // Business methods
  public void select(String userid, Book item) throws FinderException{
    try{
      CartLocal cart = getCart(userid);
      cart.add(item);
    }
    catch (Exception e){
      e.printStackTrace();
      throw new EJBException(e);
    }
  }
```

```
public void remove(String userid, Book item) throws FinderException{
  try{
    CartLocal cart = getCart(userid);
    cart.remove(item);
  }
  catch (Exception e){
    e.printStackTrace();
    throw new EJBException(e);
  }
}

public int pay(String userid, int creditCardNumber){
  // Initiate payment of bill
  // Then remove the cart bean
  try{
    CartLocal cart = getCart(userid);
    cart.remove();
  }
  catch(Exception e){
    e.printStackTrace();
    throw new EJBException(e);
  }
  return 12324;
}

public double balance(String userid){
  double result = 0.0;
  try{
    TillLocal till = getTill();
    CartLocal cart = getCart(userid);
    Book[] items = cart.returnItems();
    result = till.total(items);
  }
  catch (Exception e){
    e.printStackTrace();
    throw new EJBException(e);
  }
  return result;
}

public Book[] returnItems(String userid){
  Book[] result = null;
  try{
    CartLocal cart = getCart(userid);
    result = cart.returnItems();
  } catch (Exception e) {
```

```
        e.printStackTrace();
        throw new EJBException(e);
      }
      return result;
    }
    // Utility methods
    private TillLocal getTill() throws Exception{
      InitialContext ctx = new InitialContext();
      Object obj = ctx.lookup(till_ref);
      TillLocalHome tillHome =
        (TillLocalHome)PortableRemoteObject.narrow(obj,
            store.TillLocalHome.class);
      TillLocal till = tillHome.create();
      return till;
    }

    private CartLocal getCart(String userid) throws Exception{
      CartLocal cart = null;
      InitialContext ctx = new InitialContext();
      Object obj = ctx.lookup(cart_ref);
      CartLocalHome cartHome =
        (CartLocalHome)PortableRemoteObject.narrow(obj,
            store.CartLocalHome.class);
      try{
        cart = cartHome.findByPrimaryKey(new CartPK(userid));
      }
      catch(FinderException fe){
        // Didn't already exist so create a new one
        cart = cartHome.create(userid);
      }
      return cart;
    }
  }
```

15.3 The Environment Naming Context (ENC)

One of the aims of J2EE, and EJBs in particular, is to support deployment flexibility by decoupling components that form J2EE applications. An example might be a payroll application that needs to interoperate with an accounting application. Let's assume that both were developed for, or at least made accessible through J2EE. The payroll application will need to locate the accounting package at runtime. A JNDI lookup would be undertaken to find the relevant accounting life cycle interfaces. The lookup pathnames could be hard-coded in the payroll application. However, this is a problem if the payroll application source is not accessible. Changing the source would be dangerous anyway. In this situation the vendor of the software will have to provide an external way of configuring the lookup pathnames. J2EE provides a mechanism to enable such external configuration. Within the application, hard-coded, logical lookup pathnames can be used. However, within the `ejb-jar.xml` file these logical pathnames can be mapped onto appropriate, environment-specific pathnames; that is, the actual JNDI pathnames used when deploying the accounting EJBs. This makes it easy to redeploy the personnel application to another environment where the accounting application is deployed using different pathnames. This mapping of names is undertaken on an EJB by EJB basis, and is termed the EJB's environment naming context.

Let's see how this decoupling can be achieved within the bookstore application. To achieve maximum deployment configuration flexibility we wanted to decouple the EJBs from each other as much as possible. Figure 15.5 illustrates the use of ENC mapping for each of the bookstore EJBs. It presents a conceptual view of the JNDI directory space rather than the actual directory structure.

There are five EJB life cycle interfaces that are deployed and bound to the JNDI directory. Listing 15.3 contains the JBoss-specific deployment descriptors that define each of the pathnames. The dashed lines and circles represent the ENCs for two EJBs. The `Purchase` EJB has an ENC that consists of a JNDI `Context` node child accessed via the `ejb` link. In turn, the `ejb` node has the `tillBean` link to the `Till` EJB, and the `cartBean` link to the `Cart`

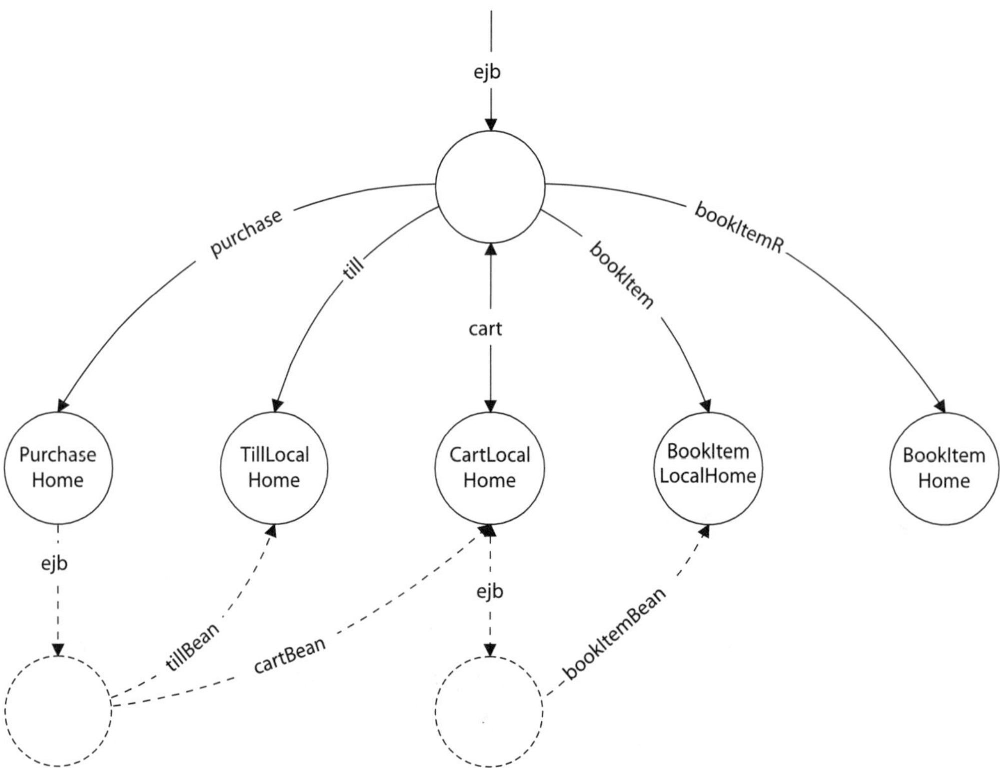

Figure 15.5 JNDI directory space for the bookstore EJBs.

EJB. The Cart EJB has an ENC that consists of the ejb Context node and the bookItemBean link to the BookItem EJB (its local life cycle interface).

Listing 15.3 jboss.xml file for the bookstore.

```
<?xml version="1.0"?>
<jboss>
  <enterprise-beans>
    <entity>
      <ejb-name>Cart</ejb-name>
        <local-jndi-name>ejb/cart</local-jndi-name>
    </entity>
    <entity>
      <ejb-name>BookItem</ejb-name>
      <jndi-name>ejb/bookItemR</jndi-name>
      <local-jndi-name>ejb/bookItem</local-jndi-name>
    </entity>
    <session>
      <ejb-name>Till</ejb-name>
      <local-jndi-name>ejb/till</local-jndi-name>
    </session>
    <session>
      <ejb-name>Purchase</ejb-name>
      <jndi-name>ejb/purchase</jndi-name>
    </session>
  </enterprise-beans>
</jboss>
```

If the Purchase EJB needs to obtain the local life cycle interface for the Till EJB then it does a JNDI lookup using the path java:comp/env/ejb/tillBean (see the getTill method in Listing 15.2). The java:comp/env prefix instructs JNDI to use the calling EJB's ENC namespace, in this case jump directly to the location ejb/purchase and then search for ejb/tillBean relative to that location. If you are familiar with Unix, then the tillBean part of the name is rather like a symbolic link. In Windows the analogy would be a shortcut reference. Note that the ENC directory space for an EJB is private to that EJB. No other EJB can access another EJB's ENC.

This mapping between logical names and actual deployment names is established in the ejb-jar.xml file, as shown in Listing 15.4.

Listing 15.4 The ejb-jar descriptors used to define ENC references to other EJBs.

```
<ejb-jar>
  <enterprise-beans>
    <!-- Other descriptors omitted -->
    <session>
      <ejb-name>Purchase</ejb-name>
```

```
      <!-- Other descriptors omitted -->
      <ejb-local-ref>
        <ejb-ref-name>ejb/cartBean</ejb-ref-name>
        <ejb-ref-type>Entity</ejb-ref-type>
        <local-home>store.CartLocalHome</local-home>
        <local>store.CartLocal</local>
        <ejb-link>Cart</ejb-link>
      </ejb-local-ref>
      <ejb-local-ref>
        <ejb-ref-name>ejb/tillBean</ejb-ref-name>
        <ejb-ref-type>Session</ejb-ref-type>
        <local-home>store.TillLocalHome</local-home>
        <local>store.TillLocal</local>
        <ejb-link>Till</ejb-link>
      </ejb-local-ref>
    </session>
  </enterprise-beans>
  <!-- Other descriptors omitted -->
</ejb-jar>
```

For each reference to the local life cycle interface of another EJB from the Purchase EJB we have included an <ejb-local-ref> tag. If an ENC remote reference is required use the <ejb-ref> tag instead. The <ejb-ref-name> tag's body contains the logical pathname that is used by the Purchase EJB when performing a JNDI lookup. It is also necessary to specify the type of the target EJB and its life cycle and business logic interfaces. The <ejb-link> tag is optional, its body identifying the deployment descriptor entry for the target EJB; it refers to the target's <ejb-name> value. This enables the deployment tools to discover the real JNDI name for the target, in this case by looking at the Till's jboss.xml entry. If the <ejb-link> tag is omitted then vendor-specific deployment descriptors must define the mapping to the actual JNDI name.

The ENC can be used to define logical pathnames to other kinds of resource, not just to EJBs. These include data sources (see Chapter 29), message queues and topics (see Chapter 16), and environment entries. The latter enables you to define configurable initialization data within the ejb-jar file that can then be accessed via JNDI within an EJB implementation object. We can illustrate this by extending the bookstore application. Let's assume that we wanted to calculate and then add the purchase tax to the price of the books in the shopping cart. A simple approach might be to change the total business method within the Till EJB. The tax rate could be provided to this EJB via an environment entry. Listing 15.5 contains the descriptors required to do this.

Listing 15.5 Defining an environment entry within the Till EJB.

```
<ejb-jar>
  <enterprise-beans>
    <!-- Other descriptors omitted -->
    <session>
```

```
      <ejb-name>Till</ejb-name>
        <!-- Other descriptors omitted -->
        <env-entry>
          <env-entry-name>taxRate</env-entry-name>
          <env-entry-type>java.lang.Double</env-entry-type>
          <env-entry-value>17.5</env-entry-value>
        </env-entry>
    </session>
  </enterprise-beans>
  <!-- Other descriptors omitted -->
</ejb-jar>
```

The `<env-entry-type>` can be any of the standard primitive wrapper classes, or `java.lang.String`. The modified `Till` EJB might have the code shown in Listing 15.6. Again, the prefix "`java:comp/env`" directs JNDI to the EJB's ENC. The `taxRate` link is followed and the `Double` object returned.

Listing 15.6 Obtaining the `taxRate` environment entry within the `Till` bean's `ejbCreate` method.

```
public void ejbCreate(){
  try{
    InitialContext jndiCtx = new InitialContext();
    Double tRate = (Double)jndiCtx.lookup("java:comp/env/taxRate");
    taxRate = tRate.doubleValue() / 100.0;
  }
  catch(Exception e){
    throw new EJBException(e);
  }
}
```

15.4 Some Design Issues to Consider When Gluing EJBs Together

In this section we examine three issues that you should think about when developing EJBs within multi-tier application. Some design issues are explored in more depth in Chapter 34. However, we wanted to introduce some basic "rules of thumb" at this stage in the book.

15.4.1 Session EJBs as Façades

It is recommended practice to reduce the degree of coupling between the client or Web tier and the business logic tier. Reducing the number of access points has several advantages:

- It simplifies the client code: it need only obtain, cache and operate on one EJB rather than several.

- Insulating the client from the majority of EJBs provides greater maintenance flexibility on the server side. The developer may add, remove or change the interfaces of the majority of EJBs without affecting the client.
- It helps avoid the temptation of inserting business logic code within the client/web tier. If the client code needs to access several EJBs as part of a transaction, then the code that ties those EJBs together may well contain business rules that should be restricted to the business tier. Why? Well, imagine trying to replace one client user interface with another, or worse still having multiple user interfaces to support the same operation. You would have to ensure that the business code is accurately copied to the new user interface classes. You are trying to maintain the user interface, but are also having to maintain business code. This is particularly dangerous if the team for maintaining the user interface is not the same as the team maintaining the business tier.
- Where coupling is high, you may be forced to manually start and complete transactions within the client code, rather than relying on automatic transaction handling in the business tier. This is because you are more likely to want to maintain transactions across multiple client calls.
- There might be multiple network calls rather than a single call required when handling multiple EJBs from the client/web tier. Each remote call requires an expensive interaction over RMI-IIOP. Minimizing such interactions will improve performance. Also, it is likely that more information needs to be transferred across the network to be cached in the client/web tier rather than the business tier.

We can achieve such decoupling by introducing an intermediate session EJB, which is typically stateful; that is, it can cache client-specific information (see Chapter 30). This is shown diagrammatically in Figure 15.6.

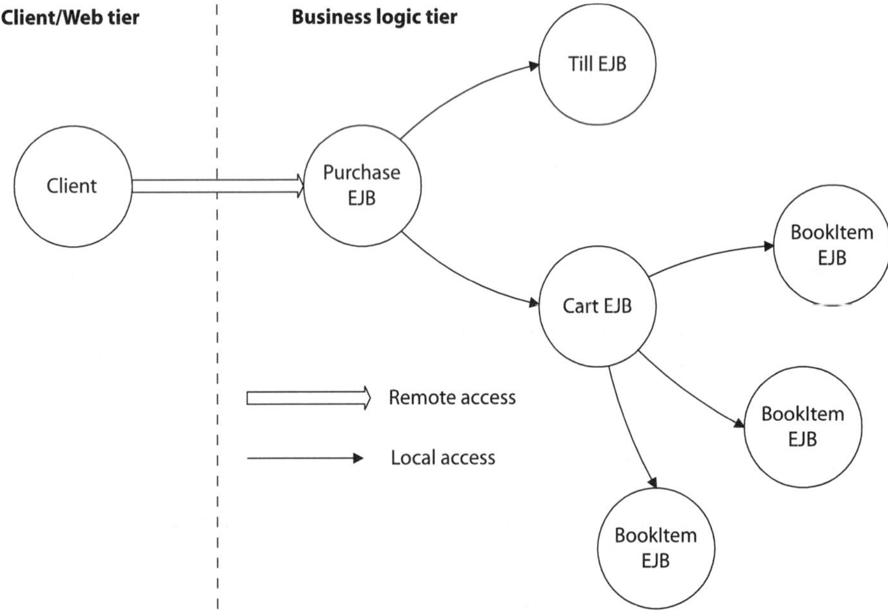

Figure 15.6 Use of the Purchase EJB as a façade.

Here the client only "knows" about the Purchase EJB. The other EJBs are hidden from the client. Each Purchase EJB operation need only run in its own transaction; it is unnecessary for transactions to span Purchase business methods.

Without the Purchase EJB, the client would have to operate on the Till and Cart EJBs directly. In this case a transaction might be required to span operations performed on both the Till and Cart to fulfil a business operation such as obtaining the balance. More seriously, the business code for coordinating the interactions needed would now reside in the client. Changing the interfaces of the Cart or the Till would impact on the client. Also, for the balance operation the number of remote interactions between the tiers would be doubled.

15.4.2 Using JNDI From an EJB

It is often necessary for one EJB to find or create other EJBs. Clearly, to do either the source EJB needs to obtain the appropriate life cycle interfaces. As normal, this is achieved using JNDI's InitialContext class. This can be seen in getTill and getCart in Listing 15.2. Rather than repeatedly calling the lookup method to obtain these interfaces, an optimization would be to store the life cycle interfaces within private instance variables. This could even be done for the stateless version of the Purchase EJB, where lookup is called once each for CartLocalHome and TillLocalHome from the Purchase EJB's ejbCreate method.

Where possible, cache references to business logic interfaces, thereby reducing the need to repeatedly find or "create" EJBs. Some care needs to be taken here, since stateless session EJBs must not cache client-sensitive data (which might include references to entity or stateful session EJBs). For our stateless Purchase EJB it would be sensible to modify the code to cache the Till stateless EJB, but not the client-sensitive Cart EJB. If we used a stateful Purchase EJB, then as we will see in Chapter 30, both can be cached.

Another issue related to using JNDI is to avoid hard-coding the absolute location and context of the JNDI service (e.g. the URL and service provider). The no-parameter version of the InitialContext constructor should be used when calling it from EJBs, since the container has already provided appropriate default values. Hard-coding such values will make your EJBs less portable.

15.4.3 When not to Use Entity EJBs

Performance considerations often have an impact on design decisions. The presentation of large amounts of data to clients is one such case. For example, the bookstore manager may wish to print a report of all books available through the online bookstore, or may wish to display a list of client carts. Since both of these operations would probably generate a large amount of data, it is important to choose a design that is scalable from a space performance point of view. The following will illustrate why entity EJBs may be a poor design choice for this kind of operation.

Figure 15.7 illustrates the consequences of defining a findAllCarts finder method on the Cart EJB's remote life cycle interface. This is defined to return a Collection of remote Cart business logic interface stubs. When called (message 1), the container-generated findAllCarts method will execute a SELECT statement on the underlying Cart table. For each row found, the container could create a business logic interface object (we say *could*, since the container may be able to share a single interface object for all the rows found). In

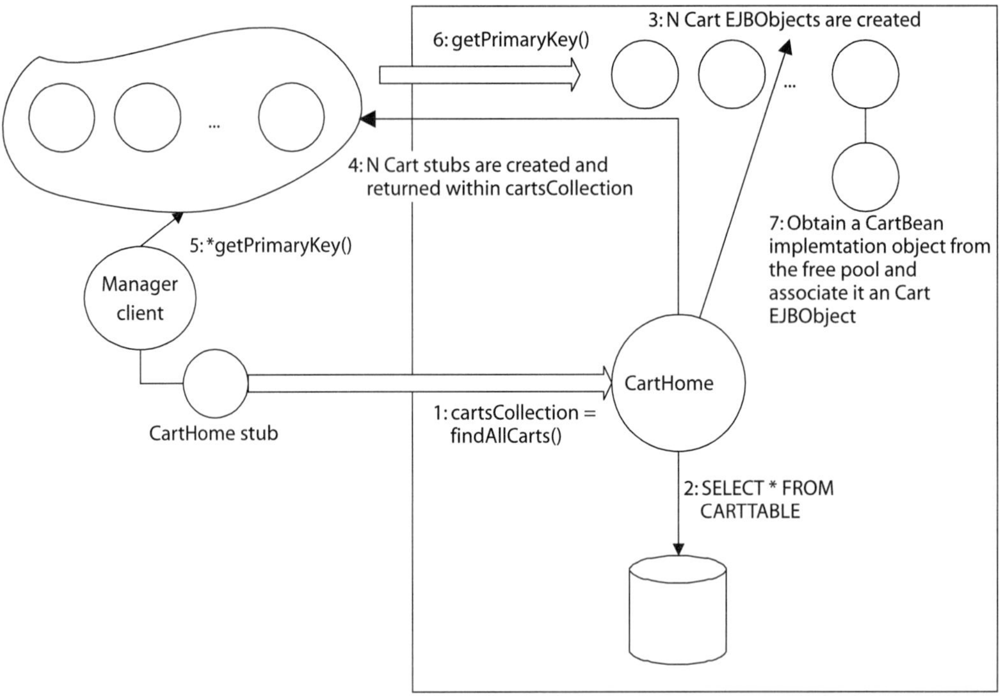

Figure 15.7 Unfortunate consequences of implementing a report operation using an entity finder method.

turn, the container will return a `Collection` of stubs, again one for each row found. If there are thousands of shopping carts, then a large amount of network traffic may be generated. Even worse, the manager client still needs to obtain information about each of the carts, in this case the primary key. The asterisk in message 5 represents the iterative calling of `getPrimaryKey` on each of the returned stubs. Calling `getPrimaryKey` may also lead to a `CartBean` object being grabbed from the free pool and associated with one of the `Cart`'s `EJBObjects`. This will certainly be the case where the `Cart`'s business methods need to be called. Clearly, this is not an efficient way of obtaining a report, especially since it is likely that the majority of `Cart` EJBs will not be required immediately to service other operations. By following this design we could blow the container VM's available memory.

Where this kind of listing behaviour is required, an alternative design approach would be to define a new session EJB (for example, a `CartReporter` EJB) that has `find` methods that you implement with JDBC calls to the `Cart` table. This provides several advantages:

- You decide what kind of information is returned to the client. You are not forced to return a `Collection` of stubs; rather, you return relevant data directly, avoiding the need for further client-to-EJB communication.
- You could define an iterator-style interface akin to that provided by the `java.util.Collection` interface. However, this could provide methods to allow client code to obtain pages

of data, rather than a single item at a time, thereby optimizing communication over the network. A design pattern that addresses this is mentioned in Chapter 34.

- The container does not need to create multiple `Cart` business logic interface objects or grab and associate with them `Cart` component objects.

The disadvantage is that the data cached by the `ReportManager` session EJB in its JDBC `ResultSet` may become out of date if a client subsequently creates or removes a shopping cart. In many applications this is acceptable, since the report represents a snapshot in time of the state of the database. If this behaviour is unacceptable, then you could arrange for the `Cart`'s `ejbPostCreate` and `ejbRemove` methods to schedule a refresh operation on any listening reporter session EJBs. You would probably have to do this via an asynchronous message queue or topic, since the container will not remove the database entry until after `ejbRemove` completes.

15.4.4 Compile-Time Checking of the Component Class's Conformance to its Business Logic Interface

One of the problems with component classes that do not directly implement their business logic and life cycle interfaces is that there is no compile-time checking of method conformance. For example, we can define business methods in the `BookItem` interface and then fail to implement them in `BookItemBean` or give them incorrect signatures. The compiler will not detect this, since we don't use Java's `implements` keyword. Instead, we will be "told" about problems during deployment. Such deployment messages are often difficult to understand, and considerably less clear than compiler messages.

How can we improve on this? We are not able to directly implement the interfaces, since their super-interfaces define methods that will be generated automatically by the deployment tools (e.g. `getHomeHandle`). Figure 15.8 provides one solution. For simplicity we have omitted the life cycle interface. We have introduced a new interface, namely, the `TillBLI`. This is where all the business methods are defined, the `Till` interface remaining empty.

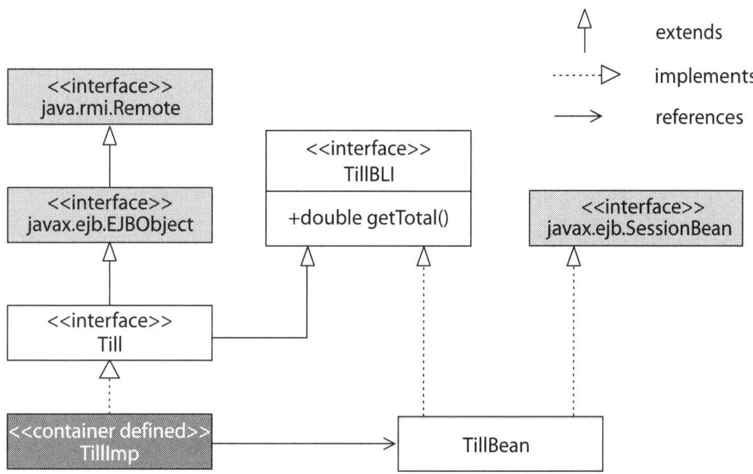

Figure 15.8 Use of an extra interface to force compile-time checking.

However, notice that Till inherits these method definitions. We now get TillBean to implement both the SessionBean interface, as before, and the new TillBLI interface. The compiler will check that TillBean contains the getTotal method.

Compile-time checking for life cycle methods is more problematic. This is because life cycle interface methods map to methods with different names in the implementation class and we believe that this technique is really only suitable for business methods. The main disadvantage with this technique is that you are forced to maintain yet another interface. Some tools that maintain consistency between the BLI and the component class may also be confused.

15.4.5 Improving Performance Through the Use of Bulk Accessor/Updator Methods

In Chapter 14 we presented the BookItem entity EJB. The local BLI contained a set of business methods allowing fine-grained access to fields within the EJB. Such fine-grained access would be a performance hit for remote clients. Each remote call requires marshalling and unmarshalling of data, a call through the transport stack, and the sending of data across the network (even if the two objects are on the same machine). To stop the potential for such poor performance, we have defined a remote business logic interface for BookItem that has just two methods (Listing 15.7). The methods can be referred to as bulk accessor/updator methods since they obtain or set all the book data in one operation. Rather than call several get methods, the remote client would call the single getData method, obtaining the data as a Book object.

For entity EJBs, such methods are also useful for another reason, and for both local and remote interfaces. Each time a call is made on the entity EJB there is the possibility that the container will synchronize the EJB data with the underlying database. We discussed this issue in Chapter 14. Providing bulk accessor/updator methods allows clients to make the minimum number of calls. However, make sure that, if clients need to get just one part of the EJB's data, you provide a suitable fine-grained accessor method as well as the bulk accessor method.

Listing 15.7 BookItem remote business logic interface.

```
package store;

import javax.ejb.EJBObject;
import java.rmi.RemoteException;
/**
 * Remote business logic interface for the BookItem EJB.
 * @author Chris Loftus
 * @version 1.0
 */
public interface BookItem extends EJBObject {
  /**
   * Resets the data for a particular BookItem
   * @param bookData All the fields except the ISBN will be
   * written to the BookItem
   * @exception RemoteException is thrown if there's a communication
```

```
    * failure
    */
   public void setData(Book bookData)throws RemoteException;
   /**
    * Gets the data for a particular BookItem
    * @return The BookItem's data is returned within a Book object
    * @exception RemoteException is thrown if there's a communication
    * failure
    */
   public Book getData() throws RemoteException;
}
```

15.5 The Cart EJB Listings

Listings 15.8–15.14 complete the code required to run the bookstore application example. The example will be enhanced further in subsequent chapters. The code for the BookItem EJB and some of the Cart deployment descriptors were shown in Chapter 14. The code for the Till EJB was shown in Chapter 13.

Listing 15.8 The CartLocalHome local life cycle interface.

```
package store;

import java.util.Collection;
import javax.ejb.EJBLocalHome;
import javax.ejb.CreateException;
import javax.ejb.FinderException;
/**
 * Local life cycle interface for the Cart EJB.
 * @author Chris Loftus
 * @version 1.0
 */
public interface CartLocalHome extends EJBLocalHome {
   /**
    * Finds the local business logic interface object
    * @param pk Must contain a valid primary key
    * @return The business logic interface object
    * @exception FinderException is thrown if the cart cannot be found
    */
   public CartLocal findByPrimaryKey(CartPK pk) throws FinderException;

   /**
    * Creates a new cart EJB, and corresponding entry in the database
    * @param param Must contain a valid primary key value
```

```
     * @return The business logic interface object
     * @exception CreateException is thrown if param is null, or
     * the EJB with that key already exists.
     */
     public CartLocal create(String param) throws CreateException;
}
```

Listing 15.9 The CartHome remote life cycle interface.

```
package store;

import javax.ejb.EJBHome;
import javax.ejb.CreateException;
import java.sql.SQLException;
import java.rmi.RemoteException;
import javax.ejb.EJBException;
import javax.ejb.FinderException;
/**
 * Remote life cycle interface for the Cart EJB.
 * @author Chris Loftus
 * @version 1.0
 */
public interface CartHome extends EJBHome {
  /**
   * Finds the remote business logic interface object
   * @param pk Must contain a valid primary key
   * @return The business logic interface object
   * @exception FinderException is thrown if the cart cannot be found
   * @exception RemoteException is thrown if there is a communication
   * problem
   */
  public Cart findByPrimaryKey(CartPK pk) throws FinderException,
    RemoteException;

  /**
   * Creates a new cart EJB, and corresponding entry in the database
   * @param param Must contain a valid primary key value
   * @return The business logic interface object
   * @exception CreateException is thrown if param is null, or
   * the EJB with that key already exists.
   * @exception RemoteException is thrown if there is a communication
   * problem
   */
  public Cart create(String param) throws CreateException,
    RemoteException;
}
```

Listing 15.10 The `CartLocal` local business logic interface.

```
package store;

import javax.ejb.EJBLocalObject;
import javax.ejb.FinderException;
/**
 * Local business logic interface for the Cart EJB.
 * @author Chris Loftus
 * @version 1.0
 */
public interface CartLocal extends EJBLocalObject {

  /**
   * Adds a book to the shopping cart.
   * @param item The item to be added to the cart.
   * @exception FinderException is thrown if the book's ISBN does not
   * correspond to a book sold by the store.
   */
  public void add(Book item) throws FinderException;

  /**
   * Removes a book from the shopping cart.
   * @param item The item to be removed from the cart.
   * @exception FinderException is thrown if the book's ISBN does not
   * correspond to a book in the cart.
   */
  public void remove(Book item) throws FinderException;

  /**
   * Returns a copy of the contents of the cart.
   * @returns an array of Book objects.
   */
  public Book[] returnItems();

  /**
   * Adds a number of books to the shopping cart.
   * @param items An array of books to be added to the cart.
   * @exception FinderException is thrown if one of the books' ISBNs does not
   * correspond to a book sold by the store. If required, it is the
   * responsibility of the caller to roll-back the transaction to abandon
   * any partial updates.
   */
  public void addAll(Book[] items) throws FinderException;

  /**
```

```
   * Removes a number of books from the shopping cart.
   * @param items The book items to be removed from the cart.
   * @exception FinderException is thrown if one of the books is not
   * contained in the cart. If required, it is the responsibility of the
   * caller to roll-back the transaction to abandon any partial updates.
   */
  public void removeAll(Book[] items) throws FinderException;
}
```

Listing 15.11 The Cart remote business logic interface.

```
package store;

import javax.ejb.EJBObject;
import javax.ejb.FinderException;
import java.rmi.RemoteException;

/**
 * Remote business logic interface for the Cart EJB.
 * @author Chris Loftus
 * @version 1.0
 */
public interface Cart extends EJBObject {
  /**
   * Adds a book to the shopping cart
   * @param item The item to add
   * @exception FinderException thrown if the book's ISBN is unknown
   * @exception RemoteException thrown if there's a communication failure
   */
  public void add(Book item) throws FinderException, RemoteException;

  /**
   * Removes a book from the shopping cart.
   * @param item The item to remove
   * @exception FinderException thrown if the book's ISBN is unknown
   * @exception RemoteException thrown if there's a communication failure
   */
  public void remove(Book item) throws FinderException, RemoteException;

  /**
   * Returns all the items current in the shopping cart.
   * @return Book[] the items held by the cart
   * @exception RemoteException thrown if there's a communication failure
   */
  public Book[] returnItems() throws RemoteException;
```

```
  /**
   * Adds an array of books to the shopping cart
   * @param Book[] the array of books to add to the cart
   * @exception FinderException thrown if the book's ISBN is unknown
   * @exception RemoteException thrown if there's a communication failure
   */
  public void addAll(Book[] items) throws FinderException, RemoteException;

  /**
   * Removes the array of books from the cart
   * @param Book[] the array of books to remove from the cart
   * @exception FinderException thrown if the book's ISBN is unknown
   * @exception RemoteException thrown if there's a communication failure
   */
  public void removeAll(Book[] items) throws RemoteException;
}
```

Listing 15.12 The CartBean component class.

```
package store;

import util.DebugSender;
import java.util.*;

import javax.ejb.EntityBean;
import javax.ejb.EntityContext;
import javax.ejb.EJBException;
import javax.ejb.CreateException;
import javax.ejb.FinderException;
import javax.naming.InitialContext;
import javax.rmi.PortableRemoteObject;

/**
 * The cart entity bean is a simplified shopping cart as used by many
 * online shops.
 * It is possible to add items to a shopping cart, remove them
 * determine how they cost, etc.
 * @author John Hunt & Chris Loftus
 * @version 2.0
 */
abstract public class CartBean implements EntityBean {
  protected EntityContext ctx;
  private BookItemLocalHome itemHome;

  // Environment naming context lookup names for the cart and till beans
  private static final String BOOK_ITEM_REF =
```

```
    "java:comp/env/ejb/bookItemBean";
  private BookItemLocal lnkBookItemLocal;

  // Container managed fields follow (defined in ejb-jar.xml)
  abstract public String getId(); // Key
  abstract public void setId(String id);

  // Container managed relationships (defined in ejb-jar.xml)
  abstract public Collection getCartItems();
  abstract public void setCartItems(Collection items);

  public void setEntityContext(EntityContext context){
    ctx = context;
  }

  public void unsetEntityContext(){
    ctx = null;
  }

  public void ejbActivate(){
    this.itemHome = this.getItemHome();
  }

  public void ejbPassivate(){
    this.itemHome = null;
  }

  public void ejbRemove(){
  }

  public void ejbStore(){
  }

  public void ejbLoad(){
  }

  public CartPK ejbCreate(String customerId) throws CreateException{
    this.setId(customerId);
    this.itemHome = this.getItemHome();
    return null;
  }

  public void ejbPostCreate(String param){
  }

  // Business methods
```

```
/**
 * Adds a book to the shopping cart
 * This actually involves adding the book to the cartItems many-to-many
 * relationship. We need to find the item from the BookItem table first
 * and then add it to the cartItems Collection.
 * @param item the item to add
 * @exception FinderException thrown if the book's ISBN is unknown
 */
public void add(Book item) throws FinderException{
  try{
    BookItemLocal bookItem = itemHome.findByPrimaryKey(item.getIsbn());
    Collection items = this.getCartItems();
    items.add(bookItem);
  }
  catch(FinderException fe){
    throw fe;
  }
  catch(Exception e){
    throw new EJBException(e);
  }
}

/**
 * Removes a book from the shopping cart.
 * Need to remove the item from the cartItems relationship
 * @param item the item to remove
 * @exception FinderException thrown if the book's ISBN is unknown
 */
public void remove(Book item) throws FinderException{
  try{
    BookItemLocal bookItem = itemHome.findByPrimaryKey(item.getIsbn());
    Collection items = this.getCartItems();
    items.remove(bookItem);
  }
  catch(FinderException fe){
    throw fe;
  }
  catch(Exception e){
    throw new EJBException(e);
  }
}

/**
 * Returns all the items current in the shopping cart.
 * @return Book[] the items held by the cart
 */
```

```
public Book[] returnItems(){
  Book books[] = null;
  try{
    Collection items = this.getCartItems();
    books = new Book[items.size()];
    Iterator it = items.iterator();
    int i = 0;
    BookItemLocal bookItem = null;
    while(it.hasNext()){
      bookItem = (BookItemLocal)it.next();
      books[i++] = new Book(bookItem.getTitle(),
                            bookItem.getAuthor(),
                            bookItem.getPrice(),
                            bookItem.getIsbn());
    }
  }
  catch(Exception e){
    throw new EJBException(e);
  }
  return books;
}

/**
 * Adds an array of books to the shopping cart
 * @param items The array of books to add to the cart
 * @exception FinderException thrown if the book's ISBN is unknown
 */
public void addAll(Book[] items) throws FinderException{
  for (int i=0; i<items.length; i++){
    add(items[i]);
  }
}

/**
 * Removes the array of books from the cart
 * @param items The array of books to remove from the cart
 * @exception FinderException thrown if the book's ISBN is unknown
 */
public void removeAll(Book[] items) throws FinderException{
  for (int i=0; i<items.length; i++)
    remove(items[i]);
}

// Private utility methods

private BookItemLocalHome getItemHome(){
```

```
      try{
        InitialContext jndiCtx = new InitialContext();
        Object obj = jndiCtx.lookup(BOOK_ITEM_REF);
        return (BookItemLocalHome)PortableRemoteObject.narrow(obj,
            store.BookItemLocalHome.class);
      }
      catch(Exception e){
        throw new EJBException(e);
      }
    }
  }
```

Listing 15.13 The CartPK class.

```
package store;

import java.io.Serializable;

public class CartPK implements Serializable {

  public String id;

  public CartPK() {
  }

  public CartPK(String id) {
    this.id = id;
  }

  public boolean equals(Object o){
    if (o instanceof CartPK) {
      CartPK otherKey = (CartPK)o;
      return (id.equals(otherKey.id));
    }
    else
      return false;
  }

  public int hashCode(){
    return id.hashCode();
  }

  public String getId(){
    return id;
  }
}
```

Listing 15.14 The cart deployment descriptors in `ejb-jar.xml`.

```
<ejb-jar>
  <enterprise-beans>
    <entity>
      <ejb-name>Cart</ejb-name>
        <local-home>store.CartLocalHome</local-home>
          <local>store.CartLocal</local>
          <ejb-class>store.CartBean</ejb-class>
          <persistence-type>Container</persistence-type>
          <prim-key-class>store.CartPK</prim-key-class>
          <reentrant>False</reentrant>
          <cmp-version>2.x</cmp-version>
          <abstract-schema-name>cartschema</abstract-schema-name>
          <cmp-field>
            <field-name>id</field-name>
          </cmp-field>
          <ejb-local-ref>
            <ejb-ref-name>ejb/bookItemBean</ejb-ref-name>
            <ejb-ref-type>Entity</ejb-ref-type>
            <local-home>store.BookItemLocalHome</local-home>
            <local>store.BookItemLocal</local>
            <ejb-link>BookItem</ejb-link>
          </ejb-local-ref>
      </entity>
      <!-- Other descriptors omitted -->
  </enterprise-beans>
  <!-- Other descriptors omitted -->
</ejb-jar>
```

15.6 The Timer Service

Introduced in EJB 2.1 (J2EE 1.4), the Timer Service allows you to register any kind of EJB to receive time-based event notifications. Although we have not shown it, each of the life cycle state diagrams shown for EJBs in other chapters can have an extra transition, a timeout caused by a `Timer` object expiring.

There are many business applications that require notification at a particular point in time or after an elapsed period of time. An example might be a stock-feed EJB that every *N* seconds needs to obtain the latest stock quotes from a stock exchange source. You might also want to interrupt a business process that is taking too long. For example, the bookstore application might communicate with a parcel delivery Web service using JAX-RPC. If a reply is not received within a certain period of time, we assume a problem with the communication link. Here a timer can notify our application if this is the case and we can abort the transaction. However, the Timer Service is not an appropriate mechanism to support hard real-time system requirements.

The Timer Service is a reliable and transactional notification service for timed events. Multiple timers can be established for any kind of EJB. For stateless and message-driven EJBs, the event notification is sent to an arbitrary EJB instance in the free pool. For entity and stateful EJBs the event notification is sent to the EJB that registered the event. Events may be cancelled prior to their expiration.

An EJB that "wishes" to create a timer must first obtain a `TimerService` (Listing 15.15) reference. This is obtained through the `EJBContext` interface's `getTimerService()` method.

Listing 15.15 The `TimerService` interface.

```
public interface javax.ejb.TimerService {
  public Timer createTimer(long duration,
      java.io.Serializable info);
  public Timer createTimer(long initialDuration,
                           long intervalDuration,
                           java.io.Serializable info);
  public Timer createTimer(java.util.Date expiration,
                           java.io.Serializable info);
  public Timer createTimer(java.util.Date initialExpiration,
                           long intervalDuration,
                           java.io.Serializable info);
  public Collection getTimers();
}
```

The `createTimer` method is overloaded to allow you to create timers that expire after a relative amount of time (specified in milliseconds) after the point of creation, or to create timers that expire at a particular date and time. The last is particularly useful for calendar- or diary-based applications. The info parameter can be obtained by the notified EJB and provides it with application-specific information. For example, an appointment-based application might provide information about an imminent appointment. The actual parameter must be serializable, since timers can be saved, and must survive container crashes. The overloads also allow for an initial notification followed by the repeated notification every `intervalDuration` milliseconds. The `getTimers` method will return all the timer objects that are associated with the calling EJB.

In order for an EJB to register itself with the Timer Service, it must implement the `TimedObject` interface:

```
public interface javax.ejb.TimedObject {
  public void ejbTimeout(Timer timer);
}
```

On timer expiration your EJB's `ejbTimeout` method will be called. The call to this will be interleaved with business method and other life cycle method calls. A consequence of this is that there is no guarantee that the ejbTimeout method will be called at the precise point of timer expiration. Indeed, there is no guarantee that several timers that are due to expire at similar times will result in ejbTimeout being called in the expected order. Transaction attributes (see Chapter 27) can be assigned to the ejbTimeout method. Indeed, treat the method as another business method, one that is time-based. By default there is no security context (see Chapter 28) associated with the method call, since the container makes the call. If you need the method to have an associated security principal then use a <run-as> tag in the deployment descriptors.

The Timer interface is shown in Listing 15.16.

Listing 15.16 The Timer and TimerHandle interfaces.

```
public interface javax.ejb.Timer {
  public void cancel();
  public long getTimeRemaining();
  public java.util.Date getNextTimeout();
  public javax.ejb.TimerHandle getHandle();
  public java.io.Serializable getInfo();
}
public interface javax.ejb.TimerHandle extends java.io.Serializable {
  public javax.ejb.Timer getTimer();
}
```

An active timer is cancelled using the cancel method. If the timer has already expired, and is a one-event timer, calling cancel will result in a NoSuchObjectLocalException being thrown. The TimerHandle interface enables you to serialize timers and then reactivate them. Note that timers must not be passed through the EJB's remote interface or Web service interface.

Finally, let us examine timers and transactions a little further. You may wish to come back to this after reading Chapter 27. What happens to a timer if the transaction that created it rolls back? If the timer was created within the scope of a transaction, then on rollback, the timer creation is also rolled back, that is, as if it didn't occur. What if the timer was cancelled prior to roll back? At the point of transaction rollback the container will rescind the cancellation. If the timeout would have occurred (if it had not been cancelled) then the container will then immediately call ejbTimeout at least once. By the way, it is recommended that ejbTimeout method is assigned the RequiresNew attribute so that it operates in a distinct transaction. If this transaction rolls back, the container will retry the timeout at least one more time.

Timers are durable across container crashes. When the container is restarted, any timers that expired during the crash will cause their associated EJBs' ejbTimeout method to be called at least once. Those that have not expired will have their internal times adjusted to take into account the downtime interval.

Chapter 16

Message-Driven EJBs

16.1 Introduction

A major feature missing from EJB 1.1 was a bean that could receive messages via an intermediate queue; sessions and entity EJBs could only be called synchronously via their business logic and life cycle interfaces. EJB 2.0 introduced the message-driven EJB to rectify this problem, an EJB that is able to communicate with other EJBs and clients in an asynchronous manner.

Message-driven EJBs simply tap into existing J2EE technologies, primarily the Java Messaging Service (JMS). We discussed JMS in Chapter 7, which we assume you have read. In this chapter we explore how message-driven EJBs are developed and used, and how they integrate with JMS. From here on we refer to message-driven EJBs as MDBs (message-driven beans).

Unlike other EJBs, MDBs only have a component class; they do not have business logic or life cycle interfaces. This is because all communication with an MDB is via a JMS queue or topic, no direct synchronous interaction is allowed. In the following sections we examine MDB life cycle states, the MDB component class and MDB deployment descriptors. We extend the bookstore application to illustrate the use of an MDB. A `DebugMonitor` MDB is presented that will receive debug messages from clients (other EJBs, web clients and application clients).

16.2 Message-Driven EJB Life Cycle

The life cycle of the MDB is straightforward. Figure 16.1 shows that the MDB can be in two states, *does not exist* and *ready pool*. At the point of deployment the deployed MDB will have no instances, corresponding to the *does not exist* state. The container will at some time after deployment, create one or more instances of the MDB component class, these instances thereby entering the *ready pool* state. The size of this pool of MDB instances will depend on deployment information provided in vendor-specific deployment files. In many applications it makes sense

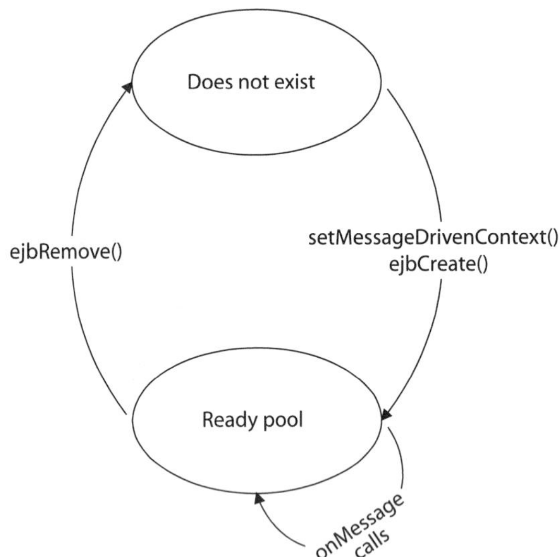

Figure 16.1 The message-driven EJB life cycle.

to have only a single instance of the MDB. This is true of our `DebugMonitor` MDB, since it represents a central point of collection for debugging information.[1]

During the transition from the *does not exist* state to *the ready pool* state the container will call the `setMessageDrivenContext` and `ejbCreate` methods on the component object. The former provides a reference to a `MessageDrivenContext` object that enables you to obtain information about the state of the MDB. The latter gives you the opportunity to obtain references to other EJBs or external resources. Similarly, during the transition in the opposite direction, the container will call `ejbRemove`. Here, you can close connections to external resources. This transition is instigated by the container if it "wishes" to reduce the size of the free pool, perhaps to optimize resource utilization within the container. It may also remove MDB instances if the queue or topic that they are attached to is made unavailable.

The `onMessage` method is called by the container when messages become available on the queue or topic associated with the MDB. Figure 16.2 illustrates an external client sending messages to a JMS `Destination` (this could be a JMS `Queue` or JMS `Topic`). When received, the container, with the aid of the JMS framework, will read the message from the head of the queue or topic and deliver it to one or more MDB instances, via their `onMessage` methods. If the `Destination` is a queue then the message will be sent to an arbitrarily selected MDB instance. If it is a topic, then a duplicate of the message will be sent to all MDBs that subscribe to the topic. Unlike synchronous communication, the client will not have to wait for a method return of control. It simply sends the message to the `Destination`

---

1 Although you could argue for specialised debugging monitors, where each instance of the MDB listens for a particular kind of debugging information.

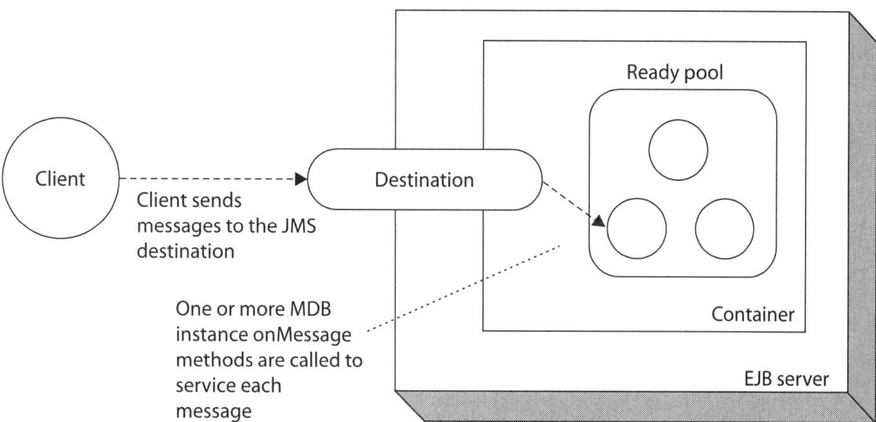

Figure 16.2 Interactions between a client and an MDB via a JMS destination.

and continues its execution. The diagram shows a single external client, but equally there could be any number of EJBs or client/web tier applications acting as clients.

16.3 The Component Class

We illustrate the use of MDBs with a `DebugMonitor` MDB. We will illustrate this MDB working with both queues and topics. For both, a single instance of the `DebugMonitor` listens for debug messages sent to either a JMS queue or a JMS topic (JMS destination). Debug messages are placed on the JMS destination by EJBs in the bookstore application that we wish to debug. In this case, the `Cart` EJB has been updated to send messages to the JMS destination. The MDB implementation is identical for both versions; only the deployment descriptors and client code need to vary.

Listing 16.1 shows part of the code for the `DebugMonitor` MDB. We decided to place the debug-related classes in the `util` package rather than the `store` package, since these classes are not application-specific. An MDB must implement the `javax.ejb.MessageDrivenBean` interface. This defines two methods:

```
public interface MessageDrivenBean extends EnterpriseBean{
  public void ejbRemove() throws EJBException;
  public void setMessageDrivenContext(MessageDrivenContext ctx)
    throws EJBException;
}
```

The `ejbRemove` method was described earlier. The `setMessageDrivenContext` method provides your MDB with a reference to the container-managed `MessageDrivenContext` object. In a similar way to other kinds of EJB, you may wish to use this to obtain further information about the MDB. This interface defines no methods of its own, but inherits methods from `EJBContext` (described in Chapter 13). The only methods that can be called from an MDB are `setRollbackOnly`, `getRollbackOnly` and `getUserTransaction`. We have omitted several deprecated methods from this list. If called, the others will throw `IllegalStateException`. These transaction and security methods will be examined in Chapters 27 and 28, respectively.

The MDB must also provide the `ejbCreate` method that takes no parameters. This is rather like the `ejbCreate` method defined for a stateless session EJB, it is called by the container immediately after the MDB's creation. Use this method to establish connections to external resources or to obtain references to other EJBs.

Listing 16.1 Part of the `DebugMonitorBean`.

```
package util;

import javax.ejb.*;
import javax.jms.*;
import java.io.*;

/*
** This class enables the central monitoring of debugging
** information. It will either write the debug information to
** the standard output or to a specified log file.
** @author Chris Loftus
** @version 2
*/
public class DebugMonitorBean
  implements MessageDrivenBean, MessageListener{

  private MessageDrivenContext mContext;

  private boolean done = false;

  private String currentOutputFile;
  private PrintWriter out;
  // The following two methods are required by the EJB spec but
  // implementations are not required for this class

  public void ejbRemove(){}

  public void setMessageDrivenContext(MessageDrivenContext ctx){
    mContext = ctx;
  }
  public void ejbCreate(){
  }
```

The MDB must also implement the `javax.jms.MessageListener` interface. This defines a single method, namely the `onMessage` method. Listing 16.2 shows the implementation of this method. The comments in the code describe its operation. A utility class called DebugUtil defines several constants used when creating or interrogating debug messages. We will examine this class in Section 16.5. Note that your MDB can reply to a message by using the JMSReplyTo header value. In this case, your MDB needs to identify whether the reply-to destination is a Queue or Topic by using Java's instanceof operator. Once this has been discovered, your code can obtain and use the appropriate kind of JMS message producer, namely TopicPublisher or QueueSender.

The utility method writeOutput is called by onMessage after it has extracted the message properties and contents. If a file pathname is provided with the message then a log file is opened (with write append). This is only done if the current output filename is null or its pathname differs from the new pathname. The MDB will write to standard output if an empty file pathname is provided. This makes it very easy for the client to direct debug messages to specific debug log files, e.g. one for the Cart EJB, another for the Purchase EJB, or to create client-specific log files.

Listing 16.2 The onMessage method.

```
/**
 ** Receives messages sent to an associated JMS queue or topic.
 ** others will be ignored. The TERMINATE_MONITOR message will
 ** be ignored, since we rely on the container to decide when to
 ** terminate this object. Extracts the message properties
 ** CLIENT_NAME, FILE_PATHNAME, CLASS_NAME and METHOD_NAME.
 ** If FILE_PATHNAME contains a non-empty string, this is used
 ** to create or append to a log file with that name.
 ** @param message The JMS message
 */
public void onMessage(Message message){
  // Check if a TextMessage
  if (message instanceof TextMessage){
    String contents = null;
    String clientName = null;
    String filePathname = null;
    String className = null;
    String methodName = null;

    try{
      TextMessage msg = (TextMessage)message;

      // Correct JMSType will be checked automatically using
      // <message-selector> descriptor
      // Get the message contents
      contents = msg.getText();
      if (contents.equals(DebugUtil.TERMINATE_MONITOR)){
        // Ignore this request. It is up to the container to decide
        // when a message driven bean should be terminated
```

```
        }
        else{
          // Get the properties
          clientName = msg.getStringProperty(DebugUtil.CLIENT_NAME);
          filePathname = msg.getStringProperty(DebugUtil.FILE_PATHNAME);
          className = msg.getStringProperty(DebugUtil.CLASS_NAME);
          methodName = msg.getStringProperty(DebugUtil.METHOD_NAME);

          writeOutput(clientName, filePathname, className,
            methodName, contents);
        }
      }
      catch (Exception e){
        // Will force rollback for container-managed transactions
        // where transaction attribute is Required
        throw new EJBException(e);
      }
    }
  }

  private void writeOutput(String clientName,
                           String filePathname,
                           String className,
                           String methodName,
                           String contents) throws IOException{
    // If a filePathname specified then see if current name
    // If yes then write to the current stream
    // Else close old stream

    if (filePathname == null || filePathname.length() == 0){
      System.out.println("client:\t" + clientName);
      System.out.println("class:\t" + className);
      System.out.println("method:\t" + methodName);
      System.out.print(contents); System.out.println();
    }
    else{
      if (currentOutputFile == null ||
          (!currentOutputFile.equals(filePathname))){
        // Close the old stream and open a new one. Append data.
        if (out != null) out.close();
          out = new PrintWriter(
                new BufferedWriter(
                new FileWriter(filePathname, true)));
          currentOutputFile = filePathname;
        }
        // Write the message
```

```
            out.println("client:\t" + clientName);
            out.println("class:\t" + className);
            out.println("method:\t" + methodName);
            out.print(contents); out.println(); out.flush();
        }
    }
}
```

16.4 The Deployment Descriptor Files

There are both standard and vendor-specific deployment descriptors used to define MDBs and their properties. For JBoss there are two JBoss-specific files we need to consider, namely `jboss.xml` which defines non-standard deployment descriptors for the MDB, and `jboss-destinations-service.xml` where JMS queues and topics can be defined.[2]

16.4.1 The `ejb-jar.xml` File

Listing 16.3 shows the standard deployment descriptors for the `DebugMonitor` MDB. An MDB is declared using the `<message-driven>` tag. As with other EJB declarations, this may be followed by several optional description and icon tags. These must be followed by an `<ejb-name>` tag, identifying the EJB. This must be followed by an `<ejb-class>` tag. A fully qualified package name for the component class must be given. Notice that, unlike other kinds of EJB, there are no business logic or life cycle interface tags; all access being through the JMS destination queue or topic.

The `<message-selector>` tag is optional. It is used to filter messages sent to the JMS destination. In this case we only want to allow messages with the "`DEBUG`" `JMSType` property. The selector constraint language was described in Chapter 7. The advantage of using this tag is that we do not need to hard-code message selection checks in our component class. The tag makes it very easy to control the behaviour of the MDB.

The `<transaction-type>` tag is mandatory. As with other kinds of EJB, this tag either has the value `Container` or `Bean`. The former requests that the container handles transactions (starts, commits or rolls them back). The latter requires you to code the transaction handling explicitly, as we will see in Chapter 27.

The optional `<acknowledge-mode>` tag can have the values `Auto-acknowledge` (the default if the descriptor is missing) or `Dups-ok-acknowledge`. The tag only influences the container where bean-managed transactions are being used (so it will be ignored in our example). Where container-managed transactions are used, the container will always auto-acknowledge the message receipt during transaction commit (which is managed by the container). For bean-managed transactions, the `Auto-acknowledge` value forces the container to acknowledge the message automatically on its arrival. The `Dups-ok-acknlowledge` allows for lazy acknowledgment of incoming messages, and can lead to the

2 Note that this was the name of the file used in JBoss 3.0. This could change in later versions.

sending of duplicate messages. However, it provides a performance enhancement avoiding the overhead otherwise required to prevent duplicates. Use it only if your application can handle duplicate messages.

The optional `<message-driven-destination>` tag specifies whether the MDB is to be tied to a JMS topic or queue. Future versions of the EJB specification might well allow for other types of messaging system, not just JMS.

Two `<resource-ref>` tags are included for the `Cart` entity EJB. As we will see later, the `CartBean` component code has been modified to send debug messages to a debug queue. JMS resources (queues, topics and connection factories) are published via the JNDI directory namespace. The `<resource-ref>` tags enable us to decouple the actual JNDI pathnames used in an environment from the logical lookup names used in our EJBs. The `Cart` EJB obtains a `QueueConnectionFactory` object using the logical name `jms/factory`. It also obtains the debug queue with the name `jms/debugDestination`. As we will see, these logical environment naming context (ENC) names are mapped onto actual JNDI names in `jboss.xml`. This is another use of the ENC (see Chapter 15) that provides decoupling between the actual location of resources and the logical location names used within our code. If we move the `Cart` EJB to another server where the JMS resources have different location names, we need only change the vendor-specific deployment descriptors to map to these new names; no code needs to be modified.

Finally, the `<env-entry>` tag (see Chapter 15) is included so that we can pass a boolean flag to the `Cart` EJB. As we will see in Section 16.5, this flag enables the `Cart` to decide whether to send debug messages to a `Queue` or to a `Topic`.

Listing 16.3 `ejb-jar.xml` file highlighting message-driven EJB-related descriptors.

```
<ejb-jar>
  <enterprise-beans>
    <!-- Some descriptors omitted -->
    <entity>
      <ejb-name>Cart</ejb-name>
      <!-- Some descriptors omitted -->
      <resource-ref>
        <res-ref-name>jms/factory</res-ref-name>
        <res-type>javax.jms.QueueConnectionFactory</res-type>
        <res-auth>Container</res-auth>
      </resource-ref>
      <resource-ref>
        <res-ref-name>jms/debugDestination</res-ref-name>
        <res-type>javax.jms.Queue</res-type>
        <res-auth>Container</res-auth>
      </resource-ref>
      <env-entry>
        <env-entry-name>debugByQueue</env-entry-name>
        <env-entry-type>java.lang.Boolean</env-entry-type>
        <env-entry-value>true</env-entry-value>
      </env-entry>
```

```
    </entity>
    <!-- Some descriptors omitted -->
    <message-driven>
      <ejb-name>DebugMonitor</ejb-name>
      <ejb-class>util.DebugMonitorBean</ejb-class>
      <message-selector>JMSType = 'DEBUG'</message-selector>
      <transaction-type>Container</transaction-type>
      <acknowledge-mode>Auto-acknowledge</acknowledge-mode>
      <message-driven-destination>
        <destination-type>javax.jms.Queue</destination-type>
      </message-driven-destination>
    </message-driven>
  </enterprise-beans>
  <!-- Some descriptors omitted -->
</ejb-jar>
```

16.4.2 The `ejb-jar.xml` file (for EJB 2.1)

The EJB 2.1 specification has changed the way MDBs are configured. Listing 16.4 provides the EJB 2.1-compliant version of Listing 16.3.

Listing 16.4 `ejb-jar.xml` file highlighting tags new to EJB 2.1.

```
<ejb-jar>
  <enterprise-beans>
    <!-- Some descriptors omitted -->
    <entity>
      <ejb-name>Cart</ejb-name>
      <!-- Some descriptors omitted -->
      <resource-ref>
        <res-ref-name>jms/factory</res-ref-name>
        <res-type>javax.jms.QueueConnectionFactory</res-type>
        <res-auth>Container</res-auth>
      </resource-ref>
      <message-destination-ref>
        <message-destination-ref-name>
          jms/debugDestination
        </message-destination-ref-name>
        <message-destination-type>
          javax.jms.Queue
        </message-destination-type>
        <message-destination-usage>
          Produces
        </message-destination-usage>
        <message-destination-link>
          DebugQueue
```

```
        </message-destination-link>
      </message-destination-ref>
      <env-entry>
        <env-entry-name>debugByQueue</env-entry-name>
        <env-entry-type>java.lang.Boolean</env-entry-type>
        <env-entry-value>true</env-entry-value>
      </env-entry>
    </entity>
    <!-- Some descriptors omitted -->
    <message-driven>
      <ejb-name>DebugMonitor</ejb-name>
      <ejb-class>util.DebugMonitorBean</ejb-class>
      <activation-config>
        <activation-config-property>
          <activation-config-property-name>
            messageSelector
          </activation-config-property-name>
          <activation-config-property-value>
            JMSType = 'DEBUG'
          </activation-config-property-value>
        </activation-config-property>
        <activation-config-property>
          <activation-config-property-name>
            acknowledgeMode
          </activation-config-property-name>
          <activation-config-property-value>
            Auto-acknowledge
          </activation-config-property-value>
        </activation-config-property>
        <activation-config-property>
          <activation-config-property-name>
            destinationType
          </activation-config-property-name>
          <activation-config-property-value>
            javax.jms.Queue
          </activation-config-property-value>
        </activation-config-property>
      </activation-config>
      <transaction-type>Container</transaction-type>
      <message-destination-link>
        DebugQueue
      </message-destination-link>
     </message-driven>
  </enterprise-beans>
  <application-assembly>
    <!-- Some descriptors omitted -->
```

```
      <message-destination>
        <message-destintation-name>
          DebugQueue
        </message-destination-name>
      </message-destination>
    </application-assembly>
  </ejb-jar>
```

The types of configuration and their values remain unchanged. However, EJB 2.1 provides a new way of declaring them. The `<activation-config>` tag packages up all the configuration properties. Each such property is declared using an `<activation-config-property>` tag. The `<activation-config-property-name>` tag declares the kind of property and the `<activation-config-property-value>` tag provides an appropriate value.

Another change is the way Queues and Topics are added to the environment-naming context of other EJBs. There is now a `<message-destination-ref>` tag. Two of the sub-tags require further explanation.

The `<message-destination-usage>` tag indicates the role the EJB will play with respect to the Queue or Topic. In this case the `Cart` will act as a producer and send messages to the queue. However, it could be declared to be a consumer or both a producer and consumer.

The `<message-destination-link>` tag provides a way of tying the ENC name to the MDB that services the Queue or Topic. Notice that `DebugMonitor` also has the same tag, and the `<assembly-descriptor>` tag has a sub-tag called `<message-destination>`. It is this latter tag that ties together the `Cart` with `DebugMonitor` by referring to the same message link name.

16.4.3 The JBoss `jboss.xml` File

One role of the `jboss.xml` file is used to map logical JMS resource location names onto their real location names. In Listing 16.5, the `Cart` descriptors include `<resource-ref>` tags that do this mapping. The MDB is represented by the `<message-driven>` tag. This has an `<ejb-name>` that must correspond to the name used in the `ejb-jar.xml` file. The `<configuration-name>` tag refers to a set of JMS-specific container configuration descriptors, in this case defined in a standard JBoss configuration file. Optionally, you can override the standard configuration using a `<container-configurations>` tag in the `jboss.xml` file (see the JBoss documentation). Some optional configuration information has been included under the `<message-driven>` tag. The `<container-pool-conf>` tag can be used to specify the maximum and minimum number of MDB instances. Here, we want to ensure that one and only one instance of the `DebugMonitor` MDB is created.

Listing 16.5 `jboss.xml` file highlighting JMS resource mappings and JMS pool configuration.

```
<?xml version="1.0"?>
<jboss>
  <enterprise-beans>
    <entity>
      <ejb-name>Cart</ejb-name>
      <local-jndi-name>ejb/cart</local-jndi-name>
```

```
      <resource-ref>
        <res-ref-name>jms/factory</res-ref-name>
        <jndi-name>ConnectionFactory</jndi-name>
      </resource-ref>
      <resource-ref>
        <res-ref-name>jms/debugDestination</res-ref-name>
        <jndi-name>queue/debugger</jndi-name>
      </resource-ref>
    </entity>
    <!-- Some descriptors omitted -->
    <message-driven>
      <ejb-name>DebugMonitor</ejb-name>
      <configuration-name>
        Standard Message Driven Bean
      </configuration-name>
      <destination-jndi-name>queue/debugMonitor</destination-jndi-name>
      <container-pool-conf>
        <MaximumSize>1</MaximumSize>
        <MinimumSize>1</MinimumSize>
      </container-pool-conf>
    </message-driven>
  </enterprise-beans>
</jboss>
```

16.4.4 The JBoss `jboss-destinations-service.xml` file

JMS queue and topics can be defined in the standard JBoss configuration file: `jboss-destinations-service.xml`. In JBoss 3, this file is located in the directory `jboss-3.0.0/server/default/deploy`. The `<mbean>` entry we used for the debugger queue is:

```
<mbean code="org.jboss.mq.server.jmx.Queue"
      name="jboss.mq.destination:service=Queue,name=debugger">
  <depends optional-attribute-name="DestinationManager">
    jboss.mq:service=DestinationManager
  </depends>
</mbean>
```

16.4.5 `DebugMonitor` Connected to a JMS Topic

In this section we explore the changes we need to make to the descriptors if we decide to use a `Topic` rather than a `Queue`. We might want to use a `Topic` if we have several different MDBs each of which subscribes to and receives messages sent to the `Topic`. Listings 16.6 and 16.7 show the changes made to `ejb-jar.xml`, with changes shown in bold. Clearly, we need to specify that we are now using `Topic`-related classes. The `debugByQueue` value is set to `false`, to indicate to the

Cart that it should send messages to a Topic rather than a Queue. We have also specified that the Topic must be durable, that is, if the server crashes then messages sent to the Topic will persist. If the <subscription-durability> tag is omitted, then the Topic is assumed to be non-durable. The tag can take the values Durable and NonDurable.

Listing 16.6 ejb-jar.xml revised for topics (for EJB 2.0).

```
<ejb-jar>
  <enterprise-beans>
    <!-- Some descriptors omitted -->
    <entity>
      <ejb-name>Cart</ejb-name>
      <!-- Some descriptors omitted -->
      <resource-ref>
        <res-ref-name>jms/factory</res-ref-name>
        <res-type>javax.jms.TopicConnectionFactory</res-type>
        <res-auth>Container</res-auth>
      </resource-ref>
      <resource-ref>
        <res-ref-name>jms/debugDestination</res-ref-name>
        <res-type>javax.jms.Topic</res-type>
        <res-auth>Container</res-auth>
      </resource-ref>
      <env-entry>
        <env-entry-name>debugByQueue</env-entry-name>
        <env-entry-type>java.lang.Boolean</env-entry-type>
        <env-entry-value>false</env-entry-value>
      </env-entry>
    </entity>
    <!-- Some descriptors omitted -->
    <message-driven>
      <ejb-name>DebugMonitor</ejb-name>
      <ejb-class>util.DebugMonitorBean</ejb-class>
      <message-selector>JMSType = 'DEBUG'</message-selector>
      <transaction-type>Container</transaction-type>
      <acknowledge-mode>Auto-acknowledge</acknowledge-mode>
      <message-driven-destination>
        <destination-type>javax.jms.Topic</destination-type>
        <subscription-durability>Durable</subscription-durability>
      </message-driven-destination>
    </message-driven>
  </enterprise-beans>
  <!-- Some descriptors omitted -->
</ejb-jar>
```

Listing 16.7 `ejb-jar.xml` revised for topics (for EJB 2.1)

```
<ejb-jar>
  <enterprise-beans>
    <!-- Some descriptors omitted -->
    <message-driven>
      <ejb-name>DebugMonitor</ejb-name>
      <ejb-class>util.DebugMonitorBean</ejb-class>
      <activation-config>
        <activation-config-property>
          <activation-config-property-name>
            messageSelector
          </activation-config-property-name>
          <activation-config-property-value>
            JMSType = 'DEBUG'
          </activation-config-property-value>
        </activation-config-property>
        <activation-config-property>
          <activation-config-property-name>
            acknowledgeMode
          </activation-config-property-name>
          <activation-config-property-value>
            Auto-acknowledge
          </activation-config-property-value>
        </activation-config-property>
        <activation-config-property>
          <activation-config-property-name>
            destinationType
          </activation-config-property-name>
          <activation-config-property-value>
            javax.jms.Topic
          </activation-config-property-value>
        </activation-config-property>
        <activation-config-property>
          <activation-config-property-name>
            subscriptionDurability
          </activation-config-property-name>
          <activation-config-property-value>
            Durable
          </activation-config-property-value>
        </activation-config-property>
      </activation-config>
      <transaction-type>Container</transaction-type>
      <message-destination-link>
        DebugQueue
      </message-destination-link>
```

```
    </message-driven>
  </enterprise-beans>
  <!-- Some descriptors omitted -->
</ejb-jar>
```

The jboss.xml file must also be altered to support topics. In Listing 16.8 we have included three new tags. These tags are mandatory for durable topics, but can be omitted for non-durable topics. The <mdb-user> and <mdb-passwd> tags identify the logical user security credentials to be used by the MDB when it accesses the associated Topic. We discuss J2EE security issues further in Chapter 28. The <mdb-subscription-id> is used to tie this MDB with the durable topic defined in other JBoss configuration files. These files are jbossmq-state.xml (in directory .../server/default/conf) and jbossmq-destinations-service.xml (in directory .../server/default/deploy). The former is used to specify logical security credentials and roles that are to be used with JMS resources, such as durable subscriptions to topics. The latter file is used to declare queues and topics, and access permissions granted to logical security roles.

Listing 16.8 Revised jboss.xml file.

```
<?xml version="1.0"?>
<jboss>
  <enterprise-beans>
      <entity>
          <ejb-name>Cart</ejb-name>
          <local-jndi-name>ejb/cart</local-jndi-name>
          <resource-ref>
              <res-ref-name>jms/factory</res-ref-name>
              <jndi-name>ConnectionFactory</jndi-name>
          </resource-ref>
          <resource-ref>
              <res-ref-name>jms/debugDestination</res-ref-name>
              <jndi-name>queue/debugger</jndi-name>
          </resource-ref>
      </entity>
      <!-- Some descriptors omitted -->
      <message-driven>
          <ejb-name>DebugMonitor</ejb-name>
          <configuration-name>
              Standard Message Driven Bean
          </configuration-name>
          <destination-jndi-name>queue/debugMonitor</destination-jndi-
name>
          <mdb-user>Admin</mdb-user>
          <mdb-passwd>debug</mdb-passwd>
          <mdb-subscription-id>DurableDebugger</mdb-subscription-id>
          <container-pool-conf>
```

```
            <MaximumSize>1</MaximumSize>
            <MinimumSize>1</MinimumSize>
        </container-pool-conf>
    </message-driven>
  </enterprise-beans>
</jboss>
```

Listing 16.9 shows part of the jbossmq-state.xml file. Here we declare logical security credentials for users and roles. One of the <User> tags declares the Admin user and associates it with the DurableDebugger identifier. The <DurableSubscription> tag ties this identifier to the specific debugger Topic. The Admin user is assigned two roles, namely guest and Adminstrator. These roles are referenced in the jbossmq-destinations-service.xml file. The guest role is a default role assigned to clients that have not provided credentials. The container inserts further subscription information into the empty <DurableSubscriptions> tag at runtime; you need not provide any values.

Listing 16.9 The jbossmq-state.xml file.

```
<?xml version="1.0" encoding="UTF-8"?>
<StateManager>
  <Users>
    <User>
      <Name>Admin</Name>
      <Password>debug</Password>
      <Id>DurableDebugger</Id>
      <DurableSubscription>
        <Name>DurableDebugger</Name>
        <TopicName>debugger</TopicName>
      </DurableSubscription>
    </User>
    <User>
      <Name>guest</Name>
      <Password>guest</Password>
    </User>
    <!-- Other tags omitted -->
  </Users>
  <Roles>
    <Role name="guest">
      <UserName>guest</UserName>
      <UserName>Admin</UserName>
    </Role>
    <Role name="Administrator">
      <UserName>Admin</UserName>
    </Role>
    <!-- Other tags omitted -->
```

```
  </Roles>
  <DurableSubscriptions>
  </DurableSubscriptions>
</StateManager>
```

Listing 16.10 shows a fragment of the jbossmq-destinations-service.xml file. We have specified the JNDI name of the Topic as debugger. In fact JBoss prefixes this with the word topic giving the full JNDI name topic/debugger. The SecurityConf attribute allows us to restrict which security roles may access the topic and the privileges granted to users with those roles. Here, the Administrator can create, write and read the topic, whereas guest users may only read and write to the topic. We have allowed guest access since the Cart EJB deployment descriptors do not restrict access to specific security roles, and by default will be granted the guest role. As we will see in the next section, the Cart acting in this guest role will need to write debug messages to topic/debugger.

Listing 16.10 The jbossmq-destinations-service.xml file.

```
<mbean code="org.jboss.mq.server.jmx.Topic"
    name="jboss.mq.destination:service=Topic,name=debugger">
  <depends optional-attribute-name="DestinationManager">
    jboss.mq:service=DestinationManager
  </depends>
  <attribute name="SecurityConf">
    <security>
      <role name="guest" read="true" write="true"/>
      <role name="Administrator" read="true" write="true" create="true"/>
    </security>
  </attribute>
</mbean>
```

16.5 Accessing the EJB From Other EJBs

The MDB is not directly accessed from clients (other EJBs or application or Web clients); rather all communication is through the JMS Destination, be it Topic or Queue. Also, the MDB clients are identical to any JMS application that needs to send messages via a Destination, as discussed in Chapter 7. However, to complete the debugger example, Listings 16.11–16.13 present the client perspective.

Listing 16.11 shows parts of the modified CartBean class (modifications in bold; see Chapter 15 for the previous version). The DebugSender class is used to send debugging information via a Topic or Queue. Three ENC references are used to access JMS-related resources and information. The DEBUG_BY_QUEUE_REF is used by CartBean to obtain the byQueue environment entry. This is obtained in the setEntityContext method. This method also creates a DebugSender object, passing the factory and destination ENC values and the byQueue value to its constructor. The pathname of a log file is also passed, which is ultimately passed on to the DebugMonitor MDB.

The DebugSender class provides methods for recording the name of the class being debugged, the name of the method sending the debug message and the debug message itself.

Listing 16.11 Modified CartBean implementation class.

```
package store;

import util.DebugSender;
// Other import statements

/**
 * The cart entity bean is a simplified shopping cart as used by many
 * online shops.
 * It is possible to add items to a shopping cart, remove them
 * determine how they cost, etc.
 * @author John Hunt & Chris Loftus
 * @version 3.0
 */
abstract public class CartBean implements EntityBean {
  // Other instance variables
  private DebugSender ds;
  private boolean byQueue = true;
  // Other ENC references
  // ENC references to JMS resources
  private static final String DEBUGGER_DESTINATION_REF =
    "java:comp/env/jms/debugDestination";
  private static final String CONNECTION_FACTORY_REF =
    "java:comp/env/jms/factory";
  private static final String DEBUG_BY_QUEUE_REF =
    "java:comp/env/debugByQueue";
  private static final String DEBUG_LOG_FILE = "debug.log";

  // Container managed fields follow (defined in ejb-jar.xml)
  // Omitted

  public void setEntityContext(EntityContext context){
    ctx = context;
    // Establish the JMS connection to the DebugMontiorBean
    try{
      InitialContext ictx = new InitialContext();
      byQueue = ((Boolean)ictx.lookup(DEBUG_BY_QUEUE_REF)).booleanValue();
    }
    catch(Exception e){}
```

```
    try{
      ds = new DebugSender(DEBUGGER_DESTINATION_REF,
                           CONNECTION_FACTORY_REF,
                           "", DEBUG_LOG_FILE, byQueue);
      ds.setClassName("store.CartBean");
      ds.setMethodName("setEntityContext");
      ds.sendMessage("Completed successfully");
    }
    catch(Exception e){
      throw new EJBException(e);
    }
  }

  // Several callback methods omitted

  public CartPK ejbCreate(String customerId) throws CreateException{
    this.setId(customerId);
    this.itemHome = this.getItemHome();

    ds.setMethodName("ejbCreate");
    try{
      ds.sendMessage("customerId = " + customerId);
      ds.sendMessage("Completed successfully");
    }
    catch(Exception e){
      throw new EJBException(e);
    }
    return null;
  }

  // ejbPostCreate omitted

  // Business methods

  public void add(Book item) throws FinderException{
    try{
      ds.setMethodName("add");
      ds.sendMessage("Started. Book = " + item);
      BookItemLocal bookItem = itemHome.findByPrimaryKey(item.getIsbn());
      Collection items = this.getCartItems();
      items.add(bookItem);
      ds.sendMessage("Completed successfully");
    }
    catch(FinderException fe){
      throw fe;
    }
```

```
      catch(Exception e){
        throw new EJBException(e);
      }
    }
    // Other business methods omitted
  }
```

Let's take a look at the DebugSender class (Listing 16.12). The comments within the code describe its operation. However, it is worth highlighting a few points. The second constructor establishes a connection with the queue or topic using the DebugUtil class. A TextMessage object is created once and then reused by the sendMessage method, rather than being repeatedly recreated. The terminateMonitor method sends a special DebugUtil.TERMINATE_MONITOR message. This gives a debug monitor the opportunity to terminate. In our example, the DebugMonitor MDB ignores this message.

Listing 16.12 The DebugSender class.

```
package util;

import javax.jms.*;
/**
 ** This class provides methods that support construction
 ** and sending of debug messages via JMS Queues or Topics.
 ** Each message sent will set the JMSType header to DebugUtil.DEBUG_TYPE
 ** and the message properties:
 ** <p>
 ** <ul>
 **   <li>DebugUtil.CLIENT_NAME   <t> A name to help distinguish messages
 **   <li>DebugUtil.FILE_PATHNAME <t> The name that can be used for a log
 **                                   file
 **   <li>DebugUtil.CLASS_NAME    <t> The name of the class sending the
 **                                   message
 **   <li>DebugUtil.METHOD_NAME   <t> The name of the method sending the
 **                                   message
 ** </ul>
 ** @author Chris Loftus
 ** @version 1.0
 */
public class DebugSender{

  private String destinationName;
  private String factoryName;
  private String clientName;
  private String filePathname;
  private String className;
  private String methodName;
```

```
private boolean byQueue;

private QueueConnection queueConnection;
private QueueSender queueSender;
private QueueSession queueSession;
private TopicConnection topicConnection;
private TopicPublisher topicPublisher;
private TopicSession topicSession;

private TextMessage debugMessage;

/**
 ** Establishes a JMS Queue or Topic connection, session
 ** and sender or publisher. As part of this it obtains the
 ** JMS Queue or Topic via JNDI.
 ** @param destinationName Contains the JNDI name for the JMS Destination
 ** @param factoryName Contains the JNDI name for the JMS connection factory
 ** @param byQueue If true, DebugSender will establish a Queue connection
 **        else if false a Topic connection
 ** @exception Exception Is thrown if there's a problem interacting with
 ** JMS
 */
public DebugSender(String destinationName,
                   String factoryName,
                   boolean byQueue) throws Exception{
  this(destinationName, factoryName, "", "", byQueue);
}

/**
 ** Establishes a JMS Queue or Topic connection, session
 ** and sender or publisher. As part of this it obtains the
 ** JMS Queue or Topic via JNDI.
 ** @param destinationName Contains the JNDI name for the JMS Destination
 ** @param factoryName Contains the JNDI name for the JMS connection factory
 ** @param clientName Used to record a client name for each message sent
 ** @param filePathname Used to record a debug log pathname for each
 **    message sent
 ** @param byQueue If true, DebugSender will establish a Queue connection
 **      else if false a Topic connection
 ** @exception Exception Is thrown if there's a problem interacting with
 ** JMS
 */
public DebugSender(String destinationName,
                   String factoryName,
                   String clientName,
                   String filePathname,
```

```
                    boolean byQueue) throws Exception{
    DebugUtil dUtil = new DebugUtil();
    try{
      if (byQueue){
        QueueConnectionFactory queueConnectionFactory =
          (QueueConnectionFactory)dUtil.getJNDIObject(factoryName);
        queueConnection =
          queueConnectionFactory.createQueueConnection();
        queueSession =
          queueConnection.createQueueSession(false,
                                        Session.AUTO_ACKNOWLEDGE);
        Queue queue = (Queue)dUtil.getJNDIObject(destinationName);
        queueSender = queueSession.createSender(queue);

        // Might as well create this once and then reuse each time
        // we send a message
        debugMessage = queueSession.createTextMessage();
      }
      else{
        // Assume it's a topic
        TopicConnectionFactory topicConnectionFactory =
          (TopicConnectionFactory)dUtil.getJNDIObject(factoryName);
        topicConnection =
          topicConnectionFactory.createTopicConnection();
        topicSession =
          topicConnection.createTopicSession(false,
                                        Session.AUTO_ACKNOWLEDGE);
        Topic topic = (Topic)dUtil.getJNDIObject(destinationName);
        topicPublisher = topicSession.createPublisher(topic);

        // Might as well create this once and then reuse each time
        // we send a message
        debugMessage = topicSession.createTextMessage();
      }
      // Set its JMSType to "DEBUG"
      debugMessage.setJMSType(DebugUtil.DEBUG_TYPE);
    }
    catch(Exception e){
      System.err.println("Connection problem: " + e.toString());
      if (byQueue){
        if (queueConnection != null){
          try{
            queueConnection.close();
          }
          catch (JMSException ee) {}
        }
```

```
    }
    else{
      if (topicConnection != null){
        try{
          topicConnection.close();
        }
        catch (JMSException ee) {}
        }
      }
      // Really ought to throw application-specific exception
      // that is more user-friendly
      throw e;
    }

    // Set the instance variables
    this.destinationName = destinationName;
    this.factoryName = factoryName;
    this.byQueue = byQueue;
    this.clientName = clientName;
    this.filePathname = filePathname;
}
/**
 ** Obtains the Destination JNDI name
 ** @return The Destination JNDI name
 */
public String getDestinationName(){
  return destinationName;
}
/**
 ** Obtains the Factory JNDI name
 ** @return The Factory JNDI name
 */
public String getFactoryName(){
  return factoryName;
}
/**
 ** Are we supporting queues or topics?
 ** @return true if queues, else false
 */
public boolean isByQueue(){
  return byQueue;
}
/**
 ** Resets the client name
 ** @param clientName The new client name
 */
```

```
public void setClientName(String clientName){
  this.clientName = clientName;
}
/**
 ** Obtains the client name
 ** @return The client name
 */
public String getClientName(){
  return clientName;
}
/**
 ** Resets the log file pathname
 ** @param filePathname The new pathname
 */
public void setFilePathname(String filePathname){
  this.filePathname = filePathname;
}
/**
 ** Obtains the log file pathname
 ** @return The debug log file pathname
 */
public String getFilePathname(){
  return filePathname;
}
/**
 ** Resets the class name
 ** @param className The new class name
 */
public void setClassName(String className){
  this.className = className;
}
/**
 ** Obtains the class name
 ** @return The class name
 */
public String getClassName(){
  return className;
}
/**
 ** Resets the method name
 ** @param methodName The new method name
 */
public void setMethodName(String methodName){
  this.methodName = methodName;
}
/**
```

```
 ** Obtains the method name
 ** @return The method name
 */
public String getMethodName(){
  return methodName;
}

/**
 ** Populates the message with data and sends/publishes it
 ** @param message The debug message
 ** @exception Thrown if the message cannot be sent/published
 */
public void sendMessage(String message) throws Exception{
  debugMessage.setStringProperty(DebugUtil.CLIENT_NAME,
                                 this.clientName);
  debugMessage.setStringProperty(DebugUtil.FILE_PATHNAME,
                                 this.filePathname);
  debugMessage.setStringProperty(DebugUtil.CLASS_NAME, this.className);
  debugMessage.setStringProperty(DebugUtil.METHOD_NAME,
                                 this.methodName);
  debugMessage.setText(message);
  if (byQueue){
    queueSender.send(debugMessage);
  }
  else{
    topicPublisher.publish(debugMessage);
  }
}
/**
 ** Closes the JMS connection
 */
public void close(){
  try{
    if (byQueue){
      queueConnection.close();
    }
    else{
      topicConnection.close();
    }
  }
  catch(Exception e){}
}

protected void finalize() throws Throwable{
  super.finalize();
  this.close();
```

```
    }

    private void terminateMonitor() throws Exception{
      debugMessage.setText(DebugUtil.TERMINATE_MONITOR);
      if (byQueue){
        queueSender.send(debugMessage);
      }
      else{
        topicPublisher.publish(debugMessage);
      }
    }
  }
```

The final piece of the puzzle is shown in Listing 16.13. This provides some useful constants and the getJNDIObject method used by DebugSender. Again you are encouraged to scan the comments for an explanation of its purpose.

Listing 16.13 The DebugUtil class.

```
package util;

import java.util.Properties;
import javax.naming.*;
/**
 ** A set of constants and a method to assist with the use of
 ** JMS as a means of sending debug messages
 */
public class DebugUtil{
  /** Intended to be used as a JMSType value */
  public static final String DEBUG_TYPE = "DEBUG";
  /** Intended to be used as part of a special terminate message */
  public static final String TERMINATE_MONITOR = "TERMINATE";
  /** Property names */
  /** Used if you need to distinguish between messages sent by
   ** different clients
   */
  public static final String CLIENT_NAME = "clientName";
  /** The property that will hold the optional log file pathname */
  public static final String FILE_PATHNAME = "filePathname";
  /** The property that will hold the class name */
  public static final String CLASS_NAME = "className";
  /** The property that will hold the method name */
  public static final String METHOD_NAME = "methodName";

  private InitialContext jndiContext;
```

```
  /**
   ** Uses InitialContext and lookup to obtain a JNDI object
   ** @param jndiName The JNDI lookup name
   ** @return The object retrieved from the JNDI directory space
   ** @exception Exception Thrown if a problem is encountered using JNDI
   */
  public Object getJNDIObject(String jndiName) throws Exception{
    if (jndiContext == null){
      jndiContext = new InitialContext();
    }
    return jndiContext.lookup(jndiName);
  }
}
```

Part 3

Servlets and JSPs

Chapter 17

Web Applications in Java

17.1 Introduction

What is a Java Web Application? This chapter sets out to clarify what is meant in the Java Servlet and JavaServer Pages (JSPs) specification about Web Applications. It introduces the concept of a Web Application, how they are defined, structured, implemented and deployed. It does this using a very simple servlet that displays a welcome message and the current date. In doing so it also introduces the concepts behind servlets and how they work.

17.2 What Are Servlets?

Java has primarily been a language used to implement browser-side programs, also known as applets, when it comes to the Web. However, with the Java Servlet API, the power of Java can be applied to server-side software as well as the client, browser-side software. This chapter tells you how servlets are written, what they are used for and how they interact with browser requests.

Just as applets are (at least conceptually) small applications, in the same way as a piglet is a little pig, servlets are programs that run on the Web server. Of course, just as with applets, the size of a servlet is not restricted and it may be anything from a few lines of code to many thousands (or more) lines of code.

The key is that a servlet runs on the server and will respond to requests from a client either from HTML pages or indeed applets. The server needs to be a Java-enabled Web server. For example, Apache can be Java-enabled using a servlet engine such as Tomcat. More recent versions of the servlet specification have introduced the concept of a Web container running a Web application. The Web application is then comprised of all the elements that make it up, such as HTML pages, image files and servlets (and JavaServer Pages as well). Thus what we really mean when we say a "Java-enabled Web server" is one that understands the concepts of a Web application as specified by the Java Servlet specification (see references at the end of this chapter).

17.3 Web Applications

The Servlet 2.2 specification defined the notion of a Web application, which has been further refined in the 2.3 and 2.4 specifications. Each Web application has:

- an identity (a name and a root URL, welcome pages etc.)
- its own servlet context (an object shared among all servlets in the Web application that can be used for application data)
- all resources needed for the application in the Web-tier: servlet classes, JSP files, gif files, HTML files, deployment descriptors
- XML deployment descriptors used to define the application and how logical resources should be mapped to actual environment resources
- the option of specifying a security domain and indicating which parts of the Web application are to be included in the server security domain
- a specific directory structure that is used to allow the Web container to find the various elements of the Web application

17.4 Structure of a Web Application

The structure of a Web Application as laid out in the servlet specification is illustrated in Figure 17.1. The boxes highlighted in dark grey are compulsory (although the `META-INF` directory and the `Manifest.MF` file are automatically created if you jar this structure up (into a Web ARchive or WAR file) and are not required if you use the structure in its expanded form with, for example, Tomcat). The boxes in light grey are application-specific.

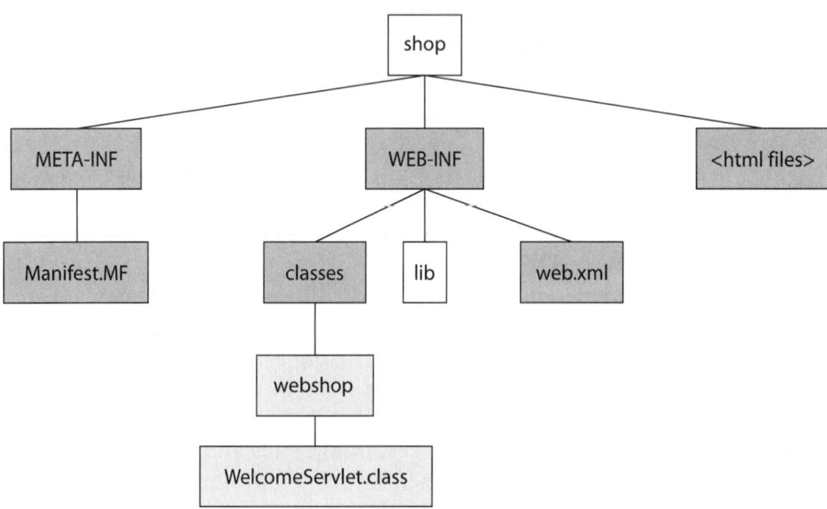

Figure 17.1 The Web Application structure.

The elements presented in Figure 17.1 define the Web application to the Web container (for example Tomcat). The elements are:

- `shop` The root directory for the Web application. The name of this directory is defined in the Web application context in Tomcat.
- `<html files>` All HTML files located at the Web application root are visible to the external Web.
- `WEB-INF` The contents of this directory is hidden from the Web server and contains the class files defining the servlets and any supporting classes. Any jar files used by the Web application should be placed within the `lib` directory. If the class files are not jar'ed up then they must be placed within the classes subdirectory: for example, in Figure 17.1, the webshop package containing the `WelcomeServlet` class.
- `web.xml` This file is an XML file that defines mappings between URLs and servlets and JSPs. It can also specify filters to apply, security domains, session timeouts etc.

17.5 How Servlets Work

Servlets work in the following manner (illustrated in Figure 17.2).

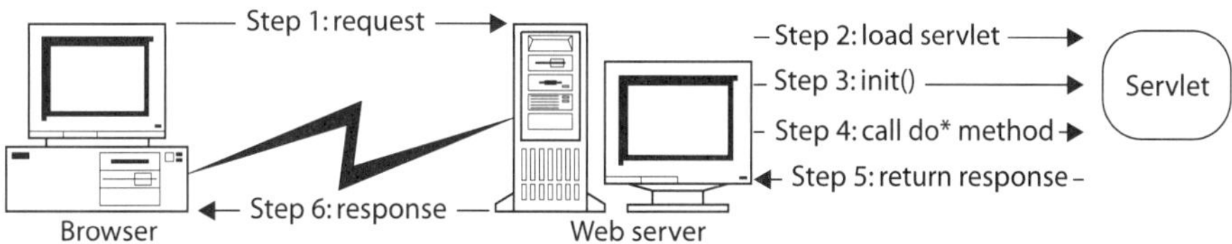

Figure 17.2 Browser–server–servlet interaction.

Step 1: A user using a Web browser requests some information from the Web server via an HTTP request.

Step 2: The Web server receives the request. If the request is for a straightforward HTML page then the appropriate HTML file will be loaded. If the request is to a servlet, then the Web container will load and initiate the servlet (unless it was already running). This is done by running the servlet on a Java Virtual Machine (JVM).

Step 3: The servlet's `init()` method is then executed. This method is the equivalent of the `init()` method defined for applets. That is, it is executed only once, when the servlet is first created. It should be used in the same way as the `init()` method for applets; that is, as the servlet's initialization method (rather than defining a constructor). The `init()` method must complete before any requests are handled.

Step 4: The servlet will receive the HTTP request and perform some type of process. Each request is handled by its own thread (lightweight Java process). Depending upon the request, one of the following methods will be called to handle the request:

- `doGet` – handles `GET`, conditional `GET` and `HEAD` requests.
- `doPost` – handles `POST` requests.
- `doPut` – handles `PUT` requests.
- `doDelete` – handles `DELETE` requests.

Step 5: The servlet will return a response to the Web server from one of the above methods.

Step 6: The Web server will forward the response to the client.

Step 7: When requested, the Web server will terminate the servlet. This may be done by the Web server administrator. At this time the `destroy()` method is called. This method runs only once and is used to "tidy" up any system resources used by the servlet etc. For the servlet to be run again, it must be reloaded by the Web server.

There are five things to note to note about servlets as opposed to applets.

1. The servlet and its environment are completely under the control of those deploying it. That is, you have control of which JVM is used and that this is independent of the browser used by the user. This is important, as it removes concerns associated with the so-called "browser wars".
2. A servlet is not constrained by the applet sandbox. This means that a servlet can reside behind a firewall and can communicate with any and all systems that it needs to. For example, JavaIDL can be used to connect to a CORBA-compliant Object Request Broker (ORB) or sockets to connect to legacy systems (for example implemented in C).
3. The client Web browser does not communicate directly with the servlet. Rather, the browser communicates with the Web server, which in turn communicates with the servlet. Thus if the Web server is secure behind a firewall, then the servlet is also secure.
4. A single servlet can process multiple user requests. That is, one instance (by default) of a servlet is loaded into the Web server and this instance services all user requests. This does not mean that each request is queued. Rather it means that each request is handled by a separate thread (of execution) that uses the same servlet instance. This is illustrated in Figure 17.3.
5. As each servlet is shared among multiple users care must be taken with user-specific data. For example, this means that sensitive user information should not be stored in an instance variable, as the instance is shared among many users. This can be overcome by using an `HttpSession` object that can be obtained from the initial request. Each session object is linked to a single user. We will look at this in the next chapter.

17.6 Why Use Servlets

There are a wide range of situations in which you might wish to use servlets. The example given here is for processing data POSTed over HTTPS using an HTML form. This example could be extended further and could be used as the basis of an e-commerce system. For example, an order entry and processing system could be implemented in this way. The servlet could receive and

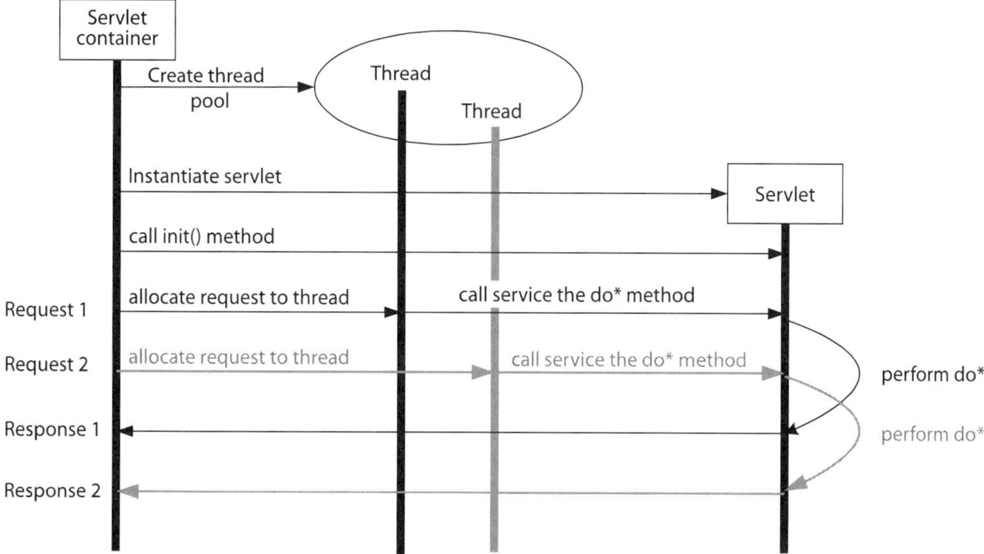

Figure 17.3 Handling multiple requests.

process the information provided. It could then generate a transaction which could be passed to the enterprise's main sales system and onto the deployment and payment systems (remember, a servlet is not restricted in what it can connect to in the way that an applet would be).

Another situation in which you might want to use a servlet is to provide real-time updates to a Web page. Rather than gaining a static Web page generated, say, the night before, the Web page viewed by the user could present the latest data. This could be used to view the current state of stocks and shares etc.

A servlet can also be used to help balance the load on a server. If a server receives a request for a service, but decides that the current server is too heavily loaded, it could forward that request to other servers and servlets. This allows a single logical service to be presented to the user that actually exploits multiple servers.

17.7 The Structure of the Servlet API

The servlet API is made up of a number of packages including the `javax.Servlet` and `javax.Servlet.http` packages. Note that these package names do not start with `java` but with `javax`. This indicates that they are a Java standard extension to the basic Java platform (a standard introduced with JDK 1.2). This means that a Java vendor does not have to support this API (although many vendors are already supporting it). You can obtain the Java Servlet Development Kit 2.0 (the JSDK 2.0) from Sun's Java Web site (see `http://java.sun.com/products/`). This development kit can be used to develop and test server extensions based on the Servlet API. Included in the development kit is the servlet source code, reference documentation and tutorial as well as a standalone server (called `Servletrunner`) that can be used to test servlets before running them in a servlet-enabled Web server.

The key classes and interfaces in the Servlet API are described below and are illustrated in Figure 17.4, along with associated classes and interfaces:

- `Servlet` This interface defines all the methods that a servlet must respond to (including `init()` and `destroy()`). Classes that implement this interface can be used as servlets.
- `HttpServlet` This is an abstract class that is intended to simplify writing HTTP servlets. It extends the `GenericServlet` base class and provides a framework for handling the HTTP protocol. The methods that are overridden by subclasses are `doGet`, `doPost`, `doPut`, `doDelete` and `getServletInfo`. The four do* methods have already been mentioned. The `getServletInfo` method provides information through a service's administrative interfaces. Note that a developer need only override one of these methods and not all of them.
- `HttpServletRequest` This is an interface specification which extends the `ServletRequest` interface. It provides a definition for an object which provides data from the client to the servlet for use in the `HttpServlet`'s methods.
- `HttpServletResponse` This is an interface specification that extends the `ServletResponse` interface. It defines the protocol for an object that manipulates HTTP protocol-specified header information and returns data to its client.

These are the main interfaces and class used by a servlet. Of course, these are not the only classes and interfaces available, but they are the key ones.

17.8 Steps for Developing and Deploying a Web Application

Step 1: Define the Web Application to the Web Container

The first thing to do is to define the Web application to the Web container; in this case define our online welcome application to the Tomcat server. This is done by adding a context XML element to the `conf/server.xml` file (located under the root Tomcat installation directory).

For example, to define a Web application called `shop` we could add a Web context entry, as illustrated in Figure 17.5. This entry indicates that the path containing the root of the Web application will be the directory `shop`. It also specifies that the document base (the location in which to find the HTML files) will also be the directory `shop`. In this case it also ensures that debugging is turned off (the default). It is also possible to force Tomcat to reloaded the Web application if it changes while Tomcat is still executing. In this case we have turned this feature off (`reloadable="false"`), as this is more efficient.

Note that the URL path and the document base do not need to be the same. For example, the `Context path` could be `/shopping` and the `docBase` could be `shop`. In this case the URL that you would enter into the Web browser would be `http://localhost:8080/shopping`, but the files would be stored under a directory called `shop`.

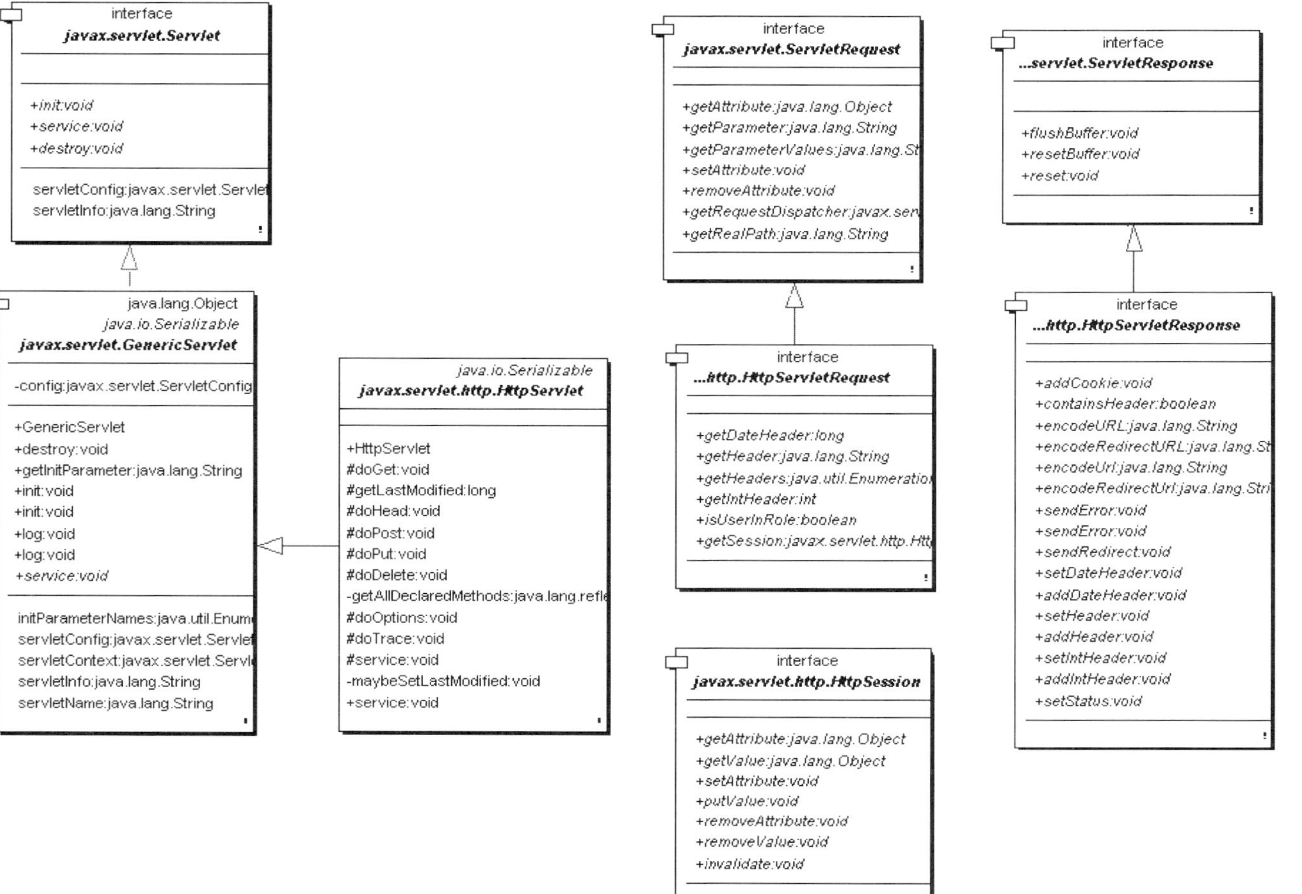

Figure 17.4 Java servlet classes and their inheritance relationships.

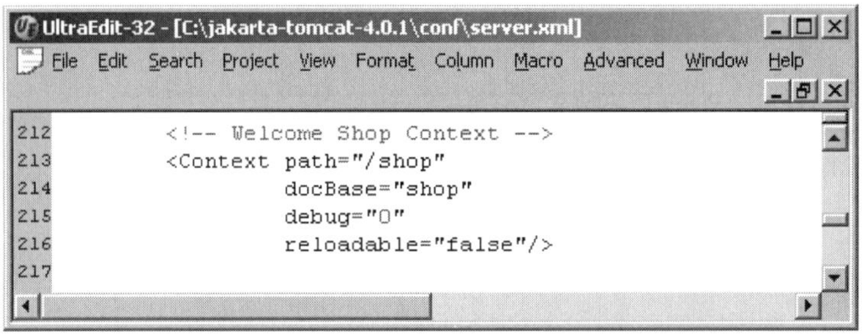

UltraEdit-32 - [C:\jakarta-tomcat-4.0.1\conf\server.xml]

File Edit Search Project View Format Column Macro Advanced Window Help

```
        <!-- Welcome Shop Context -->
        <Context path="/shop"
                 docBase="shop"
                 debug="0"
                 reloadable="false"/>
```

Figure 17.5 Configuring the Web container.

Step 2: Write the Implementation Code

We are now in a position to implement a simple servlet. We will keep things very simple and merely make our servlet generate a Web page with today's date (thus ensuring that it is, to some extent at least, dynamic).

The servlet we will write will include all the basic elements of any servlet: it will do something when it is initialized, it will generate a response to an HTTP request and it will call code in a separate class (the class `Date`).

The actual servlet is illustrated in Figure 17.6. This servlet prints a trace message when it is initialized. Note that the `init` method in a servlet must call the superclass version of the method to initialize the servlet appropriately in servlets running in pre-Servlet 2.3 specification servers). When the `doGet` method is called the servlet again prints a trace message. It then initializes the content type for the response to be `html`. It then obtains a `PrintWriter` that allows output to be generated and sent back to the user's browser. This output is simple HTML encoded as Java strings and printed to the output `PrintWriter`. Note that we could just as easily have used a JSP to do this, as this servlet does not do any real processing other than obtain the current date!

To compile this servlet you must ensure that the servlet jar is available on your classpath. Using Tomcat 4.0.1 a classpath is set as follows:

```
%CATALINA_HOME%\common\lib\Servlet.jar;..\classes
```

where `CATALINA_HOME` points at the Tomcat installation directory.

Once we have compiled this into a class file using javac, we can add it to the Web application. This is done by copying it into the appropriate subdirectory of the classes directory in the Web application directory structure. As the servlet is in a package, that package structure must be maintained in the directory structure under the `classes` directory.

Step 3: Create Web Application Deployment Descriptor

The deployment descriptor for a Web application is defined via XML in a file called `web.xml`. This file helps manage the configuration of the Web application. It must be located at the top level under the `WEB-INF` directory in order for the Web container (Tomcat in this case) to find it. The role of the deployment descriptor is:

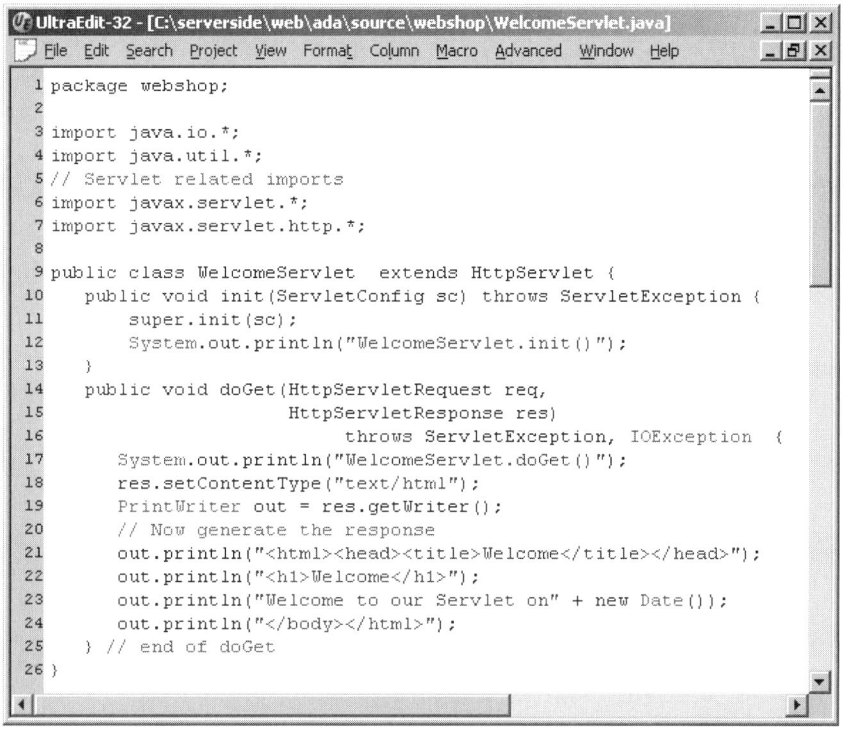

UltraEdit-32 - [C:\serverside\web\ada\source\webshop\WelcomeServlet.java]

File Edit Search Project View Format Column Macro Advanced Window Help

```
package webshop;

import java.io.*;
import java.util.*;
// Servlet related imports
import javax.servlet.*;
import javax.servlet.http.*;

public class WelcomeServlet  extends HttpServlet {
   public void init(ServletConfig sc) throws ServletException {
       super.init(sc);
       System.out.println("WelcomeServlet.init()");
   }
   public void doGet(HttpServletRequest req,
                     HttpServletResponse res)
                          throws ServletException, IOException  {
      System.out.println("WelcomeServlet.doGet()");
      res.setContentType("text/html");
      PrintWriter out = res.getWriter();
      // Now generate the response
      out.println("<html><head><title>Welcome</title></head>");
      out.println("<h1>Welcome</h1>");
      out.println("Welcome to our Servlet on" + new Date());
      out.println("</body></html>");
   } // end of doGet
}
```

Figure 17.6 The `WelcomeServlet`.

- To provide servlet/JSP definitions (including the name of a servlet, its class and description)
- To provide servlet/JSP mappings, that is to provide mappings from URLs to servlets
- To specify security, for example Web container-administered authentication
- To provide for initialization parameters for the whole Web application and for individual servlets
- To specify filters to apply to specific servlets

The `web.xml` file for J2EE SDK 1.3.1 for this simple welcome servlet is illustrated in Figure 17.7. Note the URL pattern in this figure. This means that to access this servlet it will be necessary to enter a URL of the form `http://<hostname>:8080/shop/eshop`. The `shop` part comes from the `server.xml` context specification, while the `eshop` part from the `web.xml` file. Note that port 8080 is the default port used by Tomcat. The `web.xml` file that is compatible with J2EE SDK 1.4 is presented in Figure 17.8.

Step 4: Deploy the Web Application

This can be done in compressed form or, as in this case, in expanded form. This means that we will need to copy the appropriate files to the Tomcat installation folder. On a Windows machine this can be done using the following command:

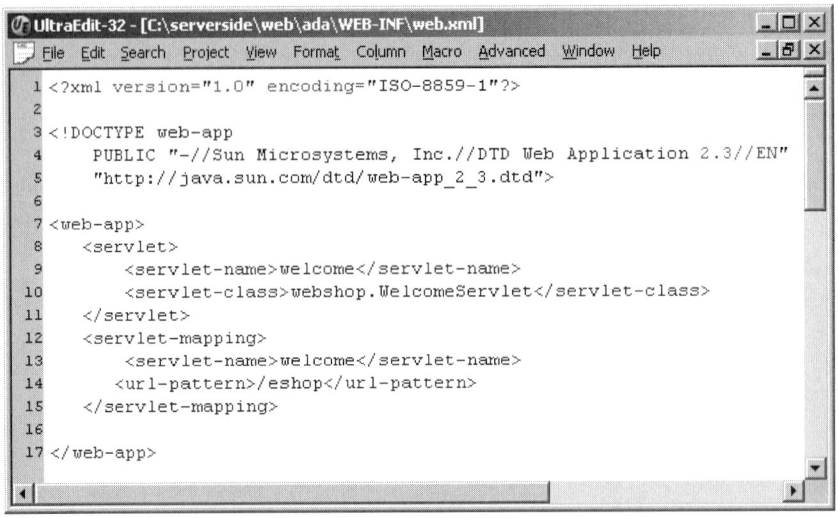

UltraEdit-32 - [C:\serverside\web\ada\WEB-INF\web.xml]

```
<?xml version="1.0" encoding="ISO-8859-1"?>

<!DOCTYPE web-app
    PUBLIC "-//Sun Microsystems, Inc.//DTD Web Application 2.3//EN"
    "http://java.sun.com/dtd/web-app_2_3.dtd">

<web-app>
   <servlet>
       <servlet-name>welcome</servlet-name>
       <servlet-class>webshop.WelcomeServlet</servlet-class>
   </servlet>
   <servlet-mapping>
       <servlet-name>welcome</servlet-name>
      <url-pattern>/eshop</url-pattern>
   </servlet-mapping>

</web-app>
```

Figure 17.7 The `web.xml` file for J2EE SDK 1.3.1.

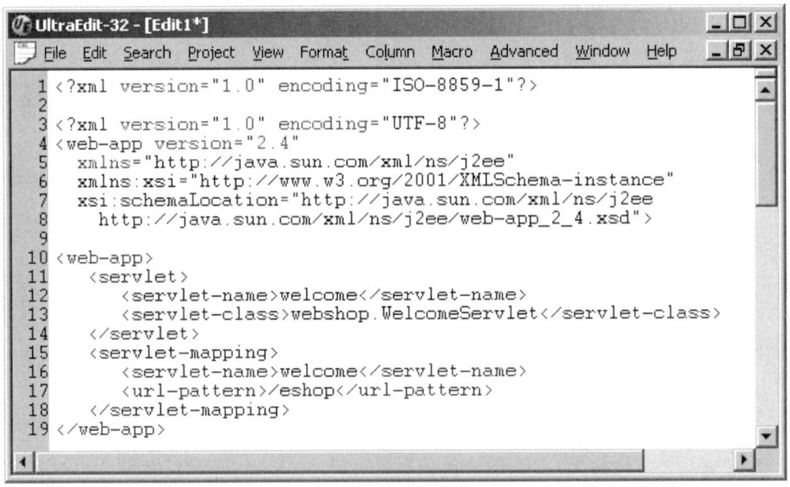

UltraEdit-32 - [Edit1*]

```
<?xml version="1.0" encoding="ISO-8859-1"?>

<?xml version="1.0" encoding="UTF-8"?>
<web-app version="2.4"
  xmlns="http://java.sun.com/xml/ns/j2ee"
  xmlns:xsi="http://www.w3.org/2001/XMLSchema-instance"
  xsi:schemaLocation="http://java.sun.com/xml/ns/j2ee
    http://java.sun.com/xml/ns/j2ee/web-app_2_4.xsd">

<web-app>
   <servlet>
      <servlet-name>welcome</servlet-name>
      <servlet-class>webshop.WelcomeServlet</servlet-class>
   </servlet>
   <servlet-mapping>
      <servlet-name>welcome</servlet-name>
      <url-pattern>/eshop</url-pattern>
   </servlet-mapping>
</web-app>
```

Figure 17.8 The `web.xml` file for J2EE SDK 1.4.

```
call xcopy /Y /E WEB-INF %CATALINA_HOME%\webapps\shop\WEB-INF\.
```

This will copy the contents of the `WEB-INF` directory to the `webapps\shop\WEB-INF` directory under the Tomcat installation directory. The `webapps` directory is the location for all Web applications. We have already specified that the directory `shop` will contain our Web application in the `conf.xml` file in the server directory of the Tomcat installation. Thus we have now copied the

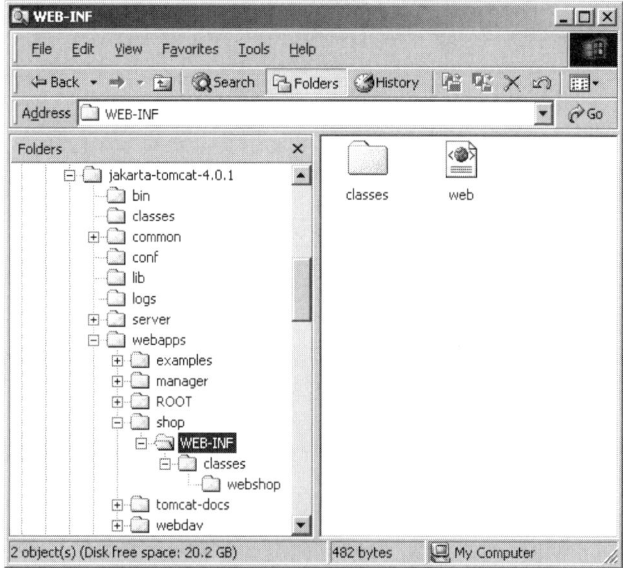

Figure 17.9 The shop Web application structure.

servlet class and the `web.xml` file to the shop directory as required. Note that if there had been HTML files at the application root we would also have needed to copy those.

The end result under the `%CATALINA_HOME%\webapps\shop` directory is illustrated in Figure 17.9.

17.9 Starting Tomcat

To test our Web application we must now start Tomcat. This is done using the `startup.bat` file (or `startup.sh` file if on Unix) found in the `bin` directory under the Tomcat installation directory. Note that you will need to make sure that the `JAVA_HOME` and `CATALINA_HOME` environment variables are set up appropriately. For Tomcat 4.0.1 they were set to the following for this example:

```
CATALINA_HOME: c:\jakarta-tomcat-4.0.1
JAVA_HOME: c:\jdk1.3.1
```

For Tomcat 5.0 you will need to make sure that the `JAVA_HOME` environment veriable points at the J2SE release appropriate for that release; for example, we are using the J2SE SDK 1.4.1 in the directory `C:\j2sdk1.4.1_01`. If you are successful in starting Tomcat a window should appear indicating that the Tomcat service has started.

You can now start a browser and enter the URL `http://localhost:8080/shop/eshop` (you can use your own server name rather than `localhost` if you wish). The Tomcat

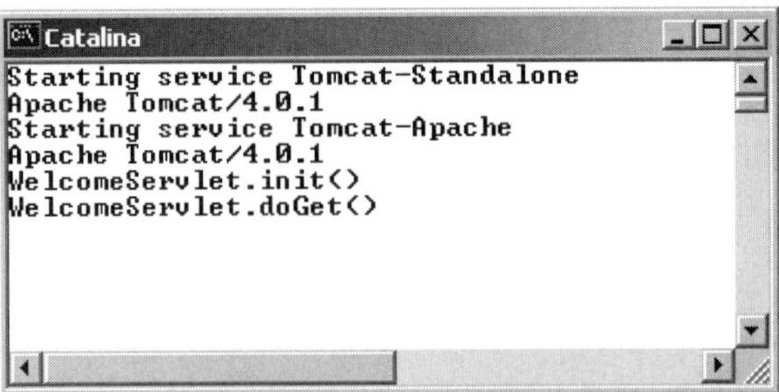

Figure 17.10 Running Tomcat.

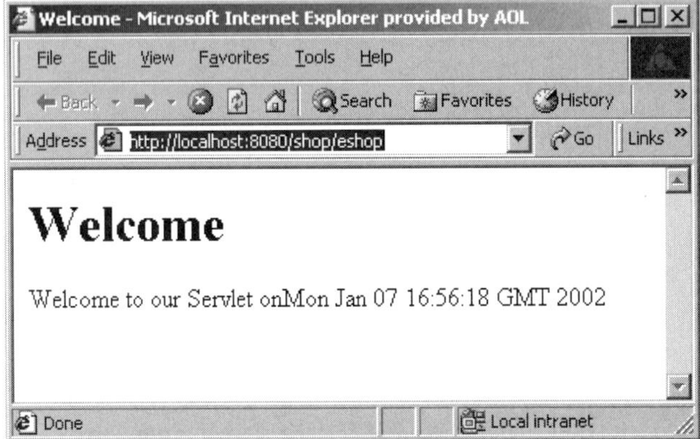

Figure 17.11 The result of running the `WelcomeServlet`.

command window (called Catalina in this release) should indicate that the servlet is being initialized and the `doGet` method called (as illustrated in Figure 17.10).

The end result in your browser should be a welcome message with the current date and time appended (as shown in Figure 17.11).

We could take this further now by adding a security domain to the Web application so that a login screen is presented before a user is able to gain entry to this servlet. Such a change would require no modifications to the servlet, merely a few additional entries in the `web.xml` deployment descriptor, as it is at the Web application level rather than at the servlet level!

17.10 A Second Example Servlet

As we have now considered how servlets work, as well as what the structure of a servlet is, we will look at a second simple implementation. This second servlet has an `init` method and this time uses the `doPost` method. Figure 17.12 presents the `AddressServlet` class. This servlet responds

UltraEdit-32 - [C:\serverside\j2ee-book\web\addresses\source\book\AddressServlet.java*]

File Edit Search Project View Format Column Macro Advanced Window Help

```
package book;

import java.util.*;
import javax.servlet.*;
import javax.servlet.http.*;
import java.io.*;

public class AddressServlet extends HttpServlet {
    private HashMap table = new HashMap();
    public void init(ServletConfig sc) throws ServletException {
       super.init(sc);
       System.out.println("init()");
       // Set up info for servlet example
       table.put("John", "Denise");
       table.put("Paul", "Fiona");
       table.put("Peter", "Karen");
    }
    public void doPost(HttpServletRequest req,
                       HttpServletResponse res)
                                 throws ServletException, IOException {
       System.out.println("doPost()");
       // Set the content type header of the response
       res.setContentType("text/html");
       // Get the output stream to write the html out to
       PrintWriter output = res.getWriter();
       // Get value passed to servlet from the html page
       String name = req.getParameter("name");
       // Generate response in HTML
       String result = (String)table.get(name);
       output.println("<html>\n<head><body>");
       output.println("<title>Example</title></head>");
       output.println("<p>");
       output.println("The partner of " + name + " is " + result);
       output.println("</p></body></html>");
       output.flush();
   }
   public void destroy() {
       super.destroy();
       // Anything specific to this application
   }
}
```

Figure 17.12 The AddressServlet class.

to POST requests for information. Essentially a user inputs a name on a Web page and "submits" the information on that page to the Web server. The Web server in turn loads and runs this servlet. The servlet responds by generating an HTML page which includes the name of the partner of the specified person.

Note that the `init()` method, although it is used to set up the hashtable of names, first calls the `super.init()` method. This illustrates one way in which the `init()` method can be overridden. That is, the `super` version of the method should be called first (`super` causes the method search to start in the parent class rather than the current class).

The doPost() method responds to requests generated by a Web client via the post option on the method parameter of the form tag (see later).

Just as with the doGet method, the doPost method takes two parameters: the request object and the response object. The request object is used to access the information provided when the client "posted" the request. In this case it will be used to access the name text field on an HTML page. In turn, the response object is used to return the result (which is probably going to be in the form of HTML).

Notice that the doPost() method throws two types of exception: the IOException and the ServletException. The IOException may be thrown during the process of reading from the request object or writing to the response object. In turn, the ServletException may be thrown if the request could not be handled.

Note that we have used an instance variable to hold the data to be accessed. In general, using instance variables in servlets is not recommended. This is because all users share the same instance of the servlet. Thus all users share the same instance variables. The result of this is that if you store an individual user's data in an instance variable then that data is available to all users. Rather, it is better to store user-specific data in the user's Session (see next chapter). In this case we can get away within using the instance variable table because we are using it in a read-only mode.

Also note that in this case, although the init() method is actually used to set up the hashtable to be used by the doPost() method, the destroy() method does not need to be included. It is presented here to illustrate how it should be overridden. That is, the super version of the method should be called first.

Having defined the servlet we now need to define an HTML page that will request services on that servlet. Figure 17.13 provides just such an HTML page. This HTML page is very simple. It uses a form to allow a user to enter a name. This name is passed to the servlet when the submit button is pressed. Notice that the form header tag specifies the action to perform when the submit button is pressed. Thus in this case it specifies the SimpleServer servlet. It does this by specifying the Web server for the servlet and the URL that will be

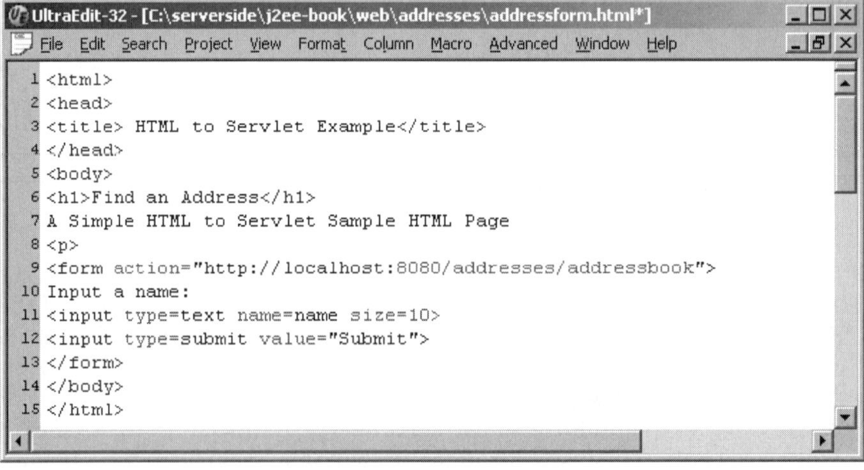


```
<html>
<head>
<title> HTML to Servlet Example</title>
</head>
<body>
<h1>Find an Address</h1>
A Simple HTML to Servlet Sample HTML Page
<p>
<form action="http://localhost:8080/addresses/addressbook">
Input a name:
<input type=text name=name size=10>
<input type=submit value="Submit">
</form>
</body>
</html>
```

Figure 17.13 The HTML form.

mapped to that servlet (in the `web.xml` file). Note that in this case the method associated with the action is POST – thus the `doPost()` method will be called on the servlet.

A form rather than an applet was used in this example as the client is significantly simpler, particularly for this very simple system. However, it is important to realize that, rather than a form, the request could have come from an applet.

The `Context` element in the `server.xml` file of the `conf` directory under the Tomcat installation is presented below for the addresses Web application:

```
<!-- Welcome Shop Context -->
  <Context path="/addresses"
    docBase="addresses"
    debug="0"
    reloadable="false"/>
```

The `web.xml` files for this example are presented in Figures 17.14 and 17.15 for J2EE 1.3.1 and J2EE 1.4 respectively. They are basically the same as that used for the first example, and so will not be discussed in any detail here.

Once the Web application has been deployed it is now possible to open the Web page with the address form. This is illustrated in Figure 17.16. Note that the Web page has been deployed along with the servlet: it is located in the root directory of the Web application. Thus it is possible to access the Web page as illustrated in Figure 17.16.

HTML forms provide a way of interacting with a Web page that requires no scripting or applet writing. In addition, almost every type of browser, from whichever vendor, support HTML forms. This makes the form a very sensible choice for Web developers. As forms are just HTML, they follow the familiar tag structure seen with other HTML constructs. They possess a start tag and an end tag. Between these tags you can use standard HTML to lay out

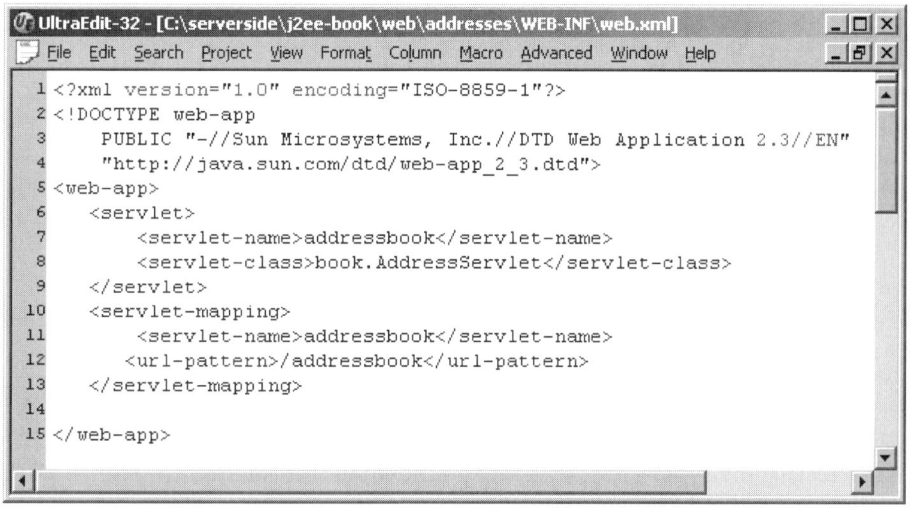

UltraEdit-32 - [C:\serverside\j2ee-book\web\addresses\WEB-INF\web.xml]

File Edit Search Project View Format Column Macro Advanced Window Help

```
<?xml version="1.0" encoding="ISO-8859-1"?>
<!DOCTYPE web-app
    PUBLIC "-//Sun Microsystems, Inc.//DTD Web Application 2.3//EN"
    "http://java.sun.com/dtd/web-app_2_3.dtd">
<web-app>
   <servlet>
       <servlet-name>addressbook</servlet-name>
       <servlet-class>book.AddressServlet</servlet-class>
   </servlet>
   <servlet-mapping>
       <servlet-name>addressbook</servlet-name>
      <url-pattern>/addressbook</url-pattern>
   </servlet-mapping>

</web-app>
```

Figure 17.14 The deployment descriptor for the `addresses` Web application: J2EE 1.3.1.

```
<?xml version="1.0" encoding="ISO-8859-1"?>

<?xml version="1.0" encoding="UTF-8"?>
<web-app version="2.4"
  xmlns="http://java.sun.com/xml/ns/j2ee"
  xmlns:xsi="http://www.w3.org/2001/XMLSchema-instance"
  xsi:schemaLocation="http://java.sun.com/xml/ns/j2ee
    http://java.sun.com/xml/ns/j2ee/web-app_2_4.xsd">

<web-app>
   <servlet>
      <servlet-name>addressbook</servlet-name>
      <servlet-class>book.AddressServlet</servlet-class>
   </servlet>
   <servlet-mapping>
      <servlet-name>addressbook</servlet-name>
      <url-pattern>/addressbook</url-pattern>
   </servlet-mapping>
</web-app>
```

Figure 17.15 The deployment descriptor for the `addresses` Web application: J2EE 1.4.

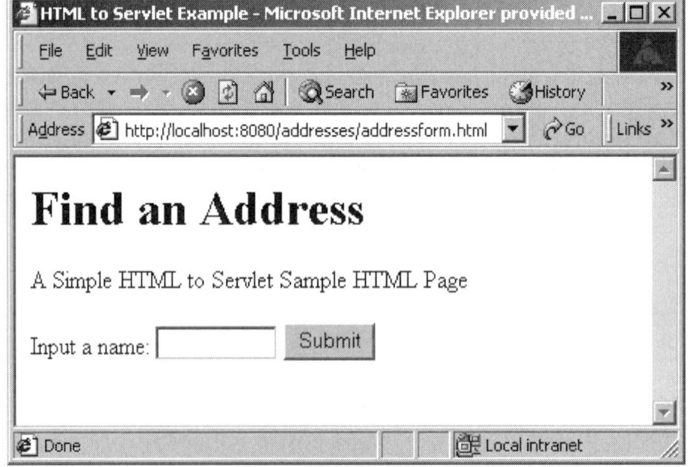

Figure 17.16 The HTML page used to access the servlet.

your form, as well as special form tags to provide for interactivity. These form tags include buttons, text fields and text areas, selection boxes etc.

One button used with a form is of particular interest: the submit button. This button (illustrated in Figure 17.16) invokes a Web server side action by requesting some service. This service could be provided by a CGI script, or as in this case by a servlet. The effect of the user selecting the submit button is that all the input information (in Figure 17.12 the information entered into the text field) is collected together and sent to the to the server along with the service requested. In our çase this results in the server loading and

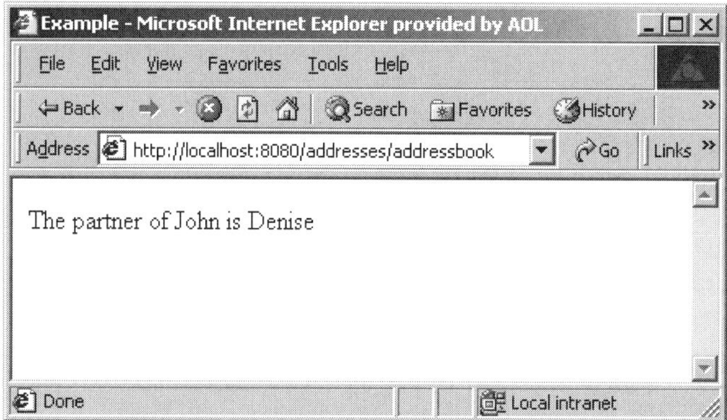

Figure 17.17 The result of querying the servlet.

initializing the servlet and then invoking the `doPost()` method. The information collected from the form is provided to the servlet via the `HttpServletRequest` object.

Once the `AddressServlet` processes the request it returns a response in terms of HTML, as described earlier. The resulting Web page is illustrated in Figure 17.17.

17.11 Should You Use doGet or doPost?

An interesting question which the two examples in this chapter may raise for you is whether you should use the `doGet` approach or the `doPost` approach. In this section we will highlight the pros and cons of each approach.

The use of `doGet` (and thus the `get` communication mechanism) might be considered to be quick and possibly nasty (which is probably a bit unfair). Part of the problem with using `GET` is that the data is sent as part of the URL, for example:

```
http://localhost:8080/addresses/addressbook?name=John
```

Thus security is compromised, as anyone can see the data being transferred. This is true even of people looking over the user's shoulder, as the information is displayed in the location field of a browser! There is also a limit on the amount of data that can be encoded into a URL in this way, and therefore `GET` is not appropriate if a large amount of data must be sent. However, it is excellent as a cheap way of testing a servlet, as the test data can be encoded in the URL and there is no need to create any HTML pages to drive the tests!

The use of `POST` in contrast provides much higher levels of security as the data is sent as part of the HTTP request body rather than as part of the URL. Thus not only is it hidden from prying eyes it is also possible to encrypt the request body using, for example, HTTPS. In addition there is no limit on the size of the data to be sent and thus large amounts of information can be transferred. However, `POST` is only available from a form and may take slightly longer to send from the browser.

17.12 Tomcat

Tomcat is a Web container that supports the latest version of the Servlet and JSP specifications released by Sun. At the time of writing the latest full version of Tomcat is 4.0.3, with the J2EE 1.4 version (Tomcat 5.0) currently under development. Tomcat is part of the Jakarta project conducted under the auspices of the Apache organization. It is also Sun's designated reference implementation for the Servlet 2.3 and JSP 1.2 specifications. This means that the Java 2 Enterprise Edition (J2EE) SDK 1.3 comes with a version of Tomcat bundled in. However, note that the version provided may not be the latest release (again at the time of writing J2EE SDK 1.3 came with Tomcat 4.0 not 4.0.3). Tomcat can be used with the J2EE environment, as it comes with all the necessary jar files when downloaded from the Apache Web site, and this can be used to create Web applications that do not need such niceties as Enteprise JavaBeans.

Although Tomcat can serve up standard Web pages it is more normal for Tomcat to be used in conjunction with a Web server, such as Apache or IIS. The Web server then handles requests for HTML pages and the like, while Tomcat handles requests for servlets and JSPs. This is primarily due to efficiency, as Tomcat is not very efficient for serving Web pages. Also note that Tomcat can be used in conjunction with an EJB server (such as JBoss) to provide a complete J2EE stack.

17.13 Summary

The introduction of the concept of a Web application into the servlet specification has greatly enhanced the set of facilities available to the Java Web developer. In the next chapter we will look at the use of session management and life cycle monitoring.

17.14 Online References

Servlet specifications: `http://java.sun.com/products/`.
Tomcat: `http://jakarta.apache.org/`.
The ServerSide.com J2EE community: `http://www.theServerSide.com/`.
Planet Java: `http://www.planetjava.co.uk/`.
jGURU: `http://www.jguru.com/`.
J2EE: `http://java.sun.com/j2ee/`.

17.15 References

Allamaraju, S. (ed.) (2001). *Professional Java Server Programming*, J2EE 1.3 Edition. Wrox Press, Chicago, IL.

Bergsten, H. (2000). *JavaServer Pages*. O'Reilly, Sebastopol, CA.

Goodwill, J. (2000). *Pure JSP.* Sams, Indianapolis, IN.
Hall, M. (2000). *Core Servlets and Java Server Pages.* Prentice Hall, Upper Saddle River, NJ.
Hunter, J. (2001). *Java Servlet Programming.* O'Reilly, Sebastopol, CA.

Chapter 18

Session Management and Life Cycle Monitoring

18.1 Introduction

For any type of distributed application a dialogue that forms a set of exchanges between a client program and a server program is very important. This is no less true of Web-based applications that use HTML and a client browser communicating with a Java-based Web application. Indeed, in some ways it is much more important, as the underlying HTTP communications protocol used in such applications is connectionless. That is, it does not establish a connection that is used for the duration of the dialogue! Instead, each time a message is sent to the Web container from the Web browser a completely new connection is made. This means that the presence of an established connection cannot be used to represent a continuation of a dialogue (or session). Instead some other way of identifying the session is required. In this chapter we explore how Web applications support the concept of a user session.

We also look at how it is possible to monitor the life cycle of a servlet as well as how information can be shared among servlets via the servlet `Context` object.

The chapter is structured in the following manner:

- Discussion of session management
- Examination of the implementation and use of cookies
- Explore how session tracking works
- Working with `HttpSessions`
- Consider how to store session-oriented data
- Present session life cycle methods and life cycle listeners
- Explore the shared servlet `Context` object

18.2 Session Management

When using servlets (or JSPs) within a Web application a user's session can be represented using an object of the type `HttpSession`. This is actually an interface in the `javax.Servlet.http` package. This interface allows the programmer not only to identify a user across multiple HTTP requests but also to store user-specific data. Remember, as a servlet is, by default, shared among all the users using that servlet, an instance variable should not be used for private/confidential data. This is an easy mistake to make and one which some large Web application suppliers have made even in delivered software. We are aware of a company having to withdraw its new Web-based application after only a few hours due to personal user data being stored in an instance variable (and then being accessed by other users!).

The Web container is responsible for providing an implementation of this interface. The implementation represents the ongoing session between the HTTP client and the HTTP server. The session persists for a specified time period, across more than one connection or page request from the user. A session usually corresponds to one user, who may visit a site many times. The Web container can maintain a session in many ways, such as using cookies or rewriting URLs. We will look at this in more detail in the next section.

The interface (as defined by the `javax.servlet.http` package in version 2.3 of the servlet specification) allows developers to:

- Obtain the session id.
- View and manipulate information about a session, such as whether or not the session is new, as well as the session creation time and last accessed time
- Bind objects to sessions, allowing user information to persist across multiple user connections.
- Control the lifetime of the session, such as setting the session timeout and invalidating the session.

Table 18.1 lists the methods (and their purpose) in the `HttpSession` interface. When data is stored into the session object it can be retrieved by servlets in subsequent HTTP requests. The way in which the session object maintains the user data entered between calls is up to the Web container (and is hidden from the developer). The data could be held in "in-memory" data structures (although if the Web container crashes that data will then be lost). The data could be stored in files (for example via serialization) or in databases (which is the most heavyweight but most reliable). The only criterion is that if the data is to be serialized in some way then all the objects stored in the session must be serializable (that is, they must implement the `java.io.Serializable` or `java.io.Externalizable` interfaces).

An instance of the `HttpSession` interface is obtained from the `HttpServletRequest` object passed into the `doGet` or `doPost` methods. There are actually two methods that can be used to obtain a new `HttpSession` object from the request. These two methods are presented in Table 18.2. The first method, `getSession()`, takes no parameters and either returns the current session object or creates one if the session does not yet exist. The second method, `getSession(Boolean)`, takes a boolean value that indicates whether a new session should be created if one does not already exist. True indicates that a new session should be created if necessary. If false is specified then if no current session object is available, null is returned instead.

A session is only valid for the current Web application – if the user moves from the current Web application to another Web application (even in the same Web container) then a new session scope is entered and thus a new session object is created. The old session is not immediately removed. It will only be deleted if it is either made invalid (which must

Table 18.1 HttpSession interface methods.

Object	**getAttribute**(String name) Returns the object bound with the specified name in this session, or null if no object is bound under the name
Enumeration	**getAttributeNames**() Returns an Enumeration of String objects containing the names of all the objects bound to this session
long	**getCreationTime**() Returns the time when this session was created, measured in milliseconds since midnight, 1 January 1970 GMT
String	**getId**() Returns a string containing the unique identifier assigned to this session
long	**getLastAccessedTime**() Returns the last time the client sent a request associated with this session, as the number of milliseconds since midnight, 1 January 1970 GMT, and marked by the time the container received the request
int	**getMaxInactiveInterval**() Returns the maximum time interval, in seconds, that the servlet container will keep this session open between client accesses
ServletContext	**getServletContext**() Returns the ServletContext to which this session belongs
void	**invalidate**() Invalidates this session then unbinds any objects bound to it
boolean	**isNew**() Returns true if the client does not yet know about the session or if the client chooses not to join the session
void	**removeAttribute**(String name) Removes the object bound with the specified name from this session
void	**setAttribute**(String name, Object value) Binds an object to this session, using the name specified
void	**setMaxInactiveInterval**(int interval) Specifies the time, in seconds, between client requests before the servlet container will invalidate this session

Table 18.2 Obtaining a session object.

HttpSession	**getSession**() Returns the current session associated with this request, or if the request does not have a session, creates one
HttpSession	**getSession**(boolean create) Returns the current HttpSession associated with this request or, if there is no current session and create is true, returns a new session

happen inside the scope for the Web application) or the session is timed out. Thus the user can move from one Web application to another and back again without losing either session object. Of course, the reason that a session is only scoped to a Web application is security; that is, the information stored in a Web application for a user is not available to another Web application – which is exactly what we want!

18.3 Session Tracking

The HTTP communications protocol is (as mentioned earlier) a connectionless protocol. That is, no persistent connection is made that exists between calls from the client to the server. This makes it impossible to use the presence of the connection to represent the current session or set of interactions. However, in many Web applications this is exactly what is required (for example, users might be presented with a number of screens in succession into which they enter data that is then used to search a database of information and present the results. As each screen sends its data to the server, we would need to store this information until the actual search process begins. Thus we need to be able to identify users and their sessions as well as be able to store user data.

A major problem for Web applications is how the session is identified; that is, how do we know that the current user has a session somewhere and how do we know which session that is? This is referred to as session tracking. The basic idea behind all session tracking approaches is illustrated in Figure 18.1. The key concept is the some form of token or identifier is generated by the Web server the first time that the client connects to it and makes a request. This token is then returned to the client with the results of that initial request. All subsequent requests then include the token. The server can then use the token to identify not only that the user already has a session but also which session is theirs.

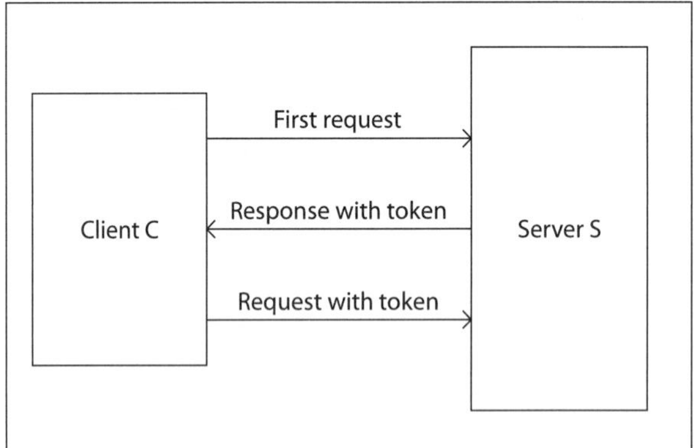

Figure 18.1 Basic session tracking concept.

The exact way in which the token is supplied to the client can vary, depending partly upon what the client allows and partly on the joint capabilities of the client and the server. There are essentially four approaches that can be taken: URL rewriting, hidden fields, SSL and cookies. We will look at each approach below.

18.3.1 URL Rewriting

URL rewriting refers to the modification of any URLs that will be used to return the client to the server in the current session. Each URL is modified so that it includes the session token. For example, if a server was to return a Web page to a user containing three URLs, then each URL would be modified to include the session token as a parameter name–value pair.

In the case of servlets the Servlet specification specifies that the parameter name to be used is `jsessionid`. Thus if a Web page contained the following URL:

```
http://www.jaydeetee.com/eshop/nav
```

this would be modified to include the `jsessionid` token as follows:

```
http://www.jaydeetee.com/eshop/nav;jsessionid=123632
```

As each user has their own session id, the URLs need to be rewritten dynamically (that is the session ids cannot be hard-coded). Thus URL rewriting only works with dynamically generated pages. Another downside to URL rewriting is that the session id can be visible to users in the location field as the information is sent to the server – this can compromise security.

18.3.2 Hidden Fields

The idea behind hidden fields is that a form can contain "hidden fields". These are fields that hold data but are not directly visible to the user in the Web browser. These fields can be used to hold the session id. Although they are not directly visible to the user they can be accessed by "viewing the source" of the Web page – once again they compromise security but are an effective way of identifying a session. As the hidden fields only work within forms, they therefore require the use of a form.

Hidden fields are not used by servlets or JSPs to identify sessions.

18.3.3 Secure Sockets Layer Sessions

Secure Sockets Layer (SSL) has been around for a while now and is an encryption technology that uses TCP/IP as its underlying communications medium. Essentially, when any data is transmitted via SSL, the data is first encrypted, then sent via TCP/IP. When the data is received it is decrypted. All this happens below the application-level protocols such as HTTP. Indeed, SSL is the technology used in the HTTPS protocol. As well as performing encryption, SSL-enabled servers can authenticate SSL enabled clients. This is particularly useful for B2B applications, as it is possible to be sure of the identity of both the client and the server. The actual process involves creating an encrypted connection during which both the client and the server generate "session keys" that are used for encrypting and decrypting the data sent back and forth. Servers based on the HTTPS protocol are then able to use the session key to identify that the client is part of an ongoing session (and which session that is). However, you should note that this is not the mechanism used by servlets or JSPs.

18.3.4 Cookies

Cookies were first introduced by Netscape, but are now a very well-established part of the World Wide Web. They are essentially textual information exchanged between a Web client and a Web server (Web container) that usually represents some information about the user. The cookie is stored in a local file on the client machine. Each file contains name–value pairs for the information stored. The information held in a cookie is exchanged via the request and response headers.

The Servlet specification specifies that if cookies are used to represent a session then the cookie should be called `jsessionid`.

However, because cookies involve writing data onto a client machine there may be practical as well as ethical problems associated with this. For example, in some organizations users are not able to store cookies on their machines (such as in shared computer labs in universities), because the machines have shared access and the necessary file stores are read-only. In other cases security concerns prohibit the use of cookies (many organizations assume a "no cookies" policy due to security fears). For more information on the perceived security issues associated with cookies see `http://www.w3.org/Security/Faq/wwwsf7.html`.

In cases where cookies are disabled most systems will use URL rewriting as a fallback option.

18.3.5 Choosing a Session Tracking Approach

Choosing which of the session tracking options to use is the responsibility of the Web container. It can use cookies, SSL or URL rewriting. The choice of which to use should be transparent to the developer and the user and will typically depend on the capabilities of the Web client and the Web server. In general, if a secure connection is required then session keys will be used; if not, the Web container will then try to use cookies first. If cookies are disabled it will then fall back on URL rewriting. Some Web containers only support cookies; in such situations you may need to exploit your own session tracking mechanism (such as hidden fields).

If the Web container needs to use URL rewriting it may then be necessary to modify any URLs generated within the servlet so that the session can be maintained. This can be done using the `encodeURL` method of the response object. For example:

```
String modifiedURL = response.encodeURL("http://www.jaydeetee.com/eshop");
```

This will append the `jsessionid` to the end of the URL (as illustrated earlier).

18.4 A Session Example

Figure 18.2 presents a very simple servlet that uses an `HttpSession` object, obtained from the `HttpServlerRequest` object, to determine whether the user is just starting a new session or whether they are already part of a session. This is done by testing the session object to see if it is a new session with the `isNew()` method. Depending upon the result of this test one of two messages is presented.

The critical statements to look at are lines 16 and 19:

Line 16: `HttpSession session = req.getSession(true);`

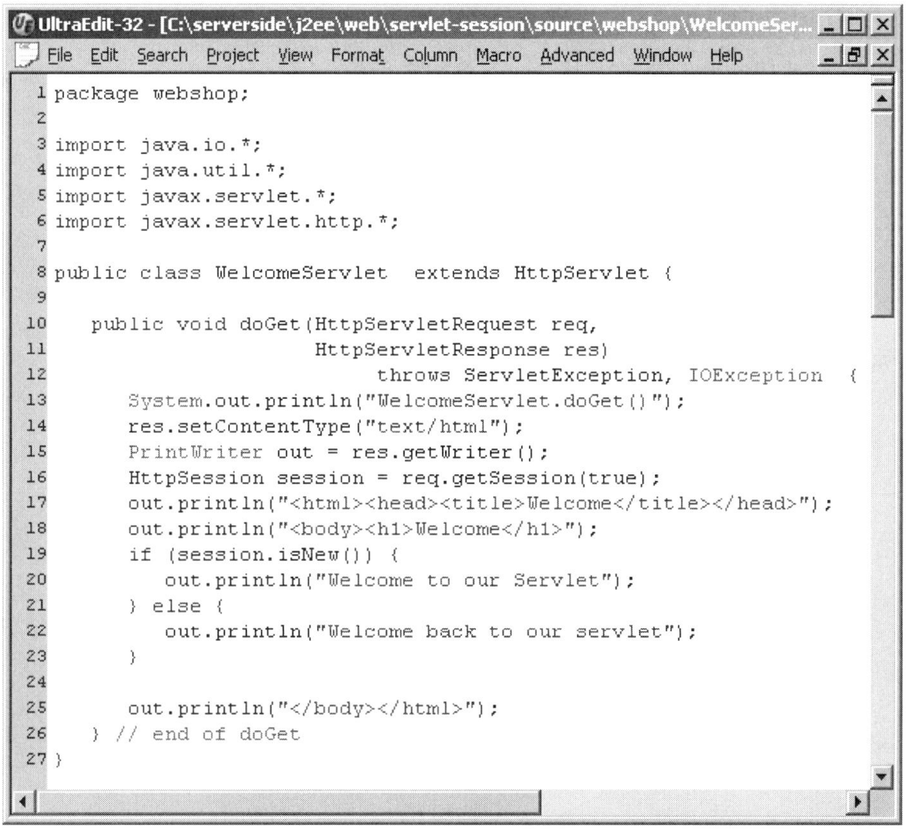

UltraEdit-32 - [C:\serverside\j2ee\web\servlet-session\source\webshop\WelcomeSer...

File Edit Search Project View Format Column Macro Advanced Window Help

```
1 package webshop;
2
3 import java.io.*;
4 import java.util.*;
5 import javax.servlet.*;
6 import javax.servlet.http.*;
7
8 public class WelcomeServlet  extends HttpServlet {
9
10    public void doGet(HttpServletRequest req,
11                      HttpServletResponse res)
12                           throws ServletException, IOException  {
13       System.out.println("WelcomeServlet.doGet()");
14       res.setContentType("text/html");
15       PrintWriter out = res.getWriter();
16       HttpSession session = req.getSession(true);
17       out.println("<html><head><title>Welcome</title></head>");
18       out.println("<body><h1>Welcome</h1>");
19       if (session.isNew()) {
20          out.println("Welcome to our Servlet");
21       } else {
22          out.println("Welcome back to our servlet");
23       }
24
25       out.println("</body></html>");
26    } // end of doGet
27 }
```

Figure 18.2 An example of using the `HttpSession` interface.

This is the line where either the `HttpSession` is created or an existing one is returned.

Line 19: `if (session.isNew()) {`

This line tests to see if the session is a new session (`isNew()` returns true). If the session existed before this request, then the result is false.

The effect of these two lines is illustrated in Figure 18.3. The left-hand browser shows the response generated the first time the servlet is called, while the right-hand browser shows the effect of subsequent calls on the servlet.

18.5 More Session Details

If you look back at Table 18.1 you will not that there are far more methods available on the `HttpSession` interface than just the `isNew()` method. These methods can be broken down into a

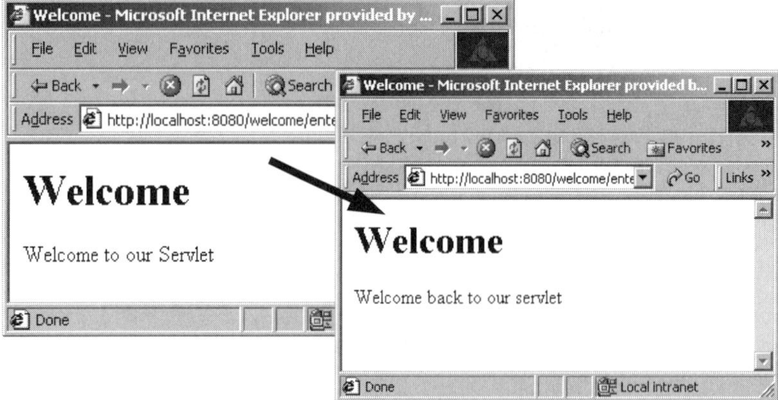

Figure 18.3 Using a session object.

number of categories, including creation time methods, session id, access time methods and invalidation. These are described in more detail below.

Creation Time Methods

- `isNew()` returns true or false depending on whether the session is new or not.
- `getCreationTime` returns the creation time in milliseconds, but can be converted into a more human friendly form using the class `Date`.

Session Id

- `getId()` returns the unique session identifier.

Access Time Methods

- `getLastAccessedTime()`; again the result is returned in milliseconds.
- `getMaxInactiveInterval()` returns the allowed time between one call and another in the session before the Web container invalidates the session. The result is in terms of seconds.
- `setMaxInactiveInterval(int)` sets the number of seconds allowed between one call and another before the Web container invalidates the session.

Invalidation

- `invalidate()` invalidates the session.

The example presented in Figure 18.4 uses almost all of these methods to illustrate their behaviour. If you are trying to run this example don't forget to ensure that you have registered your Web application with Tomcat in the `server.xml` file in the `conf` directory. In this case we are using a Web application called `welcome`.

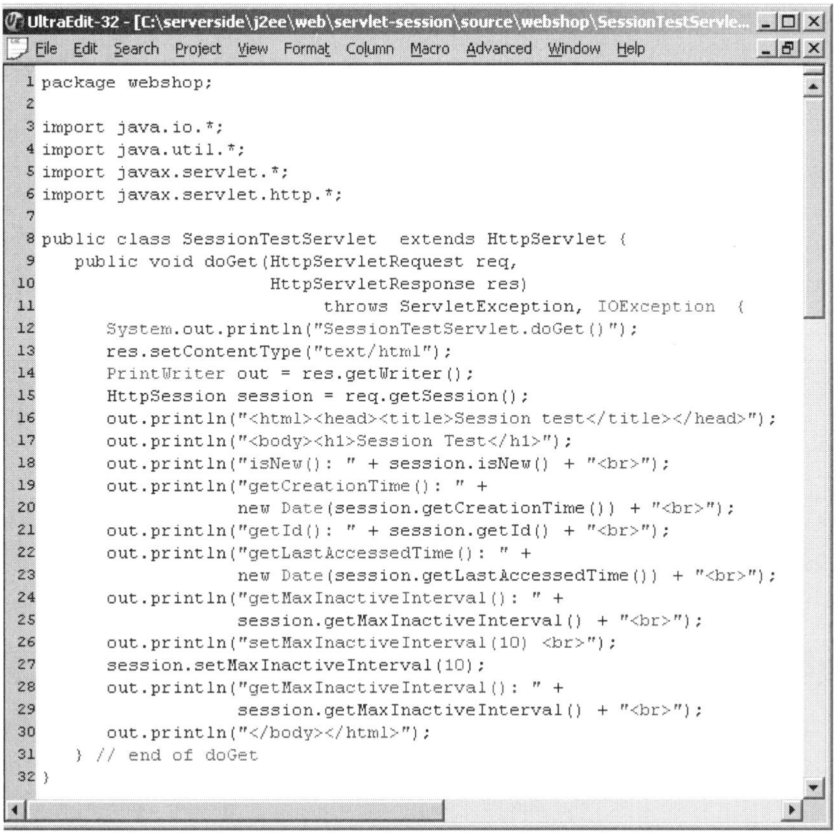

```
package webshop;

import java.io.*;
import java.util.*;
import javax.servlet.*;
import javax.servlet.http.*;

public class SessionTestServlet  extends HttpServlet {
   public void doGet(HttpServletRequest req,
                     HttpServletResponse res)
                          throws ServletException, IOException  {
      System.out.println("SessionTestServlet.doGet()");
      res.setContentType("text/html");
      PrintWriter out = res.getWriter();
      HttpSession session = req.getSession();
      out.println("<html><head><title>Session test</title></head>");
      out.println("<body><h1>Session Test</h1>");
      out.println("isNew(): " + session.isNew() + "<br>");
      out.println("getCreationTime(): " +
                  new Date(session.getCreationTime()) + "<br>");
      out.println("getId(): " + session.getId() + "<br>");
      out.println("getLastAccessedTime(): " +
                  new Date(session.getLastAccessedTime()) + "<br>");
      out.println("getMaxInactiveInterval(): " +
                  session.getMaxInactiveInterval() + "<br>");
      out.println("setMaxInactiveInterval(10) <br>");
      session.setMaxInactiveInterval(10);
      out.println("getMaxInactiveInterval(): " +
                  session.getMaxInactiveInterval() + "<br>");
      out.println("</body></html>");
   } // end of doGet
}
```

Figure 18.4 Accessing HttpSession information.

Once you have compiled this example and updated the deployment descriptor (web.xml) you can deploy your Web application onto Tomcat. Our web.xml files are presented in Figures 18.5 and 18.6 for J2EE 1.3.1 and J2EE 1.4 respectively.

The results obtained by running the SessionTestServlet are presented in the browser illustrated in Figure 18.7.

18.6 Session State

The "state" of a session is represented by the data held in the session object for the current user. This data might represent the user's previous settings, current selection, personal data etc. It is the data that represents the user's interaction. For example, if we have an application that allows a user to search through a database of online books, then the user's current data might represent the user's selections (titles, publishers, subjects etc.) as well as the paged results of any search that has been performed.

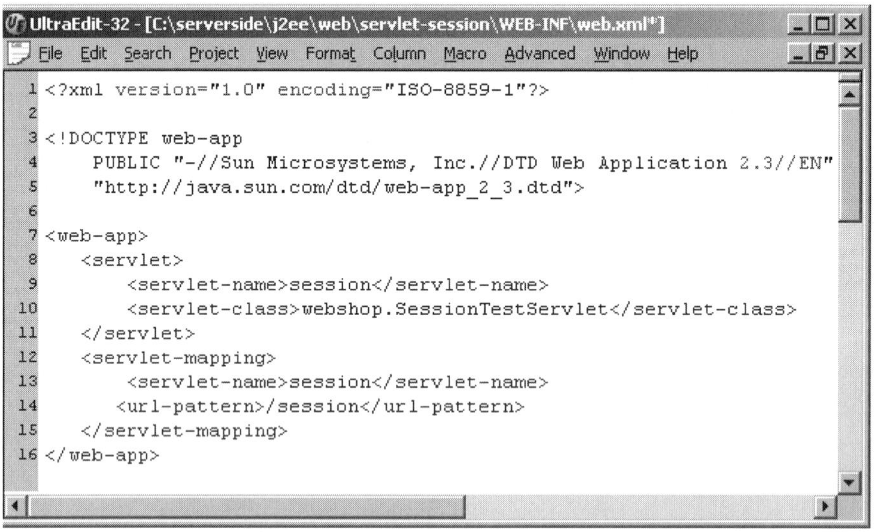

UltraEdit-32 - [C:\serverside\j2ee\web\servlet-session\WEB-INF\web.xml*]

File Edit Search Project View Format Column Macro Advanced Window Help

```
<?xml version="1.0" encoding="ISO-8859-1"?>

<!DOCTYPE web-app
    PUBLIC "-//Sun Microsystems, Inc.//DTD Web Application 2.3//EN"
    "http://java.sun.com/dtd/web-app_2_3.dtd">

<web-app>
   <servlet>
       <servlet-name>session</servlet-name>
       <servlet-class>webshop.SessionTestServlet</servlet-class>
   </servlet>
   <servlet-mapping>
       <servlet-name>session</servlet-name>
      <url-pattern>/session</url-pattern>
   </servlet-mapping>
</web-app>
```

Figure 18.5 The deployment descriptor for the `SessionTestServlet`: J2EE 1.3.1.

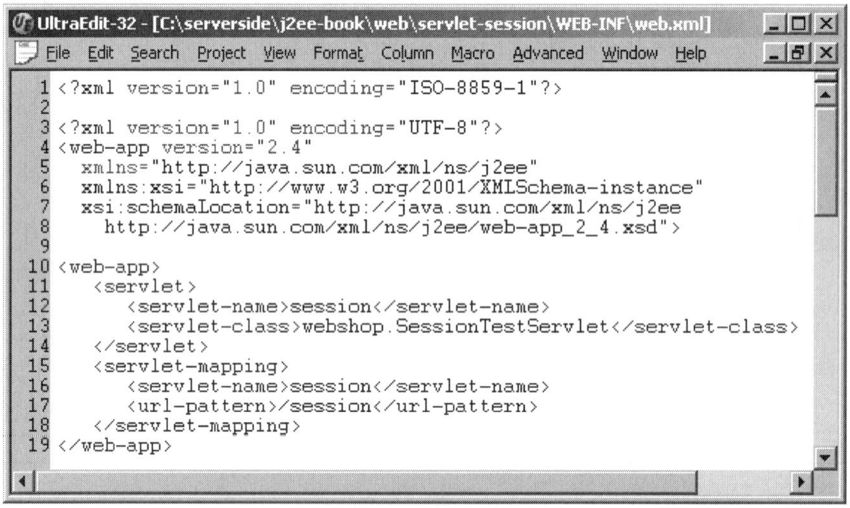

UltraEdit-32 - [C:\serverside\j2ee-book\web\servlet-session\WEB-INF\web.xml]

File Edit Search Project View Format Column Macro Advanced Window Help

```
<?xml version="1.0" encoding="ISO-8859-1"?>

<?xml version="1.0" encoding="UTF-8"?>
<web-app version="2.4"
  xmlns="http://java.sun.com/xml/ns/j2ee"
  xmlns:xsi="http://www.w3.org/2001/XMLSchema-instance"
  xsi:schemaLocation="http://java.sun.com/xml/ns/j2ee
    http://java.sun.com/xml/ns/j2ee/web-app_2_4.xsd">

<web-app>
   <servlet>
      <servlet-name>session</servlet-name>
      <servlet-class>webshop.SessionTestServlet</servlet-class>
   </servlet>
   <servlet-mapping>
      <servlet-name>session</servlet-name>
      <url-pattern>/session</url-pattern>
   </servlet-mapping>
</web-app>
```

Figure 18.6 The deployment descriptor for the `SessionTestServlet`: J2EE 1.4.

Such data must be stored in the session object as this is the only user-specific area in which we can store data. (this is because a servlet's instance variables are shared among all the users of that servlet). This data is then managed by the Web container. How it does this is hidden from the developer and the user with only the constraint that the objects that are stored into the session object should be serialization in case the Web container decided to

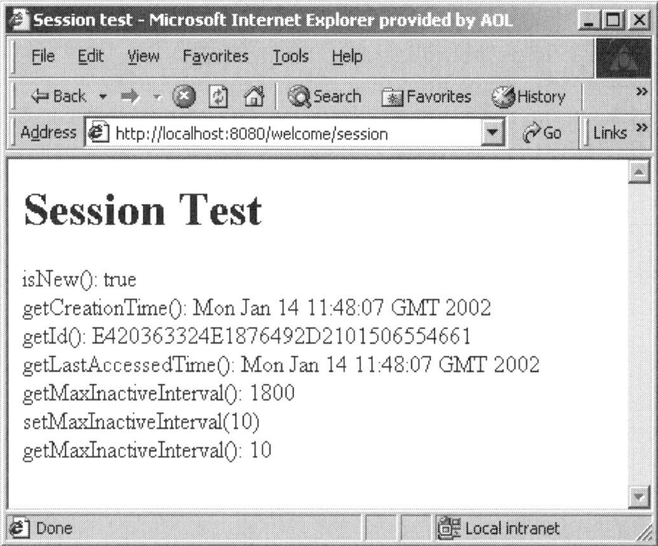

Figure 18.7 Running the SessionTestServlet.

save them to a file or a blob (binary large object) in a database etc. Note that some Web containers may be distributed (that is a Web application may be running across multiple servers). The session is serialized between these servers and thus this is another reason why the objects held in the session must be serializable.

Note that this means that the data is not sent back and forth between the server and the client; rather, the session id that identifies the session object containing the user-specific data is sent back and forth. It should also be realized that data held in a session object is not intended as a mechanism for persisting a user's data over long periods of time. It is intended for short-lived data that has a life span represented by the current "dialogue" between the client and the server. Long-term persistent data should be stored via another mechanism (such as Enterprise JavaBeans).

Within the servlet/JSP specifications the data to be held inside an HttpSession object is referred to as an attribute. The HttpSession interface provides a number of methods that support the storage, access, modification and removal of attributes from a user's session object. These are setAttribute, getAttribute, removeAttribute and getAttributeNames and are listed in Table 18.1. These methods have a simple API. For example, to set an attribute in a session object you merely need to give it an identifier or name, thus:

```
String optonObject = request.getParameter("opt");
session.setAttribute("option", optionObject);
```

To retrieve or even remove the attribute, you merely need to provide the name of the object:

```
String opt = (String)session.getAttribute("option");
session.removeAttribute("option");
```

Note that the getAttribute has a return type of Object. It is thus necessary to cast the returned object to the correct type (in the above example to a string).

It is important to note that the attribute methods on the HttpSession object are not synchronized, and thus if more than one thread is accessing the same session object there is the possibility that data will become corrupted. However, this will only happen if the developer triggers more than one thread during the processing of the same HTTP request, as each user has its own session object.

In Figure 18.8 we present an example of using the attribute methods on the HttpSession object to store the information entered by a user. This information is provided by a form in

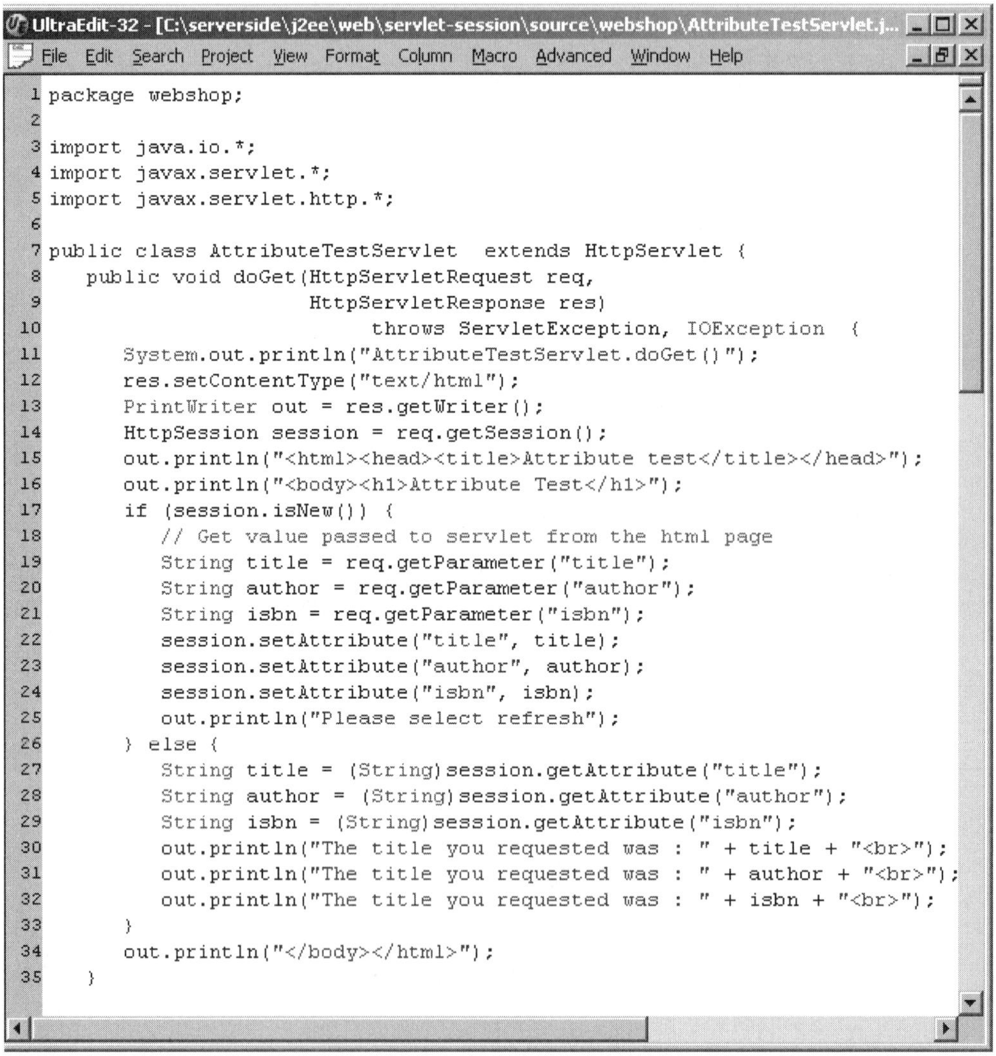

UltraEdit-32 - [C:\serverside\j2ee\web\servlet-session\source\webshop\AttributeTestServlet.j...
File Edit Search Project View Format Column Macro Advanced Window Help

```
package webshop;

import java.io.*;
import javax.servlet.*;
import javax.servlet.http.*;

public class AttributeTestServlet  extends HttpServlet {
   public void doGet(HttpServletRequest req,
                     HttpServletResponse res)
                         throws ServletException, IOException  {
      System.out.println("AttributeTestServlet.doGet()");
      res.setContentType("text/html");
      PrintWriter out = res.getWriter();
      HttpSession session = req.getSession();
      out.println("<html><head><title>Attribute test</title></head>");
      out.println("<body><h1>Attribute Test</h1>");
      if (session.isNew()) {
         // Get value passed to servlet from the html page
         String title = req.getParameter("title");
         String author = req.getParameter("author");
         String isbn = req.getParameter("isbn");
         session.setAttribute("title", title);
         session.setAttribute("author", author);
         session.setAttribute("isbn", isbn);
         out.println("Please select refresh");
      } else {
         String title = (String)session.getAttribute("title");
         String author = (String)session.getAttribute("author");
         String isbn = (String)session.getAttribute("isbn");
         out.println("The title you requested was : " + title + "<br>");
         out.println("The title you requested was : " + author + "<br>");
         out.println("The title you requested was : " + isbn + "<br>");
      }
      out.println("</body></html>");
   }
```

Figure 18.8 The AttributeTestServlet.

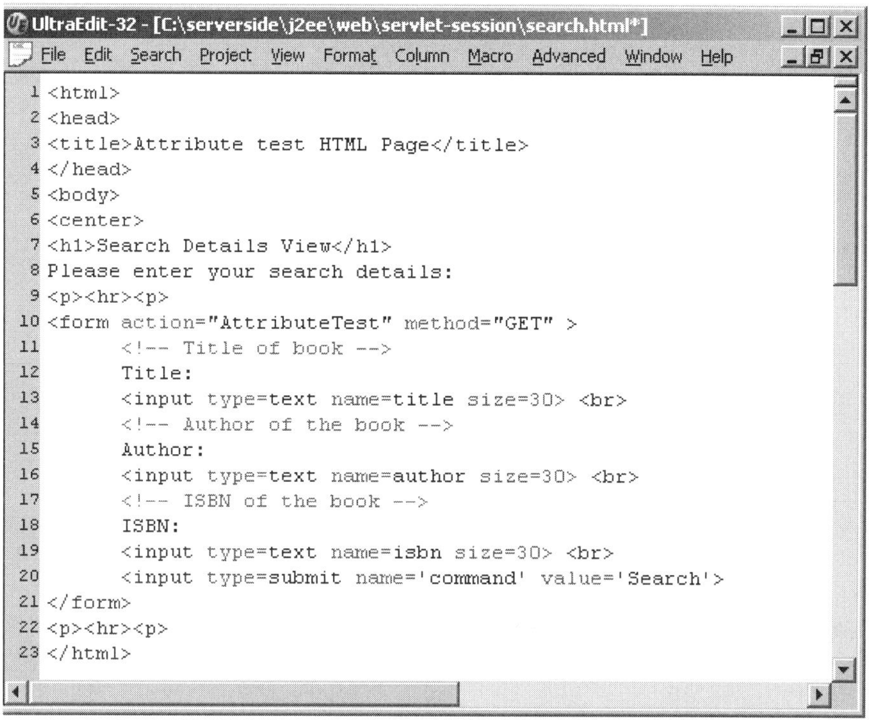

```
<html>
<head>
<title>Attribute test HTML Page</title>
</head>
<body>
<center>
<h1>Search Details View</h1>
Please enter your search details:
<p><hr><p>
<form action="AttributeTest" method="GET" >
      <!-- Title of book -->
      Title:
      <input type=text name=title size=30> <br>
      <!-- Author of the book -->
      Author:
      <input type=text name=author size=30> <br>
      <!-- ISBN of the book -->
      ISBN:
      <input type=text name=isbn size=30> <br>
      <input type=submit name='command' value='Search'>
</form>
<p><hr><p>
</html>
```

Figure 18.9 The `search.html` Web page.

the `search.html` Web page presented in Figure 18.9. The `search.html` Web page, along with the `AttributeTestServlet`, will both be installed in the `welcome` Web Application. The `web.xml` files for this example are presented in Figures 18.10 and 18.11.

Once the Web application has been deployed on Tomcat it is possible to open the `search.html` file. This can be accessed via the Web application document root (as long as it has been placed at the document root). For example, if we install it under the `welcome` directory in the `webapps` directory of Tomcat we can access the HTML page by specifying a URL `http://localhost:8080/welcome/search.html`. This is illustrated in Figure 18.12. We can now enter some information into the form displayed.

When the user selects the submit button the three items of information input are sent to the `AttributeTestServlet`, where they arrive in the `doGet` method. The `doGet` method then extracts the information from the `HttpServletRequest` object and stores the information in the `HttpSession` object also obtained from the `request` object. The HTML page returned to the client merely asks the user to refresh the page. The refresh will happen within a separate HTTP connection, but the information previously entered in the HTML form will still be available in the `HttpSession` object. This allows the servlet to extract that information and create a Web page to send back to the client with that information in it. This is illustrated in Figure 18.13.

UltraEdit-32 - [C:\serverside\j2ee\web\servlet-session\WEB-INF\web.xml*]

File Edit Search Project View Format Column Macro Advanced Window Help

```
<?xml version="1.0" encoding="ISO-8859-1"?>

<!DOCTYPE web-app
    PUBLIC "-//Sun Microsystems, Inc.//DTD Web Application 2.3//EN"
    "http://java.sun.com/dtd/web-app_2_3.dtd">

<web-app>
   <servlet>
       <servlet-name>attributes</servlet-name>
       <servlet-class>webshop.AttributeTestServlet</servlet-class>
   </servlet>
   <servlet-mapping>
       <servlet-name>attributes</servlet-name>
      <url-pattern>/AttributeTest</url-pattern>
   </servlet-mapping>
</web-app>
```

Figure 18.10 The `web.xml` file for the `AttributetestServlet`: J2EE 1.3.1.

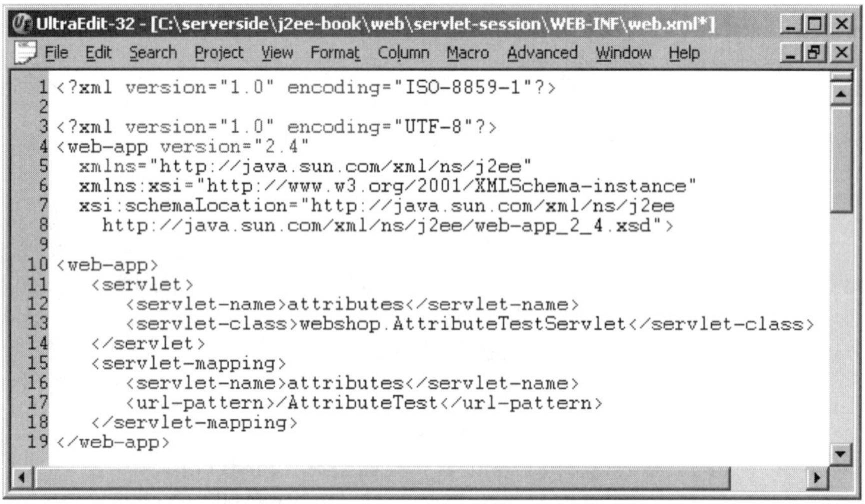

UltraEdit-32 - [C:\serverside\j2ee-book\web\servlet-session\WEB-INF\web.xml*]

File Edit Search Project View Format Column Macro Advanced Window Help

```
<?xml version="1.0" encoding="ISO-8859-1"?>

<?xml version="1.0" encoding="UTF-8"?>
<web-app version="2.4"
  xmlns="http://java.sun.com/xml/ns/j2ee"
  xmlns:xsi="http://www.w3.org/2001/XMLSchema-instance"
  xsi:schemaLocation="http://java.sun.com/xml/ns/j2ee
    http://java.sun.com/xml/ns/j2ee/web-app_2_4.xsd">

<web-app>
   <servlet>
      <servlet-name>attributes</servlet-name>
      <servlet-class>webshop.AttributeTestServlet</servlet-class>
   </servlet>
   <servlet-mapping>
      <servlet-name>attributes</servlet-name>
      <url-pattern>/AttributeTest</url-pattern>
   </servlet-mapping>
</web-app>
```

Figure 18.11 The `web.xml` file for the `AttributetestServlet`: J2EE 1.4.

18.7 Session Life Cycle Monitoring

When an application stores an object in, or removes an object from, a session, the session checks whether the object implements `HttpSessionBindingListener`. If it does, the servlet notifies the object that it has been bound to or unbound from the session. Notifications are sent after the binding method completes. For sessions that are invalidated or expire, notifications are sent after the session has been invalidated or expired.

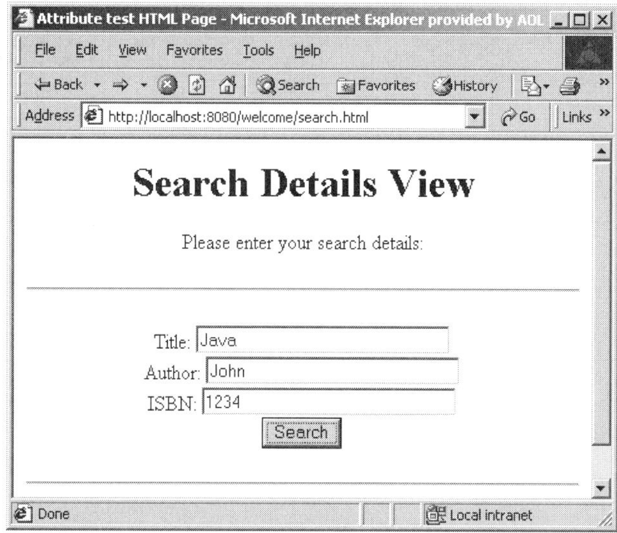

Figure 18.12 The `search.html` page viewed in a browser.

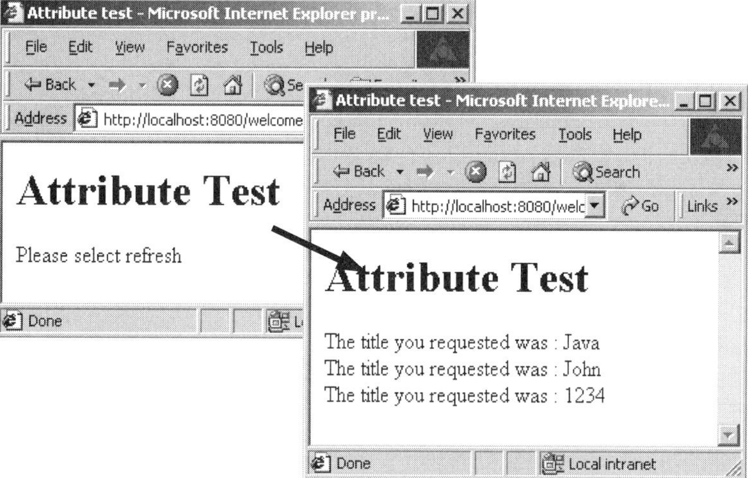

Figure 18.13 Working with session attributes.

When a container migrates a session between JVMs in a distributed container setting, all session attributes implementing the `HttpSessionActivationListener` interface are notified.

A servlet should be able to handle cases in which the client does not choose to join a session, such as when cookies are intentionally turned off. Until the client joins the session, `isNew` returns true. If the client chooses not to join the session, `getSession` will return a different session on each request, and `isNew` will always return true.

18.8 Servlet Context

In many situations it is useful to be able to share information between servlets. However, servlets are called via the Web container in response to HTTP requests from clients. How then can information be shared? One way is via the `ServletContext` object.

The `ServletContext` is, however, more than just a global blackboard for a Web application: it is the servlet's view of the Web application that it is part of. It provides access to resources and facilities that are common to all servlets (Table 18.3). Prior to the 2.1 verison of the Servlet specification the `ServletContext` only provided information about the environment within which the `Servlet` was executing (such as `getServerInfo`). However, the role of the `ServletContext` has grown such that it now acts as a shared repository for the whole Web application. Thus one `Servlet` can put data into the `ServletContext` and another `Servlet` can access that data. Note that this is per Web application and not per user (as is the case of the `HttpSession` object).

Note that each Web application has its own `ServletContext` (they are not shared among Web applications). Thus data stored in the `ServletContext` for one Web application is not available in another. If a Web application is distributable (see the chapter on deployment and configuration of Web applications) then we can extend the statement that each Web application has a single servlet context to each Web application in a JVM has a `ServletContext` (as a distributable Web application can be executing on more then one JVM for performance reasons).

The `ServletContext` is actually an interface defined in the `javax.servlet` package (and not the `javax.servlet.http` package!). It is the responsibility of the Web container to provide an implementation for the `ServletContext` interface. Again, exactly how it maintains the data held in it is hidden from the developer and could be via in-memory data structures, serialization or some other form of storage (e.g. a database).

There are two ways in which to obtain a reference to the `ServletContext`. The first is to use the `ServletConfig` object passed into the `init` method when the Servlet is initialized. The second is via the public `ServletConfig getServletConfig()` method defined on the servlet interface that is implemented by all servlets (including HTTP servlets). Thus if you need to obtain a reference to the `ServletContext` within a `doGet` or `doPost` method this can be done by merely calling `getServletConfig()` and retrieving the `ServletContext` from the `ServletConfig` object returned (via the `getServletContext()` method).

Just as with the `HttpSession` interface, the large set of methods on the `ServletContext` interface can be broken down into several categories. The categories are server environment information, servlet configuration information, shared attributes and logging. These categories are discussed below.

Server Environment Information

This category of method provides information on the environment in which the servlet is executing, such as the major and minor versions of the servlet API that the Web container corresponds to, the name and version of the server and the mime type for a file etc, for example:

- `getMimeType(String filename)`
- `getServerInfo()`
- `getMajorVersion()`
- `getMinorVersion()`

Table 18.3 Methods on the `ServletContext` interface.

`Object`	**`getAttribute`**`(String name)` Returns the servlet container attribute with the given name, or `null` if there is no attribute by that name
`Enumeration`	**`getAttributeNames`**`()` Returns an `Enumeration` containing the attribute names available within this servlet context
`ServletContext`	**`getContext`**`(String uripath)` Returns a `ServletContext` object that corresponds to a specified URL on the server
`String`	**`getInitParameter`**`(String name)` Returns a `String` containing the value of the named context-wide initialization parameter, or `null` if the parameter does not exist
`Enumeration`	**`getInitParameterNames`**`()` Returns the names of the context's initialization parameters as an `Enumeration` of `String` objects, or an empty `Enumeration` if the context has no initialization parameters
`int`	**`getMajorVersion`**`()` Returns the major version of the Java Servlet API that this servlet container supports
`String`	**`getMimeType`**`(String file)` Returns the MIME type of the specified file, or `null` if the MIME type is not known
`int`	**`getMinorVersion`**`()` Returns the minor version of the Servlet API that this servlet container supports
`RequestDispatcher`	**`getNamedDispatcher`**`(String name)` Returns a `RequestDispatcher` object that acts as a wrapper for the named servlet
`String`	**`getRealPath`**`(String path)` Returns a `String` containing the real path for a given virtual path
`RequestDispatcher`	**`getRequestDispatcher`**`(String path)` Returns a `RequestDispatcher` object that acts as a wrapper for the resource located at the given path
`java.net.URL`	**`getResource`**`(String path)` Returns a URL to the resource that is mapped to a specified path
`InputStream`	**`getResourceAsStream`**`(String path)` Returns the resource located at the named path as an `InputStream` object
`Set`	**`getResourcePaths`**`(String path)` Returns a directory-like listing of all the paths to resources within the Web application whose longest sub-path matches the supplied path argument
`String`	**`getServerInfo`**`()` Returns the name and version of the servlet container on which the servlet is running
`String`	**`getServletContextName`**`()` Returns the name of this Web application corresponding to this ServletContext as specified in the deployment descriptor for this Web application by the display-name element
`void`	**`log`**`(String msg)` Writes the specified message to a servlet log file, usually an event log
`void`	**`log`**`(String message, Throwable throwable)` Writes an explanatory message and a stack trace for a given Throwable exception to the servlet log file
`void`	**`removeAttribute`**`(String name)` Removes the attribute with the given name from the servlet context
`void`	**`setAttribute`**`(String name, Object object)` Binds an object to a given attribute name in this servlet context

Servlet Configuration Information

It is possible to pass information to a servlet when it starts up in a similar way to that possible when passing command line arguments to an application. This is done by defining the initalization parameters in the deployment descriptor file and accessing them via the `ServletContext` via the method `getInitParameter(String name)`.

Shared Attribute Methods (not Synchronized)

As with `HttpSession` objects, the data that is held in the `ServletContext` is referred to as attributes. The methods for setting, removing, obtaining and listing attributes are very similar to those found in the `HttpSession` interface and are listed below:

- `getAttribute(String name)`
- `setAttribute(String name, Object attribute)`
- `removeAttribute(String name)`
- `getAttributeNames()`

Logging

It is possible to write messages to standard log files via the `ServletContext`. The name and type of the servlet log file are specific to the servlet container. Two versions of the logging method are available: one for simple strings and one for messages associated with an exception (`Throwable`).

- `log(String message)`
- `log(String m, Throwable cause)`

18.9 `ServletContext` Example

The following example uses some of the above features of the `ServletContext` object. This example, called `ContextTestServlet` (and illustrated in Figure 18.14) creates a Web page with four sections, one for each type of method in the `ServletContext` interface.

The `web.xml` file for this servlet has an additional element in it to those presented in this chapter. This element is the `context-param` element, which allows an initialization parameter to be passed through to the servlet. In this case the parameter is called option and the value specified in the deployment descriptor is "full". This is illustrated in Figures 18.15 and 18.16. Configuring a Web application and servlets will be covered in more detail in a later chapter of this book. Note the position of the `context-param` element – this must be before any servlet tags.

Once the class and `web.xml` file are deployed, the result of accessing the servlet is presented in Figure 18.17.

The one aspect of this example not yet examined is the logging used. In the example we called the `log` method on the `ServletContext` at the end of the `doGet` method. The effect of this depends on the server. In Tomcat there is a `logs` directory under the Tomcat home directory. This contains several logs, including the log for the localhost. It is to this log that the information is

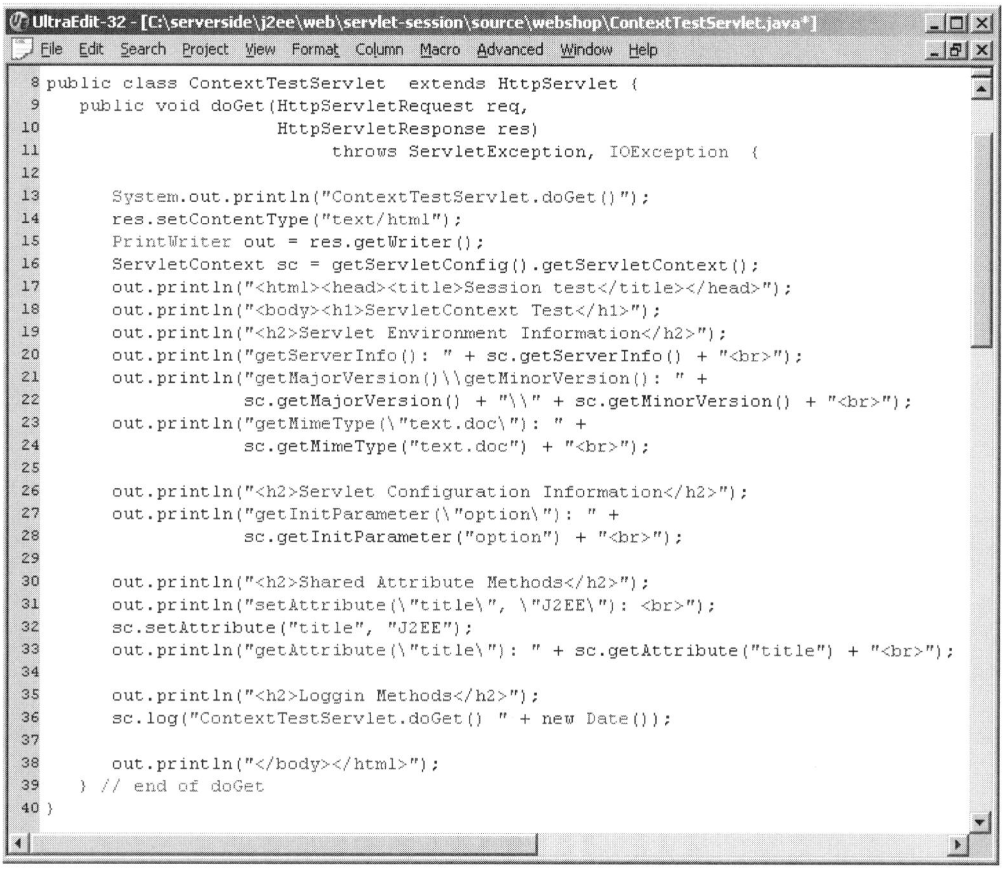

UltraEdit-32 - [C:\serverside\j2ee\web\servlet-session\source\webshop\ContextTestServlet.java*]

File Edit Search Project View Format Column Macro Advanced Window Help

```
public class ContextTestServlet  extends HttpServlet {
  public void doGet(HttpServletRequest req,
                         HttpServletResponse res)
                                throws ServletException, IOException  {

    System.out.println("ContextTestServlet.doGet()");
    res.setContentType("text/html");
    PrintWriter out = res.getWriter();
    ServletContext sc = getServletConfig().getServletContext();
    out.println("<html><head><title>Session test</title></head>");
    out.println("<body><h1>ServletContext Test</h1>");
    out.println("<h2>Servlet Environment Information</h2>");
    out.println("getServerInfo(): " + sc.getServerInfo() + "<br>");
    out.println("getMajorVersion()\\getMinorVersion(): " +
                     sc.getMajorVersion() + "\\" + sc.getMinorVersion() + "<br>");
    out.println("getMimeType(\"text.doc\"): " +
                     sc.getMimeType("text.doc") + "<br>");

    out.println("<h2>Servlet Configuration Information</h2>");
    out.println("getInitParameter(\"option\"): " +
                     sc.getInitParameter("option") + "<br>");

    out.println("<h2>Shared Attribute Methods</h2>");
    out.println("setAttribute(\"title\", \"J2EE\"): <br>");
    sc.setAttribute("title", "J2EE");
    out.println("getAttribute(\"title\"): " + sc.getAttribute("title") + "<br>");

    out.println("<h2>Loggin Methods</h2>");
    sc.log("ContextTestServlet.doGet() " + new Date());

    out.println("</body></html>");
  } // end of doGet
}
```

Figure 18.14 The main body of the `ContextTestServlet`.

written. For example, when the above example was run the following line was written to the `localhost_log.2002-01-14` file:

```
2002-01-14 15:21:58 ContextTestServlet.doGet() Mon Jan 14 15:21:58 GMT 2002
```

18.10 Servlet Life Cycle Events

The 2.3 version of the Servlet specification introduced a new feature into the armoury of the servlet developer. It allowed the developer to monitor life cycle events on either the whole Web application or individual servlet sessions. For example, it is now possible to monitor the creation, destruction and modification of the `ServletContext` object (for the whole Web application) or the `HttpSession` object.

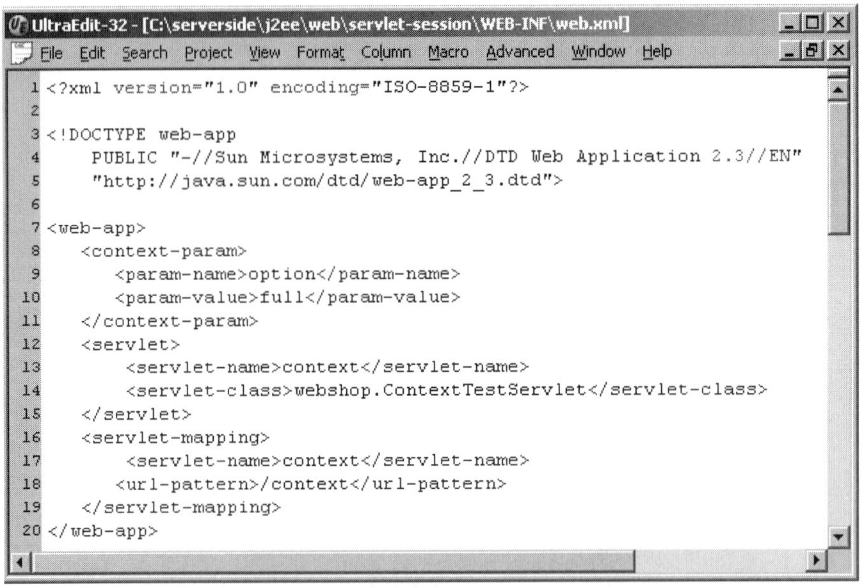

UltraEdit-32 - [C:\serverside\j2ee\web\servlet-session\WEB-INF\web.xml]

File Edit Search Project View Format Column Macro Advanced Window Help

```
<?xml version="1.0" encoding="ISO-8859-1"?>

<!DOCTYPE web-app
    PUBLIC "-//Sun Microsystems, Inc.//DTD Web Application 2.3//EN"
    "http://java.sun.com/dtd/web-app_2_3.dtd">

<web-app>
   <context-param>
      <param-name>option</param-name>
      <param-value>full</param-value>
   </context-param>
   <servlet>
       <servlet-name>context</servlet-name>
       <servlet-class>webshop.ContextTestServlet</servlet-class>
   </servlet>
   <servlet-mapping>
       <servlet-name>context</servlet-name>
      <url-pattern>/context</url-pattern>
   </servlet-mapping>
</web-app>
```

Figure 18.15 The deployment descriptor file for the `ContextTestServlet`: J2EE 1.3.1.

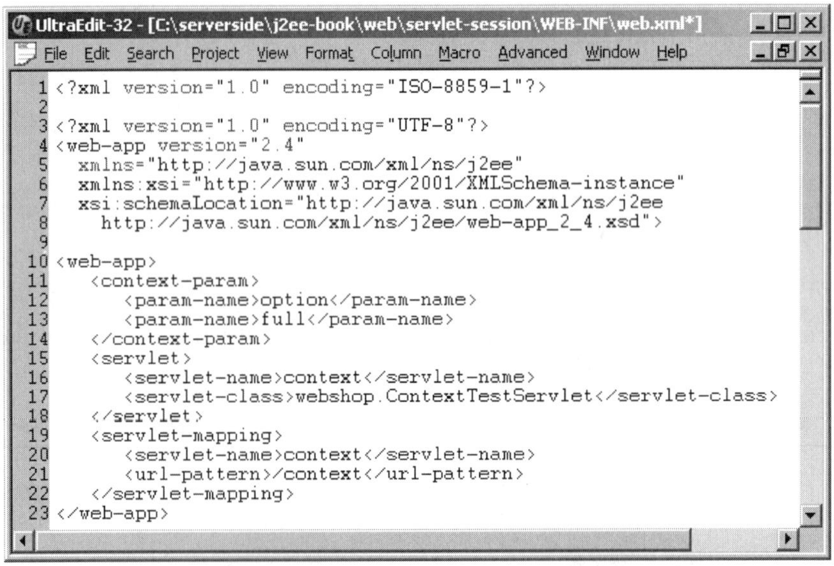

UltraEdit-32 - [C:\serverside\j2ee-book\web\servlet-session\WEB-INF\web.xml*]

File Edit Search Project View Format Column Macro Advanced Window Help

```
<?xml version="1.0" encoding="ISO-8859-1"?>

<?xml version="1.0" encoding="UTF-8"?>
<web-app version="2.4"
  xmlns="http://java.sun.com/xml/ns/j2ee"
  xmlns:xsi="http://www.w3.org/2001/XMLSchema-instance"
  xsi:schemaLocation="http://java.sun.com/xml/ns/j2ee
    http://java.sun.com/xml/ns/j2ee/web-app_2_4.xsd">

<web-app>
   <context-param>
      <param-name>option</param-name>
      <param-name>full</param-name>
   </context-param>
   <servlet>
      <servlet-name>context</servlet-name>
      <servlet-class>webshop.ContextTestServlet</servlet-class>
   </servlet>
   <servlet-mapping>
      <servlet-name>context</servlet-name>
      <url-pattern>/context</url-pattern>
   </servlet-mapping>
</web-app>
```

Figure 18.16 The deployment descriptor file for the `ContextTestServlet`: J2EE 1.4.

The way in which this monitoring works is based on the event delegation model used extensively in the AWT and Swing components of the Java 2 Standard Edition. If you are unfamiliar with the event delegation model, have a look at any good book on the standard edition version of Java, including Hunt (1999).

Figure 18.17 Running the `ContextTestServlet`.

As this monitoring or notification process is based on the Event Delegation model, what happens is that one class must implement one or more listener interfaces. The methods specified in these interfaces are then called when certain events occur.

There are four listener interface that can be implemented, depending what information you wish to monitor. For monitoring the `ServletContext` the listener interfaces are the `javax.servlet.ServletContextListener` and the `javax.servlet.ServletContext-AttributeListener`. For the `HttpSession` object the interfaces are the `javax.servlet.http.HttpSessionListener` and the `javax.servlet.http.HttpSession-Listener`. Each of these interfaces is described in more detail in Table 18.4.

There are four different types of event object that are used with the interfaces in Table 18.4: one for each listener interface. These events provide information on what has just happened. The event classes are listed in Table 18.5.

Registration of the classes implementing the various listener interfaces with the Web container, so that they are notified of the events, is handled via the deployment descriptor. A new element must be added to the `web.xml` file. This new element is the `listener` element. The listener element takes one or more listener classes via a `listener-class` tag. The Web container then creates instances of these classes and uses reflection to determine which interfaces they implement. It then registers them as appropriate.

Table 18.4 The life cycle monitoring interfaces.

javax.servlet.ServletContextListener	Implementations of this interface recieve notifications about changes to the servlet context of the Web application they are part of. The methods defined by the interface are **contextInitialized**(ServletContextEvent se) and **contextDestroyed**(ServletContextEvent se)
javax.servlet. ServletContextAttributeListener	Implementations of this interface recieve notifications of changes to the attribute list on the servlet context of a Web application. The methods defined on this interface are **attributeAdded**(ServletContextAttributeEvent s), **attributeRemoved**(ServletContextAttributeEvent s) and **attributeReplaced**(ServletContextAttributeEvent s)
javax.servlet.http.HttpSessionListener	Implementations of this interface may are notified of changes to the list of active sessions in a Web application. The methods defined in this interface are **sessionCreated**(HttpSessionEvent se) and **sessionDestroyed**(HttpSessionEvent se)
javax.servlet.http.HttpSessionListener	This listener interface can be implemented in order to get notifications of changes to the attribute lists of sessions within this Web application. The methods specified for this interface are **attributeAdded**(HttpSessionBindingEvent se) **attributeRemoved**(HttpSessionBindingEvent se) and **attributeReplaced**(HttpSessionBindingEvent se). All these methods are called after the change to the session object

Table 18.5 The Event classes.

javax.Servlet.ServletContextEvent	This class provides a single method getServletContext() which returns the ServletContext that changed
javax.Servlet.ServletContextAttributeEvent	This class has two methods, getName() and getValue(). getName() returns the name of the attribute that changes and getValue() returns either the old value (if it was removed or replaced) or the new value if it was added
javax.Servlet.http.HttpSessionEvent	This class defines only a single method getSession() that returns the session that changed
javax.Servlet.http.HttpSessionBindingEvent	This class provides three methods, getSession(), getName() and getValue(). getSession() returns the session that changed, getName() the attribute that changed and getValue() returns either the old value (if it was removed or replaced) or the new value if it was added

To illustrate the use of these interfaces we will look at a simple ServletContextHandler class. This class implements the ServletContextListener and is illustrated in Figure 18.18. There are only two methods that must be implemented: one used to notify that the Web application's ServletContext has been initialized and one to notify that it has been destroyed. Once this class is compiled and the .class file deployed to the same directory as the servlets on Tomcat we can then modify the web.xml file so that the Web container knows about the listener class.

To add this class to the Web application we need to provide a listener element after the context-param element but before any servlet elements. This is illustrated in Figure 18.19.

Using this example, once we have deployed the new web.xml file and the new Handler class, when we now start up Tomcat the following is displayed in the CATALINA command window:

```
Starting service Tomcat-Standalone
Apache Tomcat/4.0.1
ServletContextHandler.contextInitialized()
javax.servlet.ServletContextEvent[source=org.apache.catalina.core.
ApplicationCon
text@580e6d]
Starting service Tomcat-Apache
Apache Tomcat/4.0.1
```

```
package webshop;

import javax.servlet.*;

public class ServletContextHandler implements ServletContextListener{

   public void contextInitialized(ServletContextEvent sce) {
      System.out.println("ServletContextHandler.contextInitialized()");
      System.out.println(sce);
   }

   public void contextDestroyed(ServletContextEvent sce) {
      System.out.println("ServletContextHandler.contextDestroyed()");
      System.out.println(sce);
   }
}
```

Figure 18.18 The simple ServletContextListener class.

```
<web-app>

   <context-param>
      <param-name>option</param-name>
      <param-value>full</param-value>
   </context-param>
   <listener>
       <listener-class>
          webshop.ServletContextHandler
       </listener-class>
   </listener>
   <servlet>
       <servlet-name>welcome</servlet-name>
       <servlet-class>webshop.WelcomeServlet</servlet-class>
   </servlet>
   <servlet>
```

Figure 18.19 The web.xml file with a listener class defined.

There are also two additional listener interfaces. The first allows objects that are to be stored in an `HttpSession` object to be notified if the session object is to be passivated or that it has just been activated. By passivation or activation we refer to the processes associated with serialization, such as storing to a file, storing into a database or being sent via a socket from one JVM to another. If an object implements the `javax.Servlet.HttpSessionActivationListener` then it will be notified of these events. The methods defined on this listener are `sessionDidActivate(HttpSessionEvent se)` and `sessionWillPassivate(HttpSessionEvent se)`.

The final listener interface allows objects to be notified when they are being registered with a session object etc. This interface, `javax.Servlet.http.HttpSessionAttributeListener`, was discussed earlier in this chapter.

18.11 References

Hunt, J. (1999). *Java for Practitioners: an Introduction to Object Orientation and Java*. Springer-Verlag, London.

Chapter 19

Java Server Pages

19.1 Introduction

First there were servlets, then there were Java Server Pages (also known as JSPs). Both can serve up data on request, and, in the case of HTTP servlets, both can serve up Web pages on demand. So why have two approaches? The primary problem with servlets is that if you don't already know Java, it is very difficult to write a servlet!

Servlets mix presentation with processing – that is, an HTTP servlet both generates the HTML to be rendered by the client browser and contains the logic that generates that HTML. The end result of this is that the servlet developer must know both Java and HTML (and possibly scripting languages such as JScript, the use of DHTML etc.).

In general, Web designers and Java developers are not the same people, yet the servlet approaches assumes that they are (or at least that they can work closely together to produce the necessary results). The core issue here is that the presentation (the HTML) and the processing (what should be done to generate that HTML) are mixed into one single entity – the servlet.

JSPs are a direct extension to servlets that attempt to separate out the presentational aspects from the logical aspects. That is, a JSP focuses on the presentation (i.e. the HTML tags) while the Java code called from the JSP deals with the business logic.

A JSP is essentially an HTML file that uses a `.jsp` extension and provides some additional JSP tags. These tags are defined by a tag library that can be extended for custom applications.

19.2 What Is a JSP?

The main aim of the JSP framework is the separation of presentation from application logic. That is, it aims to allow non-Java developers to design the JSP pages using:

- HTML markup
- XML-like tags known as JSP tags

These JSP tags can then access server-side Java code that adheres to the JavaBeans naming conventions. In addition, JSPs can also access Enterprise JavaBeans. Thus the separation of concerns is achieved by allowing Java developers to focus on standard JavaBeans and Enterprise JavaBeans and Web designers to concentrate on HTML, DHTML and the JSP tags.

The JSP tags are very powerful. They allow the developer to:

- instantiate JavaBeans
- access Java code
- request services of Enterprise JavaBeans
- cause applets to be downloaded
- include the output of additional JSPs
- cause servlets to be executed

In turn, servlets can trigger JSPs.

It is useful to consider what happens to a JSP when a client requests a JSP and its relationship to servlets (remember above we noted that JSPs were a direct extension to servlets).

Figure 19.1 illustrates the steps that occur the first time a user requests a JSP. These steps are described in more detail below (but note that the end result is that the JSP is translated into a servlet that is then compiled and loaded into the Web server):

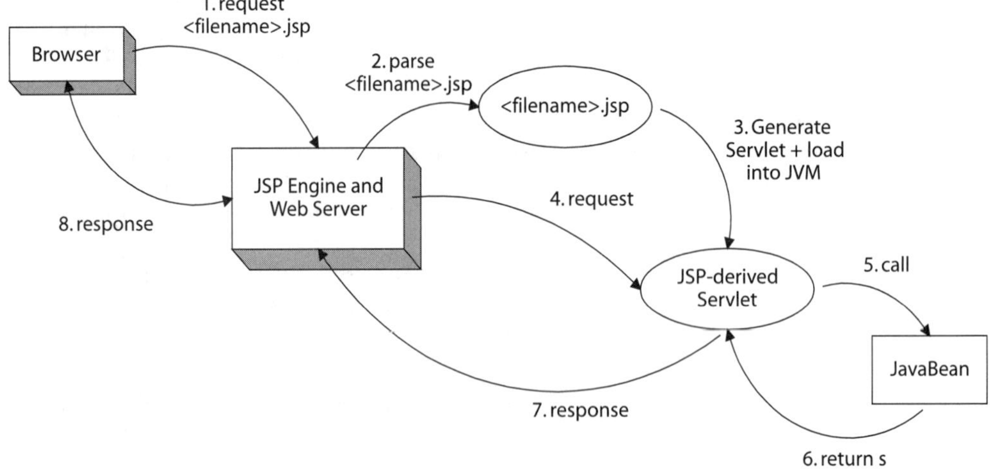

Figure 19.1 Translating a JSP into a servlet.

1. Request `<filename>.jsp`. The first step is that the client browser must request the JSP file from the JSP-enabled Web server. This may be done directly or via some form of mapping. For example, `www.jaydeetechnology.co.uk/welcome` may map to `www.jaydeetechnology.co.uk/home/sayhello.jsp`.

2. The Web server than passes the request onto the JSP engine (which is running within a JVM). This causes the JSP to be parsed and a servlet file to be generated. This servlet provides a direct mapping from the JSP into a servlet that supplies the HTML page defined by the JSP.
3. The generated servlet is then compiled and loaded into the JVM of the JSP engine (with is therefore also a servlet engine).
4. The Web server then passes the request on to the servlet implementation of the JSP.
5. This servlet can then call out to other Java code as required.
6. Any information provided by the Java code is appended to the HTML from the JSP as required.
7. The HTML generated is returned to the Web server.
8. The Web server returns the HTML page back to the client browser.
9. The client browser renders the response without ever seeing any Java.

There are some things to note from this description. Firstly, as a JSP is compiled into a servlet all the features available for a servlet are available to any Java code embedded in the JSP. Thus the request and response objects are available as well as the session object etc. Secondly, a JSP and a servlet end up being the same thing. Thus servlets can call JSPs and vice versa because they are essentially exactly the same type of object. Thirdly, just as with a normal servlet, once a JSP has been translated into a servlet, compiled and loaded into the JVM on the Web server, it remains in memory. Thus the second time a servlet is called the JSP file is not parsed nor is it translated and compiled. Instead, the request is passed immediately on to the servlet available within the JVM.

19.3 A Very Simple JSP

To illustrate the ideas discussed above we will look at a very simple JSP. The JSP we will define is the JSP version of Hello World. We will create a JSP that presents "Hello" followed by a `String` supplied from a Java class called `BasicHello` in a package `hello`. The JSP, saved in a file called `hello1.jsp`, is presented in Listing 19.1 and the JavaBean is presented in Listing 19.2 (note that the only thing that makes `BasicHello` a JavaBean is that we have followed the JavaBeans naming conventions for the `get` method).

Listing 19.1 A very simple JSP: `hello1.jsp`.

```
<html>
<body>
<%@ page import="hello.BasicHello" %><jsp:useBean id="hello" scope="page"
class="hello.BasicHello"/><h1>Basic Hello World</h1>
This is a simple test
<p> <hr> <p>
Hello <jsp:getProperty name="hello" property="name"/><p> <hr>
</body></html>
```

We will work through this simple JSP.

- The first two lines in the JSP are standard HTML tags.
- `<%@ page import="hello.BasicHello" %>` provides information for the whole page. In particular, it tells the JSP that the class `BasicHello` in the package `hello` will be used (note that this will be converted into a Java import statement when the JSP is translated into a servlet).
- `<jsp:useBean>` This locates and creates the specified JavaBean. Essentially it states that a new instance of the class `hello.BasicHello` will be created and made available via the "variable" `hello` that exists only for the current page (i.e. it does not persist over multiple calls to the JSP).
- The next three lines are standard HTML that provide a heading (Basic Hello World) and some simple formatting.
- `<jsp:getProperty>` This gets a property value of the JavaBean `BasicHello`. It assumes that there is a method `get<PropertyName>` available (in this case `getName()`).
- The output of `getName()` is then concatenated with HTML strings.
- The final lines are all HTML and deal with completing the HTML page.

Form this we know some things about the Java class that must implement `BasicHello`. These are that:

- It must be in a package called `hello`.
- It must provide a method `getName()` that returns a name to be added to the HTML page

However, it need not do anything else. Indeed, at present, if it does do more then those features will not be used by the JSP file. Listing 19.2 presents the simple `BasicHello` class.

Listing 19.2 The `BasicHello` class.

```
package hello;
public class BasicHello {
  public String getName() {
    return "John";
  }
}
```

As this is only an example, Listing 19.2 is very basic. The string returned by the class is hard coded to be "John". However, this string could be provided by some other Java code, read from a database or accessed from some legacy code etc.

The `BasicHello` class must be compiled using javac in the normal manner. However, rather than run the class directly the `.class` file must be installed in the appropriate place on the Web server (exactly where this is will depend on the JSP engine being used).

The end result of installing the JSP file and `BasicHello` class file correctly on your Web server is illustrated in Figure 19.2.

Although the example presented in Listing 19.1 is a very simple example, it does show a JSP that obtains some of its data from a Java class – this is the essence of all JSPs!

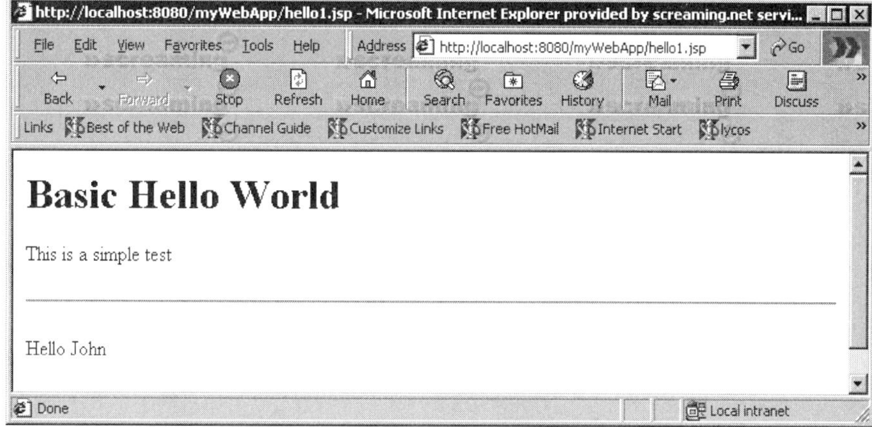

Figure 19.2 The result of running the simple JSP.

19.4 The Components of a JSP

A JSP file is make up of text, HTML tags and a number of additional components: directives, actions, implicit objects and scripts. Each of these is considered briefly below.

19.4.1 Directives

Directives are the JSP components that provide global processing instructions for a whole JSP file. the syntax of a directive is:

```
<%@ directive {attribute="value"} %>
```

For example:

```
<%@ page import="shop.BookList" %>
```

This states that the JSP should import the class `BookList` in the package `shop`. This means that the class generated from the JSP will have a normal Java import statement for this class added to it.

There are several commonly used directives:

- The `page` directive. This defines information for the current JSP page. It provides information on the scripting language to be used, the parent class for the servlet generated from the JSP, whether sessional data will be available etc. Defaults are available for these attributes and thus only those that do not use the default value need to be provided.
- The `include` directive. This is used to include text and code into a JSP at translation time.
- The `taglib` directive. This directive allows a particular tag library to be used with the current JSP.

19.4.2 Actions

Actions provide standard tasks such as creating or accessing Java objects (normally those that conform to the JavaBeans naming conventions). The JSP framework provides the following commonly used actions:

- `<jsp:useBean>` This action links an instance of a Java class (the JavaBean) with a given ID and a scope. The scope can be page, `request`, `session` or `application`. For example:

```
<jsp:useBean id="total" scope="session"
    class="com.jaydeetee.Totalizer" />
```

  - `page` scope – implies that the object only exists for the current page
  - `request` scope – indicates that the object is only available to pages processing the same request
  - `session` scope – indicates that the object exists for the current session
  - `application` scope – states that the object is available with the current Web application context; if the user requests go outside of the current Web application, the object is not available
- `<jsp:setProperty>` sets the value of a bean's property
- `<jsp:getProperty>` obtains the value of a bean's property and converts it to a `String`. This string is then concatenated with the current output stream.
- `<jsp:forward>` allows the JSP engine to forward the current request to another JSP or servlet at run time. The current JSP terminates.

19.4.3 Implicit Objects

Within a JSP there are a number of "implicit" objects that are available to the developer. In general these are available through the Servlet that the JSP will be translated into. For example, the request and response objects are available. There is also a session object and the `ServletContext` (available via a variable called `application`). There is also a variable `out` that the `JspWriter` object linked to the response object is maintained in. This provides methods such as `print` and `println`.

19.4.4 JSP Scripting

JSP scripting allows code fragments to be directly embedded in the JSP page. There are three elements that make up JSP scripting: declarations, expressions and scriptlets. We shall assume that Java is being used as the scripting language within the JSP – remember that this is server side and that the JSP will be converted into a Java servlet).

Declarations

These are used to declare variables and methods in the scripting language. The syntax of a declaration is:

```
<%! declaration %>
```

For example:

```
<%! String name = "John"; %>
<%! public String getName() { return name; } %>
```

Expressions

These allow fragments of code to be written whose result will be added to the output of the JSP. The syntax of an expression is:

```
<%= expression %>
```

For example:

```
Hello <%= getName() %>
```

Scriptlets

Scriptlets can contain any code that is valid in the scripting language. They can use the variables and methods defined in declarations, implicit objects, JavaBeans etc. The syntax for a scriptlet is:

```
<% scriplet %>
```

For example:

```
<% out.println("Hello " + hello.getName()); %>
```

19.5 Making JSPs Interactive

Data can be obtained from `request` attributes in the same way that it can be obtain from the `request` object in servlets. However, it is not necessary for the developer to code this; instead, by using the correct actions and directives in the JSP the necessary code can be automatically generated. This leaves the JSP designer to concentrate on the presentation issues and not the code of the Java servlet.

For example, a common scenario is for a JSP to generate a form that actions the same JSP. The first time the JSP is called it generates the HTML form; however, the second time it is called it retrieves the information entered into the form and triggers some behaviour (within the related Java code). As a simple example, consider the JSP file presented in Listing 19.3.

Listing 19.3 Interactive servlet: `hello2.jsp`.

```
<html><body>
<%@ page import="hello.Hello" %>
```

```
<jsp:useBean id="hello" scope="session" class="hello.Hello" />
<jsp:setProperty name="hello" property="*"/>
<h1>Hello World</h1>
  <p>Bean has been accessed <jsp:getProperty name="hello"
    property="count"/> times.
  <p><hr><p>
<% if (!hello.hasName()) { %>
    This is a simple form:  <p>
    <form method="get" action="hello2.jsp">
    What's your name? <input type="text" name="name">
    <input type="submit" value="Submit">
</form>
<% } else { %>
    Hello <jsp:getProperty name="hello" property="name"/> <p><hr>
<% } %> </body></html>
```

The servlet in Listing 19.3 has a number of features worth noting. Firstly, `<jsp@setProperty name = "hello" property="*"/>` action specifies that we want the `hello` bean (that is, the Java object referenced by the id "hello") and to automatically set the properties on this bean within the form. That is, we tell the set property action to search the request object for parameter names that match the properties of the `hello` bean. If there are any matches, then the action will set the bean properties to those values.

The next thing to note from this JSP is that we have embedded some Java within the JSP. This is indicated by:

```
<% if (!hello.hasName()) { %>
```

This is an example of a scriptlet described earlier. This code will be extracted and incorporated into the underlying servlet. Thus this is a piece of Java that will be used by the servlet to determine what should happen when the servlet executes. Note that the scriptlet contains part of a Java if statement, the else part is further down in the listing and the final closing bracket is at the start of the final line of the listing. Thus you can embed any Java into your JSP as required. This of course muddies the separation of presentation from content, but does provide a great deal of flexibility and power. For example, it is possible to embed into the JSP a section of Java code that will use JDBC to access a database and retrieve information that can be directly incorporated into the JSP itself. However, in doing this you end up with the same issues as exist for servlets – presentation and logic being mixed!

The Java class (`hello.Hello`) is presented in Listing 19.4.

Listing 19.4 The `Hello` Java class.

```
package hello;
public class Hello {
  private String username;
  private boolean flag = false;
  private int count = 0;
```

```
public String getName() {  return username;  }
  public void setName(String name) {
    username = name;
    flag = true;
  }
  public boolean hasName() {   return flag;   }
  public int getCount() {   return ++count; }
}
```

The result of running this "Web application" (i.e. the combination of the JSP and the Java class) is illustrated in Figure 19.3. The Web page on the left illustrates the result of running the JSP the first time. The Web page on the right is the result of selecting Submit on the first Web page – i.e. the result of running the JSP a second time.

Figure 19.3 The effect of running the Web application.

19.6 Why Use JSPs?

A question that is worth considering is why use JSPs at all – we already have servlets and for those who are Java developers there is less to learn! The main answer relates to the motivation behind JSPs that was mentioned at the start of this chapter – JSP designers don't need to know Java (as much). That is, the JSP is oriented around HTML and XML-like (and thus HTML-like) JSP tags. It is thus easy for an HTML Web site designer to get familiar with the JSP concepts and structures etc. It is also possible for developers to extend the JSP tag library with project-specific tags that will provide easy access to project-specific resources (again hiding the non-HTML parts from the JSP designer). Certainly it's a lot easier to produce sophisticated HTML-based pages using JSP than straight servlets.

19.7 Problems With JSPs

The main problem with JSPs is that although the aim in JSPs is to separate presentation from the application logic, they don't completely succeed. Indeed, if the developer wishes to the presentational aspect of JSPs can be heavily mixed with embedded scripts that contain extensive Java code. As an example consider the following JSP page that might form part of an online bookstore:

```
<html>
<body>

<%@ page import="com.jaydeetee.shop.Basket" %>

<jsp:useBean id="basket" scope="session" class="com.jaydeetee.shop.Basket" />

<h1>Welcome to the online shop</h1>

<%
  if (basket.isEmpty())
    String user = request.getParamter("user");
    String passwd = request.getParamter("password");
    if (user != null) {
      if (passwd != null) {
        if (basket.checkUser(user, passwd)) {
          String book = request.getParamter("title");
          String author = request.getParamter("author");
          double price = Double.parseDouble(request.getParamter("price"));
          basket.addBook(book, author, price);
        }
      }
    }
  } else {
```

```
      String book = request.getParamter("title");
      String author = request.getParamter("author");
      double price = Double.parseDouble(request.getParamter("price"));
      basket.addBook(book, author, price);
    }
  %>

  So far you have bought the following books:

  <%

    String [] books = basket.getAllBooks();
    for (int i=0; i<books.length; i++) {
      oup.println(books[i] + " <br> ");
    }

  %>

  If you wish to purchase another book then enter the detail in the
  following form:

  <hr>
    <form action='welcome2' method='GET'>"
      Input a book to buy<p>"
        Title:
          <input type=text name=title size=10>"
        <br>Author:
          <input type=text name=author size=10>"
        <br>Price:
          <input type=text name=price size=10>"
        <br>
          <input type=submit value='Submit'>
    </form>
  <p>
  <hr>

  </body>
  </html>
```

As this page illustrates, the scriptlet is doing a great deal of Java processing. This could be repeated many times in the JSP.

Care needs to be taken to try to refrain from this sort of mixing. One approach is to use JSPs where the majority of the result is HTML and servlets where you need to initiate a great amount of Java processing/business logic.

Chapter 20

JSP Tags and Implicit Objects

20.1 Introduction

The previous chapter introduced the concept of JavaServer Pages (or JSPs). This allowed the architecture of a JSP to be presented and the framework within which a JSP operates etc. However, a great deal of detail relating to the various building blocks of JSPs was left out to avoid clouding the discussion. This chapter fills in these details and provides a detailed review of the elements that can be used when creating a JSP. In particular, the previous chapter concentrated on the core aspects of the JSP architecture introduced with the original JSP 1.0 specification. However, the JSP specification has matured greatly since its introduction in September 1999 with JSP 1.1 and more recently JSP 1.2.

This chapter reviews the basic building blocks of JSP pages (in particular directives, scripting elements and standard actions). It will also discuss the implicit objects provided to allow JSP pages to access their environment etc.

20.2 JSP Tags

There are three categories of tags: directives, scripting elements and actions:

- **Directives.** These affect the overall structure of the underlying servlet, which as you know from the last chapter is generated from the JSP file automatically by the Web container.
- **Scripting elements.** These let you insert Java code into the JSP page. This Java code is then inserted into the underlying servlet.
- **Actions.** Actions are special tags that affect the runtime behaviour of the servlet version of the JSP. The JSP specification provides a number of standard actions (such as the `jsp:useBean` element that you have already seen.

It is also possible to write your own tags by defining a tag library. This is the subject of the next chapter. The remaining tags are each discussed in detail in the remainder of this section.

20.2.1 JSP Directives

JSP directives affect the code that is generated by the Web container for the JSP when converting it into a servlet. They can be used to:

- import Java classes (i.e. JavaBeans)
- participate in any ongoing session
- include the output from another Web resource such as an HTML file or another JSP
- specify inheritance of the JSP
- define the output content type etc.

There are three types of JSP directive: `page` directives, `include` directives and `taglib` directives.

The `page` *directive*

The `page` directive defines attributes for the whole page, for example in the previous chapter we used the `page` directive to import a class so that it could be used within the JSP:

```
<%@ page import="hello.BasicHello" %>
```

Other page directive attributes include:

- `language`: defines the scripting language to be used (this has the value Java by default)
- `extends`: defines the class that the servlet generated from the JSP page will extend (this is omitted by default)
- `import`: allows a comma-separated list of packages or classes to be imported
- `session`: indicates whether the page is part of a session or not (true by default)
- `autoFlush`: indicates whether the output buffer should be automatically flushed or not when it is full (true by default)
- `isThreadSafe`: indicates whether the JSP can handle multiple client requests at the same time (true by default)
- `info`: allows a description to be provided describing the JSP
- `errorPage`: defines the JSP to be called if an exception occurs within the JSP
- `isErrorPage`: used to indicate whether the JSP page acts as an error page for another JSP (false by default). If it is set to true then the implicit object `exception` is made available
- `contentType` is used to change the MIME type (it is `text/html` by default)

An example of using a number of different page directive attributes is presented in Figure 20.1.

The `include` *directive*

The `include` directive defines a file to be included in the JSP by the Web container during its conversion to a servlet. For example:

```
<%@ include file="copyright.html" %>
```

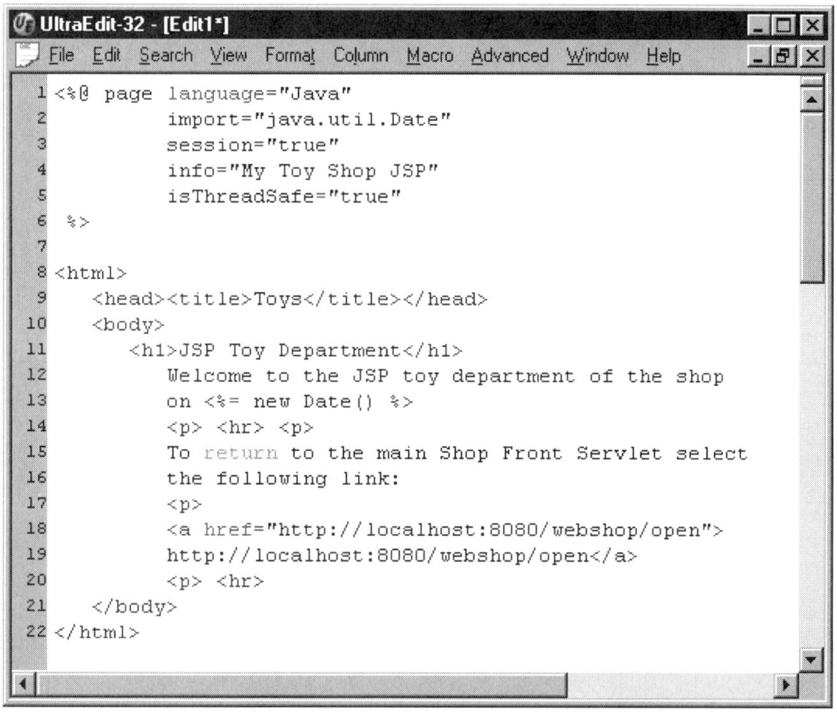

UltraEdit-32 - [Edit1*]

File Edit Search View Format Column Macro Advanced Window Help

```
<%@ page language="Java"
         import="java.util.Date"
         session="true"
         info="My Toy Shop JSP"
         isThreadSafe="true"
 %>

<html>
   <head><title>Toys</title></head>
   <body>
      <h1>JSP Toy Department</h1>
         Welcome to the JSP toy department of the shop
         on <%= new Date() %>
         <p> <hr> <p>
         To return to the main Shop Front Servlet select
         the following link:
         <p>
         <a href="http://localhost:8080/webshop/open">
         http://localhost:8080/webshop/open</a>
         <p> <hr>
   </body>
</html>
```

Figure 20.1 Using the page directive.

The included file may be an HTML file, a text file or another JSP. Note that the path name provided as the value of the file attribute is relative to the current Web application. For example:

- <%@ include file="welcome.html" %> includes the contents of the welcome.html file located in the Web applications root directory.
- <%@ include file="/WEB-INF/jsps/Footer.jsp" %> includes the output from the Footer.jsp file located in the jsps subdirectory of the WEB-INF directory of the Web application.

There a couple of things to note about the use of the include directives:

1. The value of the file attribute is a pathname and not a URL; thus the file specified does not need to be visible outside the Web application.
2. If the included file is a JSP, then what actually happens is that the file is included in the JSP file *before* it is compiled into a servlet. Thus the JSP file does not need to be a complete JSP: it can be a fragment of a JSP relying on the file it is included in to provide what it needs (such as class imports). These JSP fragments are completely valid and the JSP specification suggests that they should have an extension of .jsf or .jspf (for JSP fragment). This is illustrated in Figure 20.2.

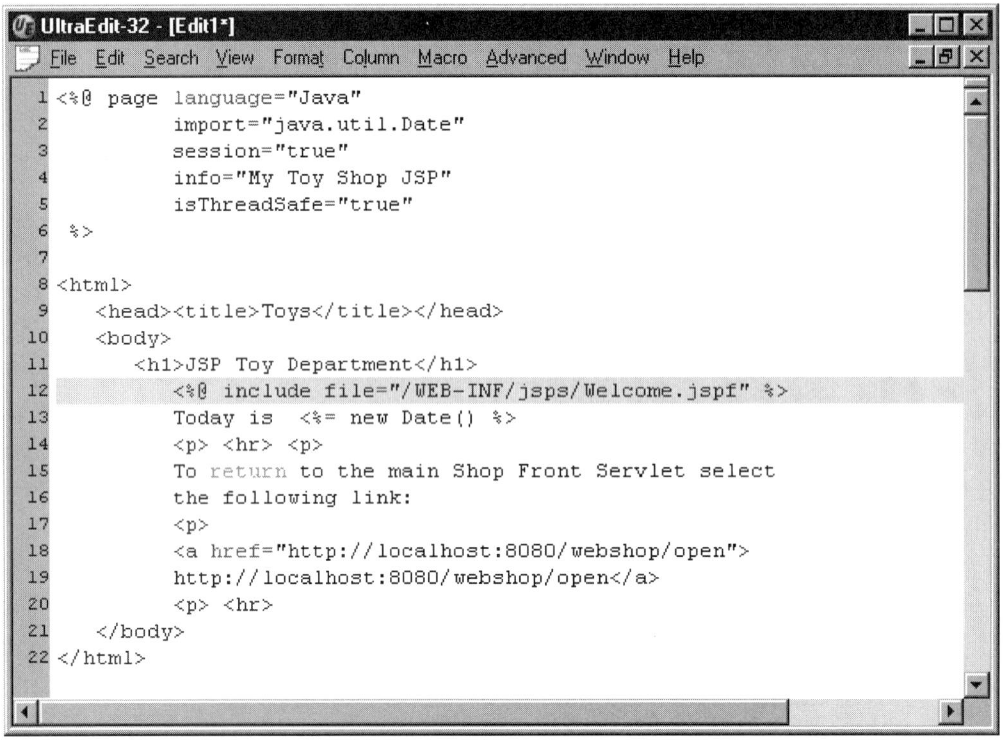

```
<%@ page language="Java"
         import="java.util.Date"
         session="true"
         info="My Toy Shop JSP"
         isThreadSafe="true"
 %>

<html>
   <head><title>Toys</title></head>
   <body>
      <h1>JSP Toy Department</h1>
         <%@ include file="/WEB-INF/jsps/Welcome.jspf" %>
         Today is  <%= new Date() %>
         <p> <hr> <p>
         To return to the main Shop Front Servlet select
         the following link:
         <p>
         <a href="http://localhost:8080/webshop/open">
         http://localhost:8080/webshop/open</a>
         <p> <hr>
   </body>
</html>
```

Figure 20.2 Including a JSP fragment.

The `taglib` *Directive*

The `taglib` directive allows tag extensions to be used. These tag extensions, also known as custom tags, allow application-specific tags to be defined and used within a JSP. The next chapter will provide more details on tag libraries.

20.2.2 Scripting Elements

Scripting elements allow Java code to be inserted into a JSP. There are three types of scripting elements: declarations, scriptlets and expressions. These are discussed in more detail below.

Declarations

Declarations are class-wide Java code that will be incorporated into the underlying Java servlet. Examples of class-wide Java code include static variables and methods as well as instance variables and methods. The variables and methods defined can then be used within the body of the JSP.

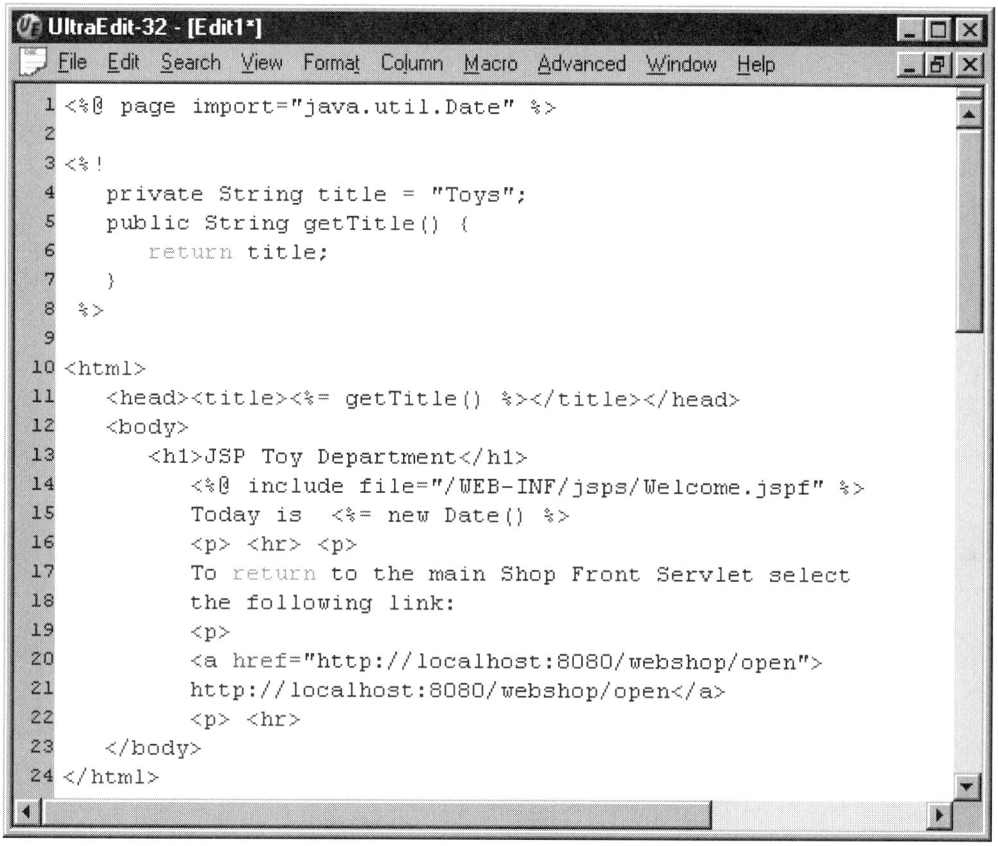

```
1 <%@ page import="java.util.Date" %>
2
3 <%!
4    private String title = "Toys";
5    public String getTitle() {
6       return title;
7    }
8  %>
9
10 <html>
11    <head><title><%= getTitle() %></title></head>
12    <body>
13       <h1>JSP Toy Department</h1>
14          <%@ include file="/WEB-INF/jsps/Welcome.jspf" %>
15          Today is  <%= new Date() %>
16          <p> <hr> <p>
17          To return to the main Shop Front Servlet select
18          the following link:
19          <p>
20          <a href="http://localhost:8080/webshop/open">
21          http://localhost:8080/webshop/open</a>
22          <p> <hr>
23    </body>
24 </html>
```

Figure 20.3 Defining an instance variable and method for a JSP.

The syntax used to define declarations is:

```
<%! variables and methods %>
```

An example of defining a simple instance variable title and a method `getTitle()` are illustrated in Figure 20.3. This example also illustrates a call to the method `getTitle()` in an expression at line 11.

Scriptlets

Scriptlets are blocks of Java code that are executed during request processing. Essentially they are incorporated to into the `GET` processing method of the servlet. A scriptlet is surrounded by `<%` and `%>`, for example:

```
<% Java code %>
```

JSP Quotes.jsp

```
<!DOCTYPE HTML PUBLIC "-//W3C//DTD HTML 4.0 Final//EN">
<%@ page import="com.luxinflecta.giza.users.HUNT.quotes.QuoteGeneratorBean" %>

<html>
<head>
<title>Quotes.jsp</title>
</head>
<body>
  <center>
    <h1>Daily Quote</h1>
      Your quote for today is:
      <p>
      <%
        try {
           QuoteGeneratorBean bean = new QuoteGeneratorBean();
           out.write(bean.getQuote());
        } catch (Exception exp) {
           out.write("No quote available today");
        }
      %>
  </center>
  <p>
</body>
</html>
```

Figure 20.4 Embedding a scriptlet in a JSP.

A JSP can have zero or more scriptlets. A scriptlet may just set up some data or it may use an implicit object to generate some output. Essentially anything you can write in Java you can place within a scriptlet. Some examples of using scriptlets include connection to databases, querying databases, connecting to EJBs and processing EJBs. An example of using a scriptlet is illustrated in Figure 11.4. This scriptlet creates an instance of a `QuoteGeneratorBean` and then retrieves a quote from that bean. The output is then written to the implicit object "`out`", which is essentially the output writer for the response object associated with the underlying servlet.

Expressions

An expression is a shorthand notation for a scriptlet that concatenates a result with the current output. If the output of the expression is not already a string then it is converted to a string. If the output is an object then this involves calling its `toString()` method. The syntax for an expression is:

```
<%= Java expression to evaluate %>
```

An example of an expression is presented at line 11 of Figure 20.3. In this example the string returned by the `getTitle()` method is concatenated with the HTML at that point (that is, it is inserted between the opening and closing title tags. A more comprehensive example of using various scripting elements is presented in Figure 20.5.

UltraEdit-32 - [D:\serverside\web\patterns\WEB-INF\jsps\NavigationPanel.jsp*]

File Edit Search View Format Column Macro Advanced Window Help

```
<html>
<head><BASE target="middle"><title>Navigation</title>

<%@ page import="webshop.constant.Commands" %>
<%@ page import="webshop.constant.Groups" %>

</head>
<body>
<h1>Navigation</h1>
<p><hr><p>
<form action="ShopFrontServlet" method="GET" name="newform">

      <input type="submit" name="command"
            value="<%=webshop.constant.Commands.SEARCH%>" target="middle">
      <p>
      <input type="submit" name="command"
             value="<%=webshop.constant.Commands.LIST%>" target="middle">
      <p>  <hr>   <p>

    <% if(request.isUserInRole("admin")) { %>
      <!-- Now only want to make edit buttons available for certain users -->
      <input  type="submit" name="command"
              value="<%=webshop.constant.Commands.NEW%>" target="middle">
      <p>
      <input type="submit" name="command"
            value="<%=webshop.constant.Commands.EDIT%>" target="middle">
       <p>
     <!-- end of if statement -->
   <% } %>

      <hr> <p>
      <input type="submit" name="command"
            value="<%=webshop.constant.Commands.ABOUT%>" target="middle">
      <p>
      <input type="submit" name="command"
            value="<%=webshop.constant.Commands.HOME%>" target="middle">
      <p>
</form>
```

Figure 20.5 Using scripting elements in a JSP.

20.2.3 Actions

Standard actions provide for common tasks that affect the runtime behaviour of the JSP. They must be implemented such that there affect is the same in all Web containers and are available by default in all JSPs. You have already seen some standard actions in the previous chapter (for example the `useBean` action). The standard actions are:

- `<jsp:useBean>`: used to access a JavaBean.
- `<jsp:setProperty>`/`<jsp:getProperty>`: used to access a JavaBean property.
- `<jsp:include>` used to dynamically include a request to an HTML file, servlet or JSP. Note that this is based on a URL and this the Web resource specified must be available and must be a valid resources (thus the included JSP may *not* be a fragment).

- `<jsp:forward>`: used to forward a request to a Web resource such as an HTML file, servlet or JSP.
- `<jsp:plugin>`: accesses a Java plug-in for an applet or bean.
- `<jsp:param>`: provides information for other tags. It is used with `include`, `forward`, `plugin` etc.

The syntax for these actions is presented below.

useBean

`<jsp:useBean id="name" scope="scope" class="class" type="type" />`	
`id`	Case-sensitive name used to identify the object in the JSP
`scope`	Scope of the bean, which can be "`page`", "`request`", "`session`" or "`application`"
`class`	The fully qualified class name
`type`	Used to specify the type of the bean (the class specified must be castable to this type and follow standard Java casting rules). This attribute is optional
`bean name`	Optionally, instead of providing a class name, it is possible to provide the name of a bean, as would be supplied to the `instantiate()` method in the `java.beans.Beans` class

It is possible to use a variant on the above syntax to allow properties of the bean to be set when it is created. This form is:

```
<jsp:useBean id="name" scope="scope" class="class" type="type" >
  Body – with JSP content, e.g. set property
</jsp:useBean>
```

setProperty

`<jsp:setProperty name="beanName" property="name" value="value" />`	
`name`	The name of the bean to be used
`property`	The name of the property being set. If the value "*" is used then the tag will automatically look through the request and extract the values for properties that have the same names as parameters sent with the request
`value`	The value to assign to the property
`param`	Optionally the name of a request parameter can be specified that will automatically be used to set the value of the property

getProperty

`<jsp:getProperty name="beanName" property="name" />`	
`name`	The name of the bean to be used
`property`	The name of the property being obtained

include

`<jsp:include page="URL" flush="true|false" />`	
`page`	The Web resource to include
`flush`	Optional parameter that indicates whether the current output buffer should be flushed before the output of the Web resource is included. It defaults to false

It is also possible to use an alternative form of the `jsp:include` element such that parameters can be passed to the called Web resource, for example:

```
<jsp:include page="URL" flush="true/false" >
  <jsp:param ... />
</jsp:include>
```

forward

```
<jsp:forward page="URL" />
```

page	The Web resource to receive the forwarded request

As with the `jsp:include` element it is possible to pass parameters to the called Web resource, for example:

```
<jsp:forward page="URL" >
  <jsp:param ... />
</jsp:forward>
```

plugin

```
<jsp:plugin type="bean|applet" code="objectCode" codebase="objectCodebase" align="alignment"
archive="archiveList" height="height" hspace="hspace" jreversion="jre" name="componentName"
vspace="vspace" width="width" nspluginurl="url" iepluginurl="url > <jsp:params>...</
jsp:params><jsp:fallback>Text</jsp:fallback></jsp:plugin>
```

type	Specifies type of component (either JavaBean or Applet)
code	As for applet syntax
codebase	As for applet syntax
align	As for applet syntax
archive	As for applet syntax
height	As for applet syntax
hspace	As for applet syntax
jreversion	The Java Runtime Environment version (e.g. 1.1, 1.2, 1.4 etc.)
name	As for applet syntax
vspace	As for applet syntax
title	As for applet syntax
width	As for applet syntax
nspluginurl	URL where the Java plugin for Netscape can be found
iepluginurl	URL where the Java plugin for IE can be found

param

```
<jsp:param name="name" value="value" />
```

name	The name of the attribute
value	The value of the attribute

20.3 Implicit Objects

The servlet that is generated from the JSP by the Web container possesses several objects that you will be familiar with from the servlet chapters earlier in this book. For example, the request and response objects are available. As the Java code you write in your JSP is not compiled until it has been incorporated into the servlet generated from the JSP you can access these objects. These objects are referred to as implicit objects (as they are there for you to use but are not explicitly declared anywhere in the JSP).

There are in fact eight such implicit objects:

- `request`: an instance of `HttpServletRequest`.
- `response`: an instance of `HttpServletResponse`.
- `pageContext`: the shared data within a page. That is, it is a single point of access to many of the page attributes and is a convenient place to put shared data within the page. It is of type `javax.Servlet.jsp.PageContext` and has page scope.
- `session`: represents the session object created for the JSP. It is of type `HttpSession`. This actually allows data created by a JSP and placed in the session object to be retrieved by a JSP or a servlet at some point in the future.
- `application`: represents the servlet context of the Web application. It is of type `ServletContext`.
- `out`: this is of type `javax.Servlet.jsp.JspWriter` (not `PrintWriter`) and is used for output to the client.
- `config`: the `ServletConfig` for the servlet generated from the JSP.
- `page`: the equivalent of `this` for the underlying servlet.

Notice that many of the above are from the familiar `javax.Servlet` and `javax.Servlet.http` packages. However, a few of the objects are of types from the `javax.Servlet.jsp` package.

20.4 Scope

The scope of a JavaBean, for example, can be one of "Page", "Request", "Session" or "Application". Each of these scope declarations has a very specific meaning:

- **Page.** Ths means that the object associated with this scope is essentially a local variable to the `GET` method created for the underlying servlet. That is, it lasts only for a single call to the JSP. Thus its scope is the current page and no more.
- **Session.** This means that the object is added to the session object associated with the current JSP. It is thus instantiated the first time the page is accessed. However, it is then stored in the `HttpSession` object and future requests to this page will use the bean obtained from the session.
- **Request.** This means that the object created is associated with the `ServletRequest` object. It can therefore be passed to other servlets and JSPs participating in the current request.

These additional servlets and JSPs can access the object using the `getAttribute()` method on the implicit request object.

- **Application.** This means that the object is available to the whole of the current Web application. It is not associated with a particular user nor with a particular request. Rather, it is a global object available anywhere in the Web application. It can be accessed using the `getAttribute` method of the implicit application object.

To illustrate the effect of different scopes on a bean object we will look at the same JSP but with different scopes applied to the bean. The bean itself is very simple and is presented in Figure 20.6. This JavaBean counts the number of times the `getCount` method is called on the same instance. It first returns the value zero, and each subsequent call on the same instance will increment the result. However, if a new instance is created then the count will of course be zero again.

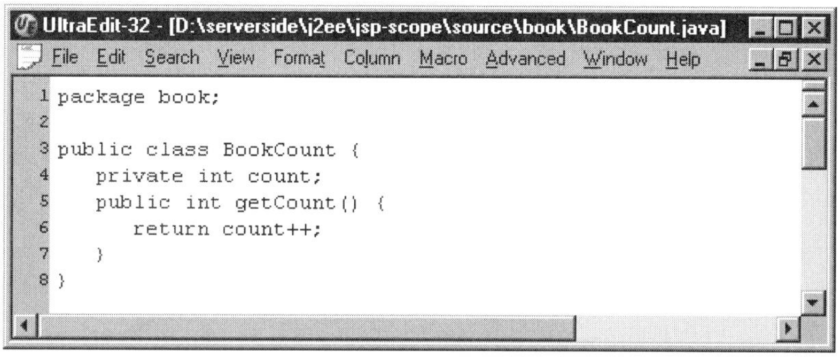

UltraEdit-32 - [D:\serverside\j2ee\jsp-scope\source\book\BookCount.java]

```
package book;

public class BookCount {
   private int count;
   public int getCount() {
      return count++;
   }
}
```

Figure 20.6 Simple JavaBean for counting calls to the same instance.

The example that uses the JavaBean with page scope is presented in Figure 20.7. The result of deploying this JSP on Tomcat and accessing it in IE 6.0 is that the count displayed always remains zero, no matter how many times the page is refreshed (see Figure 20.8).

However if the scope of the bean is changed to be session, for example:

```
<jsp:useBean id="book" scope="session" class="book.BookCount" />
```

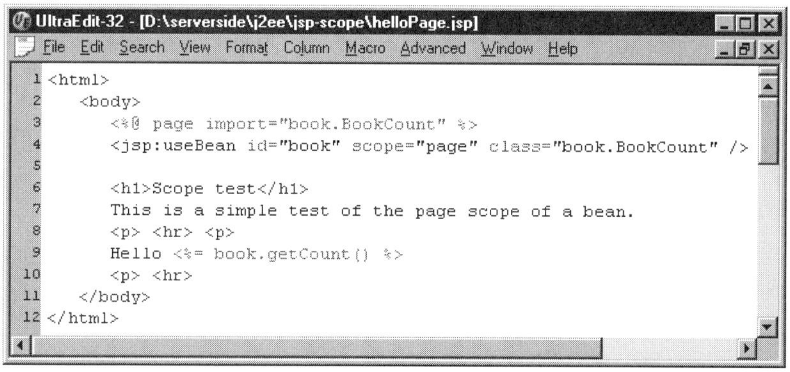

UltraEdit-32 - [D:\serverside\j2ee\jsp-scope\helloPage.jsp]

```
<html>
   <body>
      <%@ page import="book.BookCount" %>
      <jsp:useBean id="book" scope="page" class="book.BookCount" />

      <h1>Scope test</h1>
      This is a simple test of the page scope of a bean.
      <p> <hr> <p>
      Hello <%= book.getCount() %>
      <p> <hr>
   </body>
</html>
```

Figure 20.7 JSP with a page scope `BookCount` bean.

then when the page is refreshed the value returned from `getCount()` is incremented (as illustrated in Figure 20.9).

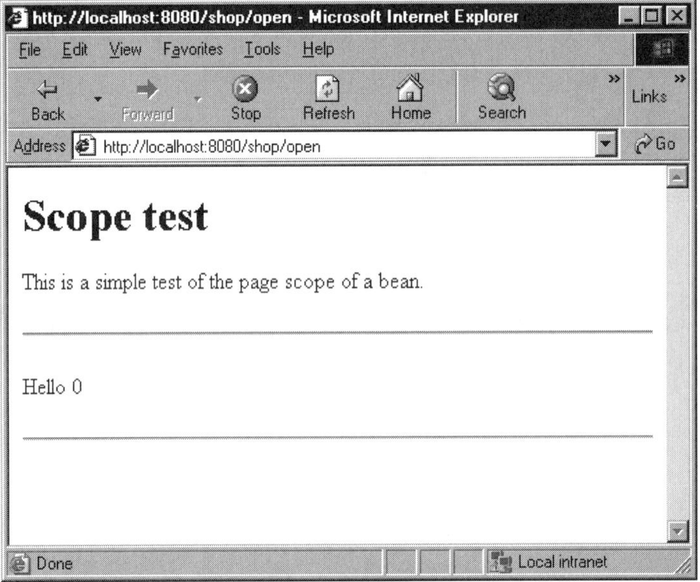

Figure 20.8 Using a page scope on the book count.

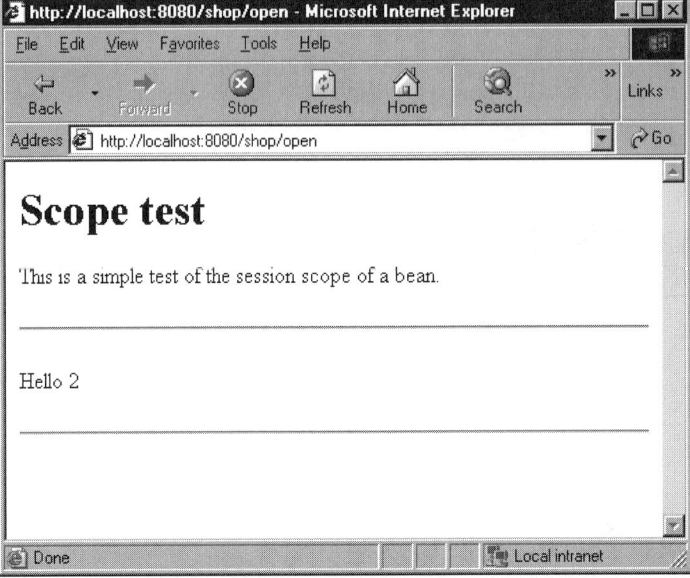

Figure 20.9 Using the session scope with the JavaBean.

Chapter 21

JSP Tag Libraries

21.1 Introduction

JSP Tag libraries were introduced in the JSP 1.1 specification. They are a very important addition to the facilities available for JSPs, as they allow much of the Java details involved in writing JSPs to be hidden from the JSP content provider. This is good, as many HTML Web designers could quite happily work with JSPs, but not with Java itself.

JSP Tag Libraries are essentially the ability to extend the set of JSP tags by creating application specific custom tags that provide some specific functionality (such as calling a JavaBean). These tags are translated at runtime into Java code that actually provides the implementation of the new tag. Thus there is a greater separation of the presentation aspects of the JSP (as represented by HTML, scripting etc.) and the business logic behind the JSP (as represented by JavaBeans and Enterprise JavaBeans).

This chapter introduces the key concepts behind tag libraries and then presents the elements required to create a custom library, including:

- Tag handler class
- The TLD specification
- Using with a Web application
- Use in a JSP

It then considers how a tag library is deployed and discusses the use of tag libraries.

21.2 Why Use Tag Libraries?

What are the benefits to be obtained from using tag libraries? In this section we will try to highlight some of the advantages of using tag libraries and why you should consider them.

- They can be used where you might have used scriptlets or expressions; therefore they remove the need for the JSP designer to know or understand either.
- They can hide complexity. The actual code behind the custom tags may be quiet complex; however, that code is accessed via a single tag element.
- They look just like other JSP tags and are thus straightforward and simple to use and do not require the user to learn a new syntax.
- They promote reusability of the Java classes without users needing to learn Java.
- They can make non-Java programmers working on JSPs more productive.
- They can introduce new scripting variables into the JSP page.
- They can provide iterative operations without resorting to scriptlets (through the use of multiple evaluation `TagBody` objects).

21.3 Key Concepts

As mentioned above, tag libraries (also known as custom tags) were introduced in the 1.1 version of the JSP specification. These custom tags or tag extensions look just like standard JSP tags; the only difference is that a developer has had to "implement" these tags in Java. Thus custom tags are merely an interface to Java classes. These Java classes must implement specific interfaces to fit into the tag library framework, but apart from that there is little that is special about the Java classes themselves. Once they are developed and deployed, the Java code can be called using custom JSP tags that completely hide the underlying implementation. Thus the tags can be used by someone with no knowledge of the Java language!

This means that custom JSP tags can be created to perform common tasks (and some are available over the Internet, either as shareware or for free, that do just that), while others can be created for project-specific activities (such as listing books currently available within a specific category). In all cases they hide the code elements from the JSP. They are thus very like the `useBean` standard action and the JavaBean linked to it. However, there are several differences, which include:

- JavaBeans may require knowledge of Java when used (for example in expressions and scriptlets) whereas JSP tags never do.
- Beans cannot access the content of the JSP page, whereas custom tags can.
- Complex operations (such as connecting to an Enterprise JavaBean) can be simplified to one or more JSP tags, whereas a JavaBean must be called to perform the correct steps within either an expression or a scriptlet.
- JavaBeans are very simple to set up and use whereas there is more infrastructure around tag libraries that must be put in place.
- Beans can be created in one JSP or servlet and then made available in the current session, the current request or the whole application depending on the scope applied to them. In contrast, JSP tags are self-contained, performing a task and terminating once completed.

Thus whether you use a JavaBean or create a custom tag depends in part on who will use the facility and what you want it to do.

There are a few basic concepts that are worth reviewing upon which custom tags rely:

- **The tag name combination.** A JSP tag is identified by its unique tag name. This is a combination of a prefix (the tag library name) and a suffix (the actual tag name). An example of this might be `<jdt:data />`. This is an example of a bodyless tag from the jdt library.
- **Attributes.** Any JSP tag may have attributes, and custom tags are no exception. These attributes use XML syntax and thus must be quoted. In general, attributes serve to customize the tag's behaviour in some way, for example:

```
<jdt:data type="today" />
```

  In this example the `jsp:data` custom tag takes an attribute `type` with a value "`today`".
- **Nested tags.** If one tag is nested inside another this can be detected at runtime and the tags can cooperate. The outer tag is referred to as the parent tag.
- **Body.** A tag can have a body. A body is some text, HTML markup etc. (excluding sub-tags) that is present between the start and end tags. This body content can be accessed by the Java classes behind the tag and manipulated as necessary.
- **Scripting variables.** Tags can create variables that can be used within the JSP page.

Custom tags are defined by creating three separate elements:

- the tag handler class that defines the Java implementation of the tag
- the tag library descriptor file that maps the custom tag name to the Java implementation
- the JSP tag directive to import a library's tags into a JSP

These elements will be considered in more detail below. You should at this point review the `javax.servlet.jsp.tagext` package, as this defines all the class and interfaces we shall be using in this chapter.

21.4 Building a Custom Tag

There are four steps to creating a custom tag:

1. Implement the Java class behind the tag.
2. Create a Tag Library Descriptor to define the JSP tag itself.
3. Map the tag library to the Web application.
4. Import the tag library into a JSP page.

Each of these is described briefly below.

The functionality of a custom tag is implemented by a Java class or classes. This class (or classes) must implement the `javax.servlet.jsp.tagext.Tag` interface (or one of its sub-interfaces). This interface defines all the methods that the JSP runtime engine (code named Catalina in Tomcat 4.0.1) calls during the execution of a tag. The class implementing the tag is known as the Tag Handler and follows JavaBean conventions.

Once the class implementing the tag has been defined, a Tag Library Descriptor (TLD) file must be created. This is an XML document describing the tag library. It provides a mapping from the tag name to the Java class implementing that tag, as well as defining the attributes on the custom tag.

Once this is completed the tag library must be added to the Web application that is going to use it. This can be done either in expanded form as part of the Web application or as a jar file that is available across one or more applications.

Finally, the JSP file (or files) that are going to use the tag library must have the tag library made available to them. This is done using a JSP declaration that imports the tag library.

21.5 The Tag Interface

A tag is implemented by a Java class that must implement the Tag interface (or a sub-interface). The Tag interface defines the basic protocol between a tag handler and JSP page implementation class. It defines the life cycle and the methods to be invoked when the start and end tags are encountered. The main methods in the interface are:

- setPageContext() and setParent(): these are called before the tag starts any processing.
- doStartTag() and doEndTag(): these methods are called when the start and end tags are encountered within a JSP page.

The full set of methods specified by this interface is presented in Table 21.1. There are also a number of constants defined on the interface that are used during the processing of the tag, and these are presented in Table 21.2.

The life cycle of a tag handler class is illustrated in Figure 21.1. This shows the steps that the handler class goes through from instantiation to destruction. The steps are described below.

- new: when the custom tag is encountered a new instance of the Java class that implements that tag is created.
- setup: next, the various setup methods are called on the new object to initialize it. These methods are setPageContext and setParent.

Table 21.1 Methods on the Tag interface.

int	**doEndTag**() Process the end tag for this instance
int	**doStartTag**() Process the start tag for this instance
Tag	**getParent**() Get the parent (closest enclosing tag handler) for this tag handler
void	**release**() Called on a Tag handler to release state
void	**setPageContext**(PageContext pc) Set the current page context
void	**setParent**(Tag t) Set the parent (closest enclosing tag handler) of this tag handler

Table 21.2 Constants on the Tag interface.

static int	**EVAL_BODY_INCLUDE** Evaluate body into existing out stream
static int	**EVAL_PAGE** Continue evaluating the page
static int	**SKIP_BODY** Skip body evaluation
static int	**SKIP_PAGE** Skip the rest of the page

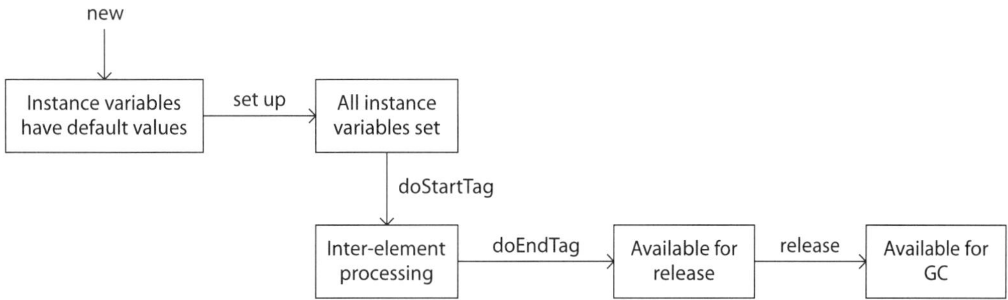

Figure 21.1 The life cycle of a tag handler class.

- doStartTag: this indicates the start of the object's role in the processing of the JSP tag. Between here and receiving notification of the end tag the object is assumed to maintain whatever state is required etc.
- doEndTag: this indicates that the end of the custom JSP tag has been encountered and the object should complete whatever processing is required. Once this is done it is available for release.
- release: this allows the tag handler class to release any resources it holds and generally perform housekeeping-style operations. There is no guarantee that this method will be called, however, as any exceptions thrown earlier will cause this method never to run. Once this method has been called the tag handler object is available for garbage collection.

Note that for performance reasons a Web container may or may not create a new tag handler object for each instance of a custom tag. Rather, it may decide to use a tag-handler pool so that free objects can be reused rather than create a new instance every time. This is at the discretion of the Web container developer and that the custom tag developer has no control whatsoever over the use of a tag handler pool. Note that tag handlers are not multithreaded, so any reuse of a tag handler object will only occur once it has been released from processing one JSP custom tag and it is free to return to the pool. Tomcat 4.0.3 does not use tag-handler pooling.

21.5.1 Other Tag Interfaces and Classes

The Tag interface has a direct sub-interface called IterationTag. The javax.servlet.jsp.tagext.IterationTag interface extends Tag by defining one additional method that controls the re-evaluation of its body. This method is called `doAfterBody()`. If this method returns `IterationTag.EVAL_BODY_AGAIN` then the body of the tag will be re-evaluated.

The `IterationTag` interface also has a sub-interface called `javax.servlet.jsp.tagext.BodyTag`. The `BodyTag` interface extends `IterationTag` by defining additional methods that let a tag handler manipulate the content when evaluating its body.

The most important class is probably the `javax.servlet.jsp.tagext.TagSupport` class. This class is a convenience class that implements the `IterationTag` interface (and thus the `Tag` interface) with default implementations. It also provides additional getter and setter methods for a tag's properties. It is intended as the base class for all tag handler classes. It has one subclass, provided in the `javax.servlet.jsp.tagext` package, called `BodyTagSupport`, which is a convenience class for tag handlers that wish to implement the `BodyTag` interface.

21.6 Creating a Tag Library

As indicated above, there are four main steps to creating and using a tag library. We will work through each step in turn; for reference the four steps are:

1. Implement the tag handler class.
2. Define the Tag Library Descriptor.
3. Map the tag library to the Web application.
4. Import the tag library into a JSP.

21.6.1 Implement the Tag Handler Class

The very simple tag we are going to start off with has no body and no attributes (we will add these later on in this chapter). The simple tag will allow us to obtain the current data and time using the `java.util.Date` class. The actual implementation, presented in Figure 21.2, is very simple. It extends the `TagSupport` convenience class and implements just two methods: `doStartTag()` and `doEndTag()`.

Note the imports to the class. These are the `javax.servlet.jsp.tagext` package, but also the `javax.servlet.jsp` package and the `java.io.IOException`. These are very common and important, and you will find them in all tag handler classes. In this case we also import the `java.util.Date` package so that we can access the `Date` class.

The `doStartTag()` method is very simple. All it does is return an integer that indicates whether the content body of the tag should be processed or not. In this case there is no body to process, so that step can be skipped. To indicate this, we return the `Tag.SKIP_BODY` value.

The `doEndTag()` method is the one that does the work. This method creates a new instance of the `Data` class and converts it to a string. This can now be written to the response output associated with the JSP. This is done by obtaining the output stream associated with the `pageContext`. This is done using the `getOut()` method on the page context variable. Note that this returns a `JspWriter`, and thus if we have more than one string to write out we could store it in a `JspWriter` variable. If something throws an `IOException`

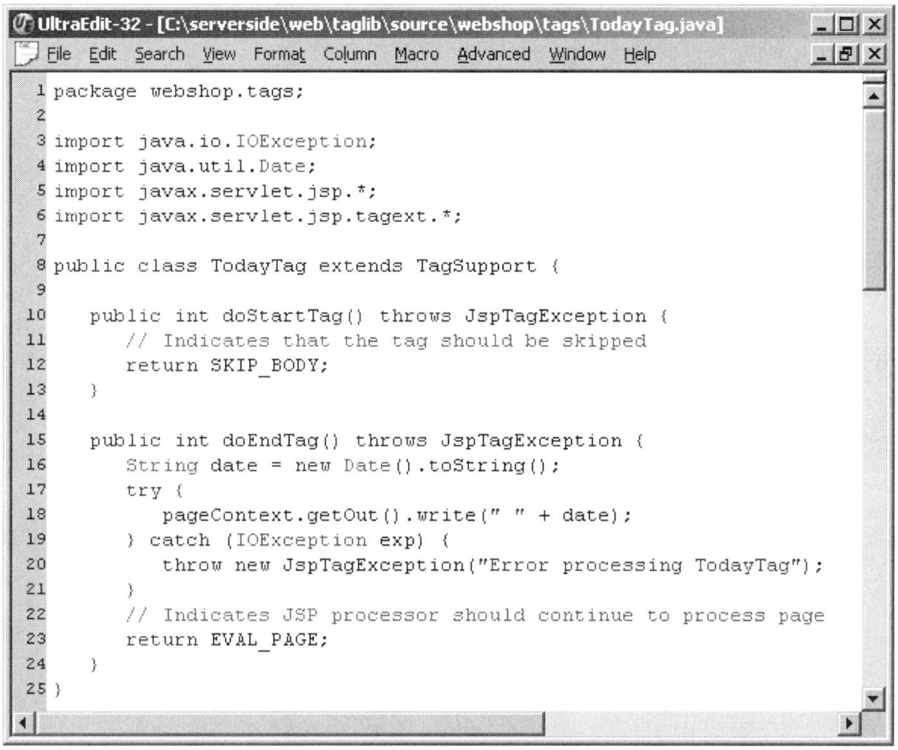

UltraEdit-32 - [C:\serverside\web\taglib\source\webshop\tags\TodayTag.java]

File Edit Search View Format Column Macro Advanced Window Help

```
package webshop.tags;

import java.io.IOException;
import java.util.Date;
import javax.servlet.jsp.*;
import javax.servlet.jsp.tagext.*;

public class TodayTag extends TagSupport {

   public int doStartTag() throws JspTagException {
      // Indicates that the tag should be skipped
      return SKIP_BODY;
   }

   public int doEndTag() throws JspTagException {
      String date = new Date().toString();
      try {
         pageContext.getOut().write(" " + date);
      } catch (IOException exp) {
         throw new JspTagException("Error processing TodayTag");
      }
      // Indicates JSP processor should continue to process page
      return EVAL_PAGE;
   }
}
```

Figure 21.2 The TodayTag tag handler class.

during this we will raise a JspTagException. Finally, the doEndTag() method must return an integer to indicate what the JSP processor should do next – in this case we indicate that it should continue to process the JSP page (using the Tag.EVAL_PAGE constant).

This class can now be compiled in the normal way. Note that the tag handler class files must be made available to the Web application, for example by being deployed under the WEB-INF directory.

21.6.2 Define the Tag Library Descriptor

Next we must define the Tag Library Descriptor file. This is an XML file that provides the mapping between the custom JSP tag and the Java class. The Tag Library Descriptor (TLD) file for the simple today tag is presented in Figure 21.3.

The Tag Library Descriptor file has a very specific structure to it, as defined by its DTD (which is illustrated in Figure 21.3). Firstly, it is necessary to specify the tag library version and the JSP version. Note that you must get these correct, as some of the XML elements in the DTD changed their names between 1.1 and 1.2. The shortname tag provides a shorthand reference to the tag library – we do not use one here.

UltraEdit-32 - [C:\serverside\web\taglib\WEB-INF\taglib.tld]

File Edit Search View Format Column Macro Advanced Window Help

```
<?xml version="1.0" encoding="ISO-8859-1" ?>
<!DOCTYPE taglib
        PUBLIC "-//Sun Microsystems, Inc.//DTD JSP Tag Library 1.2//EN"
  "http://java.sun.com/j2ee/dtd/web-jsptaglibrary_1_2.dtd">

<taglib>
  <tlib-version>1.0</tlib-version>      <!-- Tag library version -->
  <jsp-version>1.2</jsp-version>        <!-- JSP specification version -->
  <short-name></short-name>
 <tag>
    <name>today</name>
    <tag-class>webshop.tags.TodayTag</tag-class>
    <body-content>empty</body-content>
  </tag>
</taglib>
```

Figure 21.3 The TLD file for the today custom JSP tag.

In this particular Tag Library we have only one tag; therefore there is only one <tag> element in the main body of the library description. There could be any number, and normally we would expect a tag library to have more than one tag in it.

The syntax of the <tag> element is:

```
<tag>
  <name>Tag-name</name>
  <tagclass>fully-qualified-class-name</tagclass>
  <body-content>empty|JSP|tagdependent
  </body-content>
</tag>
```

The name of the tag is the name that will be used to reference the tag from within a JSP. The tag class is the name of the tag handler class. The body content indicates whether the tag will have a body and if so what to do with that body. The meaning of the three values that this element can take are:

- `empty`: there should not be a body for this tag.
- JSP: the JSP container should evaluate any body content of the tag – although it can also be left empty.
- `tagdependent`: the body content of the tag will be handled by the tag itself and it can be left empty.

The TLD file is saved in the `WEB-INF` directory of the Web application.

21.6.3 Map the Tag Library

Next we need to incorporate the tag library into a Web application. To do this we need to add another element to the deployment descriptor (the `web.xml` file) that we have seem numerous

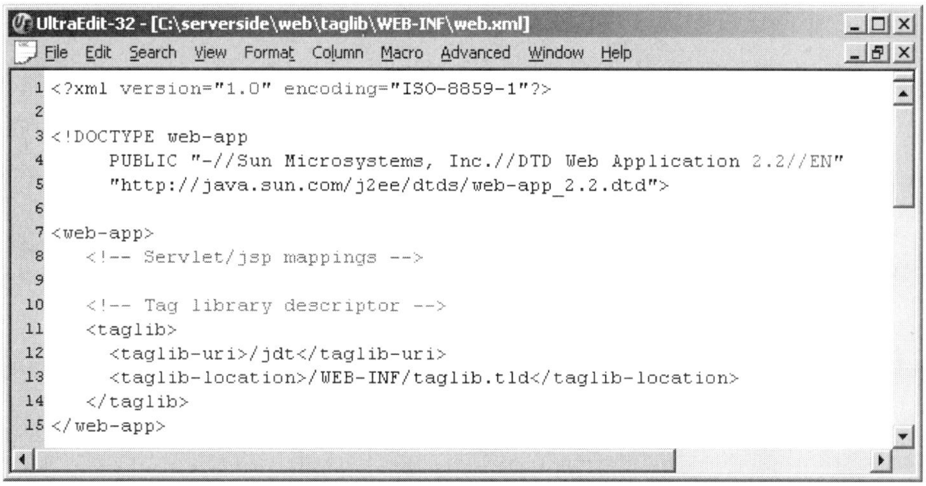

```
<?xml version="1.0" encoding="ISO-8859-1"?>

<!DOCTYPE web-app
     PUBLIC "-//Sun Microsystems, Inc.//DTD Web Application 2.2//EN"
     "http://java.sun.com/j2ee/dtds/web-app_2.2.dtd">

<web-app>
   <!-- Servlet/jsp mappings -->

   <!-- Tag library descriptor -->
   <taglib>
     <taglib-uri>/jdt</taglib-uri>
     <taglib-location>/WEB-INF/taglib.tld</taglib-location>
   </taglib>
</web-app>
```

Figure 21.4 Mapping the tag library for a Web application.

times before. The element we shall be adding is the `<taglib>` element, as illustrated in Figure 21.4.

In Figure 21.4 the Tag Library Descriptor for our tag library is referenced using the location of the TLD file within the `WEB-INF` directory. It is also given a short URI name (in this case `jdt`) that will be used within the JSP file to reference this tag library.

21.6.4 Import the Tag Library

We now need to define a JSP file that will use our tag library. An example JSP file, called `today.jsp`, is presented in Figure 21.5. We must import the tag library into the JSP in order to be able to reference the tags in that library. This is done using the `taglib` directive:

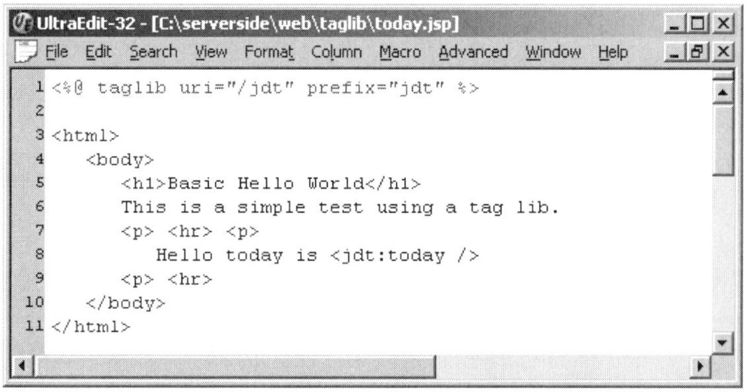

```
<%@ taglib uri="/jdt" prefix="jdt" %>

<html>
   <body>
      <h1>Basic Hello World</h1>
      This is a simple test using a tag lib.
      <p> <hr> <p>
         Hello today is <jdt:today />
      <p> <hr>
   </body>
</html>
```

Figure 21.5 A simple JSP using the `today` custom tag.

```
<%@ taglib uri="uri-name" prefix="prefix-name" %>
```

Where the `uri-name` maps to the name provided in the `web.xml` file to allow the JSP processor to find the tag library descriptor. The `prefix-name` will be used as the prefix used with all custom tags from this library to identify them uniquely as being from this library – in effect it represents a namespace.

The body of the JSP contains normal HTML markup and text with the exception of the `<jdt:today />` custom tag. Note that this could also have been written as `<jdt:today> </jdt:today>`. This will cause the class associated with the today tag in the `jdt` library to execute.

21.6.5 Run the Web Application

The effect of installing the JSP file, `web.xml` file, the `taglib.tld` file and the tag handler classes on the Tomcat 4.0.1 Web server are illustrated in Figure 21.6. This figure shows IE 6.0 being used to access the `today.jsp` file. Note that the custom JSP tag has been replaced with the current date and time.

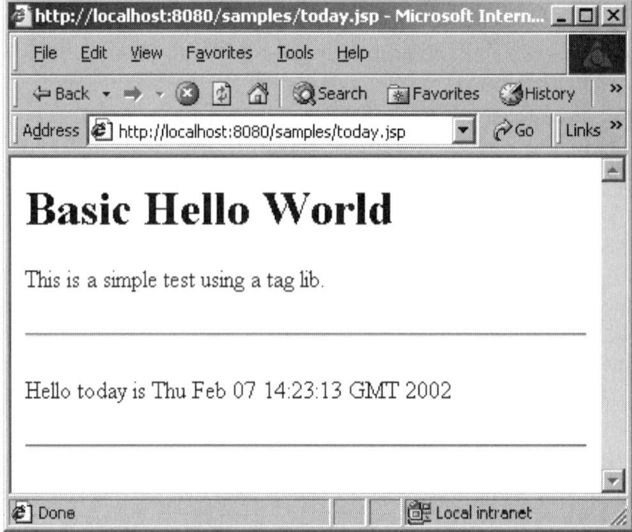

Figure 21.6 Accessing the `today.jsp` page.

21.7 Adding Attributes to a Tag

We will take the example presented in the previous section a bit further by adding an attribute to the custom JSP tag so that information used to customize the behaviour of the tag can be defined. For example, we will provide a postfix attribute that allows a different string to be added to the end of the date string. For example:

```
<jdt:date postfix="GMT" />
```

We have changed the tag to be `date` so that we do not replace the `today` tag. Thus we will have a library of two tags!

The first thing we have to do is to define the tag handler class. This class, this time called `DateTag`, is very similar to the original `TodayTag`; however, it now possesses an instance variable `postfix` and a setter method `setPostfix`. The `setPostfix` method is called during the initial configuration of the object before the `doStartTag()` method is called. The value set is whatever has been defined for the attribute `postfix` in the JSP custom tag. This is then used in the `doEndTag` to provide a postfix string to the formatted date. The `DateTag` class is illustrated in Figure 21.7. Once again this class is compiled as normal.

Next we need to update our `taglib.tld` file by adding a new tag (date) to it and specifying that this tag element will take a parameter. The parameter specification is handled by the `<attribute>` sub-element within the `<tag>` element. A custom tag can have zero or more

UltraEdit-32 - [C:\serverside\web\taglib\source\webshop\tags\DateTag.java]

File Edit Search View Format Column Macro Advanced Window Help

```
package webshop.tags;

import java.io.IOException;
import java.util.Date;
import java.text.DateFormat;
import javax.servlet.jsp.*;
import javax.servlet.jsp.tagext.*;

public class DateTag extends TagSupport {
   private String postfix;

   public int doStartTag() throws JspTagException {
      // Indicates that the tag should be skipped
      return SKIP_BODY;  // or EVAL_BODY_INCLUDE
   }

   public void setPostfix(String postfix) {
      this.postfix = postfix;
   }

   public int doEndTag() throws JspTagException {
      DateFormat df = DateFormat.getDateInstance(DateFormat.MEDIUM);
      String date = df.format(new Date());
      try {
         pageContext.getOut().write(" " + date + " " + postfix);
      } catch (IOException exp) {
         throw new JspTagException("Error processing DateTag");
      }
      // Indicates JSP processor should continue to process page
      return EVAL_PAGE;
   }
}
```

Figure 21.7 Handling an attribute postfix in the tag handler class.

attributes; thus there can be multiple <attribute> elements. Each <attribute> has the following syntax:

```
<attribute>
  <name>attribute-name</name>
  <required>true|false</required>
  <rtexprvalue>true|false</rtexprvalue>
</attribute>
```

where:

- attribute-name is the name that will be used in the custom JSP tag.
- required indicates whether the attribute will be optional or not. The default is false indicating that it is optional.
- rtexprvalue indicates whether runtime evaluation can be performed or not. That is, whether the attribute value can be the result of a JSP expression or whether it has to be a fixed value at translation time. For example, if rtexprvalue is true then you can write the following:

  ```
  <jdt:date postfix="<%= headings.getDatePostfix()%>">
  ```

  Note that the default value of rtexprvalue is false.

In Figure 21.8 the date tag has a single attribute called postfix. This attribute is not optional (require is true), but the value can be generated dynamically (rtexprvalue is true).

We do not need to make any changes to the web.xml file.

Finally we need to define a JSP page that will use the new date tag. An example hello.jsp file is presented in Figure 21.9. This page actually uses the new date tag twice. The first use has a postfix value of "GMT" while the second has a postfix value of "BST". Thus each date should have a different string after it.

The result of deploying this extended tag library and JSP on Tomcat is displayed in Figure 21.10. Here the first date is presented with a GMT extension and the second with a BST extension.

21.8 Including Body Content

So far neither of our tags has included any body content. That is, there is no content between the start tag and the end tag. However, we may wish some content to be added and for that content to be processed. There are actually two different approaches to processing the body content of a tag, depending upon whether the body needs to be evaluated once or multiple times.

- **Single evaluation.** If the body only needs to be processed once then we can use the approach we have used so far (extending TagSupport) for the tag handler class, but return

UltraEdit-32 - [C:\serverside\web\taglib\WEB-INF\taglib.tld]

```
<?xml version="1.0" encoding="ISO-8859-1" ?>
<!DOCTYPE taglib
        PUBLIC "-//Sun Microsystems, Inc.//DTD JSP Tag Library 1.2//EN"
    "http://java.sun.com/j2ee/dtd/web-jsptaglibrary_1_2.dtd">

<taglib>
  <tlib-version>1.0</tlib-version>  <!-- Tag library version -->
  <jsp-version>1.2</jsp-version>    <!-- JSP specification version -->
  <short-name></short-name>
 <tag>
    <name>today</name>
    <tag-class>webshop.tags.TodayTag</tag-class>
    <body-content>empty</body-content>
  </tag>
  <tag>
    <name>date</name>
    <tag-class>webshop.tags.DateTag</tag-class>
    <body-content>empty</body-content>
    <attribute>
      <name>postfix</name>
      <required>true</required>
      <rtexprvalue>true</rtexprvalue>
    </attribute>
  </tag>
</taglib>
```

Figure 21.8 Adding the tag `date` with an attribute postfix.

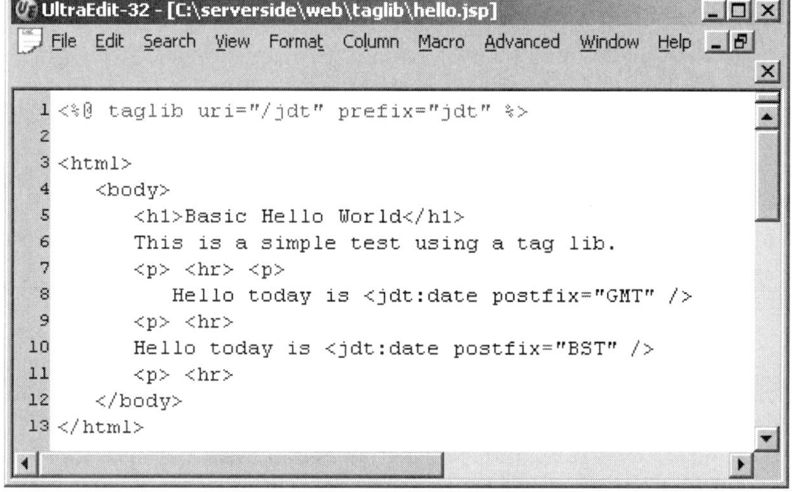
UltraEdit-32 - [C:\serverside\web\taglib\hello.jsp]

```
<%@ taglib uri="/jdt" prefix="jdt" %>

<html>
   <body>
      <h1>Basic Hello World</h1>
      This is a simple test using a tag lib.
      <p> <hr> <p>
         Hello today is <jdt:date postfix="GMT" />
      <p> <hr>
      Hello today is <jdt:date postfix="BST" />
      <p> <hr>
   </body>
</html>
```

Figure 21.9 Using the new `date` tag with an attribute.

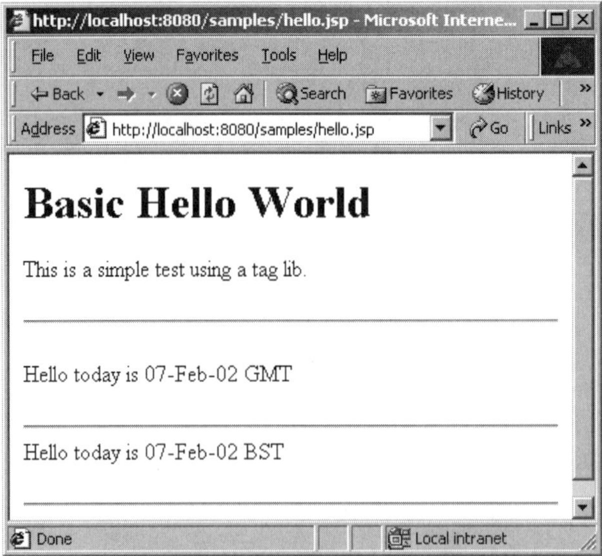

Figure 21.10 Accessing the `hello.jsp`.

`Tag.EVAL_BODY_INCLUDE` as the result of calling the `doStartTag()` method. If `SKIP_BODY` is returned then the body content is left as is and inserted into the JSP response.

- **Multiple evaluation**. If the body of the tag needs to be processed multiple times then the `BodyTag` interface must be implemented or the `BodyTagSupport` class extended. This makes available the `setBodyContent` method, the `doInitBody` method and the `doAfterBody` method. The `doInitBody` method is called just after the body is read, but before it is evaluated. The `doAfterBody` method is called after the body content has been evaluated.

For the moment we will examine a single evaluation example. We will then discuss a multiple evaluation example.

The example we will look at creates a tag that will convert any text into bold. The tag handler class is presented in Figure 21.11. Note that the only differences between this class and the previous handler classes are that the `doStartTag()` now actually generates some output and returns `EVAL_BODY_INCLUDE` and that the output added is some HTML markup.

The result of using this in a Web page is that the tag handler class mapped to the tag `<jdt:geo>` (i.e. `<jdt:geo>bold</jdt:geo>`) is presented in Figure 21.12.

This example is a very basic example of body content processing, in that we have not actually accessed the content in any way. Therefore the following example retrieves the string representing the body content and converts it to lower case. Note that we have made this class a subclass of `BodyTagSupport` purely so that we can get hold of the body content object.

The life cycle of the `BodyTag` implementing tag handler is different to that of the standard `Tag` in that the body handling methods are introduced. This is illustrated in Figure 21.13.

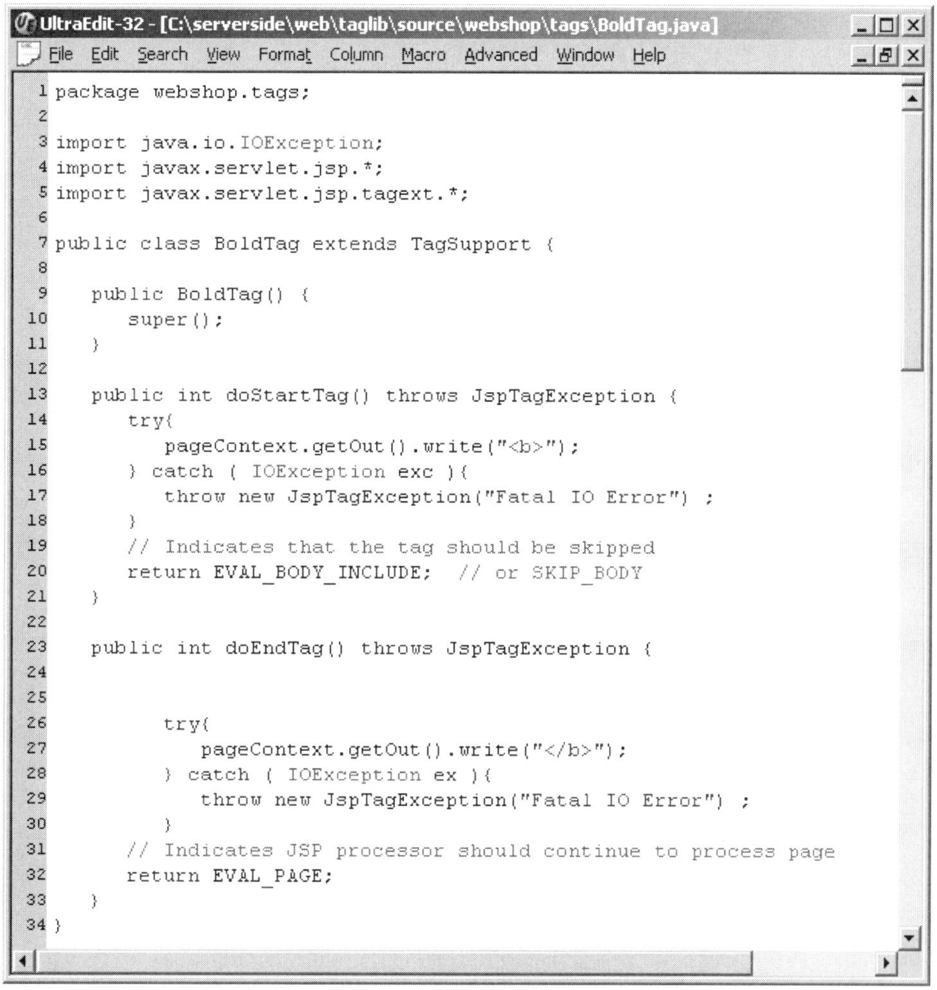

UltraEdit-32 - [C:\serverside\web\taglib\source\webshop\tags\BoldTag.java]

File Edit Search View Format Column Macro Advanced Window Help

```java
package webshop.tags;

import java.io.IOException;
import javax.servlet.jsp.*;
import javax.servlet.jsp.tagext.*;

public class BoldTag extends TagSupport {

   public BoldTag() {
      super();
   }

   public int doStartTag() throws JspTagException {
      try{
         pageContext.getOut().write("<b>");
      } catch ( IOException exc ){
         throw new JspTagException("Fatal IO Error") ;
      }
      // Indicates that the tag should be skipped
      return EVAL_BODY_INCLUDE;  // or SKIP_BODY
   }

   public int doEndTag() throws JspTagException {


         try{
            pageContext.getOut().write("</b>");
         } catch ( IOException ex ){
            throw new JspTagException("Fatal IO Error") ;
         }
      // Indicates JSP processor should continue to process page
      return EVAL_PAGE;
   }
}
```

Figure 21.11 Including body content.

The LowerCaseTag class is presented in Figure 21.14.

Note that the value returned from the doStartTag() method is now EVAL_BODY_BUFFERED. This means a BodyContent object is created to buffer the results of body evaluation. This is how the body content information is made available in the doAfterBody() method.

The BodyContent class also provides two other very useful methods:

- getEnclosingWriter: returns the JspWriter being used by the doStartTag and the doEndTag.
- getReader: returns a Reader object that can read the tag's body.

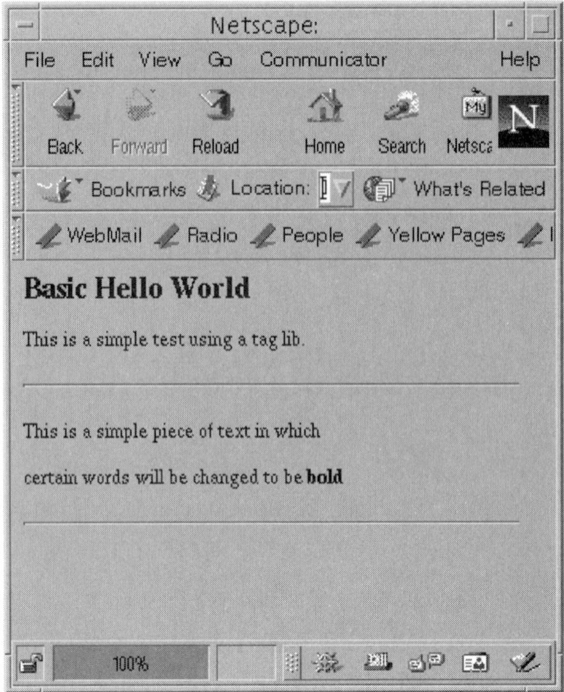

Figure 21.12 Processing the string "bold" as the body content of a custom tag.

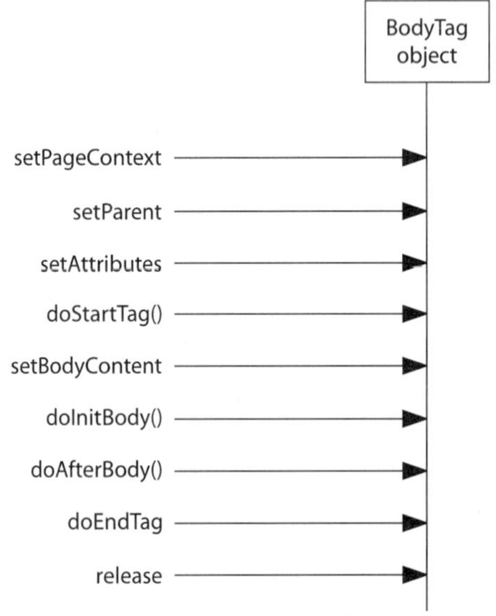

Figure 21.13 Life cycle of a `BodyTag` object.

UltraEdit-32 - [C:\serverside\web\taglib\source\webshop\tags\LowerCaseTag.java]

File Edit Search View Format Column Macro Advanced Window Help

```
package webshop.tags;

import java.io.IOException;
import javax.servlet.jsp.*;
import javax.servlet.jsp.tagext.*;

public class LowerCaseTag extends BodyTagSupport {
   public int doStartTag() throws JspTagException {
      return EVAL_BODY_BUFFERED;   // Default for BodyTagSupport
   }

   public int doAfterBody() throws JspException {
      try {
      // Get hold of the object that represents the body
      BodyContent bc = getBodyContent();
      // Get the content as a string
      String str = bc.getString();
      // get the output writer to use
      JspWriter out = bc.getEnclosingWriter();
      // Write out the string in lower case form
      out.print(str.toLowerCase());
      } catch (IOException exp) {
         throw new JspException("Error processing body");
      }
      return SKIP_BODY;
   }

   public int doEndTag() throws JspTagException {
      return EVAL_PAGE;
   }
}
```

Figure 21.14 Processing the content of the body within the tag handler class.

The `doAfterBody()` method in turn retrieves the body content, accesses the contents of the body as a string and converts it to a lower-case string before writing it out to the `JspWriter` that represents the JSPs response stream.

Note that the `doAfterBody()` method can return either the `SKIP_BODY` value (indicating that it has finished processing the body of the tag) or the `EVAL_BODY_AGAIN` value indicating that it wishes to process the body of the tag again. This causes the whole body processing behaviour to start again.

This class has been mapped to the tag name "`lower`" in the TLD file:

```
<tag>
  <name>lower</name>
  <tag-class>webshop.tags.LowerCaseTag</tag-class>
  <body-content>JSP</body-content>
</tag>
```

```
<%@ taglib uri="/jdt" prefix="jdt" %>

<html>
   <body>
      <h1>Lower Case test</h1>
      This is a simple test using a tag lib.
      <p> <hr> <p>
         <jdt:lower>Hello And Welcome to today</jdt:lower>
      <p> <hr>
   </body>
</html>
```

Figure 21.15 Using the `lower` custom JSP tag.

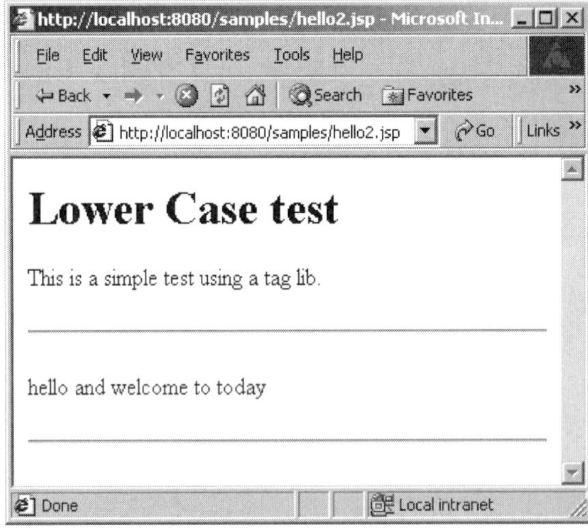

Figure 21.16 Accessing the `hello2.jsp` file.

It has then been used within a simple JSP to convert a string of words into lower case. This is presented in Figure 21.15.

The result of deploying this and accessing the JSP file is presented in Figure 21.16. Notice that the text "Hello And Welcome to today" is now all in lower case.

21.9 Guidelines for Developing Tag Libraries

The following are a relatively simple set of rules to keep in mind when developing JSP Tag Libraries:

1. Keep it simple. The more complex the tag the harder it will be to use and the less likely it is that it will be used. It will also be harder to implement and therefore more error-prone. Try to break it down into several simpler tags.
2. Make it usable. Find out what the tag needs for it to be used and tailor it around how it will be used.
3. Avoid implementing a programming language. Do not try to create a new JSP-based programming language using tags – this is not what they are for!
4. Reuse existing tag libraries. There are already several very good tag libraries available: see the Jakarta Web site (`http://jakarta.apache.org/`) for some examples and also ColdJava (`http://coldjava.hypermart.net/`).

21.10 Introducing Scripting Variables

Custom tags can introduce new scripting variables into JSP pages. In the JSP 1.2 specification there are two ways of introducing such variables. One of these approaches was introduced in JSP 1.1 and is now considered to be obsolete. We will therefore examine the newer JSP 1.2 approach, which is more intuitive and simpler to use.

There are two steps necessary to introduce scripting variables into a JSP page:

1. Add one or more `<variable>` sub-elements to the `<tag>` element in the Tag Library Descriptor.
2. Implement Java code that will add the variables to the `PageContext` object in the tag handler class.

The `variable` element is used in the `<tag>` element and has the following syntax:

```
<variable>
  <name-given>name</name-given>
  <variable-class> class </variable-class>
  <declare>true|false</declare>
  <scope>NESTED|AT_BEGIN|AT_END</scope>
</variable>
```

where:

- `name-given` defines the name of the scripting variable. An alternative form is to use `<name-from-attribute>`, which allows the name of the variable to be defined at translation time. For example, if the value for `name-from-attribute` was "`type`", then the JSP could specify that `type` would be called `car`. The scripting variable would then be named `car` in the current JSP.
- `variable-class` is the fully qualified name of the variables type, e.g. `java.lang.String`. The default for this value is `String`.
- `declare` is a boolean attribute that indicates whether a new variable should be created or whether an existing variable should be used. This attribute is optional and defaults to true.

- scope indicates the scope of the variable within the current JSP. The three values are NESTED, AT_END and AT_BEGIN. NESTED indicates that the variable is only available to this tag and any inner tags. AT_BEGIN indicates that the variable is available from the start of the tag onwards in the JSP page. AT_END indicates that the variable will only be available after this tag has been finished with but will exist for the rest of the JSP.

The tag handler class must make these variables available to the JSP page by adding them to the pageContext. This is done by calling the setAttribute method on the pageContext. For example:

```
pageContext.setAttribute("name", object);
```

Remember that pageContext is directly available if you are extending the TagSupport class (or one of its subclasses).

The new scripting variables are then available to use within scriptlets or expressions. For example, if we added to following to a <tag> element:

```
<variable>
  <name-give>date</name-given>
  <variable-class>java.util.Date</variable-class>
</variable>
```

In the associated tag handler class doStartTag() method we might add:

```
pageContext.setAttribute("date", new Date());
```

This would allow us to add the following into the JSP after the tag:

```
Today is <%= date %>
```

The result would be that the contents of the new scripting variable date would be appended to "Today is".

21.11 Nested Tags

Although you might expect that the Tag Library Descriptor and the JSP processor together could handle the specification and interaction of nested tags, you would be wrong. Rather, the tag handler classes must handle the interaction. That is, the handler classes for the nested tags must cooperate using methods such as getParent() and the static TagSupport.findAncestorWithClass() method. These methods allow an inner tag handler class to access the tag handler class of the parent tag. This is certainly a reasonable implementation choice, but there is nothing "declarative" about this interaction and it is merely represented by the runtime behaviour of the objects. Thus it places an additional burden on the designers and developers to ensure that the interactions are documented and well tested.

21.12 Tag Validation

In some cases it might be desirable to limit the combination of attributes and their values provided to a tag. For example, if attributes 1 and 2 can be combined or attribute 3 can be provided it is possible to define this. However, this is not done via the Tag Library Descriptor; nor is it done in the `web.xml` file. Instead, this is handled using either a `TagExtraInfo` class or a `TagLibraryValidator` object. The first approach was introduced in JSP 1.1 while the second was added in JSP 1.2

The `TagExtraInfo` class can be used by a JSP engine to validate the values for parameters provided by the JSP for a tag. This is done by the JSP engine invoking the `isValid(TagData data)` method at translation time. The `TagData` class will have been populated by the JSP engine with data about the attribute values given to the tag by the JSP. Both the names and values of the static attributes will be available, but only the names of attributes with runtime values will be available. Using this information a subclass of `TagExtraInfo` can implement an `isValid` method such that it can be used to determine whether the attribute values are both valid and consistent.

The `TagLibraryValidator` approach, introduced in JSP 1.2, is used to validate information for the whole tag library. It is specified in the Tag Library Descriptor using the `<validator>` sub-element of the top-level `<taglib>` element. The developer must implement a subclass of the `TagLibraryValidator` and in particular implement the method:

```
public String validate(String prefix, String uri, Page page)
```

This method is used to validate a tag's usage in the current tag library. If the tag use is acceptable null is returned. If the usage is incorrect then an error message string is returned instead. This method is called by the JSP engine at translation time every time a tag from the library is encountered in a JSP using the tag library.

21.13 Handling Tag Exceptions

If a tag handler class encounters a problem it may decide to throw an exception. This exception can be returned as the response of the JSP. Alternatively, the `javax.Servlet.jsp.tagext.TryCatchFinally` interface can be used to provide a custom exception handler for the tag handler class. This interface defines two method, `doCatch(Throwable)` and `doFinally()`, presented in Table 21.3.

The basic idea is that if an exception occurs the JSP engine will call the `doCatch` method or `doFinally` method on the tag handler class. The behaviour is as if the following was defined:

```
try{
  t = new TagHandlerClass...
  t.doStartTag();
  //....
  t.doEndTag();
```

```
} catch (Exception exp) {
  t.doCatch(exp);
} finally {
  t.doFinally();
}
```

Table 21.3 The methods in the `TryCatchFinally` interface.

void	**doCatch**(java.lang.Throwable t) Invoked if a `Throwable` occurs while evaluating the BODY inside a tag or in any of the following methods: `Tag.doStartTag()`, `Tag.doEndTag()`, `IterationTag.doAfterBody()` and `BodyTag.doInitBody()`
void	**doFinally**() Invoked in all cases after `doEndTag()` for any class implementing `Tag`, `IterationTag` or `BodyTag`

Thus if an exception occurs the `doCatch` method will be called on the tag handler class, allowing it to examine the exception and determine what to do. The `doFinally` method is called whether an exception occurs or not.

An interesting question is whether you should ever use this approach, as it is always possible to handle exceptions yourself within a `try...catch` block. The answer to this is that it depends. The API provides this feature and it will enable JSPExceptions passed out of the tag class methods to be handled in a consistent manner. However, in general it is better to try to handle the exceptions directly, as it is both more immediate and more obvious.

21.14 JSTL

The JavaServer Pages Standard Tag Library is a recent addition to the J2EE introduced in Java 2 Enterprise Edition (SDK 1.4), released in 2003.

The JavaServer Pages Standard Tag Library (JSTL) encapsulates core functionality common to many JSP applications. For example, instead of iterating over lists using a scriptlet (which is neither neat to look at nor particularly reusable) or different iteration tags from numerous vendors, JSTL defines a standard tag that works the same everywhere. This standardization lets you learn a single tag and use it on multiple JSP containers. In addition, these standardized tags may be optimized by Web application containers to improve performance.

JSTL has support for common structural tasks such as iteration and conditionals, tags for manipulating XML documents, internationalization tags, and tags for accessing databases using SQL. It also introduces the concept of an expression language to simplify page development. JSTL also provides a framework for integrating existing tag libraries with JSTL. For those of you who may have heard about or indeed used the Apache Struts library, JSTL can be used to replace the Struts logic tags.

JSTL has over 30 keywords, including facilities for accessing databases using its own query language (Table 21.4).

For example, to use the JSTL core tags in a JSP page, you declare the library using a `taglib` directive that references the TLD:

```
<%@ taglib uri="/jstl-core" prefix="c" %>
```

Table 21.4 JSTL keywords.

Area	*Function*	*Tags*	*TLD*	*Prefix*

Core	Expression Language Support	`catch`
		`out`
		`remove`
		`set`
			`/jstl-c`	`c`

	Flow Control	`choose`
		`  when`
		`  otherwise`
		`forEach`
		`forTokens`
		`if`		

	URL Management	`import`
		`  paramredirect`
		`  param`
		`url`
		`  param`		

XML	Core	`out`
		`parse`
		`set`
			`/jstl-x`	`x`

	Flow Control	`choose`
		`  when`
		`  otherwise`
		`forEach`
		`if`		

	Transformation	`transform` `  param`		
Internationalization	Locale	`setLocale`	`/jstl-fmt`	`fmt`

	Message formatting	`bundle`
		`message`
		`  param`
		`setBundle`		

	Number and date formatting	`formatNumber`
		`formatDate`
		`parseDate`
		`parseNumber`
		`setTimeZone`
		`timeZone`		

Database	SQL	`setDataSource`
		`query`
		`  dateParam`
		`  param`
		`transaction`
		`update`
		`dateParam`
		`  param`
			`/jstl-sql`	`sql`

The JSTL tag libraries comes in two versions. The TLDs for the JSTL-EL library are named *prefix*.tld. The TLDs for the JSTL-RT library are named *prefix*-rt.tld. The two versions differ only in the way they support the use of runtime expressions for attribute values. In the JSTL-RT tag library, expressions are specified in the page's scripting language. This is exactly how things currently work in current tag libraries. In the JSTL-EL tag library, expressions are specified in the JSTL expression language. An expression is a string literal in the syntax of the EL.

A primary feature of JSTL is its support for an expression language (EL). An expression language, in concert with JSTL tags, makes it possible to access application data easily and manipulate it in simple ways without having to use scriptlets or request-time expressions. Currently, a page author has to use an expression <%= aName %> to access the value of a system or user-defined JavaBeans component. For example:

```
<x:aTag att="<%= pageContext.getAttribute("aName") %>">
```

Referring to nested bean properties is even more complex:

```
<%= aName.getFoo().getBar() %>
```

This makes page authoring more complicated than it need be.

An expression language allows a page author to access an object using a simplified syntax such as

```
<x:atag att="${aName}">
```

for a simple variable or

```
<x:aTag att="${aName.foo.bar}">
```

for a nested property.

The JSTL expression language promotes JSP *scoped attributes* as the standard way to communicate information from business logic to JSP pages. For example, the test attribute of the this conditional tag is supplied with an expression that compares the number of items in the session-scoped attribute named cart with 0:

```
<c:if test="${sessionScope.cart.numberOfItems > 0}">
...
</c:if>
```

21.15 Summary

Tag libraries are one of the most powerful features of the JSP specification and are potentially of great benefit. In many ways they can revolutionize the development of JSP-based applications, providing easy to use, reusable and HTML tags that can make the construction of consistent Web-based interface simple and reliable. In this they are probably the most successful exponents yet of the separation of content from presentation ideas, which is generally accepted as good practice, to come out of the servlet/JSP specifications. Indeed, there are already a growing number of third-party tag libraries that provide for just this.

21.16 Online References

`http://www.servletsuite.com/jsp.htm`: The Coldtags suite provides 120+ custom JSP tags for common programming tasks faced by JSP developers. The suite now includes custom tags similar to Web controls in .NET.

`http://www.kobrix.com/`: a useful set of GUI components for WEB development in JSP.

Chapter 22

Request Dispatching

22.1 Introduction

In many situations it is useful to have one servlet delegate responsibility for servicing part or all of a request to another servlet (or indeed JSP). For example, you might choose to have a `FrontController` Servlet that receives all requests and then delegates those requests to other servlets as required. This can be a very good approach to use for security, auditing and logging reasons. As an example of the use of a `FrontController` see the online bookstore example presented later in this book.

In this chapter we will look very briefly at Servlet Chaining before examining in detail the more recent Request Dispatching process. Request Dispatching can be used to forward a request to another servlet (or JSP) or to include the output of another servlet (or JSP) into the current servlet. We will examine examples of each in detail.

22.2 Servlet Chaining

Servlet Chaining predates Request Dispatching (which has effectively replaced it) as a way of enabling servlets to collaborate (or communicate at least). It was at the time quite widely used and was supported by a number of servlet engines (including those from Sun). However, with the move to the J2EE model and the use of Web containers, Servlet Chaining was abandoned.

The basic idea behind servlet chaining is illustrated in Figure 22.1. Essentially, each servlet to be chained is designed and implemented independently. They are linked together via a servlet engine-specific alias that specifies the order in which the servlets will be called (note that this is outside the scope of the servlet specification and is left to the servlet engine provider to define). This is a little bit like piping the output of one program into the input of another on a Unix platform. The format was usually `<alias-name.=<comma separated list of Servlets>>`; for example "`eshop=FirstServlet,SecondServlet,ThirdServlet`".

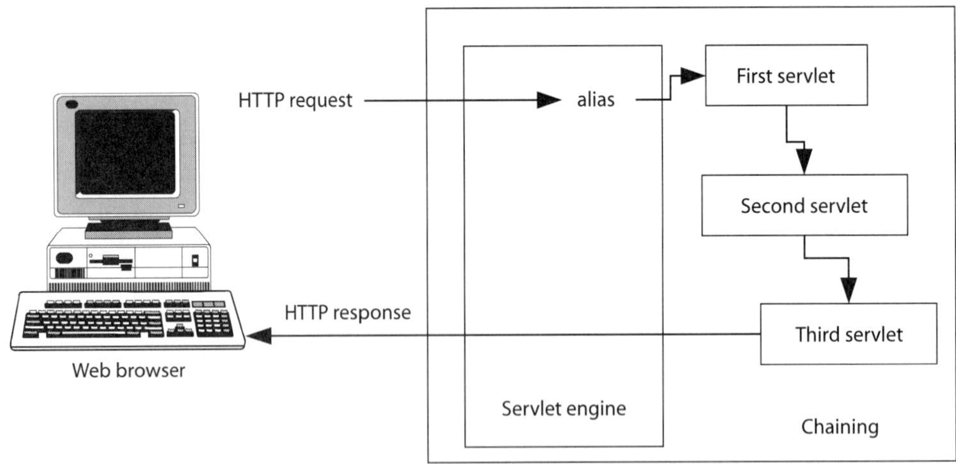

Figure 22.1 Basic Servlet Chaining concept.

When the servlet engine now receives a request for the URL that maps to the alias, it calls the servlets in the order specified in this alias.

Note that the order in which the servlets are called is predetermined when the servlet engine is configured and cannot be dynamically changed. Thus it is not possible to determine, given the current data, which servlet should receive the request next. This is one of the reasons why Request Dispatching was developed in preference to it. Request Dispatching is described in detail below.

22.3 Request Dispatching

The concept behind Request Dispatching is that one servlet can dispatch an HTTP request to another servlet (or JSP) at runtime. In fact, using Request Dispatching it is possible for a servlet to dispatch a request to any other Web resource (including servlets, JSPs, HTML pages or any other resource). There are two ways in which this can be done, either via a `forward` mechanism (in which case the resource takes full responsibility for generating the resulting response) or `include` (in which case the output of the resource is merged with the output of the current servlet). Note that if the resource being referenced is a static resource such as an HTML page, then the content of the HTML page is immediately returned. Whether it is returned to the initiating servlet (i.e. via `include`) or returned to the Web client (via `forward`) depends on the method used with the request dispatcher.

Essentially, Request Dispatching is plugging into the Web container's own dispatching mechanism. When an initial request is made by a Web client to a Web container for a servlet or JSP, the Web container identifies which resource is required and dispatches the request to that resource. In the case of servlets, for example, it creates request and response objects and calls the appropriate methods. When a servlet uses request dispatching to forward a request, exactly the same thing happens; the only difference is that instead of an external

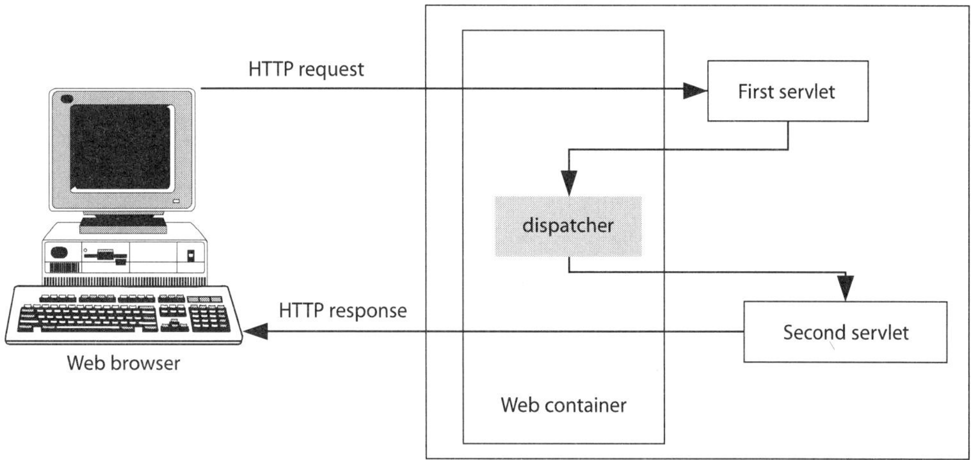

Figure 22.2 Forwarding via Request Dispatching.

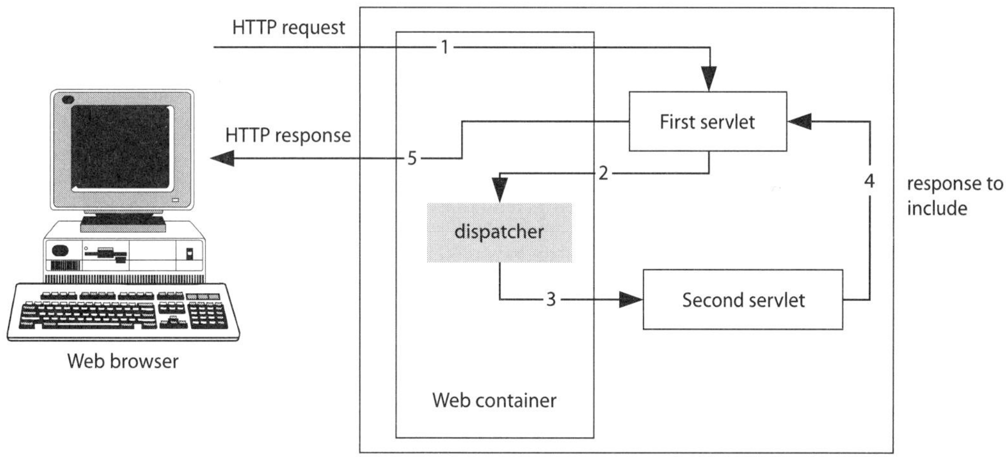

Figure 22.3 Using Request Dispatching to include a servlet.

client initiating the dispatch a servlet has done it. Things are slightly different for `includes`, as the original request and response objects can be used "as is" with the new resource.

The basic idea behind request dispatching is illustrated in Figure 22.2. In this diagram one servlet obtains a reference to a request dispatcher (represented in the diagram as the grey box inside the Web container) and uses this reference to forward the HTTP request to a second servlet. Note that this must be a forwarding example, as it is the second servlet that sends the response back to the Web browser.

We can see the difference between forwarding and including if we examine a similar diagram where the output of a second servlet is included in the output of the first servlet. This is presented in Figure 22.3.

Table 22.1 The methods in the `RequestDispatcher` interface.

void	**forward**(ServletRequest request, ServletResponse response) Forwards a request from a servlet to another resource (servlet, JSP file, or HTML file) on the server
void	**include**(ServletRequest request, ServletResponse response) Includes the content of a resource (servlet, JSP page, HTML file) in the response

22.3.1 The `RequestDispatcher` Interface

The Request Dispatching mechanism in the Servlet 2.3 API is implemented by the Web container. The Web container must therefore provide an implementation of the `javax.servlet.RequestDispatcher` interface. This interface has only two methods, listed in Table 22.1, and allow the programmer to either forward or include the output from another servlet.

Note that both the methods in this interface can throw the `ServletException` and the `IOException`.

22.4 Obtaining a `RequestDispatcher`

Whenever you use Request Dispatching you will need to perform two steps:

1. Obtain a reference to a request dispatcher for the resource you require.
2. Forward (or include) the request to the servlet.

The first of these can be done in one of three ways. You can obtain a request dispatcher from the `HttpServletRequest` object (passed into the `doGet`, `doPost` methods etc.) or you can obtain a reference to the `ServletContext` and obtain a request dispatcher that way. The third approach is to use the `getNamedDispatcher` method on the `ServletContext` interface.

We will first look at obtaining a reference to the `RequestDispatcher` using the `getRequestDispatcher` method of the `ServletContext`.

The first thing you will have to do with this approach is to obtain a reference to the `ServletContext`. This can be done using the `getServletContext()` method inherited from `HttpServlet` (and actually defined in `GenericServlet`). Once you have obtained a reference to the `ServletConext` you can obtain a `RequestDispatcher` from this using the `getRequestDispatcher(String path)` method. For example:

```
ServletContext context = this.getServletContext();
RequestDispatcher rd = context.getRequestDispatcher("/books/search");
```

However, notice that the path given the to `getRequestDispatcher` method must be an absolute path. An absolute path is a path that must start with a "/" and defines the URL required to find the servlet (or other Web resource) relative to the whole Web application. Thus if your Web application is called `eshop`, to access this servlet using a Web browser you would write:

```
http://localhost:8080/eshop/books/search
```

The absolute path is therefore the whole of the path following the Web application name.

The second approach to obtaining the `RequestDispatcher` is to use the `Http-ServletRequest` object passed into the `do*` methods. Note that this object inherits the `getRequestDispatcher` method from the `ServletRequest` class. This version of the `getDispatcherRequester` method can take either an absolute or a relative path. This is because the request object has associated with it a URL path. The Web container can use this URL path to resolve relative paths into absolute paths. Thus using the request object we can write:

```
RequestDispatcher rd = request.getRequestDispatcher("/books/search");
```

or (assuming that the current servlet has a URL that puts it in the `books` arena):

```
RequestDispatcher rd = context.getRequestDispatcher("search");
```

The final approach to obtaining a `RequestDispatcher` is to use the `getNamedDispatcher` on the `ServletContext` object. This method takes the name of a servlet (rather than a URL-type path). The name of a servlet is the name associated with it in the deployment descriptor (`web.xml` file). For example, in Figure 22.4 the name of the servlet is defined in the `<servlet-name>` element and is `addressbook`.

Therefore we could write:

```
ServletContext context = this.getServletContext();
RequestDispatcher rd = context.getNamedDispatcher("addressbook");
```

A final word about the servlet or other resource to which the request is being dispatched. You may have noticed that the `RequestDispatcher` interface is defined in the `javax.servlet` package. However, if you are dispatching `HttpServletRequest` and `HttpServletResponse`

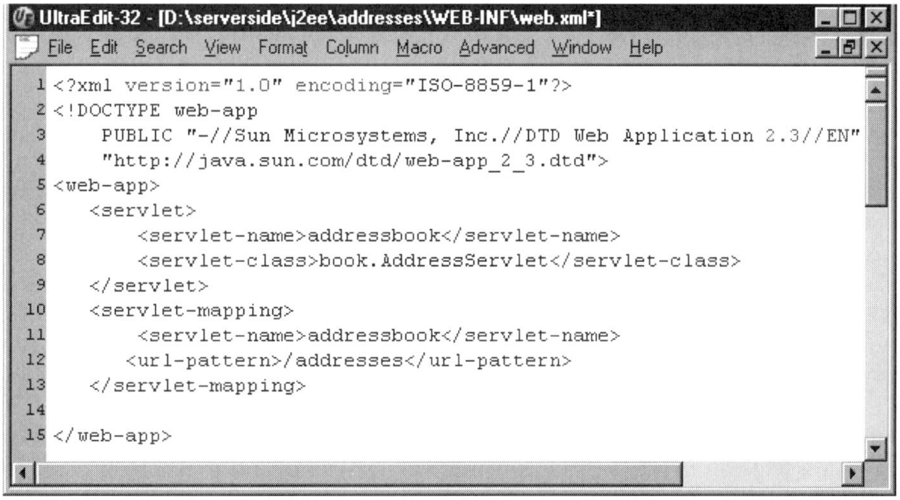

UltraEdit-32 - [D:\serverside\j2ee\addresses\WEB-INF\web.xml*]

File Edit Search View Format Column Macro Advanced Window Help

```
<?xml version="1.0" encoding="ISO-8859-1"?>
<!DOCTYPE web-app
    PUBLIC "-//Sun Microsystems, Inc.//DTD Web Application 2.3//EN"
    "http://java.sun.com/dtd/web-app_2_3.dtd">
<web-app>
   <servlet>
       <servlet-name>addressbook</servlet-name>
       <servlet-class>book.AddressServlet</servlet-class>
   </servlet>
   <servlet-mapping>
       <servlet-name>addressbook</servlet-name>
      <url-pattern>/addresses</url-pattern>
   </servlet-mapping>

</web-app>
```

Figure 22.4 A deployment descriptor illustrating a servlet name.

objects then the receiving resource must understand these (that is you cannot mix Servlets and HttpServlets – they must be of compatible types). The exceptions to this are static resources such as HTML pages etc.

22.4.1 Forwarding Requests

To forward a request to another Web resource using a request dispatcher you use the forward method, passing in the request and response object passed to the do* method being used. For example:

```
RequestDispatcher rd = request.getRequestDispatcher("/books/search");
rd.forward(request, response);
```

This will forward the HTTP request to the Web resource defined by the absolute path /books/search.

However, there are a number of points to note about the forwarding of requests, including:

- The calling servlet can write information to the request header to pass on to the called servlet.
- The calling servlet can only be forwarded if it has not committed any output to the client; otherwise IllegalStateException is thrown. It is possible to get around this by calling the reset() method on the PrintWriter used to generate the response output.
- The called servlet receives its own output stream.
- The called servlet has read/write access to the request header information.
- The calling servlet must not perform further writes on its output stream. Usually, the calling servlet will either terminate naturally or call return.
- The output of the called servlet is flushed (by the Web container) before it returns.

A final point to note is that a servlet can only forward to a static resource, such as an HTML page, in response to a GET request. This is because an HTML page can only be invoked using a GET request (and request dispatching maintains the style of request when forwarding or indeed including).

22.4.2 An Example of Forwarding

In this example we will examine a simple servlet that acts as a front controller to the webshop application. This FrontController servlet either returns a Web page containing a form that allows a user to specify which option they wish to perform or forwards the request to another resource. The resources used in this example are a JSP page, another servlet referenced by the URL backroom and an HTML page called welcome.html. The FrontController servlet is presented in Figure 22.5.

Note that in the FrontController servlet, if no option has been entered by the user the servlet generates the form, allowing an option to be provided. This is done in the createShopControllerPage method.

Obviously for this servlet to operate correctly there needs to be a JSP, a second servlet and an HTML page, all in the Web application. The JSP example is presented in Figure 22.6 for reference. As JSPs were discussed in detail earlier in this book we will leave a discussion of the content of this page as an exercise for the reader.

UltraEdit-32 - [D:\serverside\j2ee\forwarding\source\webshop\ShopController.java]

File Edit Search View Format Column Macro Advanced Window Help

```
package webshop;

import java.io.*;
import javax.servlet.*;
import javax.servlet.http.*;

public class ShopController extends HttpServlet {

   public void doGet(HttpServletRequest req,
                     HttpServletResponse res)
                        throws ServletException, IOException  {
      System.out.println("ShopController.doGet()");
      res.setContentType("text/html");
      PrintWriter out = res.getWriter();
      HttpSession session = req.getSession(true);
      String option = req.getParameter("option");
      if (option == null) {
         createShopControllerPage(out);
      } else {
         if (option.equals("1")) {
            RequestDispatcher rd = req.getRequestDispatcher("/toys.jsp");
            rd.forward(req, res);
         } else if (option.equals("2")) {
            RequestDispatcher rd = req.getRequestDispatcher("/backroom");
            rd.forward(req, res);
         } else if (option.equals("3")) {
            RequestDispatcher rd = req.getRequestDispatcher("/welcome.html");
            rd.forward(req, res);
         }
      }
   }
   private void createShopControllerPage(PrintWriter out) {
      out.println("<html><head><title>Shop Front</title></head>");
      out.println("<body><h1>Shop Front</h1>");
      out.println("You can select any of the follwing<br>");
      out.println("<ul>");
      out.println("<li>1 - for a JSP page</li>");
      out.println("<li>2 - for a Servlet page</li>");
      out.println("<li>3 - for a HTML page</li>");
      out.println("</ul><p>");
      out.println("<form action='open' method='GET'>");
      out.println("<input type=text name=option size=5><br>");
      out.println("<input type=submit value='Submit'>");
      out.println("</form></body></html>");
   }
}
```

Figure 22.5 The forwarding servlet.

The second servlet that will be accessed by the URL backroom is presented in Figure 22.7. This is a very simple servlet that presents a message and a link to take the user back to the `FrontController` servlet.

UltraEdit-32 - [C:\serverside\j2ee\web\forwarding\toys.jsp]

File Edit Search View Format Column Macro Advanced Window Help

```
<%@ page import="java.util.Date" %>
<html>
<head><title>Toys</title></head>
<body>
<h1>JSP Toy Department</h1>
Welcome to the JSP toy department of the shop
on <%= new Date() %>
<p> <hr> <p>
To return to the main Shop Front Servlet select
the following link:
<p>
<a href="http://localhost:8080/webshop/open">
http://localhost:8080/webshop/open</a>
<p> <hr>
</body>
</html>
```

Figure 22.6 A very simple JSP.

UltraEdit-32 - [C:\serverside\j2ee\web\forwarding\source\webshop\BackRoomServlet.ja...

File Edit Search View Format Column Macro Advanced Window Help

```
package webshop;

import java.io.*;
import javax.servlet.*;
import javax.servlet.http.*;

public class BackRoomServlet extends HttpServlet {

  public void doGet(HttpServletRequest req,
                    HttpServletResponse res)
                         throws ServletException, IOException  {
    System.out.println("BackRoomServlet.doGet()");
    res.setContentType("text/html");
    PrintWriter out = res.getWriter();
    out.println("<html><head>");
    out.println("<title>Shop Back Room Servlet</title></head>");
    out.println("<body><h1>Shop Back</h1>");
    out.println("<p>You are now in the shop's back room servlet");
    out.println(" - welcome.<p>");
    out.println("To return to the main shop front servlet select ");
    out.println("the following link:<p>");
    out.println("<a href='http://localhost:8080/webshop/open'>");
    out.println("http://localhost:8080/webshop/open</a>");
    out.println("</body></html>");
 }
}
```

Figure 22.7 The called servlet.

UltraEdit-32 - [D:\serverside\j2ee\forwarding\welcome.html]

File Edit Search View Format Column Macro Advanced Window Help

```
<html>
   <head>
      <title>Shop HTML Welcome
      </title>
   </head>
   <body>
      <h1>A Warm HTML Welcome to you</h1>
      <p><hr><p>
      Welcome to the HTML page of the shop <p>
      To return to the main servlet select the following link:
      <a href="http://localhost:8080/webshop/open">
      http://localhost:8080/webshop/open</a>
      <p>
      <hr>
   </body>
</html>
```

Figure 22.8 The welcome.html Web page.

The welcome.html Web page is also very simple and is presented in Figure 22.8. Notice that there is nothing special about this HTML page – it is exactly the same as any other Web page. The only difference is that it can be requested to process a HTTP request from a RequestDispatcher object.

Once all the pieces of the Web application are obtained and the two servlets have been compiled the application can be deployed on Tomcat. Note that the structure of the Web application on Tomcat is illustrated in Figure 22.9.

Of course, we must also define our deployment descriptor in the web.xml file. The deployment descriptor for this example is presented in Figure 22.10.

Once we have deployed the webshop Web application we can start Tomcat and a Web browser. The browser should point at <hostname>:8080/webshop/open. This will cause the ShopController to display the input form (as no option will have been specified). This is illustrated in Figure 22.11. Using this form we can select options 1, 2 or 3 to causes the subsequent HTTP request to be forwarded to a JSP, servlet or Web page.

Figure 22.12 illustrates the output generated when we input option 1 in the form generated by the ShopController. This output is generated from the toys.jsp JSP page. Note the URL displayed in the Address field. It indicates that the option selected was 1, but the rest of the URL was the same as that entered in Figure 22.11. This is of course correct, as all the inputs are going to the ShopController, which is then delegating the responsibility for processing the request to another resource.

Figure 22.13 illustrates the output generated when the user enters option 2. This output is generated by the BackRoomServlet.

Figure 22.14 illustrates the Web page generated when the user enters option 3. This output is generated directly from the welcome.html page.

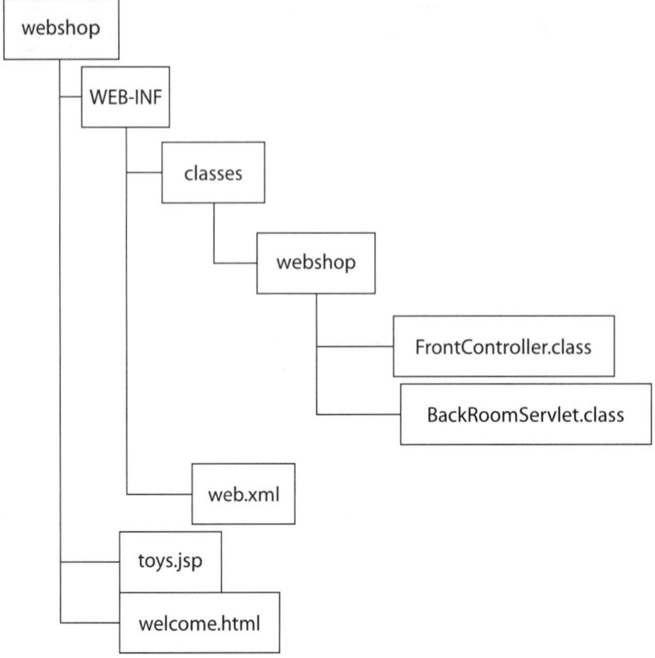

Figure 22.9 The structure of the Web application.

22.4.3 Including Via Request Dispatching

The previous section illustrated the use of the `forward` method available on the `RequestDispatcher` interface. However, rather than forwarding, this section will look at including; that is, including the output of one Web resource in the response being generated by a servlet.

To do this we will look at a servlet that generates a response as a composite of output from itself, a JSP and another servlet. The coordinating servlet is the `CompositeServlet` presented in Figure 22.15. Notice that this servlet does not try to define the scope of the Web page (the HTML body etc.). That is left to the HTML generated by the included resources. The first thing that this servlet does is to include the output of the `header.jsp` file. It then generates some HTML output itself. Finally, it uses the output of the footer servlet to finish the page off.

The very simple `header.jsp` is illustrated in Figure 22.16. This example could just as well have been an HTML page, but for interest's sake we have made it a JSP instead. Note that this JSP generates the header and the start of the body for the page.

The footer servlet (`FooterServlet`) is presented in Figure 22.17. This servlet adds some HTML to the current response and then terminates the Web page by closing the body and the HTML page element.

The deployment descriptor for this Web application is presented in Figure 22.18.

```
<?xml version="1.0" encoding="ISO-8859-1"?>
<!DOCTYPE web-app
    PUBLIC "-//Sun Microsystems, Inc.//DTD Web Application 2.3//EN"
    "http://java.sun.com/dtd/web-app_2_3.dtd">
<web-app>
   <servlet>
      <servlet-name>controller</servlet-name>
      <servlet-class>webshop.ShopController</servlet-class>
   </servlet>
   <servlet>
      <servlet-name>backroom</servlet-name>
      <servlet-class>webshop.BackRoomServlet</servlet-class>
   </servlet>
   <servlet>
      <servlet-name>Toys</servlet-name>
      <jsp-file>/toys.jsp</jsp-file>
   </servlet>
   <servlet-mapping>
      <servlet-name>controller</servlet-name>
      <url-pattern>/open</url-pattern>
   </servlet-mapping>
   <servlet-mapping>
      <servlet-name>backroom</servlet-name>
      <url-pattern>/backroom</url-pattern>
   </servlet-mapping>
   <servlet-mapping>
      <servlet-name>Toys</servlet-name>
      <url-pattern>/toys.jsp</url-pattern>
   </servlet-mapping>
</web-app>
```

Figure 22.10 The deployment descriptor for the forwarding example.

Figure 22.11 The output from the `ShopController`.

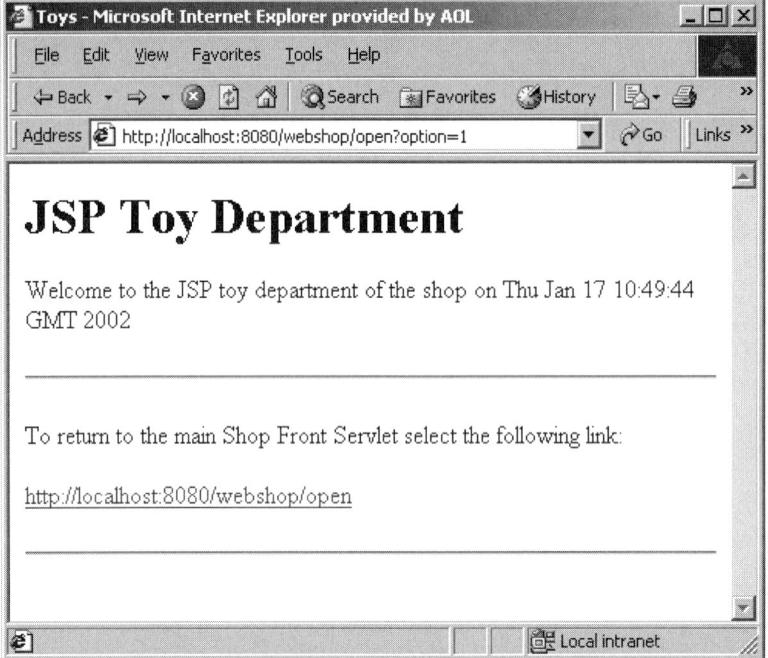

Toys - Microsoft Internet Explorer provided by AOL
File Edit View Favorites Tools Help
Back Search Favorites History
Address http://localhost:8080/webshop/open?option=1
Go Links
JSP Toy Department
Welcome to the JSP toy department of the shop on Thu Jan 17 10:49:44 GMT 2002
To return to the main Shop Front Servlet select the following link:
http://localhost:8080/webshop/open
Local intranet

Figure 22.12 The output from the JSP that receives the forwarded request.

Figure 22.13 The output from the `BackRoomServlet` that receives a forwarded request.

Figure 22.14 The `welcome.html` Web page once the `ShopController` has forwarded the request.

UltraEdit-32 - [C:\serverside\j2ee\web\including\source\webshop\CompositeServlet.jav...
File Edit Search View Format Column Macro Advanced Window Help

```
package webshop;

import java.io.*;
import javax.servlet.*;
import javax.servlet.http.*;

public class CompositeServlet extends HttpServlet {
   public void doGet(HttpServletRequest req,
                      HttpServletResponse res)
                         throws ServletException, IOException  {
      System.out.println("CompositeServlet.doGet()");
      res.setContentType("text/html");
      PrintWriter out = res.getWriter();

      // First get the header JSP
      RequestDispatcher rd1 =
                      req.getRequestDispatcher("/header.jsp");
      rd1.include(req, res);

      // Now add the content for this servlet
      out.println("This is the main body of the composite servlet.");

      // Now get the footer servlet
      RequestDispatcher rd2 = req.getRequestDispatcher("/footer");
      rd2.include(req, res);
   }
}
```

Figure 22.15 The coordinating `CompositeServlet`.

UltraEdit-32 - [C:\serverside\j2ee\web\including\header.jsp]

```
<html>
<head><title>Compositers</title></head>
<body>
<h1>Composites Department</h1>
Welcome to the Compositers toy department of the shop.
<p>
This standard header is generated by a JSP
<p> <hr> <p>
```

Figure 22.16 The very simple `header.jsp`.

UltraEdit-32 - [C:\serverside\j2ee\web\including\source\webshop\FooterServlet....

```
package webshop;

import java.io.*;
import javax.servlet.*;
import javax.servlet.http.*;

public class FooterServlet extends HttpServlet {

   public void doGet(HttpServletRequest req,
                      HttpServletResponse res)
                       throws ServletException, IOException  {
     System.out.println("Footer Servlet.doGet()");
     res.setContentType("text/html");
     PrintWriter out = res.getWriter();

     out.println("<p><hr><p>");
     out.println("Generated by the Footer Servlet");
     out.println("<p><hr><p>");
     out.println("</body></html>");
   }
}
```

Figure 22.17 The very simple `FooterServlet`.

The end result of this Web application, once deployed on Tomcat, is illustrated in Figure 22.19. The output of the three elements is clearly presented as each area is demarcated by a horizontal line.

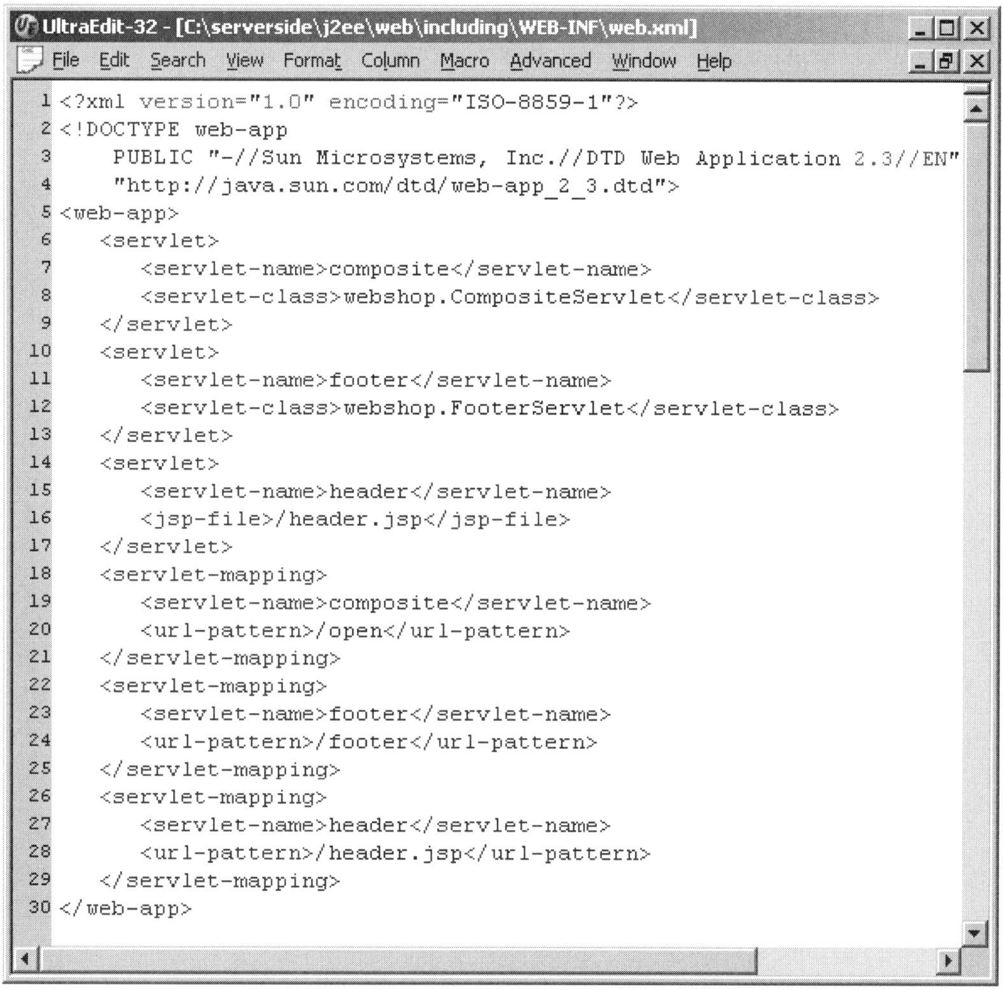

UltraEdit-32 - [C:\serverside\j2ee\web\including\WEB-INF\web.xml]

File Edit Search View Format Column Macro Advanced Window Help

```
<?xml version="1.0" encoding="ISO-8859-1"?>
<!DOCTYPE web-app
    PUBLIC "-//Sun Microsystems, Inc.//DTD Web Application 2.3//EN"
    "http://java.sun.com/dtd/web-app_2_3.dtd">
<web-app>
   <servlet>
      <servlet-name>composite</servlet-name>
      <servlet-class>webshop.CompositeServlet</servlet-class>
   </servlet>
   <servlet>
      <servlet-name>footer</servlet-name>
      <servlet-class>webshop.FooterServlet</servlet-class>
   </servlet>
   <servlet>
      <servlet-name>header</servlet-name>
      <jsp-file>/header.jsp</jsp-file>
   </servlet>
   <servlet-mapping>
      <servlet-name>composite</servlet-name>
      <url-pattern>/open</url-pattern>
   </servlet-mapping>
   <servlet-mapping>
      <servlet-name>footer</servlet-name>
      <url-pattern>/footer</url-pattern>
   </servlet-mapping>
   <servlet-mapping>
      <servlet-name>header</servlet-name>
      <url-pattern>/header.jsp</url-pattern>
   </servlet-mapping>
</web-app>
```

Figure 22.18 The deployment descriptor for the forwarding example.

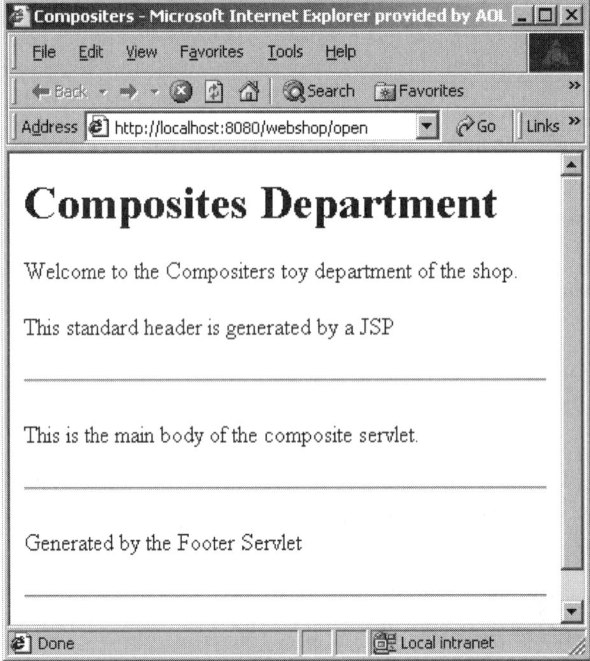

Figure 22.19 The combined output of the `CompositeServlet`.

Chapter 23

Filtering

23.1 Introduction

In this chapter we will examine in detail a new feature introduced in the Servlet Specification 2.3 called Filters. A filter is a class that wraps itself around a servlet or JSP and intercepts the call to the filter. It can then perform various pre- and post-processing tasks. It can also modify the information being passed into the servlet (or JSP) or out. We will also look at what types of operation might be performed within filters and when you might use them. We will also examine a number of example filters to see how they work.

However, it is worth noting at this point that filters are *not* servlets, and they work at a different level to servlets. Servlets, and indeed JSPs, are objects that are managed by the Web container. As a Web application developer we do not even see the HTTP request handling mechanism that leads to the execution of a servlet or JSP – indeed there is no way to obtain this or to become involved in the interactions that take place (at least not from the servlet or JSP perspective). To some extent this is where filters come in.

Filters allow the developer to provide both pre- and post-processing around a servlet or JSP, but they also allow a developer to manage the request and/or response objects such that the request information and/or the response information are processed outside of the servlet (and without the servlet's knowledge).

Note that filters are configured in the deployment descriptor (the `web.xml` file) in a declarative manner (rather than programmatically in, for example, a servlet). Also note that the servlet or JSP that is being filtered has no knowledge of this fact; nor does it ever see that it is being filtered. Thus filters, to some extent at least, sit outside the servlet and JSP world.

23.2 Filters – the Very Concept!

So what exactly are filters? Filters act as pre- and post-processors around a servlet or JSP. The general idea is that within a filter the developer can:

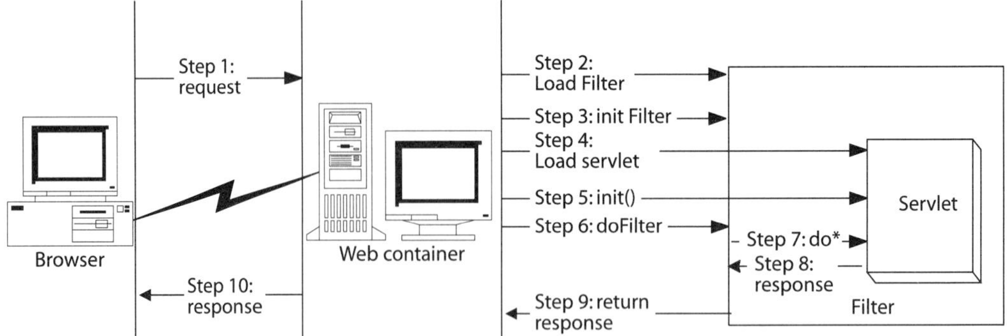

Figure 23.1 How a filter interacts with a servlet.

1. Do some pre-processing (such as examining the data sent to the servlet or performing some sort of audit)
2. Pass the request to the servlet or JSP.
3. Do some post-processing.

Thus the filter wraps around the servlet or JSP and intercepts all HTTP requests to that servlet or JSP. It is therefore now impossible to use the servlet or JSP without first passing through the filter. This idea is illustrated in Figure 23.1. Notice that the filter is instantiated and initialized some time before the servlet is instantiated and initialized (this may be at Web container startup time or at some other point before the servlet is first requested). Also note that Step 6, `doFilter`, represents the interception of the HTTP request by the filter. The filter then passes the request on to the servlet within this method. The response generated by the servlet is then returned to this method before the final response is returned to the Web container and from that back to the Web browser that initiated the original HTTP request.

Of course, in subsequent calls to this servlet neither the servlet nor the filter will need to be reinstantiated or reinitialized.

In fact, a filter can filter one or more servlets. For example, an auditing filter could be applied to every servlet in your Web application. In addition, more than one filter may be applied to the servlet. This generates a filter chain in which each filter is passed the request in turn until finally the request is passed to the servlet. In turn, the response is then passed back up the filter chain until it is finally returned to the Web container. In essence, each filter is wrapped around the inner filter. The final innermost filter is then wrapped around the servlet. This is illustrated in Figure 23.2.

In fact, although the preceding description has talked about servlets and JSPs, it is possible to filter any Web resources, including HTML pages and images as well as servlets and JSPs.

23.3 What Can a Filter Do?

We now know how filters operate, but what can they do? Or to put it another way, why bother?

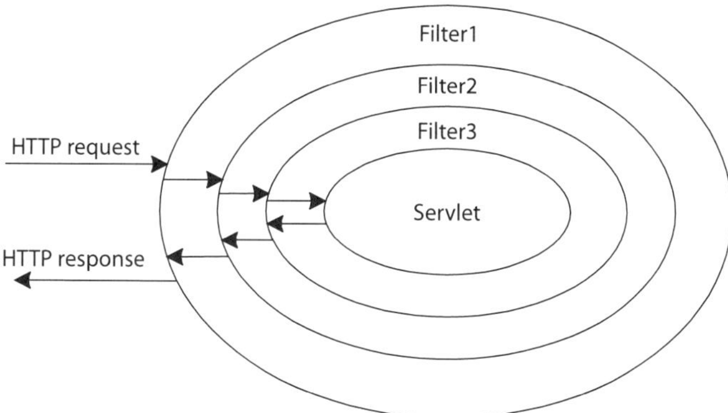

Figure 23.2 A filter chain wrapped around a servlet.

In general terms a filter intercepts a servlet's invocation. This allows it to do some preprocessing, such as examining the request object before the servlet obtains it, or to modify request headers and data if necessary. This second option is particularly useful, as it allows the filter to refine, add to or modify this data. It is also possible for the filter to wrap the request up so that the filter can provide a customized version of the request that allows additional processing etc. The filter can also wrap up the response object so that the response generated by the servlet can be processed before being returned by the filter. We will look at an example of this later in this chapter. The filter can also perform some additional post-processing after the servlet has processed the HTTP request. The filter can also decide to abort the processing of the request by not passing the request on to the next filter in the chain (or the actual Web resource). Thus filters have the option of veto on an actual HTTP request. This is very powerful and widens the scope of what a filter can be used for.

This just summarizes what has already been said. But what does that mean for everyday use in a Web application? The following list presents some of the possible uses of filters in Web applications. Remember that this is just intended to give an idea of the sort of things that a filter could be used for, and is by no means exhaustive.

- **Logging**: a filter could be used to log all requests to one or more servlets. We will look at a logging filter later in this chapter.
- **Auditing**: in a similar manner to logging, we can create a filter that creates audit trails that allow us to determine who accessed what and when, and what the changes were.
- **Data compression**: a filter could be used to decompress information before a servlet receives it or compress the information before it is sent back to the client. In this way the compression/decompression functionality could be generalized and extracted from the servlet or JSP logic.
- **Encryption**: as a variation on the data compression application, a filter could be used to decrypt and encrypt data being sent from and to the client. Again it generalizes this functionality and hides it from the actual servlet or JSP.
- **Validation**: a filter can examine the data being sent to the servlet or JSP. This means that a filter could examine this data and ensure that it is valid.

- **Authorization:** a filter can also be used to check to see whether a client should be allowed to access a particular Web resource or not. This can be used to implement fine-grained access control following the use of user authentication, as described in the next chapter.
- **XML processing:** as a filter can wrap the response object up in a custom wrapper, it is possible for a filter to provide a response wrapper that can convert XML into HTML. In this way the servlet or JSP can focus on generating XML data; then a filter can apply an appropriate transformation (for example using an XSLT stylesheet) to convert it into HTML. Thus different outputs can be generated merely by changing the filter. We shall see an example of this at the end of this chapter.

23.4 The Filter API

There are essentially three interfaces that comprise the filter API. These are:

- `javax.servlet.Filter`: this is the interface that all filter classes must implement. The methods in this interface are listed in Table 23.1. The most important method is the `doFilter` method. This is where the filter can perform any "filtering" that it needs to do.
- `javax.servlet.FilterChain`: a `FilterChain` is an object provided by the servlet container to the developer giving a view into the invocation chain of a filtered request for a resource. Filters use the `FilterChain` to invoke the next filter in the chain, or, if the calling filter is the last filter in the chain, to invoke the resource at the end of the chain. The `FilterChain` interface defines a single method `doFilter(ServletRequest request, ServletResponse response)`. This is called within the `doFilter` method of the `Filter` object when the filter wishes to pass the request to the next element in the chain.
- `javax.servlet.FilterConfig`: a filter configuration object used by a servlet container used to pass information to a filter during initialization. That is, it is the object passed into the `init` method of the `Filter` object. The `FilterConfig` interface defines the methods in Table 23.2.

At this point it is useful to review the life cycle of a filter; that is, the stages that it goes through when being used in a Web application. The Web container is responsible for managing this life cycle, which has the following stages:

Table 23.1 Methods in the `Filter` interface.

`void`	**`destroy`**`()` Called by the Web container to indicate to a filter that it is being taken out of service
`void`	**`doFilter`**`(ServletRequest request, ServletResponse response, FilterChain chain)` The `doFilter` method of the filter is called by the container each time a request/response pair is passed through the chain due to a client request for a resource at the end of the chain. Note that the parameters passed to this method are of the type `ServletRequest` and `ServletResponse`. If you are filtering on an `HttpServlet` or a JSP the request and response can be cast to the Http version; for example `HttpServletRequest` and `HttpServletResponse`
`void`	**`init`**`(FilterConfig filterConfig)` Called by the Web container to indicate to a filter that it is being placed into service

Table 23.2 Methods in the `FilterConfig` interface.

`String`	**`getFilterName()`** Returns the filter name of this filter as defined in the deployment descriptor
`String`	**`getInitParameter`**`(java.lang.String name)` Returns a `String` containing the value of the named initialization parameter, or `null` if the parameter does not exist
`Enumeration`	**`getInitParameterNames()`** Returns the names of the servlet's initialization parameters as an `Enumeration` of `String` objects, or an empty `Enumeration` if the servlet has no initialization parameters
`ServletContext`	**`getServletContext()`** Returns a reference to the `ServletContext` in which the caller is executing

- **Stage 1: Instantiation** The Web container must instantiate all filters before they are required. Exactly when this happens is at the discretion of the Web container. It could be done when the Web container starts up or some time later. In the case of Tomcat the filters are initialized when Tomcat starts up. Just as with servlets, the Web container will create one instance of a filter per Web application. Thus one filter processes all the requests for all the Web resources that it is filtering.
- **Stage 2: Initialization** The Web Container next calls the `init` method on the filter, passing in the `FilterConfig` object.
- **Stage 3: Filtering** The filter is now ready to start filtering requests. The Web container calls the `doFilter` method each time a request is to be sent to a Web resource that the filter is filtering.
- **Stage 4: Destruction** Just prior to the removal of the filter from service the Web container calls the `destroy` method on the filter object. This allows it to do any housekeeping tasks. Note that you cannot guarantee that this method will execute, as the Web container may never formally remove the filter from service.

23.5 Implementing a Simple Filter

In this section we will consider the implementation of a very simple filter. All that this filter does is to print out a message before and after a simple servlet is invoked. However, it will take us through all the steps involved in filtering a Web resource.

The first thing we must do is define a class that implements the `Filter` interface. This means that our filter class (`SimpleFilter`) must implement three methods. The intialization and destruction methods will merely print out a message. However, the `doFilter` method will print out two messages and pass the call on to the next element in the filter chain (in this case the Web resource).

If we look at the `doFilter` method it is worth noting the following points:

- It is called each time a "filtered" servlet receives a request.
- `FilterChain` contains any other filters to be applied.
- It must call `doFilter(req, res)` on the chain to pass the request on.
- `FilterChain` holds the final reference to the servlet.

- It must be called, or the servlet will not get a request.
- By not calling it, the servlet can be bypassed altogether.

The `SimpleFilter` class is presented in Figure 23.3.

The servlet to be filtered is presented in Figure 23.4. This servlet merely generates a welcome message at the front of an online bookstore application.

Having implemented the filter and the servlet we now need to define our deployment descriptor. Remember that it is in the deployment descriptor that we declare the filter and the Web resource that it is filtering. Thus we must add a new element to our `web.xml` file. This is the `<filter>` element. Each filter is declared using a filter element that takes the name of the filter and the class implementing the filter. We must then provide a `<filter-mapping>` element to map the filter to a servlet. This can be done based on either a URL or the name of a servlet. It is also possible to pass parameters to the filter at initialization time by providing an `<init-param>` element in the `<filter>` element. This element has `<param-name>` and `<param-value>` sub-elements. Examples of all of these formats are provided in Figure 23.5. The actual deployment descriptor for this Web application is presented in Figure 23.6.

UltraEdit-32 - [C:\serverside\j2ee\web\filters\source\filters\SimpleFilter.java]

File Edit Search View Format Column Macro Advanced Window Help

```
package filters;

import java.io.*;
import javax.servlet.*;
import javax.servlet.http.*;

public final class SimpleFilter implements Filter {
    public void init(FilterConfig filterConfig)
                                    throws ServletException {
      System.out.println("SimpleFilter.init()");
    }

    public void doFilter(ServletRequest request,
                         ServletResponse response,
                         FilterChain chain)
                            throws IOException, ServletException {
      System.out.println("SimpleFilter.doFilter()");
      System.out.println("SimpleFilter> Pre processing message");
      chain.doFilter(request, response);
      System.out.println("SimpleFilter> Post processing message");
    }

    public void destroy() {
       System.out.println("SimpleFilter.destory()");
    }
}
```

Figure 23.3 The `SimpleFilter` class.

UltraEdit-32 - [C:\serverside\j2ee\web\filters\source\webshop\ShopFrontServlet.jav...

File Edit Search View Format Column Macro Advanced Window Help

```
package webshop;

import java.io.*;
import javax.servlet.*;
import javax.servlet.http.*;

public class ShopFrontServlet  extends HttpServlet {
   public void doGet(HttpServletRequest req,
                     HttpServletResponse res)
                         throws ServletException, IOException  {
      System.out.println("ShopFrontServlet.doGet()");
      res.setContentType("text/xml");
      PrintWriter out = res.getWriter();
      HttpSession session = req.getSession(true);

      out.println("<html><head><title>Welcome</title></head>");
      out.println("<h1>Free Books Online</h1>");
      out.println("Welcome to our Filtered Servlet");
      out.println("</body></html>");
   } // end of doGet
}
```

Figure 23.4 The filtered servlet.

UltraEdit-32 - [Edit1*]

File Edit Search View Format Column Macro Advanced Window Help

```

<filter>
  <filter-name>filter</filter-name>
  <filter-class>filters.SimpleFilter</filter-class>
</filter>
<filter>
  <filter-name>filter</filter-name>
  <filter-class>filters.OtherFilter</filter-class>
  <init-param>
     <param-name>total</param-name>
     <param-value>10</param-value>
  </init-param>
</filter>
<filter-mapping>
  <filter-name>filter</filter-name>
  <servlet-name>welcome</servlet-name>
</filter-mapping>
<filter-mapping>
  <filter-name>filter</filter-name>
  <url-pattern>/books/childrens/</servlet-name>
</filter-mapping>
```

Figure 23.5 The filter-related elements in the deployment descriptor.

UltraEdit-32 - [C:\serverside\j2ee\web\filters\WEB-INF\web.xml]

```
<?xml version="1.0" encoding="ISO-8859-1"?>
<!DOCTYPE web-app
    PUBLIC "-//Sun Microsystems, Inc.//DTD Web Application 2.3//EN"
    "http://java.sun.com/dtd/web-app_2_3.dtd">
<web-app>
   <filter>
        <filter-name>filter</filter-name>
        <filter-class>filters.SimpleFilter</filter-class>
    </filter>
    <filter-mapping>
        <filter-name>filter</filter-name>
        <servlet-name>welcome</servlet-name>
    </filter-mapping>
   <servlet>
       <servlet-name>welcome</servlet-name>
       <servlet-class>webshop.ShopFrontServlet</servlet-class>
   </servlet>
   <servlet-mapping>
       <servlet-name>welcome</servlet-name>
     <url-pattern>/start</url-pattern>
   </servlet-mapping>
</web-app>
```

Figure 23.6 The deployment descriptor for the filter application.

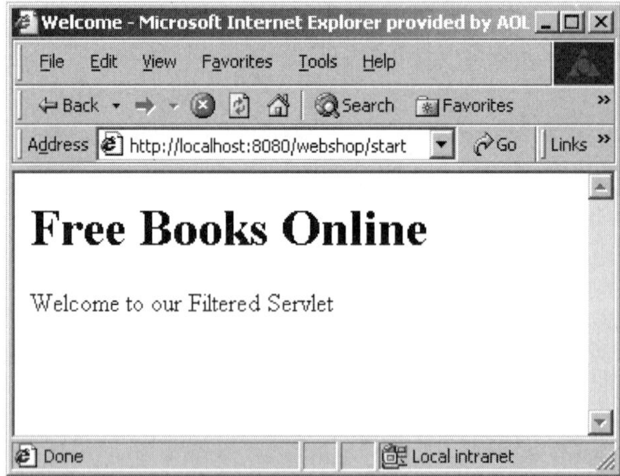

Figure 23.7 The output from the filtered `ShopFrontServlet`.

The result of accessing the filtered servlet `ShopFrontServlet` in a Web browser is presented in Figure 23.7. This would actually be exactly the same whether it was filtered or not.

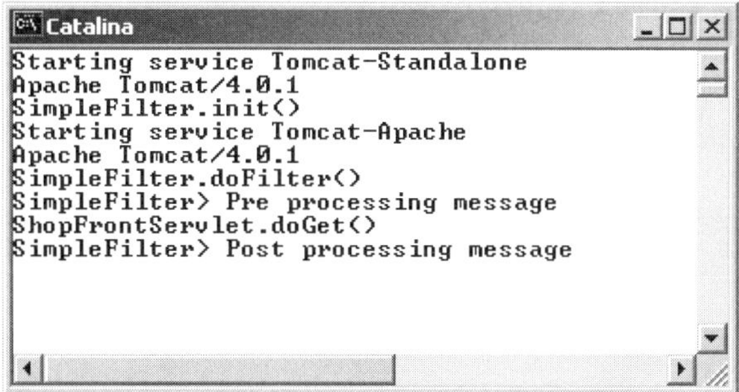

Catalina
Starting service Tomcat-Standalone
Apache Tomcat/4.0.1
SimpleFilter.init()
Starting service Tomcat-Apache
Apache Tomcat/4.0.1
SimpleFilter.doFilter()
SimpleFilter> Pre processing message
ShopFrontServlet.doGet()
SimpleFilter> Post processing message

Figure 23.8 The output in the Catalina window for the simple filter example.

The output in the Catalina window is presented in Figure 23.8. This illustrates the SimpleFilter being initialized just after Tomcat starts up. It then shows the doFilter method being called before a message is printed out from the SimpleFilter. The SimpleFilter then passes the request down the chain, which causes the ShopFrontServlet doGet() method to execute (and print a message). Once this terminates, control returns to the filter and a post-processing message is printed.

Of course this example only illustrates the use of a single filter and not a filter chain. We can define another filter (BasicFilter) and add that to our application. Assuming that we define the filter mappings in the order SimpleFilter and then BasicFilter as illustrated in Figure 23.9 we get the output generated in Figure 23.10. However, if we reverse the order of the mappings we get the output generated in Figure 23.11.

23.6 The Logging Filter Example

The examples presented in the previous section illustrate the basics of how a filter works; however, they do not use the request and response objects passed into the doFilter method. It is worth looking at these objects, not least because they are defined for the method as being of class ServletRequest and ServletResponse. However, if we are dealing with HttpServlets and JSPs (which we are here) then the objects are actually instances of the HttpServletRequest and HttpServletResponse classes. This means that there is a lot of information available to the servlet regarding the request passed in.

The LoggingFilter presented in Figure 23.12 illustrates how these objects can be used to perform some logging-style operations. This filter interrogates the request object to find out information, such as the remote host, the server name, the server port and whether the request is secure or not. Once it has cast the object to the HttpServletRequest class it also obtains the original query string, the name of the remote user, the current session id (if there is one) etc. It also logs how long the user spent inside the Web resource being filtered.

The deployment descriptor for this Web application is illustrated in Figure 23.13 and the output from the filter is shown in Figure 23.14. Note that we are using the same servlet as before, so we will not show the output from this servlet (see Figure 23.7 instead). Also note

```
<?xml version="1.0" encoding="ISO-8859-1"?>
<!DOCTYPE web-app
    PUBLIC "-//Sun Microsystems, Inc.//DTD Web Application 2.3//EN"
    "http://java.sun.com/dtd/web-app_2_3.dtd">
<web-app>
   <filter>
        <filter-name>simplefilter</filter-name>
        <filter-class>filters.SimpleFilter</filter-class>
    </filter>
    <filter>
        <filter-name>basicfilter</filter-name>
        <filter-class>filters.BasicFilter</filter-class>
    </filter>
    <filter-mapping>
        <filter-name>simplefilter</filter-name>
        <servlet-name>welcome</servlet-name>
    </filter-mapping>
    <filter-mapping>
        <filter-name>basicfilter</filter-name>
        <servlet-name>welcome</servlet-name>
    </filter-mapping>
   <servlet>
       <servlet-name>welcome</servlet-name>
       <servlet-class>webshop.ShopFrontServlet</servlet-class>
   </servlet>
   <servlet-mapping>
       <servlet-name>welcome</servlet-name>
      <url-pattern>/start</url-pattern>
   </servlet-mapping>
</web-app>
```

Figure 23.9 Multiple filters deployment descriptor (`SimpleFilter` first).

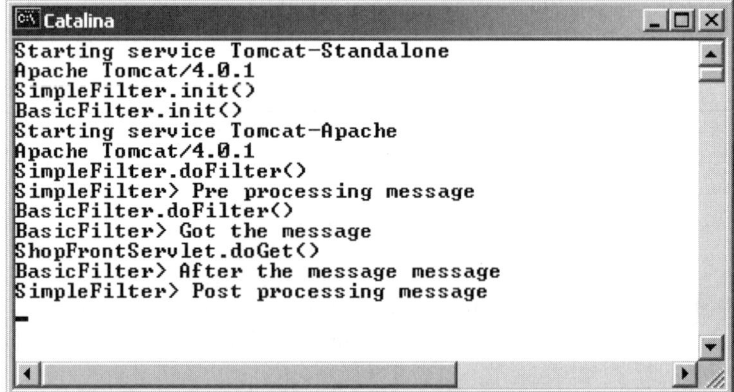
Catalina
Starting service Tomcat-Standalone
Apache Tomcat/4.0.1
SimpleFilter.init()
BasicFilter.init()
Starting service Tomcat-Apache
Apache Tomcat/4.0.1
SimpleFilter.doFilter()
SimpleFilter> Pre processing message
BasicFilter.doFilter()
BasicFilter> Got the message
ShopFrontServlet.doGet()
BasicFilter> After the message message
SimpleFilter> Post processing message

Figure 23.10 Output from two filters when the `SimpleFilter` mapping is first.

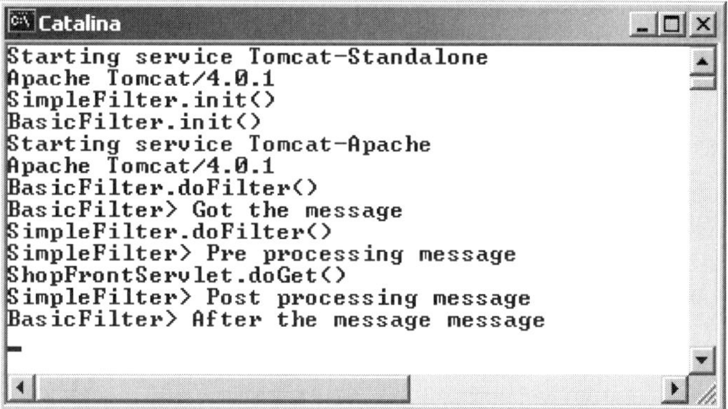
Catalina
Starting service Tomcat-Standalone
Apache Tomcat/4.0.1
SimpleFilter.init()
BasicFilter.init()
Starting service Tomcat-Apache
Apache Tomcat/4.0.1
BasicFilter.doFilter()
BasicFilter> Got the message
SimpleFilter.doFilter()
SimpleFilter> Pre processing message
ShopFrontServlet.doGet()
SimpleFilter> Post processing message
BasicFilter> After the message message

Figure 23.11 Output from two filters when the `BasicFilter` mapping is first.

UltraEdit-32 - [C:\serverside\j2ee\web\filters\source\filters\LoggingFilter.java]

File Edit Search View Format Column Macro Advanced Window Help

```
package filters;

import java.io.*;
import javax.servlet.*;
import javax.servlet.http.*;

public final class LoggingFilter implements Filter {
    public void init(FilterConfig filterConfig) throws ServletException {
      System.out.println("LoggingFilter.init()");
    }
    public void destroy() { System.out.println("LoggingFilter.destory()");    }
    public void doFilter(ServletRequest request, ServletResponse response,
                         FilterChain chain) throws IOException, ServletException {
      System.out.println("LoggingFilter.doFilter()");
      System.out.println("---------------------------------------------");
      System.out.println("remoteAddr=" + request.getRemoteAddr());
      System.out.println("remoteHost=" + request.getRemoteHost());

      System.out.println("serverName=" + request.getServerName());
      System.out.println("serverPort=" + request.getServerPort());
      System.out.println("isSecure=" + request.isSecure());
      if (request instanceof HttpServletRequest) {
         System.out.println("---------------------------------------------");
            HttpServletRequest hrequest = (HttpServletRequest) request;
         System.out.println("queryString=" + hrequest.getQueryString());
         System.out.println("remoteUser=" + hrequest.getRemoteUser());
         System.out.println("requestedSessionId=" + hrequest.getRequestedSessionId());
         System.out.println("requestURI=" + hrequest.getRequestURI());
      }
      System.out.println("---------------------------------------------");
      long startTime = System.currentTimeMillis();
      chain.doFilter(request, response);
      long stopTime = System.currentTimeMillis();
      System.out.println("LoggingFilter servicing servlet took : " +
                         (stopTime - startTime) + " milliseconds");
    }
}
```

Figure 23.12 The `LoggingFilter`.

UltraEdit-32 - [C:\serverside\j2ee\web\filters\WEB-INF\web.xml]

```
<?xml version="1.0" encoding="ISO-8859-1"?>
<!DOCTYPE web-app
    PUBLIC "-//Sun Microsystems, Inc.//DTD Web Application 2.3//EN"
    "http://java.sun.com/dtd/web-app_2_3.dtd">
<web-app>
   <filter>
        <filter-name>loggingfilter</filter-name>
        <filter-class>filters.LoggingFilter</filter-class>
   </filter>
    <filter-mapping>
        <filter-name>loggingfilter</filter-name>
        <url-pattern>/start</url-pattern>
    </filter-mapping>
   <servlet>
       <servlet-name>welcome</servlet-name>
       <servlet-class>webshop.ShopFrontServlet</servlet-class>
   </servlet>
   <servlet-mapping>
       <servlet-name>welcome</servlet-name>
      <url-pattern>/start</url-pattern>
   </servlet-mapping>
</web-app>
```

Figure 23.13 Defining the LoggingFilter in the deployment descriptor.

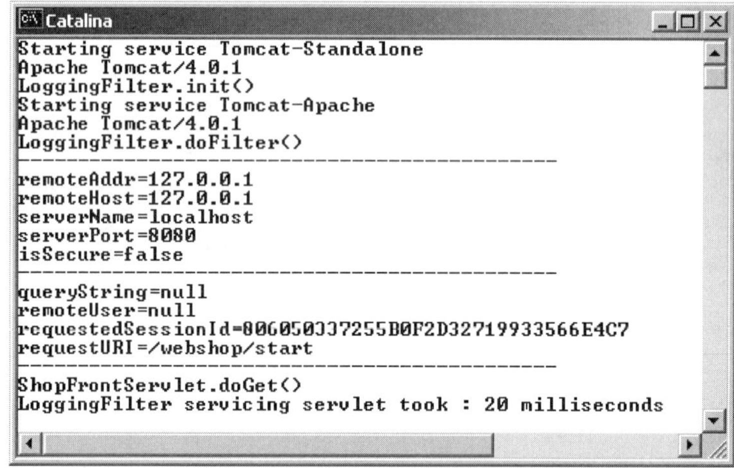

Catalina
Starting service Tomcat-Standalone
Apache Tomcat/4.0.1
LoggingFilter.init()
Starting service Tomcat-Apache
Apache Tomcat/4.0.1
LoggingFilter.doFilter()
remoteAddr=127.0.0.1
remoteHost=127.0.0.1
serverName=localhost
serverPort=8080
isSecure=false
queryString=null
remoteUser=null
requestedSessionId=806050337255B0F2D32719933566E4C7
requestURI=/webshop/start
ShopFrontServlet.doGet()
LoggingFilter servicing servlet took : 20 milliseconds

Figure 23.14 The output from the logging filter.

that we are using the <url-pattern> element to define what the servlet will filter on. This allows a URL to be specified rather than the name of the servlet. However, note that you cannot mix the <servlet-name> with <url-pattern> as the <url-pattern> takes priority and the <servlet-name> mapping is ignored.

23.7 Wrapping Request and Response Objects

As well as being able to perform pre- and post-processing around the execution of a servlet, filters can also wrap the request and response objects up such that they can modify or customize either (without the servlet or JSP being aware of it).

There are four classes that make up the Wrapping API. These are the `javax.servlet.ServletRequestWrapper`, `javax.servlet.ServletResponseWrapper`, `javax.servlet.http.HttpServletRequestWrapper` and `javax.servlet.http.HttpServletResponseWrapper`. These classes implement the respective interfaces (e.g. `ServletRequest`, `ServletResponse`, `HttpServletRequest` and `HttpServletResponse`) and can thus be used anywhere that these interfaces are specified. Most notably they can therefore be used inside a filter to wrap the actual request or response object up so that the filter can control either the data accessed or generated by the servlet or JSP.

A particular use of these wrappers is to perform some pre- or post-processing of the data being used or generated by the servlet so that the servlet does not need to know about this processing. For example, if a servlet generates XML data we need some way to convert this XML into the HTML generally expected by browser. Note that although some browsers can now process XML, it is not aimed at presentation (it is a markup language). Thus when XML is displayed in a browser it is not in a very usable form. However, HTML is ideally suited to presentation on the Web and thus converting XML into HTML for presentation purposes is a good idea.

Of course, there are many ways in which we could carry out this conversion. For example we could do it manually in a program of our own design, we could do it using an XSL stylesheet and a browser that understands XML and stylesheets (such as the later versions of IE). We could also use the translation features of JAXP to convert the XML into HTML on the server side inside our servlet or JSP. However, this is really about presentation, and our servlet is aimed at generating the data to present – it could handle the presentation work of course, but if other servlets need this same facility it would be useful to have a generalized solution. One way of providing this generalized solution is to have a filter create a response object wrapper that converts XML into HTML.

This is the example presented in the next section.

23.8 Filtering XML to Generate HTML

In this section we will examine a more complex use of filters. We will look at a servlet that does not generate HTML directly. Instead it generates XML output. It is then the responsibility of the filter to convert that XML into HTML that any browser can understand. The XML-generating servlet (presented in Figure 23.15) is very simple: a string array holds a set of strings that provide the XML output. When a `GET` request is sent to the servlet the `doGet` method sets the response type to `text/xml` and then prints out the strings in the XML string array to the response `PrintWriter`. Although this is not a particularly sophisticated servlet it does represent the behaviour of an XML-generating servlet. When this servlet is deployed we will wrap a filter that will convert this XML into HTML. This will be done in the deployment descriptor.

UltraEdit-32 - [C:\serverside\j2ee\web\xmlfilters\source\webshop\XMLGeneratingServlet.java]

```
package webshop;

import java.io.*;
import javax.servlet.*;
import javax.servlet.http.*;

public class XMLGeneratingServlet  extends HttpServlet {
   String [] xml = {
     "<books><book>",
      "<author>John Hunt</author>",
      "<title>Corba for Java programmers </title>",
      "<price>25.50</price>",
      "<isbn>123490</isbn>",
      "</book>",
      "<book>",
      "<author>Chris Loftus</author>",
      "<title>XML for Everyone </title>",
      "<price>19.50</price>",
      "<isbn>2034211</isbn>",
      "</book>",
    "</books>",
   };

   public void doGet(HttpServletRequest req,
                     HttpServletResponse res)
                          throws ServletException, IOException  {
      System.out.println("XMLGeneratingServlet.doGet()");
      System.out.println("XMLGeneratingServlet.doGet() Response " + res);
      res.setContentType("text/xml");
      PrintWriter out = res.getWriter();
      System.out.println("XMLGeneratingServlet.doGet() Response " + res);

      for (int i=0; i<xml.length; i++ ){
          System.out.println(xml[i]);
          out.write(xml[i]);
      }
   } // end of doGet
}
```

Figure 23.15 The XML-generating servlet.

The structure of the XMLFilter and its related classes is presented in Figure 23.16. The XMLFilter uses two supporting classes, XMLServletResponseWrapper and XMLResponse-Stream, to help it convert XML into HTML. These are all described below.

The filter we shall be using is called XMLFilter and is applied to the /start URL pattern (Figure 23.17). This is the URL pattern used to access the XMLGeneratingServlet. The XML filter is more complex than any of the filters we have examined so far because it wraps the response object passed into the doFilter method inside an XmlServlet-ResponseWrapper (see Figure 23.18). In turn the XMLServletResponseWrapper object uses an XMLResponseStream to actually handle the XML to HTML conversion.

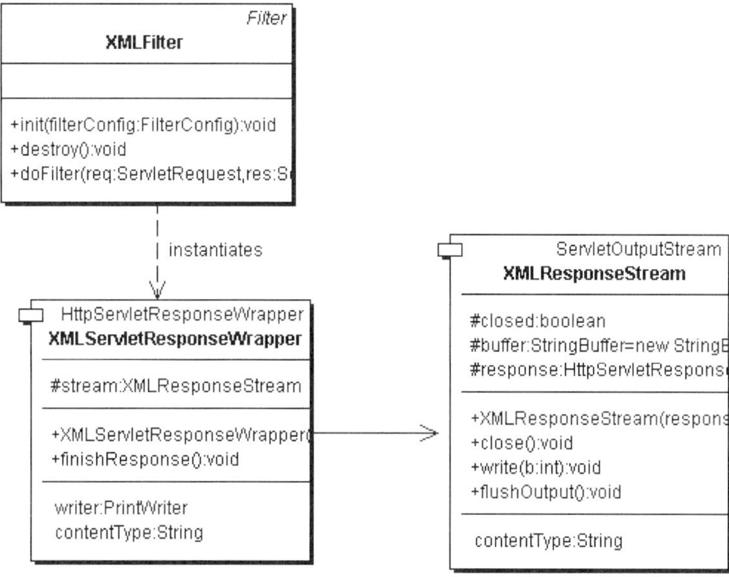

Figure 23.16 The class diagram for the `XMLFilter`-related classes.

UltraEdit-32 - [C:\serverside\j2ee\web\xmlfilters\WEB-INF\web.xml]

File Edit Search View Format Column Macro Advanced Window Help

```
<?xml version="1.0" encoding="ISO-8859-1"?>

<!DOCTYPE web-app
    PUBLIC "-//Sun Microsystems, Inc.//DTD Web Application 2.3//EN"
    "http://java.sun.com/dtd/web-app_2_3.dtd">

<web-app>
   <filter>
        <filter-name>XML Filter</filter-name>
        <filter-class>filters.XMLFilter</filter-class>
    </filter>
    <filter-mapping>
        <filter-name>XML Filter</filter-name>
        <url-pattern>/start</url-pattern>
    </filter-mapping>
   <servlet>
       <servlet-name>welcome</servlet-name>
       <servlet-class>webshop.XMLGeneratingServlet</servlet-class>
   </servlet>
   <servlet-mapping>
       <servlet-name>welcome</servlet-name>
      <url-pattern>/start</url-pattern>
   </servlet-mapping>

</web-app>
```

Figure 23.17 Deployment descriptor for the `XMLFilter` application.

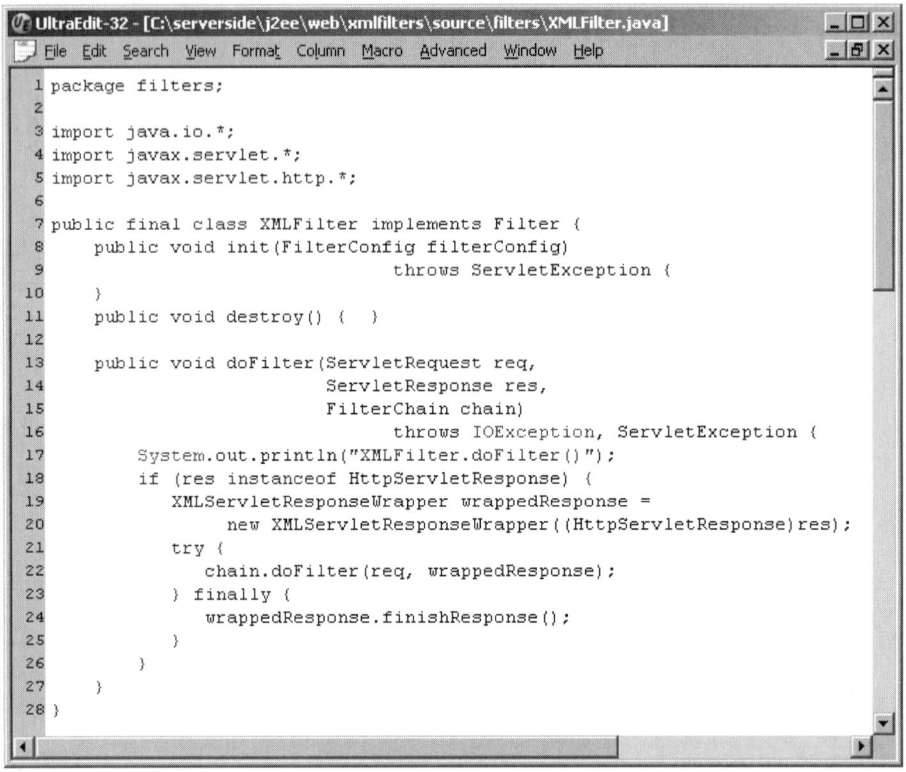

UltraEdit-32 - [C:\serverside\j2ee\web\xmlfilters\source\filters\XMLFilter.java]

File Edit Search View Format Column Macro Advanced Window Help

```
package filters;

import java.io.*;
import javax.servlet.*;
import javax.servlet.http.*;

public final class XMLFilter implements Filter {
    public void init(FilterConfig filterConfig)
                                throws ServletException {
    }
    public void destroy() {  }

    public void doFilter(ServletRequest req,
                         ServletResponse res,
                         FilterChain chain)
                                throws IOException, ServletException {
        System.out.println("XMLFilter.doFilter()");
        if (res instanceof HttpServletResponse) {
           XMLServletResponseWrapper wrappedResponse =
                new XMLServletResponseWrapper((HttpServletResponse)res);
           try {
              chain.doFilter(req, wrappedResponse);
           } finally {
              wrappedResponse.finishResponse();
           }
        }
    }
}
```

Figure 23.18 The XMLFilter class.

If we now examine the XMLFilter class in more detail we can step through the actions it performs (see Figure 23.18). The first thing it does is to check to see that what it has been given is an instance of the HttpServletResponse class (which it should be if we are using HttpServlets). Once it has checked this it wraps the response up inside the XMLServletResponseWrapper object. Remember that wrappers have the same API as the actual response, but can intercept any calls to the response, deciding whether to pass the call directly to the actual response or to handle it itself. Once it has done this wrapping, the request and the wrapper object are passed on down the filter chain via the doFilter method on the chain object. The receiving filter (or in this case servlet) will have no idea that it is being passed a wrapped response rather than the actual response object. Note that we have introduced the convention that the wrappedResponse object will be notified when the servlet has completed its task. This will allow the wrapper to notify the writer to close itself (which will mean that all the XML has been provided and that it can now be translated into HTML).

The XMLServletResponseWrapper object (presented in Figure 23.19) provides a constructor and three methods. The constructor provides the actual response object to the parent class and then wraps it inside an XMLResponseStream object. This is where the actual XML to HTML conversion will take place. The three methods provided are the finishResponse() method mentioned above, the setContentType() method that allows

UltraEdit-32 - [C:\serverside\j2ee\web\xmlfilters\source\filters\XMLServletResponseWrapper.ja...

File Edit Search View Format Column Macro Advanced Window Help

```
package filters;

import java.io.*;
import javax.servlet.*;
import javax.servlet.http.*;

public class XMLServletResponseWrapper extends HttpServletResponseWrapper
   protected PrintWriter writer = null;
   protected XMLResponseStream stream;

   public XMLServletResponseWrapper(HttpServletResponse response) {
      super(response);
      System.out.println("XMLServletResponseWrapper constructor ");
      try {
         stream = new XMLResponseStream(response);
      } catch (IOException exp) {
         exp.printStackTrace();
      }
    }

    public void finishResponse() {
       System.out.println("XMLServletResponseWrapper.finish()");
       if (writer != null)
          writer.close();
    }

    public PrintWriter getWriter() throws IOException {
        System.out.println("XMLServletResponseWrapper.getWriter()");
        if (writer == null)
           writer = new PrintWriter(stream);
        return writer;
    }

    public void setContentType(String type) {
       stream.setContentType(type);
    }
}
```

Figure 23.19 The `XMLServletResponseWrapper` class.

the content type to be passed to the `XMLResponseStream` and the `getWriter()` method. This is really the key method, as it returns a `PrintWriter` to the servlet using the `XMLServletResponseWrapper` object. However, this `PrintWriter` is wrapped around the `XMLResponseStream` (rather than the underlying stream). Thus anything written to the `PrintWriter` is first sent to the `XMLResponseStream`.

We shall look at the `XMLResponseStream` in two parts. The first part will examine the constructor and methods such as `write`. The second part will examine the conversion of XML to HTML.

The `XMLResponseStream` is based on the idea of building up a buffer of the XML written to it. Once this buffer is complete it can be used as the XML document for translation. This means that the write method (see Figure 23.20) appends each character written to it to the string buffer. Thus what happens when the servlet writes a string to the `PrintWriter` is illustrated in Figure 23.21.

In turn, when the servlet has finished writing all the strings to the `PrintWriter` and control returns to the filter, the `close` method triggers the `flushOutput` method that extracts the information from this buffer. This sequence of events is illustrated in Figure 23.22.

UltraEdit-32 - [C:\serverside\j2ee\web\xmlfilters\source\filters\XMLResponseStream.java]

File Edit Search View Format Column Macro Advanced Window Help

```
package filters;

import java.io.*;
import javax.servlet.*;
import javax.servlet.http.*;
import org.w3c.dom.Document;
import javax.xml.transform.*;
import javax.xml.transform.stream.*;
import javax.xml.transform.dom.DOMSource;
import javax.xml.parsers.*;

public class XMLResponseStream extends ServletOutputStream {
    protected boolean closed;
    protected StringBuffer buffer = new StringBuffer();
    protected HttpServletResponse response;

    public XMLResponseStream(HttpServletResponse response) throws IOException{
        System.out.println("XMLResponseStream constructor");
        closed = false;
        this.response = response;
    }

   public void close() throws IOException {
     System.out.println("XMLResponseStream close");
     if (closed)
        throw new IOException("Output stream already closed");
     flushOutput();
     closed = true;
   }

    public void setContentType(String type) {
      System.out.println("XMLResponseStream.setContentType(" + type + ")");
      response.setContentType(type);
    }

    public void write(int b) throws IOException {
        if (closed)
            throw new IOException("Cannot write to a closed output stream");
        buffer.append((char)b);
    }
```

Figure 23.20 The first part of the `XMLResponseStream` class.

Figure 23.21 The sequence of method calls following on from the `write` method in the servlet.

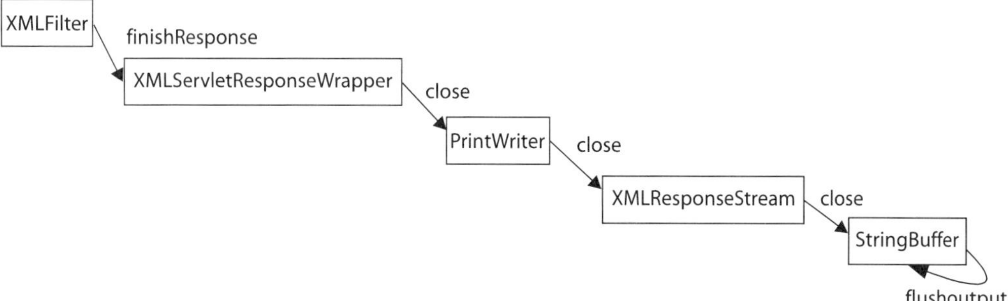

Figure 23.22 The sequence of events causing the buffer to flush.

Of course, the use of the intermediate string buffer may not be particularly efficient for very large XML documents or for a very large number of users; however, it is simple enough to illustrate the ideas presented in this section. Also note that the `setContentType` method acts as a pass-through method for the actual response object.

Once all the XML is written to the buffer and the `close` method is called on the `XMLResponseStream` (by the `PrintWriter` in response to close being called on it by the `XMLFilter` object) the `flushOutput` method is called.

The `flushOutput` method illustrated in Figure 23.23 uses the XSL translation technology described in Part 1 of this book to convert this XML into HTML using the XSL stylesheet presented in Figure 23.24. Note that the stream source for the new transformer

UltraEdit-32 - [C:\serverside\j2ee\web\xmlfilters\source\filters\XMLResponseStream.java]

```
   public void flushOutput() throws IOException {
      try {
         System.out.println("XMLResponseStream.flushOutput()");
         // Create an XML Document
         DocumentBuilderFactory dbf = DocumentBuilderFactory.newInstance();
         DocumentBuilder db = dbf.newDocumentBuilder();
         Document doc = db.parse(
                             new StringBufferInputStream(buffer.toString()));
         // Transform source xml to pathname destination file
         // We transform directly from the DOM tree
         TransformerFactory factory = TransformerFactory.newInstance();
         Transformer transformer =
                     factory.newTransformer(
                                new StreamSource(
                                  "http://localhost:8080/webshop/books.xsl"));
         StringWriter sr = new StringWriter();
         transformer.transform(new DOMSource(doc), new StreamResult(sr));
         PrintWriter pw = response.getWriter();
         pw.println(sr.toString());
         pw.flush();
      } catch(Exception exp) {
         exp.printStackTrace();
      }
   }
}
```

Figure 23.23 The second part of the `XMLResponseStream`.

UltraEdit-32 - [C:\serverside\j2ee\web\xmlfilters\books.xsl]

File Edit Search View Format Column Macro Advanced Window Help

```
<?xml version='1.0'?>
<!--XML Declaration -->
<xsl:stylesheet version="1.0"
     xmlns:xsl="http://www.w3.org/1999/XSL/Transform">
   <xsl:output indent="yes" omit-xml-declaration="no"/>
<!--declaration that the document is a stylesheet and that it
    is associated with the xsl: namespace -->
  <xsl:template match="/">
<!--Apply template to everything starting from the root node-->
   <HTML>
      <BODY>
        <TABLE BORDER="1">
<!--Set up header row -->
          <TR>
            <TD><b>Author</b></TD>
            <TD><b>Title</b></TD>
            <TD><b>ISBN</b></TD>
            <TD><b>Price</b></TD>
          </TR>
          <xsl:for-each select="books/book">
<!--set up a loop where for each occurance of the pattern defined
    in the "select", do the following -->
            <TR>
              <TD><xsl:value-of select="author"/></TD>
<!--"value-of" pulls the value of the contents specified in the
    "select" attribute -->
              <TD><xsl:value-of select="title"/></TD>
              <TD><xsl:value-of select="isbn"/></TD>
              <TD><xsl:value-of select="price"/></TD>
            </TR>
          </xsl:for-each>
<!-- close for-each loop -->
        </TABLE>
      </BODY>
   </HTML>
  </xsl:template>
<!-- close template tag -->
</xsl:stylesheet>
```

Figure 23.24 The `books.xsl` stylesheet.

specifies a URL for the XSL file that indicates that the XSL file is a Web resource deployed with the Web application (i.e. `http://localhost:8080/webshop/books.xsl`). This XSL file creates a table for the books' XML data. Each book has its own row. Each row is comprised of four columns: `Author`, `Title`, `ISBN` and `Price`.

When this particular Web application is deployed both the `webshop` package and the filter package are both deployed under the `WEB-INF` directory of the `webshop` application.

When the Web application is then accessed from a Web browser a standard HTML table is generated, as illustrated in Figure 23.25. The trace outputs from the various elements in the Web application are illustrated in Figure 23.26. Notice that the printout from the servlet clearly shows that it is XML that it is returning, whereas the Web browser clearly indicates that it is HTML that is received by the client.

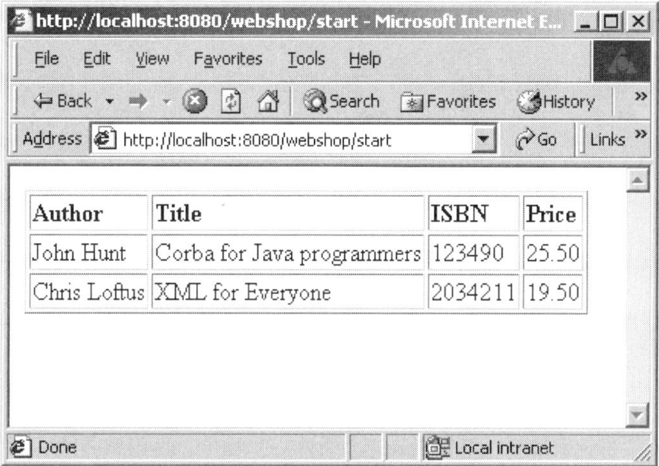

Figure 23.25 The Web output from the `XMLFilter` application.

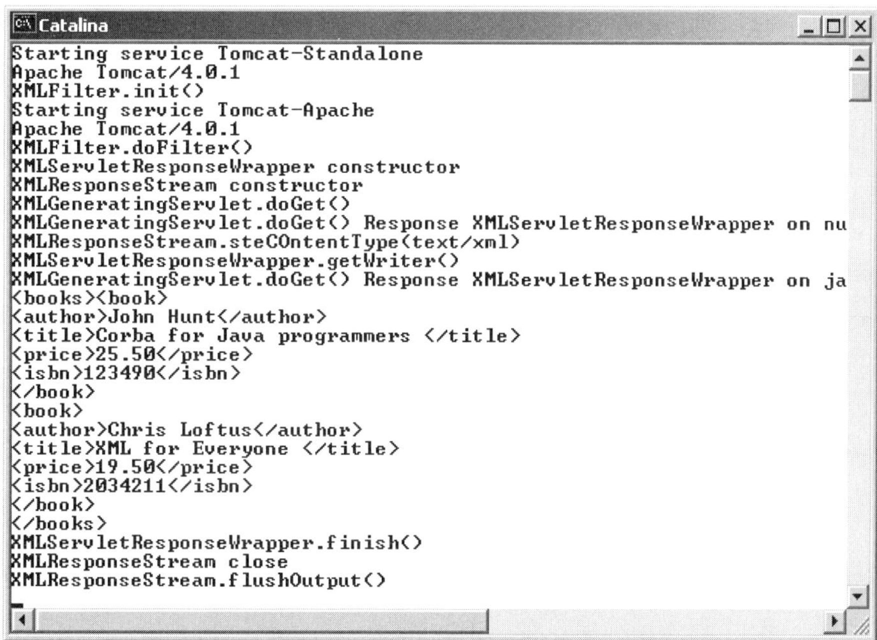

Figure 23.26 The `system.out` trace for the `XMLFilter` application.

Chapter 24

Securing Web Applications

24.1 Introduction

For many Web sites security is a primary concern. This is certainly no less true for a Java J2EE Web application (and is probably even more true!). Traditionally, security for such Web sites has been controlled either programmatically by the developer or by the Web server. With the advent of the Java Servlet 2.3 specification declarative Web container-managed security has been introduced. This greatly enhances the developer's ability to secure and control access to a Java Web application in a Web container- and operating system-independent manner.

In this chapter we will first examine traditional approaches to securing Web applications. We will then examine the features of Java Servlet 2.3 container-managed security. We will explore the purpose and implementation of security realms, we will consider configuring a Web application to protect Web resources (such as servlets and JSPs) and we will look at user authentication. We will also briefly explore the programmatic facilities provided by servlets to allow additional runtime security checks.

24.2 Traditional Approaches

24.2.1 Use the Web Server

In many cases the facilities provided by the Web server that may front the element of a server system that ran the Java code (the Java servlet engine) could be used to handle user authentication. That is, the user and their password could be verified by the Web server before the user could get near the Web application. This setup is illustrated in Figure 24.1.

However, there are a number of problems related to relying on the Web server fronting the Web application to handle authentication. These are:

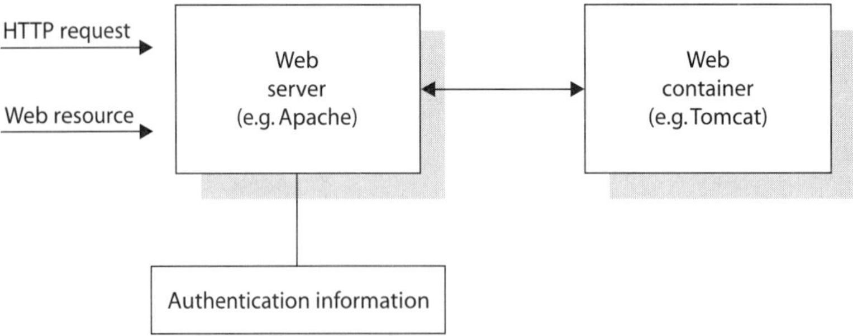

Figure 24.1 Using a Web server to authenticate users.

1. Each Web server does it differently; thus to deploy on a new Web server requires learning and implementing the authentication mechanism it provides.
2. The actual access control elements for the Web application are defined on the Web server, completely separately from the rest of the Web application. This can lead to configuration and deployment issues.
3. The user id and password information are not available to the Web application should the Web application require them.

In many cases this has led Java Web application developers to adopt a more do-it-yourself approach. This is discussed below.

24.2.2 Do-It-Yourself

In general the most common way in which Web applications were secured (prior to the Servlet 2.3 specification) was to use login forms and Secure Sockets Layer (SSL) communication. The basic idea was that when a user accessed a particular Web resource that needed to be secured, the designer of the system would ensure that the first time they did so, a login form was presented to the user. The user would then enter login information into this form (such as their user id and password). This information would then be sent to the server normally over HTTPS. HTTPS is a variation on the HTTP protocol that uses SSL to encrypt the data being transferred. This, therefore, ensures that the user id and the password are encrypted during transmission and are thus protected from unwanted scrutiny.

Once the server received the user id and password, it could then determine whether the user was known to it or not and whether the password was correct. Exactly how it did this was up to the server to determine and implement. For example, one approach might be to create a password and user id table in a database. Then when a user's details were sent to the server it could query the database table and compare the user id and password stored there with those just entered. Another approach might be to confirm that the user has access rights to some other system (such as a database system). If they succeed in logging into this second system then they can use the Web application.

Once the login process was successfully completed the server could forward the user to the appropriate Web resource. If authentication was unsuccessful then a login error page could be returned. The whole of this process could be (and indeed often was) implemented by a dedicated servlet that would handle all such logins, for example a `LoginServlet`.

Of course, because we are dealing with Web resources the designer of the system must also consider what happens if the user attempts to access the secured resource directly rather than via a `LoginServlet` etc. In general two approaches were adopted. The first was to record the fact that the user has logged in somewhere (for example in an `HttpSession` object associated with the user). If the user did not have this login token in their session then all secured resources would reject the request. This could be done either by sending the request to the login servlet or by rejecting the request. The second approach is always to use the `LoginServlet`. Thus all requests go via the `LoginServlet`.

This approach has been used successfully by many Web-based applications. However it has some significant drawbacks:

1. Every Web application re-invents the same wheel.
2. There are numerous chances for security weaknesses to be introduced if the developer makes a mistake.
3. Every servlet or JSP has to have the security checking code added to it.

For these reasons the Servlet 2.3 specification introduced container-managed security, which performs much the same role as that described above, but which is implemented by the Web container (e.g. Tomcat) and thus is both standardized and reusable. It can also be applied declaratively when the application is deployed, leaving the Web developer to concentrate on the application logic rather than the security concerns.

24.3 Container-Managed Security

A third approach to securing a Web application is to use the security features added to the Servlet 2.3 specification and often referred to as container-managed security. This approach relies on the Web container to handle user authentication and access control. Exactly what Web resources are to be secured is handled declaratively in the deployment descriptor (the `web.xml` file). By *declaratively* we mean that it is explicitly stated what URL patterns should be secured and what users can access them. In fact, this is further refined by having two layers. The first layer is for user authentication. In this layer all users must have a user id and password defined. In addition, users can be assigned roles. These roles can then be used to provide fine-grained access control to the Web resources available once the users have logged in.

The way in which the Web container obtains the user information is via a security realm. A realm is an authentication system provider. In Tomcat a realm is in fact a Java interface called `org.apache.catalina.Realm`. Note that Catalina is the codename for the servlet engine used within Tomcat.

The `Realm` interface is implemented by different authentication implementations. These implementations can then be "plugged" into the Web container as required. In the case of Tomcat 4.0.3 three different realms are provided by default. These are an in-memory security realm (which is the default), a JDBC-based one and a JNDI-based system that allows any directory

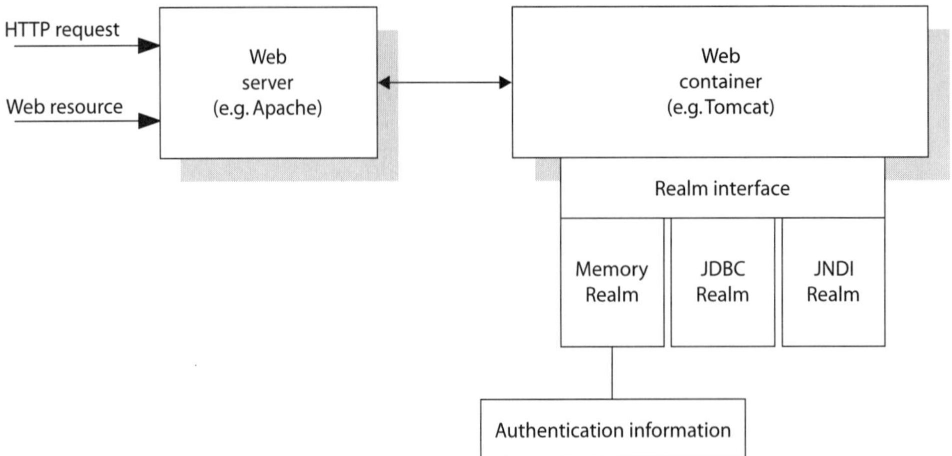

Figure 24.2 Realms in Tomcat 4.0.1.

service that can be accessed via JNDI to be used (for example LDAP or Kerberos). This is illustrated in Figure 24.2 and discussed below:

- **In-memory realm.** This is an in-memory data structure that is created using information provided in an XML fie. The default XML file is the `conf/tomcat-users.xml` file. This file can have users, their passwords and roles defined in it. Alternatively, separate XML files can be created for individual applications. Again they can define users, passwords and roles, but these are only available for a specific Web application. They are defined using the context element in the `conf/server.xml` file of the Tomcat home directory. Note that as the XML file defining the users is loaded once when the server starts up, if new users are added to the file or details of existing users are changed then these changes will not take affect until the Tomcat server is restarted.
- **JDBC realm.** This is really a basic authentication system and interface to any JDBC-compliant data source. That is, anything that provides a JDBC driver can be used as the repository for the authentication system information. If the JDBC realm is being used, then tables need to be created in a database system that contain the user id and password and the user id and roles. The JDBC realm will then query the database via JDBC to obtain the user ids, passwords and roles. This is a much more preferable solution than the in-memory approach, for two reasons. Firstly user data is only loaded as and when needed. Secondly, tools already available for the database system can be used to administer user ids, passwords and roles etc. In addition, Java-based tools can be provided to provide application-specific support. Note that once a user's data is loaded it is not reloaded from the database. Thus if a user has logged into the Web applications, any subsequent changes to that user's authentication profile will only take effect the next time the server is restarted. However, if a new user's details are added to the database they are available immediately.
- **JNDI realm.** The JNDI realm is the equivalent of the JDBC realm, but for resources that can be accessed via JNDI. Examples of such resources include LDAP and Kerberos. This realm

operates in a similar manner to the JDBC realm. Thus new users are available immediately, but changes to users who are already logged in will only take effect the next time the server is restarted.

In general, the in-memory realm is suitable for small applications and prototypes. However, larger real-world applications will need to use the JDBC or JNDI realms. Another option is to implement the `Realm` interface yourself and define your own realm.

24.3.1 Defining Users

In the remainder of this chapter we will use the in-memory realm to access user data defined within the default `tomcat-users.xml` file. This is primarily because it is the simplest approach and therefore the easiest to follow. The basic idea will be the same for the other two realms supported by Tomcat. To learn about how to define the database tables required for the JDBC realm, or the entries required in a directory services for the JNDI realm, see the Tomcat Web site.

All users have a user id, a password and one or more roles associated with them. For example, Figure 24.3 illustrates the `tomcat-users.xml` file with the users "`jjh`" and "`dec`" added. The user "`jjh`" has the password "`pop`" and the role "`eshopUsers`". The user "`dec`" has the password "`bang`" and the roles "`eshopUsers`" and "`administrator`". Note that these roles are case-sensitive and that "`eShopUsers`" is not the same role as "`eshopUsers`"!

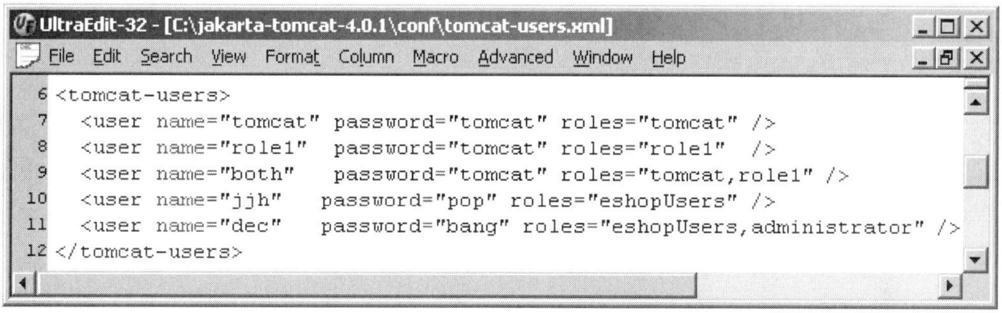

UltraEdit-32 - [C:\jakarta-tomcat-4.0.1\conf\tomcat-users.xml]

File Edit Search View Format Column Macro Advanced Window Help

```
<tomcat-users>
  <user name="tomcat" password="tomcat" roles="tomcat" />
  <user name="role1"  password="tomcat" roles="role1"  />
  <user name="both"   password="tomcat" roles="tomcat,role1" />
  <user name="jjh"   password="pop" roles="eshopUsers" />
  <user name="dec"   password="bang" roles="eshopUsers,administrator" />
</tomcat-users>
```

Figure 24.3 The `tomcat-users.xml` file.

To use a different XML file for our Web application (and thus the users, passwords and roles would only be available to that Web application) we can configure the `Context` element for the Web application.

The `Context` element of the Web application is defined in the `conf/server.xml` file. It allows the document base of the Web application to be defined, the location of the Web application to be specified, whether the application is reloadable by Tomcat and the realm to use. For an example, see Figure 23.4.

This figure indicates that the `webshop` Web application will use the standard in-memory realm, but that the file defining the users for this application is the `webshop-users.xml` file found in the `WEB-INF` directory of the `webshop` application.

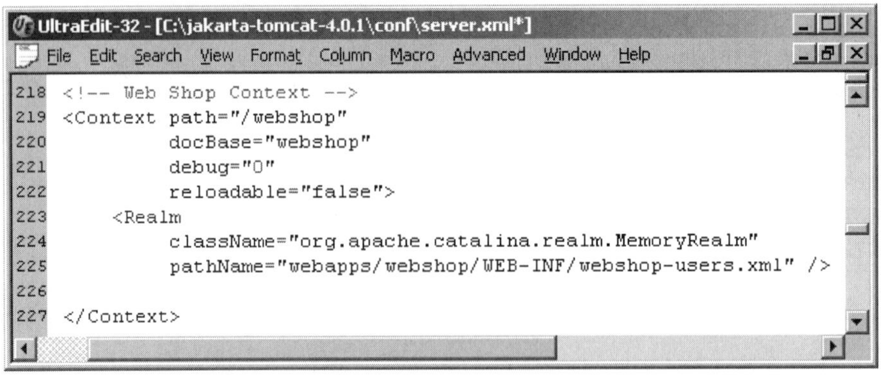

UltraEdit-32 - [C:\jakarta-tomcat-4.0.1\conf\server.xml*]

File Edit Search View Format Column Macro Advanced Window Help

```
<!-- Web Shop Context -->
<Context path="/webshop"
         docBase="webshop"
         debug="0"
         reloadable="false">
     <Realm
         className="org.apache.catalina.realm.MemoryRealm"
         pathName="webapps/webshop/WEB-INF/webshop-users.xml" />

</Context>
```

Figure 23.4 Defining an alternative user XML file.

24.3.2 Configuring Access to Web Resources

Configuring the Web resources that are secured by the authentication system is handled by the deployment descriptor file (web.xml) defined for the Web application. This declarative specification allows the developer to specify the scope of the security domain, the users who can access the secured resource and any data transfer protocols to be applied once inside that security domain. This is done using two main elements: the security constraint element and the login configuration constraint.

- **The security constraint** (<security-constraint>) element includes specification of the resources being protected, the method of access being protected (e.g. GET and POST), the users who can access the resources (based on role names), and the data that should be transmitted.
- **The login configuration** (<login-config>) element defines how authentication should be performed. There are a number of options available, the simplest being BASIC and the others being FORM, DIGEST and CLIENT.

We will examine an example of these tags before proceeding to discuss the different types of authentication available.

Figure 24.5 illustrates an example of the <security-constraint> and <login-config> elements. Note that the servlet and JSP declarations must come before the security details in the web.xml deployment descriptor. In this particular case the XML declarations state the following:

The first part of the <security-constraint> element is the <web-resource-collection>. This element specifies that everything with the URL pattern starting webshop and fb will be part of the security realm for GET and POST operations. Thus the URL http//localhost:8080/webshop/enter will be within the secured area, as its URL starts with the pattern webshop. Note we could have specified a single URL pattern, a complete path for a URL, just one HTTP method or all four HTTP methods etc. Next we need to state who can access these resources. This is done using the <auth-constraint> element. This element has one or more <role-name> subelements that specify the roles that are allowed to use these resources. In the example presented

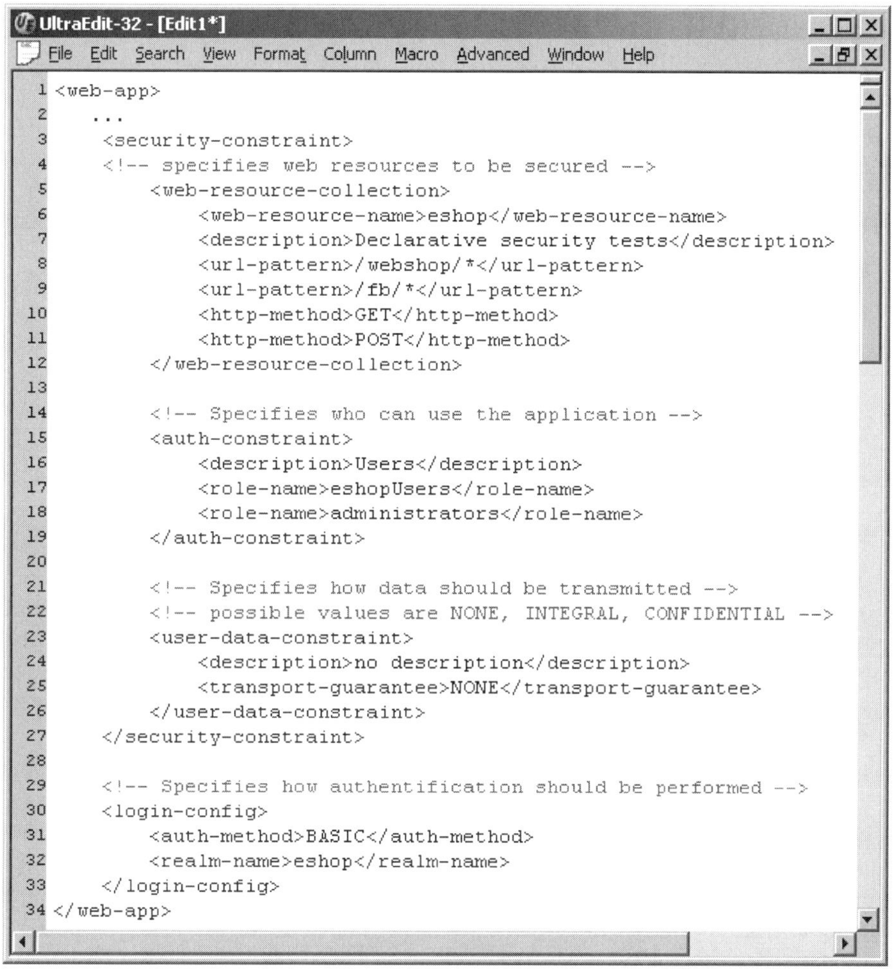

```
<web-app>
   ...
    <security-constraint>
    <!-- specifies web resources to be secured -->
        <web-resource-collection>
            <web-resource-name>eshop</web-resource-name>
            <description>Declarative security tests</description>
            <url-pattern>/webshop/*</url-pattern>
            <url-pattern>/fb/*</url-pattern>
            <http-method>GET</http-method>
            <http-method>POST</http-method>
        </web-resource-collection>

        <!-- Specifies who can use the application -->
        <auth-constraint>
            <description>Users</description>
            <role-name>eshopUsers</role-name>
            <role-name>administrators</role-name>
        </auth-constraint>

        <!-- Specifies how data should be transmitted -->
        <!-- possible values are NONE, INTEGRAL, CONFIDENTIAL -->
        <user-data-constraint>
            <description>no description</description>
            <transport-guarantee>NONE</transport-guarantee>
        </user-data-constraint>
    </security-constraint>

    <!-- Specifies how authentification should be performed -->
    <login-config>
        <auth-method>BASIC</auth-method>
        <realm-name>eshop</realm-name>
    </login-config>
</web-app>
```

Figure 24.5 Sample security constraint and login configuration specifications.

in Figure 24.5, `eshopUsers` and `administrators` are allowed to access these resources. Thus any user with the role `eshopUsers` or the role `administrators` (or both) can access the resource indicated by the URL `http//localhost:8080/webshop/enter`. Finally, we need to indicate how information to be transferred between the client's browser and the Web container. This is done using the `<user-data-constraint >` element. This element allows three values to be specified: `NONE`, `INTEGRAL` and `CONFIDENTIAL`.

- The value `NONE` indicates that data can be sent as is.
- The value `INTEGRAL` indicates that the underlying data transmission should guarantee the integrity of the data during transmission; that is, it cannot be altered in transit.
- The value of `CONFIDENTIAL` indicates that the data should be not be observable during transmission.

Figure 24.6 Basic login form.

In practice, INTEGRAL and CONFIDENTIAL usually both map to SSL transmission of the data.

The <login-config> element allows the authentication method to be specified by the <auth-method> element and the <realm-name> to be specified. The authentication method can be one of BASIC, FORM, DIGEST and CLIENT (discussed in the next section). In the case of a basic form, a simple login form similar to that presented in Figure 24.6 is displayed. This is an auto-generated form that uses a standard layout. The realm name is the name used when presenting the auto-generated login form to the user.

24.3.3 Four Types of Authentication

As has previously been mentioned there are four types of authentication method available when using container-managed security as specified by version 2.3 of the Servlet Specification. These are basic authentication, digest authentication, HTTPS client authentication and form-based authentication. Each of these will be discussed in more detail below.

- **Basic authentication** relies on the Web browser to generate a login form for the user when requested by the Web container. The user then enters their user id and password into a simple dialog box that is only customizable via the realm name. An example of the type of dialog generated by IE 5.5 is presented in Figure 24.6. No encryption is used for the user id or password, but it can be combined with the <user-data-constraint> element of the security constraint to use SSL.
- **Digest authentication** is essentially the same as basic authentication except that the password is encrypted before transmission. This encryption is performed using a hashing algorithm such as MD5. This approach is more secure than basic authentication, as the password is not sent in plain text form. However, it is a weak form of encryption.
- **HTTPS client authentication** relies on the use of public key certificates and HTTPS to authenticate client systems. This approach is most appropriate in business-to-business (B2B) systems. Using this approach the client and server must both prove who they are by using a digital certificate. The subsequent communication of information is then performed using

HTTPS. In this approach there is not even any need for a login screen as such, as the login information is sent automatically.

- **Form-based authentication** is similar to basic authentication. The difference is that it allows developers to define their own login and error forms.

We have already seen an example of basic authentication; therefore we will now have a look at an example of form-based authentication.

Figure 24.7 illustrates a `web.xml` deployment descriptor configured to use form-based authentication for the `webshop` Web application. This is done inside the `<login-config>` element using the `<auth-method>` element. If this element is used then a second element must also be provided that defines the login and error page forms. This is the `<form-login-config>` element. For example:

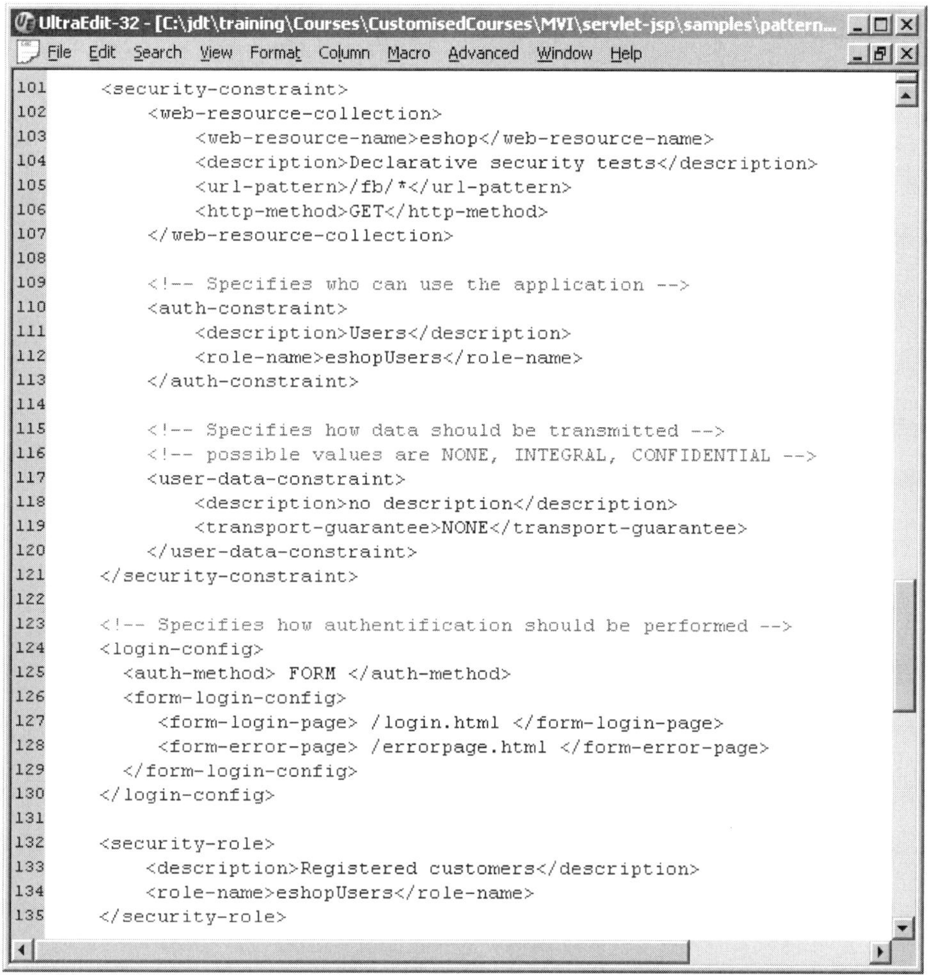

UltraEdit-32 - [C:\jdt\training\Courses\CustomisedCourses\MVI\servlet-jsp\samples\pattern...

File Edit Search View Format Column Macro Advanced Window Help

```
    <security-constraint>
        <web-resource-collection>
            <web-resource-name>eshop</web-resource-name>
            <description>Declarative security tests</description>
            <url-pattern>/fb/*</url-pattern>
            <http-method>GET</http-method>
        </web-resource-collection>

        <!-- Specifies who can use the application -->
        <auth-constraint>
            <description>Users</description>
            <role-name>eshopUsers</role-name>
        </auth-constraint>

        <!-- Specifies how data should be transmitted -->
        <!-- possible values are NONE, INTEGRAL, CONFIDENTIAL -->
        <user-data-constraint>
            <description>no description</description>
            <transport-guarantee>NONE</transport-guarantee>
        </user-data-constraint>
    </security-constraint>

    <!-- Specifies how authentification should be performed -->
    <login-config>
      <auth-method> FORM </auth-method>
      <form-login-config>
         <form-login-page> /login.html </form-login-page>
         <form-error-page> /errorpage.html </form-error-page>
      </form-login-config>
    </login-config>

    <security-role>
        <description>Registered customers</description>
        <role-name>eshopUsers</role-name>
    </security-role>
```

Figure 24.7 Using form-based authentication.

```
<auth-method> FORM </auth-method>
<form-login-config>
  <form-login-page> /login.html </form-login-page>
  <form-error-page> /errorpage.html </form-error-page>
</form-login-config>
```

In this example the login page is provided by the file `login.html` and the error page by the file `errorpage.html`. Note that both could be HTML pages or both could be servlets or JSPs.

Although there are no constraints on the format of either page, the form used to submit the login details does have some constraints specified in the Servlet 2.3 specification. These are that:

- The user id must be defined as a field of type `text` and called `j-username`.
- The password must be defined as a field of type `password` and be called `j-password`.
- The action associated with the form must be `j_security_check`. In fact, `j_security_check` is a resource within the Web container that implements the authentication. This is illustrated in Figure 24.8.

```
<form method="POST" action="j_security_check">
<center>
<table border=0>
   <tr>
      <td colspan=2>
         <p align="center">
            <img SRC="/eshop/jdt.gif">
            <p>
            <h1>Free Books on the Net</h1>
            Welcome to Free Books! <p> please enter name and login
      </td>
   </tr>
   <tr><td>
         <p align="right"><b>Name:</b>
      </td>
      <td>
         <p><input type="text" name="j_username" value="" size=15>
      </td>
   </tr>
   <tr><td>
         <p align="right"><b>Password:</b>
      </td>
      <td>
         <p><input type="password" name="j_password" value="" size=15>
      </td>
   </tr>
   <tr>
```

Figure 24.8 Part of the login form in the `login.html` Web page.

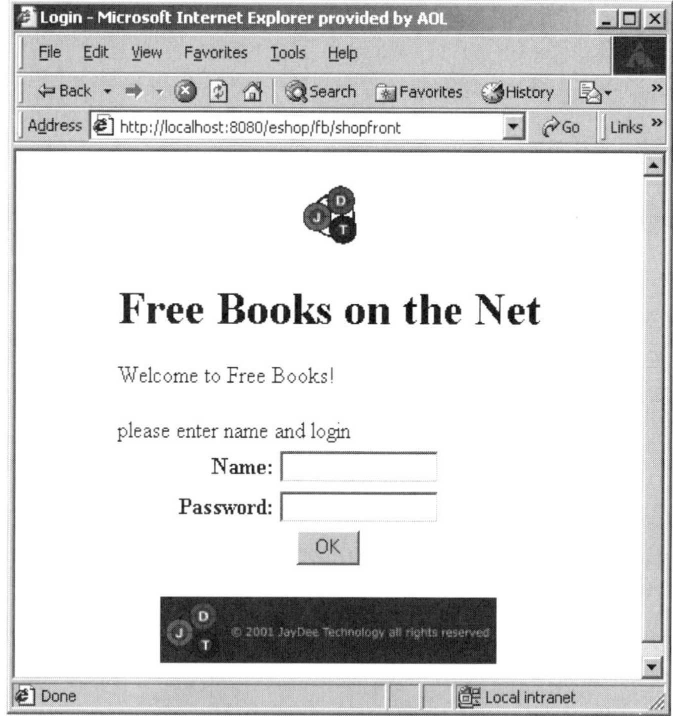

Figure 24.9 The custom login page.

The result of accessing the URL protected by this login screen is presented in Figure 24.9.

For reference, the result of incorrectly entering a user id or password is that `errorpage.html` is presented. This is presented in Figure 24.10.

24.4 Programmatic Security

It is also possible to provide addition programmatic security to a Web application. For example, inside a Web application it might be useful to determine what roles a user can play and to generate a menu based on those roles. For example, if a user does not have authority to modify specific data then do not give the user that option on a particular Web page. This sort of fine-grained programmatic security can be achieved using four methods provided by the `HttpServletRequest` interface. These methods are listed in Table 24.1. They are supported by the constants defined in the interface which are presented in Table 24.2.

As an example of actually using this feature within a JSP, consider Figure 24.11. In this example, the two input options `NEW` and `EDIT` will only be added to the form that will be

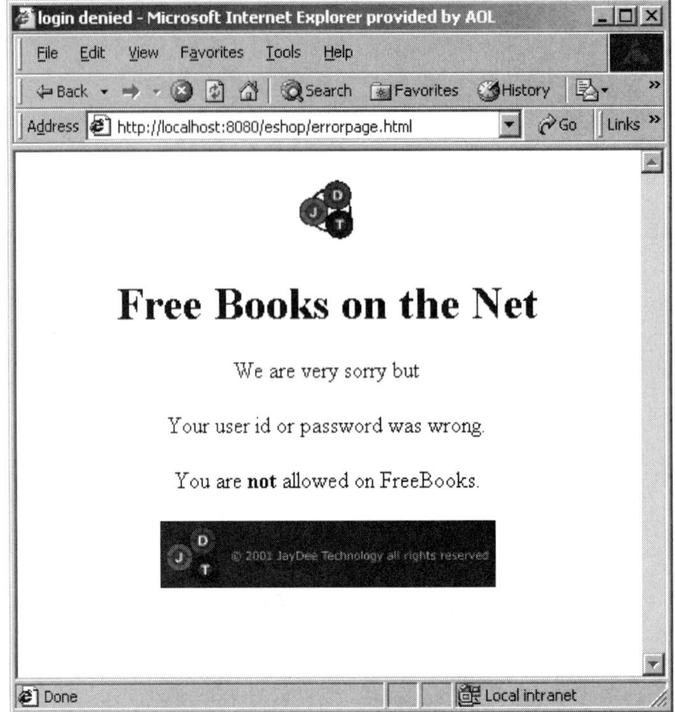

Figure 24.10 A sample error login page.

Table 24.1 Security methods on the `HttpServletRequest` interface.

`String`	**`getAuthType()`** Returns the name of the authentication scheme used to protect the servlet
`String`	**`getRemoteUser()`** Returns the login of the user making this request, if the user has been authenticated, or `null` if the user has not been authenticated
`Principal`	**`getUserPrincipal()`** Returns a `java.security.Principal` object containing the name of the current authenticated user
`boolean`	**`isUserInRole(String role)`** Returns a boolean indicating whether the authenticated user is included in the specified logical "role"

Table 24.2 Constants defined on the `HttpServletRequest` interface.

`static String`	**`BASIC_AUTH`** String identifier for Basic authentication
`static String`	**`CLIENT_CERT_AUTH`** String identifier for Basic authentication
`static String`	**`DIGEST_AUTH`** String identifier for Basic authentication
`static String`	**`FORM_AUTH`** String identifier for Basic authentication

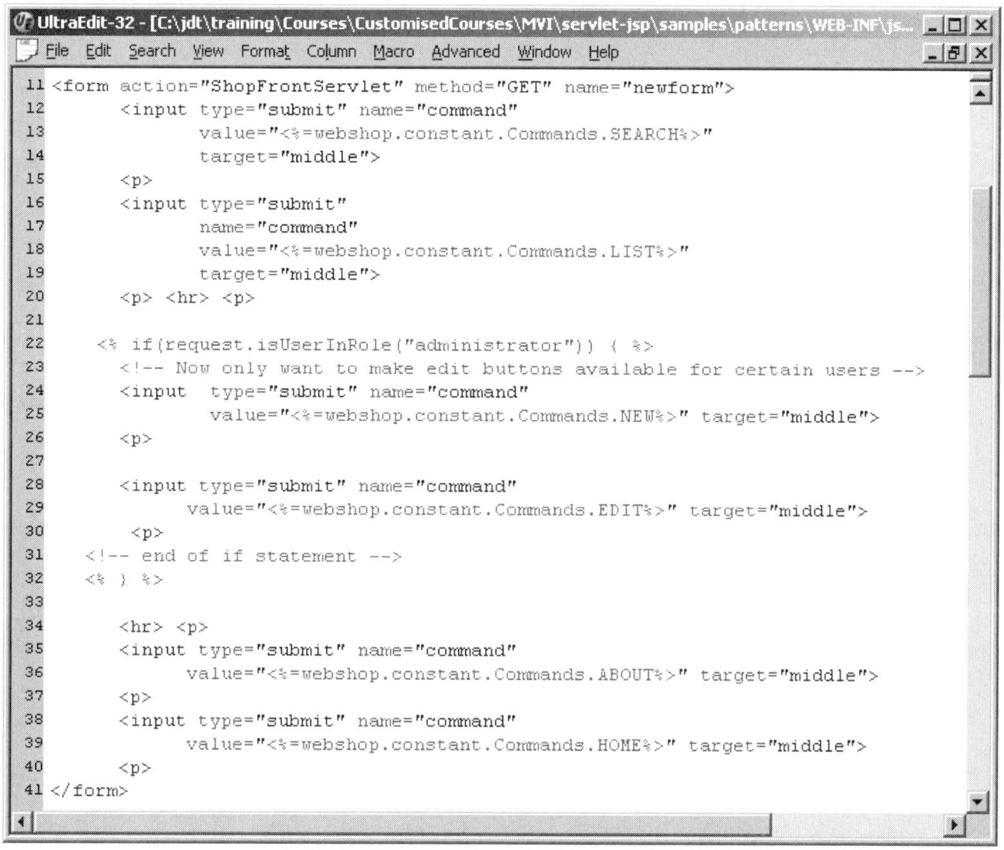

UltraEdit-32 - [C:\jdt\training\Courses\CustomisedCourses\MVI\servlet-jsp\samples\patterns\WEB-INF\js...

File Edit Search View Format Column Macro Advanced Window Help

```
<form action="ShopFrontServlet" method="GET" name="newform">
      <input type="submit" name="command"
             value="<%=webshop.constant.Commands.SEARCH%>"
             target="middle">
      <p>
      <input type="submit"
             name="command"
             value="<%=webshop.constant.Commands.LIST%>"
             target="middle">
      <p> <hr> <p>

    <% if(request.isUserInRole("administrator")) { %>
      <!-- Now only want to make edit buttons available for certain users -->
      <input  type="submit" name="command"
              value="<%=webshop.constant.Commands.NEW%>" target="middle">
      <p>

      <input type="submit" name="command"
            value="<%=webshop.constant.Commands.EDIT%>" target="middle">
       <p>
   <!-- end of if statement -->
   <% } %>

      <hr> <p>
      <input type="submit" name="command"
            value="<%=webshop.constant.Commands.ABOUT%>" target="middle">
      <p>
      <input type="submit" name="command"
            value="<%=webshop.constant.Commands.HOME%>" target="middle">
      <p>
</form>
```

Figure 24.11 Using programmatic security within a JSP.

displayed from this JSP if the user is in the role "`administrator`". This is tested by referencing the implicit object `request` in the JSP and calling the `isUserInRole` method on it. Thus if the user does not have the role "`administrator`" the HTML within that `if` statement will not be sent back to the client.

The partial JSP presented in Figure 24.11 actually provides the implementation for a navigation frame for a sample bookstore application. The effect of this JSP differs depending upon the role the user plays. This is illustrated in Figure 24.12.

It is worth noting that programmatic security, such as that presented in this example, is not as flexible as declarative security, as it must be defined at implementation time. If any changes are made within a servlet then that servlet will need to be recompiled. In addition, the security aspect of the system is now being intertwined with the business logic once again – avoiding this was of course one of the motivations behind creating a container-managed security architecture!

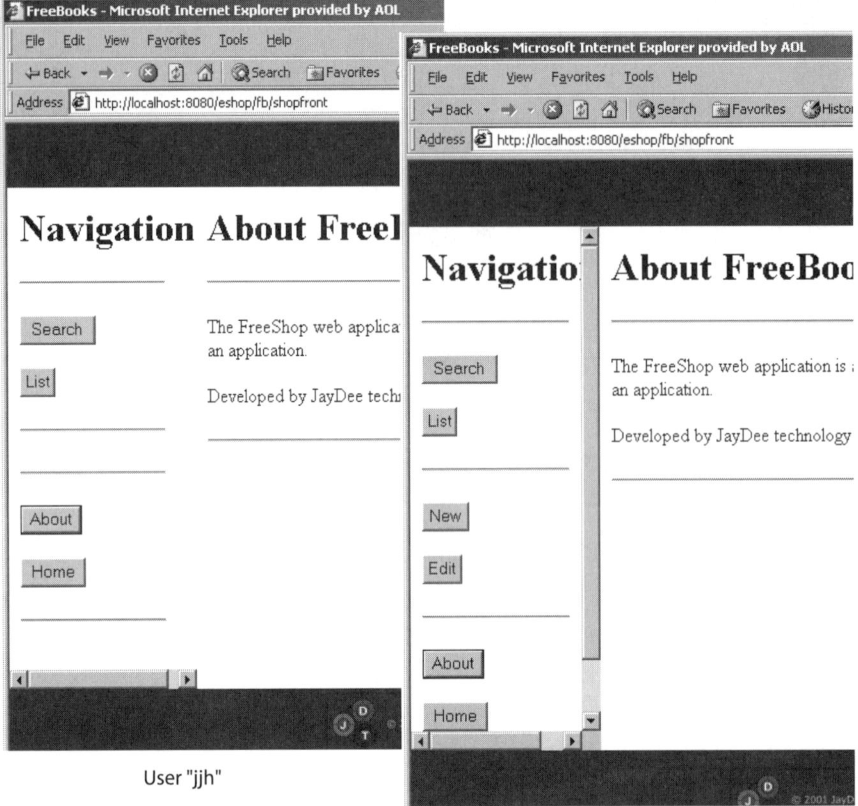

User "jjh"

User "dec" (includes role as an administrator)

Figure 24.12 Programmatically determining user roles.

24.5 JSP Configuration

A Web application can include general JSP configuration information in its `web.xml`. The information is described through the `jsp-config` element and its sub-elements.

The `jsp-config` element is a sub-element of `web-app` that is used to provide global configuration information for the JSP files in a Web application. A `jsp-config` has two sub-elements: `taglib` and `jsp-property-group`, defining the `taglib` mapping and groups of JSP files respectively.

A JSP property group is a collection of properties that apply to a set of JSP files. These properties are defined in one or more `jsp-property-group` elements in the Web application deployment descriptor. All the properties correspond to page directives.

A JSP property group is defined through one or more URL patterns; all the properties in the group apply to the resources in the Web application that match any of the URL patterns.

There is an implicit property: that of being a JSP file. There is no mechanism to indicate that a resource is *not* a JSP file; that means that all `.jsp` resources are JSP files, unless overridden by the servlet mappings.

If a resource matches URL patterns in more than one group, the pattern that is most specific (following the same rules as in the servlet specification) applies.

The properties that can currently be described in a `jsp-property-group` include:

- Enabling EL evaluation
- Enabling scripting elements
- Indicating page encoding information
- Prelude and coda automatic includes

24.5.1 Enabling and Disabling EL Evaluation

You enable expression language evaluation for a group of JSP pages with the element `el-enabled`. Its valid values are `true` and `false`. If `true`, EL expressions are evaluated when they appear in template text or action attributes. If `false`, EL expressions are ignored by the container.

For example, the following fragment defines a group that activates EL evaluation for all JSP pages having the `.jsp` extension in the directory template:

```
<jsp-property-group>
  <url-pattern>/template/*.jsp</url-pattern>
  <el-enabled>true</el-enabled>
</jsp-property-group>
```

24.5.2 Enabling and Disabling Scripting

You enable scripting for a group of JSP pages with the element `scripting-enabled`. This element defines whether scripting elements are enabled (`true`) or disabled (`false`) for this property group. When scripting is disabled, scriptlets, scripting expressions and declarations will produce a translation error if present in any of the pages in the property group. Its valid values are `true` and `false`.

For example, the following fragment defines a group that disables scripting elements for all JSP pages delivered using the `.xml` extension:

```
<jsp-property-group>
  <url-pattern>*.xml</url-pattern>
  <scripting-enabled>false</scripting-enabled>
</jsp-property-group>
```

You can also enable and disable scripting on a per page basis.

24.5.3 Declaring Page Encodings

You set the page encoding of a group of JSP pages with the element `page-encoding`. Valid values are those of the `pageEncoding` attribute of the page directive. It is a translation-time error to define the page encoding of a JSP page through one value in the JSP configuration element and then give it a different value in a pageEncoding directive, but it is legal to give it the same value.

For example, the following fragment defines a group that explicitly assigns the page encoding ISO-8859-1 to all JSP pages having the .jsp extension:

```
<jsp-property-group>
  <url-pattern>*.jsp</url-pattern>
  <page-encoding>ISO-8859-1</page-encoding>
</jsp-property-group>
```

24.5.4 Defining Implicit Includes

You can implicitly include preludes and codas for a group of JSP pages with the include-prelude and include-coda elements. Their values are context-relative paths that must correspond to elements in the Web application. When the elements are present, the given paths are automatically included (as in an include directive) at the beginning and end of each JSP page in the jsp-property-group respectively. When there is more than one include-prelude or include-coda element in a group, they are included in the order they appear. When more than one jsp-property-group applies to a JSP page, the corresponding elements will be processed in the same order as they appear in the JSP configuration section.

For example, Duke's Bookstore specifies the files /template/prelude.jspf and /template/coda.jspf to include the banner and other boilerplate in each screen. The following fragment defines the group used in the Duke's Bookstore example. It indicates that all JSP pages have /template/prelude.jspf at the beginning and /template/coda.jspf at the end.

```
<jsp-property-group>
  <url-pattern>/*.jsp</url-pattern>
  <include-prelude>/template/prelude.jspf</include-prelude>
  <include-coda>/template/coda.jspf</include-coda>
</jsp-property-group>
```

Because preludes and codas can only put the included code at the beginning and end of each file, this approach has its limitations for reuse.

24.6 Conclusion

The security features added to the servlet specification in version 2.3 are a major addition to the Java Web application builder's armoury. As more Web container vendors add this support to their systems we will see this approach being used more and more by developers. Tomcat 4 provides an excellent reference implementation for these features that are likely to be mirrored in other containers.

24.7 Online Reference

The JavaServer Pages 2.0 Specification: `http://www.jcp.org/aboutJava/communityprocess/first/jsr152/index.html`.

Chapter 25

Deployment Configuration

25.1 Introduction

There are a large number of options available to the deployer of a Web application that will customize various aspects of the application. These are all available as optional elements in the deployment descriptor file (`web.xml`). In this chapter we will focus on the most important Web application configuration options, which include:

- Context initialization parameters which specify parameters used to initialize the whole Web application.
- Servlet initialization parameters that are used to provide initialization data for individual servlets.
- Servlet loading, which is used to indicate when a servlet should be loaded and what order to load it in (if an order is significant).
- Session configuration used to define the session timeout interval.
- Welcome and error pages used to provide default Web pages for the Web application.
- MIME mappings that can be used to specify MIME types for documents in the Web application.
- Distributable applications: these are used to indicate whether a Web application can be distributed over multiple (cooperating) Web containers or not.

All these options are part of Servlet Specification 2.3, and thus any 2.3-compliant Web container should support them all. The chapter concludes by discussing some aspects of the deployment descriptor itself.

25.2 Context Initialization

If you need to, you can define a set of constants that will be available to the whole Web application. These constants are referred to as context initialization parameters. For example, you could

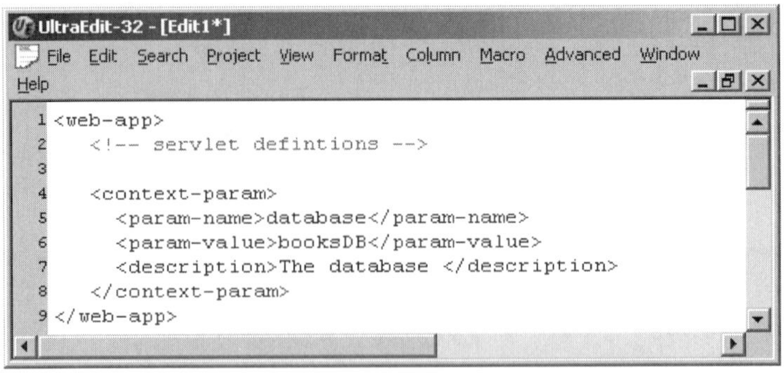

UltraEdit-32 - [Edit1*]

File Edit Search Project View Format Column Macro Advanced Window Help

```
<web-app>
   <!-- servlet defintions -->

   <context-param>
     <param-name>database</param-name>
     <param-value>booksDB</param-value>
     <description>The database </description>
   </context-param>
</web-app>
```

Figure 25.1 Defining context initialization parameters.

define a constant to declare the name of a database that all elements of the Web application should use (see Figure 25.1 for an example of doing this). It would also be possible to use context parameters to define the database driver to use, to specify global maximum and minimum values, etc.

Such context parameters are defined in the `web.xml` deployment descriptor within the `<context-param>` element. For each parameter to be defined, a `<param-name>` and a `<param-value>` must be provided. Optionally a description of the parameter can also be provided. An example context parameter is illustrated in Figure 25.1. Any Web application can have zero or more `<context-param>` elements.

Within the Web application it is possible to access the context parameter constants from the `ServletContext` interface. This interface provides two methods for this:

- `getInitParameterNames()`, which returns an enumeration of strings that represent the names of the context initialization parameters.
- `getInitParameter()`, which returns a `String` containing the value of the named context-wide initialization parameter, or null if the parameter does not exist.

Note that these constants are available to all servlets sharing the same context, that is all servlets in same Web application. The `ServletContext` is available using the `getServletContext()` method on the `HttpServlet` class (and thus inherited by all HTTP servlets).

25.3 Servlet Initialization

It is possible to set initial parameters for individual servlets rather than whole Web applications. This is done within the `<servlet>` element via the `<init-param>` element as illustrated in Figure 25.2. The format is that each servlet initialization parameter has a name and a value (just like the context parameters) and an optional description. Any servlet can have zero or more `<init-param>` tags.

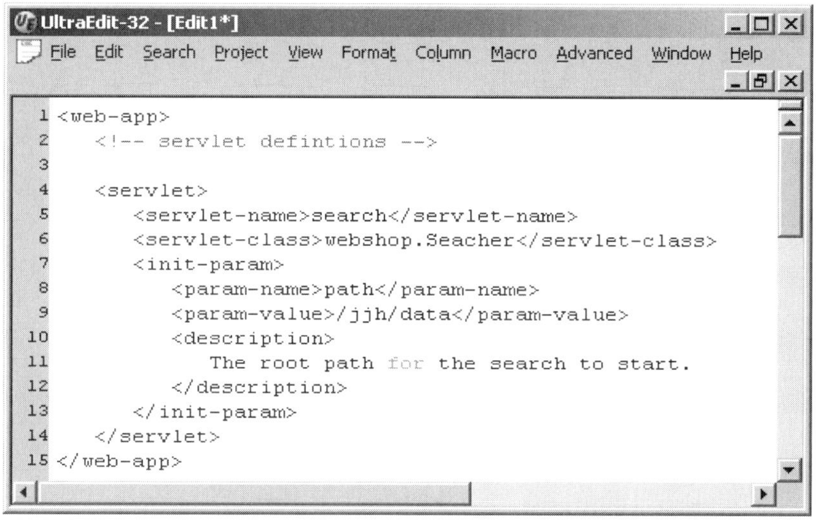

```
<web-app>
   <!-- servlet defintions -->

   <servlet>
      <servlet-name>search</servlet-name>
      <servlet-class>webshop.Seacher</servlet-class>
      <init-param>
         <param-name>path</param-name>
         <param-value>/jjh/data</param-value>
         <description>
            The root path for the search to start.
         </description>
      </init-param>
   </servlet>
</web-app>
```

Figure 25.2 Defining servlet initialization parameters.

To access the servlet initialization parameters from within the relevant servlet, the `ServletConfig` object is used (note that this is the `ServletConfig` object and not the `ServletContext` object). The `ServletConfig` object is accessible directly from within any servlet using the `getServletConfig()` method inherited from the servlet class by the `HttpServlet` class. The `ServletConfig` interface defines the following two methods to allow the developer to access any servlet initialization constants:

- `getInitParameter`, which returns a `String` containing the value of the named initialization parameter, or null if the parameter does not exist.
- `getInitParameterNames()`, which returns the names of the servlet's initialization parameters as an `Enumeration` of `String` objects, or an empty `Enumeration` if the servlet has no initialization parameters.

25.4 Servlet Loading

Normally servlets are loaded on demand by the Web container (such as Tomcat). However, it is possible to force the Web container to load servlets at startup time. It is also possible to impose an order on the loading of the servlets (should this be important). Both of these are done using the `<load-on-startup>` tag. This tag is specified within the `<Servlet>` element, as illustrated in Figure 25.3. The tag takes an (optional) integer that indicates the load order. When the tag is present for a servlet the Web container will load it at startup time. If the optional integer is present it will order the servlet loading based on this integer. If two servlets are found with the same integer, then those servlets can be loaded in any order.

```
<web-app>
   <!-- servlet definitions -->

   <servlet>
     <servlet-name>search</servlet-name>
     <servlet-class>webshop.Searcher</servlet-class>
     <load-on-startup>1</load-on-startup>
   </servlet>
</web-app>
```

Figure 25.3 Specifying the order of servlet loading at Web container startup.

25.5 Session Configuration

In general we do not want a user's session object to last forever – there needs to be some form of timeout – after a period of client inactivity. There are in fact two ways in which the session timeout for an `HttpSession` object can be specified. One is programmatically within the Web application and the other is declaratively in the deployment descriptor file.

Programmatically we can set the timeout for a session using the `setMaxInactiveInterval` method on the `HttpSession` object. The integer parameter passed to this method sets the maximum interval between client activity in terms of seconds.

Declaratively we can set the timeout interval for a session in the deployment descriptor using the `<session-config>` element as illustrated in Figure 25.4. This is done using the inner `<session-timeout>` element. Note that the `<session-timeout>` element takes the interval in terms of minutes. Thus the `HttpSession` and the `<session-timeout>` element are not consistent – one takes seconds and the other minutes!

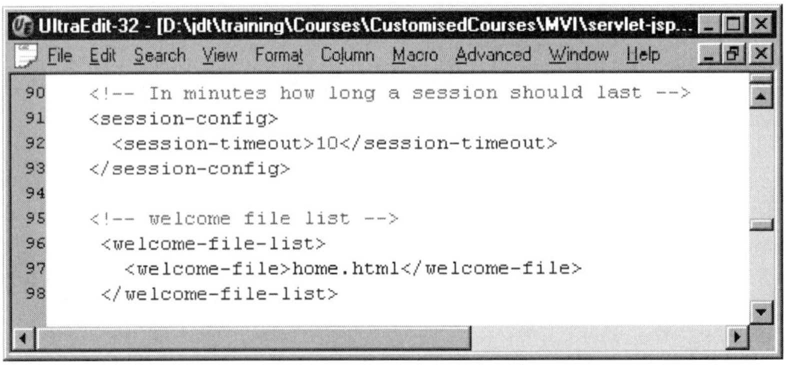

```
   <!-- In minutes how long a session should last -->
   <session-config>
     <session-timeout>10</session-timeout>
   </session-config>

   <!-- welcome file list -->
    <welcome-file-list>
      <welcome-file>home.html</welcome-file>
    </welcome-file-list>
```

Figure 25.4 Defining a 10 minute timeout for all sessions in this Web application.

Whichever approach is used, the Web container will automatically invalidate the session if the elapsed time between consecutive requests from a client is greater than the specified timeout interval.

25.6 Welcome Pages

Figure 25.4 also illustrates how a welcome file can be declared for an application. The actual default home page for a Web application is of course `index.html`. However, if you do not provide an `index.html` file and the user enters a URL that points to the whole Web application, the user will be presented with a listing of the contents of the document base of the Web application. For example, if users enter `http://localhost:8080/bookstore` then they will either get the contents of the file `index.html` or a listing of the directory if no index file is present. However, if a welcome page has been defined then this will be used instead.

It is also possible to provide a list of welcome pages rather than a single welcome page. The Web container will then supply the first that it finds. The welcome pages can be any Web resource including HTML pages and JSP pages. The format of the element is `<welcome-file-list>` which can contain one or more `<welcome-file>` elements.

25.7 Error Pages

Even in the best designed Web application errors and exceptions can occur (which can be beyond the control of the Web application – such as the failure of the intranet etc.). In many cases the Web application can be implemented in such a way as to handle the problem directly and produce a sensible response to send back to the user.

However, in some cases we may not want the Web application Java code to handle the exception. Rather, we want the Java code to send an error back to the Web container and request that it handle it – this may be because the user has entered some incorrect information (such as an invalid URL) and we wish the Web application to handle this in a standard manner. Such errors can be generated in two ways, either via normal Java exceptions or programmatically via the `sendError` method on the `HttpServletResponse` object.

If a servlet throws an exception and this exception is not handled by the Web application then the exception will make its way back to the Web container. If the Web container has not been configured to handle the exception then the exception will be sent back to the user as a formatted Web page (you may have seen this yourself when developing your own Web applications!). However, error codes can also be used to generate errors. This can be done using the `sendError(int statusCode)` and `sendError(int statusCode, String message)` methods defined by the `HttpServletResponse` interface:

- `sendError(int sc)` sends an error response to the client using the specified status code and clearing the buffer.

- `sendError(int sc, java.lang.String msg)` sends an error response to the client using the specified status clearing the buffer and including the provided additional message.

Any error code can be sent back, such as 403 for Forbidden Access and 404 for Not Found. These codes are all defined on the `HttpServletResponse` interface; for example:

`static int`	**SC_NOT_FOUND** Status code (404) indicating that the requested resource is not available
`static int`	**SC_UNAUTHORIZED** Status code (401) indicating that the request requires HTTP authentication

Of course, the result of sending an error code back, or allowing an exception to propagate to the user, may or may not be what is required. The Servlet 2.3 specification therefore allows error pages to be defined in the deployment descriptor file. These error pages can be returned by the Web container in response to various error codes and exceptions. That is, instead of merely returning an exception, the Web container can instead return a Web page that provides a more palatable explanation of the problem for the user.

These errors and exceptions are handled by the Web container when the deployment descriptor contains one or more `<error-page>` elements. An `<error-page>` element allows the deployer to define the Web page to return when either an exception occurs or an error code is generated. This is done using two inner elements: `<exception-type>` or `<error-code >` and `<location>`. This is illustrated in Figure 25.5.

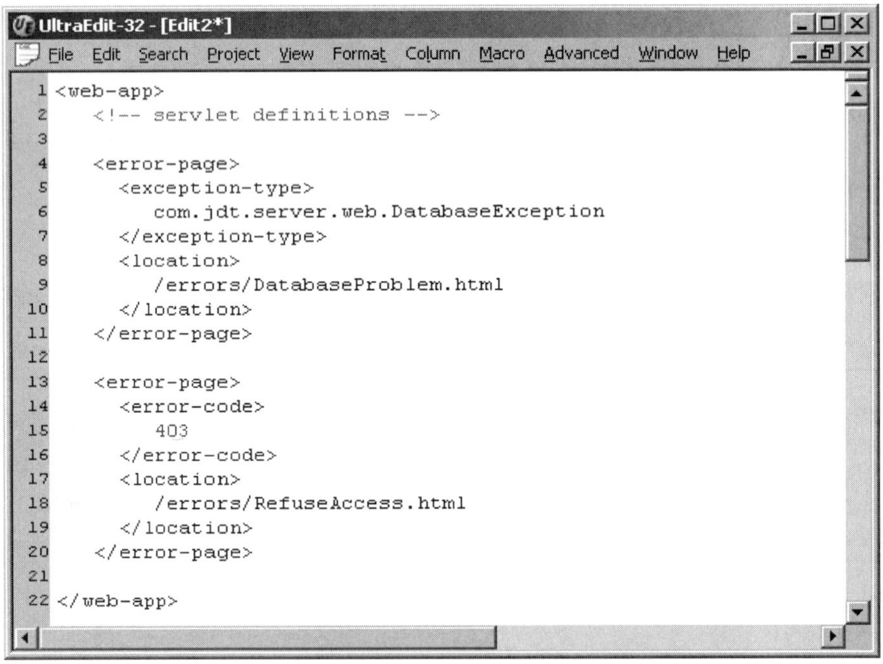

UltraEdit-32 - [Edit2*]

File Edit Search Project View Format Column Macro Advanced Window Help

```
<web-app>
   <!-- servlet definitions -->

   <error-page>
     <exception-type>
        com.jdt.server.web.DatabaseException
     </exception-type>
     <location>
        /errors/DatabaseProblem.html
     </location>
   </error-page>

   <error-page>
     <error-code>
        403
     </error-code>
     <location>
        /errors/RefuseAccess.html
     </location>
   </error-page>

</web-app>
```

Figure 25.5 Defining error pages.

Note that it is possible to associated different error pages with different error code and exceptions. Thus you are able to tailor your output depending on what error occurs. This therefore provides for graceful handling of exceptions.

25.8 MIME Mappings

As you are probably aware, the HTTP protocol uses MIME to describe the content of a HTTP response. MIME actually stands for Multipurpose Internet Mail Extensions, although it is used far more widely than just email. For example, within a servlet it is necessary to specify the content type of the response being sent back (for example `text/html` or `text/svg`). These content types are in fact MIME types. A MIME type is a string of the form `type/sub-type`. Examples of other commonly used MIME types are `text/plain`, `text/txt` and `image/gif`.

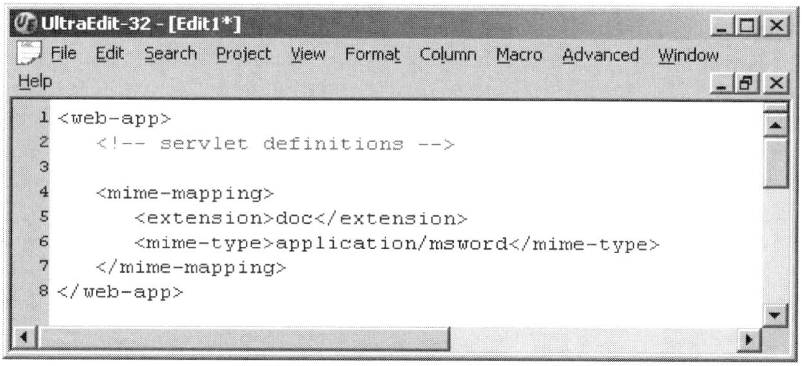

UltraEdit-32 - [Edit1*]

File Edit Search Project View Format Column Macro Advanced Window Help

```
<web-app>
   <!-- servlet definitions -->

   <mime-mapping>
      <extension>doc</extension>
      <mime-type>application/msword</mime-type>
   </mime-mapping>
</web-app>
```

Figure 25.6 Setting up a MIME mapping.

If your Web application is serving up a custom document type it may be useful to associate a particular MIME type with that type of extension. In this way the Web container and the receiving Web browser will know what type of application to associate with this document. For example, if our server is supplying Word documents directly on demand we could add the MIME mapping illustrated in Figure 25.6 to our deployment descriptor. In this way, whenever a `*.doc` document was served up the MIME type `application/msword` would be automatically associated with it.

The XML in the deployment descriptor for defining a MIME mapping is the `<mime-mapping>` element that contains an `<extension>` element and a `<mime-type>` element. The deployment descriptor file can contain zero or more MIME mappings.

Note that most browsers and Web containers will try to determine the MIME type automatically based on the extension of the document, and the `.doc` extension is normally already mapped.

25.9 Distributable Applications

In order to maximize performance and provide scalability, some Web containers can operate in a distributed manner. That is, the Web container can be replicated over a number of host machines. This Web container farm collectively handles request coming to the Web site. In this scenario one request may be handled by the Web container on one machine, while the next request from the same client may be handled by a different Web container on another machine. This is particularly useful for load balancing and reliability. In these scenarios the Web application must operate across multiple Web containers on multiple machines. This is illustrated in Figure 25.7.

However, it may not always be desirable for a Web application to operate in such an environment. It is therefore possible to indicate whether a Web container should be allowed to distribute the Web application or not. This is specified by including the `<distributable />` element in the deployment descriptor. If this entry is present then the application is distributable. For example:

```
<web-app>
  ...
  <distributable />
  ...
</web-app>
```

Note that for a Web application to be distributable, any objects stored in the `HttpSession` must be serializable, as the session object may be serialized from one machine to another.

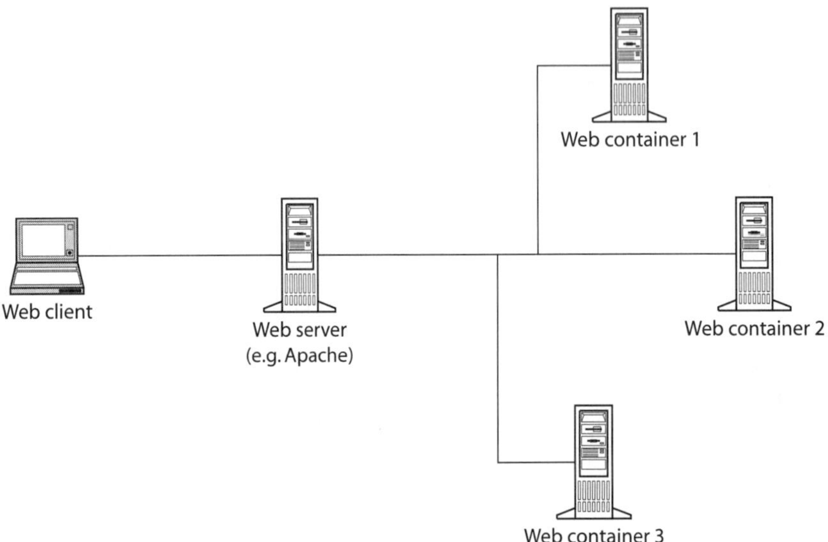

Figure 25.7 Distributed Web container.

25.10 Deployment Descriptor in J2EE 1.3

The Java Servlet Specification 2.3 specifies that the DTD that defines the deployment descriptor for a 2.3-compliant web.xml file is:

```
<!DOCTYPE web-app
  PUBLIC "-//Sun Microsystems, Inc.//DTD Web Application 2.3//EN"
  "http://java.sun.com/dtd/web-app_2_3.dtd">
```

If you wish you can examine this DTD in a Web browser. The url for the DTD is http://java.sun.com/dtd/web-app_2_3.dtd (as indicated above). An example of doing exactly this is presented in Figure 25.8. You can also read the servlet specification itself as this contains information on the deployment descriptor as well (see Chapter 13).

It is also important to follow the ensure that the order of XML elements defined in the deployment descriptor file (web.xml) is correct. If the order is wrong the Web container may reject the web.xml file. For example, this is true of Tomcat 4.0.1 (but was not true of Tomcat 3.*).

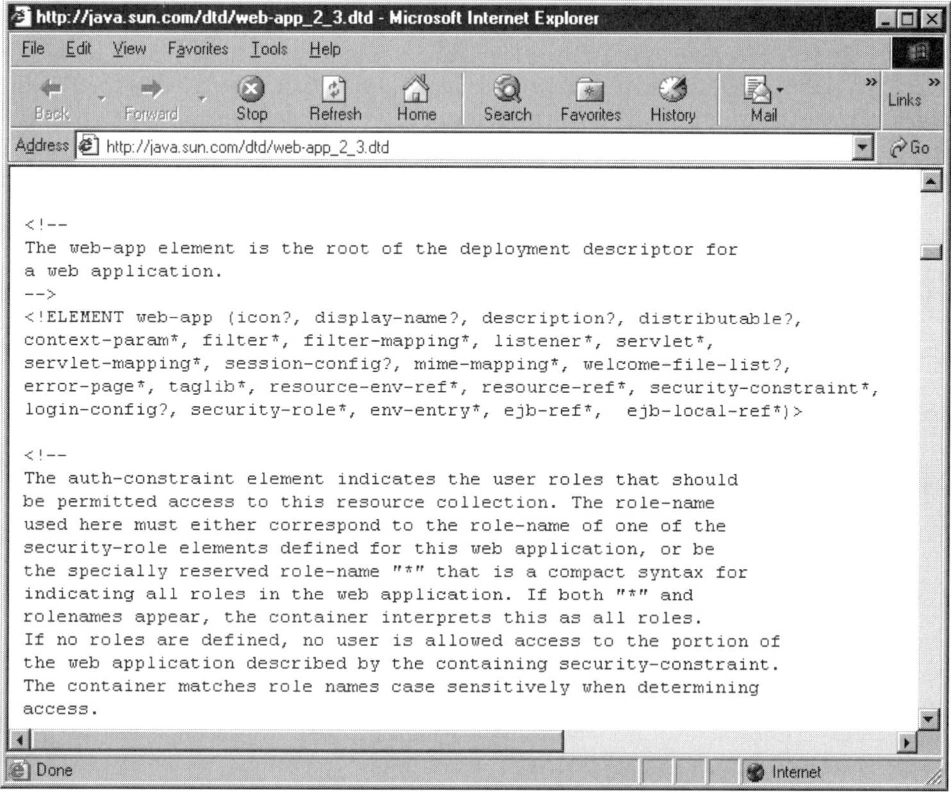

Figure 25.8 Examining the Servlet 2.3 deployment descriptor DTD in IE 6.0.

The order of the XML elements in the `web.xml` file as defined by the Servlet 2.3 specification DTD is:

- `icon?,display-name?,description?,distributable?`
- `context-param*`
- `filter*,filter-mapping*`
- `listener*`
- `servlet*,servlet-mapping*`
- `session-config?,mime-mapping*`
- `welcome-file-list?,error-page*,taglib*`
- `security-constraint*,login-config?,security-role*`
- `env-entry*,ejb-ref*,ejb-local-ref*`

where * indicates zero or more entries and ? indicates that the entry must appear once or not at all.

25.11 Deploying J2EE Applications in J2SE 1.4

Prior to the J2EE 1.4 specifications, each deployment descriptor had to be valid with respect to a specific DTD that describes the deployment descriptor. However, since the J2EE 1.4 specification, each specification requires its deployment descriptor be validated with respect to an XML schema. XML schemas are similar to DTDs in that they specify what an XML file should look like. However, they go further than DTDs in restricting the content of elements within the XML file. Note that deployment descriptors defined against previous DTDs are still supported, and thus it is possible to define a deployment description using the Servlet 2.2 or 2.3 DTD, so this should still be supported.

All J2EE deployment descriptor schemas share the namespace `http://java.sun.com/xml/ns/j2ee/`. Each schema document contains a version attribute that contains the version of the specification. For example, the XML schema document for the servlet specification contains the version attribute value "2.4", pertaining to the specific version of the specification as well as the schema document itself.

Each J2EE XML schema document's file name contains the specific version of the related specification. This is introduced for convenience to locate specific versions of the schema documents. However, deployment descriptor instances are not required to refer to a specific file. Instead, an instance must specify the version of the corresponding specification by using a version attribute. For example, connector deployment descriptor instances that must be processed with the Connector 1.5 version must indicate the version within the version attribute of the instance document, for example "1.5". The deployment descriptor processors use the version information to choose the appropriate version of the schema document(s) to process the deployment descriptor instances.

A specific version of the J2EE specification contains a set of deployment descriptor schemas to constitute the J2EE schema. The common definitions are contained in the `j2ee_<version>.xsd` document that may be included by several J2EE deployment descriptor schemas.

Some of the schemas that you will be using are presented below:

- web-jsptaglibrary_2_0.xsd: JSP Taglibrary Deployment Descriptor Schema
- ejb-jar_2_1.xsd: Enterprise JavaBeansTM Deployment Descriptor Schema
- web-app_2_4.xsd: Servlet Deployment Descriptor Schema
- jsp_2_0.xsd: JavaServer PagesTM Deployment Descriptor Schema
- j2ee_1_4.xsd: J2EE 1.4 definitions file that contains common schema components
- application_1_4.xsd: application schema
- http://www.w3.org/2001/xml.xsd: the J2EE schemas use some common definitions provided and published by W3C

For a J2EE 1.4 application the XML prolog would be

```
<?xml version="1.0" encoding="UTF-8"?>
<web-app version="2.4"
  xmlns="http://java.sun.com/xml/ns/j2ee"
  xmlns:xsi="http://www.w3.org/2001/XMLSchema-instance"
  xsi:schemaLocation="http://java.sun.com/xml/ns/j2ee
    http://java.sun.com/xml/ns/j2ee/web-app_2_4.xsd">
```

whereas for J2EE 1.3 this would be:

```
<?xml version="1.0" encoding="ISO-8859-1"?>
<!DOCTYPE web-app
    PUBLIC "-//Sun Microsystems, Inc.//DTD Web Application 2.3//EN"
    "http://java.sun.com/dtd/web-app_2_3.dtd">
```

Although the schema is stricter about the content of the resulting XML file, for a simple web application the result is the same. The J2EE 1.3 version is presented below:

```
<?xml version="1.0" encoding="ISO-8859-1"?>
<!DOCTYPE web-app
    PUBLIC "-//Sun Microsystems, Inc.//DTD Web Application 2.3//EN"
    "http://java.sun.com/dtd/web-app_2_3.dtd">
<web-app>
  <servlet>
      <servlet-name>welcome</servlet-name>
      <servlet-class>webshop.WelcomeServlet</servlet-class>
  </servlet>
  <servlet-mapping>
      <servlet-name>welcome</servlet-name>
      <url-pattern>/enter</url-pattern>
  </servlet-mapping>
</web-app>
```

whereas the J2EE 1.4 version is:

```
<?xml version="1.0" encoding="UTF-8"?>
<web-app version="2.4"
  xmlns="http://java.sun.com/xml/ns/j2ee"
  xmlns:xsi="http://www.w3.org/2001/XMLSchema-instance"
  xsi:schemaLocation="http://java.sun.com/xml/ns/j2ee
    http://java.sun.com/xml/ns/j2ee/web-app_2_4.xsd">
<web-app>
  <servlet>
      <servlet-name>welcome</servlet-name>
      <servlet-class>webshop.WelcomeServlet</servlet-class>
  </servlet>
  <servlet-mapping>
      <servlet-name>welcome</servlet-name>
      <url-pattern>/enter</url-pattern>
  </servlet-mapping>
</web-app>
```

Chapter 26

Accessing EJBs from Servlets/JSPs

26.1 Introduction

In this chapter we will look at how elements in the presentation or Web tier can access EJBs in the business tier. This is a common requirement and is therefore worthy of consideration in its own chapter. We shall look at why such an architecture is desirable. We will then consider the features in the J2EE specification that bridge the gap between the presentation tier and the EJB tier. After this we will consider issues associated with holding references to EJBs in servlets and JSPs. We will conclude by examining a simple servlet–EJB application.

26.2 Client Access to EJBs

If you refer back to the EJB sections of this book (Chapters 12–16) you will see lots of examples of clients accessing EJBs. These clients are all Java applications. However, there is nothing to stop a non-Java application accessing an EJB, for example by using CORBA and the IIOP (Internet Inter-ORB Protocol). Nor indeed is there anything to stop the client of an EJB being a servlet or JSP that is part of a Web-based application. Indeed, this is a common approach for a multi-tiered Web application. In this scenario (illustrated in Figure 26.1) the "client" application may be considered to be the element of the application running in a browser, the servlet/JSP element of the application may be considered to be the presentation tier, the business tier is implemented as EJBs that may access a database or legacy applications. This is a full J2EE stack application.

In Figure 26.1 it is important to note that the EJBs are accessed purely through the presentation tier elements (namely the servlets and JSPs and their supporting classes). The EJBs could also be accessed directly by a Java technology client, but for Web-based applications we would not normally expect this to happen.

A useful question to consider at this point is why might you want to integrate a Web-based application with a set of EJBs? There are a number of answers to this question, including:

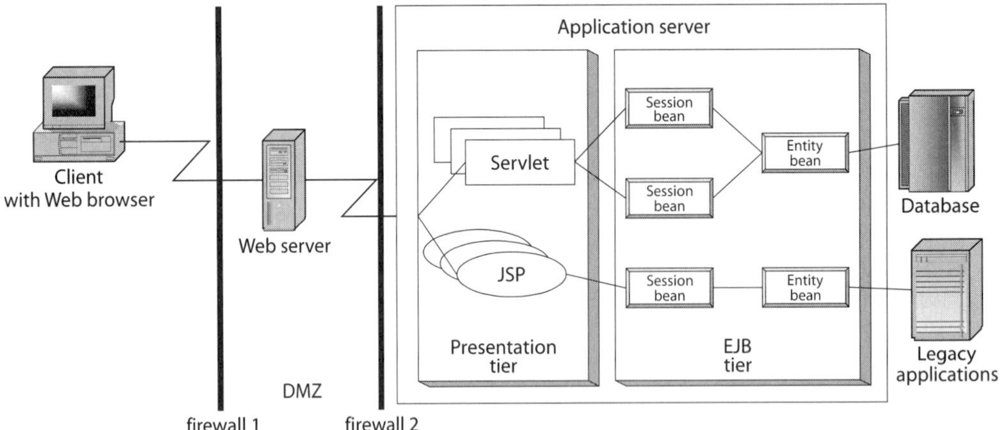

Figure 26.1 A J2EE technology application with servlets, JSPs and EJBs.

- Access to the EJBs via the Internet is enabled.
- Access to EJBs is controlled and can be limited to the servlets and JSPs only.
- The EJBS are not made available directly on the Internet, which may offer better security. For example, in Figure 26.1, they are behind a second firewall and not resident within the DMZ (Demilitarized Zone) which contains the Web server accessible from the Internet.
- Communication with the EJBs from remote clients is via HTTP and HTTPS.
- The business elements of the full application are reusable in other (possibly non-Web-based) applications.
- Transactional integrity across distributed servers is offered by the EJB tier.
- Performance optimization and load balancing is offered by the EJB tier.
- Integration with legacy systems is supported by a standardized model via the EJB tier.
- The EJB tier adds additional business logic oriented security (discussed in Chapter 28).

26.3 Accessing EJBs From a Web Application

26.3.1 The Web Archive

To access EJBs from the presentation tier (either from JSPs or servlets) there are a number of things that can be done. The first is to treat the servlet or JSP as exactly the same as any other EJB client. This makes the servlet or JSP completely separate from the EJB and requires that they use JNDI and the standard JNDI name to access the EJB.

However, the J2EE specification provides a number of improvements over this basic approach. Firstly the `web.xml` file can contain information about the EJBs that the servlet or JSPs wish to access. This local information can be linked later with actual EJBs, but buffers the presentation tier from changes in the EJB tier.

The EJB references in the `web.xml` file are defined using the `<ejb-ref>` tag. This tag is used to declare a reference to an Enterprise bean within the Web application. The tag contains six sub-elements (two of which are optional). These are `description` (optional), `ejb-ref-name`, `ejb-ref-type`, `home`, `remote` and `ejb-link` (optional). An example of such an `ejb-ref` element is presented in Figure 26.2. The meanings of the sub-elements are described below:

- `ejb-ref`: a reference to an EJB used within the presentation (Web) tier.
- `description`: an optional element used to provide a human-readable description of the EJB.
- `ejb-ref-name`: a name that the Web tier will use to look up the EJB in its own (local area) JNDI context. That is, to find the EJB name the JNDI lookup will need to reference the `java:comp/env/ejb` JNDI context.
- `ejb-ref-type`: the type of bean being reference. This can be either `Session` or `Entity` (as message-driven beans are not accessed by a home or remote interface).
- `home`: used to specify the fully qualified class name of the home interface.
- `remote`: used to specify the fully qualified class name of the remote interface.

Note that the actual bean class is not mentioned, as this is never seen by the presentation tier classes.

The `ejb-ref` element presented in Figure 26.2 represents the presentation tier view of an EJB referred to as `crfBean` (within the presentation tier). It is of type `Entity` and its `home` and `remote` interfaces are specified (the remainder of the `web.xml` file has been omitted for brevity). An equivalent `ejb-local-ref` tag can be used to refer to local EJBs, with sub-tags `local-home` and `local`.

Note that the EJB reference in `web.xml` does not directly map to an EJB JNDI name. Rather, it refers to a local name that must then be mapped to the actual EJB JNDI name. How and where this is done is server-specific. However, if we are using a JBoss–Tomcat

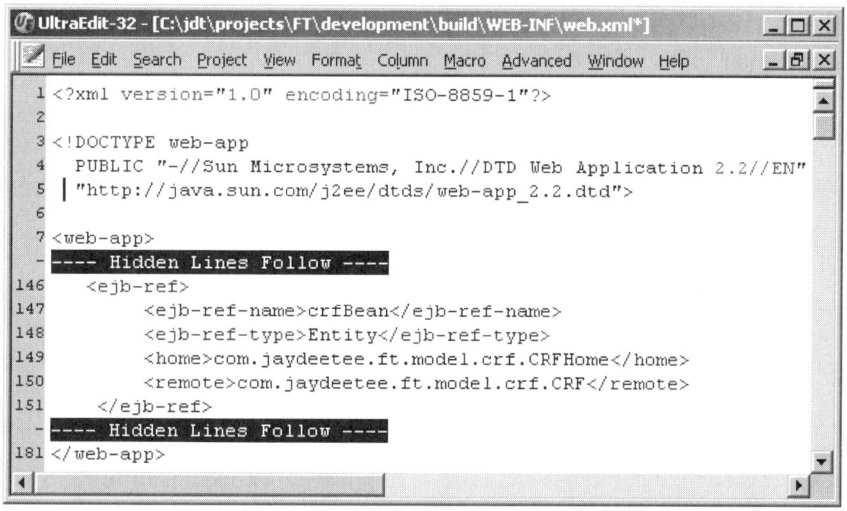

UltraEdit-32 - [C:\jdt\projects\FT\development\build\WEB-INF\web.xml*]

File Edit Search Project View Format Column Macro Advanced Window Help

```
<?xml version="1.0" encoding="ISO-8859-1"?>

<!DOCTYPE web-app
  PUBLIC "-//Sun Microsystems, Inc.//DTD Web Application 2.2//EN"
  "http://java.sun.com/j2ee/dtds/web-app_2.2.dtd">

<web-app>
---- Hidden Lines Follow ----
    <ejb-ref>
        <ejb-ref-name>crfBean</ejb-ref-name>
        <ejb-ref-type>Entity</ejb-ref-type>
        <home>com.jaydeetee.ft.model.crf.CRFHome</home>
        <remote>com.jaydeetee.ft.model.crf.CRF</remote>
    </ejb-ref>
---- Hidden Lines Follow ----
</web-app>
```

Figure 26.2 An example `ejb-ref` element in a `web.xml` file.

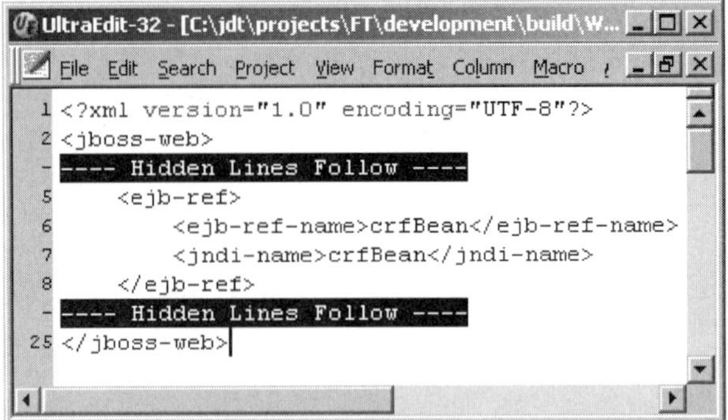

Figure 26.3 Mapping the `ejb-ref-name` to the JNDI name for an EJB.

combination to provide a complete implementation of the J2EE stack then the mapping will be done in the `jboss-web.xml` file. This file (also defined within the Web application's `WEB-INF` directory) provides the mapping from the `ejb-ref-name` to the actual JNDI name (defined for the EJB). This is illustrated in Figure 26.3.

The `jboss-web.xml` file is specific to JBoss, but other application servers (such as WebLogic) have similar structures. In the `jboss-web.xml` file the root element is `<jboss-web>`. This contains a number of elements including the `<ejb-ref>` element. This element has an `<ejb-ref-name>` element that specifies the name used for the EJB in the Web application. It also has a `<jndi-name>` element that allows the JNDI name used within the EJB tier for this EJB to be specified. If the names are the same as in this example, then no entry strictly needs to be provided (although it is still good style).

The resulting XML files and their Web application elements can now be packaged up into a Web archive (WAR) file for inclusion in an Enterprise archive. A WAR file is created using the `jar` command. For example, the following `jar` command creates a WAR file (called `ft.war`) that contains the `web.xml` and `jboss-web.xml` files from the `WEB-INF` directory, a set of HTML pages and JSPs and the classes under `com`.

```
jar cvf ft.war WEB-INF\web.xml WEB-INF\jboss-web.xml *.html *.jsp web-
inf\classes\com
```

26.3.2 The Enterprise Archive

An Enterprise archive (EAR) file is an archive file that contains all the elements required to construct a multi-tier J2EE application that exploits both EJBs and Web tier elements. Just as with a Web archive and an EJB archive there is a very specific structure defined for an Enterprise archive. The structure of an EAR file is presented in Figure 26.4.

An Enterprise archive must have a `META-INF` directory containing an `application.xml` file. This file defines the elements of the J2EE application (as opposed to its constituent elements that might be referred to as a Web application and an EJB application). The `application.xml` file declares the modules that make up this J2EE application. In the

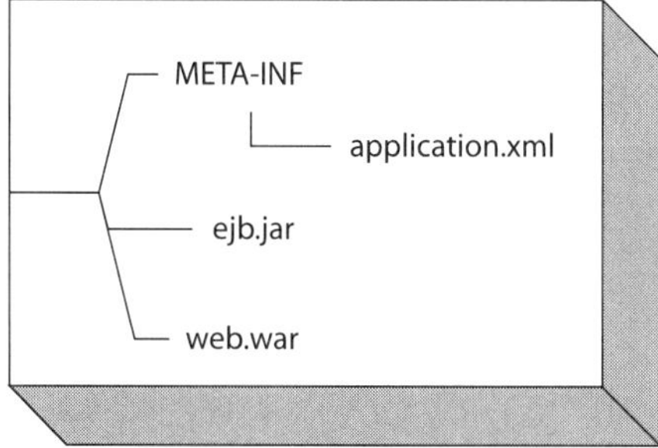

Figure 26.4 Structure of an Enterprise archive file.

example in Figure 26.4 there are two modules: one for the Web application and one for the EJB application. It can also define other aspects of the J2EE application, such as a description, icons etc.

The `application.xml` file has a root element `<application>` and five sub-elements:

- `icon` (optional): allows an icon to be specified – used with deployment tools.
- `display-name`: a name used in a deployment tool for this J2EE application.
- `description` (optional): used as a human-readable description of the J2EE application.
- `module` (one or more times): used to describe the modules that comprise the J2EE applications.
- `security-role` (optional): this contains the definition of a security role which is global to the application. The definition consists of a description of the security role, and the security role name.

UltraEdit-32 - [C:\jdt\projects\FT\development\build\META-INF\application.xml]

File Edit Search Project View Format Column Macro Advanced Window Help

```
<?xml version="1.0" encoding="ISO-8859-1" ?>
<application>
   <display-name>Fault Tracker System Version 2.1 </display-name>
   <module>
      <web>
         <web-uri>ftweb.war</web-uri>
         <!-- Context root for web application url -->
         <context-root>ft</context-root>
      </web>
   </module>
   <module>
      <ejb>ftejb.jar</ejb>
   </module>
</application>
```

Figure 26.5 A sample `application.xml` file.

The structure of the application.xml file is illustrated in Figure 26.5. The sub-elements of the <application> element provides three items of information. The first defines a display name used within deployment tools. The second and third are both <module> elements that define the Web application and EJB application that comprise this J2EE application.

The <module> element can have three different sub-elements, these are <web>, <ejb> and <java>. The <web> element is used to define a Web application module, the <ejb> element is used to define the EJB application module and the <java> element is used to define a Java application client module.

In Figure 26.5 the module defining the EJB application specifies the name of the EJB jar (in this case ftejb.jar). In turn the Web module specifies the file ftweb.war as containing the Web application. This is done in this case within the <web-uri> element. Within the Web element there is a second sub-element <context-root>. This element is used to define the root context for the Web application. For example, in this case the root context is ft; thus all URLs to this Web application will start:

```
http://<hostname>:port/ft/
```

To create an EAR file the jar command is again used. This time the jar command must specify the application.xml file and the Web archives and JAR files that make up that application. For example:

```
jar -cvf ft.ear *.war *.jar META-INF\application.xml
```

26.4 Caching EJB References

The previous section has talked about the practicalities of connecting a servlet or JSP to an EJB. However, there are additional subtleties associated with referencing EJBs from Web tier classes that are not present with standard Java clients.

For performance reasons, it is a good idea to avoid getting the InitialContext and using JNDI with every servlet request. Rather, it is better to take advantage of the HttpSession and ServletContext to store references to EJBs between requests. For example, a servlet, like any other client, can obtain EJBs via JNDI lookups and then cache them.

There are, however, a number of issues relating to this strategy. Firstly, servlets and JSPs are (by default) shared among all users of the Web application. This means that there are additional constraints that must be borne in mind when considering caching references to EJBs. These are:

- If an EJB is a stateless session bean then it can be shared by any client and, if required, can be stored in the ServletContext object as an attribute. For example:

  ```
  ServletContext sctx = servletConfig.getServletContext()
    // servletConfig is passed into init as its only parameter
  sctx.setAttribute(name, object) // provides Web application-wide scope
  ```

- If an EJB is an entity bean, then it depends. Entity beans can be shared across clients if transactions can be relied on to do the necessary synchronization. However, you must be careful if several threads from the same transaction try to access the same entity bean. This will throw a `RemoteException`, so you would need to synchronize access explicitly.
- Stateful session beans are client-specific and must not be shared. If required, store them in a `Session` object as attribute values.

Another issue associated with caching references to EJBs in the Web tier is that it is necessary to store serializable EJB handles and not the stub object themselves. This is because the application server might serialize the session/servlet objects to conserve resources or to transfer the objects between distributed JVMs.

Remote references to EJBs should not be stored directly in the session object; they do not serialize or deserialize, and an `HttpSession` may be temporarily serialized by an application server. Instead, you should get a handle for the remote or home interfaces. These can be safely serialized. This can be done by using:

- `EJBObject.getHandle()`
- `EJBHome.getHomeHandle()`

The home and remote objects can be reconstituted using:

- `remoteHandle.getEJBObject()`
- `homeHandle.getEJBHome()`

Note, however, that it is necessary to use `PortableRemoteObject.narrow()` on the objects returned by these `get` methods.

26.5 An Example

This section provides a very simple example of connecting a servlet to an EJB for the online bookstore domain. The servlet used in this application is presented in Figures 26.6–26.8. The `BookServlet` creates some trace information when instantiated (see Figure 26.6).

The main body of the `doGet` method (see Figure 26.7) either creates a new book or looks up an existing book depending upon when a book id has been entered by the end user. Note that we are not trying to do any caching of the EJB references in this example to keep things simple.

The end of the `doGet` method (presented in Figure 26.8) formats the response sent back to the end user.

As all the elements in this servlet have been described before we shall not go into any greater detail here – instead analysis of the details of the servlet is left as an exercise for the reader.

The `web.xml` file for this application is presented in Figure 26.9. This `web.xml` file defines a single servlet (`servlet.BookServlet`) used and a single `<ejb-ref>` for the `book` EJB. This is the JNDI name used within the `doGet` method presented in Figure 26.7.

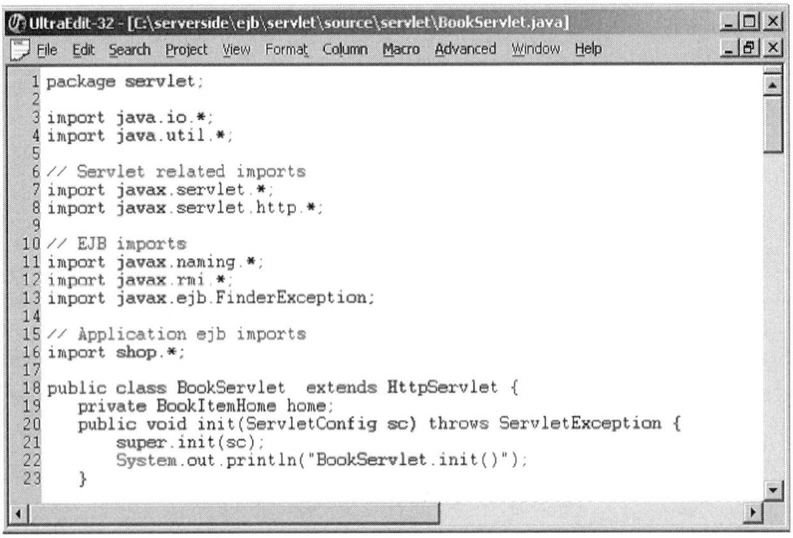

UltraEdit-32 - [C:\serverside\ejb\servlet\source\servlet\BookServlet.java]

File Edit Search Project View Format Column Macro Advanced Window Help

```
package servlet;

import java.io.*;
import java.util.*;

// Servlet related imports
import javax.servlet.*;
import javax.servlet.http.*;

// EJB imports
import javax.naming.*;
import javax.rmi.*;
import javax.ejb.FinderException;

// Application ejb imports
import shop.*;

public class BookServlet  extends HttpServlet {
    private BookItemHome home;
    public void init(ServletConfig sc) throws ServletException {
        super.init(sc);
        System.out.println("BookServlet.init()");
    }
```

Figure 26.6 The head of the `BookServlet` class.

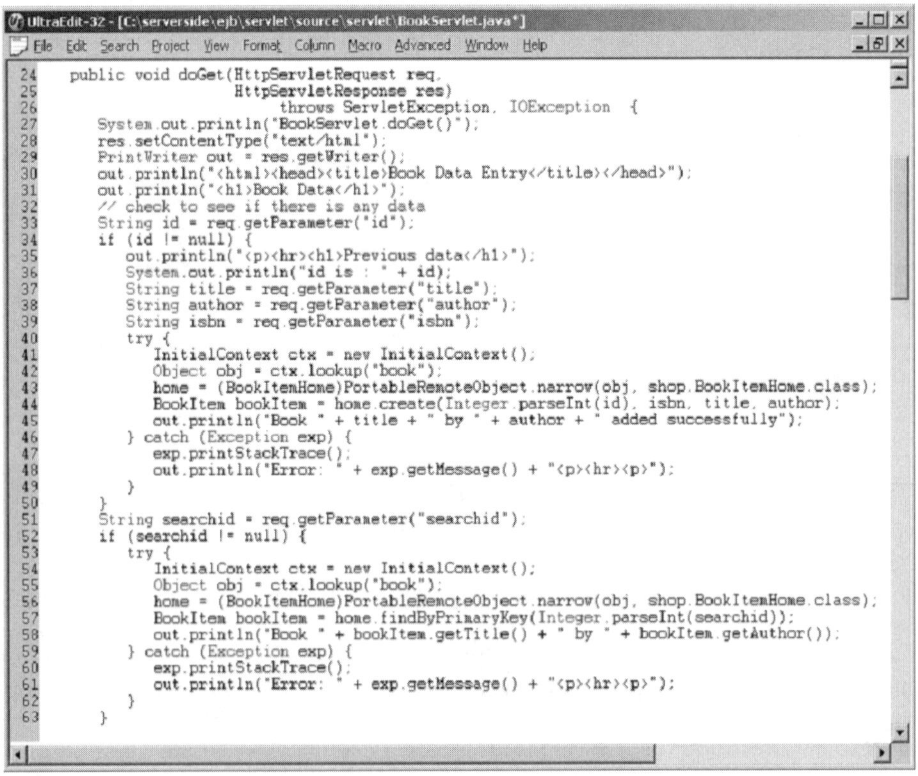

UltraEdit-32 - [C:\serverside\ejb\servlet\source\servlet\BookServlet.java*]

File Edit Search Project View Format Column Macro Advanced Window Help

```
    public void doGet(HttpServletRequest req,
                      HttpServletResponse res)
                            throws ServletException, IOException  {
        System.out.println("BookServlet.doGet()");
        res.setContentType("text/html");
        PrintWriter out = res.getWriter();
        out.println("<html><head><title>Book Data Entry</title></head>");
        out.println("<h1>Book Data</h1>");
        // check to see if there is any data
        String id = req.getParameter("id");
        if (id != null) {
            out.println("<p><hr><h1>Previous data</h1>");
            System.out.println("id is : " + id);
            String title = req.getParameter("title");
            String author = req.getParameter("author");
            String isbn = req.getParameter("isbn");
            try {
                InitialContext ctx = new InitialContext();
                Object obj = ctx.lookup("book");
                home = (BookItemHome)PortableRemoteObject.narrow(obj, shop.BookItemHome.class);
                BookItem bookItem = home.create(Integer.parseInt(id), isbn, title, author);
                out.println("Book " + title + " by " + author + " added successfully");
            } catch (Exception exp) {
                exp.printStackTrace();
                out.println("Error: " + exp.getMessage() + "<p><hr><p>");
            }
        }
        String searchid = req.getParameter("searchid");
        if (searchid != null) {
            try {
                InitialContext ctx = new InitialContext();
                Object obj = ctx.lookup("book");
                home = (BookItemHome)PortableRemoteObject.narrow(obj, shop.BookItemHome.class);
                BookItem bookItem = home.findByPrimaryKey(Integer.parseInt(searchid));
                out.println("Book " + bookItem.getTitle() + " by " + bookItem.getAuthor());
            } catch (Exception exp) {
                exp.printStackTrace();
                out.println("Error: " + exp.getMessage() + "<p><hr><p>");
            }
        }
```

Figure 26.7 The main body of the `doGet` method of the `BookServlet` class.

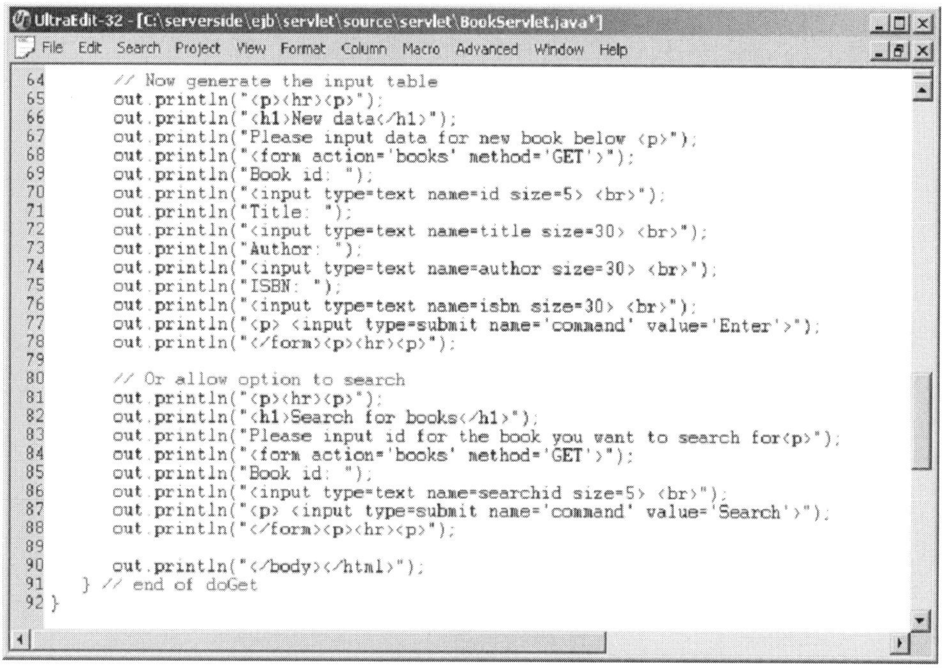

UltraEdit-32 - [C:\serverside\ejb\servlet\source\servlet\BookServlet.java*]

File Edit Search Project View Format Column Macro Advanced Window Help

```
        // Now generate the input table
        out.println("<p><hr><p>");
        out.println("<h1>New data</h1>");
        out.println("Please input data for new book below <p>");
        out.println("<form action='books' method='GET'>");
        out.println("Book id: ");
        out.println("<input type=text name=id size=5> <br>");
        out.println("Title: ");
        out.println("<input type=text name=title size=30> <br>");
        out.println("Author: ");
        out.println("<input type=text name=author size=30> <br>");
        out.println("ISBN: ");
        out.println("<input type=text name=isbn size=30> <br>");
        out.println("<p> <input type=submit name='command' value='Enter'>");
        out.println("</form><p><hr><p>");

        // Or allow option to search
        out.println("<p><hr><p>");
        out.println("<h1>Search for books</h1>");
        out.println("Please input id for the book you want to search for<p>");
        out.println("<form action='books' method='GET'>");
        out.println("Book id: ");
        out.println("<input type=text name=searchid size=5> <br>");
        out.println("<p> <input type=submit name='command' value='Search'>");
        out.println("</form><p><hr><p>");

        out.println("</body></html>");
    } // end of doGet
}
```

Figure 26.8 The formatting element of the doGet method.

Associated with the web.xml file is a jboss-web.xml file as we will be deploying this J2EE application on the JBoss–Tomcat combination Web server. In this case our jboss.web.xml file (presented in Figure 26.10) contains a single entry mapping the <ejb-ref-name> to the <jndi-name>.

We are now in a position to compile the servlet and create the Web archive file. The structure of the resulting WAR file is presented in Figure 26.11. Note that this diagram shows the WAR file containing the two XML files, a manifest file and the BookServlet class in the normal Web application structure.

Assuming that we have already constructed the EJB jar and that this jar is called book.jar; we are now in a position to create the main J2EE application Enterprise archive (or EAR file). The application.xml file for this is presented in Figure 26.12. Note that the WAR file and the JAR file are both referenced along with the application context root (eshop).

The resulting EAR file is illustrated in Figure 26.13. Note that the WAR and JAR files are listed along with the application.xml file and the EAR manifest file.

For deployment purposes we shall use the JBoss–Tomcat combination. Note that you cannot run this example using just JBoss, as it requires the Web tier as well as the EJB tier, and by default JBoss is an EJB server. However, by combining JBoss and Tomcat together you get a complete J2EE stack offering both the Web tier and the EJB tier in an integrated whole.

UltraEdit-32 - [C:\serverside\ejb\servlet\WEB-INF\web.xml]

File Edit Search Project View Format Column Macro Advanced Window Help

```
<?xml version="1.0" encoding="ISO-8859-1"?>

<!DOCTYPE web-app
     PUBLIC "-//Sun Microsystems, Inc.//DTD Web Application 2.2//EN"
     "http://java.sun.com/j2ee/dtds/web-app_2.2.dtd">

<web-app>
   <servlet>
       <servlet-name>
           books
       </servlet-name>
       <servlet-class>
          servlet.BookServlet
       </servlet-class>
   </servlet>
   <servlet-mapping>
      <servlet-name>
          books
      </servlet-name>
      <url-pattern>
          /books
      </url-pattern>
   </servlet-mapping>

<!-- ### EJB References (java:comp/env/ejb) -->
    <ejb-ref>
        <ejb-ref-name>book</ejb-ref-name>
        <ejb-ref-type>Entity</ejb-ref-type>
        <home>shop.BookItemHome</home>
        <remote>shop.BookItem</remote>
    </ejb-ref>

</web-app>
```

Figure 26.9 The `web.xml` file of the Web tier of the online bookstore example.

UltraEdit-32 - [C:\serverside\ejb\servlet\WEB-INF\jboss-web.xml]

File Edit Search Project View Format Column Macro Advanced Window Help

```
<?xml version="1.0" encoding="UTF-8"?>

<jboss-web>
    <ejb-ref>
        <ejb-ref-name>book</ejb-ref-name>
        <jndi-name>book</jndi-name>
    </ejb-ref>
</jboss-web>
```

Figure 26.10 The `jboss-web.xml` file of the Web tier of the online bookstore example.

Name	Modified	Size	Ratio	Packed	Path
web.xml	22/04/2002 11:57	812	55%	369	web-inf\
Manifest.mf	22/04/2002 13:42	68	0%	68	meta-inf\
jboss-web.xml	22/04/2002 11:58	180	43%	103	web-inf\
BookServlet.class	22/04/2002 13:42	3,894	47%	2,046	WEB-INF\classes\servlet\

Figure 26.11 The structure of the WAR file of the online bookstore.

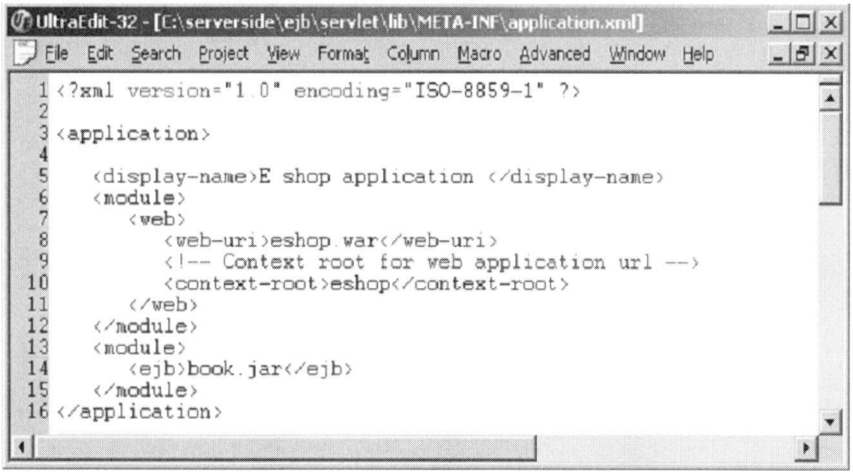

UltraEdit-32 - [C:\serverside\ejb\servlet\lib\META-INF\application.xml]

```
<?xml version="1.0" encoding="ISO-8859-1" ?>

<application>

   <display-name>E shop application </display-name>
   <module>
      <web>
         <web-uri>eshop.war</web-uri>
         <!-- Context root for web application url -->
         <context-root>eshop</context-root>
      </web>
   </module>
   <module>
      <ejb>book.jar</ejb>
   </module>
</application>
```

Figure 26.12 The `application.xml` file of the online bookstore application.

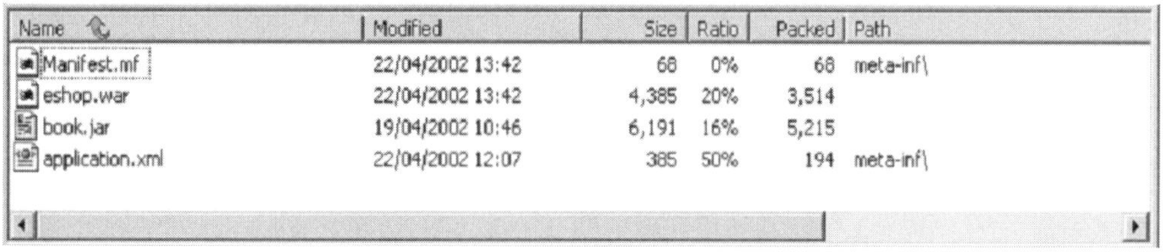

Name	Modified	Size	Ratio	Packed	Path
Manifest.mf	22/04/2002 13:42	68	0%	68	meta-inf\
eshop.war	22/04/2002 13:42	4,385	20%	3,514	
book.jar	19/04/2002 10:46	6,191	16%	5,215	
application.xml	22/04/2002 12:07	385	50%	194	meta-inf\

Figure 26.13 The structure of the EAR file of the online bookstore.

To deploy this application on JBoss–Tomcat, you merely need to copy the EAR file to the JBoss–Tomcat deployment directory (for example `%JBOSS_HOME%\server\default\deploy`, where `%JBOSS_HOME%` indicates the directory into which you have installed your JBoss–Tomcat installation). Assuming all has gone correctly you should now be able to access your J2EE application using the URL:

```
http://<hostname>:8080/eshop/books
```

This is illustrated in Figure 26.14. The important point to note is that any information retrieved and displayed within the Web page is coming from the EJB tier and that any updates performed are being made by the EJB tier.

26.6 Summary

In this chapter we have considered how elements in the presentation or Web tier can access EJBs in the business tier. We have considered the features provided by the J2EE specification to

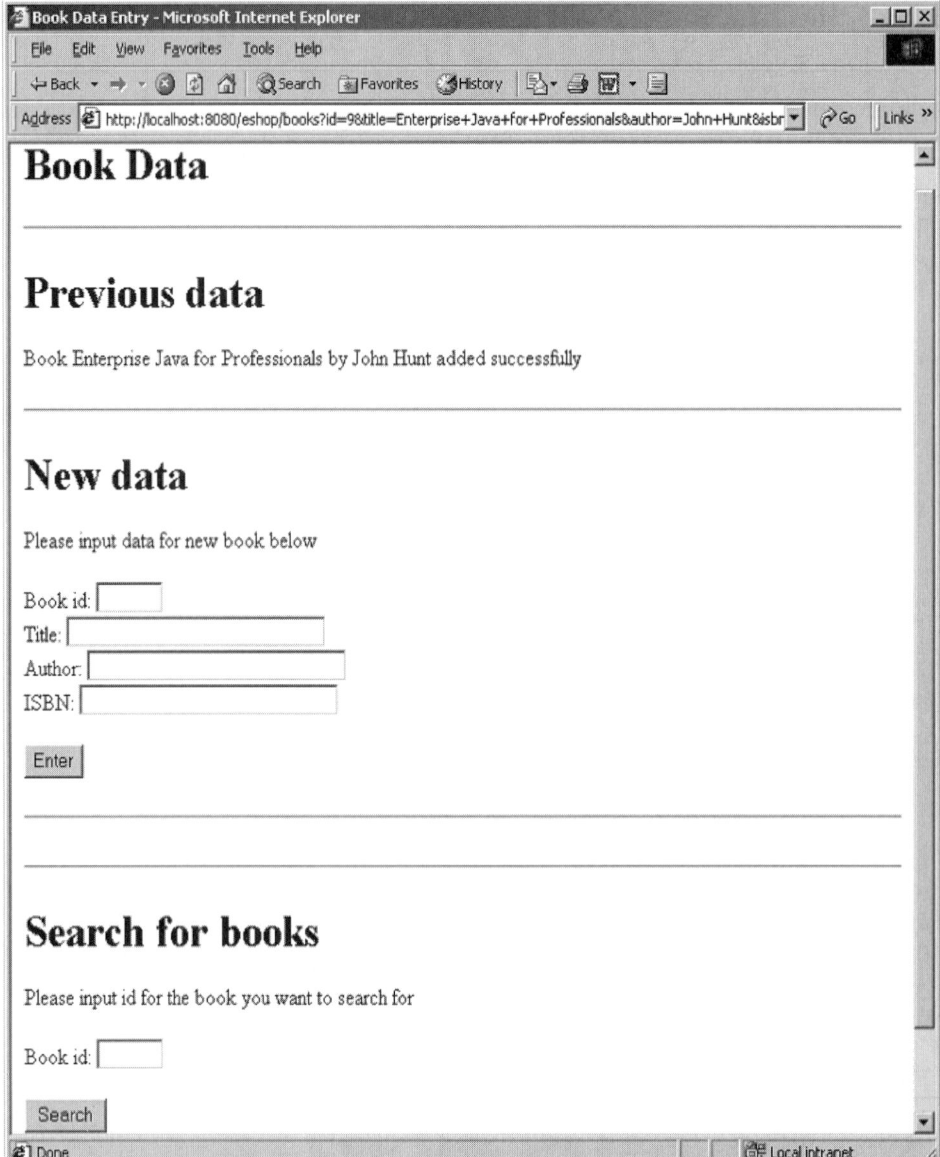

Figure 26.14 Running the online bookstore J2EE application under JBoss–Tomcat.

support such integration as well as issues associated with caching references to EJBs in servlets and JSPs. We have also examined briefly a sample application that uses a servlet and an EJB.

Part 4

Additional Technologies

Chapter 27

Deployment Issues: Transactions

27.1 Introduction

This chapter presents an overview of transaction concepts and how they relate to EJBs. We start by talking about what a transaction is both within the context of J2EE (for example, the notion of transaction scope and propagation) and more generally, such as the transaction ACID properties and the two-phase commit protocol. We examine the two kinds of transaction supported by EJB servers, namely container-managed and bean-managed transactions. To define transaction scope, the former requires the use of XML deployment descriptors. The latter requires the use of the `javax.transaction` package. Invariably, multiple transactions will operate within an application server. Managing their interactions and isolation is the subject of Section 27.6. Finally, we discuss the impact of exceptions on transaction behaviour.

27.2 Transaction Concepts

A transaction is an indivisible unit of work that either completes satisfactorily, or else is abandoned completely (see Date (1999) for a more comprehensive discussion on transactions). Normally, transactions are discussed in the context of database management systems where a transaction may lead to several updates to the database that are either committed if the transaction completes successfully or abandoned if the transaction is aborted. If committed, the updates will remain persistent, whereas if abandoned, the updates will be discarded and the database will roll back to the state it was in just before the transaction began. In J2EE, transactions can also include other data resources, such as the instance variable state of stateful session EJBs (see Chapter 30), JMS messages and, of course, entity EJBs.

In the context of J2EE a transaction will have a scope that includes all the resources "touched" by the transaction. This is illustrated in Figure 27.1, where the transaction begins at the start of the `balance` method and then completes, that is, commits or rolls back, when the `balance` method returns. The `balance` method calls methods on the `Cart` EJB

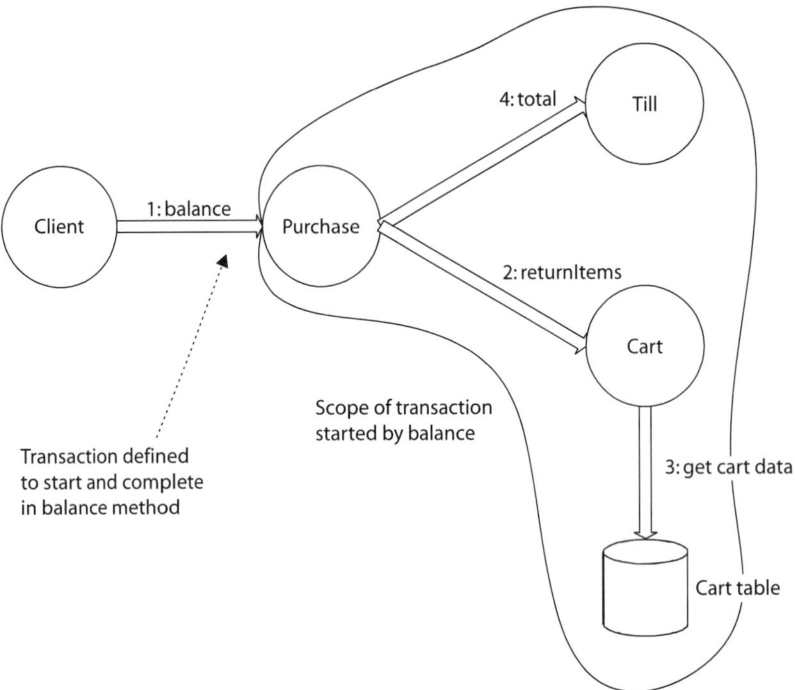

Figure 27.1 Example of transaction scope in the bookstore application.

(`returnItems`) and the `Till` EJB (`total`). Normally when this occurs, the scope of the transaction is widened to include these EJBs. Likewise, if one of these EJBs accesses other EJBs or external resources, then, usually, these EJBs and resources will also be included within the scope of the transaction. The exceptions are external resources that cannot support transactions (e.g. file-system files) and methods of other EJBs where the deployment descriptors prune the transaction propagation (more on this later).

Transaction propagation across EJBs is hidden from your code. Each transaction will have an identifier and other information associated with it. A method call on an EJB will transfer this information automatically from one EJB to another, even if they reside in separate containers or J2EE servers (although the latter might not always be supported). It is the underlying IIOP protocol that supports the transfer of such transactional context across the network.

The J2EE application server has a transaction manager (sometimes termed the transaction monitor) that keeps a record of each ongoing transaction and the EJBs and data resources associated with that transaction. This record enables the transaction manager to "know" which resources need to be committed or rolled back at the end of the transaction.

The call to `balance` does not result in an update to any resource. Consequently, if the transaction fails (for example, the EJB server fails) then there is no data to roll back to an earlier state. Figure 27.2 shows an operation that does result in an update. Here, the `add` method will cause the appropriate row in the `Cart Table` to be updated as part of the transaction. In this case, if a "problem" (and we shall define what we mean by a "problem" later)

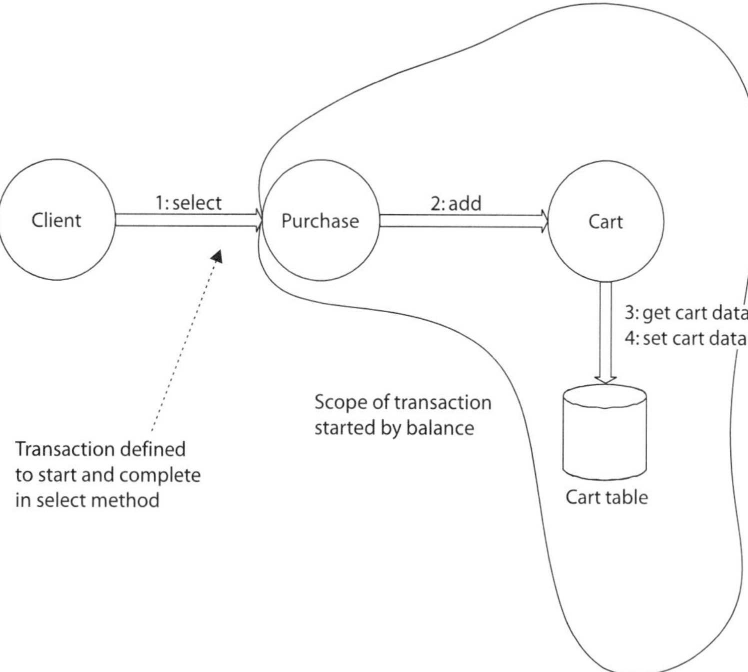

Figure 27.2 A transaction that updates data.

occurs in the Purchase or Cart EJBs or in the database, then the transaction will be rolled back, and any updates to the Cart Table carried out during the transaction will be rescinded.

In the balance example there were no updates to be unwound. So why then did we use a transaction? Transactions are also used to provide degrees of protection between multiple transactions operating on the same data, often referred to as levels of isolation. For example, while reading cart data from the Cart Table we might wish to prevent another transaction from deleting the cart or updating the contents of the cart. We may, however, be happy for other transactions to read the same data from the cart. Transactions can be configured to support varying degrees of isolation protection, locking out other transactions, depending on the kind of operation to be performed (e.g. a read, write or insert operation). We discuss this further in Section 27.6.

More formally, a transaction must support the ACID properties:

- **Atomic**: Updates to a resource are either all committed or else none are committed. Partial updates to one or more resources that form part of the transaction scope are not permitted.
- **Consistent**: Data consistency is a consequent of the other three properties. Partial updates could lead to inconsistent data. For example, in the bookstore application every time a user pays for the shopping cart contents we would record the purchase in a separate table (e.g. a PurchaseRecord table, not included in our example application). It is important that both the purchase leading to the removal of the user's cart and the purchase record are undertaken as

an indivisible operation; anything else would lead to inconsistencies between the `Cart` and `PurchaseRecord` tables. Insufficient transaction isolation could lead to several transactions overwriting each other's data, or one transaction's behaviour being incorrectly influenced by reading another transaction's uncommitted data, perhaps leading to inappropriate updates to other data. Finally, if updates are not made persistent during transaction commit, then again data may become inconsistent if the server fails during the commit operation.

- **Isolated:** Transactions should have isolation properties that isolate the data being operated on by one transaction from the operations of another.
- **Durable:** This seems obvious, but it needs to be stated. Transaction commitment is not completed until any updates made during the transaction are made persistent on backing store. This is perhaps the traditional database view of transactions. Transactions may operate on more transient resources. For example, in JMS, transaction commitment will result in the JMS messages being sent to a queue or topic. Durability also refers to the resource state prior to the start of the transaction. If a transaction is rolled back, then the transaction management system must be able to restore this previous state.

The last concept that we wish to touch on is the distributed transaction. We have already alluded to this when talking about transaction scope, including multiple EJBs and resources. These resources could include several databases, legacy information systems or JMS resources, where some of the application data resides in one resource and the remainder in another. In the bookstore application we might decide to maintain the `BookItems` table in one database resource and the `Cart` table in another. Most J2EE application servers have transaction managers that support distributed transactions; that is, they support the ACID properties across multiple data resources. Each participating resource will have its own transaction management subsystem responsible for managing its transactions. However, many resources also support a standard interface called the XA interface[1] enabling them to participate in distributed transactions; they support what is termed the two-phase commit protocol.

Here is the simplified description. In the two-phase commit protocol a central transaction manager (in this case the J2EE server's TM) interoperates with multiple database system transaction managers, via the standard XA interface. These external resources are enlisted with the TM as XA resources. During the first phase, the TM "asks" all the XA resources whether they are able to commit their bit of the transaction (often called the *prepare for commit* operation). All the XA resources are requested to roll back if no majority agreement to commit can be obtained. However, if they all "say" yes, then the TM (second phase) "asks" them all to actually commit their transactions. The protocol is not infallible since it is possible that one of the database systems could fail during the second-phase commit operation, leading to inconsistent data. The two-phase commit protocol is supported by the `javax.transaction` package that is often known as the Java Transaction API (JTA). Unless you intend to build your own transaction manager you won't need to use most of the JTA interfaces and classes. The one exception is the `UserTransaction` interface, which we will discuss later.

---

1 Defined by the X/Open CAE Specification (Distributed Transaction Processing: The XA Specification).

27.3 Types of Transaction Supported by EJB Servers

EJB servers support two kinds of transaction, namely container-managed transactions and bean-managed transactions. As with CMP, container-managed transactions are a means of insulating the application developer from having to write distribution code that detracts from the business logic, in this case the explicit management of transactions. Instead, the transaction intents of the developer, and more importantly, the application assembler and deployer, are codified within the deployment descriptor files. This gives you the opportunity to modify the transaction properties of your application without having to modify your code. During deployment, the container tools will generate code that will start, commit or abandon transactions automatically, liaising with the server's transaction manager. We discuss container-managed transactions further in Section 27.4.

Container-managed transactions are probably sufficient in most circumstances. However, there may be occasions when control over transactions needs to be undertaken programmatically. As we will see, container-managed transactions are managed at the granularity of the method, there being at most one transaction operating for, at least, the complete duration of the method. There may be circumstances where this is too coarse-grained, and you may wish to define a transaction whose scope is just part of a method. Alternatively, you may wish to create several transactions within a single method. Bean-managed transactions can be used where container-managed transactions are found to be too inflexible. The trade-off is that it is harder to change your application's transaction properties or to reuse these components in other applications or environments.

Bean-managed transactions are supported by Java's `javax.transaction.UserTransaction` interface. They are only permitted in session- and message-driven EJBs, not in entity EJBs. It was thought that bean-managed transactions would over-complicate the entity EJB life cycle. We discuss bean-managed transactions further in Section 27.5.

27.4 Container-Managed Transactions

Container-managed transactions have their scope and behaviour specified in the `ejb-jar.xml` deployment descriptor file. As we will see later, business logic and life cycle interface methods can be given one of six transaction attributes. These attributes must be specified for all qualifying methods prior to deployment, either by the developer assembling the application, or by the person responsible for deploying the application. Before looking at the deployment file, we first discuss the six attributes:

- `Required`
- `NotSupported`
- `Supports`
- `RequiresNew`
- `Mandatory`
- `Never`

For message-driven EJBs only `Required` and `NotSupported` should be used. For entity EJBs that use EJB 2.0 CMP the specification recommends that only `Required`, `RequiresNew` and `Mandatory` should be used. This is so that the container is able to rely on transaction mechanisms to ensure data consistency between the entity EJB and underlying database. Optionally, the container may support the other attributes, but use of them will reduce the portability of your EJBs. Likewise, session EJBs that implement the `SessionSynchronization` interface must not use the other attributes.

27.4.1 The `Required` Attribute

A method that is assigned this attribute must execute within the scope of a transaction. If the method's caller is operating within a transaction then this transaction's scope is propagated to include the EJB that implements the method. If not, then a new transaction is started. Figure 27.3 illustrates this.

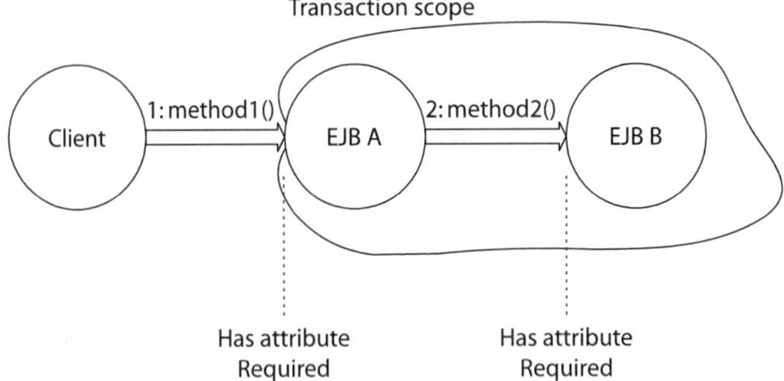

Figure 27.3 The impact of the `Required` attribute on transaction propagation.

Here, when `Client` calls `method1` a new transaction is started, since `Client` does not have its own transaction. The existing transaction is propagated when `method1` calls `method2` on EJB B. This is because `method2` has also been assigned the `Required` attribute.

The `Required` attribute is one of the most commonly used transaction attributes. It provides the flexibility of allowing an EJB containing methods with this attribute to operate either transactionally on their own or as part of a larger transaction. In most circumstances this is what you will want.

27.4.2 The `NotSupported` Attribute

A method that is assigned this attribute will effectively prevent the scope of a transaction being propagated from the caller to the EJB that implements the method. This is shown in Figure 27.4. Here, `method2` has been assigned the `NotSupported` attribute. When `method1` calls `method2`, the transaction associated with the calling thread is not propagated to `method2`. The transaction is effectively suspended and resumes when `method2` returns. Use this attribute in circumstances where EJB B uses resources that are not transactional. For example, EJB B might be a bean-managed entity EJB that is using storing data within a file-system file. A file system is not

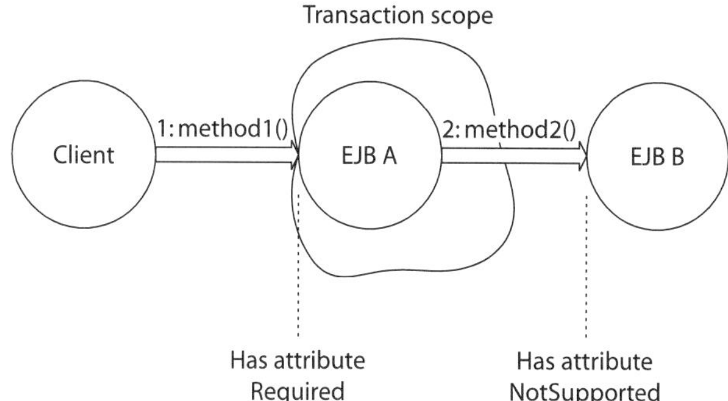

Figure 27.4 The impact of the `NotSupported` attribute on transaction propagation.

transactional, which means that a rollback cannot be supported. Consequently, there is little point in propagating the transaction to the EJB.

Another example, is where EJB B is a read-only EJB; that is, a session or entity EJB that is a data source, but not a data sink. A stock quote EJB would be an example, the EJB providing stock quote information. In this situation there is little point operating such an EJB within a transaction. Firstly, the transaction would incur an unnecessary operational overhead, and, secondly, if the isolation levels are not specified correctly, one transaction might lock out another transaction while the first transaction is accessing the EJB; clearly behaviour that is detrimental to the performance of the application.

27.4.3 The `Supports` Attribute

A method with the `Supports` attribute will propagate the transaction of a caller, if it has one. If not, it will execute in an unspecified transaction. Use this attribute with care, making sure that the EJB will execute correctly inside or outside of a transaction.

27.4.4 The `RequiresNew` Attribute

A method with the `RequiresNew` attribute will always be started in a new transaction context, irrespective of whether the caller is operating in an existing transaction or not. This is shown in Figure 27.5. This attribute can be useful where failure of one part of an application function should not jeopardize another. For example, a travel agent application's `bookAHoliday` method may require the travel agent to enter the customer's details as well as other holiday details, such as payment. If the customer decides to cancel the booking then it makes sense to preserve the customer details. One way of doing this would be to assign the `RequiresNew` attribute to the `obtainCustomerDetails` method. Even if the calling `bookAHoliday` method fails, the updates performed by `obtainCustomerDetails` will remain intact.

27.4.5 The `Mandatory` Attribute

A method with this attribute must be called by a transactional client. If not, the container will throw the `TransactionRequiredException`. Use this attribute where a business function spans

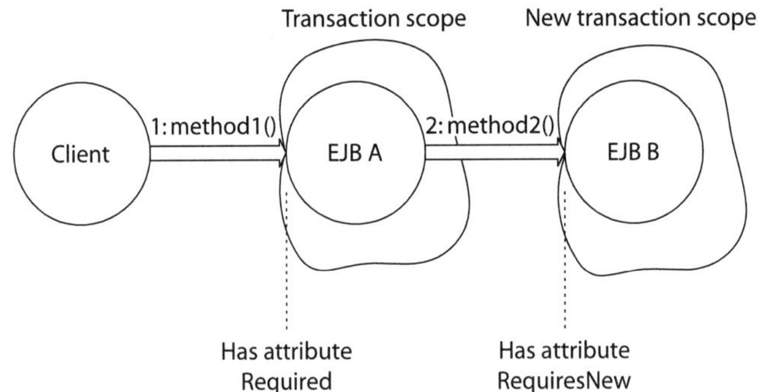

Figure 27.5 The impact of the `RequiresNew` attribute on transaction propagation.

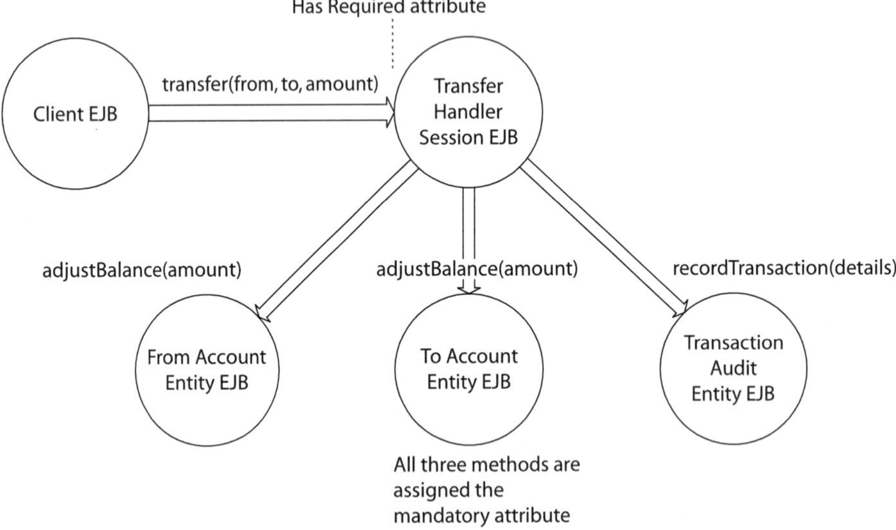

Figure 27.6 Example use of the `Mandatory` attribute.

several EJBs, and where it is important to ensure that subservient EJBs operate in the transactional context of a coordinating EJB, and not in isolation. Figure 27.6 shows an example of part of a simplified online banking application. Here, the transfer method solicits the collaboration of thee other EJBs, namely the source entity of the funds to be transferred, the target entity for the transfer, and an audit entity EJB that records bank transactions.[2] The intention of the application developer was to ensure that business methods on the subservient EJBs were never executed in isolation. Instead, they had to be executed in the context of coordinating business logic. Using the `Mandatory` attribute at least ensures that a coordinating transaction is operating

2 There is an unfortunate overloading of the term transaction here.

before adjustBalance or recordTransaction can be called. Of course, this doesn't ensure that the business logic in the TransferHandler EJB is correct, but at least it guarantees that there is a coordinating transaction.

27.4.6 The Never Attribute

A method with this attribute must never be called by a transactional client. If it is, then the container will throw a RemoteException. It may be appropriate to use this attribute with EJBs that cannot guarantee transactional behaviour and so should not be used in an application that requires such behaviour. This attribute is a stronger version of the NotSupported attribute, thereby providing more of a safeguard against the inappropriate use of a non-transactional EJB.

27.4.7 Transaction Deployment Descriptors

Listing 27.1 shows the transaction deployment descriptors for the bookstore application. Both transaction and security descriptors are placed in the <assembly-descriptor> part of the ejb-jar.xml file. This is because, in many cases, the decision concerning the most appropriate transaction and security attributes to use cannot be made until the whole application is assembled, or perhaps even as late as deployment. These attributes define behaviours that span multiple EJBs. It is rarely useful to consider the transactional properties of individual EJBs in isolation.

As shown earlier we assign transaction attributes to EJB methods. The methods that qualify depend on the kind of EJB. For session EJBs, all the business logic interface and ancestor interface methods must be assignment attributes. However, this ancestor list excludes the EJBObject and EJBLocalObject interfaces. Also, attributes cannot be assigned to the session EJB's life cycle interface methods. For entity EJBs, all the business logic and ancestor interface methods must be assigned attributes. However, the methods getPrimaryKey, isIdentical, getEJBHome, getEJBLocalHome and getHandle are excluded. Also, all the entity EJB's life cycle and ancestor interface methods must be assigned attributes. However, the methods getHomeHandle and getEJBMetaData are excluded. For message-driven EJBs an attribute must only be assigned to the onMessage method.

Listing 27.1 Transaction deployment descriptors.

```
<ejb-jar>
  <enterprise-beans>
    <!-- Descriptors omitted -->
  </enterprise-beans>
  <relationships>
    <!-- Descriptors omitted -->
  </relationships>

  <assembly-descriptor>
    <container-transaction>
      <method>
        <ejb-name>Cart</ejb-name>
```

```
        <method-name>*</method-name>
      </method>
      <method>
        <ejb-name>BookItem</ejb-name>
        <method-name>*</method-name>
      </method>
      <method>
        <ejb-name>DebugMonitor</ejb-name>
        <method-name>*</method-name>
      </method>
      <method>
        <ejb-name>Till</ejb-name>
        <method-name>*</method-name>
      </method>
      <method>
        <ejb-name>Purchase</ejb-name>
        <method-name>*</method-name>
      </method>
      <trans-attribute>Required</trans-attribute>
    </container-transaction>
    <!-- Descriptors omitted -->
  </assembly-descriptor>
</ejb-jar>
```

Transactions can be defined with one or more `<container-transaction>` tags. Each has a single `<trans-attribute>` sub-tag, the value of which defines the transaction attribute, in this case `Required`. The methods to which this attribute is applied are specified in one or more `<method>` tags. Each `<method>` tag identifies an EJB and uses one of three ways to identify the EJB's method or methods to which the transaction attribute will be applied. The first is shown in the example, consisting of a `<method-name>` tag followed by an asterisk. The asterisk is a wildcard, and denotes all the valid methods of the business logic and life cycle interfaces of the named EJB, or the `onMessage` method for message-driven EJBs. The second way is to specify the name of the method. All the EJB's methods with that name will be assigned the transaction attribute. Rarely, you may wish to assign different transaction attributes to different overloads of the same method. This can be achieved using the `<method-params>` tag as shown in Listing 27.2. Here, for each method parameter a `<method-param>` tag is used, the value of which is the fully qualified Java type-name for the parameter. If there are no parameters then there will be no `<method-param>` tags.

Listing 27.2 The third way of denoting methods using the `<method-params>` tag.

```
<method>
  <ejb-name>Cart</ejb-name>
  <method-name>add</method-name>
  <method-params>
```

```
      <method-param>store.Book</method-param>
    </method-params>
  </method>
  <method>
    <ejb-name>Cart</ejb-name>
    <method-name>addAll</method-name>
    <method-params>
      <method-param>store.Book[]</method-param>
    </method-params>
  </method>
```

Finally, in some cases you may have methods that have identical names across the business logic and life cycle interfaces. You can focus on a specific method in a specific EJB interface by using the <method-intf> tag. If for some perverse reason we wished to assign different transaction attributes to the two add method in Cart's local and remote business logic interfaces, we could do this with:

```
  <method>
    <ejb-name>Cart</ejb-name>
    <method-intf>Local</method-intf>
    <method-name>add</method-name>
  </method>
```

Other valid values for <method-intf> are Remote, LocalHome and Home. This tag can be combined with the three ways of denoting methods, as discussed above.

27.5 Bean-Managed Transactions

Bean-managed transactions (BMT) can be used when you need more control over the demarcation and granularity of transactions. With BMTs you include code in your session and message-driven beans to start and complete the transactions, rather than the business logic or life cycle interface objects starting and completing transactions based on transaction attributes. You are not permitted to use BMTs with entity EJBs.

27.5.1 The UserTransaction Interface

You control BMTs using the javax.transaction.UserTransaction interface. This is defined as:

```
public interface UserTransaction{
  public void begin()
    throws NotSupportedException, SystemException;
  public void commit()
    throws RollbackException, HeuristicMixedException,
```

```
            HeuristicRollbackException, java.lang.SecurityException,
            java.lang.IllegalStateException, SystemException;
    public void rollback()
      throws java.lang.IllegalStateException, java.lang.SecurityException,
            SystemException;
    public void setRollbackOnly()
      throws java.lang.IllegalStateException, SystemException;
    public int getStatus()
      throws SystemException;
    public void setTransactionTimeout(int seconds)
      throws SystemException;
  }
```

A transaction is started with `begin`, resulting in the current thread being registered by the transaction manager with this new transaction. The transaction manager will throw the `NotSupportedException` if the current thread is already associated with a transaction and the transaction manager implementation does not support nested transactions. Note that EJB 2.0 does not allow nested transactions. Not doing so would restrict EJB servers to only those database systems that supported nested transactions. For all the methods the transaction manager will throw `SystemException` if it encounters an unexpected error condition. Transactions, especially those that are distributed, are complex, so this exception deals with problems not foreseen by the interface designers.

The `commit` method will attempt to update durable resources during the transaction. When completed the thread is no longer associated with a transaction. A number of problems may arise. `RollbackException` is thrown if the transaction has been rolled back rather than committed. This might occur if the transaction has been marked for rollback (see below) or in a distributed transaction if one or more of the resource managers indicate that they cannot commit as part of the two-phase commit protocol. `HeuristicMixedException` is thrown to indicate that a heuristic decision was made and that some relevant updates were made but others were rolled back. This can occur within the two-phase commit protocol and may be due to one of the database systems failing during the second-phase commit, effectively forcing a rollback on that database, whereas the other databases have committed. This, of course, can lead to inconsistent data and may require separate checking to rectify any problems. A less severe exception is `HeuristicRollbackException`, which indicates a situation where some relevant updates have been rolled back, that is, although there were some valid updates to be made, for whatever reason, none were. As with several other methods, `IllegalStateException` is thrown if the thread is not associated with a transaction. `SecurityException` is thrown if the current thread does not have permission to commit the transaction.

The `rollback` method is called to roll back the transaction associated with the calling thread. This will result in the thread being unregistered by the transaction manager and any associated resources being requested to roll back also. When completed the thread is no longer associated with a transaction.

The `setRollbackOnly` method will irrevocably mark the transaction associated with the calling thread for rollback. This means that the transaction will continue, but only one outcome is possible, that is, rollback.

The getStatus method provides useful information on the status of a transaction, as defined by the javax.transaction.Status constants. Two examples are that the transaction is in the process of committing, or the transaction has been prepared for commit as part of the two-phase protocol. Status.STATUS_NO_TRANSACTION is returned if the calling thread is not associated with a transaction.

All transactions have an associated timeout value. This ensures that if you fail to explicitly commit or roll back a transaction it will, eventually, timeout, causing an automatic rollback. Transaction managers will have a default value, and most J2EE application servers will provide a mechanism for its configuration. Programmatically, the timeout for a specific transaction can be set with the setTransactionTimeout method.

27.5.2 Obtaining and using a UserTransaction object

The UserTransaction object can be obtained in two ways. The easiest is to call the method getUserTransaction from a SessionContext or MessageDrivenContext object. The method will throw IllegalStateException if the calling EJB's transactions are being managed by the container. Listing 27.3 shows a version of the Till EJB implementation class that manages its own transactions (highlighted statements), which is unnecessary for this EJB, but illustrates the use of BMT. Compared with the original in Chapter 13 we have not only included the calls to the SessionContext and UserTransaction objects, but have also inserted a try...catch block and a temporary variable for the total, to ensure that all the arithmetic operations are undertaken within the scope of the transaction. Ensure that you also change the Till EJB's <transaction-type> tag in the ejb-jar.xml file to Bean. Also remove any transaction attributes assigned to the Till EJB's methods.

Listing 27.3 Obtaining and using a UserTransaction object.

```
package store;

import javax.ejb.SessionBean;
import javax.ejb.SessionContext;
import javax.ejb.EJBException;
import javax.ejb.CreateException;
import javax.naming.*;
import javax.transaction.UserTransaction;

public class TillBean implements SessionBean {
  public double total(Book[] items){
    double cost = 0.0;
    double total = 0.0;
    try{
      UserTransaction ut = ctx.getUserTransaction();
      ut.begin();
      for (int i=0; i<items.length; i++) {
        cost += items[i].getPrice();
      }
```

```
      total += cost + (cost * taxRate);
      ut.commit();
    }
    catch(Exception e){
      throw new EJBException(e);
    }
    return total;
  }
```

The second way is to obtain the UserTransaction object using JNDI. The EJB 2.0 specification states that a BMT session or message-driven EJB may obtain this object by performing a lookup with the value "java:comp/UserTransaction". This is equivalent to using ctx.getUserTransaction, and is included to make access to the transaction manager consistent with accessing other resources, such as JMS managers or database managers.

27.6 Transaction Isolation Levels

Clearly, in many applications we will want to isolate one transaction from another. The scenario in Figure 27.7 illustrates this. This simplified business method is responsible for transferring funds between two accounts. Assume that the method is transactional. Also assume that the isolation level prevents two transactions from updating the same database row, but does not prevent a second transaction from reading an uncommitted database row. The problem that could arise is that TX1 updates the from account with funds, but just before it commits (or rolls back), a second transaction in another method might read the same row representing the from account and perform some other banking operation based on uncommitted information. If TX1 fails (rolls back) then the second transaction will act on incorrect information. What we want in this case is a degree of isolation that prevents other transactions from reading uncommitted data.

The ANSI SQL standard specifies four transaction isolation levels, which database systems support to varying degrees and interpretations:

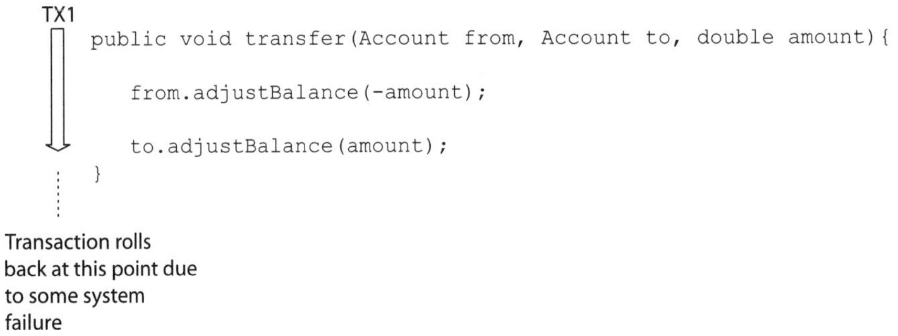

TX1

```
public void transfer(Account from, Account to, double amount){

    from.adjustBalance(-amount);

    to.adjustBalance(amount);
}
```

Transaction rolls back at this point due to some system failure

Figure 27.7 Insufficient transaction isolation.

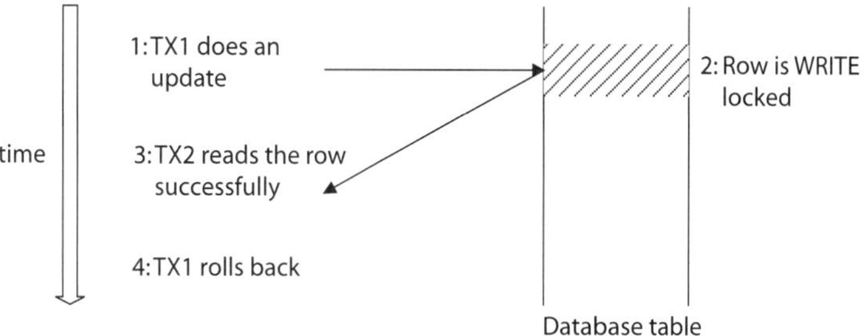

Figure 27.8 TRANSACTION_READ_COMMITTED scenario.

- TRANSACTION_READ_UNCOMMITTED
- TRANSACTION_READ_COMMITTED
- TRANSACTION_REPEATABLE_READ
- TRANSACTION_SERIALIZABLE

The degree of isolation increases from top to bottom. Let us look at each of these in turn.

The TRANSACTION_READ_UNCOMMITTED isolation level will prevent multiple transactions from updating the same data, but will allow dirty reads, as we saw in the transfer example. Figure 27.8 illustrates two transactions competing for the same resource (a more abstract case of the transfer example).

Here, TX1 performs an update operation on a database table row. The system establishes a WRITE lock on the row preventing writes by other transactions (see the discussion in Section 27.6.1 on lock modes). This lock does not prevent other transactions from reading from the row, as demonstrated by TX2. If TX1 rolls back, TX2 is left with invalid data, possibly leading to incorrect behaviour.

Dirty reads can be prevented using the TRANSACTION_READ_COMMITTED (and above) isolation level. The top diagram in Figure 27.9 shows that now TX2 is unable to read dirty data, since it is protected by a WRITE-EXCLUSIVE lock. However, this level of isolation may still allow undesirable behaviour in some applications. The lower diagram in Figure 27.9 illustrates this. Here an application cannot guarantee that the data it reads several times during a transaction will always be the same (non-repeatable reads). TX1 reads the row. TX2 then updates the row, thereby locking it against reads and writes. Eventually, TX2 commits leading to the lock being removed. TX1 can now read the row again. The issue is that the row data has changed, which might be a problem for some applications. For example, as part of a booking transaction, a travel agent application might check to see which rooms are available in a particular hotel. Whilst performing this transaction another transaction might update the room allocation table for the hotel. A room previously free might now be taken, causing the booking transaction to fail if it tries to book the room. If this is unacceptable then a higher level of isolation may be required.

The TRANSACTION_REPEATABLE_READ isolation level will ensure that reads are repeatable. Figure 27.10 illustrates this. Here, when TX1 performs a read operation, the row being

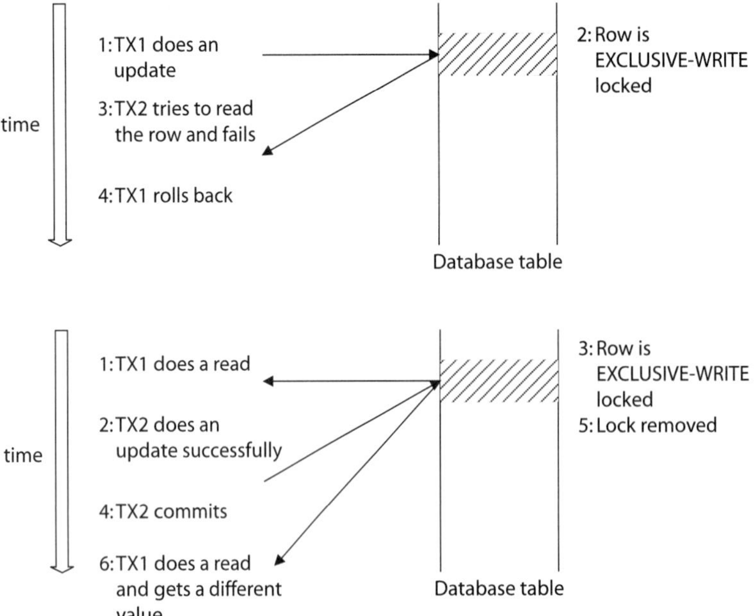

Figure 27.9 Impact of the `TRANSACTION_READ_COMMITTED` isolation level.

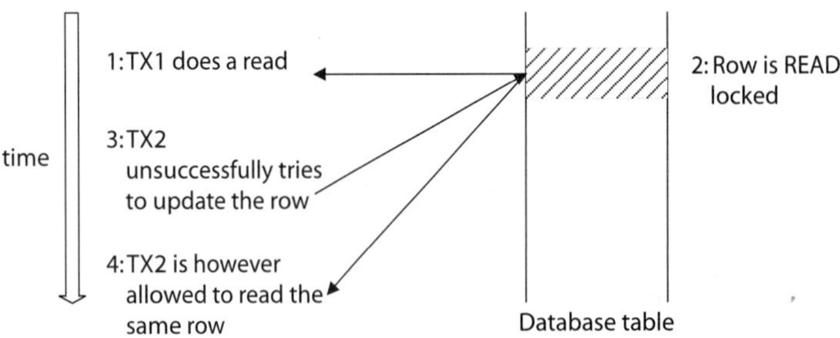

Figure 27.10 Impact of the `TRANSACTION_REPEATABLE_READ` isolation level.

read is given a READ lock.[3] TX2 is now prevented from updating the row, although it is allowed to read the same row.

There remains still one further problem to consider, namely, phantom reads. Let us say that TX1 in Figure 27.10 reads five consecutive rows of data. The `TRANSACTION_REPEATABLE_READ` level will not prevent TX2 from inserting new rows among the five rows read. When TX1 attempts to read the five rows again, it receives a phantom row, one that just

3 Don't be confused by the terminology. A `READ` lock is created as the result of a read operation. It is not a lock to prevent other read operations; rather it prevents write operations.

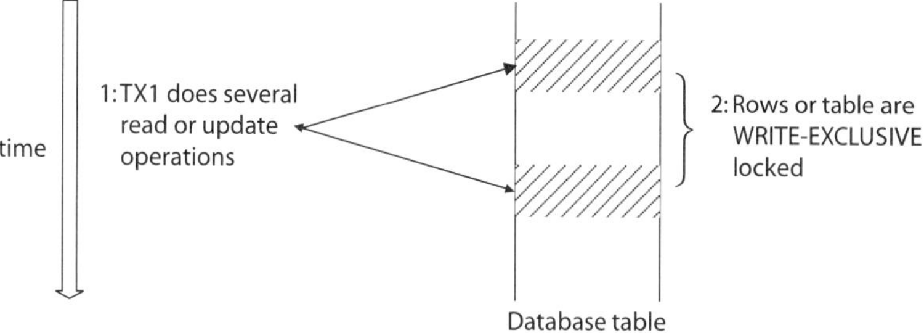

Figure 27.11 The impact of TRANSACTION_SERIALIZABLE isolation level.

appeared out of the ether. Again this might be a problem for some applications. If it is, then use the highest level of isolation, namely TRANSACTION_SERIALIZABLE. In Figure 27.11, we see that reads or updates by TX1 will effectively lock all the rows touched by TX1. Some database systems will actually lock the whole table. Neither reads, writes nor insertions are permitted by other transactions.

The semantics shown above are just one possibility. Unfortunately, different database systems may handle isolation levels in different ways. Some levels might not be supported. The above describes pessimistic locking. Some database systems employ optimistic locking, where a snapshot (copy) is made of the data being operated on, so that changes made by transactions are made on copies of the original. It is only at the point of transaction commit that checks are made to determine whether proposed updates to the original are allowed, depending on whether some other transaction got in there first. This style of operation is going to be more efficient since it is not necessary to create lots of locks and do so much checking. It can be awkward to debug though, since if a transaction is prevented from committing it might be difficult to see why. What this is saying is that transaction semantics are not portable across all database systems. You will have to read the database documentation and check to see if the described isolation levels and their semantics will impact your application.

The TRANSACTION_SERIALIZABLE level is the safest level. All transaction operations are effectively serialized; that is, TX1 will need to complete fully before TX2 gets a look in. However, there are reasons for not using this level all the time. The main reason is poor performance. A substantial part, if not all, of a table will become locked even if read operations are performed and other transactions will have to wait until the lock is removed. This can cause expensive bottlenecks. You need to analyse your application to find the appropriate level of isolation. Choose the minimum acceptable, since this will establish the least number of locks. Such analysis is not a trivial matter, as interactions between transactions can be quite subtle.

27.6.1 Lock Modes

Table 27.1 summarizes one possible interpretation of the impact of locks for various isolation levels. Take the table with a pinch of salt, since the precise semantics may vary across database implementations. In each case the lock was created by My TX.

Table 27.1 Possible set of lock modes and allowed operations for each isolation level.

	Write lock		*Write exclusive lock*		*Read lock*	
	My TX	*Other TX*	*My TX*	*Other TX*	*My TX*	*Other TX*
TRANSACTION_READ_UNCOMMITED	R/W/I	R/X/I	NA	NA	NA	NA
TRANSACTION_READ_COMMITED	NA	NA	R/W/I	X/X/I	NA	NA
TRANSACTION_REPEATABLE_READ	NA	NA	R/W/I	X/X/I	R/X/I	X/X/I
TRANSACTION_SERIALIZABLE	NA	NA	R/W/I	X/X/X	NA	NA

NA: Not applicable. The lock is not established for this mode of isolation.
R: Read operation allowed
W: Write operation allowed
I: Insert row operation allowed
X: The transaction is prevented from performing the operation.

- TRANSACTION_READ_UNCOMMITED
  Notice that the other transaction can perform dirty reads. If only rows are locked then the other TX can insert rows. The other TX is only prevented from updating the rows covered by the Write lock. Other locks do not apply.
- TRANSACTION_READ_COMMITED
  Here a write operation will create a write exclusive lock on the rows updated. This prevents other transactions from reading from or writing to those locked rows. This prevents dirty reads.
- TRANSACTION_REPEATABLE_READ
  Same behaviour as TRANSACTION_READ_COMMITED for write operations: the write exclusive lock is created. However, read operations lead to creating of a read lock (which is why it is called a read lock). It prevents updates to the locked rows by the current or other transactions. It does *not* prevent reading by other transactions. This ensures that My TX can repeatedly read the locked rows in the "knowledge" that they won't be changed. The exclusive write lock does not prevent insertion of new rows.
- TRANSACTION_SERIALIZABLE
  Both read and write operations cause a write exclusive lock to be placed on the table or area of the table being accessed by My TX. No other TX can access this area, so this prevents insertions and the possibility of phantom reads.

27.6.2 Specifying Isolation Levels

For session and message-driven EJBs that use bean-managed transactions you can set the isolation level using the JDBC API:

```
connection.setTransactionIsolation(Connection.TRANSACTION_SERIALIZABLE);
```

If you are using container-managed transactions or entity EJBs then you must use a server-specific mechanism.

27.7 Transactions and Exceptions

What happens to a transaction when an exception is thrown? If an exception escapes the boundary of the EJB component object into the container, the container will do one of two things. It will either mark the transaction for rollback and propagate the transaction to the original caller, or leave the transaction status unchanged and return control to the caller. The former occurs if the container receives a Java unchecked exception or the `java.rmi.RemoteException`. Unchecked exceptions are exceptions that don't need to be handled (caught or re-thrown), such as `ClassCastException` or `NullPointerException`. They indicate that there is a bug in your code, so the safest course of action is to force the transaction to roll back. Likewise, although a checked exception, `RemoteException` indicates that a system error has occurred and a rollback should take place.

Checked exceptions (other than `RemoteException`) do not automatically result in a rollback. Checked exceptions are those that must be handled. Examples include `SQLException` and `IllegalStateException` as well as application-specific exceptions. By simply propagating these exceptions, the container gives the caller the opportunity to deal with the exception and continue the transaction. Imagine a travel agent application where the caller calls a payment operation that fails (e.g. throws an `InsufficientFundsException`). Rather than immediately marking the transaction for rollback, the caller is given the opportunity to call the operation again, perhaps with a different set of credit card details. If the caller wishes to mark the transaction for rollback then it either calls `EJBContext.setRollbackOnly()` (for container-managed transactions) or `UserTransaction.setRollbackOnly()` (for bean-managed transactions).

You can also force the container to mark a transaction for rollback by wrapping up a checked exception within the unchecked `javax.ejb.EJBException` exception. For example, several of the methods in the `Cart` EJB in Chapter 29 wrap up `SQLException` within an `EJBException` in order to force the transaction to roll back.

27.8 Reference

Date, C. J. (1999). *An Introduction to Database Systems*. Addison Wesley, Reading, MA.

Chapter 28

Deployment Issues: Security

28.1 Introduction

From an application component developer's viewpoint, security, as with other J2EE services, is provided as a transparent service. This is to promote portability and focus on business logic. For this reason it is recommended that developers use the J2EE mechanisms rather than imposing their own through programmatic means. Indeed, only limited programmatic access to security information is provided.

The goals of J2EE security, as stated in Shannon (2001) (and reproduced here), are:

- **Portability**: the J2EE security architecture must support the Write Once, Run Anywhere™ application property.
- **Transparency**: Application Component Providers should not have to know anything about security to write an application.
- **Isolation**: the J2EE platform should be able to perform authentication and access control according to instructions established by the Deployer using deployment attributes, and managed by the System Administrator.
- **Extensibility**: the use of platform services by security aware-applications must not compromise application portability. The J2EE specification provides APIs in the component programming model for interacting with container and server security information. Applications that restrict their interactions to the provided APIs will retain portability.
- **Flexibility**: the security mechanisms and declarations used by applications under the J2EE specification should not impose a particular security policy, but facilitate the implementation of security policies specific to the particular J2EE installation or application.
- **Abstraction**: an application component's security requirements will be logically specified using deployment descriptors. Deployment descriptors will specify how security roles and access requirements are to be mapped into environment-specific security roles, users and policies. A Deployer may choose to modify the security properties in ways consistent with the deployment environment. The deployment descriptor should document which security properties can be modified and which cannot.

- **Independence**: required security behaviours and deployment contracts should be implementable using a variety of popular security technologies.
- **Compatibility testing**: the J2EE security requirements architecture must be expressed in a manner that allows for an unambiguous determination of whether or not an implementation is compatible.
- **Secure interoperability**: application components executing in a J2EE product must be able to invoke services provided in a J2EE product from a different vendor, whether with the same or a different security policy. These services may be provided by Web components or Enterprise beans.

28.2 Security Concepts and Architecture

J2EE, to varying degrees, addresses three major security facets:

- **Authentication.** This is where a user's identity is validated, for example by providing a user identifier and password in response to a login dialog box. This is required when a user accesses a security domain (see below) for the first time as part of a login session.
- **Access control (or authorization).** Once authenticated, access control constraints determine what that user is allowed to do, for example the EJB methods that can be executed.
- **Secure communication association.** Mechanisms are required to prevent unwanted snooping on or tampering with data exchanged between distributed components, clients and resources (e.g. enterprise servers). Typically such mechanisms use encryption and the exchange of cryptographic keys.

Let us examine a basic client to application server interaction scenario. This will illustrate the security steps undertaken by the server and provide a means to define security terms. Figure 28.1 shows a Web client accessing a Web server, which in turn requires access to EJBs. These also require access to an EIS.

- **Step 1.** Here the Web container has been configured to authenticate users who do not have a security principal associated with their user session (see Chapter 24 regarding Web sessions). The security principal is an object of type `java.security.Principal`. Among other things, it contains the name of the principal, in this scenario a user identifier, but it could be something else depending on the security mechanism used, for example a digital certificate. It also may contain security credentials, such as a password, again depending on the security mechanism employed. In this scenario the Web container generates and sends a login form to the Web client. A security principal may represent an individual or a group. When submitted, the data in this form is checked for validity in the environment's security domain (sometimes referred to as a security realm). The security domain defines the scope of the principal with respect to parts, or all of the application server and other environment servers. If the principal requires access to a server within another domain (for example a separate domain associated with an EIS) then a new principal will need to be created and authenticated.

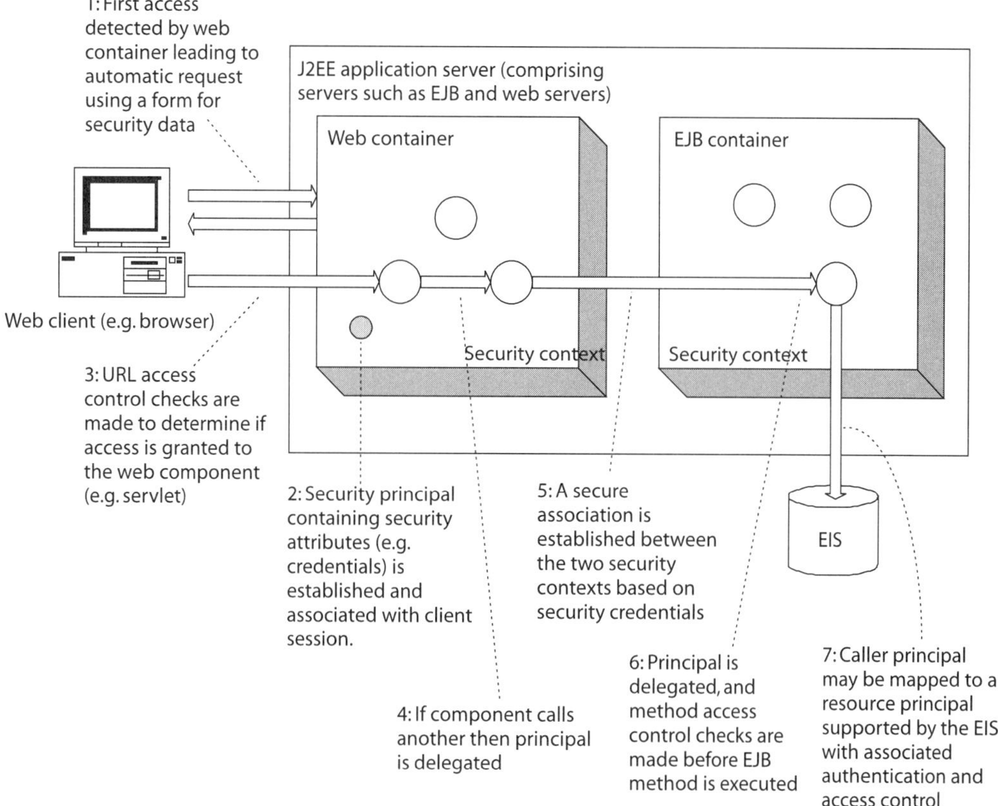
1: First access detected by web container leading to automatic request using a form for security data
J2EE application server (comprising servers such as EJB and web servers)
Web container
EJB container
Web client (e.g. browser)
Security context
Security context
3: URL access control checks are made to determine if access is granted to the web component (e.g. servlet)
2: Security principal containing security attributes (e.g. credentials) is established and associated with client session.
5: A secure association is established between the two security contexts based on security credentials
EIS
6: Principal is delegated, and method access control checks are made before EJB method is executed
7: Caller principal may be mapped to a resource principal supported by the EIS with associated authentication and access control
4: If component calls another then principal is delegated

Figure 28.1 Interaction scenario demonstrating authentication and authorization.

- **Step 2.** If authenticated, a principal is created. The security credentials might be stored in the principal object, but they might be stored elsewhere in the security context, or in a trusted third-party security server (such as an LDAP implementation). The security context will contain security constraints specific to a given J2EE container. The Web container will have security constraints defined in the `web.xml` file (see Chapter 25). The EJB container will have constraints defined in the `ejb-jar.xml` file (discussed later).
- **Step 3.** The original URL request's principal is now checked against access control constraints defined for the security context. Are we allowed to access the given servlet or JSP?
- **Step 4.** Here one component calls another (e.g. forwarding an original request). The principal is delegated (which may also be termed propagated) to the second component automatically. Again, access control checks are made.
- **Step 5.** The Web component requires access to an EJB in the same security domain, but within a separate security context. The server establishes a secure association between the two containers since the two containers probably reside in separate processes and may be physically distributed across a network. The security credentials of the calling principal may be used to establish the secure association.

- **Step 6.** By default a principal with the same name and credentials is created in the EJB container. Again this is a further example of principal delegation. The new security context has its own set of access control constraints. The principal is checked to ensure access is granted.
- **Step 7.** The called EJB method requests the services of an EIS (via the JCA). A resource principal is established at this point. Chapter 31 describes how a resource principal can be created that might or might not involve the calling principal. Authentication may be required if the EIS is in a separate security domain. The EIS will also handle access control based on the identity of the resource principal.

28.2.1 Authentication

How is authentication achieved? Although there are various mechanisms, the goal of each is to obtain and provide security identity and credentials to the security system that manages a particular security domain. Web clients can use basic authentication, SSL mutual authentication or form-based authentication (see Chapter 25 for a discussion of these mechanisms).

J2EE application clients may employ the proprietary mechanisms provided a vendor's application client container, such as the automatic pop-up of a login dialog box. Alternatively, if you provide an implementation of the `javax.security.auth.callback.CallbackHandler` interface, and refer to it within your application client deployment descriptors (see Chapter 26) then the application client container must use an object of this class to obtain security information. This forms part of the Java Authentication and Authorization Service (JAAS, now a core part of J2SE 1.4). In Section 26.4 we will briefly look at how a non-Web client can use JAAS to log into JBoss.

External resource authentication is discussed in Chapter 31.

Web containers may permit entry by unauthenticated users. In this case the container's security context's constraints permit access to Web components without the need for authentication. This is not the case for EJB containers. All calls to EJB methods must be undertaken with an authenticated principal. How can this be achieved if the calling Web component is not authenticated? One possibility is for the EJB container to provide automatically a default `guest` principal. A more portable approach is to set the `run-as` security identity in the EJB's deployment descriptors. This run-as principal will then be used from this point onwards.

Finally, clients are not allowed to change their principal identity during the course of a transaction. All transactional requests will operate in same security context. As a further restriction, stateful Session EJBs associated with a client must always be accessed with the same principal, irrespective of the transaction being used.

28.2.2 Access Control (Authorization)

J2EE uses container-based security. Each container maintains a security context containing access control constraints. These constraints determine which components an authenticated principal may access. The chief device used to achieve this is the security role. This is a logical security identity defined by an application component developer, or an application assembler within deployment descriptors (Web, EJB or application descriptors). Examples include `Manager`, `Administrator` and `ElectronicUser`. Each role is then assigned to one or more resources (in Web containers) and/or methods (in EJB containers). Only calling principals that belong to a role are permitted access to the resource *guarded* by that role. Clearly, a mapping must be established between a logical security role and the actual security identities used within the environment's security domain. This mapping is the responsibility of the deployer and is defined in a server-specific way (see Section 28.4).

In the EJB container, when a calling principal attempts to access a method, the container obtains the security identity from the principal and uses it as a key in the role mapping defined by the deployer. The key will map to zero or more logical roles. If the method being called also has one of these logical roles then the calling principal is granted access.

Security roles are defined declaratively in appropriate deployment descriptor files. As we will see, J2EE also supports limited programmatic access to security information.

Access control constraints within Web containers were discussed in Chapter 25. Section 28.3 describes how security roles are declared for EJBs.

Another more general form of access control is provided by Java's security model, for example whether an EJB is allowed to read from a file, or allowed to create a socket to a remote host. The set of security permissions are defined partly by J2EE and partly by the application server. In future you may be able to use deployment descriptors to add to this set of applied security permissions.

28.3 EJB Container-Managed Security

28.3.1 Declarative Security

For EJBs, security roles are declared within the `ejb-jar.xml` file. Listing 28.1 shows the modified `ejb-jar.xml` file for the bookstore application. Under the `<assembly-descriptor>` tag a security role has been declared with the value `Administrator`. This role is then assigned to the `BookItem` EJB's `create` and `remove` methods of its local and remote life cycle interfaces. This will ensure that only calling principals that have this role will be allowed to create new book items or remove existing book items.

We assign the role to these methods using the `<method-permission>` tag. Each `<method-permission>` tag can have one or more `<security-role>` tags or an `<unchecked/>` tag. These are followed by one or more `<method>` tags, each referring to one or more methods for a particular EJB (the form taken by the `<method>` tag is described in Chapter 27). In this way security roles can be associated with the methods that they are meant to guard. The `<unchecked/>` tag indicates that access control checks should not be made for the associated methods. This allows other authenticated and non-authenticated (where authentication was not required) users access to these methods; for the example these are all the methods defined under the second `<method-permission>` tag.

Listing 28.1 Setting method permissions for the `BookItem` life cycle methods.

```
<ejb-jar>
  <enterprise-beans>
    <!-- sub tags omitted -->
```

```
</enterprise-beans>
<relationships>
  <!-- sub tags omitted -->
</relationships>
  <assembly-descriptor>
    <security-role>
      <role-name>Administrator</role-name>
    </security-role>
    <security-role>
      <role-name>guest</role-name>
    </security-role>

    <container-transaction>
      <!-- sub tags omitted -->
    </container-transaction>

    <method-permission>
      <role-name>Administrator</role-name>
      <method>
        <ejb-name>BookItem</ejb-name>
        <method-name>remove</method-name>
      </method>
      <method>
        <ejb-name>BookItem</ejb-name>
        <method-name>create</method-name>
      </method>
    </method-permission>
    <method-permission>
      <unchecked/>
      <method>
        <ejb-name>BookItem</ejb-name>
        <method-name>addRelation</method-name>
      </method>
      <method>
        <ejb-name>BookItem</ejb-name>
        <method-name>removeRelation</method-name>
      </method>
      <method>
        <ejb-name>BookItem</ejb-name>
        <method-name>getTitle</method-name>
      </method>
      <method>
        <ejb-name>BookItem</ejb-name>
        <method-name>setTitle</method-name>
      </method>
      <method>
```

```
      <ejb-name>BookItem</ejb-name>
      <method-name>setData</method-name>
    </method>
    <method>
      <ejb-name>BookItem</ejb-name>
      <method-name>getData</method-name>
    </method>
    <method>
      <ejb-name>BookItem</ejb-name>
      <method-name>getAuthor</method-name>
    </method>
    <method>
      <ejb-name>BookItem</ejb-name>
      <method-name>setAuthor</method-name>
    </method>
    <method>
      <ejb-name>BookItem</ejb-name>
      <method-name>getIsbn</method-name>
    </method>
    <method>
      <ejb-name>BookItem</ejb-name>
      <method-name>setIsbn</method-name>
    </method>
    <method>
      <ejb-name>BookItem</ejb-name>
      <method-name>getPrice</method-name>
    </method>
    <method>
      <ejb-name>BookItem</ejb-name>
      <method-name>setPrice</method-name>
    </method>
    <method>
      <ejb-name>BookItem</ejb-name>
      <method-name>findByPrimaryKey</method-name>
    </method>
    <method>
      <ejb-name>BookItem</ejb-name>
      <method-name>findByAuthor</method-name>
    </method>
    <method>
      <ejb-name>Cart</ejb-name>
      <method-name>*</method-name>
    </method>
    <method>
      <ejb-name>Till</ejb-name>
      <method-name>*</method-name>
```

```
        </method>
        <method>
          <ejb-name>Purchase</ejb-name>
          <method-name>*</method-name>
        </method>
      </method-permission>
    </assembly-descriptor>
</ejb-jar>
```

Note that in JBoss we were forced to include entries for methods addRelation and removeRelation, even though these are not defined in any interface. We suspect that these are generated methods that maintain container-managed relationships between the Cart and BookItem EJBs.

Where a non-authenticated user attempts to access one of these unchecked methods the EJB server may provide a default principal identity, such as guest. However, this is not standard and relies on the server being configured appropriately. A standard mechanism would be to provide a <security-identity> tag within the relevant <session>, <entity> or <message-driven> tags. The <security-identity> tag can either contain a <run-as> sub-tag or a <use-caller-identity/> sub-tag. The latter requires the caller principal's identity to be propagated to the EJB. This is the default case if no <security-identity> tag is provided. The <run-as> tag indicates that a new security principal is created with an identity specified by the <role-name> sub-tag. This security role must be declared by a <security-role> tag within the assembly descriptors. In Listing 28.2, our message-driven EJB is given the Administrator run-as identity.

Listing 28.2 Example use of the <run-as> tag.

```
<message-driven>
  <ejb-name>DebugMonitor</ejb-name>
  <ejb-class>util.DebugMonitorBean</ejb-class>
  <message-selector>JMSType = 'DEBUG'</message-selector>
  <transaction-type>Container</transaction-type>
  <acknowledge-mode>Auto-acknowledge</acknowledge-mode>
  <message-driven-destination>
    <destination-type>javax.jms.Topic</destination-type>
    <subscription-durability>Durable</subscription-durability>
  </message-driven-destination>
  <security-identity>
    <run-as>
      <role-name>Administrator</role-name>
    </run-as>
  </security-identity>
</message-driven>
```

Access to methods can also be controlled with the <exclude-list> tag. This optional tag, which is placed under the <assembly-descriptor> tag, will contain one or more <method> tags, each referring to a method that cannot be called, even if that method is referenced under the `<method-permission>` tag. If we wanted to prevent all users from calling any remove method on `BookItem` we could include the following within the assembly descriptors:

```
<!-- Last element of <assembly-descriptor>-->
<exclude-list>
  <method>
    <ejb-name>BookItem</ejb-name>
    <method-name>remove</method-name>
  </method>
</exclude-list>
```

28.3.2 Programmatic Security

A limited degree of programmatic access to security information is provided under J2EE. Web containers provide the methods `getUserPrincipal` and `isUserInRole` within the `javax.servlet.http.HttpServletRequest` interface. EJB containers provide the methods `getCallerPrincipal` and `isCallerInRole` within the `javax.ejb.EJBContext` interface.

The `getCallerPrincipal` method returns the `java.security.Principal` object of the caller. This method never returns `null` since a principal must always be established in an EJB container. Calling the `getName` method on the `Principal` object can then be used to obtain the name of the principal, as a `String`.

The `isCallerInRole` method takes a security role-name as a `String` parameter and returns `true` if the caller belongs to that role, otherwise it returns `false`.

These methods give you the flexibility to deal with security at a fine level of granularity. For instance, you may use the principal name to do some form of database lookup. However, be warned: the form that a principal name takes depends on the security mechanism used in your environment, and may be different in other environments. You may end up with non-portable code if you rely on the form taken by a principal name. The `isCallerInRole` method is a useful way of checking the security role membership within your business logic. For example, in an online banking application the `transferFunds` method might allow `GoldUsers` to transfer amounts greater than a certain threshold, but other mere mortals are restricted to transferring smaller funds:

```
public void transferFunds(Account from, Account to, double amount)
  throws InsufficientFundsException, InvalidOperationException{

  if ((amount > transferLimit) && (!ejbCtx.isCallerInRole("GoldUsers")){
    throw new InvalidOperationException("Attempted to exceed transfer"
                                        + "limit of " + transferLimit);
  }
  // Remainder of method
}
```

The role-name used in the code must then be mapped to the actual security role within the deployment descriptors. This is done with a `<security-role-ref>` tag that is placed under the relevant bean tag. In the above example we might have a `TransferHandler` stateless session EJB:

```
<session>
  <ejb-name>TransferHandler</ejb-name>
  <!-- Omitted other descriptors -->
  <security-role-ref>
    <role-name>GoldUsers</role-name>
    <role-link>PreferredCustomers</role-link>
  </security-role-ref>
</session>
```

The `<role-name>` value must be the same as that used in the code. The `<role-link>` value will map the programmatic name to a logical security role name declared using a `<security-role>` tag within the assembly descriptors.

28.3.3 Stakeholder Responsibilities

A component developer may have used the `isUserInRole` or `isCallerInRole` methods, referring to a principal name. They were responsible for writing code to do fine-grained security checking. They must also expose the names they used in `<security-role-ref>` tags. However, they would not provide the `<role-link>` name. Where bean-managed authentication is required for external resources (provision of credentials and identity via `getConnection` methods) the developer must ensure that the correct values are obtained and passed to the connection factory object (see Chapter 31).

The application assembler will need to define the attributes of the application, filling out the application assembly tags, and possibly writing extra glue components to link up other application components. One of her responsibilities is to define the application's logical security roles and tie these to specific methods using `<method-permission>` tags. The assembler is also responsible for adding the `<role-link>` tags to existing `<security-role-ref>` tags, thereby tying the code version of the security role name to the actual security role defined in the assembly descriptors.

The deployer is responsible for mapping logical security role names onto environment principal names. This is achieved in an environment-specific manner. It may depend partly on the application server and partly on the security mechanisms used. We will see one example of how this is done in the next section.

28.4 Example Use of the Java Authentication and Authorization Service (JAAS)

JAAS is a security API that forms part of J2SE 1.4 and part of J2EE 1.4. To illustrate end-to-end security support we provide a brief overview and a simple Java application example that ties into JAAS and JBoss.

JAAS is a Java version of the Pluggable Authentication Module (PAM) framework (see `http://www.kernel.org/pub/linux/libs/pam/`). JBoss only uses the authentication parts of this framework; it does not use the authorization interfaces, providing instead its own mechanism. The key authentication interfaces and classes are:

- `javax.security.auth.callback.Callback`
- `javax.security.auth.callback.CallbackHandler`
- `javax.security.auth.login.Configuration`
- `javax.security.auth.login.LoginContext`
- `javax.security.auth.spi.LoginModule`

In addition, two common security interfaces are used:

- `javax.security.auth.Subject`
- `java.security.Principal`

A `Subject` represents an entity such as a person or another system that requires authentication in the current security domain. A `Subject` encapsulates `Principal` objects, public credentials (e.g. public keys) and private credentials (e.g. passwords or private keys). A `Subject` can have one or more `Principal` objects established during authentication. Each represents a calling identity for the `Subject`, such as user identifier or credit card number, or a digital signature. Credentials are also obtained during authentication. The `Principals` will be used later during authorization, as described earlier, and may also be used in combination with the credentials if further authentication is required in other security domains.

How is JAAS used to create and authenticate subjects? Listing 28.3 shows the first part of the `SetupDatabase` client for the bookstore enterprise application. This class simply creates three `BookItem` instances, thereby populating the `BookItem` table with some test data. However, it uses JAAS to obtain authentication information that is associated with a `Subject`, which is passed to the EJB server when EJB methods are called. Note that we arrange for authentication to be delayed until the call reaches the EJB server.

Listing 28.3 `SetupDatabase` main method.

```
package client;

import store.*;
import javax.naming.*;
import javax.rmi.PortableRemoteObject;
import javax.security.auth.callback.*;
import javax.security.auth.login.*;
import java.util.*;

public class SetupDatabase{

  public static void main(String[] args){
    SetupDatabase setup = new SetupDatabase();
    setup.login();
    setup.init(args);
  }
```

The login method is shown in Listing 28.4. For simplicity, the user identifier and password are hard coded. The method begins by creating an `AppCallbackHandler` object. This private inner class (Listing 28.6) implements the `CallbackHandler` interface. In this simple handler we pass the user identifier and password as constructor parameters. A more sophisticated handler would obtain this information from the environment, perhaps using a Swing GUI. The `LoginContext` class takes two parameters. The first is a security context name. In JBoss, a `Configuration` object uses this to search for a context entry in a security file called `auth.conf` (an example of which can be found in the `server/default/conf` directory). This context entry will have an associated `LoginModule` interface implementation class.[1] This class knows about a specific security mechanism, such as Kerberos or LDAP. The JBoss-provided "client-login" module's task is simply to obtain authentication data (principal name and password credential) and associate these with a `Subject`; no authentication is done in the client. An example `auth.conf` file is shown in Listing 28.5. The `LoginContext` constructor's second parameter takes the handler object. The `LoginModule` will use this to obtain authentication information.

The use of login modules decouples the application and server code from code that "knows" about a specific security mechanism. This flexibility makes it very easy to incorporate any number of modules without having to alter application or server code.

The `LoginContext.login` method then starts the login process by using the callback handler to obtain authentication data and to authenticate that data using the associated login module. If authenticated the `Subject` is created along with the principal and credential objects.

Listing 28.6 shows the `AppCallbackHandler` inner class. This implements the `CallbackHandler` interface, and as such must provide a `handle` method. This method is called for each participating `LoginModule`. It is passed an array of `Callback` objects that must be populated with the authentication information needed by the login modules. There are various standard classes that implement the `Callback` interface. The `handle` method checks to make sure that the array only contains `NameCallback` and `PasswordCallback` objects. These are the only kind of `Callback` that make sense for this client and the style of authentication it supports, namely user identifier and password. The handle method will throw `UnsupportedCallbackException` if any other kind of authentication data is requested. The `Callback` objects are populated with data using the `setName` and `setPassword` methods.

Listing 28.4 The `login` method.

```
private void login(){
  String user = "admin";
  String pass = new String("qwerty");
  try{
    AppCallbackHandler handler =
      new AppCallbackHandler(user, pass.toCharArray());

    // LoginContext is part of JAAS: javax.security.auth.login package.
```

1 It is possible to chain `LoginModule` objects where several authentication mechanisms are required when authenticating subjects.

```
      // In JBoss this will result in the
      // auth.conf file being searched for the "client-login"
      // entry which has an associated LoginModule implementation that knows
      // how to use a specific security authentication mechanism.
      // The handler is passed in since that will get the credentials
      // from the user. In this case we pass in the credentials
      // when the handler is instantiated

      LoginContext lc = new LoginContext("client-login", handler);

      // lc.login is where authentication is initiated
      lc.login();
    }
    catch (LoginException le){
      le.printStackTrace();
    }
  }
```

Listing 28.5 An example `auth.conf` file.

```
bookstore {
// A properties file LoginModule that supports CallerPrincipal mapping
  org.jboss.security.auth.spi.UsersRolesLoginModule required
  unauthenticatedIdentity="nobody";
};

// Used by clients within the application server VM such as
// mbeans and servlets that access EJBs.
client-login {
  org.jboss.security.ClientLoginModule required;
};

simple {
    // Very simple login module:
    // any user name is accepted.
    // password should either coincide with user name or be null,
    // all users have role "guest",
    // users with non-null password also have role "user"
    org.jboss.security.auth.spi.SimpleServerLoginModule required;
};
```

Listing 28.6 The `CallbackHandler` implementation.

```
// The CallbackHandler interface is implemented to obtain principal name
// and credentials (in this case username and password). This is used
// when creating a LoginContext (see above)
```

```
private class AppCallbackHandler implements CallbackHandler {

  private String username;
  private char[] password;

  public AppCallbackHandler(String username, char[] password){
    this.username = username;
    this.password = password;
  }

  public void handle(Callback[] callbacks)
    throws java.io.IOException, UnsupportedCallbackException{

    for (int i = 0; i < callbacks.length; i++){
      if (callbacks[i] instanceof NameCallback){
        NameCallback nc = (NameCallback)callbacks[i];
        nc.setName(username);
      }
      else if (callbacks[i] instanceof PasswordCallback){
        PasswordCallback pc = (PasswordCallback)callbacks[i];
        pc.setPassword(password);
      }
      else{
        throw new UnsupportedCallbackException(callbacks[i],
                 "Unrecognized Callback");
      }
    }
  }
}
```

As said earlier, the "client-login" `LoginModule` defers full authentication. After login, the `DatabaseSetup` client calls the `init` method. This method is shown in Listing 28.7. When the life cycle method, `create`, is called both the explicit Book parameter and implicit `Subject` object are passed to the EJB container. JBoss has a security interceptor object that receives this `Subject`. We have configured the deployed bookstore application to use the `bookstore` security domain, and associated `UsersRolesLoginModule`, to deal with incoming requests (Listing 28.5). This module will do the authentication of the `Subject` by checking that the principal name and password match those in a `users.properties` file (that must be on the `classpath`). It also reads a `roles.properties` file that assigns security roles to users (principals). An example `users.properties` file might contain:

```
admin=qwerty
```

which is the user identifier and associated password. An example `roles.properties` file might contain:

```
admin=Administrator
```

where admin is assigned to the Administrator logical security role. The mapping of principals to security roles is maintained within the container. If authentication fails at this point an exception is thrown back to the client. If authentication succeeds, the container will check that the calling principal is authorized to execute the create method. This is based on method permission descriptor information, as described earlier.

Listing 28.7 The init method creates three BookItem instances.

```
private void init(String [] args){
  try{
    InitialContext ctx = new InitialContext();

    Object objref = ctx.lookup("ejb/bookItemR");
    BookItemHome biHome = (BookItemHome)
            PortableRemoteObject.narrow(objref, BookItemHome.class);
    biHome.create(new Book("Java", "John Hunt", 29.50, "1234"));
    biHome.create(new Book("XML", "Chris Loftus",45.00, "1235"));
    biHome.create(new Book("UML", "Denise Cooke",19.90, "1236"));
  }
  catch(Exception e){
    e.printStackTrace();
  }
}
```

The security domain to be used by the EJB container for the bookstore application is specified in the jboss.xml file. Listing 27.8 shows two optional tags that we included. The <security-domain> tag specifies the name of the security domain to use. This is the same name used in the auth.conf file. The container will perform a JNDI lookup to obtain the appropriate LoginModule object. The other tag specifies that if a method is accessed by an unauthenticated client then a default principal with the name guest will be used.

Listing 27.8 Part of the jboss.xml file.

```
<jboss>
  <security-domain>java:/jaas/bookstore</security-domain>
  <unauthenticated-principal>guest</unauthenticated-principal>
  <enterprise-beans>
    <!-- Other descriptors omitted -->
  </enterprise-beans>
</jboss>
```

28.5 Reference

Shannon, B. (2001). *Java 2 Platform Enterprise Edition Specification 1.3*. Sun Microsystems.

Chapter 29

Bean-Managed Persistence

29.1 Introduction

In Chapter 14 we discussed container-managed persistent entity EJBs. These EJBs rely on the container to undertake operations on the database on their behalf. Deployment tools generate code that will interact with the database, probably using JDBC. You are free as a developer to focus on business logic and not worry about the plumbing to the persistent store. Bean-managed, persistent entity EJBs, on the other hand, require you to implement this code. Typically, you will write JDBC code that creates, deletes, updates and selects data within the `ejbCreate`, `ejbRemove`, `ejbStore` and `ejbLoad` methods.

Doing this removes the advantages provided by container-managed persistence, and will make your EJBs more complicated and harder to maintain. However, there are situations where the code generated to support CMP is inappropriate, either because it is too inefficient or you need access to a legacy database not supported by the container tools. For example, you might want to use a non-standard, but efficient SQL command, or to call stored procedures. Or you might want to store or retrieve data from a hierarchical or network database. BMP also grants you much more control over the object to relational mapping; for instance, you may wish to map a single entity EJB to several tables or several rows within the same table. You may also face the situation where, although you have a specialized container that supports the persistence mechanism you require, containers in other application servers don't support the same persistence mechanism. This may reduce the portability of your application to a subset of all application servers. In this case, and if portability is an important business goal, it might be wise to use BMP entity EJBs. This chapter will show you how to create BMP entity EJBs.

29.2 The Entity EJB Life Cycle Revisited

Figure 29.1 shows the entity life cycle, originally discussed in Chapter 14. The diagram is the same but the roles of the `container` and `ejb` methods are different. The differences are as follows:

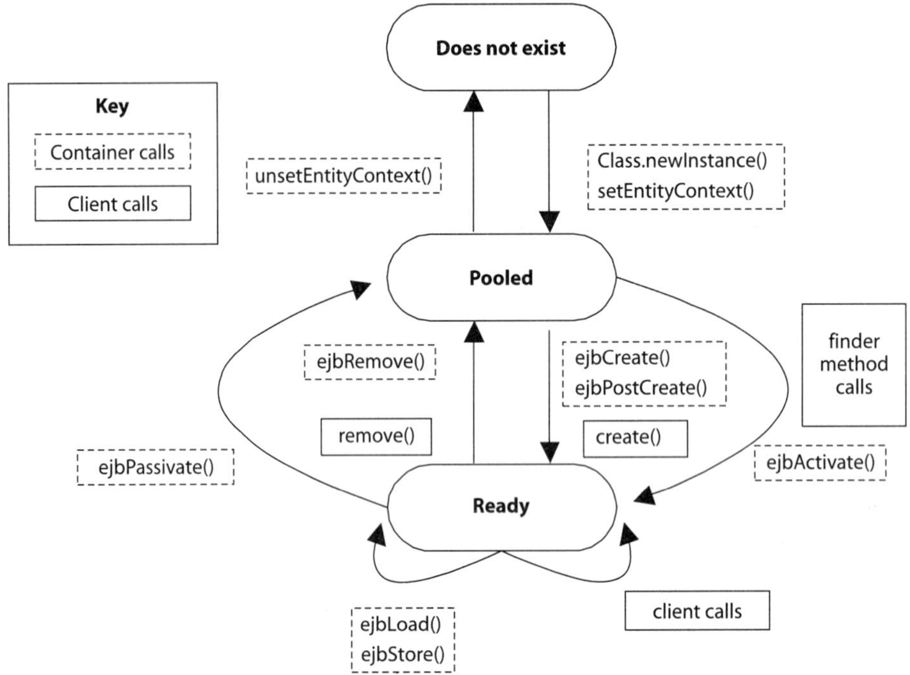

Figure 29.1 The entity EJB state diagram revisited.

- `ejbCreate`: this is required to create a new entry in the database, perhaps using JDBC. To do this `ejbCreate` will need to obtain a data source connection. We will look at this later. The other major difference is that `ejbCreate` is responsible for creating and returning a primary key object.
- `ejbRemove`: this is required to delete the database entry that represents the entity.
- `ejbStore`: this must contain code that will update the appropriate entry or entries within the database. The EJB's primary key will be used to find the relevant entries.
- `ejbLoad`: this must contain code that will retrieve data from the database and update the appropriate instance variables within the EJB.
- `ejbPostCreate`: there is less of a need to place code in this method, since you have complete control of initialization and database insertions within `ejbCreate`, unlike CMP where the container does some work after `ejbCreate` returns, and where `ejbPostCreate` may be required to complete initialization that depends on that work. However, even in BMP, the container is responsible for creating the business logic interface object after `ejbCreate` returns. If you need access to that object as part of the initialization process then you will need to do this within `ejbPostCreate`.
- `ejbPassivate` and `ejbActivate`: these continue to have the same role as with CMP, for example closing and opening the external resources.
- `ejbFindByPrimaryKey` and other finder methods and select methods: these must now be implemented explicitly, they are not generated by the container deployment tools. `select`

methods are now just treated like any other private method not exposed through the EJB's interfaces.

- setEntityContext and unsetEntityContext: these play the same role as for CMP; however, it is essential that you do save the EntityContext object in an instance variable, as we will see later.

Although you are now responsible for implementing the persistence mapping, the container will continue to call the callback life cycle methods at appropriate times; indeed, in this respect, the container makes no distinction between CMP and BMP entity EJBs.

29.3 BookItem EJB: the BMP version

We will highlight the differences between CMP and BMP by looking at the BMP version of the BookItem EJB component class, BookItemBMPBean. Note that the business logic and life cycle interfaces remain the same. Listings 29.1–29.7 present the code. As you look through this code, take a look back at the CMP version in Chapter 14. The BMP version will not work with the existing Cart EJB, since Cart has container-managed relationships to BookItem, and for this to work JBoss requires that both EJBs are container-managed. Consequently, the deployment descriptor files and test harness class all deal with the BookItem EJB in isolation.

Listing 29.1 presents the first part of the class, including the import statements, and, because we have to manage the EJB state ourselves, private instance variables for each of the fields we want to map onto an underlying database. Notice that BookItemBMPBean extends the original CMP BookItemBean. This is to make the BookItem EJB's implementation as flexible as possible. It means we can either use CMP or BMP simply by changing the deployment descriptors. In effect, we are providing the concrete subclass for BookItemBean instead of the container deployment tools. Consequently, we provide concrete implementations for the super-class's abstract getter and setter methods.

Our code needs to access one or more databases explicitly. Each database, known as a data source, is accessed using JNDI. As we did with accessing EJBs, we can use logical lookup names that are mapped to physical lookup names within the deployment descriptor files. In our EJB we need access to a single data source, and we have decided to use the name: java:comp/env/jdbc/bookstore. As we saw in Chapter 15, the java:comp/env gets JNDI to look in the calling EJB's environment naming context for the resource: jdbc/bookstore. More on this later.

Listing 29.1 Part of the BookItemBMPBean implementation class.

```
package store;

import javax.ejb.EntityBean;
import javax.ejb.EntityContext;
import javax.ejb.CreateException;
import javax.ejb.FinderException;
import javax.ejb.ObjectNotFoundException;
```

```
import javax.ejb.EJBException;
import javax.naming.InitialContext;
import javax.naming.NamingException;
import javax.rmi.PortableRemoteObject;
import javax.sql.DataSource;
import java.sql.Connection;
import java.sql.Statement;
import java.sql.PreparedStatement;
import java.sql.ResultSet;
import java.sql.SQLException;
import java.util.Collection;
import java.util.ArrayList;

/**
 * The concrete implementation class for the BMP version of
 * the BookItem EJB.
 * @author Chris Loftus
 * @version 1.0
 */
public class BookItemBMPBean extends BookItemBean {

  private static final String bookStoreDSRef =
    "java:comp/env/jdbc/bookstore";
  private Connection con;

  // Bean managed fields and their accessor methods follow
  private String isbn; // Key
  private String title;
  private String author;
  private double price;

  /**
   * Gets the ISBN primary key value
   * @return The primary key for the book
   */
  public String getIsbn(){
    return isbn;
  }
  /**
   * Sets the ISBN CMP field
   * @param isbn should be a non-null valid ISBN
   */
  public void setIsbn(String isbn){
    this.isbn = isbn;
  }
  /**
```

```
  * Gets the book's title
  * @return The title of the book
  */
 public String getTitle(){
   return title;
 }
 /**
  * Sets the title of the book
  * @param title is the new title for the book
  */
 public void setTitle(String title){
   this.title = title;
 }
 /**
  * Gets the author of the book
  * @return The author of the book
  */
 public String getAuthor(){
   return author;
 }
 /**
  * Sets the author's name for the book
  * @param author is the new author name for the book
  */
 public void setAuthor(String author){
   this.author = author;
 }
 /**
  * Gets the price of the book
  * @return The price as a double
  */
 public double getPrice(){
   return price;
 }
 /**
  * Sets the price for the book
  * @param price is the new price for the book
  */
 public void setPrice(double price){
   this.price = price;
 }
```

Listing 29.2 shows the next part of the class: the `ejbPassivate` and `ejbActivate` methods. Notice that these start by calling their superclass equivalents to ensure that any action defined in the superclass is undertaken first, although this might not always be appropriate. Since we are accessing an external resource, we have decided to close the connection during passivation and then reopen it during activation. The getConnection method is a private utility method that we will examine later. Actually, closing the connection will simply place the connection back into a free pool of database connections maintained by the container. Opening a connection will simply provide the EJB with an existing connection from the connection pool. Because of this, opening and closing connections should not be an expensive operation and will ensure that the EJB only has a connection when it needs one. This is important since the connection pool is a finite resource, and database licence restrictions may significantly curtail its size.

Listing 29.2 Roles for ejbPassivate and ejbActivate.

```
/**
 * Closes the connection while instance is back in the free pool
 */
public void ejbPassivate(){
  super.ejbPassivate();
  try{
    if (con != null) con.close();
  }
  catch(SQLException se){
    throw new EJBException(se);
  }
  finally{
    con = null;
  }
}
/**
 * Re-opens the connection for the newly associated instance
 */
public void ejbActivate(){
  super.ejbActivate();
  con = getConnection();
}
```

The ejbRemove method in Listing 29.3 now contains code to explicitly delete the appropriate row from the BOOKITEMTAB01 table. It begins by calling the superclass's ejbRemove. It then obtains the primary key using the EntityContext object, ctx. This is the only safe way to obtain the primary key in this method. It is not safe to simply use the isbn instance variable value, since this might be unset for reasons mentioned in the comments. If con is null then we get a new connection. We have hard-coded the SQL statement as part of the executeUpdate call. A better approach would be to use a data access class that decouples the database code from the implementation class. In fact, this is described by a design pattern that we mention in Chapter 34.

If executeUpdate does not return 1 then we know that the delete has failed, and we throw an EJBException. This will force any transaction to be rolled back, an issue discussed in Chapter 27. The elaborate `catch` and `finally` part of the `try` block ensures that we close unwanted resources.

Listing 29.3 The `ejbRemove` method.

```
/**
 * Deletes the relevant row from the database. Then closes
 * the connection.
 */
public void ejbRemove(){
  super.ejbRemove();

  // JDBC code to remove the item from the database. It
  // is important to obtain the key using EntityContext
  // since this method may be called while the isbn ivar
  // has an invalid value, e.g. after ejbFindByPrimaryKey,
  // but prior to ejbLoad being called.
  isbn = (String)ctx.getPrimaryKey();

  Statement stat = null;
  try{
    if (con == null)
      con = getConnection();
    stat = con.createStatement();

    if (stat.executeUpdate("delete from BOOKITEMTAB01 where ISBN = '"
                           + isbn + "'") != 1){
      throw new EJBException("Couldn't delete entry ISBN: " + isbn +
                             " from the BOOKITEMTAB01 table");
    }
  }

  catch (SQLException se){
    throw new EJBException(se);
  }
  finally{
    try{
      if (stat != null) stat.close();
      if (con != null) con.close();
    }
    catch(SQLException se){
      throw new EJBException(se);
    }
  }
}
```

Listing 29.4 contains the ejbStore and ejbLoad methods. For BMP, these methods must be implemented. As with CMP EJBs, the container will call them when it "decides" that the EJB needs to be synchronized with the underlying database. However, now your code is responsible for updating or retrieving from the database. To make the code easier to write and maintain, ejbStore uses a PreparedStatement object. Indeed, the code could be further optimized so that PreparedStatement objects are stored in instance variables and reused between method calls. Like ejbActivate, ejbLoad obtains the primary key using the EntityContext ctx object. This is the only safe way to obtain this value.

Listing 29.4 The ejbStore and ejbLoad methods.

```
/**
 * Updates the relevant database row.
 */
public void ejbStore(){
  super.ejbStore();
  // We have to update the database BOOKITEMTAB01 table
  // entry with the current value of items
  System.out.println("ejbStore");
  if (con == null)
    con = getConnection();
  PreparedStatement stat = null;
  try{
    stat = con.prepareStatement("update BOOKITEMTAB01 set TITLE = ?, " +
                                "AUTHOR = ?, PRICE = ? where ISBN = ?");
    stat.setString(1, title);
    stat.setString(2, author);
    stat.setDouble(3, price);
    stat.setString(4, isbn);
    if (stat.executeUpdate() != 1){
      con.close();
      throw new EJBException("Couldn't store book item values: " +
                            " in the BOOKITEMTAB01 table for isbn "
                            + isbn);
    }
  }
  catch (SQLException se){
    try{
      con.close();
    }
    catch (SQLException e){
      throw new EJBException(e);
    }
  }
  finally{
    try{
```

```
        if (stat != null) stat.close();
      }
      catch(SQLException se){
        try{
          if (con != null) con.close();
        }
        catch (SQLException e){
          throw new EJBException(e);
        }
        throw new EJBException(se);
      }
    }
  }
  /**
   * Refreshes the EJB with data from the relevant row in the database
   */
  public void ejbLoad(){
    super.ejbLoad();

    // We have to load from the database BOOKITEMTAB01 table
    // entry with the current ISBN

    System.out.println("ejbLoad");
    String isbn = (String)ctx.getPrimaryKey();
    Statement stat = null;
    ResultSet result = null;
    try{
      stat = con.createStatement();
      result = stat.executeQuery("select * from BOOKITEMTAB01 where "
                                 + "ISBN = '" + isbn + "'");
      if (result.next()){
        this.isbn = isbn;
        this.title = result.getString("TITLE");
        this.author = result.getString("AUTHOR");
        this.price = result.getDouble("PRICE");
      }
      else{
        if (con != null) con.close();
        throw new EJBException("Couldn't load entry " +
                               " from the BOOKITEMTAB01 table for ISBN "
                               + isbn);
      }
    }
    catch (SQLException se){
      try{
        if (con != null) con.close();
```

```
      }
      catch (SQLException e){
        throw new EJBException(e);
      }
      throw new EJBException(se);
    }
    finally{
      try{
        if (result != null) result.close();
        if (stat != null) stat.close();
      }
      catch(SQLException se){
        throw new EJBException(se);
      }
    }
  }
```

Listing 29.5 provides the code for the `ejbCreate` and `ejbPostCreate` methods. The superclass's `ejbCreate` will check that the `newBook` parameter contains appropriate values and will call the appropriate setter methods. The subclass method then obtains a database connection and uses a `PreparedStatement` to insert a new row into the `BOOKITEMTAB01` table. This will fail if the row already exists, in which case `CreateException` is thrown. Finally, the key is returned to the container, which is not the case for CMP where a `null` is returned. In our implementation, `ejbPostCreate` remains unused.

Listing 29.5 The `ejbCreate` and `ejbPostCreate` methods.

```
  /**
   * Checks that a valid book has been provided and if so
   * stores the book's details as BMP values, with an associated
   * SQL INSERT to insert a new row.
   * @param newBook The new book to add as a BookItem
   * @return Since a BMP EJB, returns the primary key.
   * @exception CreateException is thrown if newBook is null or
   * the book's ISBN is null or of length 0, or the entry
   * already exists.
   */
    public String ejbCreate(Book newBook)
           throws CreateException{

      super.ejbCreate(newBook);

    // Now we have to actually create the record in the BOOKITEMTAB01 table
      Connection con = null;
      PreparedStatement stat = null;
      try{
```

```
        con = this.getConnection();
        stat = con.prepareStatement("insert into BOOKITEMTAB01 " +
                                    "(ISBN, TITLE, AUTHOR, PRICE) " +
                                    "values (?, ?, ?, ?)");
        stat.setString(1, isbn);
        stat.setString(2, title);
        stat.setString(3, author);
        stat.setDouble(4, price);
        if (stat.executeUpdate() != 1){
          throw new CreateException("Failed to add BOOKITEMTAB01 entry "
                                    + "with fields ISBN: " + isbn
                                    + " TITLE: " + title
                                    + " AUTHOR: " + author
                                    + " PRICE: " + price);
        }
      }
      catch(SQLException se){
        try{
          if (con != null) con.close();
        }
        catch(SQLException e){
          throw new EJBException(e);
        }
        throw new EJBException(se);
      }
      finally{
      try{
        if (stat != null) stat.close();
      }
      catch(SQLException se){
        throw new EJBException(se);
      }
    }
    return this.isbn;
  }
  public void ejbPostCreate(Book newBook)
    throws CreateException {
    super.ejbPostCreate(newBook);
  }
```

Listing 29.6 shows the code for ejbFindByPrimaryKey and ejbFindByAuthor. The former is mandatory, the latter optional; it was considered a useful finder method. Both were generated automatically for the CMP version, but must be included explicitly for BMP. All the finder methods are required to return either a single key or a Collection or Set of keys to the container: the former where the finder maps to a single row; the latter where the finder may map to several rows. Use a Set if you only want to return unique entries and a Collection if duplicates are permitted. Notice that the ejbFindByAuthor creates and returns an ArrayList, since this implements the Collection interface.

When these methods return, the container will create one or more business logic interface (BLI) objects. If access was via a remote life cycle interface, then the findByPrimaryKey method will return a stub reference to the BLI object. The findByAuthor will return a Collection of stub references to BLI objects. At some later time, the container will grab EJB instances from the free pool and associate them with corresponding BLI objects. At that time the EJBs' ejbLoad methods will be invoked.

The ejbFindByPrimaryKey method must return one, and only one, value to the container. If the row does not exist then the ObjectNotFoundException must be thrown. Finders that return a Collection or Set must return an empty Collection or Set if no entries in the table qualify.

Listing 29.6 The ejbFindByPrimaryKey and ejbFindByAuthor methods.

```
/**
 * Finds the key for the relevant row in the database
 * @param isbn is the key to search for
 * @return Returns the key again if the row has been found
 * @exception FinderException is thrown if the row doesn't exist
 */
public String ejbFindByPrimaryKey(String isbn) throws FinderException{
  Connection con = null;
  Statement stat = null;
  ResultSet result = null;
  try{
    con = this.getConnection();
    stat = con.createStatement();
    result = stat.executeQuery("select ISBN from BOOKITEMTAB01 "
                             + "where ISBN = '" + isbn + "'");
    if (!result.next()){
      throw new ObjectNotFoundException("Cannot find BOOKITEMTAB01 " +
                                        " with ISBN: " + isbn);
    }
  }
  catch(SQLException se){
    throw new EJBException(se);
  }
  finally{
    try{
      if (result != null) result.close();
      if (stat != null) stat.close();
      if (con != null) con.close();
    }
    catch(SQLException se){
```

```
        se.printStackTrace();
      }
    }
    return isbn;
  }
  /**
   * Finds the books written a given author
   * @param isbn is the key to search for
   * @return Returns the key again if the row has been found
   * @exception FinderException is thrown if the row doesn't exist
   */
  public Collection ejbFindByAuthor(String author) throws FinderException{

    Collection results = new ArrayList();
    Connection con = null;
    Statement stat = null;
    ResultSet result = null;
    try{
      con = this.getConnection();
      stat = con.createStatement();
      result = stat.executeQuery("select ISBN from BOOKITEMTAB01 "
                                 + "where AUTHOR = '" + author + "'");
      while (result.next()){
        results.add(result.getString("ISBN"));
      }
    }
    catch(SQLException se){
      throw new EJBException(se);
    }
    finally{
      try{
        if (result != null) result.close();
        if (stat != null) stat.close();
        if (con != null) con.close();
      }
      catch(SQLException se){
        se.printStackTrace();
      }
    }
    return results;
  }
```

The last part of the class is shown in Listing 29.7. This contains the `getConnection` private method. The method returns a `java.sql.Connection` that is obtained using a `javax.sql.DataSource` object. The `DataSource` is similar to the `java.sql.DriverManager` class. One major difference is that its methods are non-static. You obtain the

DataSource from the JNDI directory as an object. Also, the DataSource is an interface rather than a class, which means that you are insulated from the actual implementation class provided by the application server vendor. The DataSource is now the recommended way to obtain database connections.

Listing 29.7 A method for getting connections via the DataSource object.

```
private Connection getConnection(){
  try{
    InitialContext jndiContext = new InitialContext();
    javax.sql.DataSource ds
      = (javax.sql.DataSource) jndiContext.lookup(bookStoreDSRef);
    return ds.getConnection();
  }
  catch(Exception ne){
    throw new EJBException(ne);
  }
}
// End of BookItemBMPBean class
```

For application servers, the DataSource implementation will manage a pool of connections. Also, the application server vendor, in this case JBoss, provides an implementation for the java.sql.Connection class. This means that its objects will be fully integrated with the server. An implication of this is that database access via these objects will be undertaken within the context of server-controlled transactions. Also, the close operation will return the connection object back to the connection pool rather than closing the actual database connection.

29.4 The Deployment Descriptor Files

The deployment descriptors for BMP entity EJBs are simpler than those for CMP EJBs. Listing 29.8 shows the ejb-jar.xml file for the BookItem EJB. Those descriptors that differ from the CMP version are shown in bold. Now the <ejb-class> is the concrete subclass of BookItemBean. The <persistence-type> has been changed to Bean. The other major difference is the inclusion of an entry in the EJB's environment naming context. The <resource-ref> tag enables us to define a logical ENC name for a kind of resource, in this case a DataSource (indicated by the <res-type> tag). A vendor specific mechanism is then used to map this logical name onto an environment JNDI name. In JBoss this is achieved in the jboss.xml file (Listing 29.9).

The <res-auth> tag can have the values Bean or Container. If the latter, then authorization with the external resource is undertaken automatically by the container, using security information derived from a client method call (see Chapter 28). If the former, then you must provide this authorization information when obtaining a connection to the resource. For a DataSource this would be provided as parameters to the DataSource.getConnection method.

We will look at other kinds of external resource in later chapters.

Listing 29.8 The `ejb-jar.xml` file for the `BookItem` BMP EJB.

```
<?xml version="1.0"?>
<!DOCTYPE ejb-jar PUBLIC '-//Sun Microsystems, Inc.//DTD Enterprise
JavaBeans 2.0//EN' 'http://java.sun.com/dtd/ejb-jar_2_0.dtd'>

<ejb-jar>
  <enterprise-beans>
    <entity>
      <ejb-name>BookItem</ejb-name>
      <home>store.BookItemHome</home>
      <remote>store.BookItem</remote>
      <local-home>store.BookItemLocalHome</local-home>
      <local>store.BookItemLocal</local>
      <ejb-class>store.BookItemBMPBean</ejb-class>
      <persistence-type>Bean</persistence-type>
      <prim-key-class>java.lang.String</prim-key-class>
      <reentrant>False</reentrant>
      <resource-ref>
        <res-ref-name>jdbc/bookstore</res-ref-name>
        <res-type>javax.sql.DataSource</res-type>
        <res-auth>Container</res-auth>
      </resource-ref>
    </entity>
  </enterprise-beans>

  <assembly-descriptor>
    <container-transaction>
      <method>
        <ejb-name>BookItem</ejb-name>
        <method-name>*</method-name>
      </method>
      <trans-attribute>Required</trans-attribute>
    </container-transaction>
  </assembly-descriptor>
</ejb-jar>
```

Listing 29.9 shows the `jboss.xml` file. Differences with the CMP version are shown in bold. The `<resource-ref>` tag allows us to map the logical JNDI lookup name onto the actual environment JNDI name. The value in `<res-ref-name>` must match that given in the `ejb-jar.xml` file. This is followed either by a `<res-jndi-name>` tag or, as in this case, a `<resource-name>` tag. The former would simply provide the real JNDI name. However, if you have several EJBs all referring to the same external resource, then, rather than repeating the real JNDI name, you can create yet another level of indirection using the

<resource-name> tag to a single definition of the real JNDI name. This single definition is made using the <resource-manager> tag. The <res-jndi-name> tag's value points to the true location of the DataSource object. Our version is overkill, since we only refer to the resource manager from a single entity. However, if you had several EJBs (entity EJBs, session EJBs and/or message-driven EJBs) requiring the same external resource, then this mechanism aids maintenance. Finally, since we no longer have any CMP EJBs in our application, we no longer require the jbosscmp-jdbc.xml file.

Listing 29.9 The jboss.xml file.

```
<?xml version="1.0"?>
<jboss>
  <enterprise-beans>
        <entity>
            <ejb-name>BookItem</ejb-name>
            <jndi-name>ejb/bookItemR</jndi-name>
            <local-jndi-name>ejb/bookItem</local-jndi-name>
            <resource-ref>
              <res-ref-name>jdbc/bookstore</res-ref-name>
              <resource-name>DefaultDS</resource-name>
            </resource-ref>
        </entity>
    </enterprise-beans>
    <resource-managers>
      <resource-manager res-class="">
          <res-name>DefaultDS</res-name>
          <res-jndi-name>java:/DefaultDS</res-jndi-name>
      </resource-manager>
    </resource-managers>
</jboss>
```

29.5 Accessing the BookItem BMP Entity From a Client

The life cycle and business logic interfaces for the BookItem EJB are unaffected by the change to its implementation and deployment descriptors. Consequently, you should be able to run the BookItemClient class provided in Chapter 14. Good luck!

Chapter 30

Stateful Session EJBs

30.1 Introduction

We first met session EJBs in Chapter 14. They were described as lightweight EJBs that provide mechanisms for encapsulating business logic and acting as a façade to other EJBs. However, they cannot maintain client-specific data, since they are shared among clients. Stateful session EJBs also encapsulate business logic and can also act as a façade for other EJBs. However, they also allow the storage of client-specific data. The penalty for this is that they are much more heavyweight, because unlike stateless session EJBs each stateful EJB is associated with a client for the duration of its lifetime and cannot be shared among transactions. Consequently, more instances are required to service client requests. This does not preclude the container implementation from maintaining a pool of stateful EJBs; however, they are circulated between the pool and clients less frequently.

When should you use stateful session EJBs? The main reason is if you need to store client-conversational state between client calls. An example would be an EJB that represents a client login within the business tier. At the point of login, the stateful session EJB would be created, passing in client-specific initialization data that would be stored in the EJB for the duration of the login session. Application-specific authentication could also be undertaken in such an EJB. The EJB could also act as a façade, such that all or most client tier calls to the business tier pass through this login EJB. This also provides the possibility of caching references to other EJBs. For example, an online bank might have a login session EJB for each client logged into the system. This EJB could cache references to the client's account entity EJBs and possibly even to other accounts into which transfers are to be made. Methods in the login stateful session EJB would then rely on using this cached information; they do not have to receive the information via method parameters, or rediscover the information using JNDI. Typically, stateful sessions EJBs avoid the need to maintain business logic code within the client or Web tiers. Instead, the business logic is maintained in one place within the business logic tier, thereby decoupling code concerned with the user interface from code concerned with the application logic and data.

A note of caution is needed at this point. Normally, stateful session EJBs should not be used as a replacement for entity EJBs. There is the similarity that the session data remains persistent between method calls. However, there are many differences. Firstly, stateful session EJBs can only be used by one transaction at a time, whereas entity EJBs are shareable, although one transaction's isolation level may prevent access by another transaction. An attempt to access a stateful session EJB by two transactions will result in an exception being thrown. Consequently, stateful session EJBs prevent data sharing between transactions, which is appropriate in some circumstances. More importantly, the container will not automatically synchronize an EJB's state with an underlying database, unlike entity EJBs. By default, the data lasts as long as the session EJB lasts. As we will see, there is a synchronization mechanism, but you have to explicitly program to that mechanism, and write the JDBC code to update or read from a database. Finally, a stateful session EJB can time out, at which point it will be removed, requiring re-creation if the client wishes further access. Entity EJBs never time out. However, all of this said, there are situations where it is appropriate to use stateful session EJBs instead of entity EJBs, such as supporting efficient read-only access to persistent data. This was discussed in Chapter 15.

30.2 Stateful Session EJB Life Cycle

Figure 30.1 shows part of the life cycle of the stateful session EJB. In Section 30.5 we will look at the transaction part of its life cycle. Conceptually, at the point of deployment, no session EJB instances will be created. This is represented by the *does not exist* state. However, in practice, an implementation is at liberty to create a pool of instances, but we decided not to show this on the diagram.

The EJB enters the *ready* state when a client calls a `create` method on the EJB's local or remote life cycle interface. At this point the container calls `setSessionContext` on the

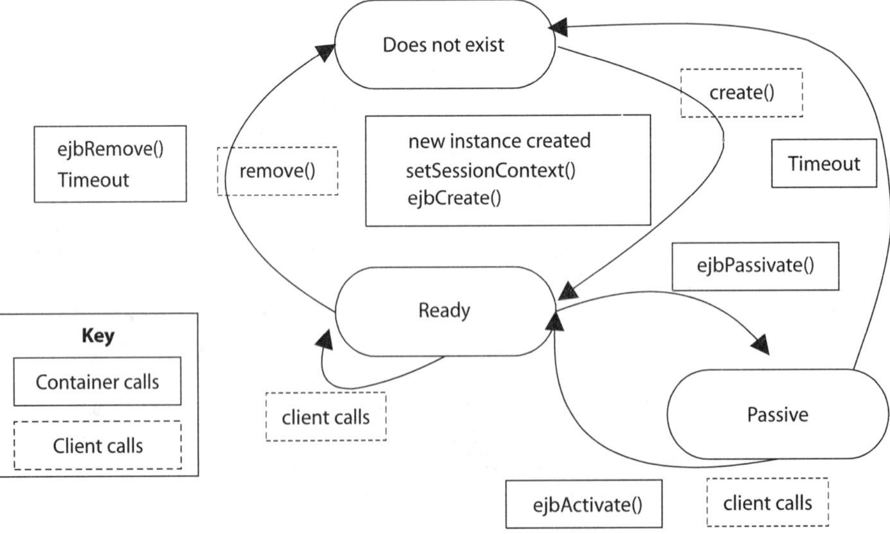

Figure 30.1 Life cycle diagram for the stateful session EJB.

implementation object in order to pass in the session context object. The container will then call the `ejbCreate` method that corresponds to the `create` method. Notice how this differs from stateless session EJBs, where `ejbCreate` is not called in response to the client calling `create`, but at the point of populating the free pool with a new instance.

The EJB now remains associated with the client until it is removed, and will service client business method calls via its local and remote business logic interface objects. Whilst in the *ready* state, three further events can occur that will cause it to change state: passivation, a request for removal by the client, or a timeout.

Passivation is the process whereby the EJB implementation instance is disassociated from its business logic interface and removed, at least conceptually, from memory. During this transition the EJB's instance variable data will be stored, usually through Java serialization. It is possible that the container implementation will store the data somewhere and reuse the EJB for another client, probably via a pool. Conceptually, however, the EJB enters a *passive* state, and can be reactivated by the client. Just prior to passivation, the container calls the `ejbPassivate` method on your implementation object. This gives your code the opportunity to close external resources, or change data to a form that can be passivated; there are certain rules discussed later concerning what can and cannot be passivated. When a client makes a business method call, the EJB is reassociated with its business logic interface object. During this reactivation, the container restores the original data to the EJB and then calls `ejbActivate`, giving your code the opportunity to re-establish connections to external resources or change data to a more convenient form.

The passivation and reactivation process gives the opportunity to the container to manage its limited resources in an efficient manner. Stateful session EJBs are heavyweight, in the sense that they are not shared between client transactions, and due to data caching may have a large memory footprint. When allocating resources the container may follow a least recently used policy, where infrequently used session EJBs are passivated. Passivation will only occur on EJBs that are not involved in a transaction.

The EJB will also leave the *ready* state if a client calls the `remove` method on the EJB's business logic or life cycle interfaces. This is only permitted if the EJB is not participating in a transaction. If it is then a `RemoveException` will be thrown. Calling `remove` transitions the EJB to the *does not exist* state. During this transition, the container will call `ejbRemove` on your implementation object. This provides your code with the opportunity to close external resources prior to instance reuse or garbage collection.

The EJB will also leave the *ready* state if the EJB's timeout is reached. Again the `ejbRemove` method will be called as part of this transition. Timeouts are specified in a vendor-specific way, usually a deployment descriptor. Timeouts support the notion that stateful session EJBs are transient, and after a given period of inactivity should be removed. These are the semantics required by many applications, for example, a login session where the client has left their connection to the business tier abandoned for a period of time. Where session EJBs are used to represent shopping carts, then abandoned carts need to be removed after a given period of time. In our application we use entity EJBs for carts so that they can be used over a long period of time and between login sessions.

If the EJB is in the *passive* state when a timeout occurs, then the EJB will transition to the *does not exist* state directly and `ejbRemove` will not be called; it does not need to be since the instance does not exist anyway, so there will not be any external resources to clean up.

30.3 Rules on Allowable Instance Variables in the Implementation Class

The EJB 2.0 specification places constraints on the types and values of instance variables to be used during passivation and activation. Allowable types and values are:

- Types that implement `java.io.Serializable`
- Primitive types (e.g. `int`, `boolean`, `double`)
- Subtypes of `EJBObject`, `EJBLocalObject`, `EJBHome` and `EJBLocalHome`
- JNDI `Context` objects where the object refers to the EJB's Environment Naming Context or any of its sub-contexts
- `SessionContext` objects
- `UserTransaction` objects
- A reference to the resource manager connection factory
- Collections of EJB references

Although other kinds of instance variables may be defined, you must either declare them as transient (discouraged) or preferably set their values to `null` in the `ejbPassivate` method. If this is not done the container will throw an exception and the EJB instance will be removed.

30.4 The Process of Developing a Stateful Session EJB

The process of developing stateful session EJBs is much the same as for developing stateless session EJBs.

30.4.1 The `Purchase` EJB Business Logic Interface

Listing 30.1 shows the code for the `Purchase` EJB business logic interface. The JavaDoc comments describe each of the business methods. However, unlike the stateless version described in Chapter 14, the methods no longer need to pass in the user's user identifier, since this can now be stored within the implementation object between client calls.

Listing 30.1 The `Purchase` EJB remote business logic interface.

```
package store;

import javax.ejb.EJBObject;
import javax.ejb.FinderException;
import java.rmi.RemoteException;
/**
 * Remote business logic interface for the Purchase EJB.
 * @author Chris Loftus
 * @version 1.0
 */
```

```
public interface Purchase extends EJBObject {
  /**
   * Selects a book ready for purchase. It is placed in a shopping cart
   * @param item The item to add. It must have a valid ISBN
   * @exception FinderException thrown if the book's ISBN is unknown
   * @exception RemoteException thrown if there's a communication failure
   */
  public void select(Book item)
    throws FinderException, RemoteException;
  /**
   * Removes a book from the shopping cart
   * @param item The item to remove. It must have a valid ISBN
   * @exception FinderException thrown if the book's ISBN is unknown
   * @exception RemoteException thrown if there's a communication failure
   */
  public void remove(Book item)
    throws FinderException, RemoteException;
  /**
   * Enables payment for the contents of the shopping cart
   * @param creditCardNumber Currently any int will do (not implemented)
   * @return A transaction number is returned
   * @exception RemoteException thrown if there's a communication failure
   */
  public int pay(int creditCardNumber) throws RemoteException;
  /**
   * Returns the current cost of the items in the shopping cart
   * @return The cost of the book items
   * @exception RemoteException thrown if there's a communication failure
   */
  public double balance() throws RemoteException;
  /**
   * Returns information about the current contents of the shopping cart
   * @return An array of book items. This will be a non-null empty
   * array if the cart is empty.
   * @exception RemoteException thrown if there's a communication failure
   */
  public Book[] returnItems() throws RemoteException;
}
```

30.4.2 The Purchase EJB Life Cycle Interface

Listing 30.2 contains the code for the Purchase EJB's life cycle interface. This differs from the stateless version in that the create method takes a parameter that contains the user identifier. This is then stored within the newly created session EJB.

Listing 30.2 The Purchase EJB life cycle interface.

```
package store;

import javax.ejb.EJBHome;
import javax.ejb.CreateException;
import java.rmi.RemoteException;
/**
 * Remote life cycle interface for the Purchase EJB.
 * @author Chris Loftus
 * @version 1.0
 */
public interface PurchaseHome extends EJBHome {
  /**
   * Creates a purchase Stateful session EJB
   * @param userid The unique account ID for the user that is used
   * to identify the user's shopping cart
   * @exception CreateException thrown if the userid has
   * already been used
   * @exception RemoteException thrown if there's a communication failure
   */
  public Purchase create(String userid)
    throws CreateException, RemoteException;
}
```

30.4.3 The Purchase EJB Component class

The component class is shown in Listing 30.3. The first point to note is that we define a set of instance variables that will cache client-specific data between client calls. All the variables conform to the passivation rules described earlier, and so will be saved and then restored during passivation and activation.

The static class constants contain the JNDI lookup names for the Cart and Till EJBs. These are used in ejbCreate via the utility method getHome, which does JNDI lookups for CartLocalHome and TillLocalHome. ejbCreate also stores the userid in an instance variable and obtains the cart and till business logic interface objects.

The methods ejbRemove, ejbPassivate and ejbActivate remain empty in this application; there are no external resources that need removing or closing.

The JavaDoc comments in the business methods describe their implementation. The only other method worth mentioning is getCart. This utility method attempts to find the Cart entity EJB. If a FinderException is thrown, then we assume that the shopping cart does not exist, and we create a new one.

Listing 30.3 The Purchase EJB implementation class.

```
package store;
```

```
import javax.ejb.SessionBean;
import javax.ejb.SessionContext;
import javax.ejb.EJBException;
import javax.ejb.CreateException;
import javax.ejb.FinderException;
import javax.naming.InitialContext;
import javax.naming.NamingException;
import javax.rmi.PortableRemoteObject;

/**
 * A stateful session bean for coordinating the purchase of items (books)
 * including obtaining current
 * balance of such items and initiating payment of thee items.
 * @author John Hunt and Chris Loftus
 * @version 3.0
 */
public class PurchaseBean implements SessionBean{
  // The EJB server is required to serialize these instance variables if
  // it decides to passivate the session object. This will only work with
  // Serializable objects and Home and Remote interface objects and
  // context objects.
  private SessionContext ctx;
  private TillLocalHome tillHome;
  private TillLocal till;
  private CartLocalHome cartHome;
  private CartLocal cart;
  private String userid;

  // Environment naming context lookup names for the cart and till beans
  private static final String cart_ref = "java:comp/env/ejb/cartBean";
  private static final String till_ref = "java:comp/env/ejb/tillBean";

  public void setSessionContext(SessionContext context){
    ctx = context;
  }

  public void ejbActivate(){
  }

  public void ejbPassivate(){
  }

  public void ejbRemove(){
  }
```

```
public void ejbCreate(String userid){
  this.userid = userid;
  // Get the CartLocalHome and the TillLocalHome. Create the TillLocal
  // and CartLocalHome objects
  try{
    InitialContext jndiContext = new InitialContext();
    cartHome = (CartLocalHome)getHome(jndiContext, cart_ref,
                                  CartLocalHome.class);
    tillHome = (TillLocalHome)getHome(jndiContext, till_ref,
                                  TillLocalHome.class);
    till = tillHome.create();
    cart = getCart();
  }
  catch(Exception e){
    e.printStackTrace();
    throw new EJBException(e);
  }
}

// Business methods

/**
 * Allows you to place a book in the shopping cart
 * @param item the item to place in the cart
 * @exception FinderException thrown if book ISBN not known
 */
public void select(Book item) throws FinderException{
  try{
    cart.add(item);
  }
  catch (Exception e){
    e.printStackTrace();
    throw new EJBException(e);
  }
}

/**
 * Allows you to remove a book from the shopping cart
 * @param item the item to remove from the cart
 * @throws FinderException if the book ISBN is unknown
 */
public void remove(Book item) throws FinderException{
  try{
    cart.remove(item);
  }
  catch (Exception e){
```

```
      e.printStackTrace();
      throw new EJBException(e);
    }
  }

  /**
   * Allows you to buy the contents of the shopping cart. This
   * will also remove the Cart bean
   * as a side effect!
   * @param creditCardNumber a number of your choice
   * @return returns a transaction id
   */
  public int pay(int creditCardNumber){
    // Initiate payment of bill
    // Then remove the cart bean
    try{
      cart.remove();  // The client will get an exception if they
                      // try to use any further purchase methods
    }
    catch(Exception e){
      e.printStackTrace();
      throw new EJBException(e);
    }
      return 12324;
  }

  /**
   * Allows you to get the balance of books in the shopping cart
   * @return The total cost of the books in the cart
   */
  public double balance(){
    double result = 0.0;
    try{
      Book[] items = cart.returnItems();
      result = till.total(items);
    }
    catch (Exception e){
      e.printStackTrace();
      throw new EJBException(e);
    }
    return result;
  }

  /**
   * Allows you to get a list of the books in the shopping cart
   * @return returns an array of Book objects
```

```
   */
  public Book[] returnItems() {
    Book[] result = null;
    try{
      result = cart.returnItems();
    } catch (Exception e) {
      e.printStackTrace();
      throw new EJBException(e);
    }
      return result;
  }

  // Utility methods
  private CartLocal getCart() throws Exception {
    try{
      System.out.println("GETCART: about to try and find existing" +
                         " cart bean for uid: " + userid);
      cart = cartHome.findByPrimaryKey(new CartPK(userid));
      System.out.println("getCart: found existing cart bean for uid: "
                         + userid);
    }
    catch(FinderException fe){
      // Doesn't already exist, so create a new one
      System.out.println("GETCART: creating new cart bean for uid: "
                         + userid);
      cart = cartHome.create(userid);
      System.out.println("getCart: created new cart bean for uid: "
      + userid);
    }
    return cart;
  }

  private Object getHome(InitialContext jndiContext,
                         String name, Class type){
    try{
      Object objref = jndiContext.lookup(name);
      return PortableRemoteObject.narrow(objref, type);
    }
    catch(NamingException ne){
      throw new EJBException(ne);
    }
  }
}
```

30.5 Transaction Synchronization Using the SessionSynchronization Interface

Session EJBs that participate within a transaction might contain data that requires updating or discarding depending on the state of that transaction. At the start of the transaction an initial set of values could be assigned to the instance variables. During the transaction, method calls on the session EJB might result in changes to these variables. If the transaction commits it might be appropriate to store the EJB's data in a database. If the transaction rolls back then we might wish to discard the data. An example might be a TravelAgent EJB that accumulates information about a holiday booking. Just before the transaction commits it might be appropriate to store details about the holiday to a database. If the transaction fails for some reason it may be appropriate to discard some or all of the data accumulated within the EJB.

A stateful session EJB that implements the SessionSynchronization interface will be informed when transaction events occur. This interface defines three methods: afterBegin, beforeCompletion and afterCompletion. The revised state diagram in Figure 30.2 illustrates when these methods are called. The EJB will enter the *ready synchronized* state when a client calls a transactional method. The EJB moves back to the *ready* state either if the transaction is aborted (rolls back) or it commits.

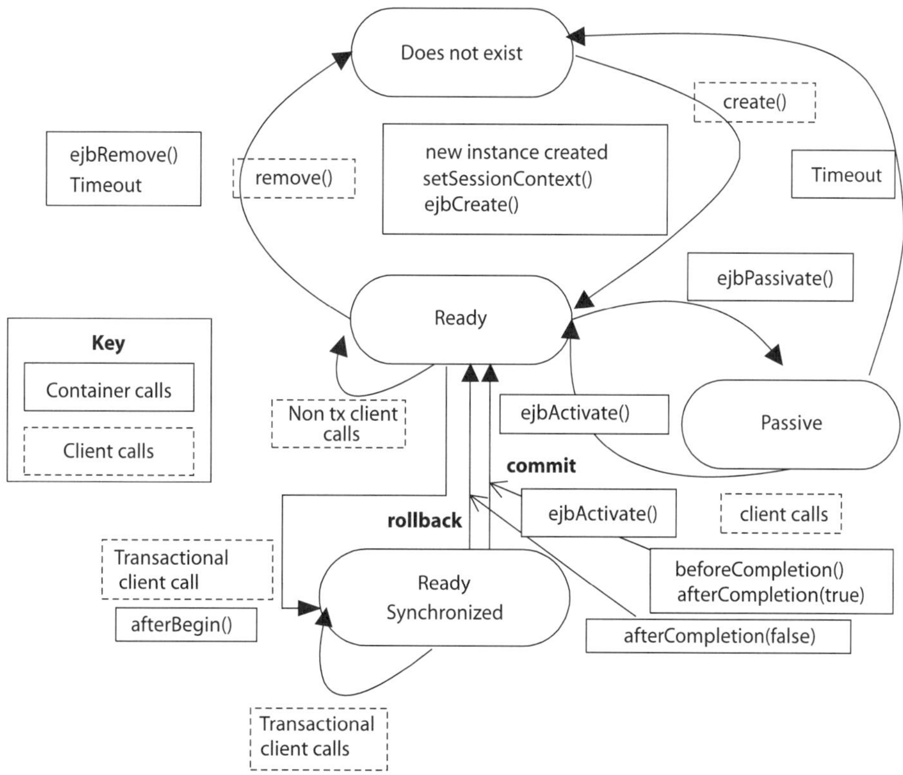

Figure 30.2 Life cycle state diagram revised to include the *synchronized* state.

During the transition from *ready* to *ready synchronized* the container will call the afterBegin method on your EJB. Use this method to reinitialize the EJB's instance variables. If a transaction rollback occurs the container will call the afterCompletion method, passing in the parameter value false. Use this method in this situation to discard any unwanted values from the instance variables. If the transaction commits the container will call beforeCompletion just before the transaction is committed. Use this method to save instance variable data within a database, as part of the existing transaction. The container will also call afterCompletion just after the transaction has committed, this time with the value true. At this point you may wish to reinitialize the instance variables.

Although not shown, the EJB can time out even when it is in the *ready synchronized* state, effectively aborting the transaction. However, the remove method must not be called while in this state. If it is, then a RemoveException will be thrown.

30.6 The Deployment Descriptor Files

Listing 30.4 shows a new version of part of the ejb-jar.xml file. The only difference from that shown for stateless session EJBs in Chapter 14 is that <session-type> is set to Stateful. The jboss.xml file remains unchanged, and so is not shown.

Listing 30.4 The ejb-jar.xml file, highlighting the stateful Purchase EJB.

```
<ejb-jar>
  <!-- Some descriptors omitted -->
  <enterprise-beans>
    <!-- Some descriptors omitted -->
    <session>
      <ejb-name>Purchase</ejb-name>
      <home>store.PurchaseHome</home>
      <remote>store.Purchase</remote>
      <ejb-class>store.PurchaseBean</ejb-class>
      <session-type>Stateful</session-type>
      <transaction-type>Container</transaction-type>
      <ejb-local-ref>
        <ejb-ref-name>ejb/cartBean</ejb-ref-name>
        <ejb-ref-type>Entity</ejb-ref-type>
        <local-home>store.CartLocalHome</local-home>
        <local>store.CartLocal</local>
        <ejb-link>Cart</ejb-link>
      </ejb-local-ref>
      <ejb-local-ref>
        <ejb-ref-name>ejb/tillBean</ejb-ref-name>
        <ejb-ref-type>Session</ejb-ref-type>
        <local-home>store.TillLocalHome</local-home>
        <local>store.TillLocal</local>
```

```
        <ejb-link>Till</ejb-link>
      </ejb-local-ref>
    </session>
    <!-- Some descriptors omitted -->
</enterprise-beans>
```

Chapter 31

J2EE Connector Architecture

31.1 Introduction

In Chapter 9 we examined the JDBC API. This API enables us to write code that interfaces to multifarious relational databases in a database-neutral fashion; that is, no matter what database system we use, we access that system through the JDBC API, and we do not access database-specific APIs. This makes our code easy to port between database systems and reduces the degree of training required by developers.

JCA is an attempt to provide a similar architecture for other kinds of enterprise information system, not just relational database systems. Examples of types of EIS are Enterprise Resource Planning (ERP) systems, mainframe transaction processing systems (e.g. IBM CICS), non-relational, legacy database systems, and relational database systems. Providing a standard way of accessing these systems reduces the amount of integration glue code that would otherwise need to be written. Before the advent of JCA, for each EIS to application server integration, experts would write a layer of code that was specific to that EIS and application server, clearly an N^2 effort. JCA (first included in J2EE 1.3 as JCA 1.0; Sharma (2001)[1]) significantly reduces the amount of effort required to integrate enterprise systems with application servers.

JCA consists of two main parts. The first consists of resource adapters that are developed by EIS vendors or third parties. These adapters are analogous to JDBC database driver classes and provide the mapping from an EIS-neutral API (either the Common Client Interface or JDBC) and the EIS-specific API. Notice that the adapter, could in fact be a relational database driver class that supports JDBC. The second consists of classes that form part of the application server, and are usually provided by the application server vendor. These classes support what are known as the system contracts. Essentially, they provide connection pooling and transaction and security management. These management services ensure that connections are managed efficiently, that transactions can be distributed

1 JCA 1.5 was in Final Draft form at the time of writing.

across multiple EIS resources, and that application-server security is integrated correctly with EIS security mechanisms.

The following sections will provide an overview of the JCA, its architecture in brief, and each of the three system contracts, connection management, transactions and security. We also examine the CCI and steps required to deploy a resource adapter. We assume that you want to understand the basic architecture and how to write client components (EJBs, Web components, applets or applications) that use the CCI to access EISs via resource adapters. We do not provide in-depth detail on the classes that support the system contracts. Although part of the JCA specification, these classes and interfaces are implemented by resource adapter and application server vendors. Developers in these roles should consult the JCA specification.

Even though we discuss the CCI, it was always the intention of those defining JCA that third-party Enterprise Integration Architecture (EIA) tools would be used to generate component code that uses the CCI on behalf of component developers. This is because the CCI is very generic and so requires complex configuration when used with various underlying enterprise systems. So even as a component developer you might never actually have to write code that talks to the CCI directly!

31.2 Architectural Overview

Figure 31.1 presents a highly abstract view of the architecture. JCA defines the classes and interfaces that comprise the CCI, and those that comprise the system contracts interface. The container–component contract is the outside the scope of JCA and consists of interfaces used by

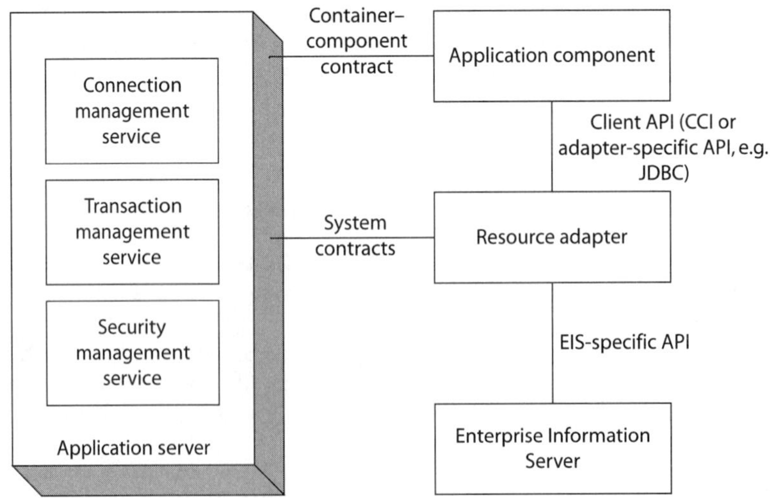

Figure 31.1 The architecture.

EJB or Web containers when accessing EJB or Web components. The EIS specific API is also outside of the scope of JCA. The internal implementation of the three system contracts services is also beyond the scope of JCA. JCA only defines the classes, interfaces and deployment descriptors and their semantics, required to enable resource adapters to be plugged into the connection, transaction and management services of an application server, and to allow client components to communicate with resource adapters.

Connection, transaction and security management are all hidden from application components. The application server and resource adapters collaborate through the system contracts API to achieve this transparency.

Each resource adapter is specific to an EIS. J2EE treats resource adapters just like any other kind of J2EE component, e.g. Web components or EJB components. This means you can deploy resource adapter components as part of an Enterprise archive (EAR), or indeed deploy them independently of other components. As with other components, you write a deployment descriptor file that describes and is used to configure the deployed resource adapter (more on this in Section 31.7). This architecture makes it easy to plug new adapters into an application server. Among others, these adapters include JDBC drivers, ERP drivers and transaction processing (TP) drivers.

There are three system contract services. The connection management service is responsible for managing connections in an efficient and scalable manner, through the use of connection pooling techniques.

The transaction management service can use a transaction manager to facilitate distributed transactions across multiple EISs, supporting two-phase commit protocol. Container-managed or bean-managed transactions will operate seamlessly with transaction coordination across multiple EISs. When a transaction spans just a single EIS the transaction service is at liberty to bypass the transaction manager and use a local transaction. This reduces the resource-tracking overhead required for distributed transactions; the application server simply relies on the local transaction mechanisms provided by the EIS. Indeed, local transactions must be used if the EIS is unable to participate in distributed (XA) transactions.

The security management service provides secure access to an EIS using the application server's JAAS implementation that interoperates with the security mechanisms supported by the resource adapter and its EIS.

JCA's Client API consists of the CCI and resource adapter-specific APIs, such as JDBC. A resource adapter is not required to support CCI, hence JDBC database drivers would typically only support the JDBC API. Despite this, it makes sense, where technically possible, for EIS vendors or third parties to provide CCI support where non-relational EISs are being used, rather than proprietary APIs.

Resource adapters can be used in either a managed or non-managed environment. Managed resource adapters are those that elicit the services of a J2EE application server via the system contracts API. Non-managed resource adapters are those used directly by a Java component that is itself not managed by the application server. For example, a Java application or applet may wish to access an EIS resource via the JCA CCI interfaces. In this case, the adapter is fully responsible for managing security, local transactions and connection management. Non-managed resource adapters are used by two-tier applications, whereas managed adapters are used by multi-tier enterprise applications.

31.3 Connection Service

Figure 31.2 displays an overview of the JCA interfaces and other major components that comprise or interact with the Connection Service. We will skip much of the detail, such as the signatures of JCA interface methods. This is because the interfaces define a contract between the adapter and the application server developers, whereas this book is aimed at business component developers.

Let us trace the flow of control from an application component that requires a connection through the system to the EIS.

The application obtains a connection factory object through a JNDI lookup. In J2EE this mechanism is identical for obtaining any kind of factory, e.g. JDBC `javax.sql.DataSource` factory (see Chapter 29), JMS `javax.jms.ConnectionFactory`

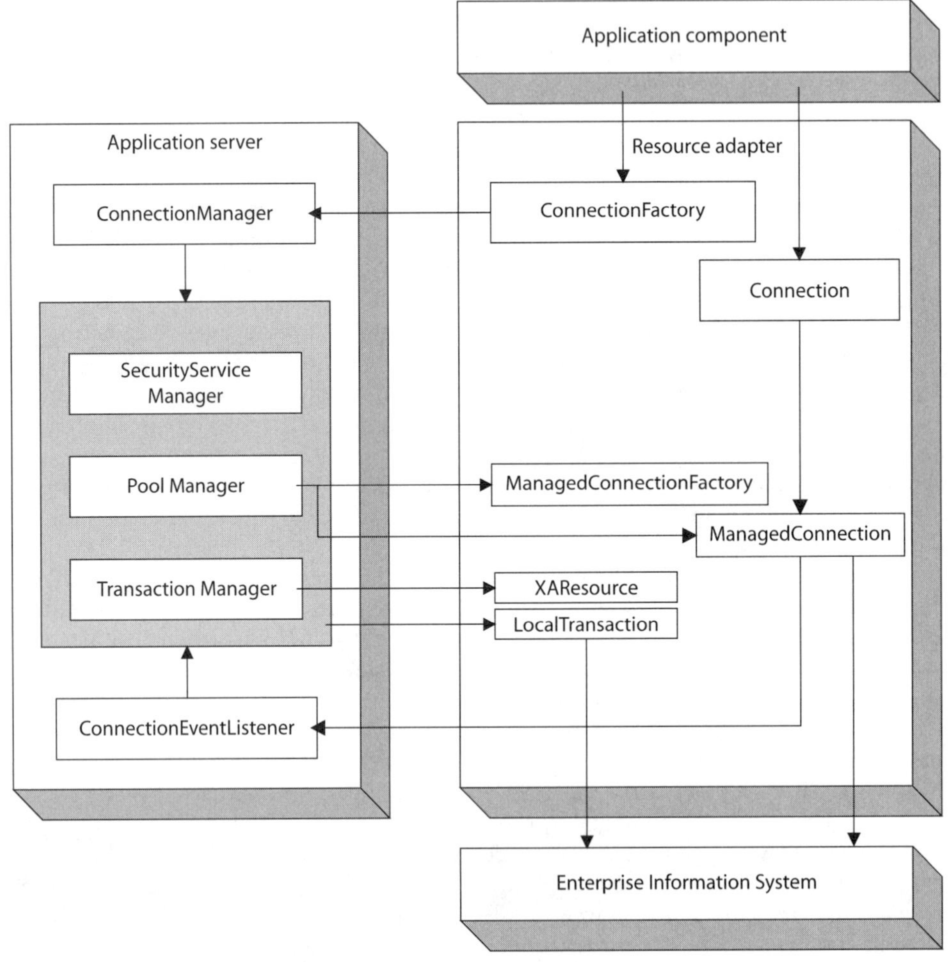

Figure 31.2 JCA in more detail.

(see Chapter 16), and CCI javax.resource.cci.ConnectionFactory. All factories provide a getConnection method.

The application calls getConnection on the factory. This method is overloaded to allow the caller, if required, to pass in data needed by the EIS, such as password and user identifier. The factory delegates the request to a ConnectionManager object in the application server.

The ConnectionManager with the aid of vendor-specific classes is responsible for maintaining one or more pools of connections. In response to a get connection request, the ConnectionManager will select a candidate set of potential connections, and with the assistance of the ManagedConnectionFactory in the resource adapter, will select, if it can, a suitable ManagedConnection.

If a suitable connection does not exist, perhaps because all the connections are currently in use, the ConnectionManager "asks" the ManagedConnectionFactory for a new ManagedConnection. This object is placed in an appropriate pool. When managing the connection pools, the ConnectionManager will solicit the support of the transaction and security services.

The ConnectionManager obtains a Connection handle from the ManagedConnection and returns this handle, via the ConnectionFactory, to the application component.

Managed connections represent physical connections to the EIS; there is a one-to-one mapping between a ManagedConnection and an EIS connection. Managed connections also maintain security context information. Some EIS connections can be shared, which means that multiple handles (Connection objects) to the same ManagedConnection can be returned to the calling application. Usually, the callers all have the same security context, although where this is not the case the EIS may support caller re-authentication.

How does the application server keep track of the state of its connections? It needs to be "told" when connections are closed or generate errors, or when local transaction events occur. Many of these events are instigated independently of the application server; for example, an application component will call close on a Connection when it no longer needs it. Relevant application server classes implement the ConnectionEventListener interface and register themselves with ManagedConnection objects. This listener interface provides methods, such as connectionClosed and localTransactionStarted, that ManagedConnection objects call when adapter events occur.

Error logging and tracing can be configured. The ManagedConnectionFactory will have a default property denoting a log file. This can be overridden using factory methods. By default, ManagedConnection objects use this same log file. However, distinct log files can be set in these objects using ManagedConnection methods.

For a non-managed environment, the resource adapter is required to provide its own default implementation of the ConnectionManager interface. This might maintain a connection pool, or else might obtain a ManagedConnection directly from its ManagedConnectionFactory.

31.4 Transaction Service

The transaction management service supports two kinds of transaction:

- Transactions coordinated by a transaction manager that is external to resource adapters. These are called XA transactions and support distributed transactions.
- Transactions managed by a resource adapter where no external transaction manager is required. These are called local transactions.

For XA transactions the adapter must have classes that implement the `javax.transaction.XAResource` interface. When a transactional thread accesses a resource adapter for the first time (when it obtains a connection) the transaction manager will record a reference to the adapter's `XAResource` object. The transaction manager will support two-phase commit protocol across all resources enlisted in this way, so that transaction commit or rollback is applied across all resources participating in the transaction (see Chapter 27 for more details on J2EE transactions).

Local transactions are represented by the `javax.resource.spi.LocalTransaction` interface. Application components can also demarcate local transactions via the `javax.resource.cci.LocalTransaction` interface. The application server may use a local transaction rather than an XA transaction if just a single resource participates in the transaction. In this way the transaction manager can be bypassed, thereby optimizing the transaction management. Alternatively, in this situation a transaction manager may still be used, but in this case would use one-phase commit rather than two-phase commit.

Both `XAResource` and `LocalTransaction` objects are obtained through the `ManagedConnection` interface.

When a transaction completes, the transaction service (possibly using a transaction manager) cleans up the affected `ManagedConnection` objects, marking them as available within appropriate connection pools. If no open `Connection` handles are associated with the `ManagedConnection` the `ConnectionManager` may also request that the `ManagedConnection` is destroyed, leading to the closure of its physical EIS connection.

Connection sharing may be allowed for a specific `ManagedConnection`. However, all the `Connection` handles that share the `ManagedConnection` must be used as part of the same transaction. If client components choose to cache these connections and use them within different transactions, then the application server must ensure that the affected connections are relocated to appropriate `ManagedConnection` objects.

31.5 Security Service

The application server's security management service provides mechanisms to protect an EIS against security threats. The three main aspects of this are:

- Identification and authentication of principals (external users: humans or other systems) to verify their identity.
- Authorization (access control) to determine what the principal is allowed to do.
- Securing the communication channel between the resource adapter and the EIS by using an appropriate security protocol, such as the secure sockets layer protocol.

The JCA 1.0 specification identifies the following goals that a security service will meet:

- Extend the end-to-end security model for J2EE-based applications to include integration with EISs based on the connector architecture.
- Support authentication and authorization of users who are accessing EISs.
- Keep the security architecture technology-neutral and enable the specified security contract to be supported by various security technologies.
- Enable the security architecture to support a range of EISs with different levels of security support and existing security environments.
- Support security configuration of a resource adapter in an operational environment.
- Keep the security model for connector architecture-based EIS integration transparent to an application component provider. This includes providing support for single sign-on across multiple EISs (Sharma, 2001).

In a managed environment, application components such as EJB and Web components are deployed within containers. When one of these components is accessed by an external (non-managed) client the container attempts to initiate an authentication procedure (such as a login form) to obtain the security credentials of the calling principal.

Internally, as components call other components the principal and its security credentials may propagate, or some form of mapping to a different principal may occur.

When a `ManagedConnection` is created, a resource adapter will establish its own resource principal for the connection; there will be a relationship to the calling principal. The precise nature of this relationship depends on the way the resource adapter is configured by the systems administrator or deployer. There are three ways in which the resource principal can be established.

- **Configured identity**. The resource principal will be assigned an identity and credentials that are independent of the calling principal. This new identity might be configured during deployment or specified dynamically by an application component during the creation of a connection (explicit provision of security information via a `getConnection` parameter).
- **Principal mapping**. The resource principal's identity and/or credentials are obtained through the use of a mapping function applied to the calling principal's identity and/or credentials.
- **Caller impersonation**. The resource principal impersonates the calling principal, using the same identity and credentials, although the security mechanism used may be quite different.

If you want to provide identity and credentials via the `getConnection` method, you will need to include a `<res-auth>` sub-tag under the EIS's resource reference deployment descriptor that has the value `Application`. If the tag has the value `Container`, then the identity and credentials will be obtained automatically using one of the three techniques mentioned above.

EIS sign-on involves three main activities. The first is to establish the resource principal, which may require authentication between the resource adapter and the underlying EIS. Depending on the mechanism used, such authentication may require two-way collaboration between the adapter and the EIS (such as the exchange of digital certificates). The principal name and credentials are obtained using one of the three mechanisms mentioned earlier.

The second activity involves authorization (access control) checking. This is to ascertain whether the requested operation on the adapter or underlying EIS is permitted for the given security principal. EIS access control will be undertaken in an EIS-specific fashion. The application server will also perform access control that is either specified declaratively within method permission deployment descriptors, or else programmatically (see Chapter 28 for more details).

The third activity is to secure the communication link between the resource adapter and the EIS. The resource adapter runs within the same address space as the application server, but the EIS does not. Unless protected, the data transferred between these two processes, possibly over a network link, is open to malicious tampering or viewing. It is important, therefore, that a secure association is established between the adapter and the EIS. Typically, this will involve the encryption of the data stream. However, for this to happen the adapter and EIS will need to authenticate one another, negotiate the level of protection required, and probably exchange cryptographic keys and message sequence information.

31.6 Common Client Interface (CCI)

The CCI provides a standard way of accessing non-relational EISs. Relational EISs should be accessed via JDBC. CCI supports a remote function-call style of interface, where function-call data (parameters and results) is encapsulated within `Record` objects.

CCI is targeted primarily towards EAI frameworks and tools, rather than for direct use by component developers. For example, Figure 31.3 shows a set of J2EE components accessing resource adapters through an EAI framework. The framework "decides" whether access is undertaken using CCI or JDBC. More generic frameworks may also interrogate a metadata repository that describes the functions and data and other capabilities of specific EISs. Figure 31.4 illustrates a scenario where an enterprise integration tool is used to generate classes that are used by application components to access EISs using the CCI on their behalf.

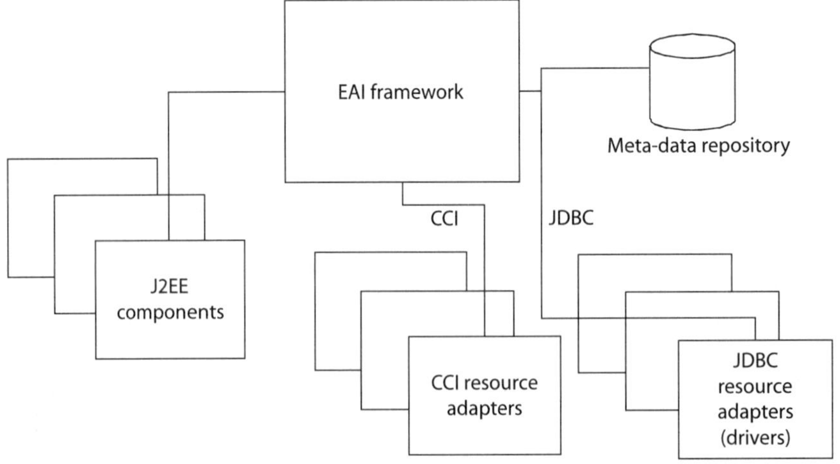

Figure 31.3 Use of an EAI framework when supporting application component to EIS integration.

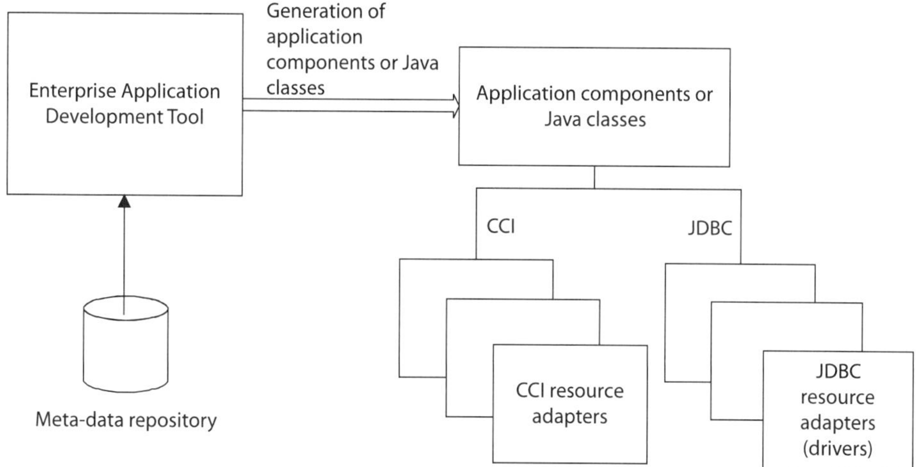

Figure 31.4 Use of development tools to generate CCI/JDBC interfacing classes.

The CCI interfaces are shown in Figure 31.5. We now look at some of the main interfaces. You are also referred to the J2EE JavaDoc API documentation.

The `ConnectionFactory` interface is used to obtain `Connection` objects (via the application server's `ConnectionManager` interface as described earlier). It is also used to obtain `RecordFactory` objects. The interface definition is as follows:

```
public interface javax.resource.cci.ConnectionFactory
  extends java.io.Serializable, javax.resource.Referenceable {
  public RecordFactory getRecordFactory()
    throws ResourceException;
  public Connection getConnection()
    throws ResourceException;
  public Connection getConnection(
               javax.resource.cci.ConnectionSpec properties)
    throws ResourceException;
  public ResourceAdapterMetaData getMetaData()
    throws ResourceException;
}
```

The `getConnection` method is overloaded to take a `ConnectionSpec` object. This can be used to programmatically pass principal identification and credential information through to the resource adapter (see J2EE API documentation). Its implementation class is implemented as a JavaBean. There are two standard properties, namely `UserName` and `Password`. The resource adapter vendor can define further properties.

The `Connection` interface represents a connection handle for a `ManagedConnection`. The definition of the interface is:

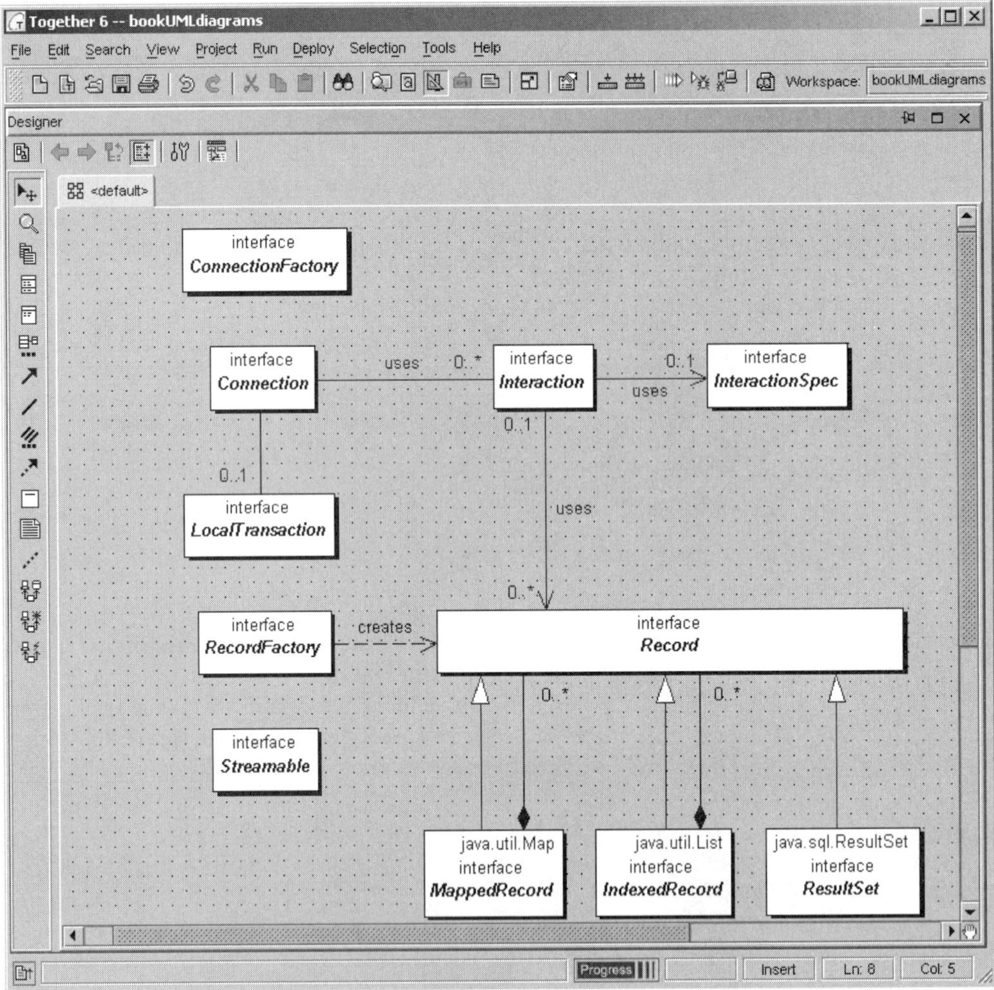

Figure 31.5 Class diagram for the `javax.resource.cci` package.

```
public interface javax.resource.cci.Connection {
  public Interaction createInteraction() throws ResourceException;
  public ConnectionMetaData getMetaData() throws ResourceException;
  public ResultSetInfo getResultSetInfo() throws ResourceException;
  public LocalTransaction getLocalTransaction()
    throws ResourceException;
  public void close() throws ResourceException;
}
```

The interface can be used to obtain `Interaction` objects. These are analogous to `Statement` objects in JDBC. The application component may also use the `Connection` interface to obtain metadata regarding connection, namely product name, EIS product version and the name of the principal using the connection. The ResultSetInfo interface enables the application component to discover the capabilities of the CCI ResultSet objects, for example, whether the objects will detect inserts by other connections to the same data, or whether changes made by the current connection will be reflected in the result set. The LocalTransaction interface enables the start, commitment or rollback of local transactions. No method is provided to set whether a transaction should auto-commit after each CCI interaction. The rule is that if a transaction is started, then auto-commit is automatically switched off. However, if an interaction is undertaken outside of a transaction, auto-commit is switched on.

The main interaction interface is Interaction, as shown below:

```
public interface javax.resource.cci.Interaction {
  public Connection getConnection();
  public void close() throws ResourceException;
  public boolean execute(InteractionSpec ispec,
                         Record input,
                         Record output) throws ResourceException;
  public Record execute(InteractionSpec ispec,
                        Record input) throws ResourceException;
  public void clearWarnings() throws ResourceException;
  public ResourceWarning getWarnings() throws ResourceException;
}
```

The getConnection method will return the Connection that controls the Interaction object. The overloaded execute methods are used to execute an interaction on a connected EIS. Both take an InteractionSpec parameter that defines the EIS function to execute. Each Record parameter or return value encapsulates the data to be sent to or received from the EIS. The first overload returns true if the interaction was successful, the second a non-null Record object. The getWarnings method enables the caller to obtain a chain of ResourceWarning exception objects. This provides a way of discovering whether and how an interaction failed or misbehaved. The clearWarnings method simply removes the warnings chain currently associated with the Interaction.

The InteractionSpec is defined as follows:

```
public interface javax.resource.cci.InteractionSpec
  extends java.io.Serializable {
  // Standard Interaction Verbs
  public static final int SYNC_SEND = 0;
  public static final int SYNC_SEND_RECEIVE = 1;
  public static final int SYNC_RECEIVE = 2;
}
```

Classes that implement this interface will support a set of properties, accessed via JavaBean getter and setter methods. Standard properties (which may or may not be supported) include:

- FunctionName: the name of the EIS function.

- InteractionVerb: the mode of interaction required with the EIS. SYNC_SEND indicates synchronous sending of information to the EIS where no result data is expected. SYNC_SEND_RECEIVE also requires the synchronous receipt of data, whereas SYNC_RECEIVE just expects result data, perhaps in response to an earlier interaction.
- ExecutionTimeout: the number of milliseconds the interaction will wait for a response from the EIS.
- FetchSize: the number of rows that should be fetched from an EIS when populating ResultSet objects.
- FetchDirection: the direction of traversal required for a ResultSet, e.g. FETCH_FORWARD or FETCH_REVERSE.
- MaxFieldSize: maximum number of bytes allowed for a ResultSet column value, or value in a Record.
- ResultSetType: an integer indicating the type of ResultSet to be returned (see ResultSet definition).
- ResultSetConcurrency: an integer indicating the concurrency type of the ResultSet returned (see ResultSet definition).

The resource adapter may provide additional properties. Some resource adapters will require you to obtain InteractionSpec objects using JNDI. Others may require you to create the object yourself.

Objects that implement the sub-interfaces of Record (see Figure 31.5) encapsulate data to be sent to or received from an EIS. The formatting and type system used to represent data within these Record objects will be EIS-dependent; there is no standard type-mapping scheme between EISs and Java. Consequently, Record implementation classes must internally "know" how to map and represent EIS specific data. This is achieved in several ways.

- The resource adapter might be packaged with Record implementation classes that perform this EIS-specific mapping and data representation.
- A tool is provided that generates appropriate Record implementation classes by interrogating a metadata repository.
- Highly generic Record implementation classes are used that interrogate a metadata repository at runtime.

From Figure 31.5 it can be seen that a Record object might actually represent a hierarchical data structure made up of IndexedRecord, MappedRecord and ResultSet objects.

The Record interface is defined as:

```
public interface javax.resource.cci.Record
  extends java.lang.Cloneable, java.io.Serializable {
  public String getRecordName();
  public void setRecordName(String name);
  public void setRecordShortDescription(String description);
  public String getRecordShortDescription();
  public boolean equals(Object other);
  public int hashCode();
  public Object clone() throws CloneNotSupportedException;
}
```

Data is inserted into an IndexedRecord using the java.util.List methods. Data is inserted into a MappedRecord using java.util.Map methods. These take key and value pairs. The ResultSet class has update methods defined in the java.sql.ResultSet class. Similarly, these super-interfaces provide accessor methods enabling you to obtain result data.

You can generate input records using the RecordFactory interface. This is defined as:

```
public interface javax.resource.cci.RecordFactory {
  public MappedRecord createMappedRecord(String recordName)
    throws ResourceException;
  public IndexedRecord createIndexedRecord(String recordName)
    throws ResourceException;
}
```

Note that only IndexedRecord and MappedRecord objects can be created. ResultSet objects are created by the resource adapter when returning results. The RecordFactory is only used for the creation of generic Record objects (those that interrogate a metadata repository). The factory uses the recordName parameter as an index into the repository. In other cases you create the instances explicitly. Note that the Record implementation class may implement the Streamable interface. This interface has read and write operations that enable the resource adapter to extract or insert data as a stream of bytes. This interface is hidden from application components. The latter use the Map, List or ResultSet methods to insert or obtain data.

A resource adapter might support the java.sql.ResultSet interface. It provides a way of returning tabular data. Refer to Chapter 9 for a description of its methods and features.

31.7 Deploying Resource Adapters

A resource adapter is a J2EE module, and as such can be deployed using the mechanisms used to deploy other modules (e.g. EJBs and Web components). If an adapter module is deployed within an enterprise archive then it will only be visible to other modules within the same archive. If an adapter module is deployed on its own, then it will be visible to any other deployed J2EE module.

A resource adapter module is packaged within a JAR file, and usually with the .rar file extension. This file will contain a META-INF/ra.xml deployment descriptor file. This is used to configure and describe the resource adapter. Java classes and native code libraries are also included within the RAR file. Java classes must be packaged within JAR files that have the .jar extension.

A resource adapter module is normally created by an EIS vendor, or a third-party vendor, rather than an application-component developer. Consequently, we will not provide a detailed description of the deployment descriptors. Please refer to the JCA specification for a definitive description (Sharma, 2001). However, the file contains the following kinds of information:

- General information: the name of the vendor and resource adapter, licensing information and version numbering.
- ManagedConnectionFactory interface: the fully qualified name of this interface.

- `ConnectionFactory` interface and its implementation class.
- `Connection` interface and its implementation class.
- Transactional support: defines the kind of transaction, if any, supported by the adapter, for example, local or XA.
- Configurable properties per `ManagedConnectionFactory` instance. Defined as name and value pairs.
- Authentication mechanism. Defines the kind of authentication mechanism supported by the adapter; for example, basic password authentication or Kerberos (`http://web.mit.edu/kerberos/www/`) authentication.
- Re-authentication support. Indicates whether a `ManagedConnection` can be re-authenticated to support different resource principals.

The application server will also need to be configured to create and bind managed objects (e.g. the `ConnectionFactory` implementation class) to the JNDI directory space, and to set other properties. For JBoss 3.0 this is done in the `jca-service.xml` or one of the other `*-service.xml` files located in the JBoss `deploy` directory. For example, JBoss 3.0 has an `hsqldb-service.xml` file that defines a JCA resource for the HSQL default database system where the JNDI name is `DefaultDS`. Without knowing it, we have been using JCA for all our bookstore entity EJB examples! In Chapter 14 the `jbosscmp-jdbc.xml` file referred to `DefaultDS`. In this case the container obtained a `DataSource` connection factory from HSQL resource adapter (which is really an SQL database driver). In Chapter 29 the `BookItemBMPBean` obtained the `DataSource` factory object through an explicit JNDI lookup. This demonstrates how seamlessly the JCA integrates with JDBC.

31.8 Reference

Sharma, R. (2001). J2EE Connector Architecture Specification, Version 1.0, Final Release. Sun Microsystems.

Chapter 32

From Java to SVG

32.1 Introduction

In many Web-based applications it is not uncommon to want to be able to generate graph-based displays from servlets and JSPs dynamically. For example, you might want to generate a graph to show how the value of a particular stock has changed over the last twelve months etc. Trying to generate GIFs or JPEGs [illegible] this is both time-consuming and inefficient. Another option that is being used more and m[illegible] Web based applications is that of SVG. SVG or (Scalable Vector Graphics) are very easy [illegible]te from Java dynamically thanks to tools such as Batik from Apache.

32.2 What is SVG?

SVG (Scalable Vector Graphics) is a new XML-based language/vocabulary created by the World Wide Web Consortium (W3C). It has been hailed as one of the most exciting developing technologies and the Web's hottest new graphics format. This may be a little strong, but it is certainly a very interesting and effective emerging technology.

So what does vector graphics mean? The most common graphics format found on the Web today is raster (or bitmap) in the form of GIF and JPEG. This format of graphic contains information about each and every pixel within it. On the other hand, vector graphics describe an image in terms of the lines, text and shapes that make up its composition. This gives the ability to create sophisticated dynamic and interactive graphics.

32.2.1 Advantages

This section lists the advantages that scalable vector graphics have over raster graphics such as JPEGs and GIFs, as well as describing other useful features.

- SVGs are smaller in size and are therefore quicker to download than raster graphics. They are smaller because they only describe what actually comprises the image – raster graphics contain information about each and every pixel in the graphic, whether they are important to the image or not.
- The text that appears on an SVG is selectable and searchable, unlike the text that appears on equivalent raster graphics.
- SVGs are clear and sharp, and can be zoomed in and out of without loss of clarity.
- SVG is an open-source technology and therefore information and examples are readily available.
- SVGs can be printed at the resolution of the destination printer.
- Every SVG element (and any of that element's attributes) can be animated.
- As an XML-based language, SVG shares the advantages of XML, including:
  - interoperability
  - internationalization
  - easy manipulation through the use of APIs such as the Document Object Model (DOM)
  - can be transformed through XML Stylesheet Language Transformation (XSLT)
- Tools for viewing SVG files are available and often free.

32.2.2 Disadvantages

The biggest disadvantage of SVG is the current lack of support in browsers such as Netscape and IE. However, this situation can be dealt with using plug-ins such as A[illegible]s SVG viewer plug-in.

32.2.3 Obtaining an SVG Viewer

The example presented in Figure 32.1 is displayed within a brow[illegible] thi[illegible] case IE 5.5). To view the SVG file IE needs an SVG plug-in. Probably the most com[illegible]used SVG viewer is from Adobe. This is an excellent, and free, SVG viewer that can be download[illegible] from the Adobe Web site.

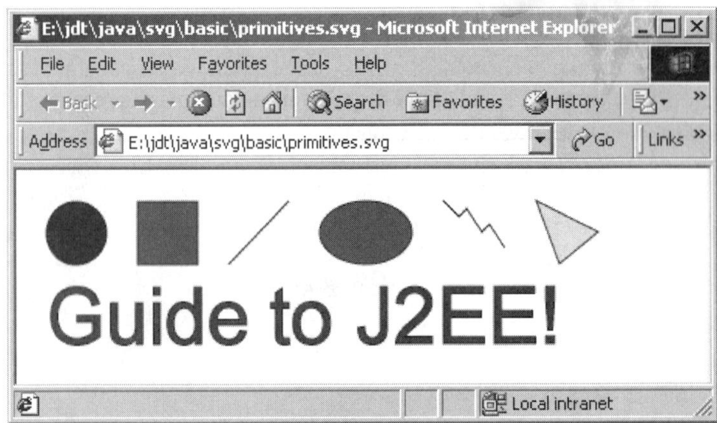

Figure 32.1

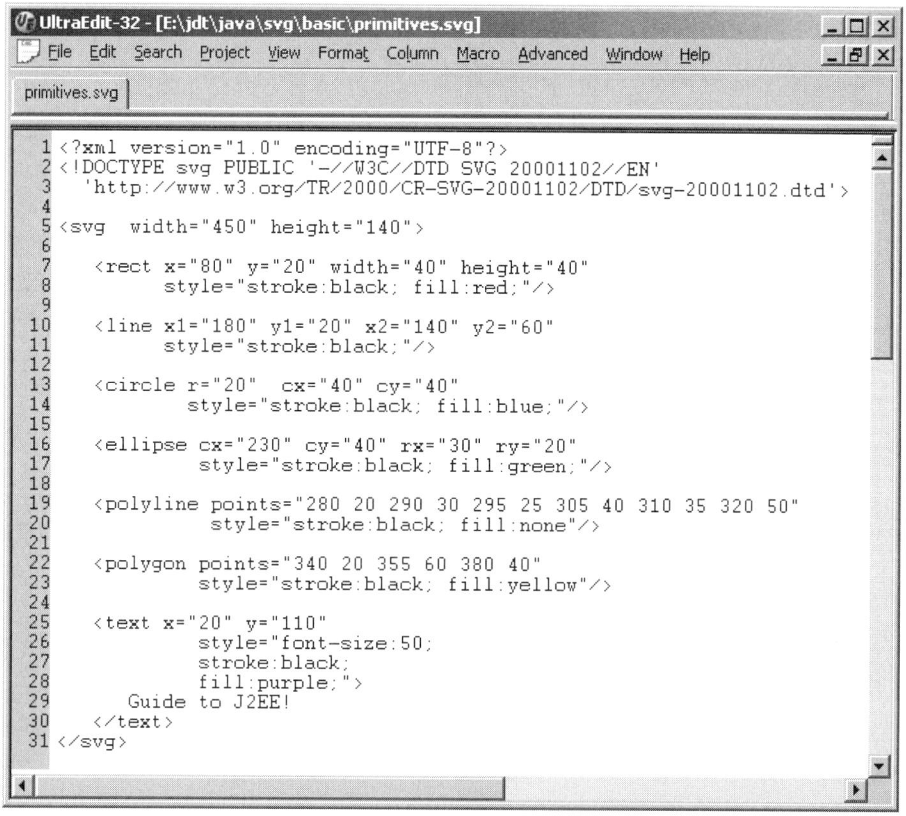

UltraEdit-32 - [E:\jdt\java\svg\basic\primitives.svg]

File Edit Search Project View Format Column Macro Advanced Window Help

primitives.svg

```
<?xml version="1.0" encoding="UTF-8"?>
<!DOCTYPE svg PUBLIC '-//W3C//DTD SVG 20001102//EN'
  'http://www.w3.org/TR/2000/CR-SVG-20001102/DTD/svg-20001102.dtd'>

<svg  width="450" height="140">

   <rect x="80" y="20" width="40" height="40"
         style="stroke:black; fill:red;"/>

   <line x1="180" y1="20" x2="140" y2="60"
         style="stroke:black;"/>

   <circle r="20"  cx="40" cy="40"
           style="stroke:black; fill:blue;"/>

   <ellipse cx="230" cy="40" rx="30" ry="20"
            style="stroke:black; fill:green;"/>

   <polyline points="280 20 290 30 295 25 305 40 310 35 320 50"
             style="stroke:black; fill:none"/>

   <polygon points="340 20 355 60 380 40"
            style="stroke:black; fill:yellow"/>

   <text x="20" y="110"
            style="font-size:50;
            stroke:black;
            fill:purple;">
      Guide to J2EE!
   </text>
</svg>
```

Figure 32.2

32.2.4 What Does SVG Look Like?

SVG looks, unsurprisingly, like XML, as it is an XML-based language (or vocabulary). An example SVG file can be seen in Figure 32.2. This SVG file renders as the image presented in Figure 32.2 using IE 5.5 with the Adobe SVG viewer plug-in.

32.3 Creating SVG Using Java

SVG files can be generated from Java in a number of ways illustrating the interest in SVG from the Java community. For example, it is possible to generate SVG merely by using the Java API for XML parsing (known as JAXP) from Sun. This is because the DOM (Document Object Model specified by the W3C) part of this API includes facilities for creating XML files (and SVG is an XML vocabulary). It is also possible to use the latest version of the JAXP API to translate an XML file into an

SVG file using a XSL translator. It can also be done using the Batik toolkit from the Apache foundation which provides a number of different modules to aid the developer. Finally, as JSPs are essentially servlets that contain XML-like tags, it is straightforward to include SVG tags in them.

32.3.1 Using the DOM API

We will first look at creating an SVG file using the DOM API as implemented by the JAXP extension from Sun or using the Batik `SVGDOMImplementation` class. The DOM API contains interfaces that model an in-memory representation of an XML document. It is possible to manipulate and update this model using the methods provided by these interfaces. As an XML-based vocabulary, an SVG file can be created using the DOM API. The following illustrates this.

Step 1: Get a DOM implementation
For this example we need to obtain an SVG-specific DOM implementation – `SVGDOMImplementation`.

```
DOMImplementation impl = SVGDOMImplementation.getDOMImplementation();
```

Step 2: Create a document from the DOM Implementation

```
String svgNS = SVGDOMImplementation.SVG_NAMESPACE_URI;
Document doc = impl.createDocument(svgNS, "svg", null);
```

or

```
Document doc = impl.createDocument("http://www.w3.org/2000/svg",
                                   "svg", null);
```

Step 3: Create a root element for the document
This is a very straightforward step that simply involves requesting an `Element` from the document.

```
Element svgRoot = doc.getDocumentElement();
```

Step 4: Set the attributes of the SVG
Two common attributes of an SVG that will need to be set here are the width and height of the graphic. Other attributes can be set in the same way.

```
svgRoot.setAttributeNS(null, "width", "200");
svgRoot.setAttributeNS(null, "height", "200");
```

Step 5: Create shape/line elements
This example creates a blue rectangle and a red circle. The code to create these is detailed below:

```
// create a rectangle
Element rectangle = doc.createElementNS(svgNS, "rect");
```

```
rectangle.setAttributeNS(null, "x", "40");
rectangle.setAttributeNS(null, "y", "50");
rectangle.setAttributeNS(null, "width", "100");
rectangle.setAttributeNS(null, "height", "100");
rectangle.setAttributeNS(null, "style", "fill:blue");
```

and

```
// create a circle
Element circle = doc.createElementNS(svgNS, "circle");
circle.setAttributeNS(null, "r", "20");
circle.setAttributeNS(null, "cx", "90");
circle.setAttributeNS(null, "cy", "100");
circle.setAttributeNS(null, "style", "fill:red;");
```

Notice that the attributes that are being set are the same as those that would be set in an SVG created manually. For example, an SVG file that creates the rectangle above would contain the following line:

```
<rect x="40" y="50" width="100" height="100" style="fill:blue;"/>
```

Step 6: Append the child element to the root
Simply use the `appendChild(Element element)` method to append the child element to the root element, for example:

```
// attach the rectangle to the svg root element
svgRoot.appendChild(rectangle);
```

Step 7: Write the document to a file
This can be done using the `PrintWriter` and the `DOMUtilities writeDocument()` method available with Batik.

```
PrintWriter writer = new PrintWriter(new FileOutputStream(filename));
DOMUtilities.writeDocument(doc, writer);
writer.flush();
writer.close();
```

The code described in the above steps generates the SVG image presented in Figure 32.3 when viewed with an SVG-enabled browser.

32.3.2 Converting XML to SVG

Generating an SVG file from an XML file and an XSL file involves the use of the `Transformer` class provided as part of the JAXP API from Sun. The XSL file provides the logic behind how the data held in the XML file should be rendered. The `Transformer` uses these rules to determine how the data held in the XML file is to be rendered. The XSL file could, for example, indicate that if

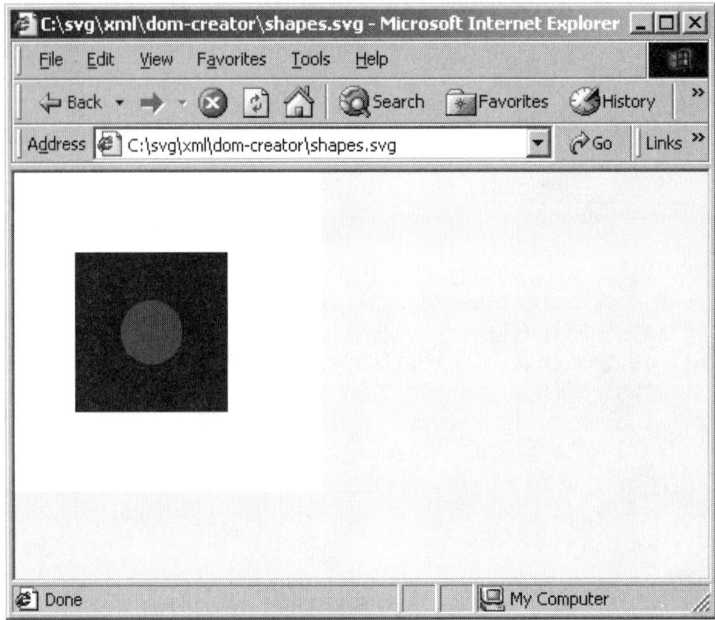

Figure 32.3

a NAME tag is found in the XML file, the value for that tag should be displayed in pink size 20 text. Alternatively, the name value could be used in a bar graph – perhaps indicating how many people have bought a book with the given name. The separation of document content from rendering information means that the same data (document) can be displayed in a number of different ways and on a variety of different media.

To illustrate how an SVG can be generated from an XML file, a simple example with an XML file called `books.xml` will be used. The example uses the data held in the XML file to create an SVG displaying a bar graph indicating how many sales each book represented in the XML file has had. The `books.xml` file contains a `<books>` element that contains a number of `<book>` elements. Each `<book>` element has three sub-elements: `<name>`, `<price>` and `<sales>`. The XSL file `books_bar.xsl` indicates how these elements should be used to build up SVG content. The `books.xml` and `books_bar.xsl` files are presented in Figures 32.4 and 32.5.

The Java code needed to convert (or transform) the `books.xml` file into an SVG file using the `books_bar.xsl` file is shown below.

```
// Create an XML Document
DocumentBuilderFactory dbf = DocumentBuilderFactory.newInstance();
DocumentBuilder db = dbf.newDocumentBuilder();
Document doc = db.parse(new File(xmlPathname));

// Transform source xml to pathname destination file
// We transform directly from the DOM tree
```

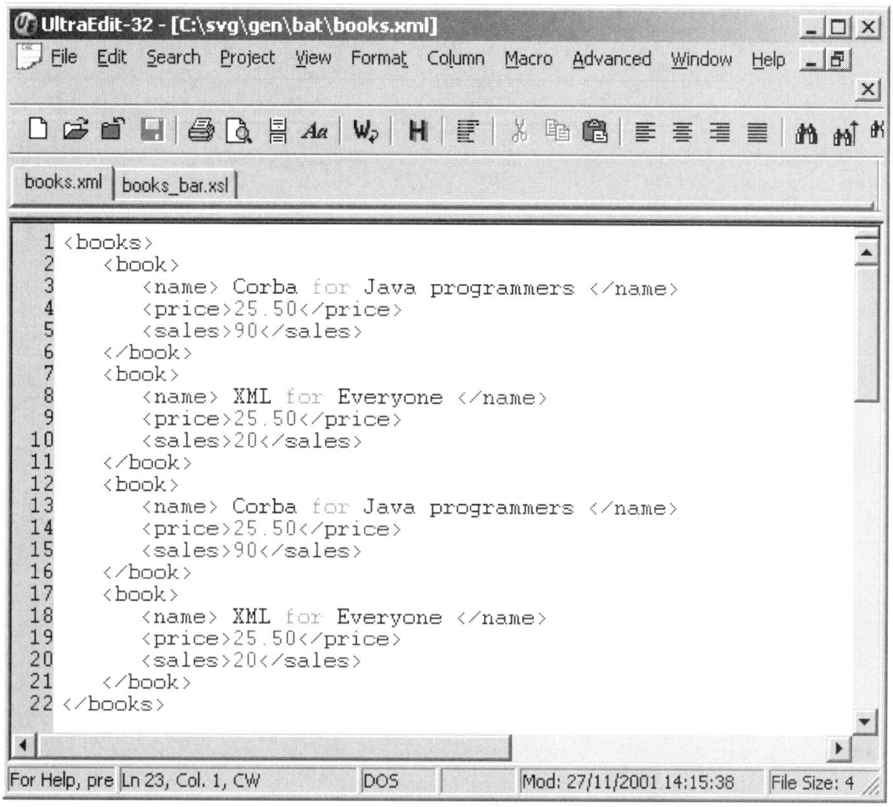

```
<books>
    <book>
        <name> Corba for Java programmers </name>
        <price>25.50</price>
        <sales>90</sales>
    </book>
    <book>
        <name> XML for Everyone </name>
        <price>25.50</price>
        <sales>20</sales>
    </book>
    <book>
        <name> Corba for Java programmers </name>
        <price>25.50</price>
        <sales>90</sales>
    </book>
    <book>
        <name> XML for Everyone </name>
        <price>25.50</price>
        <sales>20</sales>
    </book>
</books>
```

Figure 32.4 `books.xml`

```
TransformerFactory factory = TransformerFactory.newInstance();
Transformer transformer
      = factory.newTransformer(new StreamSource(xslPathname));
transformer.transform(new DOMSource(doc),
                      new StreamResult(svgfile));
```

The code follows the steps described in the list below:

1. Get a `javax.xml.parsers.DocumentBuilderFactory` instance.
2. Request a `javax.xml.parsers.DocumentBuilder` from the `DocumentBuilderFactory`.
3. Use the `DocumentBuilder` to parse the XML file (i.e. `books.xml`) into an `org.w3c.dom.Document`.
4. Get an instance of the `javax.xml.transform.TransformerFactory`.
5. Request a `javax.xml.transform.Transformer` instance from the `TransformerFactory`, passing it a new `javax.xml.transform.stream.StreamSource` object that has been created using the XSL file (i.e `books_bar.xsl`).

```
<?xml version='1.0'?>
<xsl:stylesheet version="1.0"
    xmlns:xsl="http://www.w3.org/1999/XSL/Transform">
  <xsl:output indent="yes" omit-xml-declaration="no"/>
  <xsl:template match="/">

    <svg width="600" height="550">

      <g transform="translate(70,70)">
        <text x="10" y="20" style="font-size:20">
        <xsl:value-of select="/books/publisher"/>
        </text>
        <line x1="0" y1="30" x2="500" y2="30" style="stroke:black"/>
        <xsl:for-each select="/books/book">
          <xsl:variable name="yOffset">
            <xsl:value-of select="count(preceding::sales) * 45 + 50"/>
          </xsl:variable>
          <xsl:variable name="barWidth"><xsl:value-of select="./sales"/>
          </xsl:variable>

          <rect x="40" y="{$yOffset}"
                height="15" width="{$barWidth}"
                style="stroke:black; fill:orange"/>
          <text x="40" y="{$yOffset + 30}"><xsl:value-of select="./name"/>
              ( <xsl:value-of select="./sales"/> )
          </text>
        </xsl:for-each>
      </g>
    </svg>
  </xsl:template>
</xsl:stylesheet>
```

Figure 32.5 `books_bar.xsl`

6. Create a `javax.xml.transform.dom.DOMSource` object to represent the document created in Step 3.
7. Create a `javax.xml.transform.stream.StreamResult` object and pass it the name of the destination file (i.e. `books.svg`).
8. Ask the `Transformer` instance to transform the document into an SVG file. This is achieved through calling the `transform()` method, which has two parameters. The first parameter is the `DOMSource` object created in Step 6, and the second is the `StreamResult` object created in Step 7.

The SVG file that is created from `books.xml` and `books_bar.xsl` is shown in Figure 32.6. Finally, when viewed, the SVG looks like the image presented in Figure 32.7.

The Java code for this example is straightforward and generic and can therefore be used to transform any well-formed XML file into a scalable vector graphic.

UltraEdit-32 - [C:\svg\gen\bat\books.svg]

```
<?xml version="1.0" encoding="UTF-8"?>
<svg height="550" width="600">
<g transform="translate(70,70)">
<text style="font-size:20" y="20" x="10"/>
<line style="stroke:black" y2="30" x2="500" y1="30" x1="0"/>
<rect style="stroke:black; fill:orange" width="90" height="15" y="50" x="40"/>
<text y="80" x="40"> Corba for Java programmers  ( 90 )</text>
<rect style="stroke:black; fill:orange" width="20" height="15" y="95" x="40"/>
<text y="125" x="40"> XML for Everyone  ( 20 )</text>
<rect style="stroke:black; fill:orange" width="90" height="15" y="140" x="40"/>
<text y="170" x="40"> Corba for Java programmers  ( 90 )</text>
<rect style="stroke:black; fill:orange" width="20" height="15" y="185" x="40"/>
<text y="215" x="40"> XML for Everyone  ( 20 )</text>
</g>
</svg>
```

For Help, press F1 | Ln 16, Col. 1, CW | DOS | Mod: 27/11/2001 14:41:15 | File Size: 787 | INS

Figure 32.6

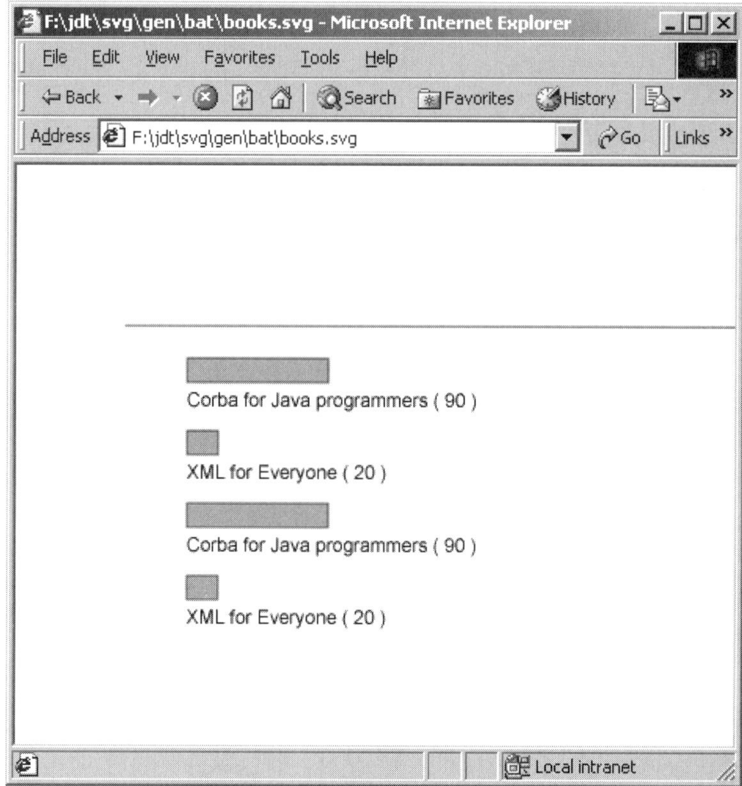

Figure 32.7

32.4 Using Batik

Batik, produced by the Apache foundation, is a sub-project of the Apache XML project. It is a Java toolkit for applications that need to work with images in the SVG format. It provides utilities for viewing, generating and manipulating SVG files. A Java application using Batik can, among other things, convert SVGs to raster format and also export its graphics in the SVG format.

Batik comes with three standalone applications: SVG Viewer, SVG Rasterizer and SVG Generator. This section will describe each of these standalone applications in brief, and the SVG Generator in more detail.

32.4.1 SVG Viewer

The SVG Viewer enables you to view SVGs. It also provides the ability to zoom into or out of the SVGs as well as allowing the viewer to rotate the graphic. This facility can be used from within any Java application as well as directly from a Web page viewed in a browser that has the SVG Viewer plug-in.

32.4.2 SVG Rasterizer

This application facilitates the conversion of SVG files to raster graphics. It can be installed onto a Web server so that users can convert their images remotely.

32.4.3 SVG Generator: Generating SVG Content from Java Graphics

The SVG Generator uses code designed for printing or drawing to the screen to export SVGs. On a Java platform, the `java.awt.Graphics2D` abstract class manages all rendering. SVGGraphics2D (the SVG Generator) is an implementation of this class that generates SVG content, which, for example, can be written out to file. The `SVGGraphics2D` class manages a tree of DOM objects. A DOM tree is an in memory representation of an XML (and therefore an SVG) document. When an application calls a rendering method on the `SVGGraphics2D` object, a new DOM object is created to represent the new SVG content, and this new DOM object is appended onto the existing DOM tree. An example of a rendering method would be the `fillRect()` method provided by the abstract `Graphics2D` class. Calling this method will result in the `<rect> ... </rect>` SVG element being appended to the SVG content.

The generation of SVG content from Java graphics can be done in four steps. These are:

1. Create a `Document` object of the appropriate type (in this case of type SVG) using a DOM implementation.
2. Create a `SVGGraphics2D` object, passing the document created in Step 1 into its constructor.
3. Invoke some rendering code on the `SVGGraphics2D` object.
4. Write the SVG content out to a file or wherever the output is desired.

These steps are illustrated in the code of Figure 32.8. The SVG generated when this code is run is as illustrated in Figure 32.9.

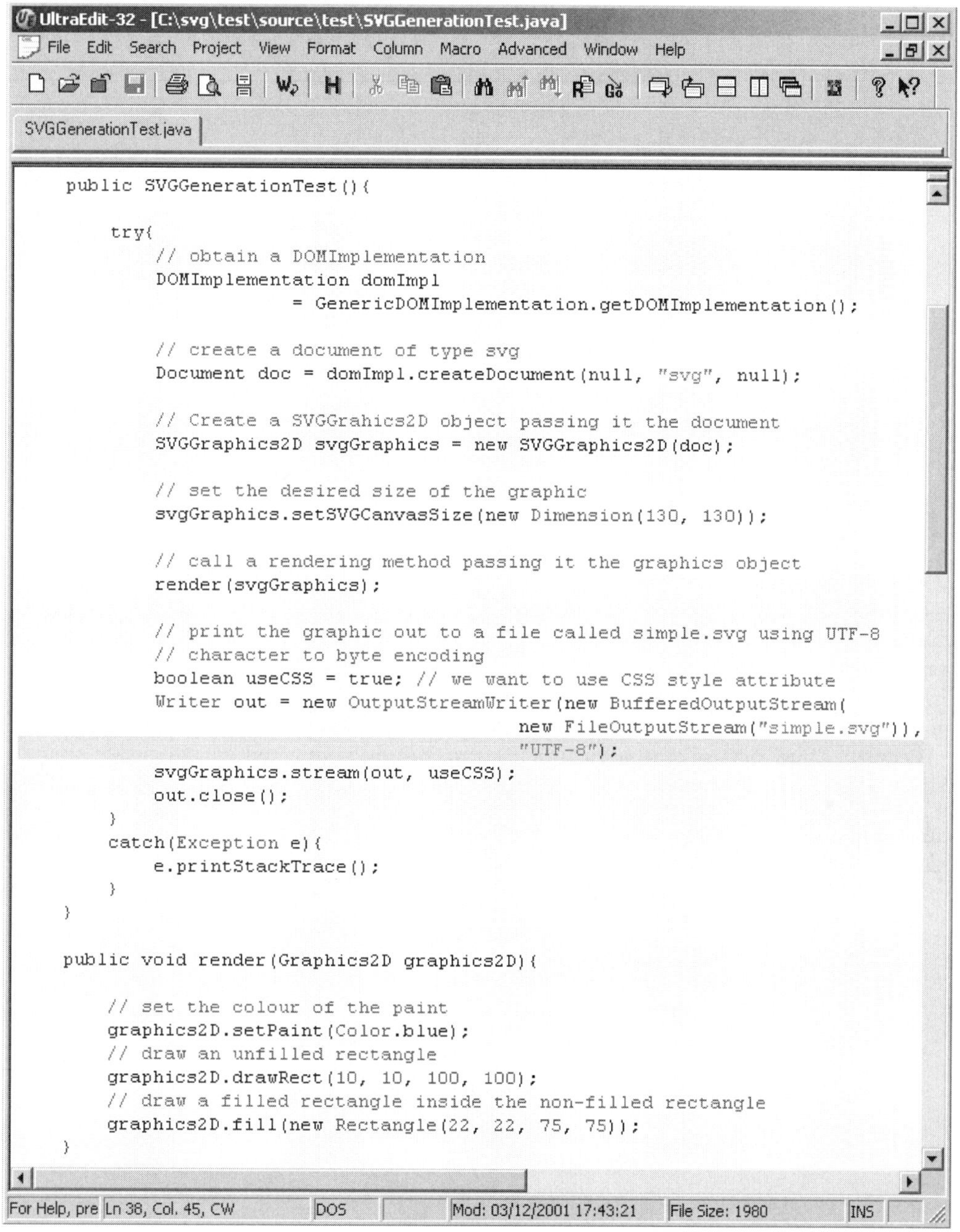

UltraEdit-32 - [C:\svg\test\source\test\SVGGenerationTest.java]

File Edit Search Project View Format Column Macro Advanced Window Help

SVGGenerationTest.java

```
    public SVGGenerationTest(){

        try{
            // obtain a DOMImplementation
            DOMImplementation domImpl
                        = GenericDOMImplementation.getDOMImplementation();

            // create a document of type svg
            Document doc = domImpl.createDocument(null, "svg", null);

            // Create a SVGGrahics2D object passing it the document
            SVGGraphics2D svgGraphics = new SVGGraphics2D(doc);

            // set the desired size of the graphic
            svgGraphics.setSVGCanvasSize(new Dimension(130, 130));

            // call a rendering method passing it the graphics object
            render(svgGraphics);

            // print the graphic out to a file called simple.svg using UTF-8
            // character to byte encoding
            boolean useCSS = true; // we want to use CSS style attribute
            Writer out = new OutputStreamWriter(new BufferedOutputStream(
                                    new FileOutputStream("simple.svg")),
                                    "UTF-8");
            svgGraphics.stream(out, useCSS);
            out.close();
        }
        catch(Exception e){
            e.printStackTrace();
        }
    }

    public void render(Graphics2D graphics2D){

        // set the colour of the paint
        graphics2D.setPaint(Color.blue);
        // draw an unfilled rectangle
        graphics2D.drawRect(10, 10, 100, 100);
        // draw a filled rectangle inside the non-filled rectangle
        graphics2D.fill(new Rectangle(22, 22, 75, 75));
    }
```

For Help, pre | Ln 38, Col. 45, CW | DOS | Mod: 03/12/2001 17:43:21 | File Size: 1980 | INS

Figure 32.8

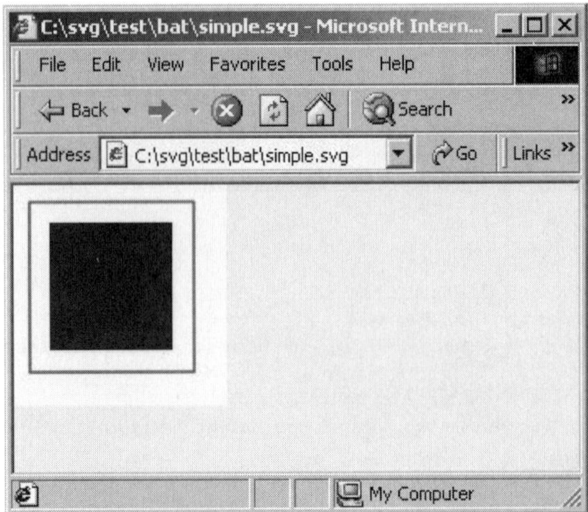

Figure 32.9

32.4.4 SwingDraw

An example of an application using the Batik toolkit is the SwingDraw program. A SwingDraw user can create a simple image on a canvas, and then request that it be converted into an SVG file. This SVG file can then be viewed and manipulated as any other SVG file. A screenshot of the simple drawing application presented in Figure 32.10 illustrates the facilities it provides.

When the "Svg" button on the SwingDraw application is selected an SVG file is created using the line-based image drawn by the user with the mouse. When viewed in an SVG-

Figure 32.10

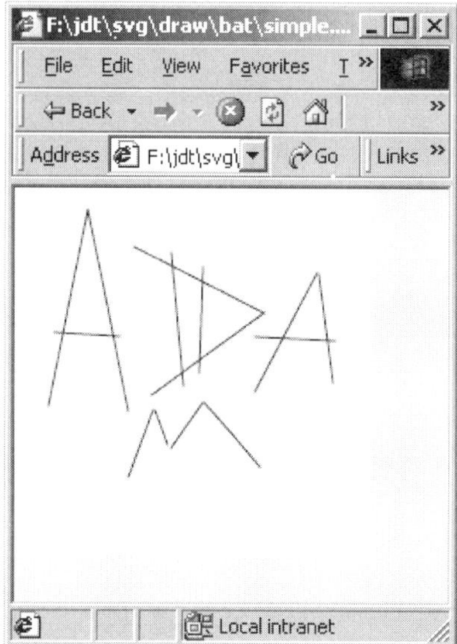

Figure 32.11

enabled browser the SVG file generated from Figure 32.10 renders as the SVG in Figure 32.11.

The process by which the SwingDraw application converts the user's diagram into a scalable vector graphic is the same as the four-step process described above.

The SVG file generated by the SwingDraw application to represent the image drawn by the user is illustrated in Figure 32.12.

32.5 Servlets and JSPs

It is very easy to generate SVG images on the Web using servlets and JSPs and the techniques described above. One important thing to remember to do is to set the content type to `image/svg-xml`. When a browser receives content to render it needs to know what plug-ins (if any) need to be invoked to display that content. This is determined by the MIME type of the content type of the response sent back to the client browser. In SVG's case, we need to display SVG content and thus the MIME/content type attribute for our JSP is set to "`image/svg-xml`". In a JSP this can be achieved through the following page directive:

```
<%@ page contentType="image/svg-xml" %>
```

Any of the techniques described in this column could then be used to generate the content of the page returned from the server to the client browser. In addition, the SVG tags could be embedded directly into the JSP.

UltraEdit-32 - [C:\svg\draw\bat\simple.svg]

File Edit Search Project View Format Column Macro Advanced Window Help

simple.svg

```
<?xml version="1.0" encoding="UTF-8"?>

<!DOCTYPE svg PUBLIC '-//W3C//DTD SVG 20001102//EN'
          'http://www.w3.org/TR/2000/CR-SVG-20001102/DTD/svg-20001102.dtd'>
<svg style="fill-opacity:1; color-interpolation:sRGB;
     color-rendering:auto; text-rendering:auto; stroke:black; stroke-linecap:square;
     stroke-miterlimit:10; stroke-opacity:1; shape-rendering:auto;
     fill:black; stroke-dasharray:none; font-weight:normal; stroke-width:1;
     font-family:&apos;Arial&apos;; font-style:normal; stroke-linejoin:miter;
     font-size:12; image-rendering:auto; stroke-dashoffset:0;" width="200" height="200">
  <!--Generated by the Batik Graphics2D SVG Generator-->
  <defs id="genericDefs" />
  <g>
    <g>
      <line x1="22" x2="8" y1="40" style="fill:none;" y2="139" />
      <line x1="23" x2="46" y1="41" style="fill:none;" y2="135" />
      <line x1="14" x2="35" y1="100" style="fill:none;" y2="97" />
      <line x1="63" x2="62" y1="43" style="fill:none;" y2="132" />
      <line x1="63" x2="93" y1="44" style="fill:none;" y2="93" />
      <line x1="94" x2="66" y1="94" style="fill:none;" y2="134" />
      <line x1="98" x2="123" y1="128" style="fill:none;" y2="46" />
      <line x1="123" x2="134" y1="46" style="fill:none;" y2="131" />
      <line x1="103" x2="139" y1="101" style="fill:none;" y2="96" />
      <line x1="16" x2="163" y1="169" style="fill:none;" y2="135" />
    </g>
  </g>
</svg>
```

For Help, press F1 | Ln 28, Col. 1, CW | DOS | Mod: 27/11/2001 14:49:38 | File Size: 1447 | INS

Figure 32.12

32.6 Summary

SVG is a powerful new technology that holds the key to fast and sophisticated dynamic images on Web sites. Its flexibility and ease of use, its advantages over raster graphics and the support available for those wanting to use it will add to the speed at which this technology is being adopted. The major drawback of SVGs is current lack of browser support, but this to some extent is already being addressed with the Adobe SVG Viewer plug-in in particular.

32.7 Online References

Overview presentation of SVGs: `http://www.w3.org/Consortium/Offices/Presentations/SVG`

Official W3C Scalable Vector Graphics Page: `http://www.w3.org/Graphics/SVG/Overview.htm8`

W3C Scalable Vector Graphics Specification: `http://www.w3.org/TR/SVG/index.html`

Adobe SVG Viewer: `http://www.adobe.com/svg/`

Adobe SVG Tutorial: `http://www.adobe.com/svg/basics/intro.html`

Sun XML XML Developer Connection – Introduction to SVG: `http://www.sun.com/software/xml/developers/svg`

Batik: `http://xml.apache.org/batik/index.html`

32.8 Appendix: SVGCreator.java

```
import javax.xml.parsers.DocumentBuilderFactory;
import javax.xml.parsers.DocumentBuilder;

import org.apache.batik.dom.svg.SVGDOMImplementation;
import org.apache.batik.dom.util.DOMUtilities;

import org.w3c.dom.Document;
import org.w3c.dom.DOMImplementation;
import org.w3c.dom.Element;
import org.w3c.dom.svg.SVGDocument;

import java.io.*;

public class SVGCreator {

  private Document doc;
  private String filename;
    private String svgNS;

  public static void main (String [] args) {

    SVGCreator sc = new SVGCreator(args[0]);
    sc.create();
    sc.save();
  }

  public SVGCreator(String file) {

    filename = file;

    DOMImplementation impl =
        SVGDOMImplementation.getDOMImplementation();
    // we are using a constant available on the SVGDOMImplementation
    // but we could have used "http://www.w3.org/2000/svg"
    svgNS = SVGDOMImplementation.SVG_NAMESPACE_URI;
    doc = impl.createDocument(svgNS, "svg", null);
  }

  public void create() {

    // get the root element (the svg element)
    Element svgRoot = doc.getDocumentElement();
```

```
    // set the width and height attribute on the root svg element
    svgRoot.setAttributeNS(null, "width", "200");
    svgRoot.setAttributeNS(null, "height", "200");

    // create a rectangle
    Element rectangle = doc.createElementNS(svgNS, "rect");
    rectangle.setAttributeNS(null, "x", "40");
    rectangle.setAttributeNS(null, "y", "50");
    rectangle.setAttributeNS(null, "width", "100");
    rectangle.setAttributeNS(null, "height", "100");
    rectangle.setAttributeNS(null, "style", "fill:blue");

    // attach the rectangle to the svg root element
    svgRoot.appendChild(rectangle);

    // create a circle
    Element circle = doc.createElementNS(svgNS, "circle");
    circle.setAttributeNS(null, "r", "20");
    circle.setAttributeNS(null, "cx", "90");
    circle.setAttributeNS(null, "cy", "100");
    circle.setAttributeNS(null, "style", "fill:red;");

    // attach the circle to the svg root element
    svgRoot.appendChild(circle);
  }

  public void save() {
    try {

      PrintWriter writer = new PrintWriter(new FileOutputStream(filename));
      DOMUtilities.writeDocument(doc, writer);
      writer.flush();
      writer.close();

      System.exit(1);
    } catch (IOException exp) {
      exp.printStackTrace();
    }
  }
}
```

Chapter 33

Web Services

33.1 Introduction

In this chapter we will look at Web services. Interest in Web services is growing at a phenomenal rate, but many are not exactly sure what a Web service is. This chapter therefore introduces the concept of Web services, before describing the technologies that underpin them. We then introduce the Axis toolkit, which is a high-level toolkit for building and interacting with Web services in the Java language. This toolkit hides much of the nitty gritty of working with Web services and provides a suitable high-level API. The chapter concludes by considering how Web services can be integrated into the J2EE architecture.

33.2 What Are Web Services?

Web services are no more and no less than distributed applications that run across heterogeneous networks using (currently) HTTP protocols and XML data formats. Of course, this is a big statement, but it illustrates the core concept. A Web services client on one machine can call a "service" on a host machine somewhere across the Internet without needing to worry about the platform, implementation language or vendor of that service. As XML transported by HTTP is used as the basis of the communication between the client and the service provider, it is also language- and platform-independent.

To support the "standardization" of Web services, various technologies have emerged. These technologies are vendor- and language-independent, and include:

- SOAP (Simple Object Access Protocol)
- SOAP with attachments
- WSDL
- UDDI

We discuss these briefly below. However, at this point a note of caution is due. Do not be put off by what you read in this section. A lot of what is happening with SOAP, WSDL and UDDI is "under the covers" if you use a tool such as Axis. This is similar to issues such as understanding how to use the `Socket` or `RMI` classes in Java. Under the covers TCP/IP protocols may be being used, but normally you do not need to know. SOAP and WSDL are a bit like TCP/IP: you may only need to understand their role and not have a detailed working knowledge of how to use them.

33.2.1 What Is SOAP?

SOAP stands for Simple Object Access Protocol (see `http://www.w3.org/TR/SOAP/`). It was originally developed by a consortium led by Microsoft and IBM. It is currently in version 1.1 (released in May 2000) with version 2.0 due soon. The W3C specification says:

> SOAP is a lightweight protocol for exchange of information in a decentralized, distributed environment. It is an XML based protocol that consists of three parts: an envelope that defines a framework for describing what is in a message and how to process it, a set of encoding rules for expressing instances of application-defined datatypes, and a convention for representing remote procedure calls and responses.

So what does this mean? SOAP is a lightweight XML-based protocol for cross-platform and cross-language communication. The basic idea is that an application written in one language can call an operation on another application, written in another language, across the network. Neither application need know how the other has been implemented. All that is required is that they both understand SOAP. Part of the key to SOAP's success is that not only does it describe the operation to perform, but it can also support the exchange of structured information between the two applications.

Figure 33.1 illustrates a scenario in which a client application and a server application communicate using SOAP messages.

When using SOAP messages to communicate between a client and a server the following steps are performed:

1. The client creates a SOAP message requesting that an operation on the server is performed.
2. The client sends the SOAP message to the server (Web service) for processing. This transmission can be performed in a number of ways, although the standard for Web services is HTTP.

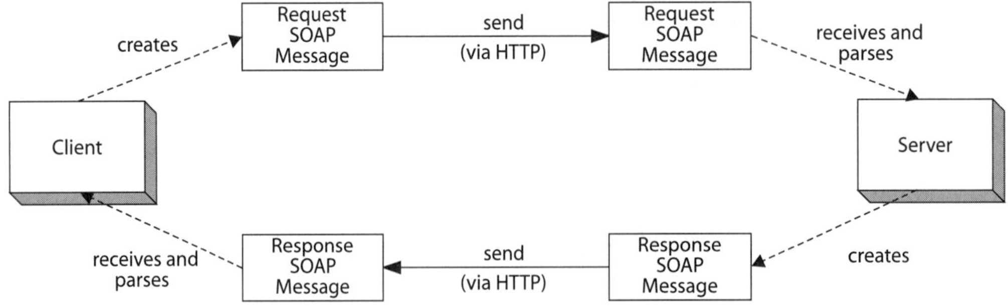

Figure 33.1 Client–server interactions using SOAP.

```
<SOAP-ENV:Envelope xmlns:xsd="http://www.w3.org/2001/XMLSchema"
                   xmlns:SOAP-ENV="http://schemas.xmlsoap.org/soap/envelope/"
                   xmlns:xsi="http://www.w3.org/2001/XMLSchema-instance">
  <SOAP-ENV:Body>
    <ns1:echoString xmlns:ns1="http://soapinterop.org/">
      <arg0 xsi:type="xsd:string">Hello Apache!</arg0>
    </ns1:echoString>
  </SOAP-ENV:Body>
</SOAP-ENV:Envelope>
```

Figure 33.2 A SOAP message.

3. The server (Web service) receives the message.
4. The server must then process the SOAP message (which is an XML document). Typically this can be done using an XML parser.
5. The server performs the request operations and generates a response.
6. The response is packaged up into a SOAP message.
7. The server transmits the SOAP message back to the client.
8. The client processes the SOAP message and extracts the result returned.

None of this is particularly novel, nor are the technologies used particularly new. However, their combination to provide a platform- and language-neutral environment within which to support distributed communication is proving extremely useful.

SOAP consists of three parts:

1. SOAP Envelope. This defines the content of the message, destination etc.
2. SOAP Encoding Rules. This defines how an application's data types should be exchanged between the client and the server application.
3. SOAP RPC Representation. This specifies a representation for remote procedure calls and responses for SOAP messages.

SOAP messages must not contain a DTD or processing instructions, but should contain two namespaces: one for the envelope and one for the encoding. An example of a SOAP request is presented in Figure 33.2. This is actually a SOAP message used with the ApacheClient described later in this chapter.

If you examine the content of Figure 33.2 you will notice that the root element is `Envelope` (from the `envelope` namespace). This element contains a `Body` element (also from the `envelope` namespace). Within the body element is the description of the requested operation. In this case the operation is `echoString` with a parameter (`arg0`) of type `string` (the type is defined by the `XMLSchema` namespace). The value of this parameter is "`Hello Apache!`".

33.2.2 SOAP With Attachments

As well as sending SOAP messages that describe the operations to perform, SOAP message can have attachments. This is referred to as SOAP with Attachments (SwA). These attachments can be images such as GIFs or JPEGs, or Word or StarOffice documents etc. SOAP 1.1 added the ability to have attachments with a SOAP message using the multipart MIME structure (see Chapter 11 for more information on MIME). The resulting message is known as a SOAP Message Package.

33.2.3 What Is WSDL?

WSDL (or Web Services Description Language) is an XML vocabulary for describing a Web service interface. That is, it:

- defines the service
- defines the set of operations on the server
- defines the format of client invocations
- acts a bit like a Java interface, but is language-independent

In other words, the WSDL describes what the contents of the SOAP message sent from the client should be. It also describes what the SOAP message sent back to the client will look like.

A WSDL document is a well-formed XML document that contains a definition element. This definition element is the root element of the WSDL document. It specifies a set of schemas used within the document. This is illustrated in Figure 33.3.

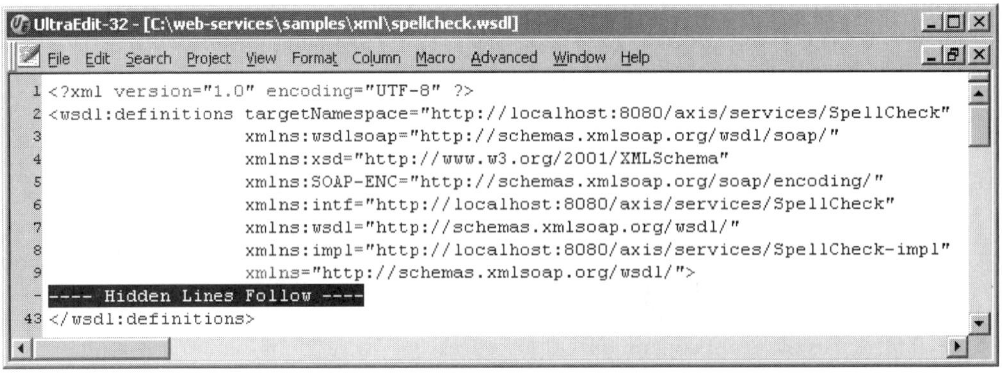

UltraEdit-32 - [C:\web-services\samples\xml\spellcheck.wsdl]

File Edit Search Project View Format Column Macro Advanced Window Help

```
<?xml version="1.0" encoding="UTF-8" ?>
<wsdl:definitions targetNamespace="http://localhost:8080/axis/services/SpellCheck"
                  xmlns:wsdlsoap="http://schemas.xmlsoap.org/wsdl/soap/"
                  xmlns:xsd="http://www.w3.org/2001/XMLSchema"
                  xmlns:SOAP-ENC="http://schemas.xmlsoap.org/soap/encoding/"
                  xmlns:intf="http://localhost:8080/axis/services/SpellCheck"
                  xmlns:wsdl="http://schemas.xmlsoap.org/wsdl/"
                  xmlns:impl="http://localhost:8080/axis/services/SpellCheck-impl"
                  xmlns="http://schemas.xmlsoap.org/wsdl/">
---- Hidden Lines Follow ----
</wsdl:definitions>
```

Figure 33.3 The root element of the WSDL document.

Within the definition element there are six major elements that describe the Web service. These are the `type`, `message`, `portType`, `binding`, `port` and `service`. The `type` element defines the data types used to describe how data will be exchanged within SOAP messages. The `message` element is an abstract description of the data being transmitted. For example, the following indicates that the response from the "`check`" service will be of type `string`.

```
<wsdl:message name="checkResponse">
  <wsdl:part name="return" type="xsd:string" />
</wsdl:message>
```

The portType describes the operations performed. For example, the following specifies that there will be an operation called "check", that takes one in parameter, and the input and output SOAP messages are described by the appropriate message element.

```
<wsdl:portType name="SpellCheck">
  <wsdl:operation name="check" parameterOrder="in0">
      <wsdl:input message="intf:checkRequest" />
      <wsdl:output message="intf:checkResponse" />
  </wsdl:operation>
</wsdl:portType>
```

The binding element defines the protocol and data format to be used for the Web service. For example, in Figure 33.4 the transport style will be XML RPC over HTTP. The operation made available is called "check" and the input and output will be encoded. This maps onto publishing an operation "check" on the SpellCheck Web service that takes a string and returns a string indicating whether the word was correctly spelt or not.

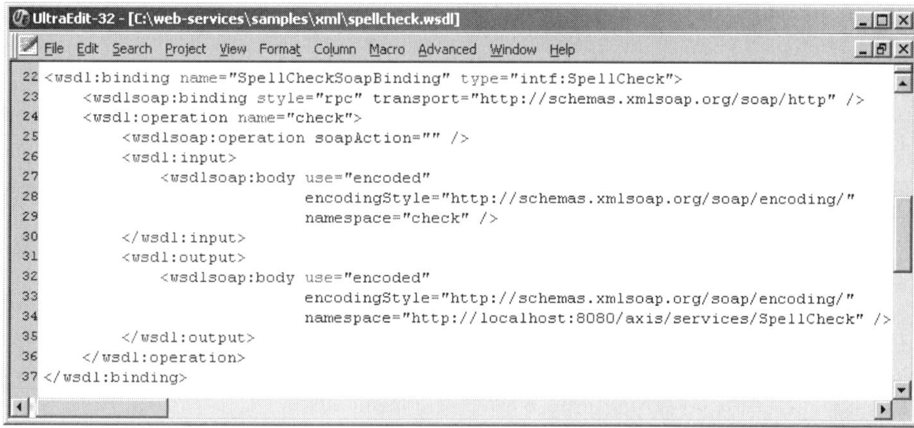
UltraEdit-32 - [C:\web-services\samples\xml\spellcheck.wsdl]
File Edit Search Project View Format Column Macro Advanced Window Help
<wsdl:binding name="SpellCheckSoapBinding" type="intf:SpellCheck">
<wsdlsoap:binding style="rpc" transport="http://schemas.xmlsoap.org/soap/http" />
<wsdl:operation name="check">
<wsdlsoap:operation soapAction="" />
<wsdl:input>
<wsdlsoap:body use="encoded"
encodingStyle="http://schemas.xmlsoap.org/soap/encoding/"
namespace="check" />
</wsdl:input>
<wsdl:output>
<wsdlsoap:body use="encoded"
encodingStyle="http://schemas.xmlsoap.org/soap/encoding/"
namespace="http://localhost:8080/axis/services/SpellCheck" />
</wsdl:output>
</wsdl:operation>
</wsdl:binding>

Figure 33.4 The binding element in a WSDL document.

Finally, the service element groups a set of related ports together. For example, the service element in Figure 33.5 describes the SpellCheckService as having a "port" SpellCheck (a destination for a Web service) that has the address http://localhost:8080/axis/services/SpellCheck.

33.2.4 What Is UDDI?

UDDI, or Universal Description, Discovery and Integration project, is a project involving very many organizations, including (but not limited to) Sun, SAP, Oracle, Microsoft and Hewlett-Packard (see http://www.uddi.org/). UDDI acts as a registry (or naming service) for Web services (much in the same was as the rmiregistry acts for RMI-based applications). Suppliers of Web services register their service with a UDDI registry. Clients of that Web service can then

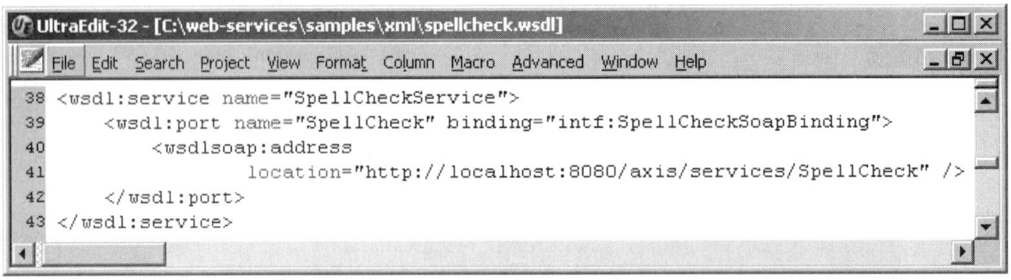

```
<wsdl:service name="SpellCheckService">
    <wsdl:port name="SpellCheck" binding="intf:SpellCheckSoapBinding">
        <wsdlsoap:address
                location="http://localhost:8080/axis/services/SpellCheck" />
    </wsdl:port>
</wsdl:service>
```

Figure 33.5 The `service` element in a WSDL document.

search the UDDI registry for services that match their requirements. A UDDI registry is accessed using XML and SOAP over HTTP in a similar manner to the way in which a client and a Web service provider interact. Thus we have a way of "finding" Web services as well as allowing clients and those Web services to interact.

33.3 What Is Axis?

Axis is a Java-based SOAP engine provided by Apache (see `http://xml.apache.org/axis/index.html`). It provides a set of classes and interfaces for constructing clients, servers, gateways etc. that process SOAP messages. To support this role AXIS provides:

- a server plug-in that allows it to be integrated into servlet engines such as Tomcat
- extensive support for WSDL (Web Service Description Language) version 1.1
- a utility (WSDL2Java) for generating Java classes from WSDL
- automatic WSDL generation from deployed services
- a utility (Java2WSDL) for building WSDL from Java classes
- preliminary security extensions, which can integrate with Servlet 2.2 security/roles
- an EJB provider for accessing EJBs as Web services

Axis does not directly support UDDI access. However, a related project to Axis is UDDI4J. UDDI4J is a Java class library that provides an API to interact with a UDDI (Universal Description, Discovery and Integration) registry. The UDDI Project is a comprehensive, open industry initiative enabling businesses to (1) discover each other, and (2) define how they interact over the Internet and share information in a global registry architecture. UDDI is the building block which will enable businesses to quickly, easily and dynamically find and transact with one another via their preferred applications. See `http://www-124.ibm.com/developerworks/oss/uddi4j/` for more information.

The use of Axis greatly simplifies the creation of Web services in Java. It shields the programmer from the lower level details of XML, SOAP, JAX-RPC, JAXP and WSDL. Indeed it makes creating Java based Web services and Java based Web service clients straight forward and little different to use any other Java framework. We will look at how to do this in the next few sections.

33.4 An Axis-Based Web Services Client

We are now in a position to start to write our first Web services client. We shall do this using a Web service on the Axis server made publicly available by Apache. This Web service, "`echoString`" receives a string and sends the string back to the client. While this may not be the most exciting Web service ever created, it does illustrate the basics of using the Axis classes in a Web client.

The client application, called `ApacheClient`, is illustrated in Figure 33.6. This application connects up to the axis server and calls the `echoString` method, passing in a string. The resulting string is returned and printed.

Lets break `ApacheClient` down into its constituent steps. These steps are:

1. Create a service object.
2. Create a call object from the service object.
3. Configure the call object
4. Invoke the call object

File Edit Search Project View Format Column Macro Advanced Window Help

```
package com.jdt.client;

import org.apache.axis.client.Call;
import org.apache.axis.client.Service;
import javax.xml.rpc.namespace.QName;

public class ApacheClient {
   public static void main(String [] args) {
      try {
         String endpoint =
             "http://nagoya.apache.org:5049/axis/servlet/AxisServlet";
         System.out.println("Creating Service object");
         Service service = new Service();
         System.out.println("Creating call object");
         Call call = (Call) service.createCall();
         System.out.println("Configuring the call");
         call.setTargetEndpointAddress( new java.net.URL(endpoint) );
         call.setOperationName(
                 new QName("http://soapinterop.org/", "echoString") );
         System.out.println("Invoking the call");
         String result =
              (String) call.invoke( new Object[] { "Hello Apache!" } );
         System.out.println("Sent 'Hello Apache!', got '"
                                   + result + "'");
      } catch (Exception e) {
         System.err.println(e.toString());
      }
   }
}
```

Figure 33.6 A simple Web services client.

Each of these steps will be considered in more detail below.

1. Create a service object. The `Service` object (from the `org.apache.axis.client` package) is Axis's JAXRPC Dynamic Invocation Interface implementation of the `Service` interface. The `Service` class should be used as the starting point for accessing SOAP Web Services. We are using the zero parameter version of the `Service` constructor. Doing this means that the Web services client will set the appropriate fields by hand rather than getting them from the WSDL. There are other constructors that take a WSDL.
2. Create a call object. This is done using one of the overloaded `createCall` methods. We are using the zero-parameter method that creates a new `Call` object with no prefilled data (the `Call` class is also from the `org.apache.axis.client` package). Again this assumes that we will configure the call as appropriate within the client application.
3. Configure the call object. We configure the call object in lines 17 and 18. Line 17 sets up the endpoint URL – this is the destination for the SOAP message. In this case it is the axis server provided by Apache. Line 18 specifies the operation (method) name of the Web service. In this case "`echoString`". It does this using the `QName` class (from the `javax.xml.rpc.namespace` package). The `QName` class represents a "qualified name" based on the "Namespaces in XML" specification. The constructor used for the `QName` takes two parameters. The first is the namespace URI for the `QName` and the second is the name of the actual operation to be performed.
4. Invoke the call. This is where we actually call the Web service, passing in the array of arguments required. In this case it is a single string. This returns another object (which is actually a string). The result is cast to a string and printed out using `System.out.println`.

To run this Web services client we must of course compile it first. To do this you will need to make sure that your classpath includes the `jaxrpc.jar` and the `axis.jar` provided with the Axis download. The setup used to compile the `ApacheClient.java` file is presented in Figure 33.7. Note that we have copied the various jars into a local `lib` directory.

One you have compiled the `ApacheClient` we can run it. To run the client another JAR needs to be added to the classpath. This is the `commons-logging.jar` used by the Axis classes themselves. The batch file used to run the `ApacheClient` is presented in Figure 33.8.

The result of running the `ApacheClient` is presented in Figure 33.9. Note that for this to work you will need to have an Internet connection, as the Web service is being hosted by

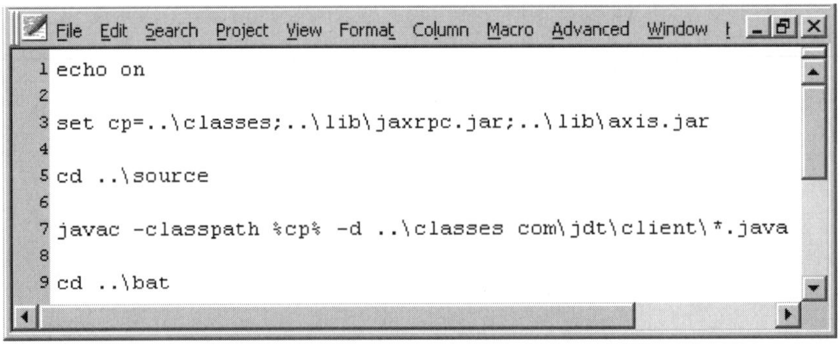

```
echo on

set cp=..\classes;..\lib\jaxrpc.jar;..\lib\axis.jar

cd ..\source

javac -classpath %cp% -d ..\classes com\jdt\client\*.java

cd ..\bat
```

Figure 33.7 Batch file used to compile the `ApacheClient.java` file.

```
echo on

set cp=..\classes;..\lib\jaxrpc.jar;..\lib\axis.jar
set cp=%cp%;..\lib\commons-logging.jar

java -classpath %cp% com.jdt.client.ApacheClient
```

Figure 33.8 Running the ApacheClient.

```
C:\web-services\samples\bat>set cp=..\classes;..\lib\jaxrpc.jar;..

C:\web-services\samples\bat>java -classpath ..\classes;..\lib\jaxr
jdt.client.ApacheClient
Creating Service object
Creating call object
Configuring the call
Invoking the call
Sent 'Hello Apache!', got 'Hello Apache!'

C:\web-services\samples\bat>_
```

Figure 33.9 Result of running the ApacheClient.

Apache. Also note that the echoString service merely echos the string sent to it back to the receiver.

So what has happened here? Well the string "Hello Apache!" has been serialized into XML and wrapped up in a SOAP envelope. The resulting XML document has then been sent over the Internet to the Axis server. There it has been received and parsed and a result has been generated. The result has then been wrapped up in XML and sent back over the Internet. It has been received locally and the Axis classes have de-serialized it into a Java string.

To see this in more detail you can use the tcpmon program to monitor the SOAP request sent out. tcpmon is a utility included with Axis in the org.apache.axis.utils package. To run it from the command line use java org.apache.axis.utils.tcpmon [listenPort targetHost targetPort]. The actual SOAP request for the ApacheClient is illustrated in Figure 33.10.

```
<SOAP-ENV:Envelope xmlns:xsd="http://www.w3.org/2001/XMLSchema"
                   xmlns:SOAP-ENV="http://schemas.xmlsoap.org/soap/envelope/"
                   xmlns:xsi="http://www.w3.org/2001/XMLSchema-instance">
  <SOAP-ENV:Body>
    <ns1:echoString xmlns:ns1="http://soapinterop.org/">
      <arg0 xsi:type="xsd:string">Hello Apache!</arg0>
    </ns1:echoString>
  </SOAP-ENV:Body>
</SOAP-ENV:Envelope>
```

Figure 33.10 The SOAP request generated for the ApacheClient.

If you examine the XML generated for the `ApacheClient` you may note a number of things:

1. The XML element which contains information specific to the call (the element within the `Body` tag) is called `echoString`.
2. The namespace URI is included in the XML at line 6.
3. The `Parameter` string passed into the `invoke` method is included at line 7 in a tag called `arg0` (a second argument would have been in `arg1` etc.).

Looking at this SOAP message you may wonder why the parameter passed to the Web service is called `arg0`. The answer to this is that we did not name the argument, and therefore it obtains a generic name, i.e. `arg0`. This can be altered if the Web service is expecting a specific argument name by using an `addParameter` method on the call and specifying the name and type of the parameter. You can also set the return type of the call in a similar manner. For example:

```
call.addParameter("testParam",
                  org.apache.axis.Constants.XSD_STRING,
                  javax.xml.rpc.ParameterMode.IN);
call.setReturnType(org.apache.axis.Constants.XSD_STRING);
```

This specifies that the first argument is called `testParam`. Note that it also declares whether the parameter is an in parameter, an out parameter or an inout parameter. Parameters in Java are by default "in" parameters so this is what we will use. The resulting SOAP message would now look like that presented in Figure 33.11. Note that the parameter is now presented within a tag called "`testParam`" and not one called "`arg0`".

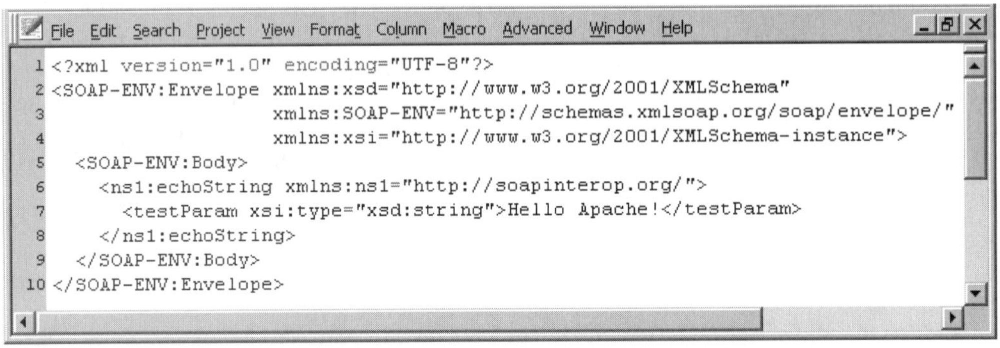

```
1  <?xml version="1.0" encoding="UTF-8"?>
2  <SOAP-ENV:Envelope xmlns:xsd="http://www.w3.org/2001/XMLSchema"
3                     xmlns:SOAP-ENV="http://schemas.xmlsoap.org/soap/envelope/"
4                     xmlns:xsi="http://www.w3.org/2001/XMLSchema-instance">
5    <SOAP-ENV:Body>
6      <ns1:echoString xmlns:ns1="http://soapinterop.org/">
7        <testParam xsi:type="xsd:string">Hello Apache!</testParam>
8      </ns1:echoString>
9    </SOAP-ENV:Body>
10 </SOAP-ENV:Envelope>
```

Figure 33.11 The modified SOAP message.

33.5 Creating a Simple Web Service Driver

33.5.1 Setting up Tomcat for Web Services

You need to set up a servlet-aware Web server with the Axis SOAP engine in order to create Axis-based Web services. You can use whatever Web server you want and the steps will be essentially the same. In our case we are going to use Tomcat (you could also use Tomcat with JBoss for this).

To install Axis first:

1. Install Tomcat.
2. Create the Axis Web application. This is done by copying the axis directory from the <axis distribution>/webapps directory to the Tomcat webapps directory. You can actually name this directory anything you want. However, whatever name you select will act as the root of the URL by which clients will access your service.
3. Start Tomcat.

You have now configured Tomcat to use Axis as the engine for handling Web services.

33.5.2 Creating a Very Simple Web Service

In this example we will do the minimum amount of work to get a Web service up and running. The service we will create will be a very simple service that will allow a client to submit a title for a book and to obtain a price for that book back. In our case we will limit this service to only three books, but the principle would be the same if we were querying a database with all books published by a particular publisher.

The basis of our service is the PriceCheck class illustrated in Figure 33.12. As can be seen from this the class holds a list of books in a HashMap. It also declares a public method lookup that takes the name of a book and returns the price (both as Strings).

```
import java.util.HashMap;

public class PriceCheck {
   HashMap map = new HashMap();
   public PriceCheck() {
      map.put("Java for Practitioners", "29.95");
      map.put("Unified Process for Practitioners", "29.95");
      map.put("Guide to J2EE", "39.95");
   }
   public String lookup(String bookname) {
      String result = (String)map.get(bookname);
      return result;
   }
}
```

Figure 33.12 The PriceCheck class.

The simplest way in which we can deploy this class as a Web service is to copy it into the Axis directory under webapps in Tomcat. The package structure needs to be preserved and the file needs to be renamed from .java to .jws (which stands for Java Web Service). For example:

```
xcopy com\jdt\server\PriceCheck.java c:\jakarta-tomcat-4.0.4-LE-
jdk14\webapps\axis\PriceCheck.jws
```

The end result of this should resemble the directory structure in Figure 33.13.

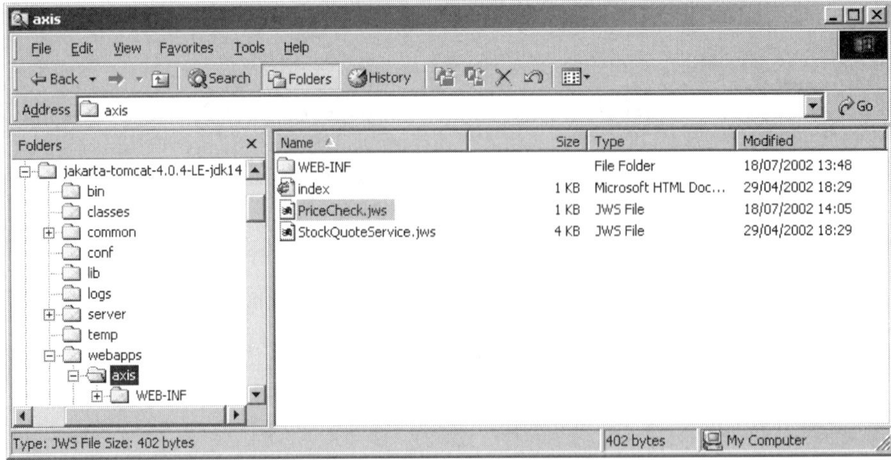

Figure 33.13 Instant deployment.

Next Axis will automatically locate the file, compile the class, and convert SOAP calls correctly into Java invocations of your service class. This is referred to by Axis as instant deployment. It is a very good way to try out a Web service easily and quickly without any overhead at all.

To try this out we will use the simple Java Web Services client presented in Figure 33.14. This is a modified version of the `ApacheClient` that connects up to the `PriceCheck` service on localhost and calls the `lookup` Web service.

File Edit Search Project View Format Column Macro Advanced Window Help

```
package com.jdt.client;

import org.apache.axis.client.Call;
import org.apache.axis.client.Service;
import javax.xml.rpc.namespace.QName;

public class PriceCheckClient {
   public static void main(String [] args) {
       try {
           String endpoint =
                   "http://localhost:8080/axis/PriceCheck.jws";
           System.out.println("Creating Service object");
           Service service = new Service();
           System.out.println("Creating call object");
           Call call = (Call) service.createCall();
           System.out.println("Configuring the call");
           call.setTargetEndpointAddress( new java.net.URL(endpoint) );
           call.setOperationName(
                   new QName("http://soapinterop.org/", "lookup") );
           System.out.println("Invoking the call");
           String result =
                (String) call.invoke( new Object[] { "Java for Practitioners" } );
           System.out.println("Sent 'Java for Practitioners', got '" + result + "'");
       } catch (Exception e) {
           System.err.println(e.toString());
       }
   }
}
```

Figure 33.14 The simple `PriceCheckClient` application.

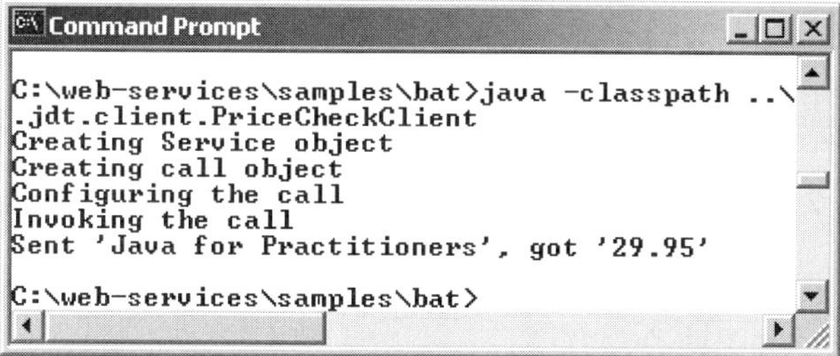

Command Prompt
C:\web-services\samples\bat>java -classpath ..\
.jdt.client.PriceCheckClient
Creating Service object
Creating call object
Configuring the call
Invoking the call
Sent 'Java for Practitioners', got '29.95'
C:\web-services\samples\bat>

Figure 33.15 Running the `PriceCheckClient` application.

The result of compiling and running this application (with the classpath set as before) is presented in Figure 33.15. As you can see from this figure, the result is that the price of the book is returned.

You have now written and deployed a Web service. So this raises a question: is this how you should deploy all your Web services? The answer is probably not! There are two reasons:

- Firstly you need to source code in order to generate the `jws` file.
- Secondly you have very little control over how your service is accessed.

For these reasons we will look briefly at how we can configure an Axis Web service manually in the next section.

33.5.3 Configuring a Web Service

In this section we will look at the Axis Web Service Deployment Descriptor (WSDD) file that allows us to define a service, how clients will connect to it and what parameters it has. It is also possible to specify the scope of an object that implements the service (this is a new instance created for each request or whether a single object supports all requests etc.).

To illustrate this we will look at another simple Web service. This Web service will act as a very simple spell checker. That is, given a `String`, it will look in its list of known words to see if the word is there. If it is, it will return true, if not it will return false. As this is just a proof of concept example the list of known words is limited to just three words. However, it could be easily extended with a spell checker package. The source code for the class that will implement this service is presented in Figure 33.16.

The WSDD file for this Web service is presented in Figure 33.17. This WSDD entry is composed of a number of parts. The outermost element tells the engine that this is a WSDD deployment, and defines the "`java`" namespace. Then the service element actually defines the service for us. A service is a *targeted chain* (see the Architecture Guide), which means it may have any or all of: a request flow, a pivot handler (which for a service is called a "provider"), and a response flow. In this case, our provider is "`java:RPC`".

We need to tell the `RPCProvider` that it should instantiate and call the correct class (e.g. `samples.userguide.example3.MyService`), and we do so by including `<parameter>` tags, giving the service one parameter to configure the class name, and another to tell the

File Edit Search Project View Format Column Macro Advanced Window Help

```java
package com.jdt.server;

import java.util.ArrayList;

public class SpellCheck {
   ArrayList words = new ArrayList();
   public SpellCheck() {
      words.add("the");
      words.add("and");
      words.add("but");
   }
   public String check(String bookname) {
      boolean result = words.contains(bookname.toLowerCase());
      return result + "";
   }
}
```

Figure 33.16 A very simple spell checker.

```xml
<deployment xmlns="http://xml.apache.org/axis/wsdd/"
            xmlns:java="http://xml.apache.org/axis/wsdd/providers/java">
 <service name="SpellCheck" provider="java:RPC">
  <parameter name="scope" value="application"/>
  <parameter name="className" value="com.jdt.server.SpellCheck"/>
  <parameter name="allowedMethods" value="*"/>
 </service>
</deployment>
```

Figure 33.17 The WSDD file for the simple `SpellChecker` Web service.

engine that any public method on that class may be called via SOAP (that's what the "*" means; we could also have restricted the SOAP-accessible methods by using a space or comma-separated list of available method names).

In the `scope` option, you add a `<parameter>` to your service like this (where "`value`" is request, session, or application).

Once the `SpellCheck.java` file has been compiled it can be deployed to the Axis server. In Tomcat this is done by copying the `.class` file to the appropriate location under the `axis` directory of the `webapps` directory of your Tomcat installation. This location is the in the `classes` directory of the `WEB-INF` directory. The package structure of your class must be maintained otherwise Tomcat will not be able to find the class file when Axis requires it (note that if you have read the servlets chapters in this book you will note that this is the location for classes used by a servlet):

```
xcopy com\jdt\server\SpellCheck.class c:\jakarta-tomcat-4.0.4-LE-
jdk14\webapps\axis\WEB-INF\classes\com\jdt\server\SpellCheck.class
```

Next we need to to send it to an Axis server in order to actually deploy the described service. We do this with the AdminClient, or the org.apache.axis.client.AdminClient class. This is done by setting up your classpath as appropriate and then calling the AdminCLient application with the name of the WSDD file (the WSDD file in Figure 33.17 is called deploy.wsdd in our case). The result of doing this is a messaging telling you that the Admin client has processed the file, for example:

```
C:\web-services\samples\xml>java -classpath %cp%
org.apache.axis.client.AdminClient deploy.wsdd
[INFO] AdminClient - -Processing file deploy.wsdd
```

You have now deployed the SpellCheck Web service.

We can now create a client that will access this Web service. Such a client is illustrated in Figure 33.18. The structure of this client is the same as the previous clients we have implemented. However, a number of items of information differ. The first is the endpoint URL. This is now:

```
http://localhost:8080/axis/services/SpellCheck
```

We could also have specified an endpoint of:

```
http://localhost:8080/axis/servlet/AxisServlet
```

That is, it points at a servlet within the axis Web application called AxisServlet. This is the object that will initially receive the request for the Web service. It will then handle initiating the SpellCheck Web service and passing data to it. It will also handle returning the result to the SpellCheckClient application. If we use the AxisServlet there is another difference. The second difference is in the data passed to the QName constructor. The first parameter to this is now the name of the published service (in this case SpellCheck) and the second parameter is the name of the operation to invoke ("check").

The SpellCheckClient is presented in Figure 33.18 (note that the operation name is of course now "check").

To run the SpellCheckClient you must compile and execute it with the appropriate classpath. The batch file used to run the SpellCheckClient is illustrated in Figure 33.19.

The result of running this client is presented in Figure 33.20.

33.5.4 Where Is WSDL?

At this point you may be wondering where the WSDL comes in? After all, we have seen the Axis buffers the developer from a lot of the low-level concerns associated with Web services, but we have been able to monitor the SOAP messages sent using TCPMON. But no mention has been made of the WSDL.

The reason we have not discussed the WSDL in our examples is that we have been using an Axis-based client to access our Axis-based Web service. This means that the use of WSDL has not been required.

```java
package com.jdt.client;

import org.apache.axis.client.Call;
import org.apache.axis.client.Service;
import javax.xml.rpc.namespace.QName;

public class SpellCheckClient {
    public static void main(String [] args) {
        try {
            String endpoint =
                    "http://localhost:8080/axis/services/SpellCheck";
            System.out.println("Creating Service object");
            Service service = new Service();
            System.out.println("Creating call object");
            Call call = (Call) service.createCall();
            System.out.println("Configuring the call");
            call.setTargetEndpointAddress( new java.net.URL(endpoint) );
            call.setOperationName(
                        new QName("http://soapinterop.org/", "check") );
            System.out.println("Invoking the call");
            System.out.println("Testing 'and': " +
                                call.invoke( new Object[] { "and" } ));
        } catch (Exception e) {
            e.printStackTrace();
        }
    }
}
```

Figure 33.18 The `SpellCheckClient` application.

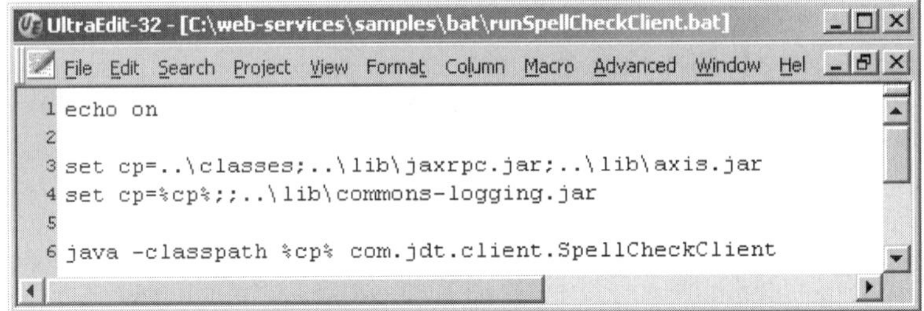

Figure 33.19 Running the `SpellCheckClient` application.

```
C:\web-services\samples\bat>java -classpath ..\cla
.jdt.client.SpellCheckClient
Creating Service object
Creating call object
Configuring the call
Invoking the call
Testing 'and': true

C:\web-services\samples\bat>
```

Figure 33.20 Output generated by the `SpellCheckClient`.

So when might you need to use the WSDL? Remember that the WSDL is a way of describing the Web service interface to a client of that Web service. Therefore if we are publishing our Web service over the Internet, those clients could be anywhere and implemented in anything. For example, the client may be a C# application running under .NET on a Windows box. Therefore the WSDL acts as the "interface specification" between our Web services and other non-Axis Web service clients.

So does this mean that you have to define the WSDL yourself? Actually no, (although you could if you wanted to). However, Axis gives you a convenience method for generating a WSDL document from a deployed Web service.

This is done by appending "?WSDL" to the end of the URL used to access the Web service. For example, if the Web service is accessed via:

```
http://localhost:8080/axis/services/SpellCheck
```

Then to generate the WSDL document you would use:

```
http://localhost:8080/axis/services/SpellCheck?WSDL
```

This is illustrated in Figure 33.21.

Axis does not stop there. It also supports the automatic generation of a WSDL file from Java code (using the Java2WSDL utility). But possibly more importantly, if a partner organization provides you with a WSDL file for its Web service, you can automatically convert that into a set of Java classes using the Axis WSDL2Java utility program. This greatly simplifies the job of interfacing to a published non-Axis Web service.

For example, if we took the WSDL document generated in Figure 33.21 and ran the WSDL2Java utility on it we would generated the Java files listed in Figure 33.22. The WSDL2Java utility is a Java application found in the `org.apache.axis.wsdl` package. To use it you need to set the classpath appropriately and then run this Java application passing in the WSDL file to process. For example:

```
>java -classpath
..\lib\jaxrpc.jar;..\lib\axis.jar;..\lib\wsdl4j.jar;..\lib\common
s-logging.jar org.apache.axis.wsdl.WSDL2Java spellcheck.wsdl
```

This will generate a directory named after the host, in the current directory, that will contain a number of Java source files automatically generated from the WSDL file. This is illustrated in Figure 33.22.

In this case `SpellCheck` is an interface defining the `SpellCheck` Web service interface (see Section 33.5.3). The `SpellCheckServiceLocator` is a class that will find and implement the client side of the Web service. The `SpellCheckService` is an interface defining what the Web service interface must provide. The `SpellCheckService` is another interface extending the RPC Service interface.

To use these classes you would create an instance of the service locator. You would then use this instance to access a reference to the actual Web service. You would then call Java methods on this "proxy" Web service that would get sent across to the actual Web service. This is illustrated in Figure 33.24 for the `SpellCheck` Web service.

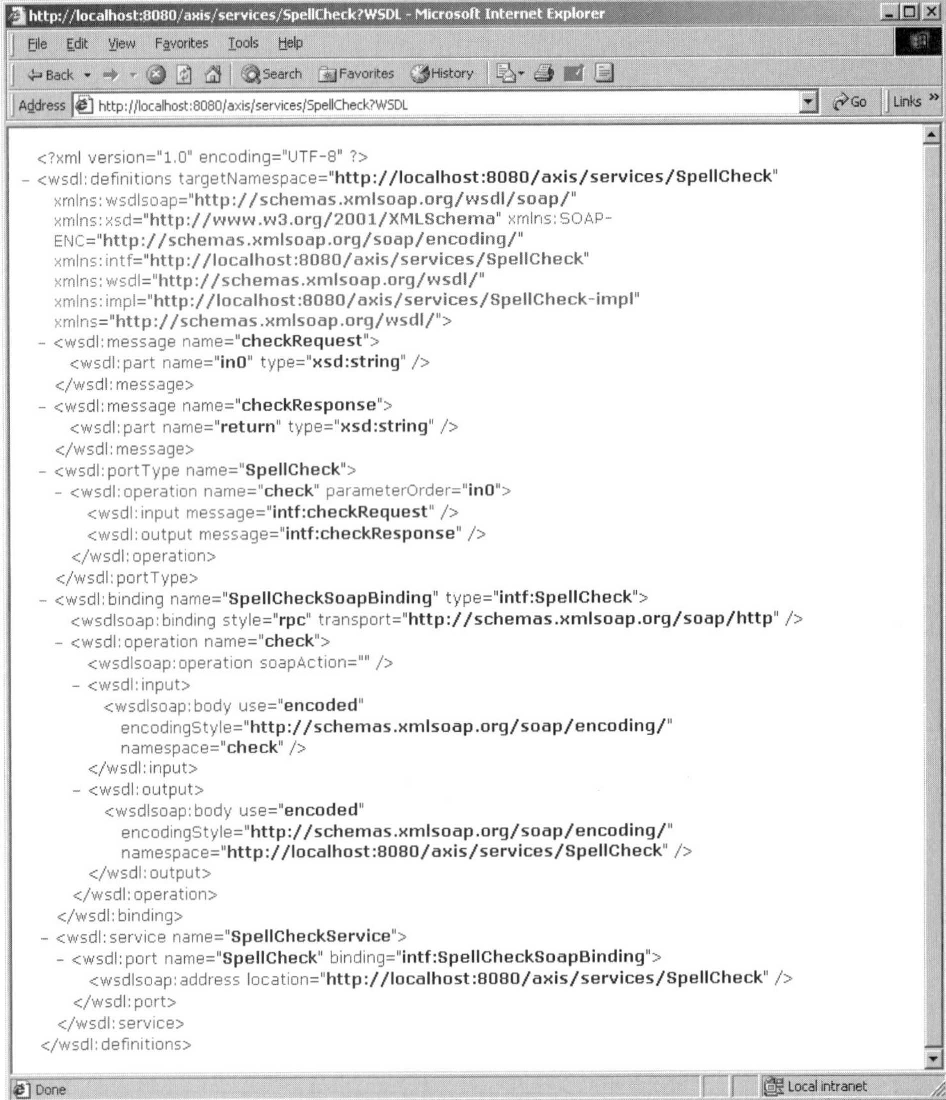
http://localhost:8080/axis/services/SpellCheck?WSDL - Microsoft Internet Explorer
File Edit View Favorites Tools Help
Back Search Favorites History
Address http://localhost:8080/axis/services/SpellCheck?WSDL
Go Links
<?xml version="1.0" encoding="UTF-8" ?>
- <wsdl:definitions targetNamespace="http://localhost:8080/axis/services/SpellCheck"
xmlns:wsdlsoap="http://schemas.xmlsoap.org/wsdl/soap/"
xmlns:xsd="http://www.w3.org/2001/XMLSchema" xmlns:SOAP-ENC="http://schemas.xmlsoap.org/soap/encoding/"
xmlns:intf="http://localhost:8080/axis/services/SpellCheck"
xmlns:wsdl="http://schemas.xmlsoap.org/wsdl/"
xmlns:impl="http://localhost:8080/axis/services/SpellCheck-impl"
xmlns="http://schemas.xmlsoap.org/wsdl/">
- <wsdl:message name="checkRequest">
<wsdl:part name="in0" type="xsd:string" />
</wsdl:message>
- <wsdl:message name="checkResponse">
<wsdl:part name="return" type="xsd:string" />
</wsdl:message>
- <wsdl:portType name="SpellCheck">
- <wsdl:operation name="check" parameterOrder="in0">
<wsdl:input message="intf:checkRequest" />
<wsdl:output message="intf:checkResponse" />
</wsdl:operation>
</wsdl:portType>
- <wsdl:binding name="SpellCheckSoapBinding" type="intf:SpellCheck">
<wsdlsoap:binding style="rpc" transport="http://schemas.xmlsoap.org/soap/http" />
- <wsdl:operation name="check">
<wsdlsoap:operation soapAction="" />
- <wsdl:input>
<wsdlsoap:body use="encoded"
encodingStyle="http://schemas.xmlsoap.org/soap/encoding/"
namespace="check" />
</wsdl:input>
- <wsdl:output>
<wsdlsoap:body use="encoded"
encodingStyle="http://schemas.xmlsoap.org/soap/encoding/"
namespace="http://localhost:8080/axis/services/SpellCheck" />
</wsdl:output>
</wsdl:operation>
</wsdl:binding>
- <wsdl:service name="SpellCheckService">
- <wsdl:port name="SpellCheck" binding="intf:SpellCheckSoapBinding">
<wsdlsoap:address location="http://localhost:8080/axis/services/SpellCheck" />
</wsdl:port>
</wsdl:service>
</wsdl:definitions>
Done
Local intranet

Figure 33.21 The WSDL document generated by Axis.

33.6 Java Web Services Development Pack

The Java Web Services Developer Pack (Java WSDP) is available both as a separate download and as part of the J2EE SDK 1.4. The Java WSDP is a package of technologies and tools for building Web services using the Java programming language and for building Java applications that access Web services.

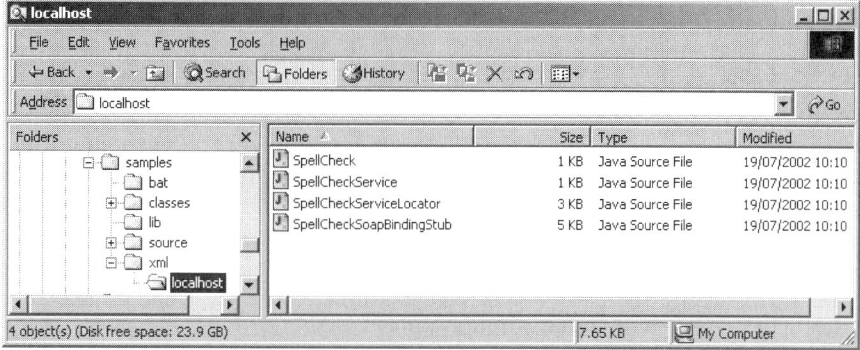

Figure 33.22 Automatically generated Java from WSDL.

UltraEdit-32 - [C:\web-services\samples\xml\localhost\SpellCheck.java]

File Edit Search Project View Format Column Macro Advanced Window Help

```
/**
 * SpellCheck.java
 *
 * This file was auto-generated from WSDL
 * by the Apache Axis Wsdl2java emitter.
 */

package localhost;

public interface SpellCheck extends java.rmi.Remote {
    public java.lang.String check(java.lang.String in0) throws java.rmi.RemoteException;
}
```

Figure 33.23 The automatically generated `SpellCheck` interface.

File Edit Search Project View Format Column Macro Advanced Window Help

```
import localhost;

public class ClientTester {
    public static void main(String [] args) throws Exception {
        // Make a service
        SpellCheckService service = new SpellCheckServiceLocator();

        // Now use the service to get a stub which implements the SDI.
        SpellCheck port = service.getSpellCheck();

        // Check spelling
        String result = port.check"and");
        System.out.println("Sent 'and' got back " + result");
    }
}
```

Figure 33.24 Using the auto-generated Java classes to access a Web service.

The technologies that comprise the Java WSDP include the Java APIs for XML, the JavaServer Pages Standard Tag Library (JSTL), the Java WSDP Registry Server and the Web Application Deployment Tool, and can run within Tomcat. A related technology is SOAP with Attachments API for Java.

It is useful to compare what the Java WSDP provides with what AXIS provides. The APIs provided by the Java WSDP allow you to build applications for Web services. In contrast, AXIS is explicitly a Web services API. That is, AXIS gives you a high-level API for constructing Web services, while the Java WSDP gives you a set of lower level building blocks that can be used to create Web services. As such, AXIS is preferable for Web service development. However, it is likely that future versions of the J2EE will extend towards a higher level API (as discussed later in this chapter).

33.7 SOAP with Attachments API for Java

SOAP with Attachments API for Java (SAAJ) was introduced in J2EE SDK 1.4 and is mainly used for the SOAP messaging that goes on behind the scenes in JAX-RPC implementations. However, it can also be used by developers who wish to write SOAP messaging applications directly rather than using JAX-RPC. The SAAJ API allows you to do XML messaging from the Java platform: by simply making method calls using the SAAJ API, you can create, send and consume XML messages over the Internet.

The SAAJ API conforms to the Simple Object Access Protocol (SOAP) 1.1 specification and the SOAP with Attachments specification. It is defined in the `javax.xml.soap` package. This package has all the API necessary for sending request–response messages

33.8 Web Services and J2EE

You may be wondering at this point how the J2EE platform might evolve to incorporate a higher level API for Web Services similar to AXIS. Although the J2EE SDK 1.4 does have some support for Web Services (as described above), let us look at how this higher level API might be integrated into J2EE components.

The J2EE architecture also provides for servlets and JSP. These are components that receive HTTP requests and return HTTP responses. Web services (currently) rely on XML-based SOAP messages being sent over HTTP between Web service clients and Web service providers (as illustrated in Figure 33.1). Therefore servlets are ideally positioned to act as the Web service provider that receives the request from a client. These servlets would receive the HTTP request containing the XML-based SOAP message. They could parse the request using the JAXP and determine what the client requires them to do. This may be a request to initiate some server-side behaviour (such as to query a database, call some operation on an EJB, send a message via JMS, access another servlet or JSP, or activate an RMI server object). This is illustrated in Figure 33.25.

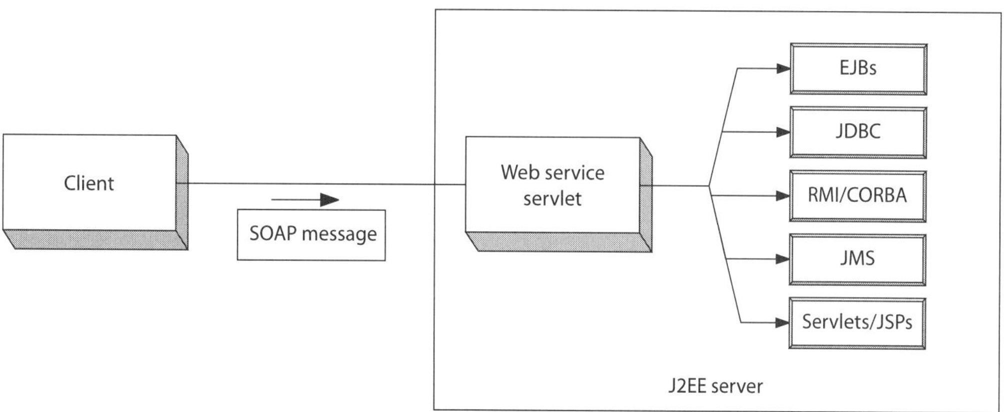

Figure 33.25 Using a servlet to handle SOAP requests.

Once the behaviour instigated by the original request has been completed, any resulting information needs to be returned. To do this, the servlet must create a new SOAP response message (again possibly by using JAXP) and send it back as the HTTP response. Servlets are therefore an ideal component with which to build Web services. Note that this is essentially the approach that has been taken with the Axis toolkit.

What does the future hold for Web services and J2EE. One possibility is the formalizing of the approach described above with direct support for creating Web service-based servlets. Another is to allow the direct invocation of EJBs from SOAP messages. This could be a very useful approach, as EJBs represent server side business logic and the Web service is server-side business logic. In this model a SOAP message would be directly mapped to an EJB. When the SOAP message is received by the EJB server it would have to map the SOAP message to an actual EJB. If the EJB is an entity bean or stateful session bean then some extra work would be needed to identify the correct context for the bean (but this would not be impossible to provide). The EJB could then execute the request operation. Any returned information would then be mapped back into a SOAP message and sent back to the Web service client. This is illustrated in Figure 33.26. At present, this model has not be introduced into the standard J2EE specification (however, many J2EE server vendors have provided this sort of functionality).

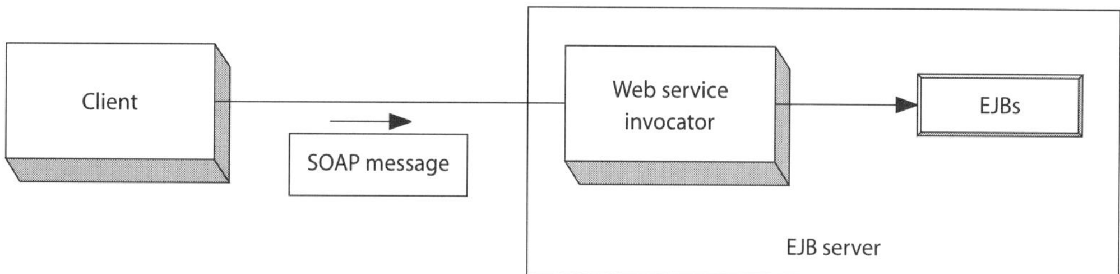

Figure 33.26 Integrating an EJB into a Web service.

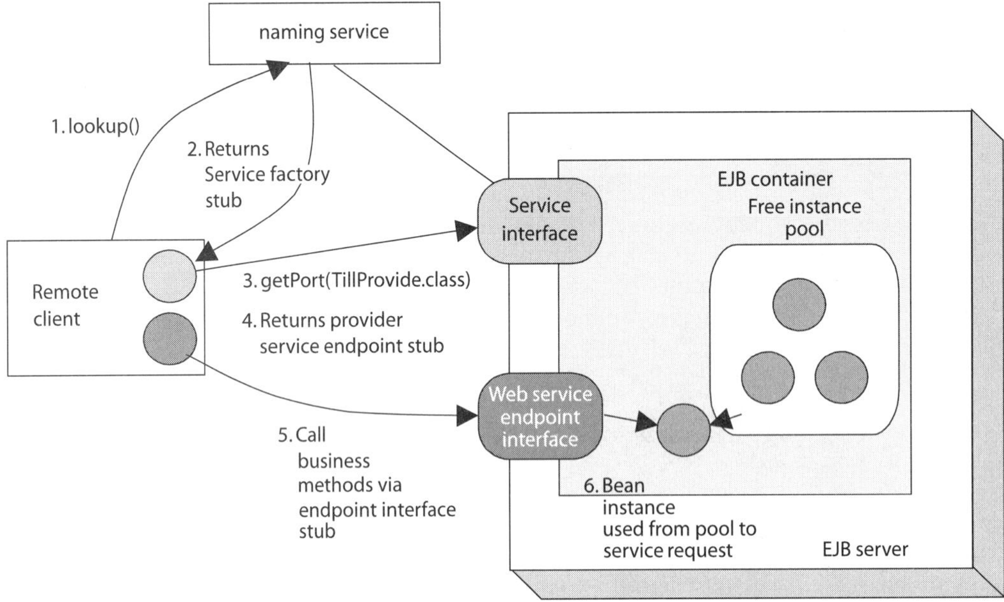

Figure 33.27 Client interaction with a Web service endpoint.

A third integration approach (for asynchronous) Web services is to map SOAP requests to a message server accessed via JMS. In this approach, a SOAP message is added to the message queue and is serviced by either a message-driven bean or a standalone JMS client.

Stateless session EJBs have the unique ability amongst EJBs to act as Web service endpoints. Effectively, this means that they can receive messages via JAX-RPC (Java's support for SOAP 1.1 over HTTP or HTTPS). Web service endpoints are described as part of a Web service client view within WSDL documents. This abstract document can then be mapped to Web service endpoint interfaces in a particular language that conform to the description. An existing stateless session EJB can provide such an interface.

Figure 33.27 illustrates how clients may access Web service endpoints. The client first needs to obtain a factory object of type `javax.xml.rpc.Service`. This factory can deliver required Web service endpoint stubs that "know" how to use JAX-RPC to communicate with the remote endpoint via SOAP. We refer the reader to JAX-RPC 1.0 (see References) for details regarding the service interface, WSDL and generation of service endpoints based on WSDL.

Listing 33.1 shows example client code accessing a `TillProvider` Web service endpoint. Here we want to gain access to a Till Web service that provides a `getTotal` method that can be accessed via SOAP. In this case we are accessing the service from a J2EE container-managed client, for example another EJB or a servlet. Consequently, we use the environment naming context lookup name for the service. More on this later.

Listing 33.1 Example client code.

```
...
Context ctx = new InitialContext();
```

```
BookstoreService bss = (store.BookstoreService)
  ctx.lookup("java:comp/env/service/BookStoreService");
TillProvider tp = bss.getTillProviderPort();
Double cost = tp.getTotal(books);
...
```

Notice that the lookup delivered a store-application specific service factory. Its getTillProviderPort can then be used to deliver a stub to the Till service endpoint. The getTotal call will map onto the Till component class getTotal method.

To advertise the Till as a service endpoint the <service-endpoint> tag should be included within the stateless session EJB's deployment descriptor, for example:

```
<ejb-jar>
  <enterprise-beans>
    <session>
      <ejb-name>Till</ejb-name>
      <home>store.TillHome</home>
      <remote>store.Till</remote>
      <ejb-class>store.TillBean</ejb-class>
      <service-endpoint>store.TillProvider</service-endpoint>
      <session-type>Stateless</session-type>
      <transaction-type>Container</transaction-type>
    </session>
  </enterprise-beans>
  ...
</ejb-jar>
```

Note that if a stateless session EJB has a service endpoint interface, you may, if you wish, omit the EJB's other client interfaces. If that is the case, the EJB can only be accessed through SOAP.

A container-managed EJB or servlet/JSP can add a service reference to its environment naming context using the <service-ref> tag. For example:

```
<ejb-jar>
  <enterprise-beans>
    <entity>
    ...
      <service-ref>
        <description>SOAP reference to BookstoreService</description>
        <service-ref-name>service/BookStoreService</service-ref-name>
        <service-interface>store.BookstoreService<service-interface>
      </service-ref>
    </entity>
  </enterprise-beans>
  ...
</ejb-jar>
```

The `Till` EJB component class remains unchanged. However, it can access the JAX-RPC `javax.xml.rpc.handler.MessageContext` interface through the `SessionContext.getMessageContext()` method. This allows access to various SOAP properties (JAX-RPC 1.0).

The service endpoint interface must follow certain rules. It must extend `java.rmi.Remote`. Methods must only have parameters and return types that follow the JAX-RPC serialization rules. Note that remote or local interfaces, managed collections or timer objects must not be exposed as method parameter or return values. The parameter types must follow WSDL to Java mapping rules. Each method must declare that it throws a `java.rmi.RemoteException`. As with other business logic interfaces, each method must have an identical method implemented in the component class (apart from the `RemoteException` declaration).

33.9 Summary

This chapter has introduced the concept of Web services and the building blocks upon which Web services are built (such as SOAP, WSDL or UDDI). It has also presented a practical toolkit (Axis) that can be used to build Web services in a painless way in Java. It has also considered how Web services may be integrated into the J2EE architecture.

33.10 Reference

JAX-RPC 1.0 Java API for XML-based RPC (JAX-RPC) 1.0, Sun Microsystems.

Part 5

Design

Chapter 34

J2EE Patterns

34.1 Introduction

There is a growing interest in what have become known generically as patterns; to be more precise, in Design Patterns. Historically, design patterns have their basis in the work of an architect who designed a language for encoding knowledge of the design and construction of buildings (Alexander *et al.*, 1977; Alexander, 1979). The knowledge is described in terms of patterns that capture both a recurring architectural arrangement and a rule for how and when to apply this knowledge. That is, they incorporate knowledge about the design as well as the basic design relations.

This work was picked up by a number of researchers working within the object oriented field. This then led to the exploration of how software frameworks can be documented using (software) design patterns (for example, Johnson (1992) and Birrer and Eggenschmiler (1993)). In particular Johnson's paper describes the form that these design patterns take and the problems encountered in applying them.

Since 1995 and the publication of the "Patterns" book by the *Gang of Four* (Gamma *et al.*, 1995), interest in patterns has mushroomed. Patterns are now seen as a way of capturing expert and design knowledge associated with a system architecture to support design as well as software reuse. In addition, as interest in patterns has grown, their use and representational expressiveness has grown.

More recently, with the advent of the J2EE, there has been interest in identifying and formalizing design patterns that are specific to the J2EE technologies. This has resulted in the development of a J2EE Patterns catalog by Sun (see `http://developer.java.sun.com/developer/technicalArticles/J2EE/patterns`) and publication of a J2EE patterns book (Alur *et al.*, 2001).

So what are design patterns? We will look at this question in more detail later in this chapter. For the moment they are essentially useful recurring solutions to problems within designs. For example, "I want to loosely couple a set of objects; how can I do this?" might be a question facing a designer. The Mediator design pattern is one solution to this. If you are familiar with design patterns you can use them to solve problems that occur. Typically early in the design process, the problems are more architectural/structural in nature, while later in the design process they may be more behavioural. Design patterns actually provide different types of patterns some of which are at the architectural/structural level and some of which are more behavioural. They can thus help every stage of the design process.

In this chapter we will discuss the motivation behind software design patterns, what design patterns are, how they are generally documented and when to use design patterns. We will then look at what a J2EE design pattern is and review the J2EE design patterns catalog. One example pattern from this catalog will be described along with a non-Sun J2EE pattern.

34.2 The Motivation Behind Patterns

Design patterns have been adopted by many organizations, architects and developers as the basis of the systems they build. Why? What is the motivation behind this? There are in fact numerous motivations behind design patterns. These include:

1. The difficulty of designing reusable software. Finding appropriate objects and abstractions is not trivial. Having identified such objects, building flexible, modular, reliable code for general reuse is not easy, particularly when dealing with more than one class. In general, such reusable "frameworks" emerge over time rather than being designed from scratch.
2. Software components support reuse of code, but not the reuse of knowledge.
3. Frameworks support reuse of design and code, but not knowledge of how to use that framework. That is, design trade-offs and expert knowledge are lost.
4. Experienced programmers do not start from first principles every time; thus, successful reusable conceptual designs must exist.
5. Communication of such "architectural" knowledge can be difficult, as it is in the designers head and is poorly expressed as a program instance.
6. A particular program instance fails to convey constraints, trade-offs and other non-functional forces applied to the "architecture".
7. Since frameworks are reusable designs, not just code, they are more abstract than most software, which makes documenting them more difficult. Documentation for a framework has three purposes and patterns can help to fulfil each of them. Documentation must provide:
   - the purpose of the framework
   - how to use the framework
   - the detailed design of the framework
8. The problem with cookbooks is that they describe a single way in which the framework will be used. A good framework will be used in ways that its designers never conceived. Thus, a cookbook is insufficient on its own to describe every use of the framework. Of course, a developer's first use of a framework usually fits the stereotypes in the cookbook. However, once developers go beyond the examples in the cookbook, they need to understand the details of the framework. However, cookbooks tend not to describe the framework itself. But in order to understand a framework, you need to have knowledge of both its design and its use.
9. In order to achieve high-level reuse (i.e. above the level of reusing the class set) it is necessary to design with reuse in mind. This requires knowledge of the reusable components available.

The design patterns movement wished to address some (or all) of the above in order to facilitate successful architectural reuse. The intention was thus to address many of the problems which reduce the reusability of software components and frameworks.

34.3 Design Patterns

34.3.1 What Are Design Patterns?

A design pattern captures expertise describing an architectural design to a recurring design problem in a particular situation. It also contains information on the applicability of a pattern, the trade-offs that must be made, and any consequences of the solution. Books are now appearing which present such design patterns for a range of applications. For example, the Gang of Four book (Gamma *et al.*, 1995) is a widely cited book that presents a catalog of 23 design patterns.

Design patterns are extremely useful for both novice and experienced object-oriented designers. This is because they encapsulate extensive design knowledge and proven design solutions with guidance on how to use them. Reusing common patterns opens up an additional level of design reuse, where the implementations vary, but the micro-architectures represented by the patterns still apply.

Thus patterns allow designers and programmers to share knowledge about the design of a software architecture. They thus capture the static and dynamic structures and collaborations of previous successful solutions to problems that arise when building applications in a particular domain (but not a particular language).

Most systems are full of patterns that designers and developers have identified through past experience and documented good practice. The patterns movement have essentially made these patterns explicit. Thus the programmatic idioms that have previously been used are now documented as behavioural patterns. In turn there are design patterns that express some commonly used design structure, and architectural patterns which express structural patterns.

34.3.2 What They Are Not

Patterns are not concrete designs for particular systems. This is because a pattern must be instantiated in a particular application to be used. This involves evaluating various trade-offs or constraints as well as detailed consideration of the consequences. It also does not mean that creativity or human judgment have been removed as it is still necessary to make the design and implementation decisions required. Having done that the developer must then implement the pattern and combine the implementation with other code (which may or may not have been derived from a pattern).

Patterns are also not frameworks (although they do seem to be exceptionally well suited for documenting frameworks). This is because frameworks present an instance of a design for solving a family of problems in a specific domain (and often for a particular language). In terms of languages such as Smalltalk and Java, a framework is a set of abstract cooperating classes. To apply such a framework to a particular problem it is often necessary to customize it by providing user-defined subclasses and to compose objects in the appropriate manner (e.g. the MVC framework). That is, a framework is a semi-complete application. As a result any given framework may contain one or more instances of multiple patterns, and in turn a pattern can be used in many different frameworks.

34.3.3 Architectural Patterns

Architectural patterns are patterns that describe the structure of a system (or part of a system). For example the Model–View–Controller (or MVC) pattern (Hunt, 2002) describes how a user interface, the associated application and any event handlers should be structured. They can be used to help you to structure your architecture as well as to explore different possible architectures. There are a range of architectural patterns that have been documented, including:

- Distributed, in which various parts of the system reside in different processes, potentially on different processors.
- Layered, in which a system is decomposed along application specific versus application generic lines.
- Model–View–Controller, in which the display, the application and the control of user input are separated.
- Blackboard, in which a central "blackboard" acts as a communications medium for a number of cooperating agents.
- Subsumption, in which high-level components can subsume the role of those lower down in the architecture.
- Repository-centric, in which a central repository is used.

For more information on architectural design patterns see Buschmann *et al.* (1996).

34.3.4 Documenting Patterns

The actual form used to document individual patterns varies, but in general the documentation covers the following:

1. The motivation or context that the pattern applies to.
2. Prerequisites that should be satisfied before deciding to use a pattern.
3. A description of the program structure that the pattern will define.
4. A list of the participants needed to complete a pattern.
5. Consequences of using the pattern, both positive and negative.
6. Examples of the patterns usage.

The pattern templates used in Gamma *et al.* (1995) and Alur *et al.* (2001) (which are very similar) provide a standard structure for the information that comprises a design pattern. This makes it easier to comprehend a design pattern as well as providing a concrete structure for those defining new patterns. Gamma *et al.* (1995) provides a detailed description of the template; only a summary of it is presented in Table 34.1. The two books mentioned above differ slightly in their terminology (for example, Gamma *et al.* use the title **Intent**, whereas Alur *et al.* use the title **Context**).

Table 34.1 The design pattern template.

Heading	*Usage*
Name	The name of the pattern
Intent/Context	This is a short statement indicating the purpose of the pattern. It includes information on its rationale, intent, problem it addresses etc.
Also known as	Any other names by which the pattern is known
Motivation/Problem	Illustrates how the pattern can be used to solve a particular problem
Applicability/Forces	This describes the situation in which the pattern is applicable. It may also say when the pattern is not applicable
Structure	This is a (graphical) description of the classes in the pattern
Participants	The classes and objects involved in the design and their responsibilities
Collaborations/Responsibilities	This describes how the classes and objects work together
Consequences	How does the pattern achieve its objective? What are the trade offs and results of using the pattern? What aspect of the system structure does it let you vary independently?
Implementation/Strategies (for implementation)	What issues are there in implementing the design pattern?
Sample code	Code illustrating how a pattern might be implemented
Known uses	How the pattern has been used in the past. Each pattern has at least two such examples
Related patterns	Closely related design patterns are listed here

A pattern language is a structured collection of patterns that build on each other to transform needs and constraints into architecture. That is, a set of related patterns dealing with for example, 2D drawing tools, would represent a pattern language for 2D drawing tools. Some of these patterns would build on others, and together they might be considered to describe how a framework for 2D drawing tools could be constructed.

34.3.5 When to Use Patterns

Patterns can be useful in situations where solutions to problems recur, but in slightly different ways. Thus, the solution needs to be instantiated as appropriate for different problems. The solutions should not be so simple that a simple linear series of instructions will suffice. In such situations patterns are overkill. They are particularly relevant when several steps are involved in the pattern that may not be required for all problems. Finally, patterns are really intended for solutions where the developer is more interested in the existence of the solution rather than how it was derived (as patterns still leave out too much detail).

34.3.6 Strengths and Limitations of Design Patterns

Design patterns have a number of strengths including:

- providing a common vocabulary
- explicitly capturing expert knowledge and trade-offs
- helping to improve developer communication

- promoting the ease of maintenance
- providing a structure for change

However, they are not without their limitations. These include:

- not leading to direct code reuse
- being deceptively simple
- easy to get pattern overload (i.e. difficult to find the right pattern)
- they are validated by experience rather than testing
- no methodological support

In general, patterns provide opportunities for describing both the design and the use of the framework as well as including examples, all within a coherent whole. In some ways patterns act like a hyper-graph with links between parts of patterns (in a similar way that pages on the Web and the links between them make a hyper-graph of information).

However, there are potentially very many design patterns available to a designer, and a number of these patterns may superficially appear to suit their requirements. Even if the design patterns are available online (via some hypertext-style browser (Budinsky *et al.*, 1996)), it is still necessary for the designer to search through them manually, attempting to identify the design which best matches their requirements.

In addition, once they have found the design that they feel best matches their needs, they must then consider how to apply it to their application. This is because a design pattern describes a solution to a particular design problem. This solution may include multiple trade-offs which are contradictory and which the designer must choose between, although some aspects of the system structure can be varied independently.

34.4 What Are J2EE Design Patterns?

So far we have discussed design patterns in general. We will now, therefore, consider J2EE design patterns. In particular, this raises a question, "What are J2EE Design Patterns?" They are essentially "J2EE technology-based solutions to common problems". By common problems, we are not referring to common "business" or "application" specific problems. Rather we are referring to recurring issues relating to how to structure, maintain and manage applications built using J2EE technologies. For example, how should a large business-critical J2EE Web application be structured? How should the servlets and JSPs be organized? Where and when should EJBs be used? etc.

At present, the definitive reference for Sun's J2EE Patterns is the book by Alur *et al.* (2001). This book describes J2EE Patterns as being architecture-oriented patterns and categorizes them into three logical tiers:

- **Presentation tier.** This tier focuses on the objects and behaviour that are required to service requests from the client tier (where the client tier may be a Web page within a Web browser, a Java application or applet, a mobile device such as a PDA or phone etc.). The primary J2EE technologies that are part of the presentation tier are JSPs and servlets.

- **Business tier.** This tier focuses on the J2EE technologies that support the business logic initiated from the presentation tier (or in some cases directly from the client tier). The J2EE technologies that focus on this tier are Enterprise JavaBeans.
- **Integration tier.** This tier focuses on the J2EE technologies that support communication with external resources. These technologies include JMS, JDBC, J2EE connector technology etc.

Alur *et al.* note that the J2EE Patterns catalog is constantly evolving so that these categories might require refinement in time. However, at the time of writing the aim is to keep things simple and not over-complicate the issue.

Each logical tier encapsulates a set of patterns that deal with an aspect of a J2EE-based application (although the focus is on Web-based applications that may or may not use other J2EE technologies such as EJBs, JMS, JNDI etc.).

34.5 A Catalog of J2EE Patterns

The J2EE Pattern catalog has evolved over a number of years since 1999 (internally to Sun)/2000 (externally from Sun). Each pattern has be revised several times based on feedback from within the J2EE community worldwide. This is an ongoing process, and one that is likely to result in additional patterns as well as modifications to existing patterns. At the time of writing there are 15 J2EE patterns in the Sun J2EE catalog, divided between the three logical tiers:

The presentation tier patterns are:

- **Decorating Filter.** Facilitates pre- and post-processing of a request.
- **Front Controller.** Provides a centralized controller for managing the handling of a request.
- **View Helper.** Encapsulates logic that is not related to presentation formatting into Helper components.
- **Composite View.** Creates an aggregate View from atomic sub-components.
- **Service To Worker.** Combines a `Dispatcher` component in coordination with the `FrontController` and View Helper Patterns.
- **Dispatcher View.** Combines a `Dispatcher` component in coordination with the `FrontController` and View Helper Patterns, deferring many activities to View processing.

The business tier patterns are:

- **Business Delegate.** Decouples presentation and service tiers, and provides a façade and proxy interface to the services.
- **Value Object.** Exchanges data between tiers.
- **Session Facade.** Hides business object complexity, centralizes workflow handling.
- **Aggregate Entity.** Represents a best practice for designing coarse-grained entity beans.
- **Value Object Assembler.** Builds composite value object from multiple data sources.
- **Value List Handler.** Manages query execution, results caching and result processing.
- **Service Locator.** Hides complexity of business service lookup and creation; locates business service factories.

The integration tier patterns are:

- **Data Access Object.** Abstracts data sources, provides transparent access to data.
- **Service Activator.** Facilitates asynchronous processing for EJB components.

Of course you are not limited to using only these patterns, as you may identify your own J2EE patterns. These patterns may be specific to your own business areas or they may be additional "generic" patterns that suit your way of operating. For example, back in 1999 at JayDee Technology we started to develop our own patterns for J2EE technologies before we were aware of Sun's catalog. This means that we have developed a number of our own J2EE patterns that are used in-house and have explicit support within our own software libraries.

We do not have the space here to present in detail all of the J2EE Patterns from the Sun catalog, let alone the patterns we and others have also adopted. Instead we direct you to Sun's J2EE Web site (`http://developer.java.sun.com/developer/technicalArticles/J2EE/patterns/`) and to Alur *et al.* (2001).

In the remainder of this chapter we will briefly present the FrontController J2EE Pattern as an example of a pattern from the J2EE Pattern catalog and the Request-Event-Dispatcher pattern from our own J2EE Pattern catalog.

34.6 The FrontController Pattern

In this section we will present (in outline) the FrontController. For a complete description see the J2EE Pattern Catalog Web site. This section presents much the same information but provides (due to space limitations) a cut-down version of the *Strategies* section.

34.6.1 Context

This operates within the context of handling HTTP requests for a Web applications.

34.6.2 Problem

Within Web applications each JSP or servlet could be a unique point of entry to the Web application. This approach has a number of problems, including:

- Each view is required to provide its own system services, often resulting in duplicate code.
- View navigation is left to the views that may result in intertwined view content and view navigation.
- Security may be harder to enforce due to multiple entry points.
- Maintenance may be harder due to many different paths through the system.

34.6.3 Forces

- Common system services processing completes per request. For example, the security service completes authentication and authorization checks.

- Logic that is best handled in one central location is instead replicated within numerous Views.
- Decision points exist with respect to the retrieval and manipulation of data.
- Multiple views are used to respond to similar business requests.
- A centralized point of contact for handling a request may be useful, for example to control and log a user's progress through the site.
- System services and view management logic are relatively sophisticated.

34.6.4 Solution

Use a Controller as the initial point of contact for handling a request. The Controller manages the handling of the request, including invoking security services such as authentication and authorization, delegating business processing, managing the choice of an appropriate view, handling errors, and managing the selection of content creation strategies.

The Controller provides a centralized entry point that controls and manages Web request handling. By centralizing decision points and controls, the Controller also helps reduce the amount of Java code, called scriptlets, embedded in the JSP.

Centralizing control in the Controller and reducing business logic in the view promotes code reuse across requests. It is a preferable approach to the alternative – embedding code in multiple views – because that approach may lead to a more error-prone, reuse-by-copy-and-paste environment.

Typically, a Controller works in coordination with a Dispatcher component. A Dispatcher is responsible for view management and navigation. Thus, a Dispatcher manages choosing the next View to present to the user and provides the mechanism for vectoring control to this resource. A Dispatcher can be encapsulated within a Controller or can be a separate component (see the ServiceToWorker pattern). In J2EE the servlet dispatcher can play this role.

The FrontController pattern suggests centralizing handling of requests, but does not limit the number of handlers in the system. There may very well be multiple FrontControllers in a system, with each mapping to a set of distinct services.

Structure

The class diagram presented in Figure 34.1 illustrates the basic structure of a Front Controller hierarchy (it also illustrates that a Front Controller could be implemented using a servlet or a JSP).

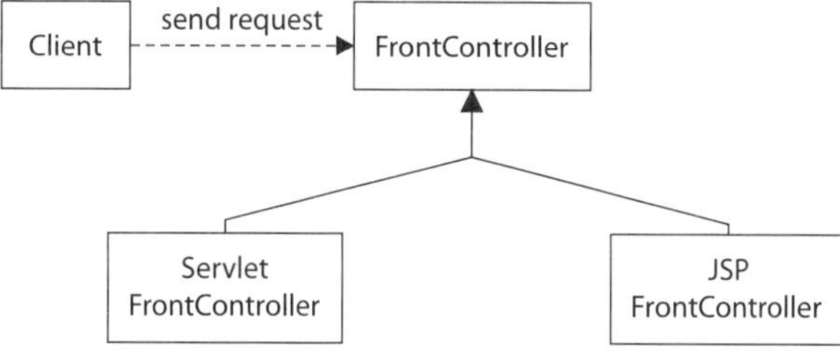

Figure 34.1 The `FrontController` class hierarchy.

Participants and Responsibilities

The sequence of events that occur when a FrontController (typically implemented as a Servlet) receives a request from a client is illustrated in Figure 34.2. It shows the FrontController receiving (the typically HTTP) request. It then determines to which View the request should be forwarded. A view is implemented as a servlet or a JSP. To initiate the receiving a view a dispatcher object is used: for example, the J2EE `RequestDispatcher` class.

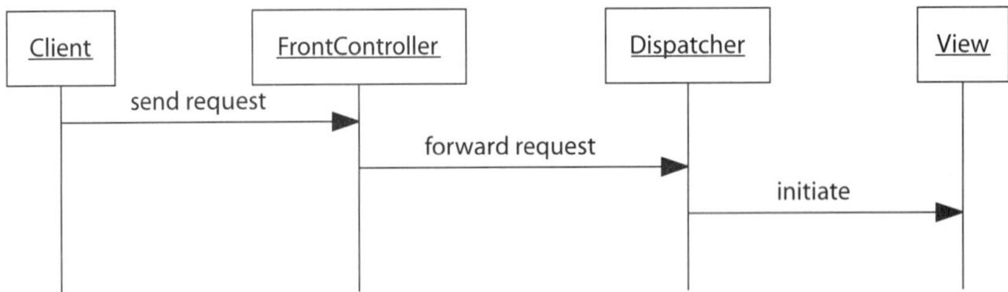

Figure 34.2 Using a FrontController to handle a request.

34.6.5 Strategies

There are several strategies relating to Controller implementation. We shall briefly mention one strategy (which has been hinted at above). For other strategies see the patterns Web site.

The implementation strategy we shall examine is known as the ServletFront Strategy. This strategy suggests implementing the FrontController as a servlet. Though semantically equivalent, it is preferred to the "JSP FrontController Strategy". The FrontController handles request processing, managing and controlling aspects of this processing. Since these responsibilities are related to, but logically independent of, display formatting, they are more appropriately included in a servlet instead of a JSP.

34.6.6 Consequences

- **Centralized control**
  This patterns defines a central point of control. This can be very good for logging application access and usage, for security and for centralizing business logic. However, it is possible to introduce a single point of failure.
- **Improved reusability**
  Allows common code to be positioned within the front controller.
- **Validation and error handling**
  The controller can also manage validation and error handling, because these operations are often done per request.

34.6.7 Related Patterns

- **View Helper pattern**
  In the View Helper pattern, the helper contains business logic that is accessed by the view. In some cases some of this business logic may be better placed within the FrontController.

- **Service to Worker**
  The Service to Worker pattern is the result of combining the View Helper pattern with a Dispatcher, in coordination with the FrontController pattern.
- **Dispatcher View**
  The Dispatcher View pattern is the result of combining the View Helper pattern with a Dispatcher, in coordination with the Front Controller pattern.

34.7 The Request–Event–Dispatcher Pattern

This pattern was developed by us to deal with a number of maintenance and management issues within an evolving Web application. Some of these were practical, related to the need to integrate work from different developers. Others related to the need to be able to adapt to changing user requirements. Actually this pattern is only one of the patterns identified to do this, another being a Web application version of the traditional Model–View–Controller architecture.

34.7.1 Context

This operates within the context of determining how to deal HTTP requests within a Web application.

34.7.2 Problem

Given a single point of entry to a Web application, we need to coordinate the delegation of these requests to appropriate parts of the application. If this is "directly" encoded into the FrontController, then to "integrate" a new feature into the Web application, the FrontController will need modification (for each and every features). Similarly, each development team would need their own separate FrontController during development. but these would need to be integrated at system build time (with any conflicts being addressed).

34.7.3 Forces

- Separation of FrontController from the implementation of various system features.
- Separate different areas of the Web application from each other.
- Ensure a standard and clean interface between the FrontController and "event" handlers.
- Ensures event handlers are not directly dependent on the FrontController.
- Ensures a standard framework for receiving and processing "request events".

34.7.4 Solution

Use a servlet to determine where to send the request, based on the event groups that handlers have registered for.

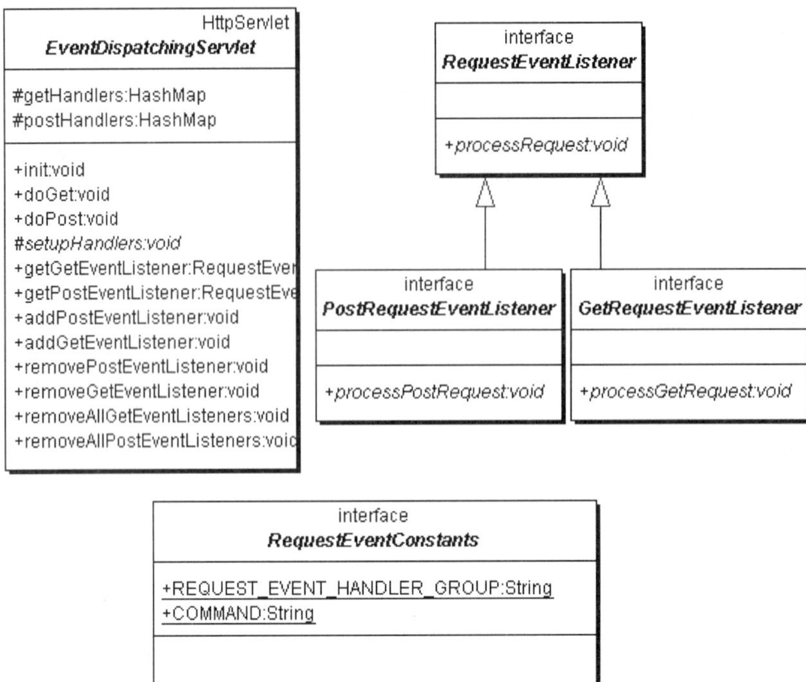

Figure 34.3 The Request Event Dispatch class diagram.

Structure

The class diagram presented in Figure 34.3 represents the interfaces and class involved in the Request Event Dispatcher pattern. Note that to use this pattern you must supply a subclass for the `EventDispatchingServlet` that implements the `setupHandler` method. A "request event" is an abstraction of an HTTP request arrival event that must be handled by a `RequestEventListener` object.

Participants and Responsibilities

Figure 34.4 shows the sequence diagram representing the Request Event Dispatching pattern. It depicts how the controller handles a request.

- **EventDispatchingServlet**
  This servlet is responsible for delegating the "request event" on to the appropriate handler. It has methods for the addition and removal of `RequestEventListener` objects.
- **RequestEventListener**
  This interface defines the method that the "handler" object must implement in order to receive "request events".

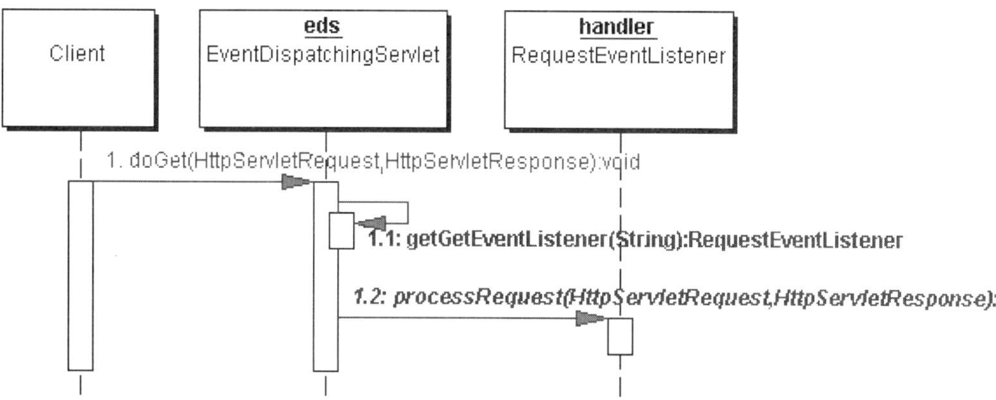

Figure 34.4 Request Event Dispatching sequence diagram.

34.7.5 Strategies

The Request-Event-Dispatcher pattern describes a framework by which a FrontController servlet can delegate request events onto other parts of a Web application in a similar manner to the Swing Event Delegation model.

Before any processing can start, the "event handler" object must be registered with the servlet. This is done using one of the two `add<Type>EventListener` methods.

The objects initially registered to handle request events are defined in the `setupHandler` method. This is an abstract method that must be implemented by subclasses that will be used as an `EventDispatchingServlet`.

During further processing additional handlers may be registered and existing handlers may be removed.

To be a handler, an object must implement the `RequestEventListener` interface or one of its sub-interfaces.

In the Request-Event-Dispatcher pattern, an `EventDispatchingServlet` receives an "event", where an "event" is a HTTP request that contains a `REQUEST_EVENT_HANDLER_GROUP` parameter. This is used to identify the "group" of handlers to receive the "request event".

The `EventDispatchingServlet` decides which `RequestEventHandler` to delegate the HTTP request to, based on the value of the `REQUEST_EVENT_HANDLER` parameter.

The `EventDispatchingServlet` looks up in a map the appropriate handlers to receive the named event. It then passes the request to this handler (by calling the `processRequest` method defined by the `RequestEventListener` interface).

The `RequestEventListener` interface is presented below:

```
public interface RequestEventListener {
  public void processRequest(HttpServletRequest req,
                             HttpServletResponse res)
    throws ServletException, IOException;
}
```

The EventDispatchingServlet class is presented below:

```
public abstract class EventDispatchingServlet extends HttpServlet {
  /** Holds list of get handler objects **/
  protected HashMap getHandlers = new HashMap();
  /** Holds list of post handler objects **/
  protected HashMap postHandlers = new HashMap();

  /**
   * Need to set up handlers in init method
   **/
  public void init(ServletConfig config) throws ServletException {
    super.init();
    setupHandlers();
  }

  /**
   * Handle get requests
   **/
  public void doGet(HttpServletRequest req,
                    HttpServletResponse res)
    throws ServletException, IOException {
    System.out.println("EventDispatchingServlet.doGet()");
    String panel =
      req.getParameter(RequestEventConstants.REQUEST_EVENT_HANDLER_GROUP);
    RequestEventListener rl = getGetEventListener(panel);
    rl.processRequest(req, res);
  }

  /**
   * Handle the post requests
   **/
  public void doPost(HttpServletRequest req,
                     HttpServletResponse res)
    throws ServletException, IOException {
    System.out.println("EventDispatchingServlet.doPost()");
    doGet(req,res);
  }

  protected abstract void setupHandlers();

  public RequestEventListener getGetEventListener(String name) {
    return (RequestEventListener)getHandlers.get(name);
  }

  public RequestEventListener getPostEventListener(String name) {
```

```
    return (RequestEventListener)postHandlers.get(name);
  }

  public void addPostEventListener(String name, RequestEventListener rl) {
    postHandlers.put(name, rl);
  }

  public void addGetEventListener(String name, RequestEventListener rl) {
    getHandlers.put(name, rl);
  }

  public void removePostEventListener(String name) {
    postHandlers.remove(name);
  }

  public void removeGetEventListener(String name) {
    getHandlers.remove(name);
  }

  public void removeAllGetEventListeners() {
    getHandlers.clear();
  }

  public void removeAllPostEventListeners() {
    postHandlers.clear();
  }
}
```

34.7.6 Consequences

- **Improves pluggablity of new features**
  It is straightforward to plug new features into a Web application in a managed and controlled manner.
- **Need to determine event group**
  Each request that is sent to the `EventDispatchingServlet` needs to include a parameter indicating the event group to use. This can be implemented as a hidden parameter in for example, a form. If this is forgotten the "request event" will not be routed appropriately.
- **Improves reusability**
  As a particular service or function of the Web application is not directly tied into other parts of the Web application, there is greater potential for reuse.

34.7.7 Related Patterns

It can be seem as another strategy for implementing a FrontController, although that is not its primary role. It can also be viewed as an implementation strategy for a Dispatcher – again, that is not its primary function.

34.8 J2EE-based Model–View–Controller

The difficulties of constructing modular, object-oriented presentation layer elements, using servlets and JSPs is well known to anyone who has ever tried to build a servlet- or JSP-based application of any size. The result can easily end up being difficult to debug, complex to understand and maintain, and certainly not reusable (except by cutting and pasting!). However, huge benefits can be obtained by separating out the user interface (i.e. HTML rendering components) from the application logic/code. This has been acknowledged for a long time and a number of approaches have been proposed over the years for separating the presentational aspect of an application from the logic of that application. In the case of J2EE Java applications used in multi-tier environments this is still true. In this section, we will explore the use of the model–view–controller architecture/pattern (or just as the MVC for short). The MVC originated in Smalltalk but the concept has been used in many places. It has been used extensively in Java Swing-based clients, but is also relevant to Web-based applications (and is the basis of the concepts in the Struts Apache project; see `http://jakarta.apache.org/struts/index.html`).

34.8.1 Context

Deals with structuring the presentation layer (servlets and JSPs) of a J2EE application.

34.8.2 Problem

It is all too easy to construct JSPs that have huge areas of Java embedded within scriptlets, making them very difficult to understand and hard to maintain, and destroying the many benefits of JSPs. It can also be hard to decide when to use a JSP and when to use a servlet.

34.8.3 Forces

- Reusability of application and/or user interface components.
- Ability to develop the application and user interface separately.
- Ability to inherit from different parts of the class hierarchy.
- Ability to define control-style classes which provide common features separately from how these features may be displayed.

34.8.4 Solution

The intention of the MVC architecture is the separation of the user display (the view), from the control of user input (mouse clicks, text entered etc.), from the underlying information/application model as illustrated in Figure 34.5 (Krasner and Pope, 1988). Note that in the figure the View and the Controller both "know" about each other, but the model knows nothing about how it is being displayed nor about how user input is being handled. This makes the model reusable with different displays.

This means that different views (interfaces) can be used with the same application, without the application knowing about it. It also means that any part of the system can be

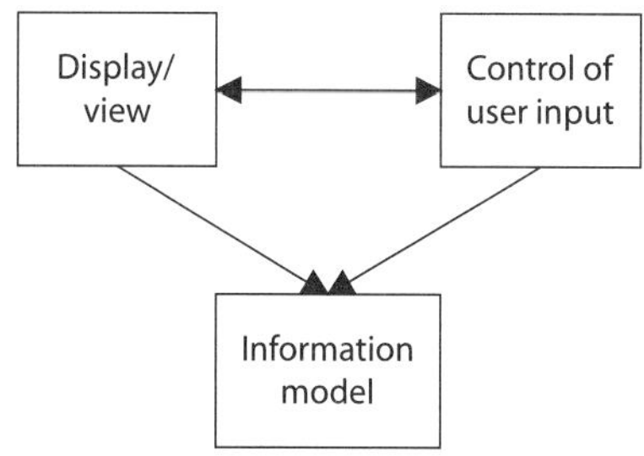

Figure 34.5 The Model–View–Controller architecture.

changed without affecting the operation of the other. For example, the way that the client (the look) displays the information could be changed without modifying the actual application or how input is handled (the feel). Indeed, the application need not know what type of interface is currently connected to it at all.

Structure

However the MVC is implemented, there will always be a Model element, a Controller element and a View element. In the case of a J2EE technology, implementation of the MVC the View may be either a servlet View or a JSP View. In general, it is most common to find that the view is implemented as a JSP as JSPs are geared towards generating the HTML that will be sent to the client tier. This is ideal in the MVC as the controller and the model should already have performed any processing and application logic before the JSP is required to generate a response back to the client. The definition of three marker interfaces for the Model, View and the Controller, along with the differing view implementations is presented in Figure 34.6.

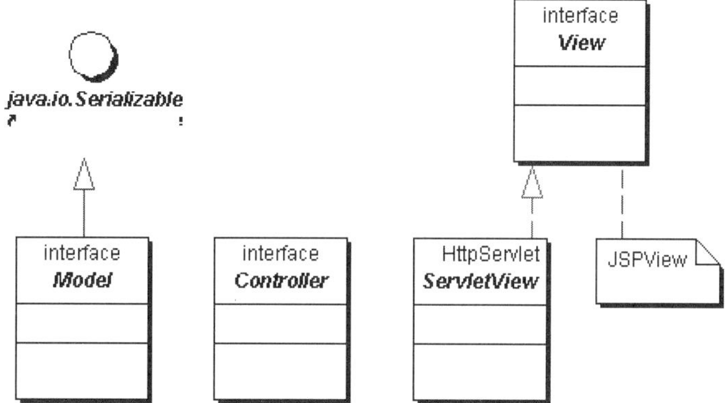

Figure 34.6 The elements of the MVC pattern.

Participants and Responsibilities

The three participants in the MVC are the Model, View and Controller. Their responsibilities are as follows:

- **Controller**
  This element is responsible for receiving the initial request for any particular operation. It must determine what should happen when this request is received. This may involve creating or accessing the model element. In a J2EE-based implementation the model may be stored for later retrieval within the `HTTPSession` object associated with the user's request. Once whatever operation is required is completed, the controller is then responsible for initiating the view. In a J2EE MVC implementation, this initiation will be performed by dispatching an appropriate JSP or HTML file (or possibly a servlet).
- **Model**
  The model represents the application logic. In a J2EE technology implementation of the MVC this may involve accessing EJBs, remote objects, databases via JDBC or any other server side components. It is really a buffer (possibly a façade) between the presentation layer and any business or application logic being invoked.
- **View**
  The view generates the response sent back to the client tier for the J2EE application. This may involve extracting information from the model (accessed via the session object) and wrapping it up within HTML etc.

34.8.5 Strategies

There are a number of strategies that can be used to implement the MVC pattern for a J2EE application. For example, if you use the Struts framework from Apache you will base the whole implementation around the use of Tags etc.

An example of a `createCRF` method from a controller based on the J2EE MVC model (taken from the Fault Tracker case study described in more detail in the next chapter) is presented below. This method is called in response to a user selecting an option on a Web page. The request is received by a handler and the `createCRF` method is called on the controlled (CRF stands for "Change Request Form"). It illustrates how the controller obtains a model from the session (or places one in the session if one is not available). It also illustrates how the model is used to initiate some business behaviour (in this case the creation of a CRF) and then how the view is generated by dispatching the request.

```
public void createCRF(HttpServletRequest request,
                      HttpServletResponse response)
  throws ServletException, IOException {
  try {
    // extract model from session
    HttpSession session=request.getSession(true);
    CrfEditingModel model= (CrfEditingModel)session.getAttribute(
        SessionConstants.CRF_EDITING_MODEL);

    // check if need to create a model
    if (model==null) {
      model=new CrfEditingModel();
      session.setAttribute(SessionConstants.CRF_EDITING_MODEL,model);
    }
```

```
      model.createCRF();

      // dispatch request onto crf editor view ("mapping registered in
      // web.xml file)
      dispatcher.dispatch("crfEditorView",request,response);
    } catch (Exception e) {
      // dispatch request onto crf operation failure view
      dispatcher.dispatch("crfOperationFailureView",request,response);
    }
  }
```

34.8.6 Consequences

The consequences of using this design pattern include:

- Reusability of parts of the presentation layer.
- The ability to inherit from different parts of the class hierarchy.
- Modularity of presentation layer code.
- Resilience to change.
- Identification of the roles of servlets and JSPs.
- Encapsulation of the presentation aspects of the application.
- Additional complexity/greater abstraction in the presentation layer.
- Increased difficulty in tracing interactions within the presentation layer (some form of logging is essential).

34.8.7 Related Patterns

Patterns related to this pattern include:

- **The Request Event Dispatching pattern.** The Handlers defined within this pattern may call methods on the controllers of the MVC pattern.
- **FrontController.** The Controller of the MVC could be implemented as or treated as a FrontController.
- **View Helper.** The model could be treated as a view helper.
- **Service to Worker.** The model may exploit an implementation of this pattern to initiate business logic.
- **Dispatcher View.** This pattern is used by the controller to initiate the JSP or Servlet associated with the controller.
- **Business Delegate.** The model may be treated as a business delegate or may use a business delegate to access business logic.
- **Value Object.** The model may use Value Objects to access information on the business tier.
- **Service Locator.** The model may use Service Locator objects to access EJBs etc.
- **Data Access Object.** The model may use a Data Access Object to obtain data from a database or back end business object.

34.9 Summary

In this chapter we have introduced the concept of Design Patterns and in particular J2EE Patterns. We have also described Sun's J2EE Pattern catalog. We have also briefly presented one of these design patterns providing an example of how you can identify your own patterns and document these. In the next chapter we will examine a larger application that makes extensive use of J2EE patterns.

34.10 Further Reading

A number of books and a great many papers have been written about patterns in recent years, the most influential of which is Gamma *et al.* (1994) by the so-called "Gang of Four": Erich Gamma, Richard Helm, Ralph Johnson and John Vlissides. There are also a series of conferences on Patterns referred to as PLoP (for **P**attern **L**anguage **o**f **P**rogram design). Two proceedings are available: Coplien and Schmidt (1995) and Vlissides *et al.* (1996).

Two further patterns books are Buschmann *et al.* (1996) (which represents the progression and evolution of the pattern approach into a system capable of describing and documenting large scale applications) and Fowler (1997) which considers how patterns can be used for analysis to help build reusable object models.

There is also a Web page dedicated to the patterns movement (which includes many of the papers referenced as well as tutorials and example patterns). The URL for the Web page is `http://st-www.cs.uiuc.edu/users/patterns/`. In addition, there is a Sun Web site dedicated to J2EE patterns: `http://developer.java.sun.com/developer/technicalArticles/J2EE/patterns/`. This is also an interest group that you can subscribe to (and participate in): see `http://archives.java.sun.com/archives/j2eepatterns-interest.html`.

34.11 References

Alexander, C. (1979). *The Timeless Way of Building*. Oxford University Press, Oxford.

Alexander, C., Ishikawa, S. and Silverstein, M. with Jacobson, M., Fiksdahl-King, I. and Angel, S. (1977). *A Pattern Language*. Oxford University Press, Oxford.

Alur, D., Crupi, J. and Malks, D. (2001). *Core J2EE Patterns: Best Practices and Design Strategies*. Prentice Hall, Upper Saddle River, NJ.

Beck, K. and Johnson, R. (1994). Patterns generate architectures, in *Proc. ECOOP'94*. Springer-Verlag, New York, pp. 139–149.

Birrer, A. and Eggenschwiler, T. (1993). Frameworks in the financial engineering domain: an experience report. In *Proc. ECOOP'93*. Springer-Verlag, New York, pp. 21–35.

Budinsky, F. J., Finnie, M. A., Vlissides, J. M. and Yu, P. S. (1996). Automatic code generation from design patterns. *IBM Systems Journal*, **35**(2).

Buschmann, F., Meunier, R., Rohnert, H., Sommerlad, P. and Stal, M. (1996). *Pattern-Oriented Software Architecture – A System of Patterns*. Wiley & Sons, Chichester.

Coplien, J. O. and Schmidt, D. C. (eds.) (1995). *Pattern Languages of Program Design*. Addison-Wesley, Reading, MA.

Fowler, M. (1997). *Analysis Patterns: Reusable Object Models*. Addison-Wesley, Reading, MA.

Gamma, E., Helm, R., Johnson, R. and Vlissades, J. (1993). Design patterns: abstraction and reuse of object-oriented design. In *Proc. ECOOP'93*. Springer-Verlag, New York, pp. 406–431.

Gamma, E., Helm, R., Johnson, R. and Vlissades, J. (1995). *Design Patterns: Elements of Reusable Object-Oriented Software*. Addison-Wesley, Reading, MA.

Hunt, J. (2002). *Java and Object Orientation: An Introduction*, 2nd edn. Springer-Verlag, London.

Johnson, R. E. (1992). Documenting frameworks with patterns. In *Proc. OOPSLA'92, SIGPLAN Notices* **27**(10), 63–76.

Krasner, G. E. and Pope, S. T. (1988). A cookbook for using the Model–View–Controller user interface paradigm in Smalltalk-80. *JOOP* **1**(3), 26–49.

Vlissides, J. M., Coplien, J. O. and Kerth, N. L. (1996). *Pattern Languages of Program Design 2*. Addison-Wesley, Reading, MA.

Chapter 35

The Fault Tracker J2EE Case Study

35.1 Introduction

In this chapter we will look at some aspects of a much larger J2EE technology application. Due to space limitations we will only be able to dip into this application. However, it should illustrate the use of some of the design patterns mentioned in the last chapter, as well as indicate the use of some of the J2EE technologies discussed in this book, including servlets, JSPs, EJBs, security restrictions etc.

35.2 The Fault Tracker Application

The Fault Tracker application is a J2EE technology application designed to support the formal problem reporting procedures and change in requirements procedures often applied to bespoke software development projects.

A Request for Change (or RFC) relates to a change by a client or customer in the agreed requirements or to a change required to the software system in response to a "bug" identified by a Problem Report Form. Monitoring, maintaining and tracing such changes are extremely important to any software engineering organization, as they have an impact not only on the end result but also on costs, testing, sign off etc.

A Problem Report (or PRF for Problem Report Form) relates to a "bug" which may be resident in any (or all) of the aspects of a software engineering project. This includes the requirements, design, UML model, code, tests or associated documentation. Monitoring, managing and tracing the progress of these "bugs" is also very important as this will affect the quality of the end product.

The Fault Tracker application manages and maintains records of all RFC and PRFs for a particular project. It is accessible via the Web using a Web browser and exploits the full J2EE multi-tier architecture. That is, it uses a Web browser to host the client aspects of the tool, servlets and JSPs for the presentation aspects of the tool, EJBs for the business logic and a relational database for the long-term storage of data.

Given that such a system can be quiet complex, it also exploits design patterns from both Sun's J2EE Pattern catalog and some additional design patterns (as described in the last chapter).

In the remainder of this chapter we will look at the domain that the Fault Tracker is applied to (i.e. managing and tracking problem reports and requests for change). We will then step through part of the Fault Tracker application. Having done this we will consider the design patterns used and examine the implementation of these patterns with the tool.

35.2.1 Requests for Change

Care should be taken when "bugs" are reported by clients that the "bug" in question is not actually a change in requirements. If a change in requirements is identified this often has implications for charging and costing, and thus must be handled in a different manner.

A change in requirements should be reported by a Request for Change (RFC) form. This form should state what it is believed that the change in requirements is (and will often need to refer to the original requirements document and additional minutes etc.).

Once generated the RFC should be handed to the Project Manager, who will confirm whether it is an RFC or a PRF. If the Project Manager accepts it as a CRF then the CRF should be entered into the Request for Change Log.

If a paper-based system is being used then completed forms are to be kept secured in a ring binder or similar. With the Fault Tracker software these forms are electronically maintained in the same format.

The use of the Fault Tracker system for recording "requests for change" is described in the following problem reporting and corrective action procedure:

1. When a Request for Change is identified (often from the bug log system), an RFC form should be completed and allocated a status of **Open.**
2. The RFC must then be given to the Project Manager, who will assign a unique RFC number to the form and who will then investigate the requirement (possibly with the aid of other team members as appropriate) and confirm that it is an RFC and determine what effort is involved in meeting this change.
3. The PRF will be updated with the results of the investigation.
4. The client must then be contacted to discuss the impact of the RFC. The status of the RFC should now be **With Client.**
5. If the RFC is accepted by the client and agreement is reached about the implications of this, the RFC should then be allocated to appropriate team members for requirements modification, design and implementation. The changes should be subject to the same control procedure as any other development, although additional care needs to be taken to ensure all affected items are included (such as user manuals etc.). The RFC should now be in **Accepted** status.

If the client rejects the RFC, either because they decide they do not need that requirement or because they do not believe that it is an RFC, then the RFC is allocated the status **Rejected.** If the latter case is true then the Project Manager and others must discuss with the client the appropriate action to take.

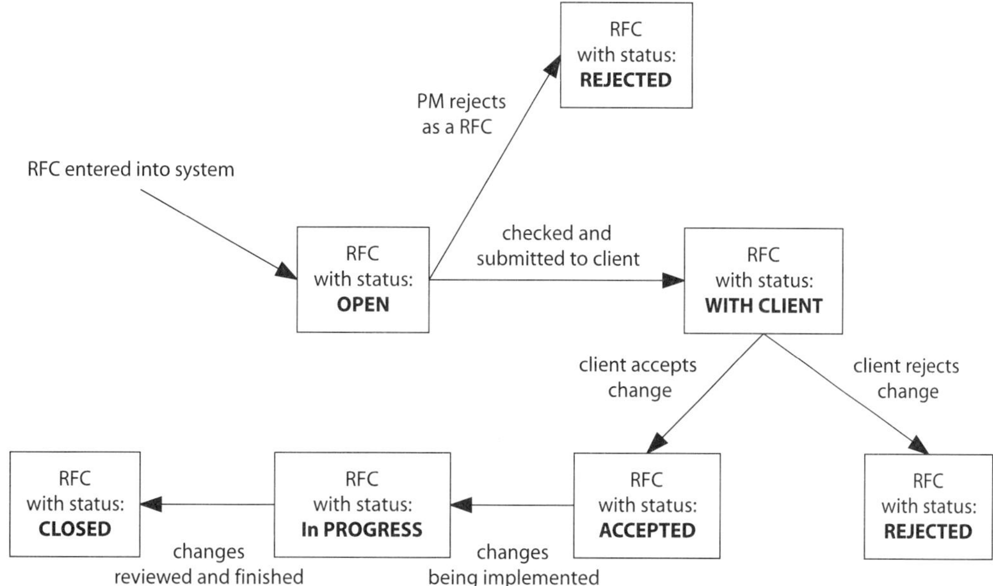

Figure 35.1 The life cycle of the RFC form.

6. Once the person or persons involved in implementing the change have completed the task (including the re-reviewing of the change and allocation of **Released** status to the items involved), the Project Manager will test the changed software to ensure that the update works. If this is the case, the RFC will be changed to **Closed** status and the binder information updated accordingly.
7. If the correction was not successful, the Project Manager will advise on further action and if necessary complete a new PRF. New forms should only be completed if a new change is identified or if the original change introduced additional problems.

The life cycle of an RFC form is presented in Figure 35.1.

35.2.2 Problem Reporting

Problems relating to configuration items, including specifications, design diagrams/models/notes, and code must go through a formal problem reporting procedure once they have reached **Release** status. In many organizations the Problem Report Form (PRF) is the basis of this process.

Completed forms are to be kept secured in a ring binder or similar, as well as online within a Problem Reporting System.

The binder should contain dividers with the following headings:

- Summary of current status (this should contain a table of the current outstanding PRFs and a table of the closed PRFs – and who they were allocated to).
- Open problems

- Closed problems
- Rejected and duplicate problems

The use of the Fault Tracker system for handling "Problem Report Forms" is described in the following problem reporting and corrective action procedure:

1. On discovery of a problem in a configuration item that has been allocated a Release status, the details of the problem should be noted on a Problem Report Form (PRF). In some cases this will happen in-house; in other cases a bug report will be filed by a client. Details of the bug must be taken from the client's report and entered into our own system. The PRF is then assigned a status of **Open**.
2. The PRF must then be given to the Project Manager, who will assign a unique PRF number to the form and who will then investigate the problem (possibly with the aid of other team members as appropriate) and identify what items need to be changed (if any). The PRF now enters an **Accepted** status.

   If the Project Manager identifies that this PRF duplicates one that already exists, the status of the PRF is made Duplicate and a link is made to the actual PRF form. No further action is taken regarding this PRF.

   If the Project Manager rejects the PRF (for example because it is not an error but the way the system works or because it is an operating system feature), then the status of the PRF is changed to Rejected.
3. The PRF will be updated with the results of the investigation. If the problem is to be fixed by another team member they will be noted as the person who will implement the fix. The PRF can now be assigned a status of **Being Corrected**. Any necessary redesign, reimplementation etc. should be subject to the same controls as the initial design and implementation. If the problem is identified as a *Request for Change*, then it should be handed over to the Change Request system.
4. Once those involved in correcting the problem have completed the task (including the re-reviewing of the change and allocation of **Released** status to the items involved), the Project Manager will test the corrected software to ensure that the correction works. If this is the case, the PRF will be changed to **Closed** status and the binder information updated accordingly.
5. If the correction was not successful, the Project Manager will advise on further action and if necessary complete a new PRF. New forms should only be completed if a new problem is identified or if the original change introduced additional problems.

The life cycle of the PRF form is illustrated in Figure 35.2.

35.3 Using the Fault Tracker

Fault Tracker is a J2EE technology-based application. This means that it is comprised of Web pages on the client tier (displayed within a Web browser such as IE), servlets and JSPs on the

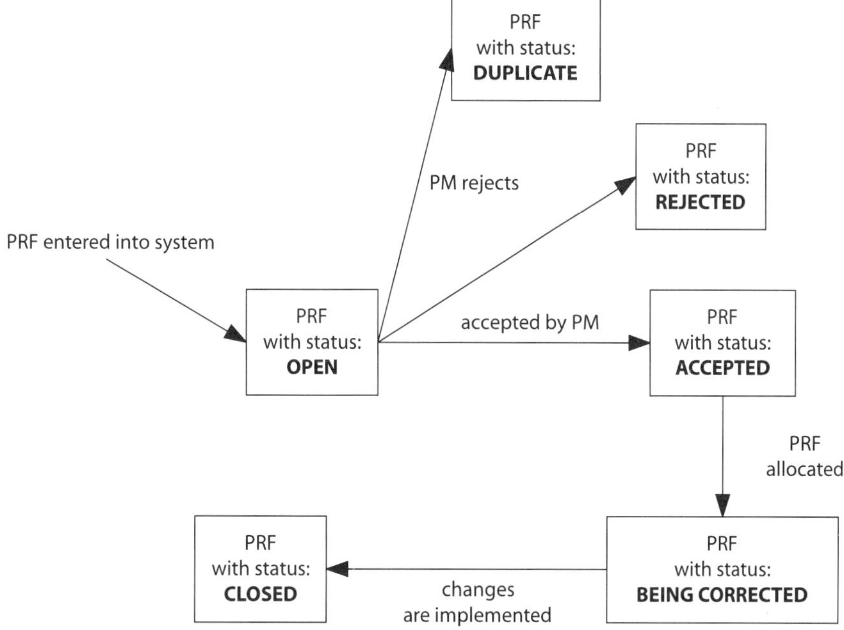

Figure 35.2 Life cycle of a PRF.

presentation tier, EJBs on the business tier and a relational database at the back. As such it is typical of many J2EE applications.

To access the Fault Tracker application a user must enter the appropriate URL in a Web browser. In this example we are running the Fault Tracker on JBoss with Tomcat on the localhost. The application is accessed using the URL `http://localhost:8080/ft`, where `ft` is the application root specified in the `application.xml` file in the EAR. The `web.xml` file in the WAR contained within the EAR specifies that the welcome page is `index.html`. This front page is presented in Figure 35.3. Note that this is the only page of the whole Fault Tracker Web application that is outside of the security control.

To use the Fault Tracker a user must be registered with the Fault Tracker. All users of the Fault Tracker system must have the security role `ftUsers`. This can be administered using the internal memory security realm or, as is the case with Fault Tracker, using an external service such as LDAP. Some users also have the role `ftAdmin`. If they are Fault Tracker administrators then various administration options are presented to them within Fault Tracker. If a user is not an administrator these options are not presented.

To access the application the user must click on the "login and select a project" link on the front page. This link takes the user into the security controlled area of the application. This causes the login screen presented in Figure 35.4 to be displayed. Note that this application is using the "BASIC" login form (i.e. no custom login page has been defined).

Once users have logged in they are presented with the "Select a Project" Web page. All "bug" or "change requests" in the Fault Tracker are associated with a particular project.

Figure 35.3 The Fault Tracker front page.

Figure 35.4 Logging into the Fault Tracker.

Therefore the first thing users must do is to select the project they wish to work with. Note that administrators are also presented with the option to carry out some administration functions at this point (non-administrators do not see this option). This is illustrated in Figure 35.5.

Figure 35.5 The Project Selection/Administration selection page.

When users select the project they wish to work with, the Fault Tracker displays the main Fault Tracker working environment. This display is broken up into four regions. There is a header and footer which frame with main display. On the left is the main menu options allowing PRFs and CRFs (which stands for Change Request Forms) to be created, edited, searched for and reports generated etc. The centre area of the display is used to display the results of any operation (such as creating a new CRF etc.). This working environment is presented in Figure 35.6.

Users can now select an option from the left-hand menu. For example, if they choose to create a new CRF (Change Request Form), then the central area displays a form with various sections to be filled in (for example see Figure 35.7).

In Figure 35.7 a user is describing a "Change Request" supplied by the end client. Once all the relevant data has been entered the user can commit the creation of the CRF (note that the CRF Number is automatically generated).

The user could then create additional forms, edit existing forms, search for forms or generate reports on different categories of form etc.

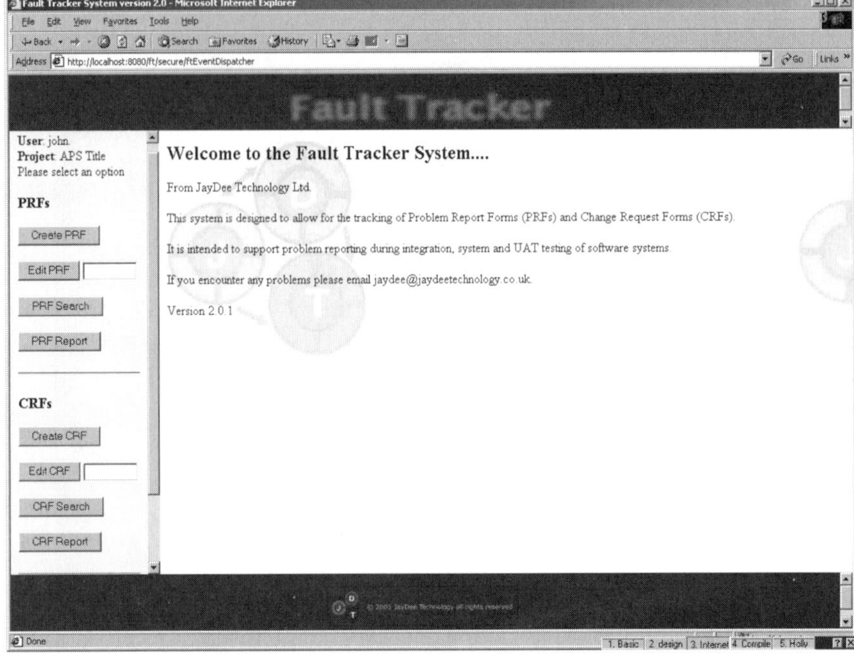

Figure 35.6 The main Fault Tracker working environment.

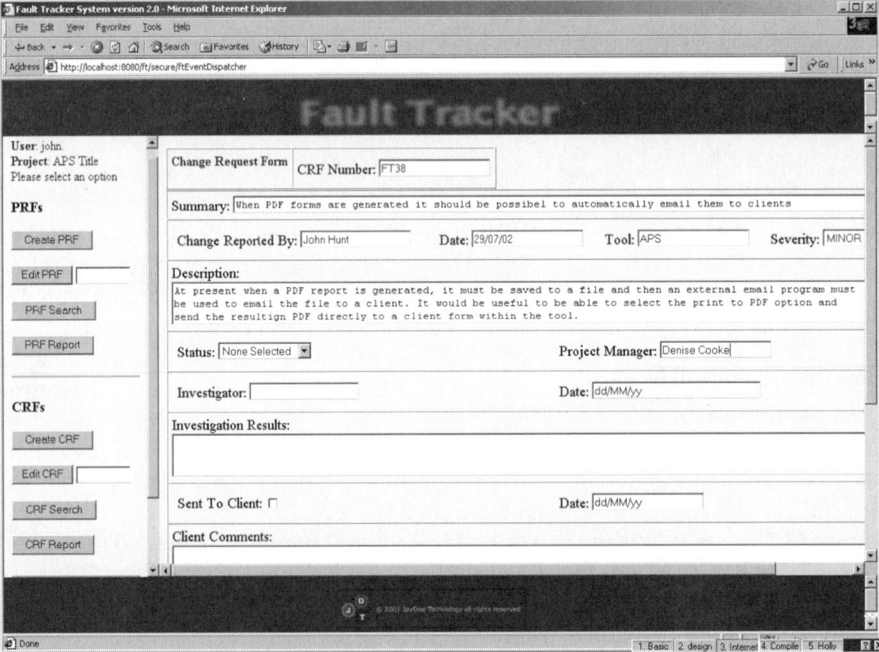

Figure 35.7 Creating a CRF.

35.4 The Design of the Fault Tracker

The design of the Fault Tracker is based on the specification of an underlying architecture that encompasses a number of the design patterns described in the last chapter. The patterns used are:

- Request Event Dispatching pattern. Used to dispatcher "request events" to the appropriate MVC structures.
- Model–View–Controller pattern. Used to manage each "view" in the application.
- Dispatcher View pattern. Used to dispatch JSP views for the MVC structure.
- Business Delegate. Used to act as a buffer between the models in the MVC presentation tier and the EJBs in the business tier.
- Service Locator. Used to allow the business delegates to locate the EJBs.

35.4.1 What Is the Architecture?

A software architecture encompasses:

- **The *overall*** plan for the structure of the system. That is, it is the blueprint for the system. It should be possible to read the architecture and gain an appreciation for how the system was structured (without needing to know detail of the structural elements).
- **The key structural elements and their interfaces.** That is, what elements make up the system, their interfaces and how they are plugged together.
- **How those elements interact (at the top level).** That is, when the various elements of the architecture interface, what they do, and why they do it.
- **How these elements form subsystems and systems.** This is a very important aspect of the architecture. Early identification of the core subsystem of the design not only helps organize future design (and implementation) work, it helps promote reuse and the comprehensibility of the system.
- **The architectural style** that guides this organization.

The intent is that within this architecture, designers are then free to work in the "spaces" left for them by the architecture. However, this is not the end of the story, as the software architecture also involves:

- How the system will be used.
- What the functionality of the final system is expected to be.
- Any performance issues that need to be addressed (these may involve more detailed development of the software architecture's implementation to assess performance constraints).
- Resilience to further development.
- Economic and technology constraints and trade-offs. The architecture can consider different solutions to the same problem, allowing different technological solutions to be aired and the most appropriate adopted (for example, CGI scripts versus Java servlets on a Web server).

The overall package structure of the Fault Tracker application is presented in Figure 35.8.

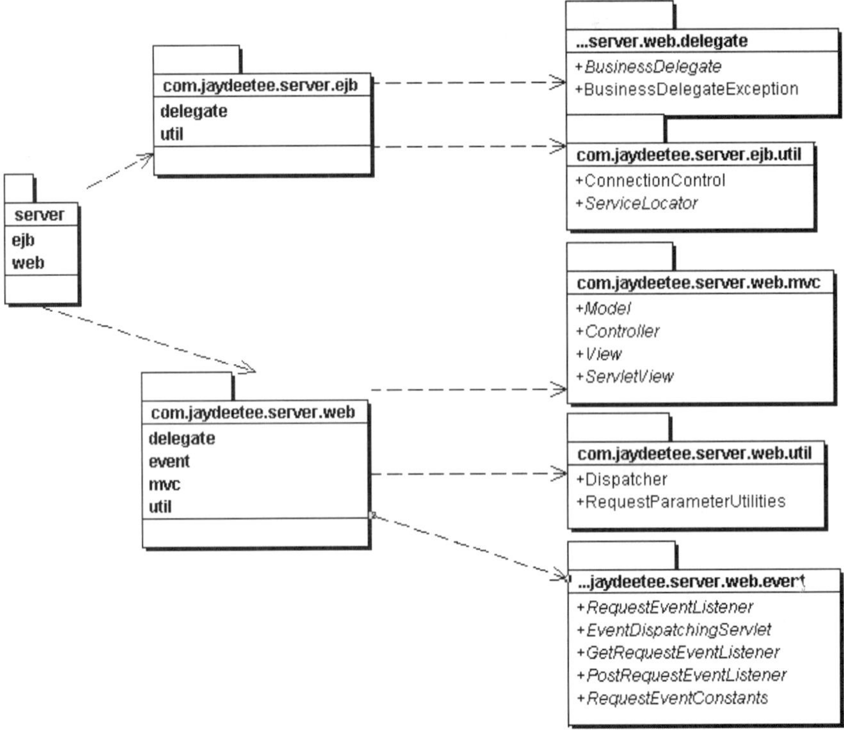

Figure 35.8 The generic frameworks used in the Fault Tracker.

As indicated by the package names, the generic frameworks used within the Fault Tracker have been divided into classes related to the EJB (or business logic) tier and classes related to the Web (or presentation) tier.

Within each package hierarchy the lowest level packages provide the classes and interfaces that support a particular framework (or pattern). For example:

- `com.jaydeetee.server.ejb.util`: this package defines the `ServiceLocator` pattern and its implementation `ConnectionControl`.
- `com.jaydeetee.server.ejb.delegate`: this package implements the `BusinessDelegate` pattern.
- `com.jaydeetee.server.web.mvc`: this package implements the infrastructure required by the J2EE implementation of the MVC.
- `com.jaydeetee.server.web.util`: this package implements the `Dispatcher` view pattern and a utilities class.
- `com.jaydeetee.server.web.event`: this package implements the `RequestEventDispatcher` pattern.

The application-specific packages are all under the `com.jaydeetee.ft` root package (see Figure 35.9). These are broken up into the EJB-oriented packages and the presentation-oriented packages. The EJB-oriented packages are:

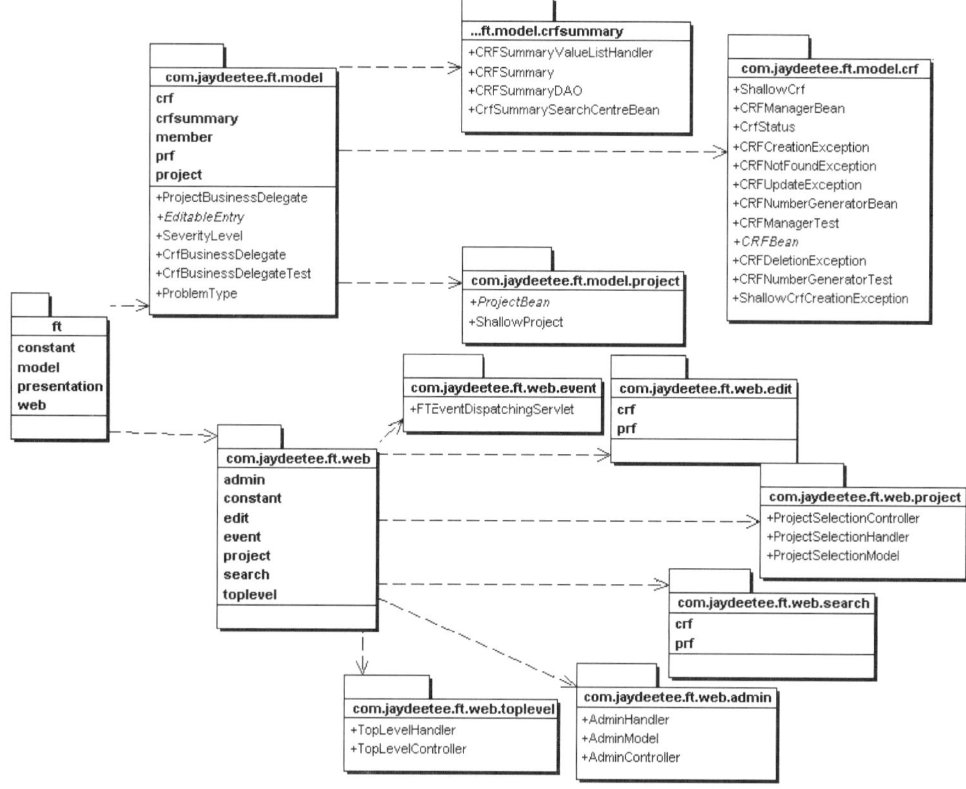

Figure 35.9 The application-specific packages in Fault Tracker.

- com.jaydeetee.ft.model: this package is the root of the packages that define the EJBs in the application. It also defines the business delegates and additional support classes.
- com.jaydeetee.ft.model.crfsummary: this package defines the EJBs that return CRF summary information used with the search operations.
- com.jaydeetee.ft.model.crf: this package defines the CRF entity EJBs and the CRFManager session beans that access the entity beans.
- com.jaydeetee.ft.model.project: this package defines the project entity bean and the representation of a project entity bean.

The presentation-oriented packages are:

- com.jaydeetee.ft.web: this package is the root of all the presentation tier packages.
- com.jaydeetee.ft.web.event: this package defines the FTEventDispatchingServlet.
- com.jaydeetee.ft.web.edit: this package contains two sub-packages one for CRFs and one for PRFs that handle editing these forms. The packages contain the presentation-oriented classes and servlets.
- com.jaydeetee.ft.web.project: this package defines the servlets and supporting classes that support the selection of a project.

- `com.jaydeetee.ft.web.search`: this package includes two sub-packages, one for CRFs and PRFs that support the search operations within Fault Tracker.
- `com.jaydeetee.ft.web.admin`: this package supports the presentation of the various administration functions within the Fault Tracker.
- `com.jaydeetee.ft.web.toplevel`: this package handles requests generated from the main menu options.

We will examine the implementation of the Request Event Dispatching pattern in more detail. This pattern requires a front controller style `EventDispatchingServlet` linked to `Handler` objects that receive the HTTP request and then initiate some server behaviour.

In the Fault Tracker the `FTEventDispatchingServlet` subclasses the `EventDispatchingServlet` class. Figure 35.10 illustrates the relationship between the `FTEventDispatchingServlet` and five of the handlers defined in the Fault Tracker system. The dependency line (dashed line) between the `FTEventDispatchingServlet` and the handlers is labelled with the event (or command) that causes the request to be sent to that handler. Note that a command is a parameter sent with the HTTP request from the "view" element.

For example, the act of selecting an option causes an HTTP request to be sent to the `FTEventDispatchingServlet` with a hidden parameter indicating the handler to initiate. The `FTEventDispatchingServlet` then delegates the request to the appropriate handler. For example, if you select to edit a CRF, then the request is forwarded to the `CrfEditingHandler` and subsequently to the `CrfEditing` MVC structure. This is illustrated in Figures 35.11 and 35.12.

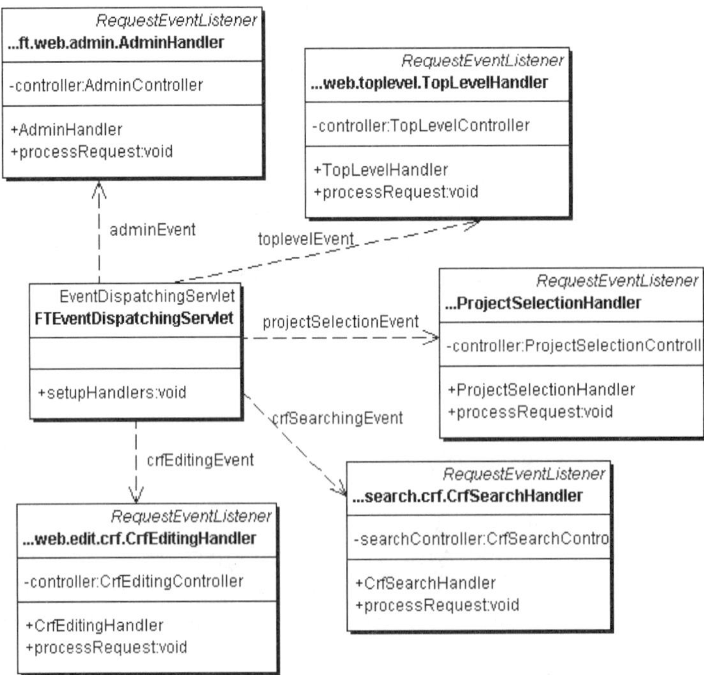

Figure 35.10 Implementing the Request Event Dispatching design pattern.

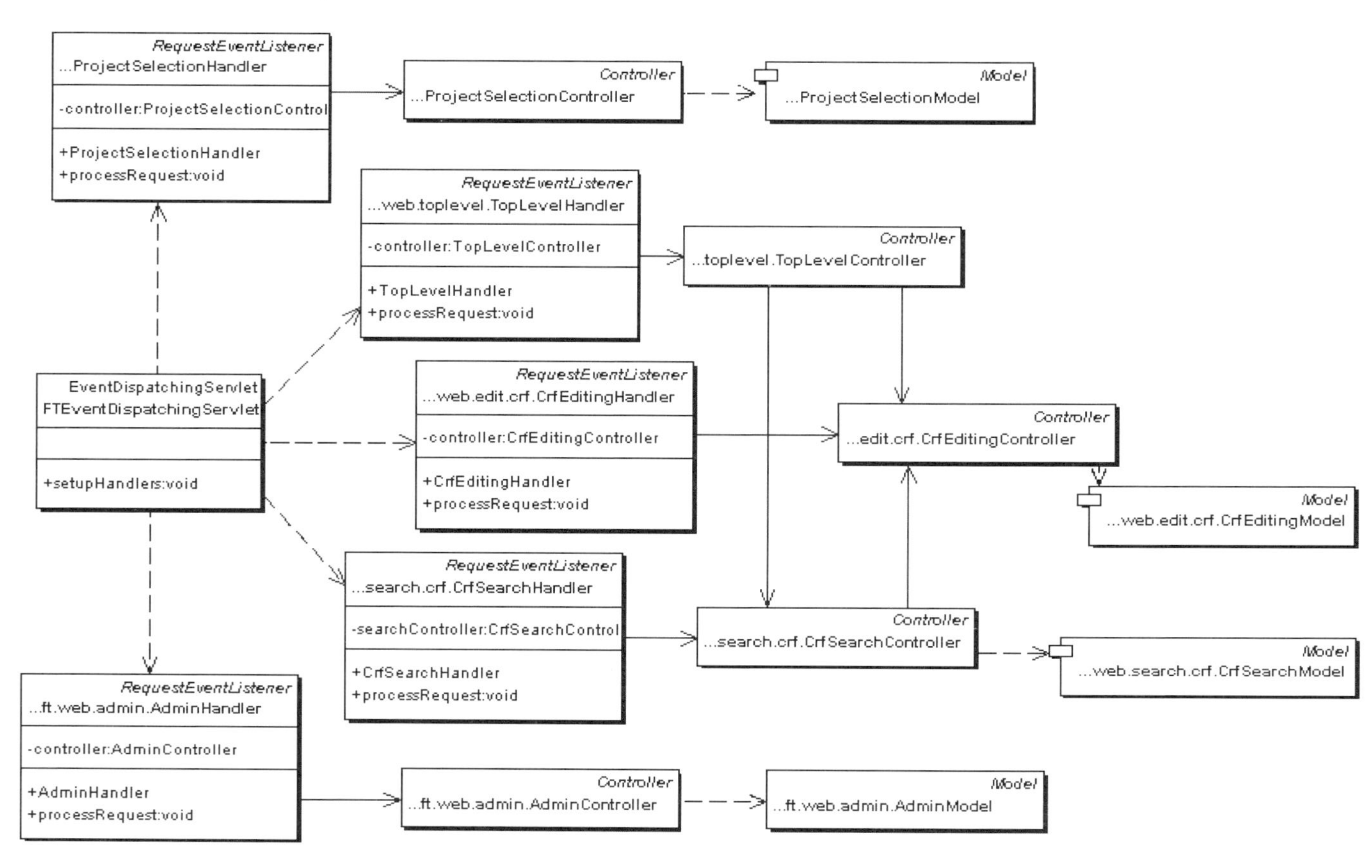

Figure 35.11 Relating the Request Event Dispatching design pattern and the Model–View–Controller pattern.

Note that in Figures 35.11 and 35.12 the dashed arrow from the controllers to the models indicates the indirect dependency between these two objects implemented by storing the model within the HttpSession.

Also note that in Figure 35.12 the controller maintains a reference to the Dispatcher object that will cause the JSP to generate a response back to the client. As a JSP is not a standard Java class it is represented in this figure by the note headed CrfEditingView.

The complete set of steps performed by the CrfEditing MVC classes in dealing with a request to edit a CRF is presented in Figure 35.13. The illustrates the following series of steps:

1. Handler receives request from FTEventDispatchingServlet.
2. Handler extracts the COMMAND from the HttpServletRequest object to determine what operation is required (in this case it is CrfEditing).
3. The editCrf method is called on the CrfEditingController.
4. The controller obtains a reference to the HttpSession from the HttpServletRequest.
5. Next the controller attempts to extract the CrfEditingModel from the HttpSession. If no model exists then one is created and added to the HttpSession.
6. The controller now calls the editCrf method on the CrfEditingModel.
7. The model then uses the CrfBusinessDelegate to access the business tier (not illustrated in this sequence diagram) to obtain the information for the CRF editing view. Note that this returns a "shallow" copy of the CRF entity beans data for use in the presentation tier.

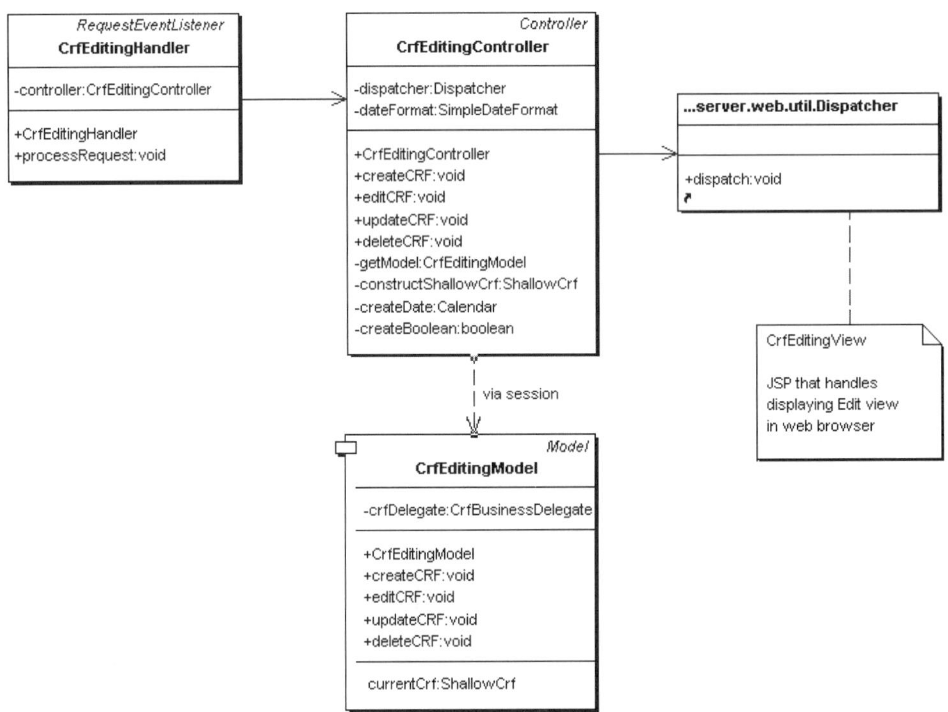

Figure 35.12 Realizing the MVC design pattern in Fault Tracker.

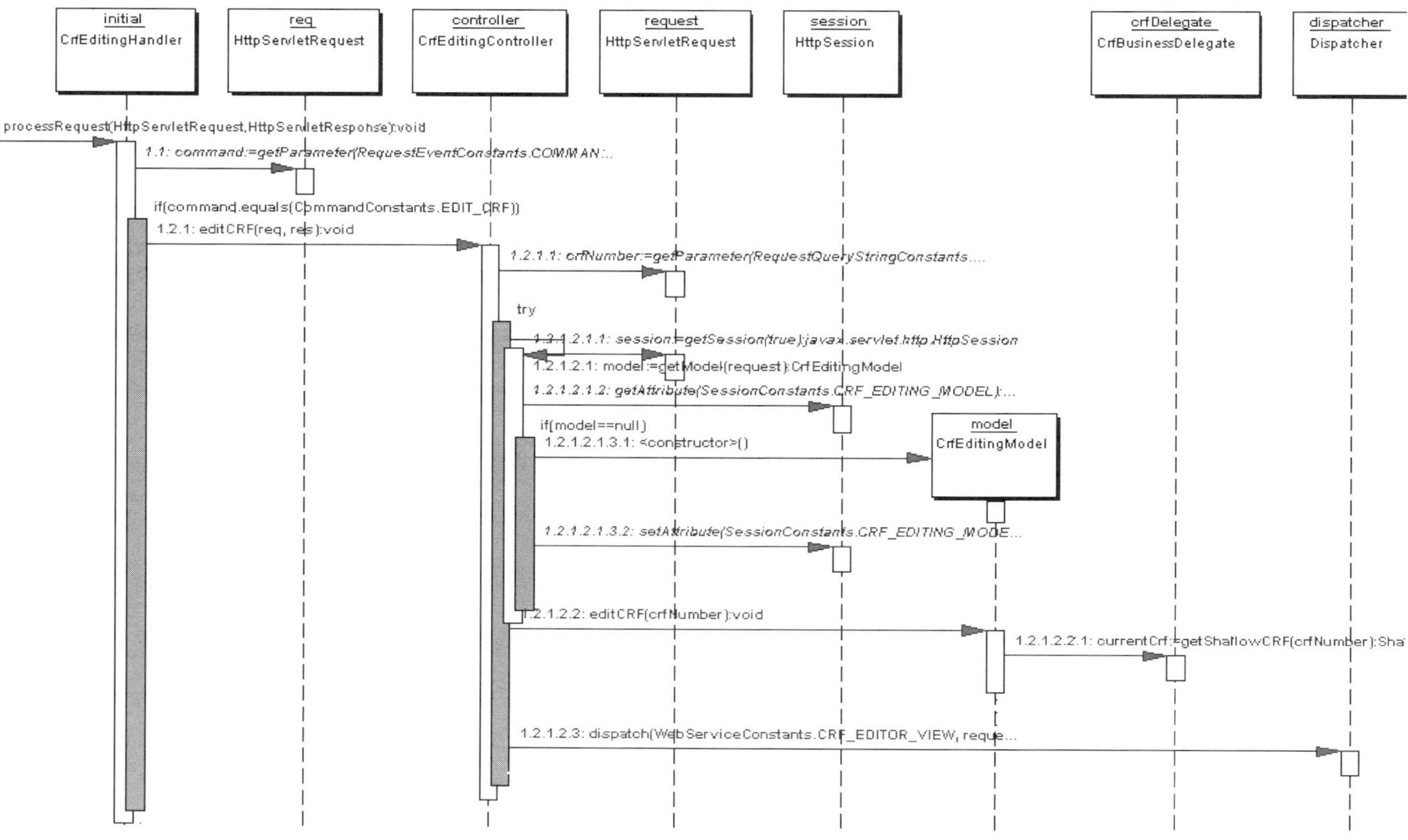

Figure 35.13 Handling a request within the MVC structure.

8. The controller then uses the Dispatcher to cause the `CrfEditingView` JSP to be displayed to allow the CRF to be edited.
9. The `CrfEditingView` JSP extracts the information to display from the `CrfEditingModel` held in the `HttpSession` object.
10. A response is then sent back to the client browser from the JSP.

The only aspect of the application this does not cover is the relationship between the model, the `CrfBusinessDelegate` and the EJB tier. This is illustrated in Figure 35.14. This diagram shows how the `CrfBusinessDelegate` object uses the `ConnectionControl` (which implements the `ServiceLocator` pattern) to access the EJB tier. The `ServiceLocator` pattern hides the API lookup (naming) services, EJB access complexities etc. from the Business Delegate. It hides, for example, the issues associated with accessing the home interface via a JNDI lookup, narrowing the resulting object and using the home interface to create the EJB object etc. It is also a generic class and can be used with any EJB.

Note that in Figure 35.14 the `ConnectionControl` accesses a `Session` bean (the `CRFManager` EJB). This acts as the buffer between the presentation layer and the entity EJBs used. In the figure, only the `CRFBean` itself is presented, although additional entity beans are also used (for example to generate a unique id for the CRF bean).

This is where the `ShallowCRF` class comes in. This class is used to extract the relevant information from the `CRFBean` without needing to make the entity bean visible to the presentation layer.

35.5 Summary and Conclusions

In this chapter we have examined some of the design patterns and structures used within a larger J2EE technology application (the Fault Tracker). What has been presented here is only part of this application, and indeed the full application has many more elements to it (including integrated email, messaging etc.). However, it should illustrate both the size and complexity of such applications. It should also illustrate how these issues can be controlled by the judicious use of well-established, as well as domain-specific, design patterns.

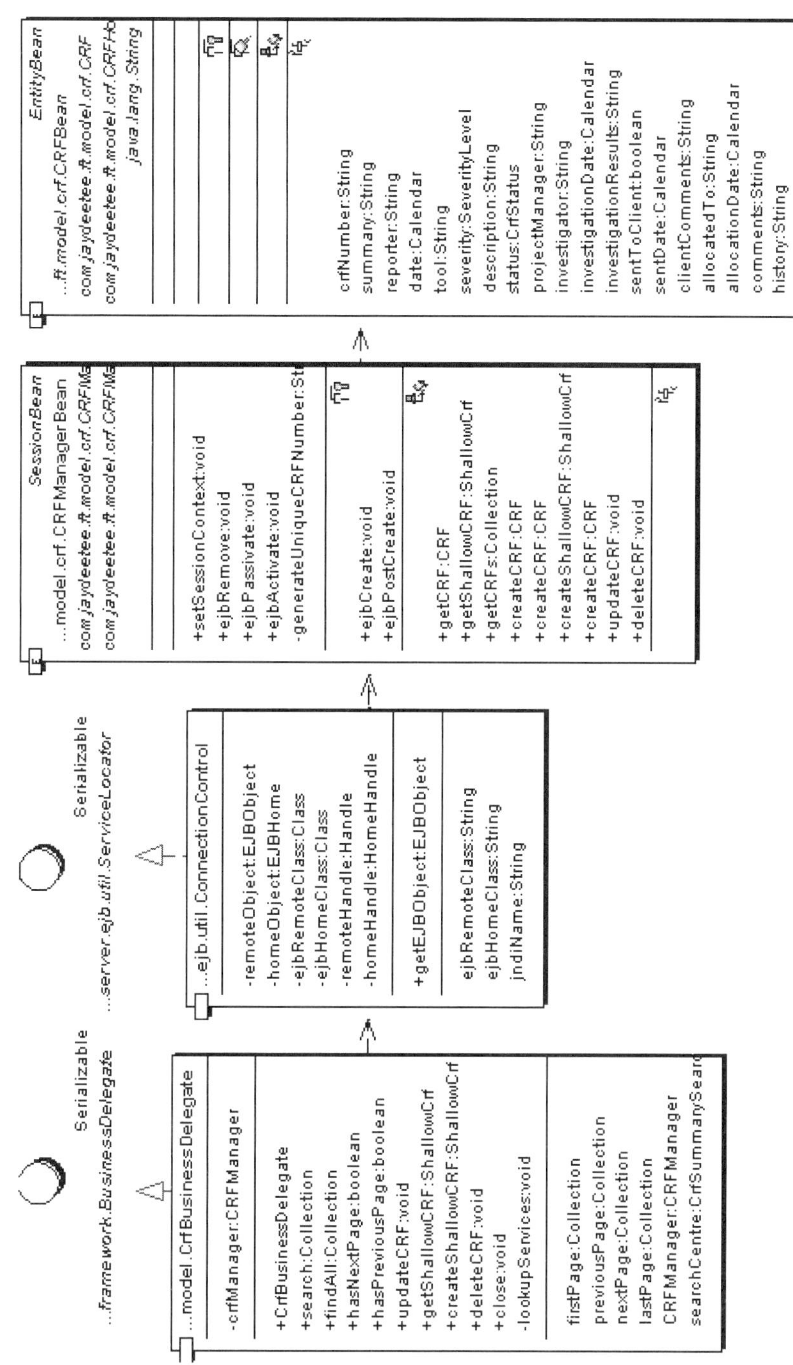

Figure 35.14 Accessing the EJB tier from the Web tier in Fault Tracker.

Index